THE
GEOGRAPHY OF
WITCHCRAFT

MONTAGUE SUMMERS

*Et infecta est terra in sanguinibus, et contaminata
est in operibus eorum.*—PSALM CV
*Non declinetis ad magos, nec ab hariolis aliquid sciscitemini,
ut polluamini per eos. Ego Dominus Deus Uester.*—

LIBER LEUITICI, XIX, 31

UNIVERSITY BOOKS   *New Hyde Park, New York*

THIRD PRINTING, FEBRUARY 1970

Library of Congress Catalog Card Number: 58-8303
Manufactured in the United States of America

DILECTO DESIDERATISSIMO

D. D. D.

AUCTOR

CONTENTS

INTRODUCTION

THE present work may be regarded as a complementary volume to, or even a second volume of, my *History of Witchcraft and Demonology*. There I spoke of general principles; here I give particulars. It is obvious that a choice must be exercised in treating of so world-wide a subject, and it is impertinent to arraign me because I have not dealt with China and Peru, with Morocco and Senegambia.

The Introduction to the previous volume clearly indicates the lines upon which I approach Witchcraft, an attitude doubtless open to criticism, as indeed are all points of view. To compile an encyclopædia is for practical reasons not now possible; to do less is to expose the joints of one's harness to every man who lists to draw a bow at a venture.

IN FESTO S. PATRIS n. IOANNIS A CRUCE Conf. et Eccl. Doctoris.
1926.

THE GEOGRAPHY OF WITCHCRAFT

CHAPTER I

GREECE AND ROME

FROM the very earliest times there were inextricably reticulated in the complex Greek systems of universal mythology and symbolistic religious ceremonial various aboriginal beliefs and curious practices of ancient superstition which formed a primitive order of magic ; in later days to be elaborated, to be augmented from Phœnicia and from Egypt, to be studied in schools, to be glossed and codified. Nature taught man the drama of the Sacrifice, some vague shadow, as it might be, of the Good Things that were to come ; some antepast of that Banquet which alone can satisfy the hunger of his soul. The Greek sacrifice, even in its crudest stages, was inevitably accompanied by ancillary rites, which, however trivial, had as their end the object either of discovering the god's will or of placating the divinity. It soon followed that there must be those who were able to acquire by intensive meditation the means of interpreting the expression of that will, of recognizing when the efforts of the worshipper had been crowned with success, when his deity was regarding him with favour and approval. And accordingly there came to be a caste of persons who made these things their principal concern, wise men (wizards), priests who from their daily and intimate communion with the god, from living in his presence, were regarded as partakers of his sanctity, protected by him, inspired by him, his friends and servants. The priests were not vagrant, not irresponsible Gyrovagi and Sarabaitæ, but stable men, dwellers in one place. Whence the locality where they abode also in its degree reflected their mysterious power, it was aureoled with supernaturalism; thither resorted the individual who wished to learn Heaven's will, and before many generations had passed these places were famous as oracles, as shrines, as centres of pilgrimage.

Naturally in the course of years the priest would take care to fix his abode in some spot which, it might be for its remoteness, the beauty or grandeur of its landscape, the loneliness of its woodland glades, the terror of its beetling crags, the reverence of its snow-capped hills, or for some accidental reason altogether, was most suited to his purpose, most impressive to the plastic mind of the inquirer, whether he came from near or far. And so we have the oracle of Dodona amid the forest of huge-girthed oaks; Apollo speaks from the chasm of legend-haunted Delphi where Parnassus towers above; horned Hammon is sought amid the sandy wastes of distant Libya; the phallic Baal upon the lonely heights of Peor in the Moabitish land.

The priests to whose charge these sanctuaries belonged were veritable sorcerers. They delivered the oracles; they chanted incantations as the smoke of sacrifice ascended; they directed, they expounded, they advised; they healed, they dispensed noxious draughts; they pretended to lord it over nature by their arts; they tamed wild beasts and they charmed serpents, as Pliny tells;[1] they controlled the winds just as the witches of Lapland and Norway were wont to do; they could avert the hail-storm (χαλαζοφύλακες),[2] or on the other hand they could cover a smiling sky with the menace of dark clouds and torrential rain (νεφελοδιῶκται);[3] "In augurum certe disciplina constat, neque diras, neque ulla auspicia pertinere ad eos, qui quamque rem ingredientes, obseruare se ea negauerint : quo munere diuinæ indulgentiæ maius nullum est. Quid ? non et legum ipsarum in duodecim tabulis uerba sunt ? ' Qui fruges excantasset.' Et alibi, ' Qui malum carmen incantasset.' "[4]

These priest-sorcerers[5] had, moreover, the power to turn human beings into brute animals; a superstition upon which S. Boethius philosophizes aptly in the Fourth Book of his *De Consolatione Philosophiæ*, when he says that man's evil passions, if uncurbed, degrade him lower than the beasts. " Euenit igitur, ut quem transformatum uitiis uideas hominem æstimare non possis. Auaritia seruet alienarum opum uiolentus ereptor ? lupi similem dixeris . . . Insidiator occultis surripuisse fraudibus gaudet ? Uulpeculis exæqua-tur.[6] Iræ intemperans fremit ? leonis animum gestare credatur. . . . Ita sit, ut qui, probitate deserta, homo esse desierit, cum in diuinam conditionem transire non possit, uertatur in belluam." This legendary power of metamor-phosis seems to be closely connected with the animal disguises ritually worn by the priest when engaged in his worship. The custom is of the remotest antiquity, for such masqued men are found even among the palæolithic drawings in France, the animal represented being the original totem of the tribe. Often the god himself was adored under the animal form, a variant which, although continually met with, is perhaps most generally known as having moulded the representation of the deities of Egypt and the Nile. This ritual disguise offers, no doubt, in part at least, an explanation of the innumerable myths of the Greek pantheon which tell how Zeus enjoyed Europa as a bull, Leda as a swan, Asterie as an eagle, Deois as a speckled serpent ; how Poseidon as a bull seduced Arne, as a ram Theophane ; how Chronos as a horse covered Philyra and begat the centaur Chiron ; and a thousand ancient legends more.

The power of transforming men to beasts particularly occurs in the legend of Circe, which, with the story of the enchantress Medea,[7] whom Diodorus[8] calls Hecate's own daughter, is amongst the earliest Greek sagas. Even so revolutionary a commentator as Kirchhoff,[9] who puts forward the view that the *Odyssey* is mainly made up with large late additions by a compiler from a number of early poems, a nucleus which he calls the " Elder Odyssey," is of opinion that this " Elder Odyssey " contains material of an almost primitive date and to this kernel belong the adventures of Odysseus with Circe. A very close analogy may be found in the Indian collection of Somadeva, which, although as a whole of the thirteenth century, A.D., comprises myths that have descended from remotest antiquity. Here the witch, after changing a company into four-footed beasts, is van-quished by a magical formula in the mouth of a young traveller, whom she then admits to her bed.

Number six of the eight epics which made up the Trojan cycle was known as the *Nostoi*, the history of the return home of certain Greek heroes, especially Menelaus and Agamemnon, after Ilium had fallen. The author of the *Nostoi*, a poem in five books, was Agias of Troezen, *c.* 750 B.C., but he is a mere name to us. In some way, as appears from the Scholiast's Argument to the *Medea* of Euripides, Medea was brought into the old epic and the incident of the restoration of Aeson to youth was therein related. Pausanias,[10] who had read the poem, tells us that it contained an account of Hades, and it may be guessed that much light would have been thrown thence on Greek magic and eschatology.

It should incidentally be mentioned that in addition to the priest-sorcerers there grew up another class of wizards, who, however, held a very inferior place in the public estimation, and who were, it seems evident, on occasion addicted to jugglery and the most bare-faced charlatanry. These were the " gœtes " (γόητες), whose name was derived from the wild shrieks and howls—Seneca's *barbaricus ululatus*—with which they chanted their incantations.[11] Yet they were feared almost as much as they were disliked, for, in spite of their impostures, it was believed that they had malevolent powers not to be despised with impunity, and they were in fact generally accredited with the most mischievous and unlucky intentions. They were the confectioners of philtres and poisons ; they peddled their craft for money ; they raised jars, jealousies, strifes, like a thick scurf o'er life. The gœtes were indeed most like the witch of the sixteenth and seventeenth centuries, the Sawyers, Demdikes, Cullenders, and the hags whom Bodin and De Lancre burned. The priests hated their tradition, and more than once laws were passed to check their activities.[12] The cynic philosopher, Oenomäus[13] (A.D. 150 ?) wrote a treatise Φώρα γοήτων (The Gœtes Unveiled) in which he exposed their frauds and quackery.

It is supposed that the gœtes were the indigenous wizards of Greece and that their arts preserved some rude aboriginal superstitions, whilst the more sober and solemn magic of the priests was if not actually in its origin, at least in its development, Oriental. Pliny (*Historia Naturalis*, XXX, 1) attributes the importation of systematized magic into Greece to Osthanes, a soothsayer who accompanied Xerxes on his expedition against the West, 480 B.C., and he tells us that Osthanes was a disciple of Zoroaster. But this is uncritical, and such an attribution must be centuries too late. " Quod certum est, hic maxime Osthanes ad rabiem, non auiditatem modo scientiæ eius, Græcorum populos egit." Pliny held Zoroaster to be in effect the first magician, but this Osthanes could not have been his pupil, inasmuch as although the Pahlavi books traditionally place this master's era between the earlier half of the seventh and the sixth century, most scholars have no hesitation in assigning him to a hundred years, or even several hundred years, before this date. Apuleius (De Magia, XXVI) mentions Zoroaster and Oromazus as the inventors of sorcery : " Do you not know that magic . . . is an art pleasing to the immortal gods . . . a science which has been noble and reverend from the very times of Zoroaster and Oromazus, who invented it, a science which is the handmaid of the lords of heaven ? "[14] He classes Osthanes with Epimenides, Orpheus, and Pythagoras " eos uero uulgo magos nominent " (whom the vulgar term magicians too).

S. Augustine, De Ciuitate Dei, VII, 35, quoting Varro, says that various kinds of divination, used both in Greece and Rome, were of Eastern origin. " For Numa himself, being not instructed by any prophet or Angel of God was fain to fall to hydromancy : making his gods (or rather his devils) to appear in water, and instruct him in his religious institutions. Which kind of divination, says Varro, came from Persia, and was used by Numa and afterwards by Pythagoras, wherein they used blood also, and called forth spirits infernal. Necromancy the Greeks call it ; but necromancy or hydromancy, whether you like, there it is that the dead seem to speak."[15]

One of the earliest and incidentally one of the most important scenes of necromancy in Greek literature is to be found in the Odyssey, Book XI. Odysseus has been advised by Circe—the witch, be it noted—to take counsel from the shade of Tiresias, the famous seer, and so he makes his way to the shores of eternal darkness, the home of the Cimmerians, where he lands and seeks the poplar groves that skirt the house of Hades.[16] Between earth and the realm of Hades is an intermediate region of ghosts, Erebus. Tartarus, the prison of the Titans, and other rebels against divine providence, is as far below Hades as he is below the earth.[17] In

the realm of Hades the spirit of the dead has the form, the
rank, and the occupations which were those of the living man.
But the spirit is a mere semblance or wraith. " The living
heart is not in it " (*Iliad*, XXIII, 103), it is " strengthless."
When Odysseus seeks to call up the spirits of the dead he
digs a pit, a cubit square, into which flows the blood of the
sheep that he sacrifices to Hades and Proserpine. A crowd
of silent shadows evoked by his prayers come up and crave
to taste the blood, but with drawn sword he keeps them at
bay until Tiresias shall appear. Even the ghost of his mother
has to be warded off from the trench. Finally the old prophet
is seen hovering near, and is allowed to drink " that I may
tell sooth." He then delivers his oracle, and further explains
that all the shades upon quaffing the blood will recover some
of the faculties of the living and be able to hold converse
awhile. The dead mother now is enabled to talk with her son,
but when they strive to embrace all is vain, he clasps the
empty air. It is interesting to observe that in this long and
fully detailed scene, where we already have much of the
ritual of mediæval and modern Witchcraft, lines 368–641
have been regarded as an " Orphic interpolation," for
Orpheus was said to be the composer of various incantations
and rhythmic charms, and fragments of the Orphic poetry
which was known to Plato still remain.

The Greek goddess of necromancy and all Witchcraft was
the mysterious Hecate. The name at least seems to be
Greek,[18] and it may be an epithet denoting " the far-off one,"
" the one who stands aloof," but whilst no explanation that
has yet been suggested is very significant, an even greater
obscurity covers the origin and character of this deity. There
is no mention of her in the Homeric epics, she has no legend,
she has no genealogy, facts which are surely not without
deep meaning when we consider the mysterious and secret
cult of this awful power. The two earliest references in
literature are the quotation in Pausanias from the κατάλογος
γυναικῶν attributed to Hesiod, which connects Hecate with
Artemis and Iphigenia ; and the well-known passage in
the *Theogony*,[19] probably the first reference in known
Greek literature. At Aegina, where she was specially
honoured, her mysteries were established at least in the fifth
century, and the tradition was locally ascribed to the Thracian

Orpheus. In Samothrace the cult was amalgamated with the occult rituals of the Cabiri. In certain parts of Caria she seems to have had eunuchs as her priests, which certainly is connected with the Corybantes of Cybele. Everything points to the fact that Thrace was the first home of Hecate, and the Thracian goddess Bendis may be Hecate venerated under another name. It should be remarked that the hound was the animal sacred to Hecate, and black dogs often precede the coming or manifestation of the divinity. The statue of Hecate Lampadephoros at Byzantium commemorated the good service of the dogs who aroused the citizens on the occasion of a night attack by Philip of Macedon.

At some period before the Peloponnesian War, Hecate had become identified with Artemis.[20] Probably in the first instance this was not because both were moon-goddesses—for such was in fact not originally the case—the usual, and rather superficial, explanation ; but rather not on account of any deep essential affinity so much as that the torches, wandering by night, hounds, and wild nature of Hecate admirably suited Artemis as well. It is true, however, that in later years both Hecate and Artemis were worshipped as lunar deities. And soon her ghostly character becomes very prominent. Euripides speaks of her as " Queen of the phantom-world " ; and on black-figured vases she is depicted in company with Persephone, Demeter, and Hermes. We find her allied with those wilder gods whose rites were mystery, who drove the impious that dare profane the orgies, mad, Pan and Cybele ; and at Tralles even with Priapus,[21] a most important fact when we remember that sexual debauchery has always been a feature of Witchcraft throughout the ages. In Lucian, *Philopseudes*, nightly Hecate is evoked by a sorcerer and she appears terrible to see, in the form of a woman, half a furlong high, snake-footed, snakes in her hair, a torch in her left hand, a mighty sword in her right.

Horror, fear, and darkness rapidly accumulated about her : at Tarentum she was adored as ἄφραττος, " the nameless one " ; at Terina and Hipponium in the fourth century as πάνδεινα, " all terrible." Her statue of triple form,[22] the queen of three worlds,[23] Selene in heaven, Artemis on earth, Persephone in hell, stood at the cross-roads, a haunted spot, where, according to Plato (*Laws* 873b), might be thrown the corpse of the murderer after execution, unwept, unburied, the prey of daws and crows. Her rites were monstrous, but to be respected and revered ; her worshippers were accursed, but to be dreaded and placated ; her prayers blasphemy ; her sacrifices impious and terrible. It was in truth the very cult of hell.

Hecate in vengeance sent spectres and ghostly phantoms which filled men's hearts with hideous fear and drove them to madness and despair.   These were the ἐπωπίδες, the silent watchers of the night.   Other of her train were the Ἐμπούσαι[24] (Empusas), monstrous hobgoblins with the feet of donkeys, who might, on a sudden, take a thousand forms to scare belated travellers; the Κερκῶπις[25] (Cercopis), a poltergeist, who haunted four cross-ways ; and, most dreaded of all, Μορμώ[26] (Mormo), a foul and loathly ghoul.

Eusebius has preserved an answer which, according to Porphyry,[27] was given by Hecate to one of her votaries. The worshipper is bidden to carve him a statue of well-planed wood according to certain mystic formulas.   The figure is to be smeared with rue, and then with a paste to be compounded of lizards,[28] myrrh, storax, and incense grains, which must be confected what time the new moon hangs a sickle in the sky. When the moon is full, " vow thy solemn vows in these words."   This phrase unfortunately has not been preserved to us.   " Build a shrine and deck it with wild laurel boughs, set therein my image which adore with fervent orison, and in thy sleep I will stand before thee."   Probably the invocation which Eusebius omitted, is that we find in the *Philosophumena*[29] of S. Hippolytus.   " Come, infernal, terrestial, and heavenly Bombo, goddess of the broad roadways, of the cross-road, thou who goest to and fro at night, torch in hand, enemy of the day, friend and lover of darkness, thou who dost rejoice when the bitches are howling and warm blood is spilled, thou who art walking amid the phantom and in the place of tombs, thou whose thirst is blood, thou who dost strike chill fear into mortal heart, Gorgo, Mormo, Moon of a thousand forms, cast a propitious eye upon our sacrifice."

As in mediæval times it was often believed that super-natural powers were the heritage of certain families, descending from one generation to another, and that all Lap women[30] in particular were born witches, so the Greeks considered that the Thessalian dames were above all other folk skilled in sorcery and enchantments. They were equally deft at brewing a love philtre or a poison, and by their litanies and charms they could draw the very moon from the skies. Pliny tells us (*Historia Naturalis*, **XXX**, ii, 2) that Menander in his comedy *Thessala* (*The Thessalian Woman*) brought on the stage a sabbat scene in which the enchantress compelled the moon to obey her magic : " Miror equidem Achillis populis famam eius in tantum adhæsisse, ut Menander quoque literarum subtilitati sine æmulo genitus, Thessalam cognominaret fabulam, complexam ambages feminarum detrahentium Lunam. Orphea putarem e propinquo primum intulisse, ad uicina usque, superstitionem ac medicinæ profectum, si non expers sedes eius rota Thrace magices fuisset." And so essential a feature of Witchcraft did this fascination of the moon become, so typical an exploit of necromancers, that Nonnus actually attributes it to the Brahmin priests.[31] Lucian, when he is to tell a story of enchantment, at once sends his hero to Thessaly, the most appropriate locale, and Apuleius, who turned the tale into finest gold, writes : " Extremely desirous of becoming acquainted with all that is strange and wonderful, I called to mind that I was in the very heart of Thessaly, celebrated by the unanimous consent of the whole wide world as the land where the spells and incantations of the art of magic are, so to speak, indigenous . . . accordingly excited in the highest degree by my eagerness and my ardent temperament I examined everything in detail with closest curiosity."[32]

The second idyll of Theocritus, the *Pharmaceutria*, gives a vividly realistic and impassioned picture of Greek sorcery. Simaetha, a proud Syracusan lady, has been forsaken by her lover Delphis, and driven to madness by the vehemence of her desire, she resorts to the terrible rites of magic to win him to her bed again. She stands at midnight upon the deserted shore, the wind has dropped and all is still, there is scarcely a ripple upon the moonlit sea, there is no sound save the gentle lap of the water that softly kisses the sand, all nature is hushed in sleep. Yet her bosom throbs with agony ; for her there is no rest, no quiet ; love has sucked her blood like a leech ; her very skin is jaundiced and sere, hot with fever, burning to the touch. A fierce fire blazes red upon the

beach, and in its light she twirls her charmed wheel, adjuring
it to bring false Delphis to her home.

ἴυγξ[33] ἕλκε τὺ τῆνον ἐμὸν ποτὶ δῶμα τὸν ἄνδρα.

Thestylis, her attendant, muffled in a mantle and shuddering
from the chilly air or with fear, casts meal upon the flames,
meal that typifies the bones of Delphis ; a green laurel bough
that crackles in the heat and stands for his supple young
limbs ; pure wax which melts as his strength shall fade and
fail.   The girl hesitates for a moment, and Simaetha upbraids
her with cold and cruel words.   New ingredients are brought ;
bran, and spurge which sets mares on heat ; the border of
the recreant's mantle is rent into shreds and scattered into
the glowing heart of the fire.   Presently Thestylis is dispatched in hot haste to smear the doors of Delphis with a
sympathetic ointment, and thrice is she to spit[34] and say
" I anoint the bones of Delphis."   Simaetha, all alone, turns
to the argent disc of the Moon, clear and calm above her,
journeying in majestic state through the Sicilian skies, and
to her she pours forth the story of her love.

φράζεό μευ τὸν ἔρωθ' ὅθεν ἴκετο, πότνα Σελάνα.

About the middle of the road, just where Lycon's house
stands, she first saw Delphis.   He was walking with his friend
Eudamippos.   Fair were their locks in the sunlight ; they
moved with the immortal grace of gods.   Then follows a tale
of hot southern passion ; gladly she yields him her virginity,
oversoon, for satiety and neglect follow on the one side,
mistrust and bitter revenge on the other.   Once he scarce
could bear to be an hour from her ; now, twelve days have
past and he has not crossed her threshold.   Can it be he loves
another ?   And will her incantations prevail ?   If not, there
are at any rate poisons swift and sure, there are phials which
she keeps in a box, drugs an Assyrian stranger once taught
her to brew, quick dispatch to the gate of hell, potions such
as were wont to be distilled by Circe, or Medea, or Perimede
of the golden hair.[35]

With the exception of a few inconsiderable circumstances
all the terrible and loathsome rites of ancient magic rehearsed
in this magnificent monodrama may be closely and immediately paralleled in the lore of modern Witchcraft.   We have

the time, midnight. The place, upon the seashore. Wax is consumed in the fire. The Aberdeen witches in 1596 assembled " att tuelff houris at eevin or thairby."[36] In the pamphlet *Newes from Scotland* (1591) the Berwick coven are represented as forgathering upon the Lothian beach at North Berwick. The use of waxen images in Witchcraft is of the highest antiquity, and there is no property, perhaps, more frequently to be met with in the records and inquiries of all ages and all countries. We know that such figures, both to do good and to do evil, were employed in the pre-dynastic days of Egypt, when the Egyptians were slowly emerging from a state of semi-barbarism into civilization. In the Western Papyrus[37] there is a story of the reign of Nebka or Neb-hau-Rā, a king of the Third Dynasty (about 3830 B.C.), in which such a model plays an important part. The wife of a certain high official, Āba-aner,[38] becomes enamoured of a soldier of the royal guard. Āba-aner, discovering this, fashions a crocodile of wax, of which material he has a supply in an ebony box, seven spans long, and having recited certain spells says : " When the man cometh down to bathe in my waters seize thou him." The crocodile is cast into the river whilst the lover is swimming there. It instantly turns into a living monster, seven cubits (about twelve feet) in length, and drags its prey down under the water. Seven days later the King and Āba-aner are walking by the stream, when the latter calls to the crocodile, which appears bringing the soldier in its mouth. Āba-aner has but to touch the reptile and lo ! there is only a small model of wax. He relates to Nebka what has happened, and when the king cries to the beast, " Take that which is thine and begone ! " the huge jaws in a moment close upon its victim and the crocodile disappears for ever into the depths of the Nile. The guilty wife was by the royal command punished with death. It should be noticed that the narrative represents Āba-aner as having by him a box of wax which he specially keeps for performing feats of magic, and that the king does not appear to attach any evil or reproach to such acts and practices.

When the famous conspiracy was formed against Rameses III, about 1200 B.C., the official account of the trials mentions that a certain high official, Hui, resorted to magic to obtain his ends. He procured from the royal library a book of spells, and then set to work to make little figures of men in wax, and so succeeded in carrying out all the "horrible things and all the wickednesses which his heart could imagine." He is more than once definitely accused of making these men of wax, which should cause the human beings they represented to become paralysed, helpless, and sick to death. The conspiracy was discovered, and Hui, who had made a wax image to bring suffering and destruction upon the king himself, was compelled by the judges to commit suicide.

Wax figures were largely employed in the liturgy of the god Amen-Rā, whose great temple was at Thebes. One feature of the daily worship consisted in elaborate ritual acts whose object was to free the Sun, deified under the form of Rā, from the attacks of a hideous human dragon named Āpep, storm-clouds and darkness. By the time of the Ptolemies there had been compiled a manual of twelve chapters *The Book of Overthrowing Āpep*. The litanies and orisons of Rā are given, the words of power, and then the rubric runs : "If thou wouldest destroy Āpep, thou shalt say this chapter over a figure of Āpep, which hath been drawn in green colour upon a sheet of new papyrus, and over a wax figure of Āpep upon which his name hath been cut and inlaid with green colour ; and thou shalt lay them upon the fire so that it may consume the enemy of Rā." This charm is to be repeated at dawn, at noon, at evening, at midnight, and oftener, every hour in fact, if deemed necessary.

Ovid's Medea employed figures of wax which she pierced with a needle :

> Deuouet absentes : simulacraque cerea figit,
> Et miserum tenues in iecur urget acus.

So writes Hypsipyle to Jason of the foreign whore her faithless lover has brought home with him. (*Heroides*, VI, 91–2.)

From ancient Egypt the magic use of wax figures passed to Greece, and thence to Rome. From Rome it passed into Western Europe. About the end of the seventh century the life of King Duffus of Scotland was attempted in this way. "A company of hags roasted his image made of wax upon a wooden spit, reciting certain words of enchantment, and basting the figure with a poisonous liquor. These women, when apprehended, declared, that as the wax melted, the body of the king should decay, and the words of enchantment prevented him from the refreshment of sleep."[39] The figure was destroyed ; the witches burned at Forres in Murray ; and the king recovered his health. The witches of North Berwick made a similar figure of James I, which was to be melted before a fire to destroy that king, who in his *Dæmonologie* (1597) ascribes such practices to the Devil, and says in describing what things witches may " effectuate by the power of their master " : " To some others at these times hee teaceth, how to make Pictures of waxe or clay : That by the rosting thereof, the persones that they beare the name of, may be continuallie melted or dryed awaie by continuall sicknesse."[40] Reginald Scot tells us that when a young girl named Stuppeny of New Romney, Kent, fell sick her parents consulted a certain Mother Baker, who at once accused a neighbour of bewitching their daughter. She said that this woman had made a wax heart and pierced it with pins to accomplish the enchantment. In order to prove the accusation Mother Baker in the meantime had concealed a wax heart in the house of the woman she accused, and then pretended to find it. But the spot she chose had been previously searched, so the malicious old crone was caught and compelled to confess her trick.[41] In 1664 the chief indictment against Christian Green and Margaret Agar of Brewham, Somerset, was that they had made "pictures" of wax into which they stuck thorns and needles, whereby those whose figures the models were languished and pined to death, being forespoken from that hour.[42]

Simaetha crushes a lizard to confect her charm ; the hags of Nogaredo in 1647 confessed that newts and lizards[43] were powerful ingredients in their hell-broth. And if her spells are of no effect, the jealous dame will have resource to some swift venom. Professor A. J. Clark, who has analysed the " flying ointments " of more modern sorceresses, writes of their three formulæ : " These prescriptions show that the society of witches had a very creditable knowledge of the art of poisoning."

The mention of the Assyrian stranger is particularly interesting. As we have seen, tradition assigned the introduction of Oriental magic into Greece to the year 480 B.C., and Theocritus was writing some two hundred years later. By that time the very name χαλδαῖος, a Chaldæan, was used as a synonym for an astrologer, a fortune-teller. So Cicero in the *De Diuinatione*, I, 2, has : " Gentem quidem nullam uideo . . . quæ non significari futura, et a quibusdam intelligi, prædicique posse censeat. Principio Assyrii . . . traiectiones motusque stellarum obseruitauerunt. . . . Qua in natione Chaldæi, non ex artis, sed ex gentis uocabulo nominati, diuturna obseruatione siderum, scientiam putantur effecisse, ut prædici posset, quid cuique euenturum, et quo quisque fato natus esset." Juvenal, also (VI, 552–4), writes :

> Chaldaeis sed maior erit fiducia : quidquid
> Dixeri Astrologus, credent a fonte relatum
> Hammonis, quoniam Delphis oracula cessant.

> (More Credit, yet, is to *Chaldeans* giv'n ;
> What they foretell, is deem'd the Voice of Heav'n.
> Their Answers, as from *Hammon's* Altar, come ;
> Since now the *Delphian* Oracles are dumb.)
>
> DRYDEN.

And again (X, 92–4), in allusion to Tiberius :

> tutor haberi
> Principis Augusta Caprearum in rupe sedentis
> Cum grege Chaldaeo.

> (And keep a prince in ward, retired to reign
> O'er Capreæ's crags, with his Chaldean train ?)
>
> GIFFORD.

Tacitus in the sixth book of the *Annals* also speaks of Tiberius, who " scientia Chaldæorum artis . . . magistrum Thrasyllum habuit." This Thrasyllus is mentioned by Suetonius, and praised by Pliny.

In English, too, the name " Chaldæan " came to be used for a soothsayer, a magician. In James Shirley's comedy *The Sisters* (8vo, 1652) III, Giovanni exclaims : " They call him a Chaldæan, a great scholar. . . . My lady hath given the Chaldæan her nativity, who is to consult with the ephemerides."[44]

The Chaldæan astrologer Berosus was said to have founded a school of astronomy and divination at Cos, and Pliny relates that the Athenians esteemed him so highly as to honour him by erecting his statue, furnished with a tongue of gold, in the public Gymnasium. "Astrologia [enituit] Berosus, cui ob diuinas prædictiones Athenienses publice in gymnasio statuam inaurata lingua statuere."[45] Other famous Chaldæans were Astrampsychos, Gobryas, and Pazalas,[46] under whose names in later days went various collections of spells and prophecies, just as in England similar chap-books were ascribed to Merlin or Mother Shipton, and in France every little *Merveilleux Trésor de la Magie* was fathered upon Cornelius Agrippa, le Petit Albert, or Nostrodamus.

Egyptian magic[47] and astrology became known to the Greeks at a comparatively early period. Some authorities find traces of Egypt among the Orphic Hymns, but from every point of view such a line of argument offers considerable difficulties.

Especially famous in Greek tradition was Nectanebus, the last native king of Egypt, about 358 B.C., and a master magician. By means of his wisdom he was lord of all the earth, and his enchantments could rule the mightiest monarchs. For if he was threatened with an invasion he sent out no soldiers to repel his foe, but retiring to a certain secret chamber, and having brought forth a great bowl kept for the purpose, he filled this with pure water. He then made small wax figures of the ships and men of the enemy, and also of his own men and ships, setting them all upon the water in the bowl, his host on one side, the fleet of the enemy opposite them. Next he robed himself in his mystic mantle and took his wand of ebony. Speaking the words of power, he summoned the winds, the subterranean demons, and the gods themselves to his aid. The wax poppets sprang into life, the ships of wax began to move, and they fought upon the water ; but the figures which represented his own men vanquished the enemy, and as the foreign vessels and warriors sank to the bottom of the bowl, so did the real ships and crews of his adversary sink to the floor of the ocean. It happened that one day certain scouts came to Nectanebus and told him that all the nations of the East had leagued against him, and were hard by the frontier, an army thick as locusts, and as the sands of the desert in number. The magician laughed scornfully awhile, and having gone into his private chamber, poured water into the bowl, and proceeded with the charm. When he looked at the wax figures, however, he saw to his dismay that the gods of Egypt were steering the enemies' navy against himself and that he could not cause their ships to founder in the usual way. Accordingly he knew that the end of the kingdom of Egypt was at hand, so hastily leaving his palace he shaved off his hair and beard, and taking with him much gold he fled, disguised in common apparel, and sailed to Pella in Macedonia, where he established himself as a physician, and as an Egyptian soothsayer, winning great renown.

In the fourth chapter of Pseudo-Callisthenes we have an account of the casting of the nativity of Olympias by Nectanebus, who also sent a dream to the queen by means of a wax figure. His object was to persuade her that she should be visited by the god Amen (or Hammon) that night. Accordingly, having collected a number of herbs, he made a wax figure of a woman upon which he wrote the name Olympias. This he anointed with the juice of the herbs, and invoked certain demons by whose power she dreamed that the god Amen came to her, and having had connexion with her, announced that from his divine embrace she should give birth to a man-child (Alexander the Great), who should avenge her on her husband Philip.

Of Alexander himself various legends are related, and one of these, possibly derived from an Egyptian source, is particularly interesting since here we have so great a name as Aristotle himself in the rôle of a wizard. The Arab writer Abu-Shâker, who lived in the thirteenth century, mentions a tradition that Aristotle gave Alexander a number of wax figures nailed down in a box fastened by a chain, and which he strictly bade him never to let go out of his hand, or at least only to entrust it to his most confidential and trusted servants. Alexander was to carry the box with him always, and whenever he took it up or set it down he was to recite a certain formula or incantation.[48] The figures were those of the various kinds of armed men that were likely to be his foes. Some of the models held leaden swords pointing backwards ; others had spears without heads ; other had bows with cut strings ; all these and many more were laid downward in the box. It is clear that in providing Alexander with these models and teaching him the words of power to say over them, Aristotle believed that he was giving his pupil the means of making his enemies become like the dummy soldiers, and so they would be unable to attack him or to withstand his arms.

Occasionally the Greek witch met with the same fate as her sister of a thousand years later, for Theoris, " the Lemnian woman," Demosthenes calls her, was publicly tried in Athens and burned for her sorceries.

From Greece Witchcraft sensibly penetrated to Rome about the third century B.C., and with it in full force came Oriental magic, although the superstitions of the East had already begun to percolate through independent channels. There were also, of course, native and indigenous traditions, such as the mysterious cults and mythology of the Etruscans, with their " Shrouded Gods," the books of Tages, and the schools of the Lucumones. There lingered, moreover, the legends and lore of yet older races and primitive civilizations. But it is now generally acknowledged that from the Etruscans the Romans derived their early belief in and solemn rites of divination, so integral a part of the official religion.

Tages was a supernatural being,[49] who, as Cicero writes,[50] once appeared suddenly in a field to a Tuscan ploughman, and taught him and all the people of Etruria the art of the haruspices. " Is autem Tages, ut in libris est Etruscorum, puerili specie dicitur uisus, sed senili fuisse prudentia . . . tum illum plura locutum multis audientibus, qui omnia eius uerba exceperint, litterisque mandauerint : omnem autem orationem fuisse eam, qua haruspicinæ disciplina contineretur : eam postea creuisse rebus nouis cognoscendis, et ad eadem illa principia referendis. Hæc accepimus ab ipsis ; hæc scripta conseruant : hunc fontem habent disciplinæ."

The fearful veneration paid to the Lemures, who were malignant spirits, with their high festival the Lemuria[51] held on the ninth, eleventh, and thirteenth of May, to propitiate the ghosts of the departed ; the cult of the Manes, the deified souls of the dead, benevolent spirits ; and the more domestic rites of the Lares, with their feast the Laralia,[52] celebrated on the first of May ; were all largely associated and mixed up with magical observances. Of these spirits S. Augustine writes : Plotinus " says also that men's souls are *dæmones*, and become *lares* if their merits are good ; if evil *lemures* goblins ; if uncertain *manes*."[53] Apuleius in his *De Deo*

Socratis Liber (XV) has the following : " I find that the human soul after it has performed its duties in the present life, and quitted the body is called in the ancient Latin language by the name of *Lemur*. Now, of the Lemures, the one who, undertaking the guardianship of his posterity, dwells in a house with propitious and tranquil influence, is called the " familiar " Lar. But those who, having no fixed habitation of their own, are punished with vague wandering as with a kind of exile, on account of the evil deeds of their life, are usually called *Larvæ*, thus becoming a vain terror to the good but a source of punishment to the bad. But when it is uncertain what is the allotted condition of any one of these, and whether it is a *Lar* or *Larva*, it is called a *God Manes;* the name God being added for the sake of honour."

The Lares belonged originally to the Etruscan religion, and were worshipped as the presiders over and protectors of a particular locality.[54] They might be patrons of a city and its suburbs, " Lares Putcolonæ ciuitatis " ;[55] of a village, " Lares uicorum " ;[56] of cross-roads, " Lares compitales,"[57] whose statues Augustus, when he became Pontifex Maximus, ordered to be decked for their festival twice a year in spring and summer with garlands of fragrant flowers ; of the road-side " Lares uiales " ;[58] lords of the sea, " Lares permarini ";[59] and one inscription even gives them the epithet " cælipo-tentes."[60] But more usually they were " familiaris " or " domestici," the guardians of one family or one home. Such is the Lar Familiaris who speaks the prologue to the *Aulularia*.

> Ego Lar sum familiaris, ex hac familia,
> Unde exeuntem me aspexistis, Hanc domum
> Iam multos annos est cum possideo, et colo
> Patrique, auoque iam huius qui nunc hic habet.
>
> (I am the Lar Familiaris of this family from whose abode ye have seen me just coming out. For many a long year have I been the guardian of this house, and I have watched over the father, ay, and the grandsire too of him who is now master thereof.)

To drive away the Larvæ, ghouls, and goblins, it was sometimes necessary to offer sacrifice with a complicated ceremonial of expiation and exorcism.[61] The ancient Italian goddess Mana (Genita Mana) or Manuana was queen of the

Manes and Summanes. As the witch goddess she is sometimes identified with Hecate, although this is merely a late
and uncritical confusion. Her worship was secret and
mysterious. To her were offered young puppies, as Pliny
tells us : " Catulos lactentes adeo puros existimabant ad
cibum, ut etiam placandis numinibus hostiarum uice uteren-
tur his. Genitæ Manæ catulo res diuina sit, et in cœnis deum
etiamnum ponitur catulira."[62] An even more awful and
shadowy figure was the dark Summanus, who hurled loud
crashing thunderbolts and sent red forked lightning through
the midnight sky.

Pliny writes, " The Tuscan rituals state that nine gods
have power o'er the levin . . . they say that Jove hurls his
bolts during the day, but Summanus wields the thunder at
night."[63] Varro tells us that the worship of this deity was
introduced by Tatius the Sabine, and here he is evidently
repeating some very ancient legend. The temple of Summanus was near the Circus Maximus, and S. Augustine says
that in later times he had few worshippers, at any rate that
is to say few acknowledged devotees.[64] The fact is this
horrid cult was conducted with such secrecy and so carefully
was his loathly ritual guarded that even the curious in such
matters could ascertain no particulars. This was the case
with Ovid, who quite frankly writes :[65]

Reddita, quisquis is est, Summano templa feruntur,
Tum, cum Romanis, Pyrrhe, timendus eras.

(A temple is said to have been dedicated to Summanus, whoever he may be, at that season when
thou, O Pyrrhus, wast our dread.)

Other authors are equally vague, but it is significant that
Martianus Capella[66] the Carthaginian, who flourished towards
the close of the fifth century of our era, identifies Summanus
with Pluto, lord of hell. Fastus speaks of cakes superstitiously
offered to Summanus, " Summanalia liba farinacea in modum
rotæ ficta " ;[67] and we known from Pliny that his rites were
accompanied by circumstances of hideous cruelty.[68] Assuredly
in the worship of Summanus we have sheer demonolatry.

Livy has preserved to us more than one legend which shows
that during the period of the kings of Rome Etruscan
divination had gained a great hold upon the growing city.[69]

Particularly striking is the account of Numa Pompilius and the nymph Egeria, with whom he was wont to commune in the hallowed grove of the Camenæ, near the Porta Capena. [70] Varro explains this story by saying that Numa practised hydromancy, divination by water, a charm of Persian origin, since Egeria was the nymph of a sacred stream.

Commenting upon which S. Augustine cries : " Necromancy, the Greeks call it, but necromancy or hydromancy, whether you like, there it is that the dead seem to speak." It is obvious that the holy doctor considers Numa to have been nothing more nor less than a wizard. Varro further relates that a certain Terentius was the owner of some fields on Mount Janiculum, which when his servants were one day ploughing they turned up, near the tomb of Numa, some old parchments and scrolls written by that monarch. Terentius took them to the Prætor, who laid them before the Senate, by whose command they were immediately destroyed. Then we have the Saint's burning words : " So either were these books filled with the Devil's bestial desires, and thereby all the politic theology that presents them such filthinesses made altogether execrable, or else the gods were shown by them, to be none but men departed whom worm-eaten antiquity persuaded the world to be gods, whereas they were devils that delighted in those obscene ministries, and under their names whom the people held divine, got place to play their impostures, and by elusive miracles to captivate all their souls." [71] Whatever we may think of Varro's suggestion— and it seems quite possible—whether there be any truth or subtratum of truth in the Numa legends at all, it is undeniable that from very early times a tradition of magic was handed down in Rome.

Malevolent spells were punished by death by the Law of the Twelve Tables [72] which the Duumvirs drew up in the fifth century B.C., and from time to time severe statutes were passed, being especially directed against those who attempted to injure crops and vines, to spread sickness amongst sheep and cattle. [73] In 139 B.C. the Prætor Cornelius Scipio Hispalus issued an edict that all Chaldeans should leave Rome and even Italy within ten days. [74] But his efforts were fruitless ; the astrologers swarmed back in even greater numbers when the first alarm was over. At the time of Marius and in the

days of Catiline, periods of civil war, intense political excitement, and lightning changes of fortune, necromancers,
diviners, soothsayers, fortune-tellers, oneirocritics, seers,
occultists, mages, infested every alley and street-corner and
the people eagerly flocked to pay their fees and drink in their
predictions. The astrologers began to compose almanacs
and books, which they openly vended up and down. Such
a one, no doubt, was the work of Nigidius, from which Varro
quotes : " Is namque numerus [septem] septemtriones
maiores minoresque facit in cælo, item Vergilius, quas
πλειάδας Græci uocant ; facit etiam stellas, quas alii erraticas,
P. Nigidius errones appellat." [75]

The witches described by the Roman writers are sometimes
mysterious and stately women, sometimes foul and filthy
hags, but both seem equally terrible and potent for evil. Of
the former class we have in Vergil the Libyan sorceress, and
the Sibyl Deiphobe, to whom have been revealed the awful
secrets of the pit, whose eyes have seen unmoved the torments
of dunnest hell. Ovid's Colchian Medea, again, is all dignity
in her despair, and her cry when she first yields to her passion
has found an echo in many a throbbing heart : [76]

> Uideo meliora proboque,
> Deteriora sequor.

Lucan's Erichtho is a ghastly figure, reeking of death and
corruption. She prowls amongst the tombs, and gathers from
the gallows-tree its obscene fruit, the rotting limbs of long-
executed criminals.

> Immersitque manus oculis ;[77] gaudetque gelatos
> Effodisse orbes : et siccæ pallida rodit
> Excrementa manus : laqueum, nodosque nocentes
> Ore suo rupit : pendentia corpora carpsit,
> Abrasitque cruces : percussaque uiscera nimbis
> Uulsit, et incoctas admisso sole medullas.
> Insertum manibus chalybem,[78] nigramque per artus
> Stillantis tabi saniem, uirusque coactum
> Sustulit et neruo morsus retinente pependit.

The Saga of Tibullus is as well versed in enchantments as
any mediæval witch, or any beldame burned under James I.
She can control the weather and evoke the dead :

> Iam ciet infernas magico stridore cateruas.[79]

(With her magic runes she can evoke the hosts of the dead.)

Ovid's Dipsas is a drunken old crone and a bawd to boot, yet

Illa magas artes, Æææaque carmina nouit.[80]

(Magic spells doth she ken, such charms as Æææan Circe knew.)

One of the most famous sabbat scenes in Latin literature is the midnight incantation of Canidia and Sagana upon the Esquiline hill before the wooden statue of Priapus.[81] Horace has spared us no hideous detail, and the extreme coarseness of certain lines seems but to add a shade of yet more revolting loathliness and disgust. Their faces pale and frightful to see, with naked feet and dishevelled hair, swathed in dingy sable cerements, the two witches uttering hoarse cries dig up the soil with their long sharp nails and begin to rend to pieces a black lamb, now and again thrusting a raw gory gobbet into their gaping jaws. The warm blood pours down into the trench ; one hag shrieks foul invocation to Hecate, the other mutters a blasphemous prayer to fierce Tisiphone. A waxen figure is melting fast before a hastily kindled fire.

That unique and inimitable fragment the *Satyricon* of Petronius contains two wonderful ghost stories told at Trimalchio's banquet, the werwolf and the witches. Niceros relates that one evening wishing to visit his mistress Melissa he persuades a soldier to accompany him on his lonesome country jaunt. The silver moon is shining at her full ; and when they have reached a spot in the road remote from the town his companion suddenly turns aside to the hedges, strips himself stark-naked (circumminxit uestimenta sua), and in a flash a huge wolf leaps with a fierce howl into the depths of the wood. Bathed in a cold sweat, Niceros, dazed and confounded, makes his way to the villa of the lady, who greets him with the tale of a wolf which has attacked the farm and torn the sheep, but it was driven off by a servant who armed with a pike dealt the animal a sharp thrust. At dawn, when the sun has fully risen, Niceros ventures back to town, and he shudders to notice a pool of blood in the place where the clothes lay by the wayside. On reaching home he finds the soldier in bed and a surgeon dressing a deep gash in his neck.

The word used by Petronius for a werwolf in this passage is " Uersipellis," one who is able to change his skin. Such an anecdote of lycanthropy is of especial interest, for it shows that the belief not only existed but was implicitly accepted in ancient Rome. In the old legend Lycaon (λυκάων, an animal of the wolf kind), father of Callisto, was turned into a wolf by Jupiter, who was worshipped under the title Lycæus. This points to the primitive cult of a wolf god in Arcadia. Pliny, *Historia Naturalis*, VIII, xxiv, 22, writes : " Homines in lupos uerti, rursumque restitui sibi, falsum esse confidenter existimare debemus. . . . Itaque Agriopas, qui Olympionicas scripsit, quod Arcades Ioui Lycæo humana etiam tum hostia faciebant, immolati pueri exta degustasse, et in lupum se conuertisse : eumdem decimo anno restitutum athleticæ, certasse in pugilatu, uictoremque Olympia reuersam." Pliny has, indeed, several anecdotes of werwolves, and it is obvious that amongst the Arcadian mountains they were shunned and feared. This superstition is, indeed, found in almost all countries, and at every period of the world's history. It is as firmly credited in modern Greece as it was in the Greece of Herodotus and Plato. Esthonia, Montenegro, Hungary, Austria, Germany, Spain, Scandinavia, Iceland, Lapland, Finland, all have an hundred legends of werwolves. In France these monsters were supposed to infest the woods and valleys of Brittany and Burgundy, the Landes, and the mountainous regions of the Côte d'Or and the Cevennes. The loup-garou when detected was sent to the stake. At Dôle in 1573 a certain Gilles Garnier was accused of this offence. Several witnesses swore that in a vineyard near the wood of la Serre he had devoured a little girl of eleven, " qu'il avait tuée et occise tant avec des mains semblans pattes qu'avec ses dents." The indictment, which was drawn up by Henri Camus, doctor of laws and Councillor of the King to the parliament of Dôle, further set forth that Garnier prowled about at night to satisfy his horrid lust, and on one occasion, eight days before the feast of All Saints, he was seen to catch another little girl with his teeth, but three country-folk rescued her, and he escaped. Fifteen days after Hallow-mas he strangled a boy ten years old, stripped him and devoured his thighs and the fleshy part of his legs. He confessed that he had also caught a boy of thirteen in a thicket near the village of Pérouse, and that he had already begun to eat his breast and arms " nonobstant qu'il fust

jour de vendredy," when he was disturbed and fled. Convicted of the "abominable crimes of lycanthropy and
witchcraft," Garnier was burned alive and his ashes scattered
to the wind on 18 January, 1573.

In 1578 the Parliament of Paris was for several days
occupied with the trial of a man named Jacques Rollet or
Roulet. Found guilty of being a loup-garou and of devouring
a little boy he was burned alive in the Place de Grêve.

In the following year a number of werwolves were discovered in the neighbourhood of Melun and sent to the stake.
In 1583 a loup-garou was burned at Orleans, and in 1588
at Riom in Auvergne the wife of a well-known citizen was
convicted of assuming the form of a beast, and executed.
One of the most remarkable cases was that of Jean Garnier
at Bordeaux in 1603. The accused, a lad of fourteen,
described as extraordinarily agile of limb, and most strikingly
handsome with dark, flashing eyes and very sharp white
teeth, gave long and detailed descriptions of the manner in
which he attacked various young children, of whom he had
eaten more than fifty. The court condemned him to death.

On 10 July, 1847, a certain Sergeant Bertrand was tried
before a military tribunal presided over by Colonel Manselon.
For many months the cemeteries in and around Paris had been
the scene of frightful violations, but in no case could the
culprit be traced. Graves were secretly dug up, coffins burst
open, the contents gnawed, nibbled, and scattered over the
ground. The watch on Père la Chaise was doubled, but to
no purpose. At last one night a number of detectives saw a
figure scale the walls of the cemetery where they had been
posted ; they fired, and a trail of blood and torn uniform
proved at least that the marauder was a soldier. Still he
could not be traced, until a grave-digger happened to hear
some sappers of the 74th Regiment say that one of their
comrades had been badly wounded a night or two before.
This was Sergeant Bertrand, who was proved to be the author
of these hideous crimes. He freely confessed his guilt,
alleging that he was driven to it by external powers he could
not resist. He tore up the soil with his nails as a wild beast
scratches the earth. He was unable to describe his sensations,
he only knew he ravened for the dead. After these nocturnal
excursions he generally fell into a deep sleep, when a change

seemed to come over him. The following evening his ghastly
desires would return, and often he passed for a short while
into a kind of trance, during which, as it appeared to him,
he underwent some strange metamorphosis. The court
interrogated him closely, and he informed them that as a
child he had always preferred to human society the company
of wild animals, over whom he possessed a magnetic power.
These obsessions, which were most marked after sunset, had
first manifested themselves when he was quite young, and,
increasing in strength, at last proved irresistible. His comrades gave evidence that amongst them he was most popular,
always showing himself good-natured to a degree, thoroughly
liked, in fact, both by officers and by men. In the end he
was sentenced to a year's imprisonment, and after his release
he immediately left the vicinity, never being heard of again.
Here we have a case of necrophily and lycanthropia, which,
although happily rare, one need not suppose unique, a case
quite sufficient to account for all the old tales of werwolves
and the loup-garou.

With regard to England, Gervase of Tilbury (c. 1150–1220)
in his *Otia Imperialia*[82] writes : " Uidimus enim frequenter
in Anglia per lunationes homines in lupos mutari, quod
hominum genus gerulphos Galli nominant, Angli uero were-
wolf dicunt." (For in England at changes of the moon we
have often seen men transformed into wolves, and these folk
the French call gerulphi, but the English were-wolves.)
Reginald Scot[83] discusses lycanthropy, and Burton[84] has
left us a passage of great interest upon the subject, in connexion with which he quotes Altomari, Weyer, Bodin, Sprenger,
and many other well-reputed authorities. He inclines to
think it a form of lunacy. In a famous scene Webster intro-
duces this horrid circumstance as the madness of Ferdinand :[85]

Pescara.	Pray-thee, what's his disease ?
Doctor.	A very pestilent disease, my lord,
	They call it licanthropia.
Pes.	What's that ?
	I need a dictionary to't.
Doc.	I'll tell you :

In those that are possess'd with't there oreflowes
Such mellencholly humour, they imagine
Themselves to be transformed into woolves,
Steale forth to church-yards in the dead of night,

> And dig dead bodies up : as two nights since
> One met the duke, 'bout midnight in a lane
> Behind St. Markes church, with the leg of a man
> Upon his shoulder ; and he howl'd fearefully :
> Said he was a woolffe : onely the difference
> Was, a woolffes skinne was hairy on the outside,
> His on the in-side : bad them take their swords,
> Rip up his flesh, and trie.

This was perhaps suggested by the following passage from Grimeston's translation (1607) of Simon Goulart's *Thrésor d'histoires admirables et memorables de nostre temps* (1606) :[86] " For there be *Licanthropes* in whom the melancholike humor doth so rule, as they imagine themselves to be transformed into Wolues . . . and all night doe nothing but runne into Churche-yardes, and about graues . . . one of these melancholike *Licanthropes* . . . carried then vpon his shoulders the whole thigh and the legge of a dead man. Beeing carefully looked vnto, hee was cured of this disease."

The reverence shown by the African negro to the fetish leopards, hippopotami, crocodiles, and other animals is closely connected with the belief in the power of *Ngoi, Moloki, N'doshi* or *Uvenwega ;* to wit, that certain possessors of evil spirits have ability to assume the shape of a beast of prey and at will return to the human form. So in Ashangoland the natives fear the wer-leopard, in Arawak the wer-jaguar, and in Malaysia the wer-tiger. No doubt this superstition is largely due to leopard and tiger societies formed by young savages to satisfy their craving for cannibalism. Dressed in skins they steal through the woods at night to attack any solitary pedestrian or an isolated household. After killing their victims they cut off those portions of the body they fancy for their eating and scoring the mutilated corpse with the signia of the society, deep scratches and wounds to imitate the tearing of claws and teeth, they retire to some secret retreat in the heart of the vast forest to devour the tit-bits at leisure.

The second weird story told at Trimalchio's table is related by the host himself. A certain lad dies, and amid the lamentations of his mother and friends is laid out for burial. On a sudden the hideous howling of the banshees (*strigæ*)[87] is heard in the courtyard of the house. A young soldier drawing his sword throws open the door and boldly leaps out, thrusting right and left. A deep groan is heard; staggering back covered with wounds and livid bruises he throws himself swooning upon a couch. They hasten to bar the door again and make it doubly fast. But when the wretched mother approached the bier to give her boy one last kiss they find the body is gone, nothing but a mere mawkin, a poppet stuffed with straw lies there, the hags have carried off the corpse to use the heart and entrails for their sabbat charms. The soldier, a few days after, expires in agony, raving mad. Surely all this might be the unvarnished evidence at a witch-trial in the sixteenth or seventeenth centuries, grimly noted down by Sebastian Michaelis, o.p., by Scipion du Pleix, or Henri Boguet.

Of immense value in the history of classical Witchcraft and of equal value in Latin literature is that superb and exquisite romance, which time has so happily spared to us, the *Metamorphoses* of Apuleius. Perverse and exotic are its pages, and—here for once one may rightly use that much overworked word—truly decadent, carrying the *nouella elocutio*, a thing of rarest beauty, to the highest point of polished perfection. Born about the year 125, Apuleius was of African origin; *semi-Numida* and *semi-Gœtulus* he calls himself. The *Metamorphoses*, his greatest work, was probably written at Rome before he was thirty, soon after he had completed his course of study at Athens. The thread of the main story is, no doubt, borrowed from that Greek tale whence also Lucian took his version, rewriting the original in his own limpid and racy style with all the wit and salt and sceptic wickedness of Voltaire. For him the supernatural was no more true and could be no more true than were the pretty adventures of *La Chatte Blanche* or *Babiole* to the graceful Comtesse d'Aulnoy. Apuleius, however, was evidently attracted by that very quality Lucian despised; the occult element with its infinite possibilities would appeal to him as a professed mystic and something more than a dabbler in necromancy and the astral sciences. " In the *Metamorphoses*," it has been admirably said, " a brooding spirit of magic is over the whole narrative."

To do anything like justice to the romance of Apuleius and to show how every page is steeped in the supernatural would demand a detailed analysis, here out of place. It must be sufficient to touch upon a few episodes. The scene opens in Thessaly, the home of magic, and after the briefest prœmium the traveller Aristomenes tells Lucius his tale. At Hypata Aristomenes has befriended Socrates, and seeks to rescue him from Meroe, " saga et diuina, potens cælum deponere, terram suspendere, fontes durare, montes diluere, manes sublimare, deos infimare,[88] sidera extinguere, Tartarum ipsum inluminare."[89] When midnight strikes the doors of the room where they are lodging fly open and two hideous beldames appear, the one carrying a naked blade, the other a sponge. Whilst his companion lies there quaking with fear, they approach Socrates, who is plunged in a hypnotic trance, and with bitter taunts drive the sword to its hilt through his neck. They catch the spouting blood in a bottle, until one hag closes the wound with the sponge, muttering : " O sea-born sponge beware lest thou cross running water." Presently they vanish, and Aristomenes attempts to leave the accursed spot. The porter, however, refuses to let him go before daybreak, and whilst they are wrangling Socrates awakes to abuse them both for disturbing his repose. In high glee Aristomenes realizes that he has suffered from a vivid nightmare, and presently the two friends cheerily set out on their journey. Nevertheless he cannot forbear to take a keen look at his comrade's neck ; but there is no red mark, no scar, no injury, no trace of a wound. Under a clump of plane trees they stop to breakfast, and Socrates eats with the keen appetite of a man who has walked briskly his eight or ten miles in the clear morning air. Feeling thirsty after the meal, he goes to the waterside and bends over to drink. No sooner do his lips touch the stream than a gaping wound bursts open in his throat, the sponge drops down, and without even a cry he falls dead upon the shelving bank.

When Lucius arrives at Hypata he is the guest of a usurer named Milo, whose wife Pamphile is a notorious witch, " maga primi nominis et omnis carminis sepulchralis magistra " (II, 5). He is warned against her enchantments, and at a supper he hears the adventures of a young student named Thelyphron, who having run through his cash undertakes for a fee to watch all night a body to preserve it against the attack of witches who are wont to tear off the nose, ears, lips, and pieces of the face from corpses to employ them in

the confection of their spells. He is told to watch with
unceasing vigilance since they may enter the room under the
form of dogs, birds, mice, and even flies or smaller insects to
effect their horrid purpose. He does indeed perceive a little
weasel, but this he scares away. In the morning the dead
man is found unmutilated, but it proves that the sorcerers
have deprived the unfortunate guardian of his nose and
ears, deftly fitting wax models in their places.

In this connexion the Rev. John Gaule's comment upon
the practices of Master Matthew Hopkins is not wholly
impertinent : " Having taken the suspected Witch, shee is
placed in the middle of a room upon a stool, or Table, crosse-
legg'd, or in some other uneasie posture, to which if she
submits not, she is then bound with cords ; there is she
watcht and kept without meat or sleep for the space of 24
hours. . . . A little hole is likewise made in the door for the
Impe to come in at ; and lest it might come in some lesse
discernible shape, they that watch are taught to be ever and
anon sweeping the room, and if they see any spiders or flyes,
to kill them. And if they cannot kill them, then they may
be sure they are her Impes."[90] A weasel was a very common
form assumed by witch or familiar. Thus in 1588 an Essex
crone confessed that she nourished three spirits, one a cat,
the second a toad, " the third like a Weasill, which she called
Makeshift. . . . There was one olde mother W. of great T.
which had a spirite like a Weasill."[91]

Whilst Milo's guest, Lucius intrigues with the wanton
Fotis, the serving-maid, who allows him to see her mistress
Pamphile change herself into a bird. In order to complete
this metamorphosis Pamphile anoints herself with ointment,
stripping naked, and smearing herself all over from head to
foot so that she may fly through the air.[92] Burning with
curiosity Lucius begs Fotis to allow him to essay the same
experiment. But the wrong unguent is used, and he is
promptly transformed into an ass, which shape he can only
lose if he eat roses, since this flower alone can dissolve the
magic. During that night the house is burgled, and the
thieves loading the ass with their prey drive him to their
mountain cave. Adventure follows adventure and episode
episode as the picaresque panorama unfolds before our eyes.
Some are of the most exquisite beauty ; some are grossly

obscene ; some are romantic as a canvas of Salvator Rosa, some are realistic in exactest detail as an interior of Gerard Terborch ; some are mere thumb-nail sketches ; some are of considerable length ; some arise directly out of the main narrative ; some are introduced almost accidentally ; all are of such surpassing interest that we feel none to be super- fluous ; there is not a dull page, not a dull line anywhere. The conclusion, the whole of the eleventh book, rises to a strain of rapturous mysticism, where the words often melt into an ecstasy of Platonic loveliness. The prayer of Lucius on the moonlit shore and the vision of the goddess " seculorum progenies initialis, summa numinum, regina manium, prima cælitum, deorum dearumque facies uniformis " (XI, 5), whose feet are swift upon the waves of the sea, whose robe is the light of the stars, whose mantle is as the beauty of nature, at morning, at noontide, and at the setting of the sun, who is all things and in whom all things live, are conceived in a strain of etherial ecstasy, and it was passages such as these which caused Apuleius to be regarded as a mighty magician in his life, and after his death in some sort as a rival of the true God, as Antichrist himself.[93] Not without reason in those dangerous days did the Fathers and early Christian writers look askance at the philosopher of Madaura and his works. " Aut indicauit aut finxit,"[94] shrewdly comments S. Augustine with reference to the *Metamorphoses*, implying that there is something more than a substratum of truth under the most extraordinary adventures. Lactantius regards Apuleius with horror. He is a worthy compeer of Apollonius of Tyana, both avowed enemies of the Cross. He was a sorcerer, of whom wonderful things are related, diabolic crafts. " Mirum quod Apuleium prætermisit, cuius solent et multa et mira memorari."[95]

The *Apologia* (*De Magia*) of Apuleius hardly permits of more than brief mention here. It is a long and elaborate literary amplification of the successful defence he made before Maximus Claudius, the proconsul of Africa, when he was accused of sorcery, of having gained the affections of the widow Pudentilla by unlawful charms, and of having poisoned his stepson Pontianus. The whole speech well repays detailed study. We have the most trifling matters mixed up with charges of the greatest gravity. Apuleius reminds the court that according to many authorities in Persian a magician " magus " means a priest, and that magic is an art dear to the immortal gods. " Nam si, quod ego apud plurimos lego, Persarum lingua magus est, qui nostra sacerdos quod tandem est crimen sacerdotem esse ? . . . auditisne magiam, qui eam temere accusatis, artem esse dis immortalibus acceptam ? "[96] He soon disposes of the suspicion that he had been buying, for magical purposes,[97] rare fish, especially the " ueretillum " and the " uirginal," upon which the prosecutors foolishly attempted an obscene play of words, trying to give infamous hints of clandestine debauchery. Thallus, a boy whom he was supposed to have bewitched, was proved to be an epileptic long before Apuleius had ever seen or heard of him, and of several other lads upon whom, as it was alleged, he had cast the evil eye not one was forthcoming. There was question of a mysterious little image, which Apuleius had ordered to be secretly made of the costliest wood for purposes of goetic ritual ; it was said to be in the form of a carious skeleton, gaunt and loathly. This he worshipped in a private chapel, calling it βασιλεύς, the King.[98] The sculptor, Cornelius Saturninus, had already been summoned and was in court ; the figure was produced and shown to be Hermes, nude and lovely in the bloom of immortal youth. From beneath his petasus curled the crisped locks, a smile was on his lips, laughter in his eyes. In fine, it seems as though from first to last Apuleius was secure of the issue ; he merely played with his adversaries, laughed at his accusers, covered them with ridicule, and availed himself to the utmost of this golden opportunity to display all the flowers of his ornate and embroidered rhetoric.

That Apuleius should have been accounted a magician is hardly surprising, but that Vergil should be regarded by the mediæval imagination as an adept in occultism is indeed an extraordinary circumstance. Yet it is not difficult to appreciate how this came about in the course of time. His undisputed supremacy in Latin literature and the mysticism of his greatest lines (VIth Æneid) soon spread the idea of a cryptic meaning in his verses, an idea which is assuredly not without foundation. Minucius Felix, Lactantius, S. Augustine, and not a few early fathers distinctly separate Vergil from all other Latin authors. Messianic prophecy was read into the Fourth Eclogue ; Vergil and the Sibyl were actually regarded as witnesses to a coming Messiah along with the Prophets of the Old Testament and the Saints of the Old Dispensation. The piety and pity for Vergil regarded him as a gentle soul who had barely missed the salvation offered by Christ. Had not S. Paul visited his tomb at Naples ? And upon the Feast of the Apostle year by year the Canons of the church of San Paolo in Mantua in the sequence at Holy Mass sang :[99]

> Ad Maronis mausoleum
> Ductus fudit super eum
>   Piæ rorum lacrymæ ;
> Quem te, inquit, reddidissem
> Si te uinum inuenissem
>   Pœtarum maxime !

Statius owed his conversion to reading the Fourth Eclogue :[100] the martyr Secundianus, venerated at Toscanella, is said to have embraced Christianity after its perusal. It was on the strength of this poem that Vergil's likeness was set among the carven seers in the Cathedral of Zamora ; it was on the strength of this poem that in the Cathedrals of Limoges and Rheims the Christmas appeal was made : " O Maro, prophet of the Gentiles, bear thou thy witness unto Christ." " In every age of Christianity," continues Mr. Myers, " from S. Augustine to Abelard, from the Christmas sermon of Pope Innocent III to the *Prælectiones Academicæ* of the late Mr. Keble, divines and fathers of the Church have asserted the inspiration of this marvellous poem." The Fourth Eclogue, in truth, formed a link between the old faith and the new.

There is also the story of S. Cadoc[101] who used to make his scholars learn Vergil by heart ; and one day whilst walking, his *Æneid* under his arm, with his friend and companion S. Gildas[102] upon the seashore at Llancarvon, the holy abbot began to weep at the thought that the poet, whom he loved so much, might perhaps never attain to the bliss of Heaven. At the moment when S. Gildas sternly reprimanded him for his " perhaps," saying that assuredly Vergil would in nowise find entrance into the kingdom of God's elect, a sudden gust of wind tossed S. Cadoc's book into the sea. " If that book return to thee," said S. Gildas,

" then will I believe that Vergil may be saved." But
S. Cadoc, who was deeply moved, withdrew to his cell, and
throwing himself upon his knees before the Crucifix, prayed,
" Lord Jesus, Thou didst die for all. I will not eat a mouthful
of bread nor drink a drop of water, until I know truly what
fate God has allotted to one who sang upon earth as the
Angels sing before His throne." And as he cried to God
a clear sweet voice said, but very softly : " Pray for me.
Pray for me. Never be weary of praying. I shall yet sing
eternally the mercy of the Lord." The next morning a
fisherman brought the abbot a mighty salmon he had taken,
and when they opened the fish they found therein, unharmed,
the book which the breeze had snatched from the Saint's
hands.

Already under the Roman empire it was common to peer
into the future and discover the secrets of fate by that peculiar
mode of divination known as the " Sortes Uergilianæ," that
is to say by opening the poems at random to find some omen
or message. There is a story that when Charles I consulted
a Vergil in the Bodleian Library at Oxford he lighted upon
the passage in the Fourth Book of the *Æneid*, which
commences (615–20) :

> at bello audacis populi uexatus et armis,
> finibus extorris . . .

Throughout the ages this strange invocation has been
addressed to Homer, Vergil, and the Bible alone, and it is
a singular illustration of the mysterious spell exercised by
the Roman poet's name that he should have kept his place
side by side with the Bible itself as an oracle of destiny.

But common tradition also represented Vergil as a wizard,
a past master of the black art. Professor Comparetti has
shown that this legend first grew out of popular Neapolitan
folklore, although curiously enough the earliest literary
accounts are not Italian.[103] The first writer to mention it is
John of Salisbury, in his *Polycraticon de Nugis Curialium et
Uestigiis Philosophorum* (1156), who describes Vergil as
fashioning for Marcellus a magic fly which would destroy all
other insects. In the letters of Conrad of Querfurt, after
wards Bishop of Hildesheim, the representative at Naples
of the Emperor Henry VI, many more details are given, the

talismans and charms wrought by Vergil are described, such as the statue of an archer whose arrow pointing to Vesuvius prevented the eruption of that mountain. These stories with many fantastic accretions occur again in the Benedictine Alexander Neckam's *De Naturis Rerum* (*c.* 1200), in the *Otia Imperialia* (1210–14), and in the French poem *Image du Monde* (1245), in which latter we first read of the famous brazen head. In the rhymed *Weltbuch* of Johann Enenkel of Vienna (1250) Vergil is represented as having found the Devil imprisoned in a glass bottle and as only releasing him when he had learned all magic. Here also occurs the extremely popular story of his assignation with a Roman lady, who fools him at the tryst, and exposes him to public ridicule by leaving him hanging half up to her window in a basket. This foolish jape was even carved on the misereres of churches. The *Roman de Cleomandes* of Adenés li Rois (*c.* 1290) first mentions Vergil's famous figure holding the mirror which showed at Rome if treason were hatching anywhere—the *Saluacio Romœ.* All the old fables are related in the French romance of the *Renard Countrefait* (*c.* 1319), whilst the German fourteenth-century poems *Reinfrit von Braunschweig* and the *Wartburg-knig* enlarge upon his compacts with the Devil in great detail. The prose *Cronica di Partenope* of Bartolomeo Caracciolo (1382) seems to be the first Italian attempt to weave together the Vergilian legends. In the *Process of the Seven Sages* (1330) the ninth tale relates the " nigromancie " of Vergil at Rome, and the same anecdotes reappear in the *Gesta Romanorum* (No. 27). Later stages of the legend are seen in *Le Myrem des Histors* written at Liege by Jean d'Outremeuse in the fourteenth century ; in the English *Lyfe of Virgilius* (1510) ; its French version, the *Faicts Merveilleux ;* and in the Spanish romance of *Virgilius* (1550).

According to the *Faicts* Vergil carried off the beautiful daughter of the Soldan of Babylon, baffled her father by sorcery, built Naples, and established a flourishing school of magic there. During the sixteenth century the legend was immensely relished by the vulgar, and we meet with such productions as a black-letter volume with the title *This boke treateth of the lyfe of Virgil, and of his death, and many other marvayles that he did in his lyfe-time by witchecrafte and negromancy, through the develles of hell.*

It is worth remark that even Horace is said to have been reputed a benevolent magician by the peasants in the neighbourhood of Palestrina.[104]

Pliny in the opening chapters of Book XXX ("Medicinæ ex animalibus per morbos digestæ") of his *Historia Naturalis* discussed magic more fully, perhaps, than any other ancient writer, only to decide that all occultism is imposture, "fraudulentissima artium." That it is so universally believed and practised is, he says, not in the least surprising, since it satisfies three imperative needs of humanity. First, it is credulously thought to have strange curative powers and to be a kind of potent medicine ; secondly, by the allurements and fascinating hopes of the future which it holds out it ministers to man's sickly craving for the supernatural, and adds "uires religionis, ad quas maxime etiamnum caligat humanum genus." Thirdly, by means of astrology it professes to discern what is to come, and is greedily embraced by those who wish to know their destiny and the luck which the years may bring. Pliny considers that Zoroaster was the first magician, and so that magic is of Persian origin. His disciple Azonaces handed on the tradition. The philosopher does not forget to point out that the *Iliad* has no reference to magic, whilst the *Odyssey* contains many allusions to Witchcraft ; Proteus, and the song of the Sirens, Circe, and the evocation of the dead. He suggests that Orpheus may have carried the superstition into Thessaly. Thence he passes on to history, to Osthanes, the wizard who accompanied Xerxes ; Pythagoras ; Empedocles ; Democritus ; Moses ; Jannes the Egyptian ;[105] and a second Osthanes who lived in the days of Alexander the Great.

The evidence of the Twelve Tables as to indigenous magic in Italy is not overlooked : "Exstant certe et apud Italas gentes uestigia [magices] in duodecim tabulis nostris." During the consulship of Cnaeus Cornelius Lentulus and Publius Licinius Crassus a law was passed "ne homo immolaretur."

But in spite of Pliny's scepticism his book is a regular storehouse of charms and magic recipes. Thus, if you have gout rub the limb with oil in which have been distilled the intestines of frogs and a dead toad burned to ashes. Or apply the Aplysia depilans to the affected part (XXXII, 26). If you have a fever, " wear as an amulet the carcass of a frog, minus the claws and wrapped in a piece of russet-coloured cloth " and you will be cured (*ibid.* 28). The liver of a dolphin will be found efficacious if there are violent symptoms, or any convulsion.

Under the early emperors " malefici " and " mathematici " were repeatedly banned, and from time to time there were sporadically severe prosecutions, but even the Cæsars themselves dabbled in magic all the while. Augustus, although he made a huge bonfire of all the grimoires in Rome,[106] was the most superstitious of men : " Whilst he was living in retirement at Apollonia in company with Agrippa he consulted a famous fortune-teller named Theogenes, who upon casting his horoscope instantly knelt before him and hailed him as emperor."

Signs and omens he regarded as infallible, and he always paid particular attention to dreams, often allowing his plans to be regulated by what he conceived to be their signification. He likewise had his lucky and unlucky days, and nothing would induce him to settle any important business or commence an undertaking on one of the latter. Livia, also, was largely guided by the advice of astrologers and diviners. Before the birth of Tiberius she employed every known mode of ascertaining the future of her child, amongst other things taking an egg from a hen that was sitting and keeping it warm in her hands and those of her maids by turns until a fine young cockerel with a large comb was hatched. When she was brought to bed the baby was at once carried to Scribonius, a famous Chaldean, who prophesied that one day the highest honours awaited him. Tiberius forbad persons to consult fortune-tellers or occultists alone without a witness.[107] But the emperor himself, although at one time he banished all public professors of astrology from Rome,[108] kept a certain Thrasyllus in constant attendance, and so great was the influence of this adept that, Suetonius says, he often checked the emperor's cruelties and persuaded him to pardon many whom he had condemned. Claudius would not repeal the decree of banishment, but even reinforced it with a further statute, " senatus consultum atrox et irritum."[109]

Under Nero Rome again swarmed with occultists of every kind, and although he repeatedly declared he had no faith in anything of the sort,[110] he anxiously consulted an astrologer named Babilus with regard to the appearance of a blazing comet, and when this man announced that such an omen must be expiated by noble blood, without hesitation he butchered half the aristocracy of the city.[111] At the same time Musonius, a Babylonian, was imprisoned on a charge of necromancy,[112] probably because he was suspected of being in the employ of the emperor's enemies. Tacitus tells us that the house of Poppæa was always thronged with packs of astrologers, whom she consulted at every turn, and that one of these, an Egyptian, Ptolemy, predicted to Otho, about the time of his Spanish expedition, that he would return to Rome as Cæsar.[113] It is certain that Otho in his short reign of ninety-five days consorted with magicians and afforded them every encouragement to exercise their arts. Vitellius, however, gave them short shrift ; there was, in fact, no class of persons whom he more heartily detested, and if they were accused before him he sent them to death without even a pretence of trial or justice. Immediately upon his arrival in Rome he had issued a proclamation ordering all astrologers to leave the city by the first of October, and during the night a mysterious bill was posted in prominent places up and down the streets, which ran : " Notice. The Chaldæans decree that on the said day of the said month Vitellius Germanicus shall be no more." This drove the emperor to madness, and he wreaked his vengeance upon all who fell into his clutches. Yet gossip said that he had been guilty of his mother's death by withholding sustenance when she was seriously ill, since long before a German witch had prophesied that if he survived his mother he would reign for many years in peace and prosperity.[114] Vespasian enforced the sentence of banishment promulgated by his predecessor, although retaining a certain Barbillus, a fortune-teller, always about his person.[115] Under Titus those who ventured to return began to be openly tolerated, whilst under Domitian they were royally encouraged.

A famous passage in the Sixth Satire of Juvenal gives a realistic and striking picture of the superstitions of Rome at this period. The lady is at her toilet, she is in haste having an assignation at the temple of Isis, and half a dozen maids are busy tiring her head. An ancient matron gravely directs and approves the anxious operation whilst curl is deftly built upon curl, and the whole attendance watch in breathless suspense as though their mistress' very life were at stake. A thundering knock at the door interrupts so serious a business. With haughty stride a tall priest of Cybele enters. Forgetful of her coiffure the lady leaps to her feet, and with clasped hands seems to hang upon his lips. Yes; he has consulted the goddess, but the omens alas ! are not altogether favourable ; there will be sickness early in September, she must avoid the autumn winds ; but there is a way, he can find a way. If she will present an hundred eggs, and also bestow some of her garments, the murrey-coloured robe will serve, he will charm the disease so that it will pass into the dress and she will clean escape the danger. Were he to bid her break the ice that coats Tiber in mid-winter and dip thrice into the shivering water at dawn, were he to bid her crawl on her tender hands and knees round the Campus Martius, or journey to Egypt to bring back a libation of hallowed lymph from the Nile at distant Meroe, all this would she do, for by the mouth of that swarthy eunuch clad in fair white linen with the nodding tiara upon his head speaks Isis herself, mystic Isis commands. Presently there creeps in cringing and courtesying a humble Jewess whose sweaty palm is crossed with a silver coin, and whose garlic breath whispers promises of luck and fortune. Or the Armenian soothsayer must be visited, but very secretly. He will deftly open a dove or a chicken with his knife and peering into the quivering entrails read whether young Postumus be false or true. Would you learn more and can you pay well, a child may be sacrificed ; it is the surer way, but it is dangerous, for the seers have been known to blackmail their wealthy clients. Best of all, by heavy fees a Chaldæan may be won to read the stars, but he must be one who has suffered for his magic skill, who was imprisoned under Nero and narrowly 'scaped death under Vitellius. He will tell you to a day how long your old mother will live, if your husband is likely to last, if that rich uncle will go off this winter, and perchance—who knows ?—the cunning man may help you with a sleepy medicine.

Lucian, with his flippant yet caustic mockery, in his *Menippus* ridicules the astrologers, sons of Zoroaster ; and

more than once takes occasion to flout the charlatans and
magic quacks with their brew of love philtres, their incantations to injure an enemy, spells to discover hidden treasure,
their talismans, their periapts, their amulets and trumpery,
but his sarcasm and laughter fell upon deaf ears. The belief
in magic was too fascinating, it had its roots too deep in the
cravings and curiosity of human nature to fall before a jest.

And soon, moreover, the occult was to take a terrible and
a darker shade. No doubt, as is hinted from time to time,
human sacrifices had been offered in remote and barbaric
districts, even in Rome itself, under conditions of inviolable
secrecy or when some crueller tyrant had brief but bloody
sway, but we find that now the human sacrifice is coming to
be regarded as the quintessence of divination, the cream of
the goetic art, a bribe whereby alone the true decrees of fate
can be wrested from the lips of dim shadowy powers. The
decadent and weary Hadrian sat upon the Imperial throne,
an unquiet dreamer of strange dreams, who in the midst of
conquests, restless travelling to and fro, and grave state-
cares, was deeply influenced by the mysterious and sym-
bolical creeds of a dimly apprehended East, and greatly
desired to see that neo-Hellenism which was already moulding
the fantastic imaginations of the Alexandrian Platonists.
Such an æsthete would undoubtedly be addicted to every
superstition, and all antiquity agreed about this trait in his
character. " In summa familiaritate," wrote Spartianus,
" Epictetum et Heliodorum philosophos, et (ne nominatim de
omnibus dicam) grammaticos, rhetores, musicos, geometros,
pictores, astrologos, habuit : præ ceteris (ut multi asserunt)
eminente Fauorino."[116] Ammianus Marcellinus spoke of
him as " futurorum sciscitationi nimiæ deditum." Tertullian
described him as " curiositatem omnium exploratorem." It
was he who established the exotic cult of Antinous, of which
Dion Cassius, who wrote less than a century after the events
related, and who in compiling Hadrian's life had beneath his
eyes the emperor's own *Commentaria* published under the
name of the freedman Phlegon, gives the following account :
" In Egypt he also built the city named after Antinous. Now
Antinous was a native of Bithynium, a city of Bithynia,
which we call also Claudiopolis. He was Hadrian's favourite,
and died in Egypt : whether by having fallen into the Nile,

as Hadrian writes, or by having been sacrificed as the truth was. For Hadrian, as I have said, was in general overmuch given to superstitious subtleties, and practised all kinds of sorceries and magic arts. At any rate he so honoured Antinous, whether because of the love he felt for him, or because he died voluntarily, since a willing victim was needed for his purpose, that he founded a city in the place where he met this fate, and called it after him, and dedicated statues, or rather images, of him in, so to speak, the whole inhabited world." Aurelius Victor, also, has the following significant phrase : " Others maintain that this sacrifice of Antinous was both pious and religious; for when Hadrian was wishing to prolong his life, and the magicians required a voluntary vicarious victim, they say that, upon the refusal of all others, Antinous offered himself." To discuss at length the mystery of the death of Antinous would be impertinent, more especially as upon a candid inquiry there is surely little mystery but much misunderstanding. I have no doubt at all that Antinous was accidentally drowned, and for this simple and straightforward view there is the authority of Hadrian himself : εἰς τὸν Νεῖλον ἐκπεσὼν are the emperor's words as quoted by Dion. I do not for a moment believe that Hadrian immolated the boy whom he so dearly loved, and, in the pathetic phrase of Spartianus, " quem muliebriter fleuit." The most important point, however, as far as we are immediately concerned is that Hadrian was so notoriously given to the black art that even when his favourite happened to slip from the royal barge to perish beneath the green waves of the Nile popular rumour soon connected the lad's death with some horrid ceremony of necromantic lore. Dion, it is true, uses the word ἱερουργηθεὶς and seems inclined to believe that Antinous fell a victim to some act of divination, whilst Aurelius Victor holds the same view in a modified form. Yet their evidence may be largely discounted in this particular. For Dion has come down to us merely in fragments and in the careless epitome of John Xiphilinos of Trapezus, a Byzantine Basilian, whose abridgement allowed of any and every kind of interpolation and abuse. Aurelius Victor (*fl.* A.D. 360) compiled his history at too distant a date to be of authoritative value, and the integrity of his work, moreover, has been gravely questioned by scholars. It is only fair to add that by a law of Hadrian, human sacrifices, ἀνθρωποθυσίαι, were most strictly forbidden throughout the Roman empire, as Porphyry tells us.

The insane Commodus (A.D. 180–92), who had himself initiated in the rites of Mithra, was deterred by no scruples, and drunk with the omnipotence of his own assumed divinity, he ordered that youths, and those not the least comely, should be selected as victims for his altars. " Sacra Mithriaca homicidio uero polluit," says Lampridius.[117] These abominations were largely practised for the sake of *extispicium*, an examination of human entrails for the sake of divining the future.

M. Didius Salvius Julianus, who bought the Roman empire of the prætorian guards, when it was put up to sale after the death of Pertinax (A.D. 193), but who only reigned two months from 28 March to 1 June, being assassinated by the soldiers, was excessively given to magic, and resorted to the same hideous sorceries.

" Julianus was also given to a particular kind of madness, the consultation of magicians before he undertook any business and the conduct of affairs under their direction, since hereby he imagined that he could either assuage the dislike the people bore him or else curb the violence of the soldiery. For his satellites were wont to offer in sacrifice victims clean contrary to any Roman custom, they also made trial of foreign spells and incantations, and dabbled in that kind of sorcery called Katoptromancy, which is to say that boys, when they have been blindfold for a while and certain runes recited over them, see the future in a mirror. Thus a boy is said to have seen the murder of Julianus and the accession of Severus."[118]

Caracalla, a sadist, whose reign (A.D. 211–17) drenched Rome in blood, continued the same horrible practices. Lampridius in his life of Heliogabalus relates how that Cæsar impurissimus was in the habit of slaying handsome and noble youths : " Cædit et humanas hostias lectis ad hoc pueris nobilibus et decoris per omnem Italiam patrimis et matrimis, credo ut maior esset utrique parenti dolor. Omne denique magorum genus aderat illi operabaturque quotidie, hortante illo et gratias diis agente quod amicos eorum inuenisset,[119] quum inspiceret exta puerilia, et excuteret[120] hostias ad ritum gentilem suum."[121] (He also slew human victims, searching throughout all Italy for the comeliest youths of high rank whose fathers and mothers were yet alive, in order (as I believe) that he might the more grieve these wretched parents. He kept swarms of sorcerers of every kind daily at his side and constantly employed their services, encouraging them in their dark crafts and often giving thanks to the gods, inasmuch, as he said, he had made friends of the friends of heaven, since he was so entirely devoted to the inspection of the entrails of human victims for purposes of divination and was wont to offer.)

Maxentius (A.D. 306–12) is credited with the same loathly mania ; νεογνῶν σπλαγχνα βρέφων διερευνομένου, are the words of Eusebius, and there can be no doubt that human sacrifices were, in blind obedience to the soothsayers and magicians, not infrequently offered by the apostate Julian (A.D. 361–3). The Byzantine emperor Constantine V, Copronymus (741–75), whose life was as filthy as his name, and whose reign is one monotonous chronicle of persecution and blood, although utterly void of religion was nevertheless addicted to necromancy and the foulest goetic superstitions. Whilst seemingly little better than an atheist, in secret he practised conjurations and ceremonial magic, and was covertly notorious as given to human sacrifices, immolating his tender victims with prolonged and most exquisite tortures.[122] Despots, for ever trembling for their lives, half-maddened by their debaucheries and cruelties, in their corroding anxiety to read the book of fate and secure their own safety have stopped at no crime to be assured of length of years and unshaken power. The *extispicium* was not unknown to princes of later centuries, to Ezzelino da Romano, Sigismondo Malatesta of Rimini, Pier Luigi Farnese, and this is certainly the true explanation of the mysterious murder of the beautiful Astorre Manfredi by Cesare Borgia in Hadrian's Mausoleum.[123] Perhaps the most striking instance of this monstrous crime is met with in Gilles de Rais, who is known systematically to have murdered several hundred children of both sexes,[124] victims of his diabolical lust, for purposes of magic. During the outbreak of sorcery (1679–82) at Paris under Louis XIV there are innumerable cases of children, generally of a tender age, being sacrificed at the blasphemy of the Messe Noire.

The abbé Guibourg, the abbé Lemaignan, the abbé Cotton, and several other priests, concerned in these foul mysteries, confessed to having killed infants during the clandestine liturgy. In 1650 at Bologna two renegade religious, two loose women and their two gallants were prosecuted for profaning the Blessed Sacrament by giving It to a goat and to a goose, and also for the slaughter of three children from whose entrails they endeavoured to read the future, thereafter distilling them in an alembic to confect a charm. Pope Innocent X was so horrified at the confessions that he directed the Roman Inquisition specially to inquire into the case.[125] In December, 1924, Fritz Haarmann, the " Hanover Vampire," was condemned to death at Berlin for twenty-four murders, seven-and-twenty being charged against him. It was believed that he was guilty of at least fifty in all. The victims were invariably young fellows between twelve and eighteen years of age, and Haarmann alleged that he attacked them whilst in a state of trance. The full details could not be generally reported, but it seems most probable that we here have a similar case to that of Gilles de Rais. Some hideous belief impelled this fiend to commit these atrocious deeds. I suggest that Haarmann and his young confederate Hans Granz, whose sentence of death was commuted to twelve years' penal servitude, were Satanists. Possibly it is not without significance that in December, 1919, the authorities broke up a gang of devil worshippers at Berlin. A numerous gathering was surprised at midnight whilst their orgies were being celebrated at the Café Kerkau. After a feeble resistance the police, who were more than a hundred strong, drew their revolvers and the whole assembly surrendered. There were present two hundred men and two hundred and fifty women, of whom the majority were nude, others being scantily draped in the most fantastic garments. All were conveyed to prison in covered motor-lorries and it is said that several army officers were among the prisoners.[126]

That, even to-day, the foul superstition of human sacrifice is sometimes attempted an extraordinary story, which comes from New York, conclusively shows. On Sunday, 17 January, 1926, the Central News (*Westminster Gazette*, 18 January) reported :

" Police, attracted by the screams of a woman, broke into

a house in Park Street, Brooklyn, yesterday, just in time to save the life of a Mrs. Parello, who was being ' sacrificed ' by a man named Joseph Musca and his wife.

"They found in a room, dimly lighted and with heavy curtains drawn across the windows, Mrs. Parello being held in a chair by a man, who was at the same time uttering an unearthly chant and stabbing at the woman with a knife, aided in his incantations and murderous work by the woman.

" In the room was an altar of strange shape and on it a lamp, while round the walls were bones and grotesque objects.

" The two fanatics were executing a ghastly dance and throwing tufts of the victim's torn-out hair on the lamp flame.

" The police seized them and pulled them back from the victim, who was by that time unconscious.

" Mrs. Parello was taken to a hospital, and is in a serious condition.   Musca and his wife are under mental examination."

It would indeed be surprising if magic had not flourished throughout the empire with the direct encouragement of Cæsars such as Commodus, Caracalla, and Heliogabalus. Even the stoical Marcus Aurelius Antoninus, " the Philosopher," favoured astrologers, resorted to them for counsel, and followed their injunctions.   For when the Empress Faustina, having fallen ill of a languishing complaint which the doctors were unable to diagnose or cure, confessed to him that she was pining for love of a certain handsome gladiator upon whom she had cast her lustful eyes, and must assuredly expire unless he were admitted to her bed, the anxious wittol hastened to the Chaldæans, since they were famous for their skill in compounding philtres to assuage amorous desire.   A remedy was promptly prescribed.   The unfortunate athlete was to be slain, and the empress was directed to bathe her body in his reeking blood.   This was accordingly done, and she forthwith declared herself cured of her passion.[127]   There can be no more striking example of the implicit trust which was put in the power of the astrologers than that at their mere word such a savage barbarity should have been enacted without scruple or hesitation and that Faustina should have agreed to so loathsome a remedy.   It is possible, of course, that Capitolinus has not told us the whole tale.   It may be the story of

Phædra and Hippolitus once more, of Joseph and Potiphar's wife, of Circe and Encolpius, and the empress was, perhaps, avenging herself for the gladiator's disdain and rejection of her favours. In any case the incident clearly shows that even a spirit such as that of Marcus Aurelius, whom Niebuhr called the noblest character of his time, could be swayed by the most degrading and horrible superstition.

Even to-day human sacrifice is not unknown, and Sir Harcourt Butler, the Governor of Burma (according to the *Daily Express*, 25 March, 1925), reports that it prevails among the wild tribes of the Naga Hills on the borderland of Assam, a people nominally under the British flag. The Nagas, even as the primitive Shans and the Singphos, who roam the dense jungles of Hukawng Valley, worship dark and terrible deities whom in times of scarcity or during an epidemic of disease of any kind they find it necessary to propitiate. When simple offerings of fruit, grain, or goat's flesh fail to move their gods, the Nagas send forth the " head-hunters " to make a human capture.

Stern efforts have been made to stamp out these hideous rites. As lately as 1917 an average of twenty boys and thirty girls were kidnapped annually from Assam and sacrificed.

Many other border tribes are infected by similar beliefs. It is not long since a Khasi cowherd of Wahumar, in the Shillong district, was tried for making a human sacrifice to a local hill deity in the belief that the rite would bring him prosperity. Orissa, on the Bay of Bengal, has been the scene of many such sacrifices, but they have been conducted with so much secrecy that the offenders have rarely been traced. At Dacca not long ago one man and thirteen women were sacrificed to appease a local deity who had smitten a village with cholera.

In spite of sternest prohibition and every precaution similar rites continue to be common almost all over Africa. Three years ago, in 1923, six chiefs of the Mashonas of the Mount Darwen district of Rhodesia were sentenced to death for sacrificing a girl who lived in a cave in the hills, in order to bring to an end a protracted drought. They urged in their defence that the day after the sacrifice abundant rain actually fell.

Instances have even occurred in Europe. In September,

1920, the Madrid authorities investigated the sacrifice of a young shepherdess in the province of Estremadura, and in October, 1921, at Hoog Soeren, in Central Holland, a religious fanatic buried two children alive in order that " the village might be saved from the wrath to come." Fortunately, the act was discovered, and the children were rescued.

Septimius Severus (193–211) fiercely attacked the Chaldæans and fortune-tellers, condemning many to death as well as executing those who had consulted them. But this was not so much that he hated occultism, as that he feared conspiracies against his power, and was suspicious lest pertinent questions should be asked and omens observed with regard to the length of his reign. " Multos etiam quasi Chaldæos aut uates de sua salute consuluissent, interemit," says Spartianus in his life of that emperor (15). And Tertullian in his *Apology* writes : " Eadem officia dependunt et qui astrologos et haruspices et augures et magos de Cæsarum capite consultant."

Less than a quarter of a century later, Alexander Severus was not only tolerating astrologers and magicians, but even helping them with gifts of money and, in some cases at least, with regular salaries for their services. " Rhetoribus, grammaticis, medicis, haruspicibus, mathematicis, mechanicis, architectis, salaria instituit."[128] Nevertheless we find the two great jurists, Ulpian, the chief adviser of the emperor, scriniorum magister, and Julius Paulus, a prominent member of the Consilium, præfectus prætorio, both formally and officially condemning the use of grimoires or books of spells, " libros improbatæ lectionis " is the phrase of Paulus.[129] And Ulpian lays down that the possession of such volumes is in itself illegal. If such are found in any house the owner is to be mulcted in a heavy fine and sent into exile ; if he be of low estate or a slave he is to be punished with death. The books themselves are to be publicly burned. The suspicion was always present that those who consulted wizards might be aiming at the prince's life, and Paulus rules : " Qui de salute principis, uel de summa reipublicæ mathematicos, hariolos, haruspices, uaticinatores, consulit, cum eo qui responderit, capite punitur."[130]

Gordian the Elder (A.D. 238) who is always accounted an excellent prince, was wont to consult astrologers on affairs of moment, although sometimes he does not seem to have taken their predictions very seriously. " When Gordian the Elder once consulted an astrologer about the birth of his son, it is said that the wise man answered ' The child will be the son of an Emperor, and himself an Emperor.' The story goes that Gordian laughed heartily, but the astrologer showed him a bright star which was then high in the heavens, and appealed to certain old books to prove that he was speaking the truth. Moreover with that unflinching confidence which is born of absolute conviction he foretold both the day and manner of their deaths to the elder as well as to the younger, nay, he named the very places where they would severally end their lives."[131]

Aurelian (A.D. 270), immediately after his election as emperor by the legions on the Danube, secretly sought certain Gaulish sybils, Druidesses, to inquire of them whether the throne would remain in his family, to which they replied that in the whole history of Rome there should be no names nobler than those of his house. A prophecy which the courtly, not to say sycophantic, historian Flavius Vopiscus sees fulfilled in Constantine. In his reign the Marcomanni, a powerful German tribe, swiftly debouched upon Italy, and the Senate in obedience to the emperor's command at once ordered the Sibylline Books to be examined, in whose cryptic pages they found that if sacrifices were offered in certain spots the invaders would be checked and overcome, and, says Vopiscus, " ita barbaris restiterunt, quos omnes Aurelianus carptim uagantes occidit."[132] The speech made on that occasion, 9 January, by Fulvius Sabinus, the Prætor Urbanus, has been preserved and commences thus :

" We commend to your attention, O Conscript Fathers, the advice of the Pontifical College and the letters of Cæsar Aurelian, wherein he gives orders that the Sibylline Books be examined since herein under divine guidance may be ascertained some prospect of concluding hostilities."[133]

When appointing his officer Saturninus commander of the Eastern frontier Aurelian with great contempt scarified the Egyptians as " uiri uentosi, furibundi, iactantes, iniuriosi, atque adeo uani, liberi, nouarum rerum usque ad cantilenas publicas cupientes, uersificatores, epigrammatarii, mathematici, haruspices, medici."[134]

It would seem that throughout these centuries there were recognized by the Romans two forms of occultism, which we may roughly define as " white magic " and " black magic," although the line of demarcation between the two was often at vanishing point. White magic was, generally speaking, allowed and often encouraged ; black magic, of which the chief exponents were the " Mathematici," was forbidden and condemned,[135] save, indeed, during the reign of an Augustus such as Heliogabalus, when all cults, pure and impure alike, were poured into the Eternal City to froth and spume there, to mix or antagonize at will. Black magic, indeed, is condemned in trenchant terms by Diocletian (A.D. 284–305) : " Artem geometriæ discere atque exercere publice interest, ars autem mathematica damnabilis interdicta est omnino."[136]

Superstition was never more rife and magic practices of every kind, from the comparatively harmless charm of healing to the foulest infamy of perverted lust and human sacrifice, were never more shamelessly and impudently pursued than in the decadent and debauched days of the later Roman empire, when the old civilization, corrupt to the core, for all its glamour and beauty, was crumbling into universal ruin. Men's bodies were old and tired with insatiate venery ; their minds were dull and heavy with agnostic philosophies and the atheism of despair ; their emotions numb and senseless ; their passions etiolated and fatigued ; hardly could the sight of blood flowing over writhing white limbs lend a fillip to their jaded appetites ; they only lived because to live was less exertion than to die. Small wonder then that they sought hope and interest in something which pointed to, even if it did not promise, other spheres of thought and action than this outworn, outmoded world. Magic was at least an adventure, and if forbidden by the law, why, that gave it an added piquancy when all else was sapless and husked long ago. The abnormal, the fascination of sheer physical dread and repulsion, the black shadows of dissolution and decay, the intangible spiritual atmosphere of unknown fear, all these were an excitement which must be essayed, and gradually the cult of magic absorbed its votaries. Just in the same way do we find to-day that Spiritism often seems the last resource of those who merely crave for some new interest. Without any very definite aim or object, if there is nothing better to do at the moment, they will for the novelty's sake attend a séance, not a little incredulous, not a little scornful at first. And then the neophyte begins to speak of his experiences with some faint warmth, and in a very short time it will be found that he is wholly wrapped up in his new pursuit, he can think and talk of nothing else, Spiritism has become an intoxication, an obsession, more often than not to his moral deterioration, the ruin of his bodily health and happiness.

Under the Roman emperors there were two great influences at work, each of which had in its way an important effect upon magic; the one being ephemeral and the nurse of enchantments, neo-Platonism with the rites of Mithra; the other eternal and the enemy of sorcery, Christianity with the Holy Sacrifice of the Mass.

Neo-Platonism was a system of idealistic and spiritualistic theosophy, deeply tinged with an indeterminate mysticism, which sought to restore the vitality of Greek thought by an essential infusion of Oriental religious conceptions. As the last effort of Hellenic ideals and ideas, it became necessary that in order to combat Christianity the intellectual world should show that paganism was not entirely bankrupt, and therefore the official polytheism of the State had to be reformed and explained by an interpretation which should be acceptable in philosophy. It derives its name from the fact that its first representatives drew their inspiration from Plato's doctrines, although it is now recognized that many of the treatises on which they relied cannot be claimed as genuine. Among the more or less eclectic Platonists who are regarded as forerunners of the neo-Platonic school are Plutarch, Maximus, Apuleius, Ænesidemus, Numeninus. Philo the Jew, who flourished in the middle of the first century, also helped to mould neo-Platonic thought, and it is not improbable that his doctrine of the mediation of the Logos had a direct influence on Plotinus. Ammonius Saccas, a public porter on the quays of Alexandria, who was born of Christian parents but who reverted to paganism, is considered to have been the true founder of the neo-Platonic school. Plotinus (A.D. 205–70) was the first systematic philosopher of neo-Platonism, and other great names are Porphyry (A.D. 233–c. 303), a bitter opponent of Christianity,

Iamblichus, his pupil (*ob. c.* A.D. 330), Proclus (A.D. 410–85), the last distinguished representative of the school, whose disciple Marinus taught Damascius, who was lecturing at Athens when the academies were suppressed by Justinian in 529. Porphyry it is, in particular, who lays great stress upon the importance of theurgic practices. Asceticism is the starting-point on the road to perfection, but as a means of further advancement the neophyte must cultivate self-contemplation, and then proceed by the consultation of oracles, divination, bloodless sacrifices to the superior gods and bloody sacrifices to the daimons or inferior power, in fact by sorcery.

The neo-Platonist had evolved a new mythology. The Supreme Being, God, the One, the Absolute, the Infinite, exceeds all the categories of human thought. But there are beneath him a multitude of supernatural powers, to whom were given the name of δαίμων, who can and do concern themselves with the affairs of men, and with whom men can establish some connexion. These δαίμονες were by the Romans often confounded with the Manes, Lares, and Genii.[137] Some δαίμονες are ἀλεξίκακοι, they protect man and watch over him, they deliver him from trouble (λύσιοι); others delight in blood, murder, and evil (προστρόπαιοι, παλαμναῖοι). Proclus is of the opinion that these wicked genii tempt men to impiety and all kinds of wickedness, and he is right, for they are indeed just devils.

The neo-Platonists, then, conceived a new hierarchy of daimons, who were in truth pagan gods under a philosophical disguise A deity was catalogued as ἀλεξίκακος or προστρόπαιος according to the general point of view from which he had been traditionally regarded, the character of his worship, his attributes and qualities. Thus Porphyry ranges the Egyptian god Serapis amongst the black daimons, since he had come to be considered as the lord of the underworld, of the dead, darkness, mystery, and night, and was to a large extent identified with Hades or Pluto. Already in Porphyry this tendency towards theogony is strongly marked ; in Proclus we find a regular demonology. Neo-Platonism, as might have been expected, soon became superstitious, one could truly say spiritistic, to a degree ; all the old magical ceremonies were preserved, half-forgotten rites rescued from oblivion, the ancient formulæ of divination studied and perpetuated, sacrifices offered anew to the infernal powers, the evocation of spirits and necromancy assiduously practised and warmly recommended. It is true that the more cultured and intellectual neo-Platonists deprecated those sorceries which might be supposed to summon evil influences and malign astral entities to assist the disciple in any criminal action or schemes of vengeance, and they thought that ill effects could be nullified by benevolent charms and incantations ; but none the less it is very certain that frequently this philosophy was embraced and exploited by many who were merely attracted owing to the thaumaturgies, or who hoped to acquire material advantages and the realization of their bad wishes by means of a mastery over spirits, who could be compelled indifferently to execute their commands whether the word was to bless a friend or to bane a foe.

Mithraism, the cult of the ancient Indo-Iranian Sun-god Mithra, entered Europe from Asia Minor, where it had taken root after the conquests of Alexander, and rapidly spread over the whole Roman empire. It seems to have been actually first introduced to the Romans through the wars of Pompey with the Cilician pirates,[138] and during the first and second centuries of the Christian era its influence was continually increased by the legionaries returning home from Eastern service. Special stress was laid by the worshippers upon the idea of fraternity, and some secret bond, with signs and passwords, " signa oris, manus, et sinus," conjoined the members and served to make them known one to another. Of these we know little or nothing, and it is only natural to suppose that such significant gestures and shibboleths would have been safeguarded with the utmost secrecy. There were seven degrees of initiation, the first being " mystes " and the last " pater." These " fathers " conducted the worship, and their chief, who was called " Pater Patrum " or " Pater Patratus," always lived at Rome. The members below the degree of pater called one another brother, and all social distinctions were forgotten in Mithraic unity. It should be remarked that these communities allowed no women to enter their ranks. No woman might be present at or have any knowledge of the mysteries of Mithra. The theosophy of the cult was an elaborate and involved system. Mithra, the friend and saviour of man, was born with the Phrygian cap on his head and a knife in his hand. In some sense he is identified with the Sun, his father or comrade, for he was worshipped as Ἥλιος Μίθρας. The central dogma of Mithraism was his struggle with the bull, whom Mithra pursued, overcame, dragged to his cave, and sacrificed by plunging his steel into its throat. This was said to be symbolic of man's life of labour and effort on earth. The bull, resigning itself to death, was transported to the heavenly spheres. The exact ritual of initiation is unknown, but it included lustration and bathing, branding with a red-hot iron, and above all the taurobolium. This ceremony consisted in the sacrifice of a bull, the blood of the animal being allowed to flow down through a floor riddled with eyelets and holes, so that it streamed in a drenching rain upon the worshippers in the chamber beneath ; which was deemed a purification of sacramental power and efficacy. These mysteries were always performed in caves, of which a large number have been found. There were no less than five at Ostia alone, but they were small and could perhaps hold at most two hundred persons. In the entrance to the cave stood the stone sculpture of Mithra, a handsome curly-headed youth in Phrygian dress and cap, slaying the bull. There were other symbols and paintings which represented the heavens, constellations, zodiacal signs, the seasons, and various grotesque personifications. In its later developments Mithraism borrowed much from Christianity ;[139] Mithra, for example, was a mediator between God and man ; Mithraism celebrated a sacred banquet of bread and wine ; Mithra saved the world by the sacrifice—of a bull ; it is, in truth, hardly possible to conceive a wider gulf than that between the imaginary Mithra taurochtonos[140] and Christ Crucified.

Before the triumph of Christianity the cult of Mithra vanished. It is true that under Julian it had once more a short lease of life, but the laws of Theodosius the Great finally closed its mystic caves. It has been contended that Mithraism was originally a pure and noble form of worship, although it is hard to see how this can ever have been the case, and it is beyond question that it eventually became permeated with theurgic ideas and was not slow to incorporate magical ceremonies and the foul dregs of occultism. There is, I think, more than a suspicion of gross immorality. Human victims were offered in these esoteric assemblies, and it was not the blood of bulls alone that sprinkled the neophyte in his subterranean shrine. Both Theodoret[141] and S. Gregory of Nanzianus[142] accuse Julian of having immolated youths and children during his secret celebrations of the Mithraic rites at Charres. S. Cyprian of Antioch,[143] after his conversion and renunciation of sorcery, confessed that he had taken part in the worship of Mithra. He describes the abominations, which were commonly practised at that time by the wizards and astrologers, who stole small children or enticed boys to their lairs that they might cut them to pieces upon their demoniac altars and make oblation of their blood to the fiends.[144]

It was this goetic Mithraism upon which neo-Platonism, in some of its developments at any rate, relied to combat Christianity.[145] But magic was also beginning to join hands with heresy. Gnosticism, in all its myriad branches, had eagerly absorbed a thousand occult fantasies and interwoven them with the fabric of its own delirious philosophy, further commingled with shreds and scraps of Christian doctrine. So when Witchcraft was under one aspect wellnigh exterminated by the destruction of paganism, it had by this time already been deeply planted in another fertile soil to bear its rank crop of evil in the days that were to come.

By the famous Edict of Milan in A.D. 313, it might have seemed for a while that religious toleration was to prevail and the equality of almost all forms of worship would be allowed. In 319–21, however, a number of laws were passed against astrology and magic which struck hard at the very essentials of paganism. It is true that heathen emperors had, as we have noted, often legislated in the same way, but the edicts of Constantine were different in their interpretation from any statutes which had ever been enacted before. Constantine forbids the diviners or haruspices to enter for the exercise of their art any private house under pain of death. Whoever persuaded a haruspex to break the law should suffer at the stake. Whosoever desired to follow non-Christian usages must do so openly. He was by no means let or forbidden in any way, but he must go in the broad noon to the public altars and sacred places and there perform the ancient rites. " Let no haruspex on any account frequent any house other than his own ; all friendship, of howsoever long a date, with men of this avocation must be repudiated ; the haruspex who frequents the house of another shall die at the stake."[146]

Any sorcerer who attempted by his charms the life of a citizen, or who essayed to tempt a youth or maiden to impurity was to be visited with the severest penalties. " Eorum et scientia punienda et seuerissimis merito legibus uindicanda, qui magicis accincti artibus aut contra salutem hominum moliti, aut pudicos animos ad libidinem deflexisse detegentur " : " The craft of magic is to be penalized and deservedly punished with the utmost rigour of the law. This is to say the science and practice of those who in any way attempt human life or health, or are discovered to have enticed the innocent by their philtres to the allurements of lust. None the less by this statute are in no wise let remedies which may be confected for bodily ailments, or those precautions whereby in country districts the ripe vintage may be in seemly wise protected from showers of rain or the violence of hailstorms ; those traditional invocations are also held to be allowable whereby no man is hurt in person or repute, but which essay to prevent the good gifts of God and the toil of man's hands from injury or harm."[147]

A most important edict, and one which throws considerable light upon the estimation in which sorcerers were held. But Libanius bears witness (*Oratio pro Templis*) that certain forms of divination were still permitted, κατὰ νόμους.

Constantius (337–61), in 353, directed a law against sacrifices at night. Those sacrifices at night which were permitted by Magnentius, are to cease entirely, " henceforth let all such abominations be suppressed."[148] In 357 he absolutely forbad all divination of whatsoever kind. " There shall be no more divination nor curious inquiries, nevermore. Whosoever shall dare disobey this statute shall lose his head by the avenging sword of the executioner."[149] The various kinds of sorcerers were explicitly named : " Let no man consult any haruspex, let no man consult any astrologer : fortune-tellers, augurs, seers, and the whole dark fraternity shall exercise their arts no more. We utterly and entirely suppress all Chaldæans and diviners, who, indeed, on account of their black sciences, are even now commonly regarded as evil-doers and criminal."¹⁵⁰

During the short reign of Julian, 361–3, who, assuming the duties of Pontifex Maximus, commanded all temples to reopen for pagan worship, astrologers, magicians, and soothsayers met with the warmest encouragement from emperor, patrician and plebeian, senator and dame, citizen and good wife, alike, and in a few months they appeared as many as before, nor was the number of their clients one whit diminished. Jovian, his successor, apparently, aimed at a universal toleration, which he reintroduced upon the lines laid down by Constantine in the Milan Edict of 313. In principle he forbad magical sacrifices, but divination was at any rate tacitly permitted, for in the year 363 there were at least two astrologers who enjoyed an immense reputation; a Lydian, Patricius, than whom none was more skilled to read the face of the heavens or cast a horoscope, and Hilary of Phrygia, clairvoyant, psychometrist, and teller of fortunes to every aristocrat and cyprian in Rome.

Under Valentinian I, 364, with whom by his own favour was associated his brother Valens, this state of things soon altered, and the former laws in every article of their severity were put into active operation against professing soothsayers and diviners.

The immediate occasion was the indiscreet carriage and talk of Theodorus, a prominent official of the court, who had been told both by Patricius and Hilary that he should succeed Valens on the throne. In 367 there took place at Antioch a curious anticipation of modern " spirit rapping," when a spirit asked to spell the name of him who should follow Valens was supposed to have rapped out the Greek letters ΘΕΟΔ which begin Theodorus. It is, however, more than probable that this psychic communication meant to indicate Theodosius.

The matter became known and was inquired into, the lives of all concerned were forfeited, and as a result Valens resolved once and for all to exterminate the whole race of occultists and magicians. The sanguinary crusade that followed recalls the worst days of Calvinistic Scotland, the Salem witch-trials, or the zealous prosecutions of Master Matthew Hopkins and his jackal John Stearne. There can be no doubt that many guilty, but more innocent, perished. One old crone was put to death because she was commonly reputed to be able to cure fevers by the recitation of certain magic rhymes and runes ; a youth was condemned because he was caught placing the palms of his hands upon a marble pillar and then laying them upon his breast. Meanwhile he chanted a formula that had been taught him, believing this operation would cure him of some gastric complaint.[151] A certain Palladius was commissioned to see that the laws were enforced, and the informers by whom he was constantly surrounded are said to have bribed servants to secrete parchments upon which were written spells and other similar objects in the houses of wealthy merchants, so that when the official searchers came to examine the premises, these documents and amulets were soon discovered, and no mean blackmail could be safely levied. Large numbers of persons destroyed their books and many other possessions lest some matter for accusation might be traced amongst them. A hideous panic swept through the Eastern world. Each man mistrusted his neighbour, his friends, his relatives, his slaves, those of his own household.

The attack even menaced philosophers and the most distinguished names in literature.[152] Libanius and Iamblichus were charged with having plotted against the emperor's life, and with having attempted to discover his successor by means of that mode of divination known as alectromancy.[153] It is said that the latter poisoned himself rather than face the consequences of so terrible and fatal a charge. Sozomen[154] tells us that many persons who had been wont to wear the fringed cloaks so generally favoured by philosophers, hastily discarded these in dread of their lives, lest they should be accused of sorcery on that account alone. It must be remembered that in spite of his adopted Roman gentile name Valens was a rough and brutal barbarian. He had been born in Pannonia, and at the time of his elevation to the throne was an ignorant pagan. A wild and savage heathen he remained all his life, for although he was baptized by the Arian patriarch of Constantinople, Eudoxius, it was impossible that he should have learned from this source even the elements of Christianity.

The laws of Gratian (367), and Valentinian II (375) who

was never much more than a nominal ruler, again forbid the
uetita sacrificia, the necromantic sacrifices, and this reiterated
prohibition shows that the evil thing still persisted in spite
of continued repression and legislature. Gratian, the first
emperor to refuse the title and insignia of Pontifex Maximus,
further enforced the laws of his predecessors, and pagan
sorcery was soon, as such, to become extinct and wholly to
merge itself in the pest of heresy.

Theodosius (379–95) by an edict of 20 December, 381,
sternly prohibits any nocturnal sacrifice or meetings at night
in old temples, where the Sabbat was secretly celebrated.
Ten years later he commands that all pagan sanctuaries shall
be definitely closed. On 25 May, 385, he had forbidden magic
sacrifices and *extispicium* on pain of an ignominious death.

Let no one defile himself by offering sacrifice, let no one
slay an innocent victim, let no one dare to enter the temples
and venerate those images and pictures which mere mortal
hands have made, lest by so doing he be adjudged a criminal,
accounted guilty by all laws, human and divine. So runs
the law of 391.[155] Honorius (395–423) by a statute of 399
recapitulates the penalties directed against those who offer
unhallowed sacrifices, the pagan altars are to be destroyed,
but the temples or any objects of beauty may remain as
public monuments. Valentinian III (425–55), on the other
hand, directs his laws in all their rigour against the Manichees,[156] declaring them guilty of sacrilege, and forbidding
them to dwell in cities. Only a brief space of five-and-twenty
years more and the imperial line of the empurpled Cæsars,
lords of the known world, was to flicker out in failure and
feebleness. Romulus Augustulus, a lad of fourteen, last
ruler of the Western Roman empire, trembling and fearful
awaited Odoacer at Ravenna, and the Goth was content to
send him to live in rustic retirement upon his estate in
Campania. The old paganism was dead, a thing of the past,
vanished utterly.[157] Witchcraft was no longer the science
of the heathen, but the portion of the heretic.

NOTES TO CHAPTER I

[1] Crates Pergamenus in Hellesponto circa Parium, genus hominum fuisse
tradit, quos Ophiogenes uocat serpentium ictus contactu leuare solitos et
manu imposita uenena extrahere corpori. Uarro etiamnum esse paucos ibi,
quorum saliuæ contra ictus serpentium medeantur. (Crates of Lavinium tells
us that there dwelt in the neighbourhood of Parium on the Propontis [now

Kamares] a certain tribe of men whom he calls Ophiogenes. These were wont to heal the bites of serpents by stroking the place, and to draw out the viperous venom from the bodies of those who had been wounded. Varro, moreover, says that there were folk in those districts who could cure the bite of a snake by their spittle.) *Historia Naturalis*, VII, 2.

[2] Seneca, *Quæstiones Naturalis*, IV, 6.

[3] S. Justin Martyr, *Quæstio a l Orthodoxos*; ascribed by Harnack to Diodorus of Tarsus; by the Constantinople MS. to Theodoret, an unlikely attribution.

[4] Pliny, *Historia Naturalis*, XXVIII, 2.

[5] Apuleius, *De Magia* (XXV), writes : Nam si, quod ego apud plurimos lego, Persarum lingua magus est, qui nostra sacerdos, quod tandem est crimen sacerdotem esse et rite nosse atque scire atque callere leges ceremoniarum, fas sacrorum, ius religionum ? (For if, as I have read in many authors, a magician means, in the language of the Persians, the same thing that the word *Priest* does in ours, what crime can there be, pray, in being a magician ? What is the crime in thoroughly knowing and clearly understanding, and being well versed in the laws of ceremonial, the due order of the sacred ritual, and holy ordinances of the gods ?)

[6] So in Greek fable Lycaon was changed into a wolf ; Alopis became a fox. Cf. Milton's *Comus*, ll. 51–77.

[7] Certe quid non repleuere fabulis Colchis Medea, aliæque, in primis Itala Circe, diis etiam adscripta ? (Are there not in truth a thousand legends of Medea the Colchian witch, and many others, amongst whom one of the most famous is our Italian Circe, a kinswoman of the gods ?) Pliny, *Historia Naturalis*, XXV, 5.

[8] IV, 45.

[9] *Die Homerische Odyssee.*

[10] X, 28, 7. Wilamowitz Moellendorff (*Homerische Untersuchungen*) quite gratuitously casts grave doubt on the veracity of Pausanias, which there is, as a matter of fact, no reason whatsoever to suspect.

[11] Γοητεία δέ καλεῖται ἀπὸ τῶν γόων καί θρήνων. Cedrenus.

[12] Plato, *Leges*, XI.

[13] Apud Eusebium, *Præparatio Euangelica*, V, 10.

[14] audistisne magiam . . . artem esse dis immortalibus acceptam . . . a Zoroastro et Oromazo auctoribus suis nobilem, cælitum antistitam ? "

[15] Healey translation, 1610.

[16] In Homer, Hades " the Unseen " is always a proper name denoting the god Pluto.

[17] So Vergil, *Æneid VI*, 577–9 :

Tum Tartarus ipse
bis patet in præceps tantum tenditque sub umbras,
quantus ad ætherium caeli susceptus Olympum.
(Then Tartarus with sheer descent
Dips neath the ghost-world twice as deep
As towers above earth's continent
The height of heaven's Olympian steep.) Conington.

[18] Preller and Welcker are inclined to believe in a foreign origin.

[19] The lines can scarcely be the composition of the author of the κατάλογος γοναικῶν.

[20] From the fifth century onwards. Euripides, *Phœnissæ*, 108. Παῖ Λατοῦς Ἑκάτα.

[21] An inscription. *Bull. de Corr. Hell.*, 1880, p. 337. Πριάπιον καὶ Ἑκατέου αὐλή. (2nd or 3rd century A.D.)

[22] The genius of Alcamenes finally decided this type.

[23] Although disputed, this still seems the likeliest interpretation.

[24] Aristophanes, *Ranæ*, 293 ; *Ecclesiazusæ*, 1056. The Empusa is Ὀνοσκελίς, Ὀνοκώλη.

[25] Suidas.

[26] *Equites*, 890. Lucian, *Philopseudes*.

[27] Porphyry apud Eusebium, *Præparatio Euangelica*, V, 8.

[28] So Theocritus, II, 58 :

σαύρον τοι τρίψασα κακὸν ποτὸν αὔριον οἰσῶ.

[29] Κατὰ πασῶν αἰρέσεων ἔλεγχος. Some MSS. name Origen as the author of the first book. Photius attributes the work to Caius, a priest of Rome in the third century. Others think that either Tertullian or Novatian may be the author.

[30] The dramatists, Fletcher, The Chances, V ; Mrs. Behn, The Dutch Lover, V ; Congreve, Love for Love, III, and many poets (Paradise Lost, II, 666) have constant reference to this proverbial tradition.

[31] Dionysiaca, XXXVI, 27 seqq.

[32] " Nimis cupidus cognoscendi quæ rara miraque sunt, reputansque me media Thessaliæ loca tenere, quo artis magicæ natius cantamina totius orbis consono ore celebrentur . . . suspensus alioquin et uoto simul et studio curiose singula considerabam." Metamorphoseon, II, 1.

[33] " O wryneck, draw thou him whom I love swiftly to my house."

The wryneck, so called from its cry, whilst the English name comes from the jerky movements of its head. The ancient witches used to bind it to a wheel, which they turned round, believing that they drew men's hearts along with it, and charmed them to obedience. Hence it was much used to recover unfaithful lovers. This operation was called ἕλκειν ἴυγγα ἐπί τινι, to set the magic bird or wheel a-going against some. Xenophon, Memorabilia, III, xi, 17.

[34] Ter cane, ter dictis despue carminibus. Tibullus, I, ii, 56.

[35] Propertius II, iv, 7.

Non hic herba ualet, non hic nocturna Cytæis,
Non Perimedea gramina cocta manu.

The scholiast says that Perimede is the witch whom Homer calls Agamede, the daughter of Augeias, granddaughter of the Sun God, and spouse of Moulios.

Μούλιον αἰχμητήν· γαμβρὸς δ' ἦν Αὐγείαο,
πρεσβυτάτην δὲ θύγατρ' εἶχε ξανθὴν Ἀγαμήδην,
ἣ τόσα φάρμακα ἤδη ὅσα τρέφει εὐρεῖα χθών.

Iliad, XI, 739–41.

[36] Spalding Club Miscellany, I, p. 97.

[37] Ed. Erman, pp. 7 and 8.

[38] He is described as Kher heb, the priestly official who performed the funeral ceremonies. He was always a man of great learning, and generally of high rank.

[39] C. K. Sharp, Witchcraft in Scotland, London, 1884, p. 21.

[40] Second Booke, Chapter V.

[41] Discoverie of Witchcraft, pp. 258–9.

[42] Glanvil, Sadducismus Triumphatus, London, 1681, II, pp. 137–8 and 164.

[43] So in Macbeth, IV, 1, a " Lizard's leg " is thrown into the caldron " For a charm of powerful trouble." In Middleton's The Witch Heccat compounds " lizard's-brain " in a charm.

[44] Licensed by Sir Henry Herbert, 26 April, 1642. First printed with separate title, 1652, in Six New Playes, 8vo, 1653.

[45] Historia Naturalis, VII, 37.

[46] Diogenes Lærtius, Proœmion, 2. Proclus, In Timæum, IV, 285.

[47] All important as Egypt is in the History of Magic, to say that Egypt was the Source of Magic and religion, a thesis propounded by Mr. W. J. Perry in his The Origin of Magic and Religion, London (Methuen and Co.), 1924, is not merely a gross and impossible exaggeration, but unscholarly and uncritical to a degree.

[48] The Greeks used incantations very early. For an example see Pindar, Pythia, IV, 213. This poet lived in the first half of the fifth century before Christ.

[49] " Si autem homo ille Tages fuit quonam modo potuit terra oppressus uidere ? unde porro illa potuit, quæ docebat alios, ipse didicisse ? " De Diuinatione, II, xxiii, 51.

[50] De Diuinatione, II, xxiii, 50.

[51] Ovid derives the name of this festival from the solemnities celebrated by Romulus at the death of Remus, and says that Remuria became Lemuria. *Fasti*, V, 421–2, 451 *sqq.*, and 483 *sqq.*

Ritus erit ueteris nocturna Lemuria sacri :
Inferias tacitis Manibus illa dabunt.

.   .   .   .   .

Romulus obsequitur, lucemque Remuria dixit
Illam, qua positis iusta fenentur auis.
Aspera mutata est in lenem tempore longo
Littera, quæ toto nomine prima fuit.
Mox etiam Lemures animas dixere silentum,
Is uerti sensus, uis ca uocis erat.

(There will be the rites of your ancient ceremonial feast of the Lemures ; this feast will present the offerings to the silent shades. . . . Romulus obeyed, and he called that day on which the prescribed rites are performed in honour of the buried dead " Remuria." The harsh letter, which was the first in the entire name, in lapse of time was changed to one of softer articulation. After-wards they called the ghosts of the silent shades *demures ;* this was the meaning of the word ; this did the expression import.)

[52] Festus, ed. Karl Ottfried Müller, p. 253.

[53] *De Ciuitate Dei*, IX, 11, trans. Healey (1610).

[54] " Lares " was in old Latin " Lases." Etruscan " Lalan," or " Laran."

[55] *Inscriptiones*, J. G. Orelli, No. 1670.

[56] Arnobius, III, 41.

[57] Suetonius, *Augustus*, XXI. Also called " Lares compitalicii," Philargus ad Vergilium. *Georgicon*, II, 381.

[58] Plautus, *Mercator*, V, 11, 24, where Charinus exclaims :

Inuoco
Uos, Lares uiales, ut me bene iuuetis.

[59] Livy, XL, 52.

[60] Tertullian, *De Spectaculis*, V.

[61] Dionysus Halicarnassus, *Antiquitates Romanæ*, V, 54.

[62] Pliny, *Historia Naturalis*, XXIX, xiv, 4.

[63] Pliny writes : " Tuscorum litteræ nouem deos emittere fulmina existi-mant . . . diurna adtribuentes Ioui, nocturna Summano." *Historia Naturalis*, II, liii, 52.

[64] *De Ciuitate Dei*, IV, 23.

[65] *Fasti*, VI, 731–2.

[66] II, 161.

[67] Festus, ed. Karl Ottfried Müller, pp. 348–9.

[68] *Historia Naturalis*, XXIX, xiv, 4.

[69] The story of the Etruscan augur Attus Navius and Tarquinius Priscus I, 36.

[70] Since Egeria was also worshipped at Aricia, according to one account it was here that Numa met her. Ovid, *Fasti*, III, 259 *sqq.*

[71] *De Ciuitate Dei*, VII, 34, 35.

[72] " Quid ? non et legum ipsarum in duodecim tabulis uerba sunt ? " " Qui fruges excantasset." Et alibi, " Qui malum carmen incantasset." Pliny, *Historia Naturalis*, XXVIII, 4.

[73] Livy, IV, 50 ; XXV, 1 ; XXXIX, 16.

[74] Valerius Maximus, I, iii, 2.

[75] *Apud* Aulum Gellium, III, x.

[76] *Metamorphoseon*, VII, 21,

[77] *Pharsalia*, VI, 541–9.

[78] Clauos ferreos, quibus fixi, qui in cruce pendebant.

[79] I, ii, 49.

[80] *Amores*, I, viii, 5.

[81] *Sermonum*, I, 8.

[82] Written 1210–14. *Monumenta Germaniæ historica*, XXVII, ed. Pauli and Liebermann.

[83] *Discouerie of Witchcraft*, V, chap. i, 6. 1584.

[84] *Anatomy of Melancholy*, Part I, Sect. i, Mem. 1, Subs. 4.

[85] *The Dvtchesse of Malfy*, V. 2. 4to. 1623.

[86] I have used the 1620 edition of the *Thrésor*, Genève, Samuel Crespin, 4 vols., 8vo. In Vols. I and II we have : Apparitions sataniques (p. 45) ; Démoniaques, illusions sataniques (p. 142) ; Efficace étrange de Satan (p. 178) ; Sorcellerie, illusions de Satan (p. 464) ; Enchanteurs et Magiciens punis (p. 718) ; Lycanthropie (pp. 720–1) ; Fureur du Malin Esprit (p. 790) ; and in volumes III and IV : Fantôme avertisseur (p. 191) ; Magiciens punis (p. 273). There is another edition of the *Thrésor, Paris, Houzé*, 1618, 2 vols., 12mo.

[87] The *Glossarium Philoxeni* defines *striga* as γυνὴ φαρμακίς, but the word means more than that here, and, I think, " banshee " or " ghoul " expresses the meaning as accurately as may be.

[88] This is the reading of V (codex Vaticanus). F (codex Florentinus) has " infirmare."

[89] I, 8. *Metamorphoseon*. Recensuit J. van der Vliet, Lipsiæ, Teubner, 1897.

[90] John Gaule, *Select Cases of Conscience Touching Witches and Witchcraft*, London, 1646, pp. 78–9.

[91] George Gifford, *Dialogue concerning Witches*, 1603.

[92] With which compare the " flying ointment " of the later witches. Queverdo's picture *Le Départ pour le Sabbat* represents this operation.

[93] Father Martindale (article *Paganism*) has well written : " A pure mysticism and sublimity of emotion barely to be surpassed had been achieved ; in the *Metamorphoses* of Apuleius the syneretistic cult of the Egyptian goddess expresses itself in terms of tenderness and majesty that would fit the highest worship, and in the concluding prayer of the Apuleian Hermes, an ecstatic adoration of God is manifested in language and thought never equalled, still less surpassed, save in the inspired writers of the Church."

[94] *De Ciuitate Dei*, XVIII, 18. Either he told a true tale or gave us fiction.

[95] *Diuinarum Institutionum*, V, De Iustitia. It is remarkable that he has omitted Apuleius of whom many wonders are told.

[96] *Apologia*, XXV, XXVI.

[97] *Ibid.*, XXIV.

[98] Unum etiam crimen ab illis . . . de cuiusdam Sigilli fabricatione prolatum est, quod me aiunt ad magica maleficia occulta fabrica ligno exquisitissimo comparasse, et cum sit sceleti forma turpe et horribile, tamen impendio colere et Græco uocabulo βασιλέα nuncupare. (There was one charge brought by them . . . . about a certain little image, which they say I ordered to be secretly made, of the most costly wood, for purposes of black magic. They assert too that although it was the baleful and malefic figure of a carious skeleton I was wont to venerate it with honour extraordinary, saluting it by the Greek name of βασιλύές, or King. *Apologia*, XXIV.

[99]
> When to Maro's tomb they brought him
> Tender grief and pity wrought him
>   To bedew the stone with tears ;
> What a Saint I might have crowned thee,
> Had I only living found thee,
>   Poet first and without peers. (Trans. J. A. Symonds.)

[100] Much the same may be said of Father Ronald Knox. The very title of his autobiography, *Æneid*, tells its own tale. The book is steeped in Vergil. " Maria undique et undique cælum."

[101] S. Cadoc (*c.* 522–90), feast 24 January, is in the English and Gallican martyrologies. He is venerated in Brittany at Belz and S. Cadou. See Rees, *Lives of the Cambro-British Saints*, and La Villemarqué, *La Légende Celtique*.

[102] S. Gildas " the Wise," born *c.* 516, died at Houat, Brittany, 570. Feast 29 January. There were important Relics in the Cathedral (S. Pierre) at Vannes. The Saint is venerated at Bieuzy, Tonquedec, Locminé, and Carnoet, where there is a Pardon on the Feast. A commemoration of the Translation of the Relics is made on 11 May.

[103] Gabriel Naudé, *Apologie pour tovs les grands hommes* . . . *soupçonnez de magie*, Paris, Targa, 1625 (ch, 21), considers that Vergil's reputation as a sorcerer arose from the Eighth Eclogue and the Sixth Book of the *Æneid*. It has been suggested that Vergil has been confused with S. Vergilius, Bishop of Salzburg, who died 27 November, 789, and left a great name for learning.

[104] Warton, *History of Poetry*, ed. 1824, II, 62 n.

[105] "Jannes et Mambres restiterunt Moysi." Ep. B. Pauli, Ap. *ad Timotheum*, II, iii, 8.

[106] Suetonius, *Augustus*, XXXI.

[107] Haruspices secreto ac sine testibus consuli uetuit. Suetonius, *Tiberius*, LXIII.

[108] It is said that no less than four thousand persons, magicians and their devotees, took refuge in Sardinia. Tacitus, *Annales*, II, 75.

[109] Tacitus, *Annales*, XII, 52.

[110] Pliny, *Historia Naturalis*, XXX, 5.

[111] Suetonius, *Nero*, XXXVI.

[112] Philostratus, *Uita Apollon. Tyan.*, IV, 55.

[113] *Historiarum*, I, 23.

[114] Suetonius, *Uitellius*, XIV. "Uaticinante Catta muliere." These foreign sibyls were highly esteemed. Galba had been encouraged to seize the empire owing to the predictions of a Spanish seeress.

[115] Dio Cassius, LXVI, 10.

[116] Spartianus, *Adrianus Cæsar*, 16.

[117] Lampridius, *Commodus*, 9.

[118] Fuit præterea in Iuliano hæc amentia, ut per magos pleraque faceret, quibus putaret uel odium populi deliniri, uel militum arma compesci. Nam et quasdam non conuenientes Romanis sacris hostias immolauerunt,[1] et carmina profana incantauerunt,[2] et ea quae ad speculum dicunt fieri,[3] in quo pueri præligatis oculis incantato uertice respicere dicuntur, Iulianus fecit. Tuncque puer uidisse dicitur et aduentum Seueri et Iuliani decessionem.[4]

[119] "Nam ueram magiam Persarum Plato pronuntiat θεῶν θεραπείαν" Casaubonus in Lampridium ad locum.

[120] Salmasius prefers the MS. reading "excruciaret."

[121] Lampridius, *Antoninus Heliogabalus*, 8.

[122] Giorgius Cedrenus, V, ii. p. 1., ed. Bekker, Bonn, 1838–9.

[123] 1501. Guicciardini writes : "Astorre, che era minore di diciotto anni e di forma eccellente . . . condotto a Roma, saziata prima (secondo che si disse) la libidine di qualcuno, fu occultamente insieme con un suo fratello naturale privato della vita." Nardi (*Storie Fiorentine*, lib. iv, 13) plainly states that Cæsar Borgia violated and murdered the boy.

[124] Most authorities say about eight hundred. In the official process at his trial one hundred and forty were named, but it is recognized that this only represents a tithe of the whole.

[125] *Histoire veritable des crimes horribles commis . . . sur le S. Sacrament de l'Autel, . . . et sur trois enfans. . . .* Iouxte la copie imprimée à Paris, 1651, 4to, 7 pp.

[126] *The Daily Express*, 9 December, 1919. Surely in a case such as this an expert theologian should sit as assessor at the trial.

[127] Capitolinus, *M. Antoninus Philosophus*, 19. The Chaldæans advised "ut occiso gladiatore, sanguine illius sese Faustina sublauaret [τὴν φύσιν], atque ita cum uiro concumberet. Quod quum esset factum, solutum quidem amorem, natum uero Commodum gladiatorem esse non principem." Human blood was often used for healing purposes. Pliny (*Historia Naturalis*, XXVIII, 1) says :

---

[1] Pueros multos mactauit. *Casaubon.*

[2] Magicas ἐπῳδὰς uocat *carmina profana :* ut Romanis sacris non conuenientia sed Barbaricis. *Ibid.*

[3] John of Salisbury, *De uestigiis philosophorum*, I, 12, writes : "Specularios uocant, qui in corporibus leuigatis et tersis, ut sunt lucidi enses, pelues, cythi, speculorumque diuersa genera, diuinantes curiosis consultationibus satisfaciunt." (Scryers (specularii) is the name given to those who by gazing at some shining and polished object, it may be a bright sword, a glittering basin, a cup, and any kind of reflecting mirror, divine and thuswise satisfy the anxious inquiries of those who consult them as to the future.)

[4] Spartianus, *Didius Julianus*, 7.

"Thus epileptics even drink theblood of gladiators, and indeed out of living goblets. . . . They consider it the most effective method of cure to swallow down the blood, when it is still warm, still bubbling, out of the man himself." Scribonius Largus (First Century) the author of *Medicamentorum Compositiones*, recommends human blood as a cure for epilepsy. Physicians of the Byzantine period (third to sixth centuries) such as Aëtius and Alexander of Tralles give the same prescriptions.

[128] Lampridius, *Alexander Seuerus*, 44.

[129] Julius Paulus, *Sent. recept*, V, xxiii, 17, 18. Apud, *Jurisperiti Antejustiniani* (p. 511), ed. Schulting, Lipsiæ, 1728.

[130] *Seut. recept.*, V, xxi, 3.

[131] Quum senior Gordianus mathematicum aliquando consuleret de genitura huius [Gordiani tertii], respondisse ille dicitur hunc et filium imperatoris, et ipsum imperatorem futurum. Et quum senior Gordianus rideset, ostendisse constellationem mathematicum ferunt, et de libris ueteribus dictasse, ita ut probaret se uera dixisse. Qui quidem et seni et iuueni et diem et genus mortis, et loca quibus essent perituri, obstinata constantiæ ueritate prædixit. Capitolinus, *Gordianus Iunior*, 20.

[132] Vopiscus, *Diuus Aurelianus*, 18.

[133] Referimus ad uos P. C. Pontificum suggestionem et Aureliani principis literas, quibus iubetur ut inspiciantur fatales libri quibus spes belli terminandi sacrato deorum imperio continetur. Vopiscus, *Diuus Aurelianus*, 19.

[134] Vopiscus, *Saturninus*, 7. During the reign of Probus (A.D. 276–82) Saturninus was proclaimed Emperor at Alexandria, but he was soon slain by the soldiery.

[135] I have tried to generalize as far as possible, but exception might be taken even here as Alexander Severus helped the "mathematici" with money. Or, perhaps, in this instance Lampridius is using the word loosely. In Cicero and Seneca "mathematicus" means a mathematician, but in later Latin it always signifies an astrologer, a wizard. Cf. the use of the English word "Geometry," as in Mrs. Behn's *The Luckey Chance*; or, *An Alderman's Bargain*, 4to, 1687, IV, 1, when Gayman says :

> By Magick Art I was conducted—I know not how
> To an inchanted Palace in the Clouds,
> . . . .
> But for the amorous Devil—the old *Proserpine*
> . . . .
> She was laid in a Pavilion, all form'd of gilded Clouds, which hung by Geometry.

[136] *Cod. Justin.*, L. IX, tit. xviii, 2 ; *The Twelve Tables*, 10 ; Beugnot, *Histoire de la destruction du paganisme en Occident*, Paris, 2 vols. 8vo., 1835.

[137] Quos Græci δαίμονας appellant nostri opinor lares. Cicero, *De Universo* (*Timœus*). Lactantius, *Diuinarum Institutionum*, II, 14, speaks of "spiritus contaminati ac perditi . . . sibi geniorum nomen assumunt. Sic enim Latino sermone dæmonas interpretantur. In inscriptions *Diis Manibus* is termed by Δαίμοσιν εὐσεβέσιν. Maffei, *Museum Ueronense*, CCCXVI.

[138] Plutarch, *Pompeius*, 24.

[139] It is hardly worth noting that some unscholarly and unscientific writers have endeavoured to show that the Church borrowed from Mithraism.

[140] In reality a mere abstraction ; a personification, not even of the sun, but of diffused daylight.

[141] *Historia Ecclesiastica*, III, 27.

[142] *Orationes*, IV, 92.

[143] Martyred 26 September, 304.

[144] Bollandists, *Acta Sanctorum*, 26 September.

[145] To Tertullian Mithra was a demon, and the adaptation of Christian rites by his worshippers simply devilish. *De Præscriptione Hœreticorum* (c. 200), XL ; S. Justin holds much the same view, *Apologia*, XVI.

[146] Nullus haruspex limen alterius accedat, nec ob alteram causam ; sed huiusmodi hominum, quamuis uetus, amicitia repellatur : concremando illo haruspice, qui ad domum alienam accesserit. *Codex Theodosianus*, Lib. IX, tit. xvi, l. 1.

[147] Nullis uero criminationibus implicanda sunt remedia humanis quæsita corporibus, aut in agrestibus locis, ne maturis uindemiis metuerentur imbres, aut ruentis grandinis lapidatione quaterentur, innocenter adhibita suffragia, quibus non cuiusque salus, aut existimatio læderetur, sed quorum proficerent actus, ne diuina munera et labores hominum sternerentur. *Codex Theodosianus*, Lib. XI, tit. xvi, l. 3.

[148] Aboleantur sacrificia nocturna, Magnentio auctore permissa, et nefaria deinceps licentia repellatur. *Codex Theodosianus*, Lib. XVI, tit. x.

[149] Sileat omnibus perpetuo diuinandi curiositas. Etenim supplicium capitis feret, gladio ultore, prostratur quicumque iussis obsequium denegauerit. *Ibid.*, Lib. IX, tit. xvi, l. 4.

[150] Nemo haruspicem consulat, aut mathematicum nemo, hariolum, augurem et uatem, praua confessio conticescat ; Chaldæi, et magi, et ceteri quos maleficos ob facinorum magnitudinem uulgus appellat. *Ibid.*

[151] Ammianus Marcellinus, XXIX, 2.

[152] Zosimus, *Historiæ Nouæ*, IV, Oxonii, 1679.

[153] Joannes Zonaras, *Annales*, XIII, 16.

[154] *Historia Ecclesiastica*, VI, 35.

[155] Nemo se hostiis polluat, nemo insontem uictimam cædet, nemo delubra adeat, templa perlustret et mortali opere formata simulacra suscipiat ne diuinis atque humanis sanctionibus reus fiat. *Codex Theodosianus*, Lib. XVI, tit. x, l. 10.

[156] They had previously been banned by Valentinian I, Theodosius, and Honorius, but it is during the reign of Valentinian III that they may be said to be overtly regarded as wholly antagonistic to Christianity as paganism once was. In fact, Manichæism in some sense took the place of paganism.

[157] This is, of course, a generalization ; as such, true. In obscure localities pagan superstitions lingered for long centuries. Thus S. Benedict (*ob.* 543) destroyed the ancient chapel upon the crest of Monte Cassino where the foolish and simple country folk worshipped Apollo and built there oratories of S. John and S. Martin.

CHAPTER II

ENGLAND

THE word Witchcraft itself belongs to Anglo-Saxon days, although magic played an important part in the Druidic mysteries, and certain obsolete superstitions are possibly to be referred back through the centuries to their ancient and cryptic lore. According to Whitely Stokes the Irish Druids were never even a hierarchy or separate priestly clan as in Britain, but were merely regarded as enchanters and medicine-men. Strabo the geographer in the first century[1] writes : φησὶν εἶναι νῆσον πρὸς τῇ βριττανικῇ καθ᾽ἥν ὅμοια τοῖς ἐν Σαμοθράκῃ περὶ τὴν Δήμητραν καὶ τὴν Κορὴν ἱεροποιεῖται. (They say that there is an island near Britain, where Demeter and Kore are worshipped with rites similar to the orgies of Samothrace.) As has been before noted Samothrace was the chief seat of the worship of the Cabiri, Κάβειροι, with whose occult ritual was closely associated the cult of Hecate.[2]

In the seventh century was composed the *Liber Pœnitentialis* of S. Theodore, seventh Archbishop of Canterbury,[3] the earliest collection of ecclesiastical disciplinary laws for England. No less than the whole of one section is concerned with magic practices and ceremonies, a penance being duly assigned for each offence. The thirty-seventh Book has as its rubric, " Of Idolatry and Sacrilege, and of those who pay divine honours to certain Angels, and evil-doers, sooth-sayers, poisoners, charmers, diviners, and those who vow their vows otherwise than to Holy Church, and the man who on the Kalends of January goeth about in the masque of a stag or a bull-calf, as also of astrologers, and those who by their craft raise storms."[4] There are six-and-twenty heads, and of these many are so important that the more significant provisions of the principal enactments must at least be given. " If anyone sacrifices to demons, one year of penance if he be a clown of low estate, if he be of higher degree, 10 years. If anyone sacrifice a second or a third time to demons he shall do penance for 3 years. If anyone commits sacrilege, that

65

is if he consulteth soothsayers who divine by birds or in any other forbidden way he shall do penance 3 years, and of these one shall he fast on bread and water. It is unlawful for any, cleric or layman, to exercise the craft of a seer or a charmer, or to make philtres, and all such as practise such arts or use them we order to be expelled from the church. If anyone by evil spells hath slain another. . . . If anyone hath poisoned another from jealousy and yet hath not slain him. <. . . If anyone hath procured abortion. . . . If anyone frequents seers, whom men call diviners, or hath practised any charms, for this is devilish. . . . If anyone hath made a trial of those lots, which are wrongly called the Holy Lots, or hath cast any lots at all, or hath with evil intent cast lots, or hath divined. . . . If any woman hath divined or hath used devilish evocations. . . . If any woman hath placed her son or daughter upon the house-top or in the oven in order to ensure them health. . . . If anyone hath burned wheat upon the spot where a man hath died in order to ensure the health and prosperity to his household. . . . If anyone in order to ensure health to his young son hath passed the baby upwards through some cavity in the earth, and then hath closed fast the hole behind him with thorns and brambles . . . anyone who hath had resource to diviners and cleaveth to the traditions of the heathen, or hath brought men of this craft into his house in order to find out some secret by their evil science, or in order to expiate some wrong. . . . If anyone hath vowed a vow and hath fulfilled the same at a clump of trees, or a spring of water, or at certain rocks, or at a spot where boundaries meet, or at any other place whatsoever, save in God's house, the church, he shall do penance fasting on bread and water for 3 years, since this is sacrilege, and verily devilish. Who hath eaten or drunk in honour of idols one year shall he do penance fasting on bread and water. If anyone at the Kalends of January goeth about as a stag or a bull-calf, that is, making himself into a wild animal, and dressing in the skins of a herd animal, and putting on the heads of beasts ; those who in such wise transform themselves into the appearance of a wild animal, let them do penance for three years, because this is devilish. If anyone be a wizard, that is, if by the invocation of demons he hath wrought upon any man's mind. . . . If anyone hath raised

storms by his evil craft. . . . If anyone hath tied the knot
(*ligaturas fecerit*) because this is devilish."[5] S. Augustine
(*In Ioannem*, VII) uses the word *ligatura* for an amulet bound
about one, and by " ligaturas facere "[6] we are here to understand sexual magic, *nouer l'aiguillette*. The *ligatura* was both
used for casting a spell upon a man, or for freeing him from
the effects of a charm. So in Petronius, *Satyricon*, 131, the
old witch in order to restore Encolpius " took out of her
bosom a hank of various colours and bound it round my
neck."[7] Upon which passage Turnebus (1512–65) glosses :
" In spells and charms hanks or threads of various colours
are employed, not only to bind and make fast a spell as in
the *Pharmaceutria* but also to loose and undo as here, whence
these threads are called ligatures (*ligatura*)."[8] George Erhard
notes : " This little old woman was skilled in magic spells,
and so she undertook to cure the sexual frigidity of Polyaenus
[Encolpius], whose virility was, as he himself acknowledged,
cold and dead. Witches can heal diseases by ligatures . . .
especially venereal complaints. . . . These hanks (*Licia*) the
writers of the Middle Ages call ligatures (*ligaturas*)."[9]

Maurus in a letter to Bonosus quotes the following phrase
of Mark of Rheims with reference to the repudiation of his
queen Thietberga by the licentious Lothair II in 860 : " Ad
hæc non pertinent ligaturæ exsecrabilium remediorum, quæ
ars medicorum commendat, siue in præcantationibus." A
slight variation of the same erotic charm is alluded to in
Vergil's famous lines :

Terna tibi hæc primum triplici diuersa colore
licia circumdo, terque hæc altaria circum
effigiem duco ; numero deus impare gaudet.
Ducite ab urbe domum, mea carmina, ducite Daphnim.
Necte tribus nodis ternos, Amarylli, colores ;
necte, Amarylli, modo et " Ueneris " dic " uincula necto."[10]

(Around his waxen Image first I wind
Three woollen Fillets ; of three Colours join'd :
Thrice bind about his thrice-devoted Head,
Which round the sacred Altar thrice is led.
Unequal Numbers please the Gods : My Charms,
Restore my *Daphnis* to my longing Arms.
Knit with three Knots the Fillets, knit 'em straight ;
Then say, These Knots to Love I consecrate.
Haste, *Amaryllis*, haste ; Restore, my Charms,
My lovely *Daphnis* to my longing Arms.   DRYDEN.)

The clause in S. Theodore's *Penitential* which forbids anyone at the Kalends of January to go about as a stag or a bull, that is, making himself into a wild animal and dressing in the skins of herd animals and putting on the heads of beasts, and assigns three years of penance to those who in suchwise transform themselves into the appearance of a wild animal, since the practice is devilish, is of especial importance and interest, since here we probably have the explanation of the greater part of these accounts which record that the Demon appeared as a goat, a rampant bull, a huge black ram, whilst his satellites particularly favoured the shape of monstrous cats. The individual clad in a beast-skin or mask is the worshipper putting himself by personal contact under the influence and protection of his deity. In Italy, in Gaul, in parts of Germany, in England, and in Spain men decked themselves for licentious assemblies and obscene rites which they performed at Christmas and early in the New Year, shielding themselves under the kindly ægis of the Church's festivals. They clad themselves in hairy and horned skins, in hides with immense tails, they smutted their faces or bedaubed them with filth, and donned the most hideous masks imagination could conceive. These performances seem, indeed, almost universal, and they are denounced again and again. " Lo, the day is close at hand," writes Severian, " yea, the Kalends are here, and the whole devilish procession will come forth, the very fountain-head and workshop of idols will go in full parade. The New Year is hallowed by old blasphemies. They appear as Saturn, they show us Jupiter, they display Hercules, they present Diana with her huntress train, they exhibit Vulcan spouting the vilest obscenities, and many more beside, whose names I will not utter, for they are monstrous lewd. Of a verity those beastlinesses which are unknown to nature do they endeavour to fashion by their craft and purblind skill, abnormal, epicene. Moreover men are dressed like herd animals, they turn men into women, I say, they laugh at decency, they break all laws, they laugh at public opinion, they riot and roister whilst the whole world looks on, and those who commit these abominations declare 'tis but a jest. No jest, forsooth, but black sin and shame. Men are transformed into idols. And, if it be a crime to resort to idols, what think ye is it to become an idol ? . . .

For when they would assume the likeness of these heathen gods, if pigments and charcoal, wherewith to caulk and smear their faces, are found to be lacking, that they may make their appearance more quaint and horrid, they not only tire themselves in hides, in rags and tatters, but deck themselves out with straw and bedaub their countenances all over with excrement or any other filthy ordure which they can light upon anywhere."[11] S. Maximus of Turin (c. 412–65) repeatedly reprobates similar ceremonies : " Are not indeed," he cries, " all those rites and ceremonies which the devil's own servants enact on those days frantic folly ? . . . What is it but frantic folly when men created by God and in the image of God transform themselves to herd animals or to wild beasts or to some monstrous shapes ? . . . These gecks and losels say that they are observing omens and judging of the length of their lives from some empty and idle signs, for how shall the events of the coming year be ascertained by the vague betokenings of beast or bird."[12] S. Peter Chrysologus (406–50), Doctor of the Church, writes in the same strain : " The man who puts on the guise of an idol has no wish to be in the image and likeness of God. Who jests with the Devil cannot rejoice with Christ. . . . Wherefore let the father strive to convert his son, the master his servant, the kinsman his relation, the citizen his fellow-citizen, each man his fellow-man, and the Christian all, all who have masqueraded in the likeness of animals, who have metamorphosed themselves as draught-cattle, who have assumed the shape of herd animals, who have turned themselves into devils."[13]

S. Caesarius of Arles (470–542) is not one whit less emphatic: " Is there any sensible man," he asks with biting irony, " who could ever believe that there are actually rational individuals willing to put on the appearance of a stag and to transform themselves into wild beasts ? Some dress themselves in the skins of herd animals ; others put on the heads of horned beasts ; swelling and wildly exulting if only they can so completely metamorphose themselves into the animal kind that seem to have entirely abandoned the human shape." And again he warns the faithful: "Wherefore if ye abhor any participation in their sins, ye will not suffer these human stags or bull-calves or other monsters to approach you, nay,

not so much as to come nigh your dwellings."[14] And again
he warns the faithful: "Et ideo si in peccatis eorum participes
esse non uultis, ceruulum uel iuuencam,[15] aut alia quælibet
portenta, ante domos uestras uenire non permittatis."[16] He
also writes : " I would fain believe that so foul a tradition,
so evil a custom . . . hath been abolished ; but if ye know
of any who practise this most heinous abomination of guising
themselves as a roebuck or a musonned stag . . . do ye
chastise such with sore stripes."[17]

In spite of the denunciations of the Fathers and Doctors
these buffoon but evil rites persisted, although shorn to some
degree of their primitive offence, and they are found inter-
mixed with the mediæval Feast of Fools, *festum stultorum* or
fatuorum, the Feast of Asses, *asinaria festa*, with which the
inferior clerics in cathedrals and collegiate churches were
wont riotously to usher in the New Year. At these outrageous
and extraordinary festivals hideous and repulsive masks were
often worn, *personæ*, or *monstra lauarum* as they are termed
by Pope Innocent III, who issuing a decretal to the archbishop and bishops of the province of Gnesen in Poland,
directed that all such grotesque clowning should be at once
discontinued.[18] No doubt there were beast-masks, furnished
with the most fantastic corniculate projections, a remnant
of the actual skins and hides of animals. Some writers have
found an Oriental origin for the Feast of Fools, but this does
not seem probable, although similar mock revels were held
in Constantinople, and in the twelfth century the Patriarch
Balsamon unavailingly combated an ancient custom which
the clergy of S. Sophia refused to abandon. They claim the
right at Christmas and Candlemas to wear masks, and to
enter the sanctuary in the guise of soldiers, or of monks, or
of four-footed beasts, " ἀλλὰ καί τινες κληρικοὶ κατά τινος
ἑορτὰς πρὸς διάφορα μετασχηματίζονται προσωπεῖα, καὶ ποτὲ μὲν
ξιφήρεις ἐν τῷ μεσονάῳ τῆς ἐκκλησίας μετὰ στρατιωτικῶν ἀμφίων
εἰσέρχονται, ποτὲ δὲ καὶ ὡς μοναχοὶ προοδεύουσιν ἢ καὶ ὡς ζῶα
τετράποδα."[19] There was no abuse amid all the indecorum
of these burlesque celebrations which was reproved with
greater severity and visited with sterner censure by the
Church, and this, no doubt, because such a masquerade was
definitely traceable to the old superstitions of Witchcraft,
although the evil of the connexion had in actual fact and

practice entirely disappeared, and on the face of it at worst it was mere ribald mumming.

S. Aldhelm of Malmesbury and Sherbourne (c. 639–709), writing about 685, has : " Et ubi pridem eiusdem nefandæ natricis ermuli[20] ceruulique cruda fanis colebantur stoliditate in profanis, uersa uia discipulorum gurgustia (imo almæ oraminum ædes) architecti ingenio fabre conduntur."[21]

The Laws of Withraed, King of Kent, in 690, ordain : " If a theow make an offering to devils let him make a bot of vi shillings, or his hide."[22]

In the Confessional of Ecgberht, Archbishop of York[23] (734–66) the following significant clauses appear : " 27. If any woman practise any magic arts, or spells, and work evil charms, let her fast for a twelvemonth, or for three canonical fasts, or for xl days : let the heinousness of her offence be computed. If she has slain any one by her evil charms, let her fast for vii years. And 32. If anyone be found who hath offered sacrifice to devils, no matter on howsoever trifling an occasion let him fast for 1 year. If he hath made any precious offering let him fast x years."[24] And in the law of the Northumbrian priests it is ordered : " If anyone be found that shall henceforth practise any heathenship, either by sacrifice or by fyrt, or in any way love witchcraft, or worship idols, if he be a king's thane let him pay x half marks ; half to Christ, half to the king."[25]

In the ninth century the Penitential of Pseudo-Theodore renews these prohibitions. This *Pœnitentiale* has been quoted by Tille[26] and other authors as being English, although it is really Frankish, and to some extent, although not in these sections, based upon the genuine Penitential of S. Theodore. It may be remarked that verymany Penitentials[27] particularly denounce and forbid the masquerade of the *Ceruulus and Uetula*. Their ultimate authority may be the Council of Auxerre, held under S. Annacharius in 578 (or 585),[28] a canon of which directs : " It is forbidden to masquerade as a bull-calf or a stag on the first of January or to distribute devilish charms, but if gifts are to be given on that day let them be bestowed as on other days."[29]

The Venerable Bede, Doctor of the Church (died 735), in his great *Historia Ecclesiastica Gentis Anglorum* mentions devil-worship, and says that Redwald, King of the East

Saxons, and his court " in eodem fano et altare haberet ad sacrificium Christi, et arulam ad uictimas dæmoniorum."[30] (" In the same temple had an altar to sacrifice to Christ, and another small one to offer victims to devils.")

Again in the Laws of Edward and Gunthrun of the tenth century (after 901) it is enacted : " If witches or diviners, perjurers, or *morth*-workers, or foul, defiled, notorïous adulteresses, be found anywhere within the land ; let them be driven from the country and the people cleansed, or let them totally perish within the country, unless they desist, and the more deeply make *bōt.*" In those of King Æthelstan, "And we have ordained respecting witchcrafts and *lyblacs* and *morth-dœds :* if any one should be thereby killed, and he could not deny it, that he be liable in his life. But if he will deny it, and at the threefold ordeal shall be guilty, that he be cxx. days in prison : and after that let his kindred take him out, and give to the king cxx. shillings, and pay the *wēr* to his kindred, and enter into *borh* for him, that he evermore desist from the like."

The ecclesiastical statutes of King Edgar, 959, direct " that every priest zealously promote Christianity, and totally extinguish every heathenism ; and forbid well worshippings, and necromancies, and divinations, and enchantments, and man worshippings, and the vain practices which are carried on with various spells, and with frith-splots, and with elders and also with various other trees, and with stozes, and with many various delusions, with which men do much of what they should not. . . . And we enjoin, that on feast days there be complete abstinence from heathen songs and devil's games."

This enactment is repeated in the laws of King Ethelred and in those of Cnut. The latter adds, " and we earnestly forbid every heathenism. Heathenism is, that men worship idols ; that is, that they worship heathen gods, and the sun or moon, fire or rivers, water-wells or stones, or forest-trees of any kind ; or love witch-craft, or promote *morth*-work in anywise ; or by *blot*, or *fyrht*, or perform anything pertaining to such illusions."

The fearful prevalence of Witchcraft in England, and the survival of heathen superstitions which it so readily adopted and moulded to its own evil, could not more plainly be demonstrated than in this catena of ordinances, both ecclesiastical and civil, extending from the seventh to the eleventh centuries. There is no doubt that from the time that S. Augustine landed on the Isle of Thanet in the spring of 597 the Christian monks and missionaries had continually to battle with the dark opposing powers, who were not easily to be driven from the fair land of Britain, whose inhabitants already knew and dreaded their influences, as is shown by the fact that King Æthelberht immediately suspected the Roman stranger himself to be some mighty magician and insisted that their first meeting should take place under a spreading oak tree where no incantations could prevail.

Although Witchcraft in England had not even by the eleventh century become so elaborated and organized as in later years, nevertheless we clearly distinguish in Anglo-Saxon days far more than the germ which soon developed so systematically and so rapidly when it was fostered and given a terrible impulse by the Satanism of the Gnostic heretics who appeared in parts of Europe as early as 1038. Professor Notestein, who seeks to differentiate between the earlier and later Witchcraft, remarks that in Anglo-Saxon days " Nothing is yet said about the transformation of witches into other shapes, and there is no mention of a compact, implicit or otherwise, with the Devil."[31] But he has either overlooked the anathematization of the *Ceruulus* and *Uitula,* or else ignored the signification of these prohibitions in the Penitentials, whilst surely such an alliance with the Devil is overtly expressed in the worship of demons. " There is no allusion," he continues, " to the nocturnal meetings of the Devil's worshippers and to the orgies that took place on these occasions ; there is no elaborate and systematic theological explanation of human relations with demons." Demonology had not, from the very nature of things, been studied in such scholastic detail and so judicially codified as by Sprenger and Bodin, but there are continual references in the Fathers to man's commerce with the demon, which is, for example, discussed at some length by S. Augustine in the twenty-third chapter of the fifteenth Book of his *De Ciuitate Dei.*

With reference to the nocturnal meetings and orgies there is a decree of a General Council of Ancyra, which passed into the *De ecclesiasticis disciplinis* ascribed to Regino of Prüm

(906), and thence to the canonists S. Ivo of Chartres and Johannes Gratian. Section 364 of the Benedictine Abbot's work relates that " certain abandoned women turning aside to follow Satan, being seduced by the illusions and phantasms of demons, believe and openly profess that in the dead of night they ride upon certain beasts with the pagan goddess Diana and a countless horde of women, and that in these silent hours they fly over vast tracts of country and obey her as their mistress, while on other nights they are summoned to pay her homage."[32] John of Salisbury, who died in 1180, in his *Policraticus*[33] speaks of the popular belief in a witch-queen named Herodias, who called together the sorcerers to meetings by night when they had feasting, sacrificed babes to ghouls and ghosts, and gave themselves up to blasphemies and debauchery, in a word the Sabbat. He writes : " Quale est quod noticulam quandam uel Herodiadem, uel præsidem noctis dominam, consilia et conuentus de nocte asserunt conuocare : uaria celebrari conuiuia : ministeriorum species diuersis occupationibus exerceri : et nunc istos ad pœnam trahi pro meritis, nunc illos ad gloriam sublimari. Præterea infantes exponi lamiis, et nunc frustratim discerptos edaci ingluuie in uentrem trajectos congeri, nunc præsidentis miseratione rejectos in cunas reponi."

There are indeed many allusions to Herodias, or Diana, or Habundia, queen of the Sabbat, and the *good-women*,[34] as they were euphemistically called, who attended her. Thus in *Le Roman de la Rose* (l. 18,624), which was written in the thirteenth century, occur these lines :

Maintes gens, par lor folie,
Cuident estre par nuit estries
Errans avecques dame Habonde ;
Et dient, que par tout le monde
Li tiers enfant de nacion
Sunt de ceste condicion,
Qu'il vont trois fois en la semaine,
Si cum destinée les maine,
Et par tous ces ostex se boutent,
Ne elés ne barres ne redoutent,
Ains s'en entrent par les fendaces,
Par chatières et par crevaces,
Et se partent des cors les ames,
Et vont avec les bonnes dames

Par leus forains et par maisons ;
Et le preuvent par tiex raisons,
Que les diversités veues
Ne sunt par en lor liz venues.

The following passages from a manuscript *De Sortilegis* seemed worth transcribing at some length, as not only do they speak of Herodias and of hags, who mounted upon beasts fly through the air during the dark watches of winter nights, but it also preserves some curious ecclesiastical superstitions not unworthy of notice : " With regard to priests and religious from whom holy vessels, church ornaments, or similar furniture have secretly been stolen ; or even with regard to lay folk from whom property has secretly been stolen ; may they inquire into these matters by using the astrolabe or some such instrument ? All authorities agree in their answer to this question, namely, that if there be any invocation of demons or any other superstitious rite, such inquiry is wholly unlawful and he who attempts it sins most grievously. Indeed if anyone even in the ignorance of youth and with the best intentions has thus sought a reply he shall be suspended from his function and his benefice. If, however, such an inquiry be made merely by astronomy, if there be no invocation of any demon and no superstitious rite performed, then perchance, as some say, although it seem barely consonant with the ecclesiastical decrees, it is allowable, and yet these astrological sciences inasmuch as they contain much dubious matter should not be too closely studied and ensued. Again, we must consider the case of priests who on account of some private grief, denude the altar of its coverings, or clothe it in some sad-coloured frontal, or extinguish the sanctuary lamps and the altar candles, or perchance hang the altar and the crucifix with thorns and briars.

" What are we to say with regard to those who with a full intent and wilfully sing a solemn requiem or set a catafalque in the midst of the church and sing the Office of the Dead, inserting the names of those whom they hate, or perform some similar funereal ceremony, that their enemies may die swiftly and soon ? The reply to this is that if a priest performs any of these rites in such circumstances and with such object as we have just rehearsed on account of a private quarrel he sins mortally and unless he do canonical penance he should be deprived. If, however, he performs any of these rites for some just reason, as, for example, if the person devoted be any enemy to the Faith, or a public enemy, or one who will plunder the church, then by no means does he sin, because it is indeed his humility which is apparent through his placing the event in God's hands rather than any resentment or anger. This is plainly according to the mind of the Church, since we sing Psalm lxxviii, *Deus uenerunt Gentes*, and on Good Friday we strip our altars in token of mourning. Yet this distinction will not cover those who knowingly and of purpose celebrate the Office of the Dead for the living. For such, if they be discovered, assuredly must be deprived and must do condign penance, both the priest himself and he who incited the priest to chant the dirge, they must be condemned to exile, a sentence not to be rescinded, or confined within some monastic house. The Council of Toledo expressly lays this down in the twenty-sixth canon.

"We next inquire concerning certain wicked crones who believe and profess that in the night time they ride abroad with Diana, the heathen goddess, or else with Herodias, and an innumerable host of women, upon certain beasts, and that in a silent covey at the dead of night they pass over immense distances, obeying her commands as their mistress, and that they are summoned by her on appointed nights, and they declare that they have the power to change human beings for better or for worse, ay, even to turn them into some other semblance or shape. Concerning such women I answer according to the decrees of the Council of Alexandria that the minds of the faithful are disordered by such fantasies owing to the inspiration of no good spirit but of the Devil. For the Devil when wishing to win over any soul by evil superstition of this kind transforms himself into an angel of light, and changes himself into the semblance and shape of various individuals so that he deludes and mocks the mind, deceiving a person by many subtle sleights, nor ought any man or woman to be so blindly besotted as to believe all this, which can only happen in dreams and sick imagination, actually takes place in the body, when Blessed Paul would not assert that he was in rapture in the body. [I know a man in Christ above fourteen years ago, whether in the body, I know not, or out of the body, I know not ; God knoweth, such a one caught up to the third Heaven. 2 Corinthians xii. 2.] Wherefore if any man believe such follies or maintain them, out of all question he is a heretic and worse than a heathen. For when, as has recently been laid down, we declare that no faith must be put in auguries, the casting of lots, and any other kind of divination whatsoever, although since much which is thus foretold may not infrequently come to pass, and although charmers may often heal the sick or even send diseases, S. Augustine who has discussed this problem conclusively settles it, for the holy doctor says that these wonders happen by divine permission, since all who see or hear them may approve their faith and glorify God. This he proves by the authority of Deuteronomy : If there arise in the midst of thee a prophet or one that saith he hath dreamed a dream, and he foretell a sign and a wonder, and that come to pass which he spoke, and he say unto thee : Let us go and follow strange gods, which thou knowest not, and let us serve them : thou shalt not hear the words of that prophet or dreamer : for the Lord your God trieth you, that it may appear [that is to say to those who are thus and to other men, not to God, since He knows all things before they come to pass] whether you love Him with all your heart, and with all your soul or not. (xiii. 1–3.) " [35]

The witch of Berkeley, who inspired Southey's ballad, is traditionally said to have lived about the middle of the ninth century. She is a shadowy figure enough, although she is still well remembered in the West-country, and it is just possible there may have been some such person about whom the legend encrusted. She had been wealthy, but on her death-bed she confessed that her riches were derived from a compact with the Devil. Accordingly she bids them sew her body in the hide of a stag[36] and place her in a stone coffin, binding it with heavy chains of iron. Fifty psalms are to be sung each night, and fifty masses to be said each morning, and if her body can be thus kept safe for three nights, upon the fourth day they may bury it deep in the churchyard, the Devil will have sought and not have found.

The bier is laid before the high altar, and on the first night monks and nuns chant their nocturns, whilst the demons wail and howl outside the church. On the second night the fiends grow more powerful and burst open the doors and invade the cloister, but prayer prevails. On the third night the monastery is shaken to its foundations by a hideous tempest, the religious white to the lips and trembling with fear can scarce intone the dirge, the yells of the demons sound fiercer and nearer, until at length with an awful crash the gates fly open and a devil, more terrible than any who had yet been seen, stalks up the aisles to where the wretched woman lay. In a voice of thunder he bids her rise and follow him. Piteously she pleads she cannot, she is held by the iron bands. In a moment he snaps them as if they were burned thread, and wrenches open the coffin. Livid and stark, in sore affright, the stiffening corpse uprose, and the Devil taking her by the hand led her to the door, where stood a gigantic black horse, impatiently pawing the ground and breathing flame. Like a flash he vaults into the saddle and throws her across before him ; away they speed swifter than the wind, whilst earth and heaven ring with the hopeless shrieks of the tortured soul.[37]   An idle story, and grossly immoral, since evil triumphs over repentance and prayer.

The narrative told by William of Malmesbury in his *Gesta regum* (1125), who says he had it from an eye-witness, is also found in Olaus Magnus and in the *Nuremburg Chronicle.* It is also contained in the *Flores Historiarum*[38] *sub anno* 852. but is generally better known owing to Southey's ballad.[39] The pseudo Matthew of Westminster's account, not without a certain vigour and grim power, runs as follows : " A.D. 852.   At that time, there is said to have lived in the village, which is called Berkeley, a certain woman of evil life, a glutton and wanton, pursuing her wickedness and practising the black art even in her old age, persisting in her whoredoms until the hour of her death.   On a day as she sat at meat, her pet crow began to chatter something or the other, where-upon the knife fell from her hand, and her face grew ghastly white.   'Alas ! ' she cried, ' to-day some sore hurt will hap to me ; to-day my plough hath turned its last furrow.'   Even as she said these words a messenger bearing ill-tidings entered the room, and when she asked what news he brought, ' Thy son is dead,' he replied, ' and his whole household also, since the four corners of his house and the roof-tree were smitten, and fell upon them, so they are not.'   The woman, vexed to the soul at his words, forthwith went up to her bed,

and lay very sick. When she knew furthermore that this
sickness was to death, she caused letters to be sent calling
her two surviving children, to wit a monk and a nun. To
whom she spake with bitter tears and grievous lament, saying,
' Alack, my children, this doom have I surely deserved owing
to my long continuance in wizardry ; I am the sink and
sewer of all evil, I was the mistress of all whoredoms. Yet
I ever placed as my succour between me and the wickedness
I wrought the buckler of your holy profession, whereby
I comforted my unhappy soul : to you do I look to defend
me mightily against the demons ; ye are my champions
against my cruel and most fierce foe. Now therefore inasmuch
as I am come to the end of my life, I beseech you by the
womb that bare ye, that ye should try to deliver me from
my torment. When I am dead sew my body in the hide of
a stag, place it in a sarcophagus of stone, which make fast
with iron and molten lead, binding around the stone three
iron chains of the stoutest forge. Let fifty chauntry priests
sing Dirige for three days, and let as many priests say
exequial masses for the repose of my soul, in order that the
dread onset of mine enemies may be driven back, and if
I lie for three nights in peace unharmed, on the fourth day
ye shall bury me in the ground.'

" It was done as she had commanded. Alack the day !
Nor prayer, nor tears, nor did the stout chains avail. On the
first and second nights, indeed, whilst the quiristers and
clerics were singing their office, a host of Demons, gathering
without the church, burst open the door which was fast shut
with bolts and bars, and rushing up to the bier broke asunder
the two chains which bound the coffin, albeit the third chain
baffled their rage. On the third night, however, a hideous
spectre, a devil of gigantic form and baleful countenance,
shivered the church doors into fragments with a violent blow.
Both priests and people were sore afraid so that their hair
bristled with fear and the psalm died in their throat. The
devil, approaching the tomb with a haughty and mocking
gesture, calling the woman by name, bade her come forth.
And when she replied she could not seeing she was bound
fast by the chain, ' I will release thee from that hindrance,'
quoth he, and presently he brake the chain which had
withstood the strength of the howling fiends as though

it were a thread of tow. The covering of the sepulchre he spurned aside with his cloven foot, and in the sight of all raised up the wretched woman, drawing her to the church door where stood a coal-black steed that neighed lustily, all beset, as it seemed, with huge iron hooks, gaunche-like, and great nails, upon which he flung his miserable burthen, and both vanished clean away from the eyes of all that were present. But they say that for wellnigh four miles shrieks of agony were heard, and cries for help.

" In truth this story which is told cannot be accounted other than true, for blessed Gregory has written in one of his dialogues that a man, who was buried in a church, was cast out of the holy place by a horde of devils. Charles Martel, too, King of the Franks, a hero of no mean prowess, who drove back into Spain the Saracens when they invaded France, is said to have been buried, when he had finished his course, in the cathedral of S. Denis. But since he had grievously sinned in that he robbed nearly all the churches of France of their revenues and tithes to pay his soldiers, his body was torn from its resting-place by devils in most horrid wise, and it hath not been found even unto this day."[40]

During the reign of King John, in 1209, a case of Witchcraft came before the courts, when Agnes, the wife of Odo, a substantial merchant, charged with this crime a certain Galiena, who, however, was acquitted when tried by the ordeal of hot iron. " Placita apud Westmonast. in octab. Sancti Hilarii anno regni regis Iohannis decimo. Norf. Agnes uxor Odonis mercatoris appelauit Galienam de sorceria, et ipsa liberta est per iudicium ferri. Et ideo Agnes remanet in misericordia."[41]

In 1279 a man accused of killing a witch, who had assaulted him in his house, was fined, but he had already fled from justice.

Less than a quarter of a century later, in 1303, a great noise was made by the charges brought against one of the chief men in the realm, Walter Langton, Bishop of Lichfield and treasurer of Edward I. He was accused before Boniface VIII of demonolatry and of paying shameless homage to the Devil, with whom he held long midnight conferences and consultations, " erat in regno Angliæ et alibi publice defamatus quod diabolo homagium fecerat et eum fuerat osculatus in tergo eique locutus multotiens." The Pope commanded that a searching inquiry should be made, but the incriminated prelate was able successfully to clear himself with the compurgators.

Two very important cases of Witchcraft loom largely in the legal records of 1324. In the first of these no less than twenty-seven defendants were tried at the King's Bench for murder by fashioning and tormenting a wax image. Upon the eve of All Hallows, Richard Latoner, Geoffrey Frebern, Robert Palmer, Adam Wolreston, Henry Hinton, and a number of their friends, Coventry men, went privately to the house of a famous " nigromauncer," John of Nottingham, who was living in their town, and having bound him and his man, Robert Marshall from Leicester, to closest secrecy, paid him a large sum of money to undertake the slaying of King Edward II ; the two le Despensers, father and son ; the Prior of Coventry ; his steward Nicholas Crump ; his maniple; and various other officials, who, as they asserted, ground them to the earth under imposts and heaviest taxation. Nothing loath, John the wizard and his servant commenced operations. They were well fed from time to time, and provided with seven pounds of wax and two ells of superfine canvas to make the various images as required, the king with a crown on his head, and the rest. The confession of Marshall who betrayed the whole gang to the authorities, gives ample details of their sorceries. A remote old manor-house under Shorteley Park, about half a league out of Coventry, was put at the service of Master John, and there he and Marshall, worked assiduously to fashion there puppets, " from the Monday after the Feast of S. Nicholas," 6 December, until " the Saturday after Ascension Day," which seems an extraordinarily long time, and suggests that they could not have been very proficient at their modelling. In any case they resolved that they would first make trial of the efficacy of their enchantments upon the image of a hated courtier, Richard de Sowe. Accordingly at midnight on the Friday preceding the Feast of Holy Rood (3 May) Master John gave Marshall a long leaden pin and bade him thrust it boldly two inches deep into the forehead of the figure representing their intended victim. The next morning, the servant being dispatched to de Sowe's house to see how he fared, found him writhing on his bed in agony, uttering piercing cries, with burning pains in his head, and frantically delirious. And so he lingered, until some days later the wizard drew the pin from the brow and struck it into the heart of the image. Whereupon de Sowe expired, and Marshall, who it is plain was by now thoroughly frightened, confessed what had been going on, which immediately resulted in the arrest of Master John and all concerned, those who were not able to find substantial bail being held in custody. Richard Latoner and his friends soon produced sureties, good men and true, but the " nigromauncer " was not so lucky, and, indeed, he died in prison before the day of the trial. Marshall stuck to his story, but the accused strenuously denied the allegations in every particular and were honourably acquitted. The unlucky wight who blabbed seems to have come off worst in the end, for " quibusdam certis de causis " he was sent back to jail by the court.

The trial is so full of interest that it will assuredly not be impertinent to give an extract from the *Parliamentary Writs* [42] of the time. " On Wednesday, the Vigil of All Hallows, in the eighteenth year of the reign of King Edward, Robert Marshall of Leicester confessed before Simon Crozier, deputy magistrate of our Lord the King, that when he was dwelling in the house of Master John of Nottingham, who practised magic and dwelt at Coventry, there came thither Richard Latoner, Geoffrey Frebern, Robert Palmer, Adam Wolreston, Henry Hinton, Hugh Tuwe, John Sifflet, William Gloucester, John Stoneley, Richard Taylor a hosier, John Waller servant to Alice la Honte, Henry Pake, Robert Stowe, Robert Lichfield, Robert Mercer, who is married to the daughter of Adam Lyndsay, Piers Baron, Philip Hosier, Walter Chubbock, Roger Bray, John Frebern, Reynold Alesleye, William Waller, Richard Grauntpé, John the son of Hugh de Merington, a page at the court, William Russell, Richard Greene, and John Redeclerk, a hosier of Coventry, and that these on the Wednesday next before the feast of S. Nicolas in the seventeenth year of our Lord the King, came to Coventry to the aforesaid Master John of Nottingham and Robert Marshall, and inquired of them whether they would conceal what was to be unfolded to them, whence they would derive great profit. And Master John faithfully promised them that he would discover nothing ; and the aforesaid Robert promised the aforesaid Master John that he would keep counsel. When this compact had been made between them, the aforesaid Richard Latoner and others informed the aforesaid Master John and Robert that they could not live on account of the hard treatment which the Prior of Coventry had dealt them and was daily dealing them, and on account of the favour and support that our Lord the King, Monsieur Hugh Despenser Earl of Winchester, and Monsieur Hugh Despenser his son, gave to the said Prior to their great hurt and the great hurt of the city of Coventry, wherefore they prayed Master John if at their entreaty he would undertake to kill the King, Monsieur Hugh Despenser Earl of Winchester, the Prior of Coventry, and others whom they named, by his nigromancy and his art. And he said Yes, and agreed thereto ; whereupon they made a covenant with him, that he should have xx pounds sterling, and his lodging in any house of religious which he desired to appoint in England, and that the aforesaid Robert should have xv pounds sterling to aid and abet them in the aforerehearsed crimes, of which sum the aforesaid Richard and others paid to Master John at Coventry eleven marks, on the Sunday next after the feast of S. Nicolas in the seventeenth year of our Lord the King, as part payment of the aforesaid xx pounds, and to the said Robert four pounds of the aforesaid xv pounds on the same day of the same year at the same place, by the hands of John son of Hugh de Merington and John Redeclerk at the house of Richard Latoner, and seven pounds of wax and two ells of canvas, of which wax the said Master John and Robert made seven figures, one of our Lord the King crowned in wax, another of the Earl of Winchester, the third of Monsieur Hugh, the fourth of the Prior of Coventry, the fifth of the Cellarer, the sixth of Nicholas Crump the Prior's seneschal, and the seventh of a courtier named Richard de Sowe, by experimenting upon whom with the image made in his likeness, they wished to essay the other images whether they were efficacious or impotent and this they did with the full assent of the said Richard and the others. And the said Robert hath confessed that he and the said Master John began to perform their craft in the aforesaid manner on the Monday next after the feast of S. Nicolas, in

the xviith year, with the assent of the aforesaid Richard
Latoner and the others in an old house about half a league
from the town of Coventry, under Shorteley Park, and there
they abode wholly occupied with their work until the
Saturday next after the following Ascension Day. Moreover
he confessed that as the aforesaid Master John and he were
at the aforesaid old house busy upon their work on the Friday
next before the Feast of Holy Cross, about midnight the said
Master John gave the said Robert a curious pin wrought of
sharp lead, and bade him thrust it two inches deep into the
forehead of the image made in the likeness of Richard de Sowe,
by which proof they were to try the others ; and he did as
he was bid ; and on the morrow morn the said Master John
sent the said Robert to the house of the said Richard de Sowe
to see how he fared, and the said Robert found the said
Richard shrieking and shouting without being able to recognize any man, for his memory was distraught, and so the
said Richard pined and waxed weaker until the Sunday before
the feast of the Ascension, when the said Master John drew
the said leaden pin out of the forehead of the said image
made in the likeness of the said Richard, and thrust it into
the heart. And so the said pin remained in the heart of the
said image until the next Wednesday following, upon which
day the said Richard died. This trial was made of the said
Richard in the way aforesaid with the full assent of the
aforesaid Richard [Latoner] and others, and they were fully
cognizant of all these proceedings."[43]

It is pretty clear, I think, that in spite of their stout
denials and the fact they were acquitted a very elaborate
conspiracy against the King and his friends was being brewed.
It is most noticeable how frequently politics are mixed up
with Witchcraft.

A little more than a century later we have another striking
example of this in the reign of Henry VI, the prosecution of
the Duchess of Gloucester ; the connexion of Francis Stewart,
Earl of Bothwell, with the North Berwick witches and their
plots to kill James I (VI) were notorious ; the conspiracy of
Giacinto Centini against Urban VIII involved the fashioning
of a wax image of that pontiff which was repeatedly stabbed
with a sharp knife to cause his death by sympathetic magic ;
the black masses of the abbé Guibourg and his fellow-

Satanists had as their object the perpetuation of Madame de Montespan's ascendancy over Louis XIV, whom indeed they at one time thought to poison ; and very many more cases might be cited from every country and every century to show how repeatedly those who sought the death of the sovereign had resource to the black art to achieve their ends. Robert Marshall's story bears the stamp of truth. In 1324 rebellion against Edward II was already seething furiously, and not for the first time ; his favourite Hugh le Despenser was bitterly hated ; the barons were rousing themselves effectually to pull his throne from under him ; and it is very certain that these well-pouched burgesses of Coventry, who could not openly take the field against their liege lord went their own tortuous way to work. When their dark deeds were discovered money tactfully placed here and there secured their safety ; their tool, the warlock, conveniently died in prison, perhaps not without some helping draught to speed him forth, whilst the unfortunate varlet, poor and friendless, was left to face the consequences as best he might, the veriest scapegoat for worthy Richard Latoner, Robert Palmer, and their wealthy friends. Thus it happens again and again : Dr. Fian is tortured and burned, Bothwell goes free ; La Vigoureaux expires on the rack, La Voisin is executed, but the Comtesse de Soissons retires from court, and Madame de Montespan's name must not so much as be breathed in connexion with the accused.

During the late spring of 1324, constant reports came to the ear of Richard de Ledrede, a Friar Minor, Bishop of Ossory,[44] that sorcery was being practised in his diocese, and accordingly the accused were presently haled before the spiritual court. Upon inquiry a round dozen individuals proved to be implicated, some being of quality and no little reputation. The chief witches were Dame Alice Kyteler " domina diues " of Kilkenny,[45]—Kyteler is apparently her maiden name— William Outlawe her son, a banker " amicos sibi faciens de mammona iniquitatis " ; and Robert of Bristol,[46] a cleric in minor Orders. With them were concerned Alice, wife of Henry Faber, John Galrussyn, Helen Galrussyn, Syssoh Galrussyn, Petronilla de Meath and her daughter Sarah,[47] William Payne de Boly, Eva de Brounestoun, and Annota Lange.

Dame Alice Kyteler was indicted on various counts, and

very amply detailed are the accusations brought against her. Both she and her accomplices in order to obtain their ends by means of black magic had renounced the Christian faith, absenting themselves from Mass, in some cases for months at a time, in others for a whole year, refusing to adore the Most Holy Sacrament, ay, even to enter a church door, never taking the blessed bread,[48] nor using holy water. Further they had sacrificed to the Demon live animals whom they tore limb from limb, *diuidebant membratim,*[49] and offered them at the cross-ways to a spirit who bade them call him " son of Art," *qui se facit appellari Artis Filium.* It would be interesting indeed to discover the identity of this mysterious personage. They had practised divination and sought oracular responses from evil spirits, casting spells upon those whom they sought to injure by cursing them and naming each separate member, holding the while candles in their hands which they extinguished at the end of the ceremony, in mockery of ecclesiastical excommunication. Moreover, they confected love charms and made certain unguents from loathsome ingredients, the flesh of unbaptized babes, the hair of criminals who had been hanged, the nails of dead men's fingers, the intestines of animals, and noxious herbs. Dame Alice herself entertained a familiar, *a quo cognosci carnaliter se permittit,*[50] who was named " Son of Art " and sometimes " Robin, son of Art." He appeared to her in various guises, as a cat, as a large black shock-dog, as a huge negro with two gigantic attendants, one of whom carried an iron rod, *in specie cuiusdam æthiopis cum duobus sociis ipso maioribus et longioribus, quorum quilibet uirgam ferream portat in manibus,* and to him she had devoted herself body and soul, since she averred that it was he who was the source of all her wealth and good fortune. Dame Alice had been married four times, first to William Outlawe of Kilkenny, a banker and rich money-lender, who was dead before 1302 ; secondly to Adam le Blund of Callan (Le Blond or Le White he is sometimes called), who was dead before 1311 ; thirdly to Richard de Valle (or *Wall*); and in 1324 she was wife to Sir John le Poer. At least two of her husbands had been widowers with children, and these sons and daughters now loudly accused their stepmother before the Bishop of having killed their fathers by Witchcraft, whilst John le Poer was himself wasting away under a terrible and unnatural sickness during which the nails dropped from his fingers and feet, and the hair from his head. A maidservant, however, had opportunely given him something more than a hint of what might be going on, and violently possessing himself of his wife's keys, which he actually wrenched from her hands in spite of her struggles and resistance, he promptly opened the boxes and chests in her bower, to find the mysterious vials and elixirs, strange instruments and ghastly relics of mortality, the whole of which he packed up and dispatched to the Bishop under the charge of two trusty friars.

All this detailed contemporary evidence is of the first importance. It has not infrequently been stated that the various practices of Witchcraft which loom so largely in the Elizabethan and Stuart trials, as well as in French and other continental records, which are reiterated again and again, the commerce with familiars, sacrifices to the Demon, the making of potions and lotions from obscene and foul recipes, the slaying of enemies by lingering disease, and many black secrets beside, were hardly known amongst us until the reign of Elizabeth, when sorcery took on a darker and more criminal colour. The trial of Dame Alice Kyteler is demonstrative proof of the contrary.

Raphael Holinshed in his *Chronicle of Ireland* (London, 1587, p. 69) gives the following account of these proceedings, wherein will be noticed even further particulars.

" 1323. In the eighteenth yere of King Edward II, his reigne, the Lord John Darcie came into Ireland, and to be lord justice, and the Kings lieutenant there. In these daies lived in the diocesse of Ossorie the Lady Alice Kettle, whom the bishop asscited to purge herselfe of the fame of inchantment and witchcraft imposed unto hir and to one Petronill and Basill hir complices. She was charged to have nightlie conference with a spirit called Robert Artisson, to whome she sacrificed in the high waie nine red cocks and nine peacocks eies. Also that she swept the streets of Kilkennie betweene compleine and twilight, raking all the filth towards the doores of hir sonne William Outlawe, murmuring secretlie with hir selfe these words :

" To the house of William my sonne,
Hie all the wealth of Kilkennie towne.

At the first conviction they abjured and did penance, but shortlie after they were found in relapse, and then was Petronill burnt at Kilkennie, the other twaine might not be heard of. She at the hour of hir death accused the said William as privie to their sorceries, whome the bishop held in durance nine weeks, forbidding his keepers to eat or to drink with him, or to speake to him more than once in the daie. But at length, thorough the sute and instance of Arnold le Powre then seneschall of Kilkennie, he was delivered, and after corrupted with bribes the seneschall to persecute the bishop ; so that he thurst him into prison for three moneths. In rifling the closet of the ladie, they found a wafer of sacramental bread, having the divels name stamped thereon in steed of Jesus Christ, and a pipe of ointment, wherewith she greased a staffe, upon which she ambled and gallopped thorough thicke and thin, when and in what manner she listed. This businesse about these witches troubled all the state of Ireland the more, for that the ladie was supported by certeine of the nobilitie, and lastlie conveied over into England, since which time it could never be understood what became of hir."

Although it has been suggested that Holinshed immediately derived his account from the Latin *Annales Hiberniæ*, which probably received their ultimate form in the fifteenth century, they incorporate, at least, much contemporary matter, and there can scarcely be any doubt that the above is an excerpt from the actual testimony of witnesses at the trial. Two very prominent particulars at once call for notice : the Host stamped with some mysterious evil name ; the staff which was greased with magic ointment. The Devil's wafer impressed with strange characters or of grotesque shape is frequently mentioned in the witch trials. Bocal and Migalena, two apostate priests of the Basses-Pyrénées, confessed that they celebrated Mass with triangular hosts whilst the diabolists at the elevation cried " Corbeau noir ! Corbeau noir ! " ; Gentien le Clerc, condemned at Orleans in 1614, frequented Sabbats " quand il veut leuer l'Hostie & le Calice, qui sont noirs " ; Thomas Boullé, who was executed on 21 August, 1647, and his superior l'abbé Picard, parish-priest of Mesnil-Jourdain, had both used blood-red hosts at their profane celebrations ; in the Mass of S. Sécaire the host is triangular with three sharp points, and black. Similar abominations are not unknown among the Satanists to-day, so Dame Alice Kyteler is linked up with the twentieth century.

The staff, and the riding thereon, a hobby-horse ritual which has survived, innocently enough, in the Mummers' Play, is the familiar broomstick, the magic weapon of the witch throughout all ages. In the Plough Monday play of Cropwell,[51] Nottinghamshire, as in the Lutterworth variety, Beelzebub himself actually appears and, what is very significant, he bears a besom.

It must be noticed that throughout the whole of the Kyteler trial considerable emphasis is laid upon the heresies of the accused, showing that earlier than the fourteenth century heresy and sorcery were inextricably commingled. They are termed " hæretici sortilegæ quamplures, diuersis utentes sortilegiis, quæ sapiebant diuersas hæreses." Alice Kyteler is "hæresibus uariis irretitam." Again, when the Bishop is pressed to stay the proceedings for a while, he pertinently replies : " Si perpendere possint hæretici processus ecclesiæ contra ipsos, fugient ad partes alias sine mora." Dame Alice's advocate, Roger Outlawe,[52] and his juniors " allegarunt quod in crimine tam detestabili sicut est crimen hæresis non tenebatur ipsa personaliter, sed sufficiebat per procuratorem comparere." Alice Kyteler is expressly described as " sortilega et hæretica " ; she is excommunicated for forty days " in causa hæresis " ; she and her companions are " personæ de hæresibus notatæ," and the Archbishop of Dublin sends a mandate to Kilkenny directing the attachment of " Alicia Kiteler, mater Willelmi Outlawe, Willelmus Outlawe filius eiusdem, Iohannes Galrussyn, etc., [qui] super criminibus hæreticæ prauitatis coram ipso [episcopo Ossoriensi] sunt irretiti." The account in the *Annales Hiberniæ* commences : " Richardus Lederede episcopus Ossoriensis citauit dominam Aliciam Ketyll de hæretica prauitate et ipsam coram se comparere fecit."

The trial, however, did not take place without serious delays and difficulties, the chief obstacles being the extraordinary influence brought to bear on behalf of William Outlawe, whose great wealth won him many adherents, both high and low, until it seemed as if he were almost able to defy justice. At length, however, the Bishop, who was not easily turned from his purpose, seized the haughty and purse-proud banker, whom he kept in durance until his prisoner, broken and humbled, begged to be reconciled and released. Pardon was not too easily granted, but at length Outlawe was permitted publicly to recant and adjure his heresies in the Cathedral Church of S. Mary, Kilkenny, when he was formally reconciled, *sub conditionibus*, of which one was that he should roof the Cathedral with lead, and another that he should go on a pilgrimage to the shrine of S. Thomas at Canterbury, fasting every Tuesday[53] until he had duly per-formed that penance.   Dame Alice Kyteler herself, who on 2 July was found guilty,[54] " propter sortilegia diuersa et hæresim multimodam et sacrificia dæmonibus immolata," had already taken ship for England having with her Basilia (Sarah) de Meath.[55]   The rest of the coven[56] were not so lucky.   Some were burned, others publicly whipped in the market-place and through the streets of Kilkenny, others banished and declared excommunicate.

Petronilla de Meath, " hæretica, una de sodalibus dictæ dominæ Aliciæ," was burned on Saturday, 3 November.[57] She had confessed her misdeeds in full. She had renounced the Christian faith, and on three occasions sacrificed to the Devil ; she had brewed philtres composed of adders, spiders, the herb cinquefoil, the brains of an unbaptized babe, and other ingredients for love or hate ; she had consulted and commerced with demons and familiar, actually being present when Robin, son of Art, had copulated with the Lady Alice, " et post tantum scelus locum turpitudinis cum kaneuacio lecti sui manu propria tersit " ; she had performed diabolical ceremonies with a ritual of lighted candles and spittings to cast a spell upon her enemies, ay, even upon her own husband. She boasted that she was a mere novice in comparison with Dame Alice, who had taught her every secret of this evil craft, and than whom she averred there was not a more powerful and cunning witch in the realm of England itself, not in the whole wide world.   Glorying in her iniquities, refusing the Sacrament of Penance, spurning priest and friar who sought to assoil her, this unhappy witch was burned at the stake, "cum debita solemnitate" in the presence of an immense and awe-struck throng.   " Et hæc est prima sortilega hæretica inter tot et tantas quæ unquam combusta fuit in Hybernia," concludes the old chronicler.

The most singular and significant figure throughout the whole proceedings, however, is not Dame Alice Kyteler, nor William Outlawe, but the mysterious familiar, the incubus, Robin, son of Art.[58] Who, we might well ask, was he ? He visits Dame Alice in various animal disguises, as a cat, a big black dog, or again as a tawny Ethiop with two attendants who carry iron rods—probably some kind of javelin or other weapon. Petronilla de Meath bawds for him ; the noble and wealthy dame prostitutes herself to him ; they offer him sacrifice, and regard him with the utmost veneration as the author of all their good. The most intensive and prolonged study of the evidence has not afforded a single clue, and yet beyond a doubt here is the key to the situation. He is said to be " ex pauperioribus inferni." If we suggest that Robin was some lusty young peasant that line is full of difficulties. He must have been possessed of keenest wit and resource to keep outside the trial, for Bishop Ledrede threw his net wide ; he must have been endowed with remarkable strength of character and fascination for his followers were true to him to ruin and death. Surmise is useless ; we can only confess ourselves baffled ; and indeed there are not sufficient data to enable us to arrive at any conclusion.

The records of sorcery in Ireland are scanty, and it may be convenient here to pass them briefly in review. The Statute Rolls of the Parliament (ed. H. F. Berry) for the year 1447 contain remonstrances drawn forth by the fact that some man of rank had been accused of the intent to do grievous harm to his enemy by unholy spells. John, Archbishop of Armagh and others declare that by such charges which are nothing save " the subtle malice and malicious suits of certain persons slandering a man of rank this land was entirely slandered, and still is in such slanderous matters as never were known in this land before, as in ruining or destroying any man by sorcery or necromancy." The Kyteler scandals had been forgotten, or were at any rate conveniently unknown.

No further cases of Witchcraft are to be traced until 1544 when we have the following entry in the table of the red council book of Ireland : *A letter to Charles Fitz Arthur for*

sendinge a witch to the Lord Deputie to be examined. The red
council book has been lost, and we possess but an abstract
of the contents, so further details of this witch cannot be
ascertained. In 1578 a trial for sorcery took place at Kilkenny,
though, here again, nothing but the bare fact can be known.
In November of that year sessions were held by Lord Justice
Drury and Sir Henry Fitton, who in a letter to the Privy
Council upon the 20 of the said month report : " Thirty-six
persons were executed, amongst whom were some good ones,
a blackamoor and two witches by natural law for that we find
no law to try them by in this realm."[59]   An omission soon
to be remedied, since in 1586 a Statute " against the practices
of the wicked offences of conjurations, and of invocations of
evill spirites, and of sorceries, enchantments, charms, and
witchcrafts," was passed by the Irish Parliament, all who
were found guilty of destroying any person by spells or
charms being condemned to suffer paines of death as a felon
or felons.   Those who hurt or lamed, or sought treasure by
goetic crafts were to be punished in the pillory upon the first
conviction, but if twice found guilty were to be executed.
An Act of 1634 also makes mention of Witchcraft as one of
the recognized methods by which one man may take the
life of another.   It would seem, indeed, from incidental
notices in writers of the latter half of the sixteenth century
that sorcery was regarded as very prevalent in Ireland about
that period.   Barnabe Rich, for example, says in his description of Ireland : " The Irish are wonderfully addicted to give
credence to the prognostications of Soothsayers and Witches."
Stannihurst, again, writes that in his day (1547–1618) there
were many sorcerers and warlocks among the Irish.

Gerald, sixteenth Earl of Desmond, the " Great Earl," who
was betrayed and killed in 1583, has largely passed from the
clear vision of history to the mystic clouds of legend.   He is
supposed yet to lie enchanted at the bottom of Lough Gur,
a lonely lake some miles from Limerick.   Once in seven years
he rises and rides by night upon his white horse round Lough
Gur.   The steed is shod with silver shoes, and when these are
worn out the spell will be dissolved and the Earl will regain
possession of his vast estates and semi-regal power.   In the
early years of the nineteenth century a blacksmith named
Teigue O'Neill claimed to have seen the ghostly cavalcade,

which actually stopped at the door of his lonely forge that overlooked the waters of the lake.

In 1606 " on the Saturday next after the three weeks of Easter " John Aston, a clergyman, " late of Mellifont, Co. Louth," was examined before the King's Court upon a charge of having used certain conjurations and invocations to recover a stolen silver cup, to obtain certain treasures of gold concealed in the earth at Mellifont and Cashel, and to ascertain where Hugh, Earl of Tyrone, was abiding. The prisoner " by warrant of the Lord King was sent into England,"[60] but nothing further has been traced concerning him.

Holy Cross Abbey, the famous Cistercian house, about three miles south-west of Thurles, Tipperary, was enriched with a shrine of the Holy Cross, the Relic, which had been presented by a Plantagenet queen,[61] being one of the most considerable throughout all Christendom. For three and a half centuries this pillared shrine in the north transept was assuredly the favourite pilgrimage place in Ireland. Although suppressed in 1536 under the evil fiat of the godless Henry VIII the Abbey still maintained its existence in some sort, for Holy Mass was said or sung there as late as 1633, and 1632 seems to have been the last date when the Relic was solemnly exposed for public veneration. In 1609 Anastasia Sobechan, a pilgrim from Callan, Kilkenny, who had long been tortured by magical spells (*ueneficiis incantationibus collisa*), worshipped at the shrine, when the Lord Abbot Bernard [Foulow] placed a girdle which had touched the Wood of the Cross about her body. At that moment by virtue of the Rood of Calvary she was cured and set free from every vexation.[62]

The Rev. Alexander Colville, D.D., who was ordained in Episcopal orders in 1622, and subsequently held the vicarage of Carnmoney, the prebend of Carncastle, and the Precentorship of Connor, common gossip held to be a wizard of no mean powers who had made a compact with the Devil and choused the old enemy at last by a subtle sleight. He was a man of considerable wealth, which rumour attributed to a demoniac source. The truth is simple. As a prominent member of the Establishment Dr. Colville was known to be a stout and stalwart enemy to the Presbyterianism at that

time vermiculating all Ulster.   Indeed he opposed the
sectarians with all his might, and in return his opponents
whose empty heads were always teeming with noisome and
morbid stories of hell's influence, quickly sowed lies right and
left accusing him of communion with evil spirits and
Assyrians.

In 1661 we have one of the most important cases in the
history of Irish sorcery, the extraordinary tale of Florence
Newton, the witch of Youghal and her cantrips.   The details
are in truth exactly similar to those which were so meticu-
lously rehearsed time after time in the majority of English
cases, and as the reports are redundant even to excess it is
hardly needful to do more than epitomize the events and
the evidence.   The beldame seems to have been indicted
upon two separate counts, viz. with bewitching Mary Longdon, serving-maid to John Pyne, a man of some importance
who was Bailiff of Youghal in 1664, and with causing the
death by occult arts of David Jones.   She had been committed to prison by Richard Mayne, Mayor of Youghal, on
24 March, 1661, and she was tried at the Cork Assizes, on
11 September following, before Judge Sir William Aston, who
had borne arms for King Charles I, and on 3 November, 1660,
was appointed senior puisne Judge of the Chief Place.[63]
Such comment had been excited by the proceedings that the
Attorney-General himself went down to prosecute.

It should be remarked that there was at Youghal a coven
of suspected witches, two of whom, Goody Halfpenny and
Goody Dod, were confronted with the afflicted girl, who,
however, identified Gammer Newton as the author of her
sickness.   About Christmas, 1660, Florence Newton presented
herself at the house of John Pyne and demanded a piece of
beef out of the powdering (pickling) tub, which was refused,
whereupon she tottered away mumbling curses.   A week or
two later she met Mary Longdon, whom she suddenly grasped
tightly and kissed with some violence saying, " Mary, I pray
thee let thee and I be Friends."   Within a few days Mary
Longdon was vexed by strange visions.   A woman in a veil
stood by her bedside, and when the veil was removed she saw
it was old Mother Newton.   Next she was taken with fits,
trances, cramps, and vomitings, whilst uncanny poltergeist
tricks began to take place in the house, stones flying about

and hurting her, the furniture being shifted from room to room without visible cause, feather beds being thrown at her as though to stifle her beneath them. In her paroxysms she cried out on Florence Newton, who when requested to visit the house curtly refused. The matter became serious and was presently investigated by the authorities. The mayor ordered the suspected woman to be brought to Pyne's house and taken into the wench's chamber. When this was done the convulsions and chorea were redoubled until the patient twisted and writhed as in an agony with foaming lips and set sightless eyes. The mayor upon examining the case and hearing various witnesses committed Florence Newton to Youghal Prison, 24 March, 1661. In the April following, however, she bewitched one David Jones to death by kissing his hand through the bars of the gate. Elinor Jones, the widow, at Cork Assizes, alleged that her husband and Francis Besely had watched the woman one night in her prison, and that when her husband, who had desired to teach Newton the Lord's Prayer, stood by the grate, resting his hand on the bars, the hag suddenly kissed his hand. He returned home restless and ill, and greeted his wife with " She hath kiss'd my Hand, and I have a great pain in that arm, and I verily believe she hath bewitch'd me, if ever she bewitch'd any Man." All that night and thereafter he grew sicker, complaining of strange numbness in his arm. At the end of seven days the agony increased, and he then kept his bed, grievously afflicted, and crying out against Florence Newton. Fourteen days later he died.

Valentine Greatrakes, the well-known healer or " stroker," was one of the witnesses at the trial. In the company of two persons of local prominence, Edward Perry and Mr. Blackwall, they essayed certain approved tests upon the witch, and were soon convinced that the charges brought against her were only too just. Unfortunately there seems to be no record of the result of the trial, but if Florence Newton were found guilty, and there can be little doubt that such was the case, she would have been sentenced to death under the Elizabethan statute of 1586.

There are not a few stories of enchantments, but these belong to færy rather than to sorcery; we have accounts of meetings with the Devil or his henchmen, apparitions, banshees, and a dozen other such spectres, but to meet the actual witch in Irish records is rare indeed. In 1670, an Irish clergyman, the Rev. James Shaw, Presbyterian minister of Carnmoney, " was much troubled with witches, one of them appearing in his chamber and shewing her face behind his cloke hanging on the clock-pin, and then stepping to the door, disappeared . . . he sickens and dyes ; his wyfe being dead before him, and, as was supposed, witched."

About the same time " In Ireland there was one Thomas Moor, who had his wife brought to bed of a child, and not having made use of her former midwife, who was *malœ famœ*, she was witched by her so that she dies." In 1685-6, at Cork, when the son of Christopher Crofts fell sick with a convulsion of eight or nine hours, his mother and several others were of opinion that he was bewitched by old Gammer Welsh, a notorious hag who had been recently committed to Bridewell by Crofts. In a letter to Sir John Perceval, however, the father avows " I have not faith to believe it was anything but the hand of God."[64]

A witch is said to have been apprehended, condemned, strangled at the stake, and burned to ashes at Antrim in 1699 for casting a spell upon a young girl some nine years old.[65]

The last instance of witches being tried and convicted in Ireland as offenders against the laws of the realm is the celebrated Island-Magee case. In September, 1710, Mrs. Anne Haltridge, widow of the Rev. John Haltridge, late Presbyterian minister of Island-Magee, whilst staying in the house of her son James Haltridge, suffered continual vexations at night by the throwing about her room of turf from the heath and stones. No visible agent could be traced, and she was obliged to seek another chamber. In December, as she sat before the fire, a little boy of some twelve years, having an old black bonnet on his head with his face concealed in a torn blanket he wrapped about him, suddenly entered and took his place near her. When she questioned him in surprise he made no answer, but nimbly leaped about the room and then ran out of the house, not, however, before the servants saw him and ran after him, only to find he had vanished. On 11 February, 1711, the disturbances were renewed. Books were snatched from the hands of readers and found stowed away in odd corners. Stones were flung, windows broken, the clothes suddenly snatched from the beds and thrown in a heap, and other phenomena, not unusual in this kind of disturbance, were experienced. Several persons of repute visited the house to investigate such extraordinary happenings. Not unnaturally trickery was suspected, but no amount of watching or inquiry could trace anything of the kind. One night Mrs. Haltridge, who had gone to bed as usual in the haunted room, uttered a loud cry and screamed out that she had been stabbed by a knife. The violent pain never left her and at the end of the week, 22 February, she died.

Some ten days later, a girl about seventeen years of age, Miss Mary Dunbar, came to stay with Mrs. Haltridge to keep her company after the death of her mother-in-law. On the night of her arrival her trunk was secretly burst open and the contents scattered over the house. An apron was found to be tied up by a string which had nine curious knots fastened in it. This was a baleful charm, the witches' ladder, *la ghirlanda delle strege*. It seems at once to have operated, since Miss Dunbar was seized with hideous convulsions in which she cried out that three women were tormenting her. About midnight another fit succeeded, and she gave the names of seven or eight hags whom she saw mocking her and consulting over the progress of her disorder. She also added a close description of their persons. They were Janet Liston, Elizabeth Cellor, Kate M'Calmont, Janet Carson, Janet Mean, Jane Latimer, and one who was termed Mrs. Ann. Without the knowledge of Miss Dunbar, Jane Latimer was brought to the house, whereupon the ailing girl was thrown into the most alarming paroxysms, and shrieked out that Latimer was torturing her. At one time, moreover, she singled one of her tormentors from among thirty women who had been collected to see if she could be deceived either in the name or description. Between the 3 and 24 of March depositions relevant to various aspects of the case were sworn to by various persons, and the Mayor of Carrigfergus issued a warrant for the arrest of all those suspected. Seven were at once taken : Janet Mead, of Braid Island ; Jane Latimer, of Irish quarter, Carrigfergus ; Catherine M'Calmont, of Island-Magee ; Janet Liston, *alias* Sellar ; Elizabeth Sellar ; Janet

Carson ; and Margaret Mitchell of Kilroot, who proved to be the Mrs. Ann, so dubbed by the rest of the coven. The accused were brought up for trial before Judges Antony Upton and James Macartney at Carrigfergus, 31 March, 1711. The proceedings commenced at six in the morning and lasted until two in the afternoon. Judge Upton was of opinion that the prisoners could not be brought in guilty upon the sole testimony of Miss Dunbar's trances, but Judge Macartney differed from him altogether, and thought that the jury might well return a verdict of guilty. This was accordingly done and in accordance with the existing statute the gang, one and all, were sentenced to a year's imprisonment and to stand in the pillory four times during that period.

Almost a century after, in March, 1818, Mary Butters, the notorious " Carnmoney witch," was put forward for trial at the Spring Assizes of Carrigfergus. A tailor, Alexander Montgomery, whose cow had in his opinion been bewitched, applied to Mary Butters, well known in the district as a "wise-woman," to raise the spell. Mary Butters ordered Montgomery and a young man named Carnaghan to watch in the cow-house, whilst she herself, an old woman named Lee, Montgomery's wife and son, remained indoors to confect the counter-charm. Montgomery and his companion kept vigil until dawn, when, becoming alarmed at receiving no summons, they knocked loudly at the door of the house. No answer was given, and peering through the kitchen window they beheld the four inmates lying on the floor as dead. Admittance was at once forcibly gained, and it was found that the wife and son had actually expired, Margaret Lee only survived a few minutes. Mary Butters was thrown out by the roadside and shortly recovered. The house was filled with a fetid stench, and on the fire a large pot wherein were found milk, needles, pins, crooked nails, with other ingredients, was smoking furiously. At the inquest held at Carnmoney on 19 August the jurors gave as their opinion that the three victims had been suffocated owing to Mary Butters having made use of some noxious gallimaufry, which she cooked as a charm to recover a sick cow. Her story was that a gigantic blackamoor had appeared before them armed with a huge bludgeon, and in a moment he had killed the three persons by his blows, stunning herself. She was brought up at the

Assizes but discharged by proclamation. The affair caused much talk, and a racy lilting ballad, composed by some resident in the district, which jestingly describes the scene, was long sung up and down the countryside.[66]

That Mother Butters merely used the traditional and old practised method of delivering the cow is shown by a case which occurred at Newtownards in January, 1871. A farm-hand brought an action against his master for wages alleged to be due. In the course of the evidence it transpired that on one occasion he had been set to drive away the witches who were harming the cattle. All left the house except the operator, who, having locked himself in, closed the windows and stopped up every crack and crevice, even blocking the chimneys with sods. He then placed upon the peat fire a large pot of new milk, into which he threw three rows of pins which had never been used and three packets of bright needles. All these boiled fast for an hour, and, as there was no outlet for the smoke, the man narrowly escaped being choked by the fume.[67]

In June, 1890, at Dungannon Quarter Sessions, before Sir Francis Brady, one farmer sued another for breach of warranty in a cow. It was stated that the animal had been " blinked " or bewitched, and the defendant described how a visit had been paid to a wise-woman, who instructed him in an elaborate curative charm.

In 1892 a man related that a friend of his dwelling in the Aran Islands was stricken by an incurable disease, and having been given over by his doctor, he sought the services of a *cailleach*, an old woman able by her occult power to transfer the malady from the sufferer to some healthy person who would ail fast and die in consequence. Her method was to go to a field adjoining the highway, and here to pluck certain herbs from the ground, gazing up the public road as she did so. The first passer-by upon whom her malignant glance lighted would in twenty-four hours take the sick man's illness and swiftly die, the patient mending apace as the unconscious victim languished.

" Burying the sheaf," a practice of the black art, was still used in 1893, in Co. Louth. The person essaying the charm first visits the chapel, where facing withershins, with back mockingly turned to the altar, as witches use, certain words are muttered. A sheaf of wheat is selected and shaped like the human body, the heart being made of plaited straw. Into this and at the various joints pins are deeply thrust, and with horrid invocations of the Devil the sheaf is buried near the house of the individual whose death is desired. As the wheat rots the victim will languish, to expire when it has wholly decomposed. If the sheaf be buried in damp ground it will fast rot, and so the forespoken wight will fade fast ; but if the victim is to perish slowly and linger on in pain a dry spot should be chosen for the sepulture of the moppet. A case where one woman tried to kill her rival by this magic came to light during certain police court proceedings at Ardee in 1893.[68]

The terrible Baltyvadhen tragedy which was heard at Clonmel in 1895, and which is continually referred to as a " witch-burning," is wholly misnamed. The poor woman who was placed upon the kitchen fire by her own family and burned so that she died was not tortured because she was a witch, but in the belief that the real wife had been taken away and a fairy changeling substituted in her place ; when the latter was subjected to the ordeal of fire it would vanish, and the wife would be restored.

In 1911 an unhappy old creature was tried for killing another such crone, an old-age pensioner, in a fit of insanity. One of the witnesses deposed that on the morning of the murder he met the accused in the highway. She was muttering to herself : " I have the old witch killed. . . . She came to me at three o'clock yesterday, and told me to kill her, or I would be plagued with rats and mice." To another person she said : " We will all be happy now. I have the devils hunted away. They went across the hills at three o'clock yesterday."[69]

One authority tells us that the law against Witchcraft lasted in Ireland until 1821,[70] but another authority writes that " though the Statutes against witchcraft in England and Scotland were repealed (the latter very much against the will of the clergy), it is said that that passed by the Irish Parliament was not similarly treated and consequently is, theoretically, still in force. Be that as it may . . . witchcraft is still [1913] officially recognized in Ireland as an offence against the law. In the Commission of the Peace the newly appointed magistrate is empowered to take cognizance of amongst other crimes " Witchcraft, Inchantment, Sorcery, Magic Arts."[71]

To return to the ample annals of English sorcery, in the forty-fifth year of the reign of Edward III, 1371, there was brought before the King's Bench, in circumstances which might have been thought to be absolutely incriminating, a Southwark man discovered with not only a dead man's head in his possession but a grimoire to boot. Accordingly he was arrested on suspicion of black magic, but discharged on swearing he would never be a sorcerer. " In Trinity term of the xlvth year of the reign of Edward III. Note, a man was arrested at Southwark with a skull and the head of a corpse, and with a book of spells in his wallet, and brought before Sir J. Knivet the king's justice of peace, but no official indictment was charged against him, wherefore the magistrates made him swear that he would never practise sorcery, and he was released from prison, and the head and book were burned in Tothill fields."[72] Two hundred years later he would almost certainly have been hanged, and it is astonishing that the ecclesiastical courts did not take up the matter. Their powers were considerably increased and quickened by the statute *De hæretico comburendo* passed in 1401, which was mainly the work of Archbishop Thomas Arundel, the primate, although in fact nothing more than the application to England of the general law of Christendom.

When the so-called " Good Parliament " met in April, 1376, one of the first persons against whom they concentrated their attacks was the lovely Alice Perrers, the royal favourite. They were manifestly determined to put an end to her "dyshonest malapertnes," and the accusations they brought forward were many and grave. Her exhortations and rapacity were cited ; a special statute was passed to prevent her interference with the course of justice ; she had brought dishonour to the King's soul and disease to his body, they said, by her lewdness. Her power over Edward was attributed to Witchcraft, and orders were issued for the apprehension of the necromancer who aided her wiles. Some members of Parliament declared that the lady had long maintained in her house a mysterious Dominican, " whoe in outwarde show professed physicke & practised the same arte, but he was a magician, gaven to wicked enchantments, by whose experiments Ales allured the Kynge to her unlawfull love, or els, as I may trulyer say, into madnes, for a young man riotous syneth, but an olde man lecherous outragiously dootethe." This friar, following the lore of an Egyptian wizard, named Vertebanus, had made pictures of Edward and Alice, which, with the help of herbs and incantations, gave her complete power over her lover. He had also made rings of memory and forgetfulness, the virtue whereof was to keep the King ever mindful of his mistress.

It was decided that the magician must be had before the Parliament, but as it was difficult, if not impossible, to seize him in Alice's house, he was lured thence by two knights who feigned to be sick and offered large sums for their cure, and his person promptly attached. " And when without remedye he lamented hys taikynge, a certayne mayd sayd unto hym : What ys the matter, father, that you so lament ? what have you now cause to feare ? could you not fore see these thyngs, that were accustomed to tell unto others thynges to come ? to whom he answered, I dyd foresee trewely these thynges, but when they sholde chaunce I wist not, for I tolde of a Parliament to come, wherein both I & my mystres sholde suffer many adversatyes." Brought before the Council he could say little to defend himself, and it seems that he would have suffered at the stake had it not been for the opposition of the mild and gentle Archbishop of Canterbury, Simon of Sudbury.[73] This prelate very properly handed over the accused to the Superiors of his own Order, by whom he was relegated under strict supervision to a distant house. " Ales Peres, whoe alwayes before had prefered wantownesse to servitude, hearynge of the apprehension of her frere, bigan vehemently to feare, & her colour wanied." Although the other charges against Alice Perrers were pressed at the moment, that of sorcery was not pursued, especially since the triumph of the " Good Parliament " was short-lived, and the lady, after a brief exile from court, returned to the King's side to punish her foes.

In 1406 when Henry IV was informed that the diocese of Lincoln was infested by sorcerers, wizards, magicians, necromancers, diviners, and soothsayers of every sort, he sent a letter dated 2 January to the Bishop, Philip Repington, his own chaplain and confessor, requiring him to search for any such occult practisers and straightway commit them to prison.

On the 7 May the King addressed a letter to John Colepeper and Robert Passemer bidding them immediately to arrest and bring before the Privy Council a Dominican friar of Worcester, Thomas Northfield, and to seize all his books pertaining to magic, his curious instruments, and similar furniture. The result of this examination does not appear to be recorded. The letter, printed in Rymer's *Fœdera*[74], is as follows :

The King. To his well-beloved and faithful John Colepeper and beloved Robert Passemere, his esquire, Greeting. Ye know that for certain particular reasons which were laid before Us and before Our Council, We did bid you, jointly and severally, attach and arrest Thomas Northfield, professor of theology, of the Order of Preachers, now dwelling in the city of Worcester, and furthermore that ye should attach, seize, impound, and closely examine, all his books treating of the evil science of magic, and that with all possible dispatch ye should bring Brother Thomas himself with any and every suspect book, safe and sound, before Our Council, that he may answer to these charges which there and then will be objected to him, and that moreover he may make such satisfaction and receive such sentence as We and Our Council deem fitting in this matter : and therefore We do command you that with all diligence ye perform this business and that ye execute and carry it out in the prescribed form : Wherefore We require Our Knights of the Shire, Our justices, bailies, apparitors, and all other officers, summoners, constables, and all within Our jurisdiction, collectively and severally, all and each, as well within as without the liberties, by the tenour and mandate of these presents, to lend you furtherance, assistance, and aid, as often as, and whensoever, they shall be called upon by one of you, or both, to do Us service, and shall be duly and officially advised of the same. In which, &c. In the presence of Us, the King. Given at Westminster, on the seventh day of May.[75]

In connexion with the measures taken against Witchcraft in the reign of Henry IV, it may not impertinently be remembered that this monarch was active in the suppression of the Lollard nuisance, and by their abuse of the Sacraments and all things holy—Our Lady of Walsingham was blasphemously termed the Witch of Walsingham by these miscreants—there seems little doubt that their practices were akin to Satanism.

On the 9 May, 1432, Walter Hungerford, the Constable of Windsor, brought before the Privy Council three persons suspected " pro sorcerye," whose operations had been performed within his jurisdiction, namely, Margery Jourdemain, a married woman ; John Virley, a cleric ; and John Ashwell, a Crutched Friar.[76] They were all dismissed ; Margery Jourdemain upon being bailed by her husband, and the two men upon giving security.[77]

Nine years after, in 1441, a much more important case was brought before the ecclesiastical courts, " the duchesse of Gloucestre was arested and put to holt, for she was suspecte of treson." The hand of the enemies of Duke Humphrey is, of course, to be seen in such an attack. Their first move was to arrest a member of the duke's household, Roger Bolingbroke, an astrologer, " for werchyrye of sorcery against the king." It was declared that he had cast the horoscope of the Duchess with a view to ascertain her chances of succeeding to the throne, which he had plotted to secure for her by bewitching Henry VI to death according to the orthodox fashion of melting a waxen image of the monarch. With Bolingbroke were implicated Thomas Southwell, a canon of S. Stephens ; Sir John Hume or Hun, a priest ; and one William Wodham. Margery Jourdemain was also charged, and this time she received short shrift, being burned in Smithfield on 27 October. On the 18 November, Bolingbroke, who had been compelled to ask pardon at Paul's Cross, was hanged at Tyburn, beheaded, and quartered, his head being set on London Bridge, and his body being distributed to Hereford, Oxford, Cambridge, and York, to deter those who were inclined to mix treason and Witchcraft. Thomas Southwell died in prison.

Eleanor Cobham was first brought before " certayne bisshoppis of the kyngis," and there closely examined by Robert Gilbert, Bishop of London ; William of Alnwick, Bishop of Lincoln ; and Thomas Brown, Bishop of Norwich. By these three prelates she was found guilty of high treason and sorcery, and condemned to do public penance. On a Monday, barefoot and bareheaded, carrying a taper of two pounds weight, she was landed at the Temple, whence she walked through Fleet Street to S. Paul's and there offered up her taper at the High Altar. On the Wednesday she landed at the Swan in Thames Street and proceeded by way of Bridge Street and Gracechurch Street to Leadenhall. On Friday she passed from Queenhithe down Cheapside to S. Michael's, Cornhill. On each occasion she was accompanied by the mayor and sheriffs. She was then imprisoned for life at Chester, or more probably at Peel Castle in the Isle of Man.

Ladies of high estate seem to have been particularly implicated in accusations of Witchcraft, obviously for political reasons, and we find that in 1478 Jaquet, Duchess of Bedford, complains to the Privy Council concerning the rumours which are being spread abroad to the effect that she was a witch and by her enchantments had fascinated the King, causing him to dote on her daughter Elizabeth, whom he had made his queen, although he had actually been troth-plight to Eleanor Butler, daughter of the Earl of Shrewsbury. The Privy Council clears the lady and orders their decision to be officially recorded. The original documents (*Rolls of Parliament*, 9 Edward IV) present features of considerable interest :

" Edward by the grace of God, kyng of Englond and of Fraunce, and lord of Irland, to the reverent fader in God Robert byshope of Bathe and Wells, oure chaunceller, greting. Forasmoche as we send unto you within these oure lettres the tenure of an acte of oure grete counsail, amonge othir thinges, remaynyng in thoffice of oure privé seal, in fourme as folowith : In the chambre of the grete counsaill, callid the parliment-chambre, within the kyngs paleis att Westminster, the x. day of Februarie, the ixth yere of the regne of oure soveraygne lord the kyng Edward the IIIIth, in the presence of the same oure soveraigne lord, and my lordis of his grete councail, whos names ben under writen, a supplicacion addressed unto oure said soveraygne lord, on the behalf of the high and noble princesse Jaquet duchesse of Bedford, and two sedules in papier annexed unto the same supplicacion, were openly, by oure saide soveraygne lordis commaundement, radde ; and aftirward his highnes, by thavis of my said lordis of his grete counsaill, acceptyng eftsones the declaracion of my said lady specified in the said supplicacion, accordyng to the peticion of my said lady, commaunded the same to be enacted of record, and therupon lettres of exemplificacion to be made under his grete seal in due fourme ; the tenure of the supplicacion and cedules, wherof above is made mencion, hereafter ensue in this wyse. To the kyng oure soveraygne lord ; shewith and lamentably complayneth unto your highnes your humble and true liegewoman Jaquet duchesse of Bedford, late the wyf of your true and faithfull knyght and liegeman Richard late erle of Ryvers, that where shee at all tyme hath, and yit doth, treuly beleve on God accordyng to the feith of Holy Chirche, as a true cristen woman owith to doo, yet Thomas Wake squier, contrarie to the lawe of God, lawe of this land, and all reason and good consciens, in the tyme of the late trouble and riotous season, of his malicious disposicion towardes your said oratrice of long tyme continued, entendyng not oonly to hurt and apaire her good name and fame, but also purposed the fynall distruccion of her persone, and to that effecte caused her to be brought in a comune noyse and disclaundre of wychecraft thorouout a grete part of this youre reaume, surmytting that she shuld have usid wichecraft and sorcerie, insomuche as the said Wake caused to be brought to Warrewyk atte your last beyng there, soveraigne lord, to dyvers of the lords thenne beyng ther present, a image of lede made lyke a man of armes, conteynyng the lengthe of a mannes fynger, and broken in the myddes, and made fast with a wyre, sayyng that it was made by your said oratrice to use with the said wichcraft and sorsory, where she, ne noon for her ne be her, ever sawe it, God knowith. And over this, the said Wake, for the perfourmyng of his malicious entent above said, entreted oon John Daunger, parishe clerk of Stoke Brewerne, in the counte of Northampton, to have said that there were two other images made by your said oratrice, oon for you, soveraygne lord, and anothir for oure soveraigne lady the quene, wherunto the said John Daunger neyther coude ne wolde be entreted to say. Wheruppon it lykid your highnesse, of your noble grace, atte humble sute made unto your highnesse by your said oratrice, for her declaracion in the premisses, to send for the said Wake and the said John Daunger, commaundyng

them to attende upon the reverent fadir in God the bishop
of Carlisle, the honorable lord therle of Northumberland, and
the worshipfull lords lord Hastyngs and Mountjoye, and
mayster Roger Radclyff, to be examined by them of such as
they coude allegge and say anenst your said oratrice in this
behalf; thaxaminacions afore them had apperith in wrytinge
herunto annexed; wherof oon bill is conteyning the sayings
of Wake, and writte with his owne hand; and anothir
shewyng the saiyngs of the said Daunger, and wrete in the
presence of the said lords; which seen by your highnesse, and
many othir lords in this your grete councell, the xx day of
January last passed, then beyng there present, your said
oratrice was by your grace and theime takyn clerid and
declared of the said noises and disclaundres, which as yet
remaygneth not enacted; forsomuch as divers your lords
were then absent. Wherfor please it your highnesse, of your
most habundant grace and grete rightwisnesse, tenderly to
consider the premisses, and the declaracion of your said
oratrice had in this behalf, as is afore shewid, to commaunde
the same to be enacted in this youre said grete counsaill, so
as the same her declaration may allway remaigne there of
record, and that she may have it exemplified undir your grete
seall: And she shall continually pray to God for the pre-
servacion of your most royal estate.

"Thomas Wakes bille. Sir, this ymage was shewed and
left in Stoke with an honest persone, which delyverid it to
the clerk of the said chirche, and so shewid to dyvers neighbours, aftir to the parson in the chirche openly to men both
of Shytlanger and Stoke; and aftir it was shewed in Sewrisley
a nounry, and to many other dyvers persones, as it is said, &c.
And of all this herd I nor wist no thyng, till after it was sent
me by Thomas Kymbell from the said clerc, which I suppose
be called John Daunger, which cam home to me, and told me
as I have said to my lord of Carlille and to your maistershipp,
from which saying as by herdsay I neither may nor will vary.
And yf any persone will charge me with more than I have
said, I shall discharge me as shall accord with my trouthe
and dutee.

"John Daungers bille. John Daunger, of Shetyllanger,
sworn and examined, saith, that Thomas Wake send unto
hym oon Thomas Kymbell, that tyme beyng his bailly, and

bad the said John to send hym the ymage of led that he had, and so the said John sent it by the said Thomas Kymbell, att which tyme the same John said that he herd never noo wichecraft of my lady of Bedford. Item, the same John saith, that the said ymage was delyvered unto hym by oon Harry Kyngeston of Stoke ; the which Harry fonde it in his owne hous after departyng of soudeours. Item, the same John saith, that the said Thomas Wake, after he cam from London, fro the kyng, send for hym and said that he had excused hymsylf and leyd all the blame to the said John ; and therfor he bad the said John say that he durst not kepe the said image, and that he was the cause he send it to the said Thomas Wake. Item, the same John saith, that the said Thomas Wake bad hym say that ther was two othir ymages, oon for the kyng, and anothir for the quene ; but the said John denyed to say soo. Present my lords whos names foloweth ; that is to say, my lordis the cardinall and archebishop of Caunterbery [Thomas Bourchier], tharchebishop of York [Lawrence Booth], the byshops of Bathe, chauncellor of Englond, Elye [William Grey], tresorer of Englonde, Rouchester [John Russell], keper of the privie seall, London [Thomas Kempe], Duresme [William Dudby], and Karlill ; therls of Warrewyk, Essex, Northumberland, Shrewsbury, and Kent ; the lords Hastings, Mountjoye, Lyle, Crowmell, Scrope of Bolton, Say, &c."

These charges were revived during the troubles after the King's death, as we learn by the " Act for the Settlement of the Crown upon the King and his issue, with a Recapitulation of his Title," whence the following is taken.

" Over this, amonges other things, more specially wee consider, howe that, the tyme of the reigne of kyng Edward the iiij[th] late deceased, after the ungracious pretensed marriage, as all England hath cause soo to say, made betwixt the said king Edward and Elizabeth sometyme wife to sir John Grey knight, late nameing herself and many years heretofore quene of Englond, the ordre of all poletique rule was perverted, the lawes of God and of Gods church, and also the lawes of nature and of Englond, and also the laudable customes and liberties of the same, wherein every Englishman is inheritor, broken, subverted, and contempned, against all reason and justice, soo that this land was ruled by selfewill and pleasure, feare, and drede, all manner of equite and lawes layd apart and despised, whereof ensued many inconvenients and mischiefs, as murdres, extorsions, and oppressions; namely, of poore and impotent people, soo that no man was sure of his lif, land, ne lyvelode, ne of his wif, doughter, ne servaunt, every good maiden and woman standing in drede to be ravished and defouled. And besides this, what discords, inward battailles, effusion of christian mens blode, and namely by the destruction of the noble blode of this londe, was had and comitted within the same, it is evident and notarie thourough all this reame, unto the great sorowe and hevynesse of all true Englishmen. And here also we considre, howe that the seid pretensed mariage betwixt the above-named king Edward and Elizabeth Grey was made of grete presumption, without the knowyng and assent of the lords of this lond, and also by sorcerie and wichecrafte, committed by the said Elizabeth and her moder Jaquett duchesse of Bedford, as the common opinion of the people, and the publique voice and fame is thorough all this land; and hereafter, if and as the caus shall require, shall bee proved sufficiently in tyme and place convenient. And here also we consider, howe that the said pretensed marriage was made privatly and secretely, without edition of banns, in a private chamber, a prophane place, and not openly in the face of the church, aftre the lawe of Goddes churche, but contrarie thereunto, and the laudable custome of the church of Englonde. And howe, also, that at the tyme of contract of the same pretensed marriage, and bifore and longe tyme after, the said king Edward was and stode maryed and trouth-plight to oone dame Elianor Butteler, doughter of the old earl of Shrewesbury, with whome the same kyng Edward had made a precontracte of matrimonie, longe tyme bifore he made the said pretensed mariage with the said Elizabeth Grey, in manner and fourme abovesaid. Which premisses being true, as in veray trouth they been true, it appeareth and followeth evidently that the said king Edward duryng his lif, and the seid Elizabeth, lived together sinfully and dampnably in adultery, against the lawe of God and of his churche; and therefore noo marvaile that, the souverain lord and the head of this land being of such ungodly disposicion, and provokyng the ire and indignacion of oure Lord God, such haynous mischieffs and inconvenients, as is above remembred, were used and comitted in the reame amongs the subgects. Also it appeareth evidently and followeth that all thissue and children of the seid king Edward been bastards, and unable to inherite or to clayme any thing by inheritance, by the lawe and custome of Englond."[78]

It was now that Jane Shore was charged with sorcery by the Protector, Richard of Gloucester, who accused her before the Privy Council on the morning of 13 June, 1483. " What are they worthy to have that compass and imagine the destruction of me, who am so near of blood unto the king, and Protector of his royal person and realm ? " he cried. " It is yonder sorceress, my brother's wife, and others with her. Ye shall all see in what wise that sorceress and that other witch of her council, Shore's wife, with their kind, have by their sorcery and witchcraft wasted my body." Thereupon he pulled up his left sleeve, and exhibited " a werish withered arme and small." It was, of course, well known to all present that the duke's left arm had been so malformed from birth. And presently Lord Hastings, " a good knight and a gentle . . . a louing man and passing wel beloued," lost his head to clear the way for Richard to seize the throne. It is difficult to account for the malevolence with which the Protector regarded his brother's mistress. The unfortunate Jane Shore was tried before the court of the Bishop of London, Thomas Kempe, and one Sunday morning, clad only in her kirtle and carrying a lighted taper, she walked as a penitent to S. Paul's, after which Richard kept her a close prisoner in Ludgate jail. When released under Henry VII she was reduced to absolute penury, and, writes Blessed Thomas More in his *History of Richard III*,[79] " At this daye shee beggeth of many at this daye living, that at this day had begged, if shee had not bene." When at last she died, about 1527, she must have been nearly eighty years of age.

In 1521 the most eminent nobleman in England, Edward Stafford, Duke of Buckingham, Lord High Constable of the realm, was condemned to death on a charge of high treason simply because King Henry VIII vaguely suspected he was aiming at the succession to the throne and had determined he must die. Late in 1520 it reached Wolsey's ears that in " his fumes and displeasures " the Duke had railed not only against the Cardinal but against the King. It soon became known that Buckingham was out of favour, and enemies at once pressed forward with accusations. Robert Gilbert, his treacherous chancellor, swore that he had heard his master say that the Cardinal was an idolater and a sorcerer " taking counsel of a spirit how he might continue to have the king's favour." Another informer was John Delacourt, the Duke's chaplain, who deposed that on 24 April, 1513, the Duke had sent him from Thornbury to the Charterhouse of Hinton in Somerset to consult secretly with Nicholas Hopkins, one of the community there. Dom Hopkins seems to have had some reputation as a mage, and to have been generally credited with the gift of prophecy. At any rate Delacourt swore that the message he received for the Duke was that His Grace " should have all," and later, Buckingham himself interviewed the monk to be assured that if the King died leaving no son he should ascend the throne. Again we find divination commingled with alleged treason, and on 13 May the Duke was brought into Westminster Hall to be tried upon an indictment which rested upon the depositions of three discontented servants, fomented by Henry's savage jealousy and fears. Buckingham was allowed no counsel, he was found guilty—a foregone conclusion, and his head fell upon Tower Hill.

It is curious to note that on 29 January, 1536, the day of Queen Catherine's funeral, when the syphilitic monster who terrorized England was already growing somewhat weary of the gospel light which beamed from Bullen's eyes, he told some one in great confidence that as regards his second wife[80] he had " made this marriage seduced by witchcraft ; and that this was evident because God did not permit them to have any male issue."[81] Such a speech undoubtedly shows that Henry VIII was swayed by the meanest superstitions and incidentally how prevalent and ever present was the belief in black magic and spells. Before the birth of Elizabeth on Sunday, 7 September, 1533, a whole horde of diviners and occultists had been consulted as to the sex of the child, and when the royal mistress was delivered of a daughter it was felt to be to " the great reproach of the astrologers, sorcerers, and sorceresses,"[82] who had affirmed that the infant would be a male.

In 1541 Lord Hungerford was beheaded " for procuring

certain persons to conspire that they might know how long the King's Grace should live," and in the same year an act[83] was passed : " Where dyvers and sundrie persones unlawfully have devised and practised Invocacions and conjuracions of Spirits, . . . and also have used and occupied wichecrafts, inchauntmentes, and sorceries to the distruccion of the neighbours persones and goodes. . . . And for execucion of their saide falce devyses and practises have made or caused to be made dyvers Images and pictures of men, women, childrene, Angelles or develles, beastes or fowles . . . and gyving faithe and credit to suche fantasticall practises have dygged up and pulled downe an infinite nombre of Crosses within this Realme " all such proceedings are considered felony. This piece of legislation is absolute ; there are no gradations of offences ; the law is plain and absolutely sweeping. But within six years this statute, VIII 33 Henry VIII, was annulled. The schismatical Nicholas Ridley, who had been thrust into the see of London ; Thomas Goodrich, the protestant Bishop of Ely; the notorious Master John Scory, who called himself Bishop of Chichester; John Shypp, who uncanonically held the see of Hereford ; and their partisans could ill brook the clauses which forbade the destruction of calvaries and roods, and so the whole statute was clean repealed.

It was at the beginning of the reign of Elizabeth that definite and severe penalties were enacted for Witchcraft, conjuration, and all related arts. A bill was draughted very soon after the accession of the new queen, although actually it was not until 1563 that the measure finally passed on to the statute-book and became English law. It was enacted that those who " shall use, practise, or exercise any Witchecrafte, Enchantment, Charme or Sorcerie, whereby any person shall happen to be killed or destroyed . . . their Concellors and Aidours . . . shall suffer paynes of Deathe as a Felon or Felons." It was further declared that those by whose acts any person was wasted, consumed, or lamed, should suffer for the first offence one year's imprisonment and should be placed in the pillory four times. For the second offence death was the penalty. It was also provided that those who by Witchcraft presumed to discover treasure or to find stolen property or to " provoke any person to unlawfull love " should suffer a year's imprisonment and be pilloried at each quarter. It may not unfairly be said that with this distinctive and comprehensive legislation the prosecution of Witchcraft in England as a secular crime to all practical intents was begun. It is true that some few cases had occurred before this date, but they are comparatively unimportant : in 1558 John Thirkle " taylour, detected of conjuringe " was examined, as also were various persons who were sent to Edmund Grindall on the same charge.[84] In 1559 certain persons, probably including Lady Frances Throgmorton, were vehemently suspected and officially questioned,[85] whilst George Throgmorton and the daughter of Lady Chandos were actually imprisoned.[86] In the following year humbler game was started. Old Mother Burke of S. John's, Kent, fell under the censure of the ecclesiastical authorities ;[87] whilst at London in 1561 a company of ten men, arraigned before the Queen and council on charges of " trespass, contempt, conjuration, and sorceries," were punished with the pillory and compelled solemnly to renounce any such occult proceedings for the future.[88]

The immediate occasion of the statute of 1563 is not far to seek. At the death of Queen Mary the whole gang of seditious recalcitrants, who had taken refuge from the law in Switzerland and South Germany, swarmed back to England in full force, eager to feather their nests to the very fullest advantage. Unscrupulous and of conscience none too nice, they were just the pliant tools Elizabeth required, and they immediately became prominent in Church and State. From 24 June, 1559, the Mass and all other Catholic services were forbidden in England. Of the twenty-seven sees of England ten, including Canterbury, were vacant owing to deaths of those who had occupied them. Fifteen of the seventeen bishops then living were deposed by the Queen before 29 December, 1559, and men who would accept the new religion appointed in their place.[89] Thus Thomas Bentham,[90] who was to occupy the see of Coventry and Lichfield whence Bishop Ralph Bayne had been ejected, and John Parkhurst appointed to Norwich, had both settled in Zurich, a hot-bed of dissensions. John Scory, the new bishop of Hereford, made Geneva itself his headquarters. Richard Cox, who possessed Ely instead of Bishop Thomas Thirlby, and Edmund Grindall, who replaced Bishop Edmund Bonner in London, sojourned in Strassburg and Frankfort. Miles Coverdale, who in 1551 had been intruded into the see of Exeter, and who took no inconsiderable part in the consecration of Archbishop Parker, found Geneva under the iron tyranny of Calvin, with the companionship of sour John Knox, and the unhappy Servetus writhing in the flames as a sight to see, most agreeable to his feelings during his enforced absence from England. There can be no doubt that during their residence in such towns these divines must have become intimately familiarized with the propaganda against Witchcraft that was raging throughout this decade, a movement their old ally Martin Bucer had so urged and excited not many years before. It is natural that when they returned to England and had a large and influential share in the direction of the laws their thoughts should revert to the subject of sorcery, to them a very real and pressing danger, and beyond all question the Calvinistic John Jewel's notorious sermon, which seems actually to have brought the statutes of 1563 into force, admirably sums up and expresses the opinions of the rest.

John Jewel was born in Buden, Devon, on 2 May, 1522. In 1535 he entered Merton College, Oxford, whence four years later he removed to Corpus Christi, and in 1544 commenced master, having been admitted a fellow and appointed a tutor of that foundation. He acquired considerable influence throughout the university, and tirelessly propagated the doctrines of Luther and Zwingli. When the apostate Peter Martyr came to Oxford in 1549 he found no more fervent disciple than this rancorous polemic, and together the precious pair seem to have wrought incalculable mischief. At the time of the trials of Cranmer and Ridley, Jewel acted as their secretary, and attracted so much attention by his extreme partisanship of the accused that he was himself examined by Dr. Marshall, Dean of Christ Church and Vice-Chancellor, and obliged to sign a profession of belief. This proved to be utterly insincere, as at the first opportunity he made off in hot haste for the Continent, first visiting Frankfort, and later Strasburg and Zurich, in both of which towns he boarded in the house of Peter Martyr. Upon the death of Queen Mary (17 November, 1558) he came back to England, and was at once employed in a visitation of the western counties, whence he returned late in October, 1559.[91] His mind was already fully occupied with the horrors of Witchcraft, as is shown by a letter 2 November, where he writes in churlish strain : " We found in all places votive relics of Saints, nails with which the infatuated people dreamed that Christ had been pierced, and I know not what small fragments of the Sacred Cross. The number of witches and sorceresses had everywhere become enormous."

There is, in truth, no controversialist of the day who exceeds Jewel in the reckless violence of his abuse. His impudence, profanity, unblushing mendacity, and downright forgery are beyond belief. There are, moreover, to be discerned in the cold concentration of his hate a bitter cynicism and a mocking impiety which one can only stigmatize as devilish, and which go far to prove that the man held no faith at all. Constructive ideas he has none, he is essentially Mephistopheles, " the Spirit that Denies." When he has to speak of Holy Mass he blasphemes like a maniac, as in a letter to Peter Martyr, probably to be dated May, 1559, where he writes : " This it is to have once tasted of the Mass ! He who drinks is made mad by it. Depart from it, all ye who value a sound mind ; who drinks is made mad by it. They perceive that when that palladium is removed every thing else will be imperilled."[92] Again describing the state of England on his return he says : " No part of religion was yet restored ; the country was still everywhere fouled with the Mass," *eadem erat ubique missarum proluuvies*,[93] a phrase which seems to me the extreme of criminal blasphemy. The insincerity of the man is frankly appalling. Ten years after his death Blessed Edmund Campion wrote : " When I was young, John Jewell, the Calvinist leader in England, was impudent enough to challenge the Catholics to a proof of their respective tenets from the works of the Fathers of the first six centuries.[94] The challenge was accepted by some well-known men then in exile and poverty at Louvain. I venture to say that Jewell's craft, ignorance, roguery, and impudence, as exposed by these writers, did more good to the Catholic cause than anything within my remembrance. A proclamation was immediately posted on the doors that none of the answers should be read or kept, though they had been squeezed out by a direct challenge."[95] It is important that we should appreciate a just character of the man to whom the witch-trials in England are largely due, not that he acted from any hatred to Witchcraft and Satanists, but solely from political motives.

As early as the summer of 1559, just before his western circuit, Jewel had been nominated Bishop of Salisbury, and although his masque of narrow Calvinism demurred, or at any rate pretended to demur for bare form's sake, against the prescribed episcopal dress which he had erstwhile harshly denounced, he conveniently allowed his scruples to be overcome and was consecrated in January, 1560. His discourse against witches seems to have been delivered some time between November, 1559, and 17 March, 1560, probably in February of the latter year. At this time the ecclesiastical and civil authorities were in close touch, and no doubt the way was being laid for drastic legislation on the subject of sorcery. A sermon delivered by a famous court preacher, a newly made Bishop, would carry great weight. And Jewel vehemently urged immediate action. It was, he told the Queen, "the horrible using of your poor subjects" that forced him to be round and plain. "This kind of people (I mean witches and sorcerers) within these few last years are marvellously increased within this Your Grace's realm. These eyes have seen most evident and manifest marks of their wickedness. Your Grace's subjects pine away even unto death, their colour fadeth, their flesh rotteth, their speech is benumbed, their senses are bereft. Wherefore, Your poor subjects' most humble petition unto Your Highness is, that the laws touching such malefactors may be put in due execution."[96] Strype certainly says that this sermon was the occasion of the law passed in the fifth year of Elizabeth's reign, by which Witchcraft was again made a felony, as it had been in the reign of Henry VIII.[97]

Another important factor in the crusade against witches lay in the suspicion that sorcery was frequently mixed up with treasonable practices and plots, since it was common knowledge that magic had been constantly employed in attempts against the life of the sovereign. The accession of Elizabeth brought many violent changes of every kind, which, as might well be supposed, were not effected without much opposition, whilst her cruel tyranny bred continual discontent.

Venal poets might sing of her as Gloriana, Belphœbe, Pandora, Cynthia, Astræa, a Goddess divine ;[98] a lewd old strumpet might be acclaimed as a Virgin Queen ; her court might be blazoned with all pomp and circumstance, with wanton dames and roving buccaneers, a very galaxy of tinsel beauty and cardboard chivalry ; but there was another and a darker side to the picture, as the old fox Cecil and the gutter-rat Walsingham with their spies and butchers knew only too well. Conspiracy succeeded conspiracy, and conjuration conjuration. As early as November, 1558, Sir Antony Fortescue,[99] member of a famous Catholic family, was arrested together with several accomplices on a charge of casting the horoscope of the Queen's life. He was soon released, but in 1561 he was again in custody with several other persons of note, alleged to be implicated in an elaborate design which even involved the French and Spanish ambassadors. It was reported that two conjurers in his employ, John Prestall and Edmund Cosyn, with the assistance of a " wicked spryte," had discovered Elizabeth would shortly die a natural death. The accused were for the most part executed, but Fortescue himself, owing to influence in high places, seems to have escaped such punishment. Throughout the whole of the reign and especially during those years when the Scottish Queen was held a prisoner, 1568–87, the English Privy Council pretended to be extraordinarily anxious with regard to any sorceries that might touch the health of Elizabeth. This astute policy they adopted and widely advertised for purposes of their own. There were, of course, plots to liberate the captive Queen, but Elizabeth's life was never for a moment in danger. The Act of 1581, 23 Eliz. Cap. II, is merely a piece of diplomatic bluff : " That if any person . . . during the life of our said Sovereign Lady the Queen's Majesty that now is, either within her Highness' dominions or without, shall by setting or erecting any figure or by casting of nativities or by calculation or by any prophecying, witchcraft, conjurations, or other like unlawful means whatsoever, seek to know, and shall set forth by express words, deeds, or writings, how long her Majesty shall live, or who shall reign a king or queen of this realm of England after her Highness' decease . . . that then every such offence shall be felony, and every offender therein, and also all his aiders [etc.], shall

be judged as felons and shall suffer pain of death and forfeit
as in case of felony is used, without any benefit of clergy or
sanctuary."[100]

The new statute passed in 1563 was the beginning of a
drastic and searching prosecution by the State of witches
and all who consulted or consorted with them. In 1565
Agnes Mondaye, a Dorset witch, was to be apprehended for
casting a spell on one Mistress Chettell,[101] and in the same
year Jennet Pereson[102] was delated to the Durham ecclesiastical authorities, but the first case of any importance seems
to have taken place three years later at Chelmsford. A full
account is given in a black letter pamphlet,[103] *The examination
and confession of certaine Wytches at Chensforde in the
Countie of Essex before the Quenes maiesties Judges the xxvi
daye of July Anno* 1566. The accused Elizabeth Francis,
Alice Chandler, and old Mother Waterhouse were examined
before a distinguished court consisting of Sir John Fortescue,
keeper of the great wardrobe ; Sir Gilbert Gerrard, the
Queen's attorney ; Justice Southcote, a judge of the Queen's
Bench ; and Dr. Thomas Cole, rector of Stanford Rivers, a
parish about ten miles from Chelmsford. Elizabeth Francis
glibly confessed to many " vilanies." She freely acknowledged
that " she learned this arte of witchcraft at the age of xii
yeres of hyr grandmother whose name mother Eue of Hat-
fyelde Peuerell, disseased. Item when shee taughte it her,
she conseiled her to renounce GOD and his worde and to
geue of her bloudde to Sathan (as she termed it) whyche she
delyuered her in the lykenesse of a whyte spotted Catte."[104]
Apparently she asked this familiar for whatsoever she
required—a husband who as a matter of fact led her anything
but a quiet life, as also to avenge herself on her enemies.
After keeping the cat fifteen years she turned it over to
Mother Waterhouse : " she came to one Mother Waterhouse
her neighbour she brought her this cat in her apron and
taught her as she was instructed by her grandmother Eue,
telling her that she must cal him Sathan and geue him of
her bloude and bread and milke as before—Mother Waterhouse said, she receyued this cat of this Frances wife in the
order as is before sayde."[105] She employed it to kill the
geese, swine, and cattle of those who offended her. In some
mysterious way the cat became a toad, and this at her

command killed her husband. The woman's eighteen-year-old daughter Joan confessed that she had pledged her soul to this toad, and confirmed her mother's statements in every particular. Sir Gilbert Gerrard questioned Mother Waterhouse : " When dyd thye Cat suck of thy bloud ? " " Never," she replied, but upon inspection the witch marks upon her body where she had cut and pricked herself for the evil spirit were discovered. So she was convicted and hanged.[106]

Thirteen years later, Elizabeth Francis, whose reputation as a dangerous woman had evidently been long established, was again in trouble, and brought to trial before the judges on circuit. As before, she was ready to tell a long story and to involve others in her mischiefs. The result is not clear. Three of the accused were found guilty and executed, and of these she may have been one ; a poor drab named Elleine Smith, daughter of a woman who had been hanged for a witch, was certainly another ; whilst Mother Staunton was released because " manslaughter or murder was not objected against her."[107]

During episcopal visitations unremitting search after witches was enjoined. Thus in 1577 Whitgift inquires in the diocese of Worcester for known or suspect users of Witchcraft, charms, enchantments, or unlawful invocations for those who took on themselves to tell destinies or to find things lost. In the Lichfield diocese seven years later inquiries were especially directed against magical practices of midwives, a very significant article.[108]

The Chelmsford district in particular was a veritable hotbed of sorcery, as in 1589 there was yet a third alarm, when a beldame named Joan Cunny was convicted, largely on the evidence of a lad of some eleven years, the elder bastard of her " lewde " daughter's two illegitimate children. At the same time Joan Upney was accused of nourishing familiars in the shape of toads, and Joan Prentice, who lived in an Essex almshouse, harboured and fed her familiars as ferrets. All three were hanged.[109]

It will be seen that most of the persons concerned in these trials were the very dregs of society, " namelie leud miserable and envious poore people,"[110] many of them dependent upon organized charity, ignorant, idle, malignant, doting crones and pot-house whores.

During the forty years from 1563 to 1603 alone the details of more than two hundred cases are definitely known, a number which obviously precludes chronological treatment here, whilst the pamphlet literature, although of the greatest value, is also far too voluminous for any detailed examination. It must be remembered, moreover, that this matter only presents a tithe of what doubtless exists, and even barely to enumerate the recorded trials were no easy task, whilst to ascertain the exact sum total of witches involved in these cases rendered impossible by such entries as that relating to Samuel Cocwra (1579), who was paid for " searching for certen persons suspected for conjuracion,"[111] or in 1580 at Kent, when several persons were to be apprehended for conjuration,[112] or in Essex during the same year " sondery persons " were charged with sorcery.[113] In 1584 " the oulde witche of Ramsburg " and many " oulde witches and sorcerers " fell under grave suspicion ;[114] in 1595 several persons were committed at Bristol touching the Earl of Derby's death ;[115] in 1600 several conjurers were detected at Ipswich.

There remains, no doubt still unexamined, a whole mass of English local evidence in the municipal archives of county towns, in the jail delivery records, in old legal documents, among the MSS. to be found in private collections, and not until all these have been scrupulously searched and codified can we venture exactly to estimate the number of Elizabethan witch-trials and condemnations. When we remember that although Mother Gabley of King's Lynn was hanged in 1582–3, and Anne Kerke of Bokes-wharfe was executed at Tyburn in 1599, and hundreds such of poor wretches paid the penalty of penury and guilt, my Lady Hatton, whose heart the demon at the expiration of their contract tore from her bosom in Bleeding-heart Yard, and a score of proud court dames were dabbling in the black art and consulting sorcerers with impunity or, at least, without discovery, we realize how terrible and how widespread a plague was Witchcraft in Elizabethan days. Did not the Queen herself favour Dr. John Dee, a master of hermetic mysteries, who with his speculator, as Lilly dubs him, Edward Kelly, was wont to converse familiarly with spirits and read the future in his magic shew-stone ?[116]

The very titles of the contemporary pamphlets often give

data of considerable interest. Thus we have : *The Examination and Confession of a notorious Witch named Mother Arnold, alias Whitecote, alias Glastonbury, at the Assize of Burntwood in July,* 1574 : *who was hanged for Witchcraft at Barking* (1575). As also : *An Account of Margaret Hacket, a notorious Witch, who consumed a young Man to Death, rotted his Bowells and back bone asunder, who was executed at Tiborn,* 19 *Feb.,* 1585. (London, 1585.) And again : *The Arraignment and Execution of 3 detestable Witches, John Newell, Joane his wife, and Hellen Calles ; two executed at Barnett, and one at Braynford,* 1 *Dec.,* 1595. Another very curious pamphlet is : *The most wonderfull and true storie of a certaine Witch named Alse Gooderidge of Stapenhill, who was arraigned and convicted*[117] *at Darbie, at the Assizes there. As also a true Report of the strange Torments of Thomas Darling, a boy of thirteen years of age, that was possessed by the Devill, with his horrible Fittes and terrible apparitions by him uttered at Burton upon Trent, in the Countie of Stafford, and of his marvellous deliverance.* (London, 1597.)[118]

One of the most remarkable of all Elizabethan cases was that in 1582 of the witches of S. Oses, or S. Osyth's, a hamlet to the north-east of Chelmsford. The trouble began when Grace Thurlow, a " poore and needie woman," as she described herself, laid information before the magistrates concerning one Ursley Kemp, *alias* Gray, who had long borne a very dubious reputation, and who eked out a scanty maintenance by acting as midwife, nursing children, harlotry, and various kinds of white magic, which included " unwitching " the sick. It appeared that Grace Thurlow's son, Davy, had been taken with a strange illness and hideously convulsed. Ursley Kemp came to see him with other neighbours, and after taking the lad by the hand and muttering some mysterious words, she said to the mother : " I warrant thee, I, thy childe shall doe well enough." The boy was almost immediately restored to health, but Grace Thurlow was suspicious, and she refused to allow Ursley Kemp the nursing of a newly born baby girl. Soon afterwards the infant fell out of its cradle and broke its neck. Then a violent quarrel and a " fratch " ensued, during which Ursley threatened her with lameness, and she answered sharply enough : " Take heed, Ursley, thou has a naughtie name." But soon enough

Grace Thurlow was crippled with pain, and could scarcely drag herself along on her hands and knees. A complaint was accordingly made, Ursley Kempe was formally accused, and committed to the assizes by the justices. Here she appeared before Justice Brian Darcy, who promptly examined her eight-year-old " base son " Thomas Rabbet, and he confessed that his mother " hath foure seuerall spirites, the one called Tyffin, the other Tittey, the third Pigine, and the fourth Iacke : and being asked of what colours they were, saith that Tyttey is like a little grey Cat,[119] Tyffin is like a white lambe, Pygine is black like a Toad, and Iacke is black like a Cat. And her saith, her hath seen his mother at times to giue the beere to drinke, and of a white Lofe or Cake to eate, and saith that in the night time the said spirites will come to his mother, and sucke blood of her vpon her armes and other places of her body." He further declared that the spirits had been given to " Godmother Newman," who had carried them away in an earthen pot, and so Ales Newman was also apprehended. One Laurence then appeared to give his testimony against Ursley Kempe, who had bewitched his wife to death.

At first Ursley Kempe denied all the accusations brought against her, but presently upon Justice Darcy " promising to the saide Ursley that if she would deale plainely and confesse the truth that she should haue fauour, so by giving her faire speeche she confessed as followeth," and acknowledged that the indictment of Witchcraft and murder was correct in every particular. The death of Grace Thurlow's baby would have been easy to accomplish, and we may well suppose that Ursley Kempe, who seems to have been the chief of the St. Osees' witches, was initiated into all the secrets of poisoning, which horrid art was universally practised by the wise-women and conjurers of the day, both at home and abroad. Her story, as well as the confessions of the other witches, tallied exactly with the accusations of the witnesses, and it would clearly have been impossible that such should be so concisely the case if the narratives were mere fiction and wild romance. Ursley Kempe went on to incriminate other women who were guilty of these heinous crimes, and soon a whole coven was sought out and brought before the Justice. Among them were Ales Hunt, and her sister Margerie Sammon, who had " two spirites like Toades, the

one called *Tom,* and the other *Robbyn.*" These two were
the daughters of old Mother Barnes, a notorious witch, who
was said to have bequeathed them her familiars. Febey Hunt,
a lass of about eight years old, deposed that her stepmother
Ales Hunt, had two little things, one black and one white,
" the which shee kept in a little lowe earthen pot with woll,
colour white and black . . . and saith, that shee hath seene
her mother to feede them with milke." Elizabeth Bennet
acknowledged that she had two " spirits, one called *Suckin,*
being blacke like a Dogge, the other called *Lierd,* beeing red
like a Lion." Ales Mansfielde had lamed Joan Chester's cattle
because she was refused some curds ; Joan Robinson had
bewitched geese and a litter of pigs, drowned cows, struck
horses with spavins, and men with a wasting sickness ; Annis
Herd, according to her little " base daughter " aged seven,
had six avices or blackbirds as her imps, and six more who
lay in a box lined with black and white wool. And so the
trial proceeded with guilty confessions, accusations, bitter
recriminations, and counter-accusations until sixteen persons,
one of whom was a man, were involved, of whom thirteen, as
it was proved, were held to be guilty of murder owing to
their sorceries. It is uncertain how many were executed
According to some accounts the thirteen were put to death,
but Scot[120] who had followed the case with unusual care says
at least seventeen or eighteen paid the penalty. That the
trial excited unusual interest is plain, and both Scot and
George Gifford, the author of *A Dialogue concerning Witches,*[121]
seemed to have attended some of the hearings.

Perhaps the best summary of the trials, certainly the best
summary of what was believed at the time, is the singular
table drawn up at the end of the pamphlet, evidently written
(in part at any rate) by Justice Darcy himself, to whom it
is dedicated, and entitled :

*A true and iust Recorde of the Information, Examination, and
Confession of all the Witches, taken at St. Osees in the countie of
Essex ; whereof some were executed, and other some entreated
according to the determination of lawe. Wherein all men may
see what a pestilent people Witches are, and how vnworthy to
lyve in a Christian Commonwealth. Written orderly, as the
cases were tryed by euidence by W. W. Imprinted in London at
the three Cranes, in the Vinetree, by Thomas Dawson. 1582.*

The conspectus of the whole affair runs thus :

" The names of xiii Witches and those that have been bewitched by them.

" The Names of those persons that have beene bewitched and thereof haue dyed, and by whome, and of them that haue receyved bodyly harme, &c. As appeareth vpon sundrye Enformations, Examinations, and Confessions taken by the worshipfull Bryan Darcey, Esquire ; and by him certified at large vnto the Queene's Maiestie's Justices of Assise of the Countie of Essex, the xxix of Marche, 1582.

	The Witches.		
S. Osythes.	1. Ursley Kempe, alias Gray .	bewitched to death	Kempes wife, Thorlowes Childe, and Strettons wife.
	2. Ales Newman and Ursley Kempe . .	bewitched to death	Letherdalles childe, and Strettons wife.
Confessed by Ursley and Elizabeth.	The said Ales and Ursley Kempe . .	bewitched	Strattons Childe, whereof they Grace Thorlowe, did languish.
	3. Elizabeth Bennet . .	bewitched to death	William Byet, and Joan his wife, and iii of his beasts. The wife of William Willes, and William Wittingalle.
	Elizabeth Bennet . .	bewitched	William Bonners Wife, John Butler, Fortunes Childe ; whereof they did languish.
	Ales Newman	bewitched to death	John Johnson and his Wife, and her own Husband, as it is thought.
Confessed the cattell	4. Ales Hunt . .	bewitched to death	Rebecca Durrant and vi beasts of one Haywardes.
	5. Cysley Celles .	bewitched to death	Thomas Deaths Childe.
Little Clapton.	Cysley Celles .	bewitched	Rosses Mayde, Mary Death, whereof they did languish.
Thorpe.	Cysley Celles and 6. Ales Manfielde.	bewitched Richard Rosses horse and beasts and caused their Impes to burne a barne with much corne.
Confessed by Ales Manfield.	7. Ales Manfielde and Margaret Greuell . .	bewitched to death	Robert Chesson, and Greuell husband to Margaret.
	Ales Manfielde and Margaret Greuell . .	bewitched the widdow Chesson, and her hus band, v beasts and one bullocke and seuerall brewinges of beere, and batches of bread.
Thorpe	8. Elizabeth Ewstace . .	bewitched to death	Robert Stannevettes Childe, and Thomas Crosse.
	Elizabeth Ewstace . .	bewitched Robert Stanneuet, vii milch beasts, wʰ gaue blood in steede of milke, and seuerall of his Swine dyed.
Little Okley.	9. Annys Herd .	bewitched to death	Richard Harrisons wife, and two wives of William Dowsinge, as it is supposed.
	Annys Herd .	bewitched Cartwright two beasts, made, sheepe, and lambes xx ; West swine, and pigs ; Diborne, a brewing of beere, and seuerall other losses of milke and creame.
Walton.	10. Joan Robinson	bewitched beasts, horses, swine, and pigs, of seuerall men.

" The sayd Ursley Kemp had foure spyrites, viz. their names Tettey a hee like a gray cat, Jack a hee like a black cat, Pygin a she like a black toad, and Tyffin a she like a white lambe. The hees were to plague to death, and the shees to punish with bodily harme, and to destroy cattell.

" Tyffyn, Ursley's white spirit, did tell her alwayes (when she asked) what the other witches had done : and by her the most part were appelled, which spirit telled her alwayes true. As is well approved by the other witches confession.

" The sayd Ales Newman had the sayd Ursley Kemps spirits to vse at her pleasure. Elizabeth Bennet had two spirits, viz. their names Suckyn, a hee like a blacke dog : and Lyard, red lyke a lyon or hare.

" Ales Hunt had two spirits lyke colts, the one blacke, the other white.

" 11. Margery Sammon had two spirits lyke toads, their names Tom and Robyn.

" Cysley Celles had two spirits by seuerall names, viz. Sotheons Hercules, Jack, or Mercury.

" Ales Manfield and Margaret Greuell had in common by agreement, iiii spirits, viz. their names Robin, Jack, Will, Puppet, alias Mamet, whereof two were hees, and two were shees, lyke vnto black cats.

" Elizabeth Ewstace had iii impes or spirits of colour white, grey, and black.

" Annis Herd had vi impes or spirites, like auises and black byrdes, and vi other like kine, of the bygnes of rats, with short hornes ; the auises shee fed with wheat, barley, otes, and bread, the kine with straw and hay.

Annys Glascocke . . .	These have not confessed anything touching
12. Joan Pechey .	the hauing of spirits.
13. Joan Robinson	

Annis Glascocke . . .	bewitched to death	Mychell Steuens Childe.
		The base Childe at Pages.
		William Pages Childe."

A case, which attracted unusual attention at the time, was that which had its scene at Warboys in Huntingdonshire. Joan, the eldest daughter of Sir Robert Throckmorton, the head of a prominent county family, being a child about ten years old, was taken with sudden fits during which she " screeked " loud and long. It so happened that a neighbour, Gammer Alice Samuel, called at the house, and the hysterical girl cried : " Did you ever see one more like a witch then she is : take off her blacke thumbd cap, for I cannot abide to looke on her." " The old woman hearing her, sat still, without sáying a word, yet looked very dismally, as those that saw her remembered very well." Nothing was thought of it, however, at the time, and when Dr. Barrow, an eminent physician of Cambridge, who had treated the child without success, asked the parents if Witchcraft might not be suspected they promptly answered in the negative. Young Joan now particularly complained that Mother Samuel was trying to force a cat, a frog, or sometimes a toad into her mouth to suffocate her, obviously the hysterical ball, " palla isterica," one of the most marked and commonest somatic indications of acute hysteria. But when two or three of their other neurasthenic daughters were seized with the same strange disorder and fell into frantic convulsions, crying out that Mother Samuel was tormenting them, the suspected woman was forcibly brought into their presence by Gilbert Pickering, an uncle of the children, who thereupon instantly scratched her, as by shedding the witch's blood those who were for-spoken might obtain some temporary relief. Meantime Lady Cromwell[122] visited the Throckmortons, and found the sick girls so racked with aches and twisted with pain that she could not refrain from tears. She insisted upon seeing Mother Samuel, whose good man was a tenant of her husband, and she succeeded after a struggle in cutting off a lock of the crone's grey hair. That very night she had horrible dreams, and awoke in a panic, sweating and screaming. By day she pined and languished, at night she scarce dared seek her couch, and at length exhausted with suffering and fear she died a bare fifteen months after her interview with the witch, by whom the whole countryside believed she had been done to death. Henry Pickering, a cousin of the Throckmortons, and several Cambridge scholars, next examined Mother Samuel, it being the winter of 1591, but they merely received tart and angry replies which convinced them that she was indeed a baleful witch. And now the children could only be well when she was present, and the wretched old creature was harried on every side to confess that it was she who had wrought all this mischief. At length completely " dazed and mazed " with the screams of the hysterical girls, their sham paroxysms and wild imaginings, the threats and entreaties, the anger and the din, the shouting and ranting and exhorta-tions of that disordered household, she gave way and exclaimed : " Oh, sir, I have been the cause of all this trouble to your children." Soon both she and her daughter, Agnes, were in close custody and on their way to Dr. William Wickham, Bishop of Lincoln, before whom she made a confession, avowing that she entertained three familiars, Pluck, Catch, and White, that she had sold her soul to the Devil, that she had killed Lady Cromwell, cast a spell upon the Throckmorton family, and in fine anything else they asked her to avow. Inevitably she was imprisoned with her daughter and her husband John Samuel, who was now also accused by the children, and all three were tried before Judge Fenner at the Huntingdon assizes. The trial lasted five hours and the accused were found guilty, condemned to be hanged, and their bodies burned. The poor old woman, half crazed with her agony, set up a plea of pregnancy, though she was wellnigh fourscore years of age. The whole court was convulsed with laughter, in which the unfortunate victim herself joined as merrily as any, and this was, of course, an extra proof that she was a sorceress. The daughter was urged to make this defence, but she stoutly replied, " It shall never be said that I was both a witch and a whore." The whole family was executed on 7 April, 1593. An agreement is still preserved in the archives of the Huntingdon corporation providing that the town shall pay as bequeathed by Sir Samuel Cromwell forty pounds annually to Queen's College, Cambridge, in order that a sermon shall be preached at Huntingdon on each Lady Day by a divine of the College, who is to take Witchcraft as his theme. The annual sermon on this endowment was still being delivered in the earlier years of the nineteenth century when the preachers were wont vigorously to attack the belief in Witchcraft. The persecution of the Samuels is, in truth, one of the most sordid of tales. The evidence reeks with the hysteria of disordered, mentally unbalanced children ; a record of ignorance, trickery, lies, and imposture. " A special characteristic of hysterical persons," says Tardieu, " is instinctive dissimulation, an inveterate and unceasing impulse to lie by word and deed." " The sagacity and inconceivable tenacity," continues Charcot, " with which they deceive others is quite wonderful." " And these falsehoods," adds Richet, " are told with such audacity, indifference, and assurance as to throw you completely off your guard." The Warboys' manifestations could hardly be summed more tersely or with greater exactitude.[123]

King James I upon his accession to the throne of England gave additional impetus to the witch trials and condemnations. He had quite definite opinions with regard to the subject ; he felt very deeply on the matter ; and expressed his views with much weight and detail in his *Dæmonologie*,[124] especially penned " against the damnable opinions of two principally in our age, whereof the one called Scot an Englishman, is not ashamed in publike print to deny, that ther can be such a thing as Witch-craft : and so mainteines the old error of the Sadducees, in denying of spirits. The other called Vviervs, a German Phisition, sets out a publick apologie for al these craftes-folkes, whereby, procuring for their impunitie, he plainly bewrayes himselfe to haue bene one of that profession."[125]

Reginald Scot was a Kentish man of quiet and secluded life. He had kept several terms at Hart Hall, Oxford, but left the University without proceeding to a degree, and settling down at Scots Hall devoted himself to the management of his estate. His love for his native countryside is shown in *A Perfect Platforme of a Hoppe-Garden and necessary instructions for the making and maintaining thereof*, which first published in 1574 ran into three editions within five years. In 1584 there came from the Press his *Discoverie of Witchcraft*, a subject which he seems to have studied, and concerning which he had in a somewhat desultory fashion been collecting notes for a long period. It is obvious that the immediate occasion of publication was the S. Oses affair,[126] and the greater part of the *Discoverie* was most certainly written in 1583, in some haste, no doubt, to strike lustily whilst the iron was hot. For years before he put pen to paper he had been investigating on his account alleged cases of Witchcraft, attending trials,[127] closely questioning magistrates and divines. His mind was naturally sceptical, and in religion he would nowadays be a pseudo-scientific modernist. That is to say, he was utterly without imagination, a very dull, narrow, and ineffective little soul. When he has exposed certain egregious impostures of contemporary date, enlarged upon card tricks and prestidigitation at inordinate length, attributed the appearance of Samuel in the cave of Endor to ventriloquism, and more than hinted that possession in the New Testament merely means disease, this myopic squireen deems that the whole matter is settled once and for all. It is true that he gives us an ample bibliography, over two hundred Latin and thirty English titles, but he came to the subject with a deeply prejudiced mind and was determined not to find in any author other than what he sought. Had he dared, Scot would have openly denied the supernatural, of that I make no doubt ; and to-day he might have shone in the company of Mr. Clodd and Mr. McCabe.

Johann Weyer[128] was born in 1516 at Gran in North Brabant. He studied medicine at Paris and Orleans, and about 1545 settled as a physician at Arnheim, whence he was called to Dusseldorf, to be body-physician to Wilhelm IV, Duke of Jülich, Cleves, and Berg, to whom he dedicated his famous treatise *De præstigiis dæmonum et incantationibus ac ueneficiis*, Basel, 1563. This was followed by other works upon the same lines. No doubt there is something in these works which curbed the extravagances of the day, and although Weyer was a Protestant he is careful not to show himself too audaciously sceptical. It is true that he insinuates more than he affirms or denies, and probably in print he did not go so far as he really wished. He was safe under the protection of the Duke, who favoured him and mourned his death, which took place on a journey in Seeklenburg, 24 February, 1588.

It is natural that when King James came to England his *Dæmonologie* should have been accepted by officials as a text-book whose authority was enhanced by the sovereignty of the author. But his most direct influence was the passing of a new law, which was taken in hand by the House of Lords when his first Parliament had been but eight days in session. The Elizabethan statute made killing by Witchcraft a capital offence, whilst to inflict an injury by charm or spell meant a year's imprisonment. James felt that this in practice was but the law against murder, and did not punish the crime of Witchcraft, commerce with the Devil, harbourage and employment of familiars. Accordingly the new Bill went to a large committee which included Sir Edmund Anderson, the Lord Chief-Justice of the Common Pleas ; Sir Edward Coke, the Attorney-general; twelve bishops, and six earls. On 9 June it passed its final reading in the Lords. The Elizabethan statute was repealed and it was enacted that " If any person or persons shall use, practise or exercise an Invocation or Conjuration of any evill and wicked Spirit, or shall consult, covenant with, entertaine, employe, feede, or rewarde any evill and wicked Spirit to or for any intent or purpose ; or take up any dead man, woman, or child out of his, her, or their graue, or any other place where the dead body resteth, or the skin, bone, or any part of any dead person to be employed or used in any manner of witchcraft, enchantment, charm, or sorcerie, whereby any person shall be killed, destroyed, wasted, consumed, pined, or lamed in his or her body, or any part thereof, every such offender is a felon without benefit of Clergy." Even the finding of treasure or lost goods by Witchcraft, as well as " the intent to provoke any person to unlawfull love," and the harming of cattle, were punishable with one year's imprisonment with the pillory at each quarter, and upon a second offence, death. It is fairly obvious that most offenders must at any rate come under these latter provisions, for it is not to be supposed that a witch would only once make use of her powers.

We have recorded some fifty cases of witches executed in King James's reign. Of these about thirty suffered for causing actual death by sorcery : 1603, Yorkshire, Mary Pannel, executed for killing in 1593 ;[129] 1606, Hertford, Johanna Harrison and her daughter ;[130] 1607, Derbyshire, several witches were put to death at Bakewell ;[131] 1612, Lancaster, the famous Pendle trials, ten persons executed, Alice Nutter, Alizon Device, Elizabeth Device, James Device, Anne Whittle (Chattox), Anne Redfearne, Isobel Robey, John Bulcock, Jane Bulcock, Katherine Hewitt, whilst Elizabeth Demdike died in prison ;[132] 1612, Northampton, Agnes Browne, Joan Vaughan (or Browne), Mary Barber, Hellen Jenkenson, and Arthur Bill, were executed on 22 July for bewitching " the body of a young child to the death " ;[133] 1612, York, Jennet Preston ;[134] 1613, Bedford, Mother Sutton, and Mary her daughter, of Milton Miles, hanged ;[135] 1615, Middlesex, Joan Hunt of Hampstead, hanged ;[136] 1616, Middlesex, Elizabeth Rutter of Finchley, hanged for laming and killing three persons ;[137] 1619, Lincoln, Margaret and Philippa Flower, hanged, their mother, Joan Flower, died on the way to prison ;[138] 1619, Leicester, three women, Anne Baker, Joan Willimot, Ellen Green, accused and confessed, and were executed ;[139] 1621, Middlesex, Elizabeth Sawyer of Edmonton, " indicted for that she the said *Elizabeth Sawyer*, by Diabolical help, and out of her malice-aforethought, did witch unto death *Agnes Ratcleife*, a neighbour of hers, dwelling in the toun of *Edmonton*," hanged at Tyburn, Thursday, 19 April of the said year.[140]

The records of those condemned to suffer for Witchcraft whereby death was not actually caused are very few. In 1607 the local authorities at Rye, Sussex, would have sent to the gallows two women who resorted to spirits in order " to gain wealth," but it seems that they were discharged owing to a mandate from London.[141] In 1616 Agnes Berrye of Enfield was hanged for laming and causing to languish.[142] And in the same year Mary Smith, the wife of a Norfolk glover, Henry Smith, was hanged at King's Lynn for causing four people to languish by her enchantments.[143] A few months later nine women were hanged at Leicester on the accusation of a lad, some twelve or thirteen years old, who fell into hideous convulsions, which he said were caused by spirits whom they set on him. Six more women were in jail and would probably also have suffered had not the King in his northward progress, whilst staying in the town, examined the boy and detected imposture. What punishment was meted out to him is not stated, but the judges were disgraced.[144]

At Bristol in 1624 two witches were executed, but there are no details given of their trial.[145] Edward Poeton, also, in the *Winnowing of White Witchcraft*,[146] tells us that two women were hanged for their sorceries, but again there is merely this bare record.

These, of course, were the more serious cases, and we have a large number of minor trials in which the accused was sentenced to a year's imprisonment ; such for example was the punishment awarded to Margaret Pearson at Lancaster in 1612, and to Dorothy Magick of S. Andrew's parish, Holborn, in 1614. Very often the prisoners were acquitted. Alice Bradley of Hampstead who was arraigned in 1607 was discharged ; so also were Margaret Pilton of Warminster,

Wilts, in 1613 ; Anne Branche of Tottenham in 1617 ; Agnes Miller of Finchley in 1619 ; Anne Beaver of Middlesex in 1621 ;[147] and very many more.

When we consider that in the Valais from 1428–34 at least two hundred witches were put to death ; whilst at Briançon in 1437 one hundred and fifty were executed ; that in the year 1524 alone, according to Fra Bartolomeo Spina, the erudite Dominican, no less than a thousand persons suffered the extreme penalty for Witchcraft in the northern provinces of Italy ; that Nicolas Remy says he convicted and burned nine hundred sorcerers during a decade and a half ; and at Bamburg, in Bavaria, the executions from 1610 to 1840 were at the rate of about a hundred annually ; even if we allow for some exaggeration—although the evidence is plain and there is no need for such precaution—it will appear that the popular ideas concerning the holocausts in the reign of James I are anything but historically exact, and instead of shuddering at the large numbers who perished we may well be surprised that the executions in England were so few. Moreover it is said that towards the end of his reign the King was by no means so firm a believer in Witchcraft as he had formerly been. Fuller, in his *Church History of Britain*, has the following truly remarkable passage : " The frequency of such forged possessions wrought such an alteration upon the judgement of King James that he, receding from what he had written in his *Dæmonology*, grew first diffident of, and then flatly to deny, the workings of witches and devils, as but falsehoods and delusions."[148] Francis Osborne also writes that the King would have gone as far as to deny any such operations ; but out of reasons of State and to gratify the Church.[149]

Such a complete change of opinion is hardly credible. No doubt the King modified his belief, but it is almost impossible to accept these statements as they stand. That the author of the *Dæmonologie* should become a sceptic seems an unprecedented revolution, and we may well be excused if we feel mistrustful before we subscribe to so sweeping an assertion. Yet we may appreciate the truth that no doubt underlies the report, and the falling off of prosecutions, the numerous acquittals, towards the latter end of the King's reign, may or may not have any bearing upon this point.

By far the most important of the witch-trials under James I
was that of the Pendle coven in 1612,[150] and this not only
created a tremendous stir at the time and was to give matter
and melodrama for romance and the theatre in future days,
but it even contributed a phrase to the English language, for
The Lancashire Witches has become proverbial in its use and
popularity.

In the lonely forest of Pendle, among the wild hills of
eastern Lancashire, there eked out her wretched sustenance
a blind beggar of some fourscore years, a " wicked fire-brand
of mischiefe," generally acknowledged to be " a genrall agent
for the Deuill in all these partes," Elizabeth Southernes or
Demdike. This ancient crone had been a witch longer than
memory could serve, and she had dedicated her children and
grandchildren to the service of Satan. Her bitter rival in
age, influence, and evil was a hag named Anne Whittle, or
rather Chattox, " a very old, withered, spent, and decreped
creature, her sight almost gone ; a dangerous witch of very
long continuance ; always opposite to old Demdike ; for
whom the one fauoured the other hated deadly : and how
they curse and accuse one another in their examinations may
appear. In her witchcraft always more ready to doe
mischief to men's goods than themselves ; her lippes ever
chattering and talking ; but no man knew what. She lived
in the Forest of Pendle amongst this wicked company of
dangerous witches . . . from these two sprung all the rest in
order ; and even the children and friendes of these two
notorious witches."

There was, in fact, a deadly feud between the two families,
and both having been long exercised in supernatural practices
and devoted body and soul to the Demon, fearful was the
mischief they wrought in their angry struggles for supremacy
in wickedness. Moreover there were the usual quarrels over
petty pilferings among country-folk in ignorant hamlets.
Demdike's daughter had missed clothing, some of which, a
coif and band, had (they said) been found in the possession
of Chattox's daughter, and ceaseless disputes and brawls
took place in consequence. Even a third family was involved.
The Nutters were well-known well-to-do county gentry, but
dashing young Robert Nutter, who no doubt thought it
shame a witch should not be a whore, attempted to seduce

Chattox's comely daughter, and when to his extreme surprise his advances were repulsed he threatened one day to evict the whole family since the land where they dwelt would be his property. Old Chattox promptly set about contriving Nutter's death by witchcraft, and in less than three months he was in his grave, accusing her of his bewitchment with his latest breath. Some years before Chattox had killed John Device, the son-in-law of Demdike, in similar fashion, because he had omitted to pay her a yearly tax of " one aghen-dole of meale," which she extorted under a promise to do him and his no harm. She had slain Anne Nutter, too, for laughing at and mocking her ; as also John Morris' child whom she had caused to pine and dwindle by piercing a clay image with sharp pins. As for Demdike, the " rankest hag that ever troubled daylight," her iniquities were legion. She " brought vp her owne Children, instructed her Graundchildren, and tooke great care and paines to bring them to be Witches." Little wonder that Master Roger Nowell, an active and austere magistrate, suddenly swooped down upon this community of Satanists and in a very short space of time he had Elizabeth Demdike with three other women securely lodged in Lancaster Castle.

As might be supposed the whole witch community was now seriously alarmed, and Demdike's daughter hurriedly summoned a meeting of the gang on Good Friday, which seems to have been one of the principal dates whereon the Pendle witches were wont to foregather in full force, at her abode, the lonely Malking Tower. Here they plotted a scheme for the release of Mother Demdike, and considered how they might kill the governor and jailer and blow up the Castle. They then sat down to a hearty meal. " The persons aforesaid had to their dinners Beefe, Bacon, and roasted Mutton : which Mutton (as this Examinates said brother said) was of a Wether of Christopher Swyers of Barley : which Wether was brought in the night before into this Examinates mothers house by the said Iames Deuice, this Examinates said brother : and in this Examinates sight killed and eaten. . . . And before their said parting away, they all appointed to meet at the said Prestons wiues house that day twelve-moneths ; at which time the said Prestons wife promised to make them a great Feast."[151]

But long before that they had all been arrested, and had been put on their trial before Sir Edward Bromley and Sir James Altham, the Justices of the northern circuit, who reached Lancaster on the sixteenth of August. Mother Demdike had died in prison, but her depositions, especially as regards her familiar, who " appeared vnto her in the likenes of a broune Dogg, forcing himselfe to her knee, to get blood vnder her left Arme," had been taken down before the magistrates and covered her memory with execration. Five members of the two rival Pendle broods made ample confession.[152] Mother Chattox[153], Elizabeth Device, Alizon and Jennet, a child aged nine, her daughters ; and their brother James. They involved one another in the most hateful sorceries, and in spite of many grotesque, but not necessarily untrue, details the tale they told was foul and horrible to a degree. All the bestial malice, crass stupidity, empty revenge, and besotted superstition of the remote countryside are there compounded. Especially remarkable is the testimony of James Device, a lad who can at most have barely been out of his teens : " that vpon Sheare Thursday was two yeares, his Grand-Mother Elizabeth Southernes, alias Demdike, did bid him this Examinate goe to the Church to receiue the Communion (the next day after being Good Friday)[154] and ther not to eate the Bread the Minister gaue him, but to bring it and deliuer it to such a thing as should meet him in his way homewards ; Notwithstanding her perswasions this Examinate did eate the Bread : and so in his comming homeward some fortie roodes off the said Church, there met him a thing in the shape of a Hare, who spoke vnto this Examinate, and asked him whether he had brought the Bread." It is not surprising that he was condemned for " as dangerous and malicious a witch as ever lived in these parts of Lancashire, of his time, and spotted with as much innocent bloud as euer any witch of his yeeres."

Alice Nutter of Rough Lee was also implicated, for Elizabeth Device accused her of having assisted Old Demdike to bewitch a man to death ; she had further attended the Sabbat feast at Malking Tower. " She was," says Potts, " a rich woman, had a great estate and children of good hope." She showed herself " of good temper, free from envy and malice."

The Pendle cases were interrupted on the third day by the

trial of three women from Salmesbury, who pleaded not guilty. The charges against them chiefly rested upon the evidence of a single witness, Grace Sowerbutts, who declared that she had been tormented and vexed for three years. No " matter of witchcraft," however, was proved, and the accused were discharged. This acquittal surely shows that the judges and court were not merely actuated by the blind fury and insensate to which sentences of condemnation are usually attributed by modern historians.

Of the Lancashire coven ten were executed: Mother Chattox and her daughter Anne Redfearne; Alice Nutter; Elizabeth Device[155] and two of her children, Alizon and James; Katherine Hewit, *alias* Mouldheels, a fearful beldame; John Bulcock and his mother Jane; Isobel Roby. Mother Demdike had died in prison, and Jennet Preston, one of the gang, was some three months later sent to the gallows at York for the murder by noxious spells of Master Thomas Lister. So ended this famous trial, by some accidental chance, for there were many other cases equally interesting, equally fantastic, and equally terrible, perhaps the most famous witch-trial among English records.

It seems very dubious if the Boy of Bilston, one William Perry, a thirteen-year-old lad of Bilston in Staffordshire, was in truth the impostor he is alleged to have been. It is true that a hag named Joan Cocke was accused of having forespoken him,[156] yet even if we allow this to be fantasy the fact remains his case seems to have been one of genuine possession, whether it had any connexion with Joan Cocke's sorceries or no.

It should be remembered that our only accounts are from violently prejudiced sources. The contemporary pamphlet *The Boy of Bilston* (London, 1622) was actually prepared by Richard Baddeley, secretary to Bishop Morton,[157] and is absolutely unreliable in its presentation of the case. Arthur Wilson in his *Life and Reign of James I* (London, 1653) tells us that he heard the story " from the Bishop's own mouth almost thirty years before it was inserted here " ; most partial testimony. John Webster's *The Displaying of Supposed Witchcraft*, which mentions the incidents, was not published until 1677,[158] and in any case the man was a crass rationalist, a muddy materialist, whose conclusions are hardly worth consideration. It is obviously impossible that more than three hundred years after we can investigate the details of a case of extraordinary difficulty, and indeed delicacy, which occurred in 1620—especially when, as I believe, those details have been cleverly perverted—with any degree of exactitude and caution that will warrant us in pronouncing upon its genuineness, how far it was uncounterfeit, and in what, if any, particulars it was exaggerated or misreported. Nevertheless the impression is strongly conveyed to my mind that Bishop Thomas Morton, or more particularly perhaps Mr. Secretary Baddeley, made no fair use of young William Perry, and moulding him by threats, " for he brast out into plentiful teares " and they obviously bullied him soundly, obliged the poor lad to confess that the very truth was trickery and sleight, a cunning device indeed and a weapon meet to be employed in their anti-Catholic crusade.

The charges brought in 1622 by Edward Fairfax of Knaresborough against six women, whom he accused of sorcery and who were indicted for bewitching his children, soon fell to the ground. These women had been examined by the local magistrates, by whose command one was publicly searched for the Devil's mark, and committed to the assizes. At the April session, however, four were released, two of them on bond. Two seem to have been already allowed to return home. Fairfax was far from satisfied, and had sufficient influence to ensure that they were again brought up in August. The judge at the outset warned the jury to be very careful, and, after hearing some of the evidence, dismissed the prisoners on the ground that what was alleged " reached not to the point of the statute." This is indeed remarkable, and indicates a considerable, if temporary, change in public opinion. The case in itself is interesting owing to the fact that it is an episode in the life of the translator of Tasso, but otherwise it presents no special features which call for comment or examination.

During the reign of Charles I, which for our purpose may fairly be reckoned as not extending beyond 1642, the outbreak of the rebellion when the Puritans assumed responsibility for the government, there was only one notable witch alarm in England, whilst there are but seven recorded executions and two at least of these rest upon most insufficient evidence. In 1630 a wizard named Utley, a professed conjurer, alleged to have bewitched Richard Assheton to death, was hanged at Lancaster ;[159] in the same year a woman was hanged at Sandwich in Kent ;[160] in 1631 in Wiltshire " John Barlowes' wife " is stated to have suffered ;[161] in Somerset one person was executed ; and at Taunton, a sorcerer, probably Edmund Bull, who had been under grave suspicion in 1626, went to the gallows.[162]   In 1641 one Hammond of Westminster was tried and perhaps hanged,[163] but this is quite uncertain, as also is a story given at third hand of a woman who was put to death at Oxford.[164]   The one resounding scandal was the notorious recrudescence of the Pendle tradition in 1633–4, when young Robinson set the county aflame with his lies, and as many as seventeen suspected persons were tried and condemned only to be reprieved by the King.   The case has been discussed at length in connexion with Heywood and Brome's topical drama *The late Lancashire Witches*, produced at the Globe in 1634.[165]

Many stories are told of the necromantic powers of Dr. Lamb, who was high in the Duke of Buckingham's favour. He is said, upon what appears to be wholly insufficient evidence, to have dealt in poisons and to have been of the same fraternity as " sweet father " Foreman, who was so deeply implicated in the murder of Sir Thomas Overbury and the Somerset scandals.[166]   But the popular hate, which had impotently assailed his patron, proved fatal to Lamb. At length he could not venture to appear in the streets of London with safety, and one day in 1640 whilst walking abroad under a disguise he was recognized and hooted by some idle boys.   As he sought to escape a crowd collected and pursued him.   He was seized in Wood Street, and dragged through the kennels to S. Paul's Cross, where the brutal mob beat and stoned him to death with hideous yells of " Kill the wizard ! Kill the poisoner ! "   Charles I, hearing of the riot, rode from Whitehall to quell it, but he arrived too late to save their victim.   The City, which protested its inability to deliver up the ringleaders to justice, was very properly fined six hundred pounds for so infamous an outrage.[167]   In 1653 Anne Bodenham, who had been Dr. Lamb's servant, but then lived at Fisherton Anger in Wiltshire, was hanged at Salisbury upon an absurd and unsubstantiated charge of witchcraft.   She was accused of nourishing familiars ; and when she was searched in jail the women who performed this office swore that they had found two unnatural teats or witch-paps upon her body, the one on her shoulder, the other *in uerendis*. She was said to have made a particular contract with the Devil, by whose help she could transform herself " into the shape of Mastive Dog, a black Lyon, a white Bear, a Woolf, a Bull, and a Cat," although it does not appear how such metamorphoses would benefit her, and one might imagine that a black lion, a white bear, or even a wolf must attract considerable attention if met with in a Wiltshire lane. Such a tissue of absurdities was the evidence, and the whole trial is indeed a glaring example of judicial murder, which is perhaps hardly surprising when one considers that it took place under Cromwell's tyranny.[168]

Almost immediately upon the outbreak of the Rebellion in 1642,[169] there was, as might have been expected when England fell gradually into the hands of gloomy and grossly superstitious fanatics as cruel as Calvin and as very knaves as Knox, a hideous epidemic of blind and bloody persecution.

Now also appears upon the scene the most notorious figure in the whole annals of English Witchcraft, a worthy emissary of the rebel Parliament. Matthew Hopkins[170] was the son of James Hopkins, minister of Wenham, Suffolk. It is evident from his writings that he had received some education and was able to wield a facile and forcible enough pen in vulgarly fluent fashion. An orthodox Puritan of narrowest views,[171] which were certainly adopted for convenience rather than from conviction, he was energetic enough so far as his own pockets were concerned, and his crusade up and down the eastern counties, which created something like a reign of terror at the time, has caused his name to stink in the nostrils of all decent persons ever since.

Little is known of Hopkins' early life, but it seems probable that he practised the law, at Ipswich for a while, and afterwards at Manningtree, Essex. It was in his own town that his attention was first drawn to Witchcraft, for a whole coven was wont to meet near his house. " In *March*, 1644, he had some seven or eight of that horrible sect of Witches living in the Towne where he lived, a Towne in *Essex* called *Manningtree*, with divers other adjacent Witches of other towns, who every six weeks in the night (being alwayes on the *Friday* night) had their meeting close by his house, and had their severall solemm sacrifices there offered to the *Devill,* one of which this Discoverer heard speaking to her *Imps* and bid them goe to another Witch, who was thereupon apprehended."[172]   Elizabeth Clarke, a wretched hag, was taken into custody, she was searched, " found to have three teats about her, which honest women have not," kept " from sleep two or three nights " and on the fourth night confessed that she nourished five familiars, Holt, " a white kitling " ; Jarmara, " a fat spaniel " ; Vinegar Tom, " a long-legg'd Greyhound with a head like an Oxe with a long taile and broad Eyes "; Sack and Sugar, " a black Rabbet "; Newes " like a Polcat." No less than eight people swore they had seen these familiars. Other witches, Anne West, her daughter Rebecca, Anne Leech, and her daughter Helen Clarke, Elizabeth Gooding, were arrested and revealed the names of their imps, Elemanzer, Pyewacket, Peck in the Crown, Grizzel Greedigut, " which no mortall could invent." Hopkins continues, " in our Hundred in Essex, 29 were condemned at once, 4 brought 25 Miles to be hanged,—where their Discoverer lives, for sending the Devill like a Beare to kill him."

Elizabeth Gooding refused to acknowledge her guilt, but the others confessed so fast that ere long amid the meshes of charges and counter-charges more than twenty-three persons were involved. The accused were searched, the Devil's marks and teats discovered. The trials were held at Chelmsford on 29 July, 1645, Robert Rich, Earl of Warwick, a venomous Presbyterian, being President of the Court. In those troublous times the ordinary assizes had been suspended. Twenty-nine were condemned, four of whom were hanged at Manningtree and ten at Chelmsford, the others presumably being executed in various hamlets and villages throughout the locality. Meantime Hopkins, who had got great glory, was extending his operations into Suffolk. Four searchers were appointed, two men and two women, " who take the partie or parties so suspected into a Roome, and strip him, her, or them, starke naked."[172]   Another speciality of Hopkins' craft was the watching of witches : " Having taken the suspected Witch, shee is placed in the middle of a room upon a stool or table, crosse-legg'd, or in some other uneasie posture, to which if she submits not she is then bound with cords ; there is she watcht and kept without meat or sleep for the space of 24 hours. . . . A little hole is likewise made in the door for the Impe to come in at ; and lest it might come in some less discernible shape, they that watch are taught to be ever and anon sweeping the room, and if they see any spiders or flyes to kill them. And if they cannot kill them then they may be sure they are her Impes."[173] " Beside that unreasonable watching, they were extraordinarily walked till their feet were blistered, and so forced through that cruelty to confess."[174] But the chief test of all was swimming the witch, the water-ordeal, which indeed was popularly considered to be so supremely efficacious a test that it was still in use, albeit wholly illegal, of course, among rustics as late as the nineteenth century. The witches tied with " their thumbes and great toes . . . acrosse " and steadied by ropes— (" a roape tyed about their middles ")—were let down into the water, some running stream or pond. If she sank the suspect might be cleared ; if she swam her blackest guilt was evident. For water was a holy element, it had become instinct with life whilst the earth was yet barren and uninhabited ; and as the witch had rejected the sacramental water of Baptism, so that pure lymph would refuse to receive her into its bosom.[175] The first record of the use of the water-ordeal in England is, so far as we know, in 1612, when the Northampton witches were thus tested. It was employed officially by command of a justice, probably in compliment to King James, who so strongly recommends it in his *Dæmonologie*. The royal author also mentions the Devil's mark, and the supposition that a witch is incapable of shedding tears. He says : " I think it hath ben seldome harde tell of, that any whome persones guiltie of that crime accused, as hauing knowen them to be their marrowes by eye-sight, and not by hear-say, but such as were so accused of Witch-craft, could not be clearely tryed vpon them, were at the least publickly knowen to be of a very euil life & reputation : so iealous is God I say, of the fame of them that are innocent in such causes. And besides that, there are two other good helpes that may be vsed for their trial : the one is the finding of their marke, and the trying the insensiblenes thereof. The other is their fleeting on the water : for as in a secret murther, if the deade carcase be at any time thereafter handled by the murtherer, it wil gush out of bloud, as if the blud wer crying to the heauen for reuenge of the murtherer, God hauing appoynted that secret super-naturall signe, for tryall of that secrete vnnaturall crime, so it appeares that God hath appoynted (for a super-naturall signe of the monstruous impietie of the Witches) that the water shal refuse to receiue them in her bosom, that haue shaken off them the sacred Water of Baptisme, and wilfullie refused the benefite thereof : No not so much as their eyes are able to shed teares (thretten and torture them as ye please) while first they repent (God not permitting them to dissemble their obstinacie in so horrible a crime) albeit the women kinde especially, be able other-waies to shed teares at euery light occasion when they will, yea, although it were dissemblingly like the *Crocodiles.*"[176]

Bodin also writes : " L'autre presomption est, si la sorciere ne pleure point, qui est vne des plus fortes presumptions que Paul Grilland, & les Inquisiteurs ont remarqué pour en auoir fait executer bien grād nombre. Le Lieutenant de Ribemont [Antoine de Loan], duquel i'ay parlé cy dessus, m'a dit que l'vne des Sorcieres, aus quelles il a faict le procés, confessa qu'elles ne peuuent ietter que trois larmes de l'œil dextre : ce qui m'a semblé digne d'estre remarqué."[177]

Hopkins was accompanied in his visitations by John Stearne,[178] an unctuous rascal, who strenuously aided and seconded him, and by an assistant, Goody Phillips, whose special province lay in discovering the witch-mark on the bodies of the accused. It was a very profitable business, and it has been calculated that between them the gang netted well-nigh a thousand pounds, no inconsiderable sum. Their rapacity was recognized even at the time and towards the end of his career Hopkins was openly accused of fleecing East Anglia to fill his own pockets. It may well be asked how it was possible such knavery should continue unchecked. It must be remembered that 1644–8 England was almost in a state of anarchy, the witch-finder was a fine specimen of Puritan tyranny and he battened richly after the manner of his kind.

In Suffolk Hopkins caused an immense sensation by dis-covering that John Lowes, minister of Brandeston, an old man of eighty who had occupied the living for half a century, since the days of Elizabeth, was a foul witch. He had been a quarrelsome old fellow, it appears, misliked by many in his parish, and although at first he stoutly denied his guilt, when thoroughly taken in hand by the most approved methods, " till he was weary of his life and scarce sensible of what he said or did,"[179] he confessed his sorceries and went to the gallows at Bury.

By this time there were nearly two hundred people shut up in the county jail. In spite of the unhappy distractions of the day this state of affairs made some noise, and Parliament granted a special " Commission of Oyer and Terminer "[180] for the trials. Serjeant John Godbolt, the local justices, and two ranting divines, Samuel Fairclough and Edward Calamy (the elder), composed this special court. It is true that an end was put to the swimming tests, which must have caused Hopkins no small displeasure, but eighteen persons who " dyed . . . very desperately "[181] were hanged. The sessions however were adjourned in a hurry, as the royal forces were approaching Bedford and Cambridge. When they sat again some fifty more witches were executed.

Hopkins was now hurrying from place to place at break-neck speed and urging on trials with fatal rapidity. Before 26 July twenty witches were executed in Norfolk : he was at Yarmouth, by special demand from the corporation, in September, and again in December ; he was then at Ipswich, and shortly afterwards at Aldeburgh, whence he journeyed to Stowmarket, where he received twenty-three pounds for his services,[182] which means that no small number perished. King's Lynn and many other towns as well as the smaller villages were visited, a trail of blood and misery marking his passage throughout the countryside. Somewhere about March, 1645-6, he was active in Northamptonshire, and a little later he crossed into Huntingdon, but here in spite of the fact that the justices of the peace were not backward he met with opposition which seems to have turned the scale. Mr. John Gaule, the minister of Great Staughton, not only preached against the witch-finder but sharply criticized his proceedings. Hopkins, although he had been asked to visit Great Staughton, hesitated, and seems to have contented himself with a blustering letter[183] addressed to one of the parishioners:

" My service to your Worship presented. I have this day received a Letter, &c., to come to a Towne called Great

Staughton, to search for evil disposed persons, called Witches (though I heare your Minister is farre against us through ignorance :) I intend to come the sooner to heare his singular Judgment on the behalfe of such parties ; I have known a Minister in Suffolke preach as much against their discovery in a Pulpit, and forcid to recant it (by the Committee) in the same place. I much marvaile such evil Members should have any (much more any of the Clergy) who should dayly preach Terrour to convince such Offenders, stand up to take their parts, against such as are Complainants for the King and sufferers themselves, with their Families and Estates. I intend to give your Towne a Visite suddenly. I am to come to Kimbolton this weeke, and it shall bee tenne to one, but I will come to your Town first, but I would certainely know afore, whether your town affords many Sticklers for such Cattell, or willing to give and afford es good welcome and entertainment, as other where I have beene, else I shall wave your Shire (not as yet beginning in any part of it myselfe) and betake me to such places, where I doe, and may persist without controle, but with thanks and recompense. So I humbly take my leave and rest, your Servant to be Commanded,   MATTHEW HOPKINS."

Gaule answered with his *Select Cases of Conscience Touching Witches and Witchcrafts*, London, 1646, an utter repudiation of Hopkins' methods and an insistence upon the exercise of the utmost caution in admitting evidence. This seems to have had considerable effect, for it is clear that during the summer and autumn of 1646 Hopkins was no longer active in his pursuit of prey, indeed he might almost be said to have retired. He may have been concerned in the Ely discoveries of 1647, but if so it was his last effort. He died within the year at his old home in Manningtree. Stearne relates that he passed away " peaceably, after a long sicknesse of a Consumption."[184] But Hutchinson tells us that Hopkins himself was seized upon by the irate people, accused of being a witch, and put to the water-ordeal, when he was drowned, and this is commonly accepted. Another story[185] said that Hopkins had stolen the Devil's roll of all the witches in England, and so was casting out Beelzebub by means of Beelzebub. Probably Stearne is correct, and the other tales merely show how infamous his name had become. Butler's famous lines[186] hardly need convey more than that Hopkins had fallen from his high estate and died in obscurity and disgrace.

> Hath not this present Parl'ament
> A Lieger to the Devil sent,
> Fully impower'd to treat about
> Finding revolted Witches out ?
> And has he not within a year
> Hang'd threescore of them in one Shire ?
> Some only for not being drown'd,
> And some for sitting above ground
> Whole days and nights upon their Breeches,
> And feeling pain, were hang'd for Witches.
> And some for putting knavish Tricks
> Upon green Geese or Turkey Chicks ;
> Or Pigs that suddenly deceast
> Of griefs unnatural, as he guesst ;
> Who after proved himself a Witch,
> And made a rod for his own Breech.

Matthew Hopkins was an ideal type of the Puritan underling in power, and I should hesitate to say that he differed very much in cruelty and bigotry from the rest of his Genevan brethren. The brute instincts of primitive man are but insecurely disguised under the cloak of religious principle, and a garnish of Gospel texts may satisfy the canter but only serve more deeply to offend the impartial judge. Ireland yet remembers the tender mercies of Cromwell. The Roundheads found it their duty and their pleasure to butcher any Catholic priest who fell into their hands. An actor was to be shot through the head after he had laid down his arms upon a promise of quarter.[187] The victors of Naseby massacred in cold blood a hundred Irish women whom they found among the baggage, contenting themselves only with slashing and cutting open the faces of the English camp-followers. It was to be expected that after the fall of Oxford in 1646, which finally gave the " Good old Cause " its sovereignty, the savagery of the witch-trials should most fearfully increase. So we find that two women were burned alive at Norwich in 1648 ;[188] John Palmer and Elizabeth Knott, " two notorious Witches," were hanged at S. Albans in 1649 ;[189] whilst in July the gild of Berwick invited a common pricker, " an artist that way,"[190] a Scotchman, to assist them in discovering witches. The fellow was promised twenty shillings a witch, and soon enough he was stripping naked suspected persons, men and women, and probing them with a needle to find the insensible spot where the Devil had marked his own. Presently he went back home with thirty pounds in his pocket. But before long, March, 1649–50, he was summoned to Newcastle at the same rate together with fees for his journey to and fro. Thirty women were collected at the town-hall " and stript, and then openly had pins thrust into their bodies, and most of them were found guilty."[191] Fourteen women and one man, Matthew Bulmer, were hanged. Later the witch-finder was arrested, " indicted, arraigned, and condemned for such like villanie exercised in *Scotland*. And upon the Gallows he confessed he had been the death of above two hundred and twenty women in *England* and *Scotland*, for the gain of twenty shillings a peece, and beseeched forgiveness. And was executed."[192]

After 1642 indeed, as Eachard well remarks, " Blasphemies, Heresies, Enthusiasms, and Witchcrafts were in a full tide,"[193] and so universal were the holocausts of witches during the Commonwealth and Protectorate that it is well-nigh impossible to calculate the numbers who perished. Dr. Zachary Grey, in the notes to his edition of *Hudibras*, II, Canto iii, 143–4, says : " Dr. Meric Casaubon in his Preface to Dr. *Dee's Book of Spirits* observes ; That nine hundred Men and Women suffer'd in *Lorain* for Witchcraft in the Compass of a few Years : And *Ludovicus Paramo*, that the *Inquisition*, within the space of one hundred and fifty Years, has burnt thirty thousand Witches. *Baker's History of the Inquisition*, p. 186. But our enthusiasts much exceeded both. Mr. *Ady* says that in *Scotland* some thousands were burnt in those Times. (Dr. *Hutchinson*, p. 38.) I have somewhere seen an Account of betwixt three and four thousands, that suffer'd in the King's Dominions from the Year 1640 to the King's Restoration."[194]

The Puritans were scouting in all directions, and it must suffice to mention but some few victims of their blood lust and ignorant rage. In 1650 Joan Allen was hanged at the Old Bailey.[195] Two years later " The Witch of Wapping," Joan Petersen, was upon her trial before the Recorder of London. It is obvious that the accusation was the outcome of an almost overt conspiracy. Witnesses against her were bribed in advance ; those who might have given evidence in her favour were intimidated into staying away from the Courts ; Sir John Danvers, a member of Cromwell's council, whose interest it was to see that Mistress Petersen was found guilty, " came and sate upon the Bench at her Trial, where he hath seldom or never been for these many years " to see justice done. And so in April, 1652, Joan Petersen, who " seemed not to be much above 40 years of age, and was not in the least outwardly deformed as those kind of creatures usually are," was hanged at Tyburn tree.[196] In the following July six women, Anne Ashby, *alias* Cobley, Anne Martyn, Mary Browne, Mildred Wright, and Anne Wilson of Cranbrook, with Mary Reade of Denham, were indicted at the Maidstone assizes before Sir Peter Warburton, charged with " the execrable and diabolicall crime of witchcraft." Anne Ashby " was the chief actresse " and made a full confession. She nourished a familiar, called Rug,[197] who possessed her and used to come out of her mouth like a mouse. " Anne Ashby, Anne Martyn, and one other of their Associates, pleaded that they were with child pregnant, but confessed it was not by any man, but by the Divell. . . . Anne Ashby and Anne Martyn confessed that the Divell had known them carnally, and that they had no hurt by it."[198] When pricked neither Mary Browne, nor Anne Wilson, nor Mildred Wright, felt any pain or lost blood ; whilst Mary Reade " had a visible Teat, under her tongue, and did show it to many." They were all hanged at the common place of execution, although many were of opinion that they should have been burned alive.

In the summer of 1652, also, at Worcester was hanged Catherine Huxley of Evesham on the charge of bewitching Mary Ellins, a lass of nine years.[199] A little later in the same year Francis Adamson and one Powle were executed at Durham.[200] The following year there was an alarm in Cornwall. A hag who dwelt in a lonely hovel near Land's End was accused as a notorious and known witch. She retaliated by naming others and shortly eight persons were lodged in Launceston jail. It is uncertain how many—probably all— suffered.[201] In 1653 Elizabeth Newman of Whitechapel was hanged,[202] and in the same year Anne Bodenham, whose case has been mentioned above, was executed at Salisbury.

Bury S. Edmunds saw old Mother Boram and her daughter led to the gallows in 1655.[203] On 26 March, 1658, Jane Brooks of Shepton Mallet was hanged on the charge of having afflicted Richard Jones, " a sprightly youth of twelve," with strange disorders. Alice Coward, the witch's sister, was also involved.[204] In fact, once the deadly accusation had been launched it was impossible to say who might not be caught as the circle widened and widened throughout the little village or neighbouring market-town, nay, throughout the whole countryside.[205]

In 1658 at Salisbury an aged widow named Orchard was executed ;[206] and in the same year Mary Oliver was burned at Norwich.[207]

It is hardly surprising that amid this pandemonium of Witchcraft and terror legend should have attached the name of sorcerer to Oliver Cromwell himself. The story goes that on the morning of 3 September, 1651, Cromwell, whilst it was yet early dawn, bade a trusted officer, one Colonel Lindsey, attend him, and rode off to the confines of a lonely little wood not far from the camp. Here they alighted, and having secured their horses, walked some way down the silent glades. Presently the colonel began to shake and tremble with unwonted fear, until at length he was unable to proceed farther, and fell pale and half-swooning against a tree. A mysterious dread overcame him, but Cromwell sternly strode on muttering " Faint-hearted fool ! " At that moment there advanced from behind a huge-girthed oak a grave elderly man who held a parchment in his hand. The general eagerly approached him and they talked together awhile in low earnest tones. " This is but for seven years," cried Cromwell ; " I was to have had it for one-and-twenty." The other peremptorily answered it could be for no longer term. " It shall last fourteen years," was the reply. " Seven, and no more," returned the stranger in a voice of harsh rebuke, and seemed as if about to retire, upon which Cromwell snatched the parchment, and hurrying back to where Lindsey stood, shouted in a triumphant voice, " Now, the battle is our own ! " They left the wood, but seeking his opportunity Lindsey slipped quietly away and never drew rein until he was come into Norfolk, to the house of an intimate friend, one Master Thoroughgood, minister of the parish of Grimstone.

"How now, Colonel?" cried he. "We hear there is likely to be a battle shortly: what, fled from your colours?" "A battle," said the other, "yes, there has been a battle and I am sure the King is beaten. But if ever I strike a stroke for Cromwell again, may I perish eternally! For I am sure he has made a league with the Devil, and the Devil will have him in due time." So at Grimstone, Lindsey lay perdu until he could cross out of England. And when Cromwell died that day seven years, at three of the clock on 3 September, 1658, there had raged for many hours a fearful storm round Whitehall; the Devil had come for his own, folks said. *Aniles fabulæ*, old wives' trattles round the winter fireside ; "fashious and feckles to recite" wise King Jamie might comment. But even gossip sometimes has its value. At any rate it marks the estimation in which Cromwell was popularly held, and a fairy tale may be morally, although not literally, true.

It was not, of course, possible that the witch alarms should die away simultaneously with the Restoration, and in rural districts suspected persons were continually being haled before the justices but only to be acquitted. There were some significant happenings, however, as when Joan Bibb of Rushock in 1660 received twenty pounds damages for being ducked,[208] and in the following year Frances Bailey of Broxbourn made an official complaint before the magistrates against those who had called her witch.[209] In 1665 three persons were convicted of murder and hanged for killing a supposed witch.[210]

Several witches are said to have suffered at Canterbury in 1660, but the record is possibly in error and may refer to a slightly earlier date.[211] In 1663 Julian Cox was executed at Taunton ; the following year saw the condemnation at Bury S. Edmunds of the Lowestoft witches, Amy Duny and Rose Cullender, the most important case during this later period ; in 1674 Ann Foster was hanged at Northampton on a charge of bewitching a flock of sheep, but there was also the crime of arson proved against her, for barns and standing corn had been fired ; and in 1682,[212] at Exeter Assizes, Temperance Lloyd, Mary Trembles, and Susanna Edwards were sent to the gallows, this being almost certainly the last execution for Witchcraft in England.

In the trials of 1663–4 the evidence revealed that beyond all question a gang of Satanists flourished in Somerset, held their Sabbats, and were eager to spread their accursed propaganda.[213] They were discovered by an active magistrate named Robert Hunt, who committed them to the Taunton Assizes, where they appeared before Justice Archer. Elizabeth Style died in prison, but Julian Cox, who had met the Demon, or the Grand Master of the company, " in the shape of a black Man," who had signed a written contract with him, and attended countless Sabbats in Brewham Forest, was hanged. The Somerset gangs were especially skilled in the fashioning of clay and wax figures, which they baptized with impious rites to make the charm more deadly and more devilish.[214]

The trials at Bury S. Edmunds in 1664 are of the greatest importance and interest, largely from the position of the presiding judge, Sir Matthew Hale, chief baron of the exchequer, and one of the greatest lawyers of the seventeenth century, a period singularly prolific in famous names. On 10 March, Amy Duny and Rose Cullender, two widows of Lowestoft, were indicted for bewitching Elizabeth and Ann Durent, Jane Bocking, Susan Chandler, Elizabeth Pacy, Deborah Pacy, and William Durent, an infant. Amy Duny had long been reputed a witch and a " person of very evil behaviour." One of the chief witnesses against her was Samuel Pacy, upon whose two daughters Elizabeth, aged about eleven, and Deborah, aged nine, she had cast the evil eye. The younger girl had already been taken ill, when one morning Amy Duny came to buy some herrings, which were refused her. She turned away muttering curses and threats, whereupon " the child was taken with the most violent fits, feeling most extream pain in her stomach, like the pricking of pins, and shrieking out in a most dreadful manner, like unto a whelp, and not like unto a sensible creature." The hag was at once suspected, and when a few days later Elizabeth Pacy fell into hideous convulsions, vomiting crooked pins and broad-headed nails, the neighbours considered that sorcery was plainly at work. Both girls were seized with paroxysms of pain, during which they cried out continually that Amy Duny and Rose Cullender were tormenting them. There were strange stories, too, of spectral mice, a toad, and poultry that haunted the house, running hither and thither. Upon a warrant granted by Sir Edmund Bacon, a Suffolk justice, six women searched Rose Cullender and found the Devil's mark, and other damning proof that she had nourished familiars. Sir Thomas Browne, then Dr. Browne, who was present at the trials, being a " person of great knowledge," was " desired to give his opinion what he did conceive of them : and he was clearly of opinion that the persons were bewitched . . . for he conceived that these swooning fits were natural, and nothing else but that they call the mother, but only heightened to a great excess by the subtilty of the Devil, co-operating with the malice of these which we term witches, at whose instance he doth these villainies." The prisoners being asked what they had to say replied " nothing material to anything that was proved against them." After an absence of half an hour the jury brought the two women in guilty upon thirteen indictments. " This was upon Thursday in the afternoon 13 March, 1665." The two witches were much urged to confess, but would not ". . . no reprieve was granted : And they were executed on Monday the 17th of March following, but they confessed nothing."[215]

The Witchcraft of Ann Foster who was hanged at Northampton in 1674 may be explained by other crimes, but there seems little doubt that this vicious beldame was at any rate a witch in will if not in deed. A rich farmer had in some way offended her, and a little later thirty of his sheep were found dead with their " Leggs broke in pieces and their Bones all shattered in their Skins." Soon after his house and barns were set on fire. Ann Foster was indicted for bringing about these mischiefs by her sorceries, she made ample confession, and went to the gallows.[216]

In August, 1682, at the Exeter Assizes, Temperance Lloyd, Mary Trembles, and Susanna Edwards were indicted before Sir Thomas Raymond and Sir Francis North, the circuit judges, upon multiplied charges of sorcery. Temperance Lloyd, who long lived in the worst repute at Bideford and was looked upon as the woman that did debauch the other two, was accused of having cast a spell on Mrs. Grace Thomas, who had been seized with " sticking and pricking pains, as if pins and awls had been thrust into her body, from the crown of her head to the soles of her feet, and she lay as if she had been upon a rack." It seemed that the witch possessed a piece of leather and in this she had stuck nine pins to destroy her victim. She had, she frankly acknowledged, caused William Herbert to languish some twelve years before, and but three years since she had destroyed Anne Fellows, yet although suspected, and even arraigned, on both occasions, she managed to escape justice for the time. According to custom she was searched by Anne Wakely and the witch mark was found. " Upon search of her said body she this informant did find in her secret parts, two teats hanging nigh together like unto a piece of flesh that a child had suckt. And that each of the said teats was about an inch in length."[217] Temperance Lloyd also confessed that she had met the Devil " in the shape or likeness of a black man, about the middle of the afternoon of that day [30 September] in a certain street or lane in the town of Biddiford aforesaid, called Higher Gunstone lane." She further admitted connexion with evil spirits. Dixit enim Diabolum in forma leonis (ut putabat) domum intrasse, et secum concubuisse corpus fœdissime subigitando. Quæ cum fecisset tam uiolenter eum pudenda suxisse ut pro dolore magnos se edidisse clamores. (She saith and confesseth that the Devil hath had carnal knowledge of her body three other times. . . .)

Susanna Edwards, " did meet with a gentleman in a field called the Parsonage Close in the town of Biddiford. And saith that his apparel was all of black. Upon which she did hope to have a piece of money of him. Whereupon the gentleman drawing near unto this examinant, she did make a curchy or courtesy unto him, as she did use to do to gentlemen. Being demanded what and who the gentleman she spake of was, the said examinant answered, and said, that it was the Devil."[218] It was she who had persuaded Mary Trembles to join the coven, and they both stated that shortly after they had seen the Devil as a lion, by which no doubt a large cat is intended. Later she confessed that " there was something in the shape of a little boy which she thinks to be the Devil came into her house and did lie with her." These two seemed to the judge to be " overwhelm'd with melancholy and waking Dreams." All three were condemned on 25 August, 1682, and executed eleven days later. The case certainly presents many curious features, and there was a considerable amount of evidence which it is impossible to dismiss lightly. The witches' own confessions point to a coven, and there can be little doubt that it was only by chance many other persons were not implicated. There are three contemporary pamphlets which report the case, the fullest (40 pages) and most correct of these being *A True and Impartial Relation of the Informations against Three Witches, viz., Temperance Lloyd, Mary Trembles, and Susanna Edwards, who were Indicted, Arraigned, and Convicted at the Assizes holden . . . at . . . Exon, Aug.* 14, 1682. *With their several Confessions . . . as also Their . . . Behaviour, at the . . . Execution on the Twenty fifth of the said Month. London,* 1682.

Notestein gives it as his definite opinion that these were the last persons put to death for Witchcraft in England, and he makes out an excellent case. The witch who was condemned at York in 1687 was almost certainly reprieved,[219] as also was Margareta Young, a Wiltshire witch, two years later.[220] In 1693 the Widow Chambers of Upaston, Suffolk, was committed, but died in jail.[221] In the following year Ann Hart of Sandwich was convicted, but went free under a general act of pardon.[222] In 1712 Jane Wenham was condemned at the Hertford Assizes, but reprieved.

There remain two cases which call for more detailed comment : Elinor Shaw and Mary Phillips, " two notorious Witches," are said to have been burned at Northampton on Saturday, 17 March, 1705, for bewitching a woman and two children ; and on Saturday, 28 July, 1716, Mary Hicks and her daughter Elizabeth, aged nine, are reported to have been executed at Huntingdon. There are two pamphlets, London, 1705, which purport to relate the first case ; and one pamphlet, apparently published in 1716, is brought forward as proof of the second.

As the pamphlet is of the last rarity, the only known copy being in Bodley's Library, Oxford, the full title will doubtless be found of interest.

" *The whole Trial and Examination of Mrs. Mary Hicks and her Daughter Elizabeth, But of Nine Years of Age, who were condemn'd the last Assizes held at Hunting-ton for Witchcraft ; and there executed on Saturday the 28th of July,* 1716.

" *With an Account of the most surprising pieces of Witchcraft*

they play'd, whilst under their Diabolical Compact, the like never heard of before ; their Behaviour with Several Divines who came to converse with 'em whilst under Sentence of Death ; and last Dying Speeches and Confession at the place of Execution.
"*London : Printed by W. Matthews in Long Acre.*" 12mo, 8 *pp.*

From internal evidence it may be taken as clearly established that the Northampton pamphlets are a reworking of a pamphlet published in 1700, *The Full Tryals, Examination and Condemnation of Four Notorious Witches, At the Assizes held in Worcester on Tuesday the 4th of March,*[223] which is itself but a slightly adapted version of a witch-trial and execution at Chelmsford in July, 1645. This at once casts something more than suspicion upon the authenticity of the affair.

Miss Murray in her usual inaccurate slap-dash fashion writes : " Elinor Shaw and Mary Phillips were executed at Northampton in 1704,"[224] giving a reference to " *Witches of Northampton,* p. 6," whilst in her Bibliography she cites " *Witches of Northamptonshire.* London, 1612." Here we have confusion worse confounded, as in any case the two women are said to have suffered in March, 1705.

To turn for a moment to the Huntingdon pamphlet. Various details, small in themselves but in the aggregate not without weight, have been questioned. A " Justice Wilmot " is mentioned, who seems to have conducted the examination preliminary to the assizes. Such a magistrate would have surely belonged to a county family, or at any rate to some well-known house. No such name as Wilmot occurs among all the records and histories of Huntingdonshire so far as can be traced. Nor is Hicks to be discovered. These points are, of course, not conclusive, but they seem to make the story more improbable.

James Crossley, the scholar and a high authority on Witchcraft, writing to *Notes and Queries* (1st series, V, 514, 29 May, 1852), gives several reasons for doubting the truth of the Huntingdon narrative. In the first place Francis Hutchinson, who made a chronological table of cases, published his *Historical Essay on Witchcraft* in 1718. He had the help in his compilations of Chief Justices Parker and King, and of Chief-Baron Bury, and yet he says the last execution in

England for Witchcraft was in 1682. He spared neither pains nor time in finding out all details. He had investigated the case of Sarah Moordike, who having been before acquitted at Guildford, in 1701–2, appealed to a justice in London against her persecutor.[225] He had collected with the nicest discrimination all the evidence concerning Jane Wenham in 1712, he had even interviewed and questioned her closely. He had, in fact, made a personal inquiry into all cases and trials that could be remembered by his contemporaries. " It is scarcely possible," says Crossley when speaking of the noise of the Wenham case and the rain of pamphlets, " that in four years after two persons, one only nine years old . . . should have been tried and executed for witchcraft without public attention being called to the circumstance." Moreover, neither the *Historical Register* for 1716 nor the files of two London newspapers for that year, although enumerating other convictions on the circuit, record the supposed trials.[226]

It will be seen that the argument with reference to Hutchinson equally applies to the Northamptonshire witches. It is impossible to believe that he should have quite overlooked these executions. In the *Northamptonshire Historical Collections*, 1st series (Northampton, 1896), there is a chapter on Witchcraft in Northamptonshire, copied from the *Northamptonshire Handbook* for 1867. That chapter gives the trials in detail with copious extracts from the pamphlets. In a footnote the writers say : " To show that the burning actually took place in 1705, it may be important to mention that there is an item of expense entered in the overseers' accounts for S. Giles parish for faggots bought for the purpose." Professor Notestein, however, applied to the Reverend R. M. Serjeantson, who examined the parish register of S. Giles Church, and stated : " The S. Giles accounts briefly state that *wood* was bought from time to time— probably for melting the lead. There is *no* mention of *faggots* nor witches in the Churchwardens' overseers-for-the-poor accounts."[227] It is obvious that the compilers of the *Northamptonshire Handbook* for 1867 have blundered.

Moreover, witches in England were not burned but hanged. It is true that in 1645 at Ipswich, Mother Lakeland was burned. But this was because she had killed her husband by Witchcraft. Burning was the penalty appointed for heresy ;[228] and both for high and petty treason, *i.e.* murder of a husband by a wife, murder of a master or mistress by a servant ;[229] and several offences against the coin. Thus on the 16 July, 1546, Anne Askewe was burnt to death at Smithfield for obstinately maintaining theological opinions tantamount to a denial of Christianity. A woman was burned in 1571 and another in 1575.[230] On 10 May, 1652, Evelyn notes in his *Diary*, " Passing by Smithfield I saw a miserable creature burning, who had murdered her husband." The sentence upon Alice Lisle, who was convicted of high treason, was commuted to beheading, and she suffered at Winchester, 2 September, 1685. Elizabeth Gaunt, an Anabaptist fanatic, who was guilty of the same crime perished at the stake at Tyburn, 23 October in the same year. Culprits were generally first strangled by the executioner, although the law seems to have made no such provision. In the case of the notorious Catherine Hayes the hangman bungled and the wretched woman was actually burned alive at Tyburn, 3 November, 1726. Ann Whale, who murdered her husband by administering white mercury in gruel, was executed on Broadbridge Heath Common, near Horsham, in August, 1752. She " was led to the stake, her back chained thereto, and then strangled, and in about five minutes the fire was kindled, and her body consumed to ashes."[231] Tennyson's grandmother saw a young widow, who had killed her husband, on her way to be strangled and burned. This would be about 1760.[232] On 21 March, 1764, Mary Saunders, a servant, was burnt at Monmouth for the murder of Mrs. Jones, with whom she lived.[233] In 1776 a hag of eighty, Anne Cruttenden, who had cut the throat and mutilated the dead body of her husband, a man half her age, was sentenced at the Horsham Assizes on 5 August by Lord Mansfield. " Let her be drawn on a hurdle to the place of execution on Thursday next and there to be burnt with fire until she be dead."[234] John Baker in his *Horsham Diary*[235] says that a little after noon on 8 August she was " hanged and burnt." A woman was burned at Ipswich in 1783, and one Mary Bayley at Portsmouth in 1784. The last execution of this kind was that of Christian Bowman, the paramour of a coiner named Hugh Murphy, who was hanged. The details are given in a contemporary chap-book : " The Life and Death of Christian Bowman, alias Murphy ; Who was burnt at a Stake, in the Old Bailey, on Wednesday the 18th of March, 1789, for High Treason, in feloniously and traitorously counterfeiting the Silver Coin of the Realm. *Containing her Birth and Parentage, youthful Adventures, Love Amours, fatal Marriage, unhappy Connections, and untimely Death.*" Christian Bowman was hanging forty minutes before the faggots were fired. The law was altered by 30 George III. c. 48 (1790), which provided that after 5 June, 1790, women under this sentence should be hanged.

It is, I think, plain that the Northamptonshire witch pamphlets of 1705 dealing with Mary Phillips and Elinor Shaw are purely fictitious, as also must be accounted the Huntingdonshire narrative of 1716. During the last decade of the seventeenth century the belief in Witchcraft had fast begun to decline, and with the eighteenth century the possibility of Satanism was very generally being flouted. This is hardly surprising when we remember the flood of scepticism and polite indifference which was about to stagnate the anæmic creed and religious practice of England. Men such as Charles Blount, Toland, Anthony Collins, Tindal, Woolston, Thomas Chubb, Thomas Morgan, Peter Annet, Conyers Middleton, had no sort of use for the supernatural. There had been some extravagances and credulity at which it was so absurdly easy to mock and sneer. The reality of the darker side of the picture these narrow minds would have deemed impossible.

Now and again in some remote country districts accusations of Witchcraft were bruited, but officially these almost invariably fell through upon inquiry. At the accession of William and Mary, Sir John Holt became Chief Justice of the King's Bench and he was a notorious sceptic. His opinions were very decided ; his disbelief in Witchcraft very pronounced, and naturally from his authority and position his influence was felt far and wide. In 1694 he tried Mother Munnings at Bury S. Edmunds and secured her acquittal. In 1696 at Exeter he plainly[236] refused to accept the evidence against Elizabeth Horner, and she was brought in not guilty. His example spread throughout the country.

Thus at Launceston in 1695 Mary Guy or Daye was acquitted ; in 1698-9 Ruth Young, a Wiltshire woman, was discharged ;[237] in 1701-2 Susanna Hanover of Devonshire was acquitted, as also six years later was Maria Stevens of Somerset.

Addison, in one of his Roger de Coverley papers (*Spectator*, No. 117, Saturday, 14 July, 1711), gives a very apt description of the feelings still excited among the rustics by these crones who lay under an imputation of Witchcraft. In company with Sir Roger, Mr. Spectator visits the hovel of a hag, named Moll White. " In our Return home Sir ROGER told me, that old *Moll* had been often brought before him for making Children spit Pins, and giving Maids the Night-Mare : and that the Country People would be tossing her into a Pond and trying Experiments with her every Day, if it was not for him and his Chaplain. I have since found, upon Enquiry, that Sir ROGER was several times staggered with the Reports that had been brought him concerning this old Woman, and would frequently have bound her over to the County Sessions had not his Chaplain with much ado persuaded him to the contrary. I have been the more particular in this Account because I hear there is scarce a Village in *England* that has not a *Moll White* in it."

When he expresses himself seriously upon the question of Witchcraft Addison, as we might expect, hedges and utters vague ambiguities. " There are some Opinions in which a Man should stand Neuter, without engaging his Assent to one side or the other." This may be, but only in matters of indifference. Yet he continues : " It is with this Temper of Mind that I consider the Subject of Witchcraft. . . . In short, when I consider the Question, whether there are such Persons in the World as those we call Witches ? my Mind is divided between the two opposite Opinions ; or rather (to speak my thoughts freely) I believe in general that there is, and has been such a thing as Witchcraft ; but at the same time can give no Credit to any Particular Instance of it."[238] Which just means nothing at all.

The trial of Jane Wenham, the " Wise Woman of Walkerne," on 4 March, 1711–12, before Mr. Justice Powell at Hertford Assizes, roused extraordinary interest not only throughout the district, but in London too, for ere long the accused had become " the discourse of the town." For some years since Jane Wenham had been vehemently suspect, and when Matthew Gilson, whom she had rated and threatened, began to behave in a very odd and crazy manner, honest Farmer Chapman hailed the angry beldame as a witch. Thereupon she applied to Sir Henry Chauncy, a local justice, for a warrant against her adversary on the score of defamation. He was fined one shilling; whilst Mr. Gardiner, a well-known clergyman, read her a sound lecture upon living more peaceably, which she much resented. Anne Thorne, servant at the parsonage, next fell into fits and told a story of having been to a remote lane, where she saw " a little Old Woman Muffled in a Riding hood," who gave her a large crooked pin. Shortly afterwards the maid met Jane Wenham, who abused her roundly in the street, and presently she fell into fresh paroxysms. The reputed witch was now clapped up in custody, Sir Henry Chauncy being assisted by the rector of Walkerne, Mr. Francis Bragge, and Mr. Strutt, vicar of Audley. A few days later in the presence of the justice and three local ministers the accused made a halting and equivocal confession. The assizes were thronged. " So vast a number of People have not been together at the Assizes in the memory of Man." [239] In spite of the preliminary investigations the one charge brought was that Jane Wenham entertained a familiar in the shape of a cat. There was a curious story of cakes of small feathers set in an elaborate pattern and clotted together with some viscous matter, the Devil's unguent made of dead men's fat, which were found in Anne Thorne's pillow. From the first Justice Powell set himself against a conviction, but the evidence proved overwhelming and Jane Wenham was formally condemned, only to be reprieved forthwith and soon pardoned. After her release she was taken under the protection of Colonel Plummer of Gilston, and upon his death she was allowed a small pension by the Earl and Countess of Cowper. She lived until 1730.[240] The case provoked a pamphlet controversy and there was nothing more loudly discussed at the time. Mr. Bragge's *A Full and Impartial Account of the Discovery of Sorcery and Witchcraft, Practis'd by Jane Wenham of Walkerne in Hertfordshire, upon the bodies of Ann Thorn, Anne Street, &c. . . . till she . . . receiv'd Sentence of death for the same, March 4, 1711–12,* ran into no less than five editions within the year, 1712. It was answered by such pieces as *A Full Confutation of Witchcraft . . . proving that, Witchcraft is*

Priestcraft, London, 1712, a contemptible brochure ; and *The Impossibility of Witchcraft, Plainly Proving, From Scripture and Reason, That there never was a Witch*, London, 1712, which is sufficiently narrow and inept.[241] It seems very possible that Jane Wenham was a medium possessed of hypnotic powers, one who had attempted to meddle with dark secrets. No doubt the fright she received restrained her from any such dangerous essays in the future.

It is said that in 1717 Jane Clark and her daughter appeared at the Leicester Assizes.[242] In any case the last witch-trial— or more precisely commitment for trial—in England was that of an old woman and her son at Leicester Assizes in September, 1717, before Lord Parker. Information had also been laid against the daughter, who, however, was not committed by the Justice. There were twenty-five informants, and it was deposed that the witches were swum crosswise and " that they Swam like a cork, a piece of paper, or an empty barrell, tho : they Strove all they could to Sinck." It was asserted that several persons had been afflicted with strange diseases, but upon applying to " a Cunning man or white witch " he prescribed various counter-charms of a crude, but apparently effective, nature, such as boiling the patients' urine, which invariably brought the witches helter-skelter into the room. " Sometimes in the Shape of a cat & sometimes a dog who would run in panting as if He was upon a hard chase, and these dogs and cats would come in tho : the doors and windows were shut and all passages Except Keyholes & chimneys Stopt & could never be catch[d] but would grin furiously, and approaching near the bewitch'd persons give them great pain and so vanish." The time-honoured remedy of drawing blood from the witches was essayed, and the constable helped to hold them during these experiments. " The old woman's Skin was so tough that they could get no Blood of her by scratching so they used great pins & such Instruments for that purpose." " Searching the old witch publickly before a great number of good women in that town they deposed there were found on her Secret parts two white pieces of flesh like paps and some swore they were like the teats of an ewe, & some like the paps of a Cat." The bill was not found, and so the trial did not come on, but these MS. notes were made by Sir George Beaumont for the private use of the Judge, who preserved them with some care.[243]

At this point it may be well most briefly to pass in swift review one or two names of those who, particularly during the seventeenth century, have written in English specifically upon the subject of Witchcraft. To give detailed criticism of a vast library of authors, however interesting, were here impertinent, but some cursory mention of a few more remarkable literary men would seem to be useful. Reginald Scot, whose *Discoverie of Witchcraft*, 1584,[244] is one of the earliest and most famous of these treatises, has already been considered. He found a disciple in George Gifford, a non-comformist minister, who resolutely seconded the opposition to the prevalent belief. Three years after the publication of Scot's book he produced *A Discourse of the Subtell Practises of Devilles by Witches*, which he followed in 1593 with *A Dialogue concerning Witches*.[245] Gifford accepts the fact that there are witches, but they are deluded by the Devil, and all their practice is mere phantasmagoria. He seems to consider prosecution unjustified. Henry Holland in his *A Treatise against Witchcraft*, Cambridge, 1590, takes the same line. He does not reduce Witchcraft to a " cozening or poisoning art " as did Scot ; he allows there may be a real " confederacie with Satan himself," but he avers that— nowadays at any rate—the proof of such a bargain cannot be sustained. Thomas Potts' *The Wonderfull Discoverie of Witches in the countie of Lancaster*, London, 1613, an able book, concentrates, of course, upon the one Pendle case. *A Discourse of the Damned Art of Witchcraft*, by the well-known Calvinist minister William Perkins, was published in 1608, six years after the author's death. His point of view is mainly Biblical, and he discounts entirely such tests as the scratching of witches and the swimming ordeal. John Cotta, a Northampton physician, wrote *The Triall of Witchcraft*, 1616, to put forward what may roughly be termed the medical aspect of these cases. Thus he explains possession largely as a subject for the doctor, and although he allows there are witches, he thinks it very hard to distinguish the many impostors from the devoted bond-slave of Satan. *A Treatise of Witchcraft*, 1616, by Alexander Roberts, " minister of God's word at King's Lynn," and the Reverend

Thomas Cooper's *The Mystery of Witchcraft*, 1617, are both thoroughly conservative in their approach to the problem. Richard Bernard, the vicar of Batcombe, Somerset, shows the true Anglican caution when he published in 1627 *A Guide to Grand-Jurymen . . . in cases of Witchcraft.* He hedges and multiplies reservations, excepts and cavils, until he reaches conclusions with which he hopes no one can disagree. A most unsatisfactory attitude. Of far higher value is the Platonic Henry More's *An Antidote against Atheism : or, An Appeal to the Natural Faculties of the Mind of Man, whether there be not a God,* 1653,[246] More justly regards the phenomena of Witchcraft as part of the evidence for the reality of the unseen world. He has absolute proof of the "nocturnal conventicles" of witches. It should be superfluous, but may not be irrelevant, once again to emphasize that only the illogical and circumscribed materialist would now venture to deny these, and he is generally impervious to demonstration. Nathaniel Homes, minister of S. Mary Stayning's, was inclined to suppose that evil spirits did many of their tricks by jugglery and deception. There is much truth in his views which he elaborates in *Dæmonologie and Theologie. The first, the Malady. . . . The Second, the Remedy,* 1650. Sir Robert Filmer's *Advertisement to the Jurymen of England,* 1653, may be dismissed as a thoroughly unreliable and uncritical compilation, a thing of no account, whilst Thomas Ady's *A Candle in the Dark,* 1656, which has been much admired, although perhaps not read, by some modern sceptics, has a great many dogmatic assertions but very little evidence of impartial inquiry and investigation. A shiftless empty piece. The profound Burton in the *Anatomy of Melancholy* assuredly accepted the dark fact of Witchcraft. " Many deny witches at all," he says,[247] " or if there be any they can do no harm ; of this opinion is Wierus, *lib.* 3, *cap.* 53, *de præstig dæm.,* Austin Lerchemer, a Dutch writer, Biarmanus, Ewichius, Euwaldus, our countryman Scot, . . . but on the contrary are most lawyers, divines, physicians, philosophers, Austin, Hemingius, Danæus, Chytræus, Zanchius, Aretius, &c., Delrio, Springer, Niderius, *lib.* 5, Fornicar, Guiatius, Bartolus consil. 6, tom. 1, Bodine, dæmoniant. *lib.* 2, *cap.* 8, Godelman, Damhoderius, &c., Paracelsus, Erastus, Scribanius, Camerarius, &c."[248] And in another place he poises : " Whether by these diabolical means, which are commonly practised by the Devil and his ministers, sorcerers, witches, magicians, &c., by spells, cabilistical words, charms, characters, images, amulets, ligatures, philtres, incantations, &c., this disease and the like may be cured ? " He discusses and decides that magicians can remedy certain harms, and " *Hoc posito*, they can effect such cures, the main question is, whether it be lawful in a desperate case to crave their help, or ask a wizard's advice." The answer is : never, in no imaginable circumstances, for so to do is a mortal sin.

In 1636 was born at Plymouth Joseph Glanvill, who is undoubtedly the most able as he is the fairest-minded English writer upon Witchcraft in the seventeenth century. An undergraduate of Exeter College, Oxford, he proceeded B.A. in 1655, and having shortly after moved to Lincoln, M.A. in 1658. For a short time he was chaplain to Francis Rous, Provost of Eton, but in 1660 he was presented to the Rectory of Wimbish, Essex. In 1661 he published *The Vanity of Dogmatizing* and in the following year *Lux Orientalis*. Some three years after the formation of the Royal Society he was elected a member of that body, and in 1666 he received the important appointment of Rector of the Abbey Church, Bath. The same year saw a tentative volume *Some Philosophical Considerations touching Witches and Witchcraft*, but unfortunately the first edition almost entirely perished in the Great Fire. Immediately reprinted, it had reached a fourth issue in 1668–9 when it took a new title *A Blow at Modern Sadducism*.[249] In the spring of 1681 the work was republished as *Saducismus Triumphatus*, " or A full and plain Evidence concerning Witches and Apparitions. In Two Parts. The First treating of their Possibility ; the Second, of their real Existence. By Jos. Glanvill, late Chaplain to his Majesty, etc. With a Letter to Dr. *Hen. More* on the same Subject ; and an Authentick and Wonderful Story of Sweedish Witches, Englished by Anthony Horneck. In Octavo. Printed for J. Collins, under the Temple Church ; and S. Loundes, near the *Savoy* in the *Strand*."[250] The work became extremely popular and went through several more revisions and reimpressions (1683, 1689, 1700, 1726). It has in truth proved to be Glanvill's not unworthy and substantial title to fame. In 1672 Glanvill was appointed Chaplain in Ordinary to

Charles II, and six years later he was installed Prebendary of Worcester. On 4 November, 1680, he succumbed to a fever, and is buried in the Abbey Church, Bath.[251]

The *Sadducismus Triumphatus* is a weighty, an important, an authoritative book.[252] Even the work of obtaining and verifying the many accounts of psychic phenomena therein recorded was very laborious and long. The author was resolved to submit each narrative to the most searching scrutiny, to test it in every possible way, not to spare himself letters and inquiries of every kind which might serve to throw some light upon the problems in hand. He meets every twist and turn of the opponents' argument, and is more than ready for them at every point. How clinchingly does he argue : " Matters of Fact well proved ought not to be denied, because we cannot conceive how they can be perform'd. Nor is it a reasonable method of inference, first to presume the thing impossible, and thence to conclude that the fact cannot be proved. On the contrary, we should judge of the Action by the evidence, and not the evidence by the measures of our Fancies about the Action."[253]

And again with most topical pertinence in reply to those shallow minds who, because of many fraudulent cases in the region of psychic phenomena, with entire lack of logic and perception jump to the conclusion that all must be trickery, he remarks : " Frequency of deceit and fallacy will warrant a greater care and caution in examining ; and scrupulosity and shiness of assent to things wherein Fraud hath been practised, or may in the least degree be suspected : But to conclude, because that an old Womans Fancy abused her, or some Knavish fellows put Tricks upon the Ignorant and timorous ; that therefore whole Assizes have been a thousand times deceived in Judgments upon matters of Fact, and numbers of sober Persons have been forsworn in things wherein Perjury could not advantage them ; I say, such Inferences are as void of Reason, as they are of Charity and good Manners."[254]

To me Glanvill's line of argument and many of his particular instances appear conclusive.[255]

Meric Casaubon's *Of Credulity and Incredulity in things Natural, Civil, and Divine : wherein the denying of Spirits, Witches, etc., is confuted,*[256] is a meritorious work, which again emphasizes the fact that many cases of charlatanry do not establish a complete negative. Casaubon considers the cumulative evidence of cases which have been proven authentic to be overwhelming, as indeed it is.

John Wagstaffe, a graduate of Oriel College, Oxford, in 1669 published *The Question of Witchcraft Debated*, a sour and crooked polemic, which need not detain us. He ingenuously suggests that coincidence may account for much that is inexplicable in the witch-trials.

Professor Notestein finds " no little brilliance and insight " in John Webster's *The Displaying of Supposed Witchcraft*, 1677,[257] but I confess that these qualities entirely escape me. Personally I am conscious of a singular lack of sustained argument, not a few unsupported asseverations, and a number of suggestions which have already been fully answered by Glanvill and Casaubon. It will hardly be believed that Webster declares the impurity of Witchcraft and the abominable orgies of the Sabbat are of themselves proofs that it does not exist. " Surely even the impurity of it may be sufficient to overthrow the credibility of it, especially among Christians."[258] This fatuity shows that he has not even an elementary grasp of his subject. Does he look for purity and holiness among the bond-slaves of the Devil ? Are not rather their lusts and obscenities the very hall-mark of their profession ? As Madame Chantelouve said to Durtal : " Pensiez-vous rencontrer ici des Saints ? " It is a terrible side, and a hideous side, but it is one which the scholar and the historian may not ignore.

The prolific Baxter's *Certainty of the World of Spirits*, 1691, a stout defence of the supernatural ; John Beaumont's *Treatise of Spirits*, 1705 ; and Richard Boulton's *A Compleat History of Magic*, 1715 ; must be passed over with a bare mention. They are in the main sound treatises of a reasonably conservative tendency.

It is hardly necessary to pursue the discussion of works upon Witchcraft after the trials had themselves ceased, for any literary arguments and pamphlets must for many long years to come have merely a theoretical value.[259] Francis Hutchinson's *Historical Essay on Witchcraft* appeared in 1718, the year following the committal of the old woman and her son at Leicester, when no bill was found to go for trial. The author, who was afterwards Bishop of Conmore and Down, shows himself of unwearied industry, and his collections make his work of no small value. No doubt some of his observations are sound. There were abuses, there was cruelty, there were extravagances. But the obscurantist spirit which sweeps away all evidence is intellectually just as illogical as the fanaticism of the Parliament or the Scotch Calvinists. Hutchinson's arguments are unbalanced and oblique. Under the specious guise of common-sense they too often appeal to the half-educated, the superficial. Notestein, who is patently uncritical, writes : " Hutchinson's work was the last chapter in the witch controversy. There was nothing more to say." And yet to-day psychologists and scientists are discussing the truth of spiritistic phenomena, exploring the twilight land of those intimate half-guessed connexions between spirit and matter, are with pains and patience spending month after month, it may be, in the observation of some one extraordinary manifestation. Then we hear that as long ago as 1718 " there was nothing more to say " ! So far as actual legislation in England is concerned the Act of James I was repealed under George II in 1736, [260] when a new Act was introduced based on the assumption that there is no such thing as Witchcraft, and therefore aimed against any pretence to the exercise of a non-existent power, or in other words, against fraud. It is entitled an Act for punishing such persons as *pretend* to exercise " any kind of witchcraft, sorcery, enchantment, or conjuration," and it lays down that in order to prevent any pretences to such arts or powers, if a person pretends to exercise any kind of witchcraft, sorcery, enchantment, or conjuration, or undertakes to tell fortunes, such person is to be imprisoned for a year, and to be set in the pillory at every quarter.

Proceedings against professional fortune-tellers, palmists, and consulting mediums of any kind, are now generally taken under the Vagrancy Act of 1824, the title of which is : " An Act for the punishment of idle and disorderly persons, and rogues and vagabonds." Various classes of individuals are specified who are to be deemed " idle and disorderly " or " rogues and vagabonds " within the meaning of the Act, including " every common prostitute wandering in the streets and behaving in a riotous or indecent manner," every person lodging in any unoccupied building, or in any cart or wagon, not having visible means of subsistence and not giving a good account of himself, and every person in the possession of an instrument with intent to break into a dwelling-house.

Mixed up with these definitions are the words under which mediums are prosecuted : " Every person pretending or professing to tell fortunes, or using any subtle craft, means, or device, by palmistry or otherwise, to deceive and impose on any of his Majesty's subjects."

Having regard to the object of the statute and the collocation of the words in the above clause with the other definitions given in the Act it is reasonable to suppose that the Act was not intended to apply to anyone having no intention to deceive. It has been held, however, by the divisional court, in a comparatively recent case, that a person " telling fortunes," however honestly, commits an offence within the Statute. This it might be argued opens up the widest issues, and there is obviously need for a prompt reform of these vague Statutes. In any case impostors trading on general credulity by feigning to read the future would be punishable at Common Law, independently of any Statute.

It is plain that the repeal of the Act of the first year of James I had very little effect upon what has been well termed " the religious belief in witches." Not infrequently do we find shocking cases of peasants and country-folk having taken the law into their own hands, and having swum some old trot suspected of sorcery and harming her neighbours.

In 1751[261] there were living at Tring, in Hertfordshire, an old man, named Osborne, and his wife, Ruth, a palsied, doting couple, miserably poor, who had long been held in very bad repute as witches. Some six years previously, during Prince Charlie's '45, old Mother Osborne had begged a portion of buttermilk off a farmer named Butterfield, who dwelt at Gubblecot, and having been roughly refused, turned away muttering a curse upon the calves and hogs. Soon after the whole stock became ill, and affairs deteriorated so rapidly that Butterfield gave up his farm and opened an inn, where he hoped for better luck. He made no secret of the fact that he deemed sorcery had worked the mischief. In 1750 he himself was seized with a strange sickness, and he promptly summoned a wise man from Northamptonshire, who soon diagnosed the case as witchcraft. Shortly news flew round that certain witches would be ducked at Longmarston on 22 April. A disorderly mob assembled in the vein for any brutality. The parish officers had taken the Osbornes into the workhouse for safety, but the gates were broken open, the doors wrenched off their hinges, and straw piled against the building to burn it to the ground with all the inmates unless the witches were produced. The master in desperation pointed to their hiding-place and with horrid curses the ruffians dragged forth the old man and his wife half-dead with fear. They were stripped stark naked, tied up in the traditional manner, and hurried to a small pond or river some two miles off, where with oaths and kicks they were flung into the water. Mother Osborne did not sink, and so one of the ringleaders, a chimney-sweep, named Colley, waded into the water and thrust at her with a long pole. She was drawn out and beaten until she expired. Her husband died also, although not on the spot. The men who had been the leading spirits in this assault went among the crowd collecting money in return for the amusement. But Government took the matter up, and when a coroner's inquest was held a verdict of wilful murder was returned against Colley, who was hanged in chains, many of his friends being punished with only less severity. It will be seen that when matters were left to the mob they had hardly improved since the days of witch-finder Hopkins, and there was always danger of similar riots. Had the law been at first modified rather than repealed a better condition of things might have been obtained.[262]

When London was all agog in the year 1762 discussing the mystery of the Cock Lane ghost Hogarth produced his *Credulity, Superstition, and Fanaticism*, a confused and, indeed, hopelessly involved satire, a little disgusting and coarsely violent, one of the least satisfactory of his works. It has, however, a certain historical interest, since " To ridicule certain extraordinary occurrences that savoured of the marvellous, was the design of the print now under consideration."[263] The thermometer, which is placed upon two volumes, Wesley's Sermons and Glanvill's *Sadducismus Triumphatus*,[264] is fixed in a human heart and decorated above with a representation of "Scratching Fanny" knocking upon the wainscot of young Miss Parsons' bedchamber, being crowned by the Drummer of Tedworth. The harlequin preacher, vociferating from the pulpit—a grotesque figure— in one hand extends a puppet representing a devil holding a gridiron, in the other the figure of a witch on a broomstick, who is being sucked by her familiar as a weasel. The three panels of the pulpit represent the spectre of Sir George Villiers, who is said to have appeared three times at Windsor Castle to an officer of the King's wardrobe and foretold the Duke of Buckingham's danger from Felton ;[265] the vision of Julius Cæsar seen by Brutus at Philippi ; and the appari- tion of Mrs. Veal to Mrs. Bargrave. Upon the floor con- vulsively swoons the celebrated Mary Tofts,[266] the rabbit breeder of Godalming in Surrey. She is represented as in all the pangs of labour, whilst some friendly hand offers her a glass of cordial, which she has broken in the violence of her paroxysms. The rabbits are scampering away from beneath her petticoats. Hard by a possessed shoe-black[267] vomits forth huge nails and crooked pins. His basket, wherein appears a volume of Whitfield's *Journals*, is placed upon King James' *Dæmonologie*. I had not dwelt upon the details of this unpleasing picture were it not that it well displays the temper of the age, than which it would be, I suppose, difficult to point to a more unspiritual and indifferent a period.

John Wesley, as is well known, was a firm believer in Witchcraft, and in 1768 he writes in his *Journal :* " It is true, likewise, that the English in general, and indeed most of the men of learning in Europe, have given up all accounts of witches and apparitions as mere old wives' fables. I am sorry for it, and I willingly take this opportunity of entering my solemn protest against this violent compliment which so many that believe the Bible pay to those who do not believe it. I owe them no such service. I take knowledge that these are at the bottom of the outcry which has been raised, and with such insolence spread through the land, in direct opposition, not only to the Bible, but to the suffrage of the wisest and best of men in all ages and nations. They well know (whether Christians know it or not) that the giving up of witchcraft is in effect giving up the Bible." And again : " With my latest breath will I bear testimony against giving up to infidels one great proof of the invisible world : I mean that of witchcraft and apparitions, confirmed by the testimony of all ages.''

In 1785 a poor woman named Sarah Bradshaw, of Mears Ashby, who was accused of being a witch, in order to prove her innocence, submitted to the ignominy of being dipped, when she was immediately taken to the bottom of the pond, which was deemed to be an incontestable proof that she was no witch.[268]

Such a pamphlet (twenty-four pages, 8vo) as the following, which was published at Bristol in 1788, shows that Witchcraft and possession were still firmly believed, since the event excited considerable interest in the West Country : *A Narrative of the Extraordinary Case of Geo. Lukins, of Yatton, Somersetshire, who was possessed of evil spirits for* 18 *years ; also an Account of his remarkable deliverance at Bristol.*

An interesting passage occurs in *The Memoirs of Susan Sibbald* (London, 1926), née Mein, the daughter of Dr. Thomas Mein, R.N., born at Fowey in 1783. She paid a visit to Haslar Hospital as a schoolgirl, and vividly recalls the peculiarities of Captain Yeo, the governor.

'' He was a big, boisterous sort of man, dreadfully subject to gout, and wheeled himself about from room to room, in a chair, as fast as one could run almost. The gout had deformed both his thumbs, which made both the upper joints project forward. Now, he was a very passionate and superstitious man, and would, before he left the breakfast-room, wheel himself round the table and crush to atoms every egg shell on it. I thought this very odd, so the next day I put my egg cup back into the stand in the middle of the table. He wheeled round and round the table and made a great fuss until he got it and broke it up. I asked Mrs. Yeo in the drawing-room why he did it. ' My dear,' she said, ' the Governor thinks witches go to sea in egg shells and cause storms and shipwrecks.' One morning after we had become well acquainted, I took my egg shell off the table and said, ' I am determined a witch shall take a cruise in this that I may see what will happen.' He wheeled his chair between me and the door and came after me so quick that he got me in a corner, and although I had thrown away the egg shell, he pinched my arm with his thumb bones till he made the tears come into my eyes. I took care not to interfere with his preventive service again."

On Wednesday, 17 February, 1808, a girl named Alice Brown, living at Great Paxton, Hunts, endeavoured to cross the Ouse on very thin ice, which after she had gone a few yards gave sharply, since it had been thawing for some hours, and she was promptly immersed in the cold water, and only able to make her way with great difficulty to the bank where a frightened friend, Fanny Amey, awaited her. Alice Brown, shivering and scared, hurried back to her father's house near the river, and as soon as she reached it exhausted nature threw her into convulsions. Fanny Amey, who was subject to epilepsy, was also alarmed to such a degree that she also was seized with fits of the nature from which she suffered. Both girls now became thoroughly ill, and fell victims to acute hysteria. A credulous neighbour affirmed they were bewitched, and told a long rambling story of a town in Bedfordshire where he had recently been staying. There an old crone was more than suspected of causing a man actually to languish away by her evil spells. Accordingly he filled a vessel with his urine, and heated it in a corked bottle. The result was the old woman was seen to enter the room, she hurried wildly to and fro as in pain and vanished with a distracted air. After a few days the witch died, when her victim was completely cured.

This tale had immense effect, and it was now commonly bruited in Great Paxton that Alice Brown, Fanny Amey, and Mary Fox were bewitched. The Rev. Isaac Nicholson,[269] curate of the parish, sternly rebuked his congregation for spreading so idle and wicked a rumour, but to little effect, for a woman, named Ann Izzard, some sixty years of age, presently came in great trepidation to tell him she was being openly accused. "I am not a witch," she cried, "and am willing to prove it by being weighed against the church Bible." On Thursday, 5 May, Mrs. Izzard betook herself to St. Neots' market. Towards evening she was returning in a cart driven by her son, a lad of sixteen, when they offered a lift to a neighbour, who carelessly set her basket of grocery upon a sack of corn, where it kept jolting in no very secure manner. On going down the hill which leads to Paxton village, one of the horses became restive and by his plunging overturned the basket, ruining the contents. The irate dame to whom the goods belonged at once accused Anne Izzard of spoiling them by Witchcraft. Shortly the whole place was in an uproar, since it was reported that the local witch had overturned a loaded wagon and team " with as much ease as it had been a spinning-wheel." At ten o'clock on Sunday evening, 8 May, a disorderly crowd, taking with them the young wenches supposed to be forespoken, collected outside Wright Izzard's cottage. They broke in, dragged his wife from bed, pricked her with pins, beat her, pelted her with stones, and flung her naked in the yard. At last the unfortunate wretch was able to creep away to a neighbour's, the widow Russel, who took her in, tended her wounds, and put her to bed. Upon the next evening, however, 9 May, Ann Izzard was a second time assaulted, and plans were made to swim her the following afternoon. But she escaped her tormentors by flight, and took refuge in a village some miles away. Alice Russel, however, was subjected to bitter persecution, and so hideously was she threatened that on Friday, 20 May, she died of an illness brought on owing to her fears.

On 17 July following Mr. Nicholson delivered a discourse which was afterwards published as : *A Sermon against Witchcraft, preached in the Parish Church of Great Paxton, in the County of Huntingdon, July 17, 1808, with a brief account of the circumstances which led to Two atrocious attacks on the Person of Ann Izzard, as a reputed witch. By the Reverend Isaac Nicholson, A.M., Curate. . . . London : Printed for J. Mawman, Poultry,* 1808.[270]
There is a preface of ix pp. which commences :—

" *A brief Account of the Attack on the Person of Ann Izzard, and the Circumstances which led to it.*

" In the year 1593, an indelible mark of infamy was stamped upon the inhabitants of Warboys, in the County of Huntingdon, for their folly and wickedness in carrying to trial, and afterwards to execution, three of their unfortunate parishioners, for the alleged offence of witchcraft . . . but the following statement of facts, will convince them of their mistake, and, allowing for the difference of science and civilization, will shew that Great Paxton, in the same county, is more than upon a level with Warboys for ignorance, credulity, and barbarity."

A few special copies of this sermon have attached to them "An abstract of The Proceedings had against Joseph Harper, James Staughton, Thomas Braybrook, Mary Amey, Fanny Amey, Alice Browne, Edward Briers, Mary Hook, and Mary Fox, for assaulting Ann Izzard of Great Paxton in the County of Huntingdon, on the 8th and 9th of May, 1808, under the pretence of her being a Witch. By Isaac Nicholson, A.M., Curate. London : Printed for J. Mawman, Poultry. 1810."

The prisoners were first tried at Huntingdon Assizes, and afterwards at the Court of King's Bench, at Westminster, 23 November, 1809. Mr. Justice Grose in passing sentence animadverted most severely on their conduct, mentioning that some held the husband, Wright Izzard, whilst others assaulted the wife, piercing " her hands, arms, and other parts of her person with pins and other sharp instruments, and wounding her in a most painful manner, and causing a great disturbance in the neighbourhood, and behaving in a most outrageous manner." Edward Briers, Mary Hook, and Mary Fox were sent to the common jail at Huntingdon for one month ; James Staughton was imprisoned for two months. All were ordered to find security for their good behaviour or to be kept in durance until such security was forthcoming. Even this did not effectually stop the malice and gossip, for on 16 October, 1809, Ann Izzard appeared before Henry Pointer Standley, Esq., J.P., of Little Paxton, and lodged a complaint against a mother and daughter named Day, for assault. In default of finding bail for their good behaviour they were both sent to Huntingdon jail.

In 1829 at Monmouth several persons were tried for common assault, the ducking of a supposed witch.

About 1830 there dwelt in the Rope-walk, Hastings, an old beldame who was commonly reputed to be a witch and assiduously cultivated that foul reputation. Hideous in appearance with eyes gleaming malignantly beneath her frosted brows, a mutch covering her few grizzled locks, bearded, buckled and bent so that she was wont to use a crutched stick for support, her mouth full of blasphemy and curses, upon her walks abroad she donned a red cloak and a beaver hat, whilst there were many who would gladly turn a mile out of their way rather than meet her. It was fully believed that she could assume the form of a cat, and when the child of a woman who resided within two doors of her fell lame, the mother constantly asserted that the hated crone had bewitched her girl, a tale which was received with universal credence and sympathy.[271]

In the same town there dwelt a fisherman, who was declared to have sold himself to the Devil, and to have made his daughter a witch so that he might obtain dark power over all his fellows. He was shunned and dreaded, and it was believed that no sharp instrument could pierce his skin. It is said that the company in the alehouses he frequented would often place long needles in the cushions of a chair he was to occupy arranged in such a manner that he could not fail to be hurt, but that the result of such experiments invariably tended to confirm their faith in his supernatural anæsthesia.[272]

In the third decade of the nineteenth century a witch-doctor who lived at New S. Swithin's, Lincoln, had a large practice throughout the neighbouring counties. On one occasion he informed a patient's wife that her husband's disease, a painful abscess, was an infliction of the Devil, and that he was bewitched by his next-door neighbours, who, he stated, had made a waxen image of the sufferer and stuck it full of black pins, repeating charms which included the Paternoster said backward. To counteract this the witch-doctor prescribed certain simples and gave a charm to wear next the skin where the swelling lay. Psalms and prayers must also be repeated. The fee for this advice was a guinea. The patient actually recovered after several weeks, whilst his neighbours in great alarm lest he should persuade the wise man to punish them for their alleged Witchcraft feed another cunning man at Nottingham, who furnished them with counter-charms to protect them against any malicious attack.[273]

In 1839 there died at Cŵrt-y-Cadno (Fox's Court), a hamlet situated high up in the valley of the Cothi, one of the fairest and most remote parts of Carmarthenshire, the famous John Harries,[274] a white witch or Wise Man (*dyn hysbys*) who was consulted by persons from all over Southern Wales. Born in 1785 he had been sent by his father, a substantial yeoman, to London to study medicine, and on his return to his native village he at once set up in practice. It was rumoured that he had no ordinary gifts of soothing pain ; and that persons troubled in mind as well as in body had consulted him to their lasting benefit. He himself openly professed to derive his knowledge from astrology and from certain secrets confided to him by attendant spirits. Once every year on a particular day Harries and a chosen disciple repaired to a lonely place far from all human habitation. There he drew a large circle on the earth, and, after various ceremonies, having placed the neophyte within its bounds he opened a mysterious volume, chanting a long litany in loud, monotonous tones. It was firmly believed that spirits manifested themselves and imparted occult secrets of mighty power. Many are the stories told of the wonders he wrought. He is said to have cured lunatics, to have recovered stolen property, to have conjured up visions in a magic mirror. Incessant was the stream of clients at his door, and he was held not only in honour, but in something like veneration, throughout the whole district. From a careful study of his own horoscope he was convinced he was marked to die a violent death. Upon the day his planet became fulfilled he retired to bed early in the afternoon so that no harm should befall him, but he was aroused by a cry that the house was on fire. He hurried down to assist in extinguishing the flames, but whilst ascending a ladder to throw water on the roof, he slipped, fell and was instantly killed. He is buried in Caio churchyard, where the old headstone records " John Harries, Surgeon."

His mantle fell upon his son Henry, who specialized in astrology, and rumour had it was even a more profound adept than his father. He died in 1849. The Harries are said to have possessed a not inconsiderable occult library. There was also a secret book of magic and a crystal. One account explains that the book was really a box, always kept locked, which contained MSS., recipes, charms, and astrological calculations. There is, no doubt, a substratum of truth beneath all the legends and strange happenings. The Harries were probably shrewd folk, whose nimble brains enabled them to make many a lucky hit, but I think that unquestionably they also had a very real gift of clairvoyance and perhaps even mediumistic faculties.

In the year 1846, Commissioners were appointed by the Council (now the Board) of Education to examine into the educational condition of Wales. The Report of these Commissioners, however, extended to a general inquiry into the civilization of the Principality. The following is extremely significant : " Superstition is said to be very common among the poor of this neighbourhood. There was recently a woman in the village who gained her living by conjuring ; and there is now a conjurer at Wrexham to whom scores are said to go annually " (p. 531).

A famous white-witch named Okey or Oakley resided at Tunbridge Wells in 1830. He was at that time fully eighty years old, and had been practising his craft since the beginning of the century. The seventh son of a seventh son, as he asserted, his white locks, flowing beard, and patriarchal appearance excited the utmost respect, nay, even something of awe. He professed to be endowed with miraculous powers for the healing of diseases, especially such as might have been inflicted by sorcery and malign spells. He asked enormous fees from the wealthy for his advice, for not only were the poor among his patients, but ladies of the highest quality would send their carriages from distances of sixty or seventy miles to convey him to their seats. All his charges were amply paid on these occasions, and he was often rewarded with a handsome present into the bargain.[275]

Writing in 1861 Mrs. Lynn Linton remarks : " Even the mere vulgar belief in witchcraft remains among the lower classes ; as witness the old gentleman who died at Polstead not so long ago, and who, when a boy, had seen a witch swum in Polstead Ponds, ' and she went over the water like a cork ' ; who had also watched another witch feeding her three imps like blackbirds ; and who only wanted five pounds to have seen all the witches in the parish dance on a knoll together."[276]

But a few years earlier an epidemic of Witchcraft swept through various smaller Essex villages, and at East Thorpe the vicar of the parish was actually compelled to mount guard over the door of a miserable crone, who was violently suspect, and whom the mob were endeavouring to capture and submit to the old water-ordeal.

On Friday, 20 March, 1857,[277] at Stafford Assizes, before Mr. Justice Willes, the judge of the Oxford Circuit, James

Tunnicliff, the keeper of a small beershop, was charged with obtaining by false pretences a sum of money, about thirty pounds, from Thomas Charlesworth, a local farmer. Charlesworth, a young fellow some thirty years old, related in detail a long story of strange happenings on his land. The milk turned sour in the pail directly the cows had been milked, the butter would not come in the churn, the dairy-maid fell sick with twitchings and shooting pains in her limbs, a murrain seemed to attack the cattle, there was illness in the house; in fact, from first to last it was a pitiful tale of maladies and misfortunes. Eventually he decided Witchcraft was at work and referred the matter to James Tunnicliff, who seems to have enjoyed some repute among the rustics as a white-witch or wise-man. Tunnicliff asserted that two persons, a man named Bull of Yeaverley and a certain Cotton of Longton, by their evil spells had cast a blight upon Charlesworth's wife, children, and cattle. He set about undoing the bewitchment, a somewhat costly and lengthy process. Fee after fee was paid him. Now a book of spells had to be procured from London ; now some charm confected of rare ingredients. But in the course of time his impostures became evident, and at last he found himself in the dock. He was sentenced to twelve months' hard labour. The most striking feature in the whole case was the absolute and implicit belief in Witchcraft which prevailed throughout the countryside. The account might well be from a pamphlet of Jacobean days rather than from *The Times* newspaper seventy years ago.

It was in reference to the discussion caused by these revelations that on Friday, 3 April, 1857, a magistrate wrote to *The Times*[278] to say that on 17 November, 1856, application had been made to him by a farmer whose wife was bewitched. The husband asked that the police might be instructed to swim old Mrs. C. or at least to search her for the Devil's mark. An ancient superstition had been resorted to ; one evening urine had been warmed in a hermetically sealed bottle, and sure enough as it grew hot the witch, Mrs. C., tormented in her bladder had come to their cottage window, grinning and mowing at them through the casement. When the magistrate remonstrated the man declared that not many years before a witch named Pointer had been swum in the village pond, and it was found that she could not sink. It is certain that all the villagers believed that this farmer's wife was bewitched. One woman told the magistrate of a witch whom she had known when she was a girl, a hag named Betsy Norris, who, it was never denied, had bewitched cows, pigs, geese, and people. Old Mother Norris was swum but could not sink.

On Tuesday, 22 September, 1865, at Castle Headingham, before Mr. Bernardiston and a full Bench of Magistrates, Emma Smith, aged 36, the wife of a beershop-keeper at Ridgwell, and Samuel Stammers, aged 28, a master carpenter, were charged with having assaulted an old Frenchman called " Dummy " on the 3 August, so that he died the following day. Sixty or seventy persons were concerned, and " the whole disgraceful transaction arose out of a deep belief in witchcraft which possesses to a lamentable extent the trades-people and lower orders of the district." It appeared that " Dummy " was a deaf and dumb Frenchman, between eighty and ninety years old, who used to make energetic and grotesque gestures which were taken for cabalistic and diabolical signs. He lived in a miserable hovel and gained his living by telling fortunes and pretended Witchcraft. Those who consulted him wrote their question on a piece of paper, to which he subscribed the answers. Hundreds of these scraps were found on the floor of his hut. Such inquiries were : " What was the reason my Sun do not right ? I mean that sodger ? "   " Shall I marry ? "   " How many children shall I have ? " Emma Smith, who had been anæmic and ill for eight or nine months, continually asserted she was bewitched by Dummy. On the night of 3 August Dummy happened to be in the tap-room of the Swan Inn at Sible Hedingham, where also Mrs. Smith chanced to enter. On seeing the old man to whose sorceries she attributed her failing health, half in fear and half in anger she accosted him with violent words. The crowd of some thirty or forty frequenters of the inn seemed to have egged her on, and to have mocked Dummy by dancing round him and yelling ribaldry, until in a fury Mrs. Smith seized him, thrust him into the street, and began to belabour him with a stick, shouting : " You old Devil, you served me out and I'll serve you out." The crowd, led by Stammers, became more and more unruly, and at last dragged their unfortunate victim to a brook which ran down the side of Watermill Lane to the river and was particularly deep at that spot. Voices from the rabble cried " Put him, or swim him, on the Millhead." Stammers seems to have thrown the poor wretch into the water, which closed over him. When he was drawn out he was covered with mud, and, said a witness, Henrietta Garrod, a child of ten years, " was green and much wet all over." Dummy, who had been immersed for a quarter of an hour, died on the following day owing to shock and exposure. In her defence Emma Smith kept reiterating that she was bewitched. Stammers pleaded not guilty. Both prisoners were committed to Chelmsford jail for trial at the assizes.[279]

In 1875 Ann Turner, a reputed witch, was murdered by a man who was afterwards found to be insane. In 1879 at East Deringham in Norfolk a farmer was heavily fined for assaulting the daughter of an old woman who had charmed him by " a walking toad," her familiar.[280]

In 1886 there happened to be found hidden away in the belfry of an English country church a long cord tied in elaborate strands and interwoven with the feathers of a black hen. Obviously it had been made for some definite purpose, and presently an old woman in the village identified it as a " witch's ladder," proof positive that some persons in the neighbourhood knew something of the traditional occult lore and were trying to effect a spell.[281]

Writing to *The Evening News*, 12 December, 1924, a letter which is headed " Black Magic," Mr. Walter Britten relates a significant survival of Witchcraft in Devonshire. He tells how a friend of his who was making a stay at Sidmouth for a few months had a bicycle sent down there from London. In those days the modern cycle was still something of a novelty, and the visitor, an enthusiastic devotee of the wheel, was soon known as " the flying devil." On a certain evening he was actually waylaid by the villagers at Sudbury ; he dismounted with no small misgiving, when to his surprise the leader of the party ran a sharp pin into one of his legs, chanting : " Prickee wi' a pin, and draw his blood, an' ee can't hurt ee ! " After which the rustics at once appeared quite satisfied and friendly. This, of course, was nothing else than the scratching of the witch, so continually spoken of in the old trials and recognized by the demonologists as a powerful counter-charm to malefic spells.

In our towns never was Witchcraft more openly and more unblushingly practised than at the present time, for what is Modern Spiritism with its mediums and materializations but Old Witchcraft writ Large ? There is hardly a phenomenon of these sabbat-séances to-day that cannot be exactly paralleled in the witch-trials of the seventeenth century. The whole land teems with superstition. We have the gross obscurantism of the rationalists, the materialists, and the modernists on the one hand ; on the other the dark fanaticism of the spiritist, and his fellow-devotees of a thousand exotic cults. The nightmare theosophy of the Gnostics is taught in magazines and by lectures ; false prophets and theologasters abound. Necromancy is openly practised ; familiar spirits are consulted ; public resort is had unto wizards that peep and that mutter. Spells and charms are sought for with a perseverance and energy worthy of a better quest. It was not many months since that a lady of wealth and education, a non-Catholic, who unhappily loves one who cannot reciprocate her feelings, earnestly begged me to place a sealed and folded paper, wherin she had written the name of the man whose affection she seeks, upon the corporal under the Chalice at Holy Mass, so that God's Blood might be poured forth, as it were, over her billet, and this she felt would infallibly mean the attainment of her wish. She was amazed when I pointed out the profanity and horrid sacrilege of such a superstition, and rejoined with the hardly veiled offer of a bribe. Shocked as I was by the incident, it seems extremely pregnant.

A somewhat similar charm is mentioned by the late Monsignor Benson in a letter dated 26 July, 1905. He says : " Have you heard of the events in Paris and Venice this year ? In each case the person put the full name of an enemy into a drawer, purposely ; and the enemy died within six months. It is rather terrible."

That a firm belief in Witchcraft still obtains in many rural districts of every part of England is very certain, and from time to time this is brought to light in local police-courts or at assizes.

In Somersetshire witches are yet believed to assume the

shape of hares. It will be remembered that one of the chief charges against old Julian Cox, who was tried in 1663 at Taunton before Justice Archer and hanged for sorcery, was the tale of a huntsman. He swore that he had started a hare and chased it behind a bush. But when he came up to the thicket he only found Mother Cox there, crouched down and panting wildly all out of breath.

Round Glastonbury they have by no means lost all faith in the power of certain hags to forespeak an enemy, to blight the crops, and bring strange misfortune. As for the Abbey ruins the whole countryside knows of the curse laid upon them, nor will it ever be lifted until the Abbey, red with the blood of the martyred Richard Whiting, be delivered unto the Church again.

On Tuesday, 12 January, 1926, at Tipton, Staffordshire, two men were brought up for threatening a woman who lived in a caravan. This woman, Haddington by name, was believed in her own part of Staffordshire to possess supernatural powers, including the dreadful gift of the evil eye. She was said to have cast a spell over the wife of one of the accused men and over the sister of the other. In the case of this latter, the unfortunate creature reputed to be forespoken jumped through a window, and had been removed to a lunatic asylum. Nor were these two men the only believers in the woman Haddington's diabolical incantations. Several of the country people testified on their oath that they were afraid to go near Haddington because of the spells she could weave against them and the curses she could put upon them.[282]

Mr. G. Mitchel, the chairman of the magistrates, in binding the defendants over for twelve months, remarked : " There seems to be in the Black Country a surprising and deplorable amount of ignorant superstition."

In Norfolk the same traditional beliefs prevail, and if possible are even more strongly maintained by the peasantry.[283] Thus Merton, the village of the legend of the Babes in the Wood, holds firmly that sorcery can still work harm, that there are those who practise occult arts for malison and bane. " I have lived here," wrote the Rector of Merton, the Rev. Charles Kent, " for twenty years and so I know my people intimately. I am the rector of four parishes—Merton, Tottington, Sturston, and Thompson—and if I were to take a census of opinion in all four villages I am certain that I should find a majority seriously professing belief in witchcraft, the policy of the ' evil eye,' and the efficacy of both good and evil spells.

" My own belief in witchery, as they term it about here, is possibly not so crude as that of some of my older parishioners. Not like, for instance, that of a labourer who not so long ago parted with a hard-earned guinea to a local planet-reader for a spell to cure his wife. I believe in the actual power of hate so working on the power of faith that evil results. Witchery is hate made manifest. Here, as elsewhere, persons against whom the wicked charge of witchery is whispered are usually old women of dominant personality.

" My first experience of the kind was connected with what is known as ' The Curse of Sturston.' This story dates back to the time of Queen Elizabeth. An Elizabethan vicar of Bray was then the rector. For the country folk he held a Protestant service in the church on Sunday morning, and then recited Mass in his parlour for the Popish gentry.

" An old Protestant lady, as she lay dying, solemnly cursed this very accommodating parson-priest, his church, his rectory, and the great folks' hall. And the curse seemed to come true !

" When I came upon the scene I was asked to lay the curse, for the old hall had become a farmhouse surrounded by a few cottages and the people feared that the curse might still be working itself out. I held a public service, using an old altar tomb in the ruined churchyard as a lectern. People flocked to the service from miles around. In the sequel nothing further dreadful happened. I had laid the curse.

" Soon afterwards I was asked to visit a woman who was thought to be dying. I found the usual deathbed scene—the whole family gathered to take farewell. I offered up the ordinary Prayer Book prayers and the woman began at once to revive and eventually recovered.

" When I told her some time later that she ought to be thankful to the Almighty for sparing her life, she said ' I weren't a-dying. I was bewitched, and your prayers laid the witchery. It's an old wummin wi' a hook nose that

bewitched me. When you made the prayer I left the
witchery, reglar lifting-up like, and I fared better and
betterer.'

" Here, if you will, you have a clear case of white magic,
or faith healing. But the simple spirit of that old woman's
belief is as much alive to-day as it was then."

It is a sad fact that early in the troublous days of Elizabeth
some few country priests hoping for the restoration of the
Catholic faith did accommodate themselves to Protestantism
and used the Book of Common Prayer in public. As late as
1568 Pope S. Pius V sent the famous Laurence Vaux, who
was to die a martyr in the Clink, to England, where considerable uncertainty prevailed among the faithful as to how
far it might be lawful to conform outwardly to the new State
religion. Father Laurence was delegated to make known the
papal decision that to frequent the Established service was
a mortal sin. The Bull of Excommunication, *Regnans in
Excelsis*, which the Vicar of Christ launched against Elizabeth
in 1570, finally left no loophole for doubt or indecision. In
spite of the schismatic tendencies of the Elizabethan Rector
of Merton, and we trust that his pliancy ended before 1568,
or at least did not continue after that date, I cannot, I fear,
accept the story of the curse breathed by the old Protestant
lady. It is far more likely that the curse fell when the
Catholic worship ceased.

Merton is about ten miles north of Thetford, and it was at
Merton Rectory that Edward Fitzgerald died, 14 June, 1883,
whilst the guest of a former rector. Fitzgerald had begun
his translation of Omar Khayyám there, and the Rev.
Charles Kent tells us " In the ' Del ' in the garden he did
much of his writing in the summer. One Sunday after I had
preached a sermon on Fitzgerald our cook came to me and
said, ' I have often seen Mr. Fitzgerald, sir.' ' Pooh, nonsense,' I said. ' You were not born then.'

" ' No,' she replied, ' I was not born then, but I was born
in church time hours, and so I have the gift of second sight.
I saw my grandfather long after he was dead. I was a child
going for the groceries, and I dropped the pennies I had in
my hand and ran home all of a tremble with fright. I never
saw granddad but once. But this Fitzgerald, I have often
seen him.'

" ' Tell me what he was like,' I asked. ' He was rather fat,' she said, ' and with his clothes shoved on anyhow ' (Fitzgerald was both stout and slovenly). ' I have seen him upstairs in the little bedroom and in the pantry, too. I know the look of him as well as I know you.' "

That the spirit of the writer of a poem which, however great the beauty of its quatrains, contains in those honeyed words the most poisonous philosophy that ever crutched knock-kneed pusillanimity, does not rest in his grave I can very well believe.

In February, 1923, there were strange stories afloat concerning the haunting of a house, New Barn Farm, Gorefield, in Cambridgeshire. The farm was in possession of a Mr. Joseph Scrimshaw, who resided there with his aged mother, and his daughter Olive. For many weeks noises such as the moving of heavy weights were heard in various rooms, which upon examination proved to be empty. Furniture was then flung about and broken into a thousand pieces. These manifestations caused the greatest trouble and discomfort. Hundreds of investigators visited the place and the " Fen Fiend " was talked of far and wide. It was a clear case of poltergeist manifestations.[284]

In February, 1926, the police without success strove to trace the origin of similar happenings at a farm near Finchhampstead, Berkshire. Pictures fell clattering from the wall ; furniture was overturned with a crash, and a perambulator could not be made to stand within the house.[285]

Unhappily it cannot be denied that Satanism is practised in England at the present day. The Black Mass is said in London and in Brighton—and I doubt not in many other towns too—under conditions of all but absolute secrecy. The tabernacles of London churches, moreover, have been robbed of Hosts in circumstances which admit of no other explanation. I myself have been shown two ancient candlesticks of great value upon which in a secret place was inscribed in Hebrew characters the Most Holy Name of God, —but inverted. They had been used at the hideous celebration of a diabolic Eucharist. Now and again some gang of devil-worshippers may be broken up and dispersed, but perhaps there are few persons who realize how far-spread and how cunningly organized are these societies of evil. To the ordinary man Satanism is incredible, or at any rate a myth of the remote Dark Ages. He does not realize, and he is happy in his ignorance, the evil fires that burn but just a very little way beneath the thin and crumbling crust of our boasted modern civilization.

NOTES TO CHAPTER II

[1] *Circa* 54 B.C. to A.D. 24. *Geographia*, IV, c, iv, 6.

[2] Cf. Cicero, *De Natura Deorum*, Lib. I, xlii, 119 : Omitto Eleusinem sanctam illam et augustam ;

> Ubi initiantur gentes orarum ultimæ.
> Prætere Samothraciam, eaque quæ Lemni
> Nocturno aditu occulta coluntur
> Siluestribus sepibus densa.

[3] He was consecrated by Pope Vitalian at Rome, 26 March, 668, but did not reach his see until May, 669. He died at Canterbury. 19 September, 690.

[4] De Idolatria et Sacrilegio, et qui Angelos [*i.e.* malos] colunt et maleficos, Hariolos, ueneficos, sortilegos, diuinos, et uota reddentes nisi ad Ecclesiam Dei, et in Kalendis Ianuarii in ceruulo et in uitula uadit, et mathematicos, et emissores tempestatum.

[5] Si quis immolat dæmonibus in minimis 1 annum pœnitentiæ qui in magnis x annos. Si quis secundo uel 111° immolat dæmoniis 111 annos subiaceat pœnitentiæ. Si quis sacrilegium fecerit, id est quod haruspices uocat qui augurio colunt per aues aut quocunque auguriauerit malo ingenio 111 annos pœniteat, 1 ex his in pane et aqua. Non licet clericos uel laicos, magos aut incantatores existere aut facere philacteria, quæ animarum suarum uincula comprobentur ; eos autem qui his utuntur, ab æcclesia pelli præcipimus. Si quis maleficio suo aliquem perdiderit. . . . Si quis pro amore ueneficus sit, et neminem perdiderit . . . Si autem per hoc mulieris partum quis deceperit. . . . Si quis hariolos quærit, quos divinos uocant, vel aliquas diuinationes fecerit, quia et hoc dæmoniacum est. . . . Si quis sortes habuerit, quas sanctorum contra rationem uocant, uel aliquas sortes habuerit, uel qualicunque malo ingenio sortitus fuerit, uel diuinauerit. . . . Si qua mulier diuinationes vel incantationes diabolicas fecerit. . . . Si qua mulier filium suum uel filiam super tectum pro sanitate posuerit, uel in fornace. . . . Qui grana arserit ubi mortuus est homo, pro sanitate uiuentium et domus. . . . Si quis, pro sanitate filioli, per foramen terræ exierit, illudque spinis post se concludit. . . . Qui diuinationes expetunt, et more gentilium subsequuntur ; aut in domos suas hujusmodi homines introducunt, exquirendi aliquid arte malefica, aut expiandi causa. . . . Si quis ad orbores, uel ad fontes, uel ad lapides, siue ad cancellos, uel ubicunque, excepto in æcclesia Dei, uotum uouerit, aut exsoluerit, III. annos cum pane et aqua pœniteat ; et hoc sacrilegium est, uel dæmoniacum. Qui uero ibidem ederit, aut biberet, I. annum pœniteat in pane et aqua. Si quis in kalendas Januarii in ceruulo aut uetula uadit, id est, in ferarum habitus se commutant, et uestiuntur pellibus pecudum, et assumunt capita bestiarum : qui uero taliter in ferinas species se transformant 111 annos pœniteant; quia hoc dæmoniacum est. Si quis mathematicus est, id est, per inuocationem dæmonum hominis menten conuerterit. . . . Si quis emissor tempestatis fuerit, id est maleficus. . . . Si quis ligaturas fecerit, quod detestabile est. Benjamin Thorpe, *Monumenta Ecclesiastica*, London, 1840, pp. 292–3.

[6] Pacifico Massimo in his *Hecatelegium* uses " ligare " in a cognate sense.

[7] De sinu licium protulit uarii coloris filis intortum ceruicemque uinxit meam.

[8] In ueneficiis licia adhibebantur discoloria, non tantum illigandi incantandique gratia, ut in *Pharmaceutria* sed etiam soluendi et expiandi, ut hic, unde et *ligatura* dicuntur.

186 THE GEOGRAPHY OF WITCHCRAFT

[9] Anicula autem hæc uenefica fuit, quæ Polyæni [Enclopii] curam suscepit cuius, ut ipse loquitur, inguinum uires funeratæ erant. Morbos enim uenefici ligamentis sanabant. . . . Sed præcipue morbos inguinum. . . . *Licia* hæc mediæ ætatis scriptores *ligaturas* uocabant.

[10] Ecloga, VIII, 73–8.

[11] Ecce ueniunt dies ecce kalendæ ueniunt et tota dæmonum pompa · procedit, idolorum tota producitur officina, et sacrilegio uetusto anni nouitas consecratur. Figurant Saturnum, faciunt Iouem, formant Herculem, exponunt cum uenantibus suis Dianam, circumducunt Uulcanum uerbis haletantem turpitudines suas, et plura quorum, quia portenta sunt, nomina sunt tacenda ; quorum deformitates quia natura non habet, creatura nescit, fingere ars laborat. Præterea uestiuntur homines in pecudes, et infe minas uiros uertunt, honestatem rident, uiolant iudicia, censuram publicam rident, inludunt sæculo teste, et dicunt se facientes ista iocari. Non sunt ioca, sunt crimina. In idola transfiguratur homo. Et, si ire ad idola crimen est, esse idolum quid uidetur ? . . . Namque talium deorum facies ut pernigrari possint, carbo deficit ; et ut eorum habitus pleno cumuletur horrore, paleæ, pelles, panni, stercora, toto sæculo perquiruntur, et quidquid est confusionis humanæ, in eorum facie collocatur. The quotation is from *Homilia de Pythonibus et Maleficis.* Mai, *Spicilegium Romanum*, X, 222. The locality and date of Severian, to whom the Homily is assigned, are uncertain. Perhaps he is to be identified with Severian, Bishop of Gabala in Syria, *c.* 400, who won fame as an eloquent and prolific preacher.

[12] "An non omnia," he cries, "quæ a ministris dæmonum illis aguntur diebus falsa sunt et insana ? . . . Num quid non uniuersa ibi falsa sunt et insana, cum se a Deo formati homines, aut in pecudes, aut in feras, aut in portenta transformant ? . . . Auspicia etiam uanissimi colligere se dicunt, ac statum uitæ suæ inanibus indiciis æstimantes, per incerta auium ferarumque signa imminentis anni futura rimantur ? " *Homilia XVI de Kalendis Ianuariis.* Migne, *Patres Lat.*, LVII, 255.

[13] Imaginem Dei portare noluit, qui idoli uoluit portare personam ; qui iocari uoluerit cum diabolo, non poterit gaudere cum Christo. . . . Abstrahat ergo pater filium, seruum dominus, parens parentem, ciuem ciuis, homo hominem, Christianus omnes qui se bestiis compararunt, exæquarunt iumentis, aptauerunt pecudibus, dæmonibus formauerunt. *Sermo CLV, Patres Lat.*, LIII, 609.

[14] "Quis enim sapiens," he asks with biting irony, "poterit credere, inueniri aliquos sanæ mentis qui ceruulum facientes in ferarum se uelint habitum commutare ? Alii uestiuntur pellibus pecudum ; alii assumunt capita bestiarum, gaudentes et exsultantes, si taliter se in ferinas species transformauerint, ut homines non esse uideantur." *Sermo Pseudo-Augustin. CXXIX, de Kalendis Ianuariis. Patres Lat.*, XXXIX, 2001. The sermon has been ascribed to S. Augustine, to Faustus of Raji, and to Maxentius. For a full discussion of these points see C. P. Caspari, *Eine Augustin falschlich beilegte Homilia de Sacriligiis*, 1886.

[15] *Anulas, agniculam, anniculam*, are also read.

[16] *Sermo Pseud.-Augustin. CXX, Patres Lat.*, XXXIX, 2003. The authorship is generally held to be that of *Sermo CXXIX*, but a Fleury MS. attributes it to Bishop Sedatus of Besiers, who died in 589.

[17] Licet credam quod illa infelix consuetudo . . . iam . . . fuerit sublata ; tamen, si adhuc agnoscatis aliquos illam sordidissimam turpitudinem de hinnicula uel ceruula exercere . . . castigate. *Sermo Pseud.-Augustin.* 265, *Pitres Lat.*, XXXIX, 2239.

[18] This decretal was included as part of the permanent canon law in the *Decretales* of Gregory IX in 1234. It was strongly supported by the Paris theologians, and the Councils of Basle, Soissons, Laon, Lille. *Patres Lat.*, CCXV, 1070.

[19] Theodorus Balsamon, *In Can. LXII Conc. in Trullo., Patres Græci*, CXXXVII. 727.

[20] Ducagne *s.v.* would read *hinnuli*. Archbishop Ussher thought this passage referred to the Saxon god Irminsul.

[21] *Epistola III in Eahfridum. Patres L.*, LXXXIX, 93.

[22] *Ancient Laws and Institutes of England*, Thorpe, 1840, p. 18.

[23] Miss Murray (*Witch-Cult in Western Europe*, p. 22) ambiguously says "first Archbishop of York." But Ecgberht was appointed by King Ceolwulf to succeed Wilfrid II. There was a bishop of York in very early days. At the Council of Arles (314) "Eborus episcopus de ciuitate Eboracensis" was present. The bishops of York may have acted as diocesan prelates until Ecgberht received the pallium from Gregory III in 735, but their jurisdiction was at first hardly defined.

[24] Si mulier artem magicam, et incantationes, et maleficia exerceat, xII menses, uel tria legitima ieiunia, uel xl dies ieiunet: sciatur quantum sit flagitium. Si maleficiis suis aliquem occiderit, vII annos ieiunet. 32. Si quis dæmonibus exigui quid immolauerit annum I ieiunet; si magni quid immolauerit x annos ieiunet. *Apud* Thorpe.

[25] *Ibid.*

[26] *Yule and Christmas, Their Place in the Germanic Year*, G. Tille, 1899.

[27] See F. W. H. Wasserschleben, *Bussordnungen der abendland Kirche*; H. J. Schmitz, *Die Bussbüchen und die Bussdisciplin der Kirche.* Also P. Schaff, *History of the Christian Church* (1883–93, 2nd edition), Vol. VII, p. 321.

[28] Some writers give the date as 573–603. Many laws were made during that period and comprised under one authority. *Concilia Æui Merouingici*, Recensiut F. Maassen, 1893. Also Mansi, *Sacrorum conciliorum noua et amplissima collectio*, Venice, 1769 *sqq.*, 31 vols., folio. Dr. Ch.-J. Hefele, *Conciliengeschichte*, 2nd ed., 9 vols., 8vo., Fribourg-im-Brisgau, 1890 *sqq.*

[29] Non licet kalendas Ianuarii uetolo uel ceruolo facere uel streneas diabolicas obseruare, sed in ipsa die sic omnia beneficia tribuantur, sicut in reliquis diebus. Originally twigs plucked from the grove of the goddess Strenia, who was associated with Janus in the revels of the New Year. Later the *strena* became an omen which possessed divine influence. The force of the prohibition here lies in the adjective "diabolicas." Superstitions and evil periapts were evidently distributed. The word *strenas* survives in the French *étrennes*.

[30] *Hist. Eccl.*, ed. Plummer, Oxford, 1896, I, p. 116.

[31] *Witchcraft in England*, p. 3.

[32] *Patres Latini*, CXXXII, 352.

[33] Liber I, xvii.

[34] Cf. the Greek "Eumenides" for "Erinyes."

[35] Quid de sacerdotibus et religiosis, quibus uasa uel ornamenta ecclesiæ uel similia furtim subtracta sunt; uel etiam de laicis quibus res propriæ furto sublata sunt; numquid poterunt per inspectionem astralabii uel similia inuestigare? Ad hoc dicas secundum omnes, quod si fit ibi inuocatio dæmonum uel aliud superstitiosum, nullo modo licet, immo grauissime peccat quicunque facit, extra e. extrarum. Ubi quidam, licet iuuenili simplicitate et bono zelo fecisset, fuit tamen suspensus ab officio et beneficio. Si autem talis inspectio fieret simpliciter per astronomiam, non inuocatis dæmonibus nec alio superstitioso adiumento forte posset amicti x[to,] a contrario assensu præallegatæ dec. et di. xxxvij. si quis gramaticam, et ita dicunt quidam : tamen in eodem dec. dicitur, quod licet quadruuiales artes in se contineant mertatæ, tamen quia non sunt pietatis, non est in eis studendum. Item, quid de sacerdotibus qui causa doloris permoti, ut altare uestibus sacris exuunt, aut qualibet alia lugubri ueste operiunt, aut consueta luminaria subtrahunt, aut altare vel crucifixum spinis circumdant.

Quid etiam de illis qui pronius scienter cantant missam defunctorum, uel sub nomine illorum quos odiunt feretrum cum exequiis mortuorum in medio ecclesiæ ponunt, uel alia similia faciunt, ut illi citius moriantur ? Ad hoc dico, quod si aliquid prædictorum fiat propter odium priuatum, grauissime peccat qui facit, et nisi per legitimam pœnitentiam se purgauerit, debet deponi. Si autem propter causam communem puta, quia metuit contaminationem sacrorum ordinum uel subuersionem fidei, uel hostilitatem suffert, uel obsidionem uel diuinorum iudiciorum sententiam metuit, et ideo tale quod facit, non dicitur peccare, quia in tali facto plus humilitas qua Deus placatur, quam materiam liuoris dolositas declaratur. Hoc etiam tenet consuetudo ecclesiæ, unde solet cantare, omnes uenerunt gentes, et in signum tristitiæ in die Ueneris sancti altaria spoliare. Hoc tamen distinctio fallit in illis, qui pronis scienter celebrant officium mortuorum. Nam tales, si fuerint detecti, indistincte debent deponi, et agendam pœnitentiam, tam ipse sacerdos, quam qui eum ad hoc incitauit, debent exilii perpetui ergastulo, seu monasterio religari : hoc totum habes expresse in c. Tolletano, xxvi. q. i., quicunque.

Quid de quibusdam sceleratis mulieribus, quæ credunt se et profitentur cum Diana dea paganorum nocturnis horis, uel cum Herodiade et innumera multitudine mulierum, equitare super quasdam bestias, et multa terrarum spatia intempestæ noctis silentio pertransire, eiusque iussionibus obedire uelut dominæ, certis noctibus ad ejus seruitium euocari, asserunt etiam ab illis aliquas creaturas posse in melius uel in deterius commutari, aut in aliam speciem uel similitudinem transformari ? De hiis dico, c. Acquiren. quod non a diuino spiritu sed maligno talia fantasmata mentibus fidelium irrogantur. Diabolus enim, cum anima alicuius per talem credulitatem subjugauerit sibi, transfigurat se in angelum lucis et transformat se in diuersarum personarum species atque similitudines, mentem quasi captiuam tenet, multipliciter deludit, nec debet aliquis uel aliqua in tantam uenire stultitiam ut credat hæc omnia, quæ in sompniis et spiritu tantum fuerit, etiam, in corpore accidere, cum etiam Paulus non audeat asserere quod fuerit raptus in corpore. Quicumque ergo talia crediderit uel asseruerit, proculdubio infidelis est et pagano deterior, xxvj. q. v. episcopi. Item, cum dictum sit supra fidem non esse habendam in auguriis, sortibus, et cæteris speciebus diuinationis, quoniam ferquenter euenerint ea quæ prædicunt, quoniam etiam tales homines sæpe liberant ægros, et mittunt ægritudines, Aug. mouet hanc quæstionem et soluit, dicens, Hoc fieri permissu Dei, ut illi qui audiunt et uident probentur in quali fide sunt erga Deum. Hoc probat auctoritate Deutoronomii, Si surrexerit in medio tui propheta aut qui sompnum dicat se uidisse, et prædixerit signum atque portentum, et uenerit quod locutus est, et dixerit tibi, eamus et sequamur deos alienos quos ignoras et seruiamus eis, non audics uerba prophetæ, aut sompniatoris, quia tentat nos Deus noster, ut palam fiat, scilicet ipsis temptantur et aliis hominibus, non autem Deo, quia ipse scit omnia antequam fiant, utrum diligatis cum an non, xxvj. q. u. nec mirum circa.

³⁶ A curious detail, possibly it has some connexion with the disguise as a *ceruulus.*

³⁷ One may compare the legend of S. Bruno. At the funeral of Raymond Diocres, a learned professor of Paris and canon of Notre Dame, when the priests are chanting " Responde mihi quantas habes iniquitates," the corpse half-rising from the bier cried in a lamentable voice, " By the justice of God, I am condemned." This happened thrice, and so terrible an incident decided S. Bruno to leave the world. Le Sueur has included this fearful resurrection in the series he painted for the Chartreuse at Paris in 1649. This story is first found in a Chronicle of the Carthusian Order written about 1250, and it again occurs in the Chronicle compiled by John of Ypres in the thirteenth century. It was inserted in the Roman Breviary, but omitted in the revision under Urban VIII, approved 19 September, 1631, and issued in the following year. But it is generally recognized to-day that this reform was incomplete and is most unfortunate in many respects. Dom Innocent Masson, General of the Carthusians, in his *Annales Ordinis Carthusiani,* 1687, gives the old legend, which is defended against critics by the learned theologian Théophile Raynaud, S.J. (1583–1663), the author of ninety-two separate treatises, and by another scholarly Jesuit, Francesco Colombi, in his *Dissertatio de Carthusianorum Initiis.* The tradition is rejected, on the other hand, by Jean de Launoy, the ecclesiastical historian (1603–78), in his *Dissertatio de Recessu Brunonis* ; by Mabillon, who is often unduly sceptical ; and by the French Oratorian Dubois in his *Histoire de Paris,* Book XI, c. ii, n. 6 and 8. Dom Ambrose Mougel, O. Cart., doubts the historicity of the event, and some modern writers ascribe S. Bruno's retirement from the world to his disgust at the misrule and violence of Manasses de Gournai, Archbishop of Rheims, who was suspended from office in 1077, and ejected in 1080.

³⁸ Attributed to an imaginary monk, Matthew of Westminster. The misunderstanding is due to the blunder of a copyist.

[39] Published in *Poems*, Vol. II, 1799.

[40] A.D. 852. Circa dies istos, mulier quædam malefica, in uilla quæ Berkeleia dicitur degens, gulæ amatrix ac petulantiæ, flagitiis modum usque in senium et auguriis non ponens, usque ad mortem impudica permansit. Hæc die quadam cum sederet ad prandium, cornicula quam pro delitiis pascebat, nescio quid garrire cœpit ; quo audito, mulieris cultellus de manu excidit, simul et facies pallescere cœpit, et emisso rugitu, Hodie, inquit, accipiam grande incommodum, hodieque ad sulcum ultimum meum peruenit aratrum. Quo dicto, nuncius doloris intrauit ; muliere uero percunctata ad quid ueniret Affero, inquit, tibi filii tui obitum et totius familiæ ejus ex subita ruina interitum. Hoc quoque dolore mulier permota, lecto protinus decubuit grauiter infirmata ; sentiensque morbum subrepere ad uitalia, liberos quos habuit superstites, monachum uidelicet et monacham, per epistolam inuitauit ; aduenientes autem uoce singultiente alloquitur. Ego, inquit, o pueri, meo miserabili fato dæmoniacis semper artibus inseruiui ; ego omnium uitiorum sentina, ego illecebrarum omnium fui magistra. Erat tamen mihi inter hæc mala spes uestræ religionis, quæ meam solidaret animam desperatam ; uos expectabam propugnatores contra dæmones, tutores contra sæuissimos hostes. Nunc igitur quoniam ad finem uitæ perueni, rogo uos per materna ubera, ut mea tentetis alleuiare tormenta. Insuite me defunctam in corio ceruino, ac deinde in sarcophago lapideo supponite, operculumque ferro et plumbo constringite, ac demum lapidem tribus cathenis ferreis et fortissimis circumdantes, clericos quinquaginta psalmorum cantores, et tot per tres dies presbyteros missarum celebratores applicate, qui feroces lenigent aduersariorum incursus. Ita si tribus noctibus secura iacuero, quarta die me infodite humo.

Factumque est ut præceperat illis. Sed, proh dolor ! nil preces, nil lacrymæ, nil demum ualuere cathenæ. Primis enim duabus noctibus, cum chori psallentium corpori assistebant, aduenientes Dæmones ostium ecclesiæ confregerunt ingenti obice clausum, extremasque cathenas negotio leui dirumpunt; media autem quæ fortior erat, illibata manebat. Tertia autem nocte, circa gallicinium, strepitu hostium aduentantium, omne monasterium uisum est a fundamento moueri. Unus ergo dæmonum, et uultu cæteris terribilior et statura eminentior, ianuas ecclesiæ impetu uiolento concussas in fragmenta deiecit. Diuexerunt clerici cum laicis, metu steterunt omnium capilli, et psalmorum concentus defecit. Dæmon ergo gestu ut uidebatur arroganti ad sepulchrum accedens, et nomen mulieris modicum ingeminans, surgere imperauit. Qua respondente, quod nequiret pro uinculis, Iam malo tuo, inquit, solueris ; et protinus cathenam quæ cæterorum ferocium dæmonum deluserat, uelut stuppeum uinculum rumpebat. Operculum etiam sepulchri pede depellens, mulierem palam omnibus ab ecclesia extraxit, ubi præ foribus niger equus superbe hinniens uidebatur, uncis ferreis et clauis undique confixus, super quem misera mulier proiecta, ab oculis assistentium euanuit. Audiebantur tamen clamores per quatuor fere miliaria horribiles, auxilium postulantes.

Ista itaque quæ retuli incredibilia non erunt, si legatur beati Gregorii dialogus, in quo refert, hominem in ecclesia sepultum, a dæmonibus foras eiectum. Et apud Francos Carolus Martellus insignis uir fortitudinis, qui Saracenos Galliam ingressos, Hispaniam redire compulit, exactis uitæ suæ diebus, in ecclesia beati Dionysii legitur fuisse sepultus. Sed quia patrimonia, cum decimis omnium fere ecclesiarum Galliæ, pro stipendio commilitonum suorum mutilauerat, miserabiliter a malignis spiritibus de sepulchro corporaliter auulsus, usque in hodiernum diem nusquam comparuit.

[41] *Abbreuiatio Placitorum*, p. 62.

[42] Vol. II, Div. ii, p. 269.

[43] Robert le Mareschal de Leycestre ad reconuz devant Simond Croyser, coronner del hostiel nostre seigneur le roi, le Mescredy en la veille de Touz Seyntz, l'an du regne le roi Edward disoeytisme, q'il fust demorrant ove Mestre Johan de Nottingham, que se fist nigromauncer et demorra en Coventré, et vindrent Richard le Latoner, Geffrei Frebern, Robert le Palmere, Adam de Wolreston, Henri de Hynton, Hugh de Tuwe, Johan de Siflet, William de Gloucestre, Johan de Stonleye, Richard le Taillour hosier, Johan le Wallere que sert Alice la Honte, Henri Pake, Robert de Stoue, Robert de Lichefeld, Robert le Mercer que ad espusée la fille Adam de Lyndeseye, Piers Baroun,

Phelipp le Hosier, Wautier Chubboc, Rogier le Brai, Johan Frebern, Reynauld de Alesleye gurdeler, William le Wallere, Richard Grauntpé, Johan le filz Hugh de Merington, apprentiz de court, William Russell, Richard de la Grene, et Johan le Redeclerk, hosier de Coventré, et le Mescredy preschein devant la feste Seint Nicholas, l'an disseptisme, à Coventré à les avantditz mestre Johan de Notingham et Robert le Mareschal, et les demaunderent si il voleyent leur counseil celer et il averoient un grant profist. Et mestre Johan les assura par sa foi q'il ne les discovereit poynt ; et le dit Robert assura le dit mestre Johan de celer le counseil. La seurtée faite parentre eux, les avantditz Richard le Latoner et les autres disoient à les avantditz mestre Johan et Robert q'il ne purroient vivre pur la duresce que le priour de Coventré les avoit fait et fist de jour en autre, et pur le meintenaunce que nostre seigneur le roi, monsieur Hugh le Despenser counte de Wyncestre, et monsieur Hugh le Despenser le filz, firent au dit priour, en destruccion de eux et de la ville de Coventré, et demanderent au dit mestre Johan s'il voleit pur le leur donant enprendre de tuer le roi, le counte de Wyncestre, monsieur Hugh le Despenser, le priour de Coventré, et autres q'ils nomereint, par sa nigro-mancie et ses artz. Et il dist qe oyl, se assenti ; et sur çeo là fesoient covenant ove luy, q'il averoit xx. li. d'esterlings, et sa gareison en quelle mesoun de religioun q'il voleit eslire en Engleterre, et au dit Robert xv. li. d'esterlings, de estre eidaunt à les felonies avantdites, desqueux deners les avantditz Richard et les autres paierent au dit mestre Johan à Coventré unze mars, le Dimenge preschein après la feste Seint Nicholas l'an dissep-tisme en partie de paye de xx. li. avantdites, et au dit Robert quatre lyvers des xv. li. avantdites meismes le jour, lieu, et an, par les meyns Johan fitz Hugh de Merington et Johan le Redeclerk, à la meson Richard le Latoner, et sept lyvres de cire et deux aunes de canevace, de laquele cire les ditz mestre Johan et Robert fesoient sept images, un après nostre seigneur le roi coronné de cire, un autre après le counte de Wyncestre, le tierz après monsieur Hugh, le quart après le priour de Coventré, le quint après le celerer, le sisme après Nichol Crumpe, seneschal le priour, et le septisme après un Richard de Sowe, par qui et l'ymage fait après luy, il voleient prover les autres images s'il furent certeyns ou ne mye, par l'assent et l'acord le dit Richard et les autres. Et le dit Robert ad reconuz, qe le dit mestre Johan et lui comencerent de faire leur mestries en la fourme avant-dite, le Lundy preschein après la feste Seint Nicholas, l'an xvii., par l'assent les avantditz Richard le Latoner et les autres, en une vielle mesoun à une demie luwe de la ville de Coventré, desouz le parke de Shorteleye, et ensuit demorerent continuelment sur leur oevre, tancque le Samady preschein après l'Ascension preschein suivant en meisme l'an. Et à çeo ad reconuz qe anxi come le dit mestre Johan et lui furent en la dite vielle meson entour leur oevre, le Vendredi preschein avant la feste de la Seinte Croice l'an xvii., entour la my nuyt, le dit mestre Johan bailla au dit Robert une broche de plum acu devant, et lui comanda q'il la botast la mountaunce de deux pouz parfound en frount de l'ymage fait apres Richard de Sowe, par qui ils voleient prover les altres ; et il issi le fist : et lendemeyn matyn le dit mestre Johan manda le dit Robert à la meson le dit Richard de Sowe, pur veer en quel estat il fust, et le dit Robert trova le dit Richard brayaunt et criaunt " harrou ! " sanz avoir conissance de nul homme, et si perdi memoire, et ensuit just le dit Richard languissant tancque le Dimenge en le journant preschein avant la feste de l'Ascension preschein suivant, à quel houre le dit mestre Johan treet hors la dite broche de plum hors du frount le dit image fait après le dit Richard, et la bota tancque à quoer. Et ensi demurra la dite broche au quoer del image, tancque le Mescredi preschien suivant, quel jour le dit Richard morust. La proeve faite du dit Richard en la fourme avantdite, par l'assent les avantditz Richard et les autres, et eux sachauntz le fait.

" He had been consecrated at Avignon in 1318, by Nicholas, Bishop of Ostium, under a mandate from Pope John XXII. There were constant quarrels between him and Arnold Poer, Seneschal of Kilkenny, whom he accused of heresy. But the same charge was brought against himself by the Archbishop of Dublin, Alexander Bicknor, and he was forced to flee and appeal to the Pope for protection. Edward III in 1329 seized his temporalities, but these were soon restored. Bishop Ledrede returned from banishment in 1347-8, but it was not until 1354 that the storm blew over, and six years later he died at a very advanced age, having sat about forty-two years in his see. He is buried in his own cathedral on the Gospel side of the High Altar.

⁴⁵ For a very complete and scholarly study of this case see Thomas Wright's *Proceedings against Dame Alice Kyteler*. Camden Society, 1843.

⁴⁶ The name afterwards became Britten.

⁴⁷ Also called Basilia in some accounts of the trial.

⁴⁸ A sacramental, *Panis benedictus*, now known in France as *pain bénit*. Generally the bread is presented with some solemnity at the Offertory of the parochial Mass and the priest blesses it before the Oblation of Host and Chalice. Different customs prevail in different dioceses, although such variations are slight and unimportant. It is distributed to the faithful, who generally partake of it in church.

⁴⁹ So in Horace Canidia and Sagana at the Sabbat ;

scalpere terram
unguibus et pullam diuelleie mordicus agnam cœperunt.

Sermonum, I, viii, 25-7.

⁵⁰ Quidam dæmon incubus nomine *Robyn Artysson* concubuit cum ea. *Annales Hiberniæ*. Probably a chronicle of the fifteenth century, printed by Camden, *Britannia*, ed. 1607, p. 818.

⁵¹ Printed by Mrs. Chaworth Musters in *A Cavalier Stronghold*, 1890, p. 388, and in a French translation by Mrs. H. G. M. Murray-Aynsley in the *Rane des Traditions populaires*, IV, 605. In Cornish mummings we find a character "Hub Bub," and at Chiswick "Lord Grubb," in both cases obviously a corruption of the original name. A player with a blackened face is generally a protagonist in folk-drama, and sometimes the very name is "Little Devil Doubt " or "Jack Devil Doubt," descending from mediæval or even earlier days.

⁵² Prior of S. John of Jerusalem, appointed Lord Deputy of Ireland in 1326, and Lord Justice in 1344.

⁵³ The day of the week kept in commemoration of the Saint, upon which votive Masses were allowed.

⁵⁴ Ut hæretica inditata, probata, condemnata.

⁵⁵ The *Annales Hiberniæ* say : "Ipsa ulterius non comparuit, sed de consilio filii sui et aliorum ignotorum absconsa fuit in uilla quousque habuit uentum uersus Angliam, et sic transiuit, et sic nescitur quo deuenit." And again : "Præfata Alicia . . . cum præfata Basilia fugit, et nunquam postea fuit inuenta."

⁵⁶ John Clynn, in his *Annales*, speaks of the confederates as being "de secta et doctrina prædictæ dominæ Aliciæ."

⁵⁷ A retro actis temporibus non est uisum uel auditum quod quispiam pro hæresi pœnam mortis sustineret in Hiberniæ anti ipsam . . . non dico hæc sit quæ in hoc facinore primo peccauit, sed quæ primo passa est mortis iustum iudicium propter hæresim. Clynn, *Annales*.

⁵⁸ Miss Murray, giving a list of the Kilkenny coven (*The Witch-Cult in Western Europe*, p. 285), has : " 9. Robin, son of Artis (the Devil)," i.e. the Grand Master or Chief of the witches in that district, and we are no further.

⁵⁹ Carrigan, *History of the Diocese of Ossory*, III, p. 18.

⁶⁰ Enrolment of Pleas, 6 James I, memb. 2 (Queen's Bench).

⁶¹ Almost certainly Isabella of Angoulême, widow of King John.

⁶² *Triumphalia Sanctæ Crucis* (Register of Father Malachy Hartry, Monk of Holy Cross, 1640-9), tr. and ed. Murphy, Dublin, 1891. Holy Cross, although not one of the largest, was the loveliest of Irish Cistercian houses. It was founded in 1169 by Donald O'Brien, King of Thomond. The pillared shrine of the Relic still stands.

⁶³ He died in 1671. *Cork Hist. and Arch. Journal*, vol. VII (2nd series).

⁶⁴ Egmont MSS. (Hist. MSS. Comm.), II, 181.

⁶⁵ Sinclar in his *Satan's Invisible World Discovered* (later edition), where he quotes a pamphlet published in 1669, *The Bewitching of a Child in Ireland*. This, which was probably locally printed, does not seem to have been traced.

[66] The ballad is printed in *The Ulster Journal of Archæology* for 1908. There also exists a shorter version, which is very incorrect, and in which the wise-woman is termed Butlers.

[67] *Notes and Queries*, 4th series, Vol. VII.

[68] *Folklore*, VI, 302.

[69] *Irish Times*, 14 June, 1911 ; *Independent*, 1 July, 1911.

[70] George Ives, *A History of Penal Methods*, 1914, p. 68.

[71] S. John D. Seymour, *Irish Witchcraft and Demonology*, 1913, pp. 247–8.

[72] De termino Trinitatis anno xlv. regni Edwardi tertii. Nota, Que un home fust prise en Southwark ovesque un test et un visage d'un home mort, et ovesque un livre de sorcery en son male, et amesné devant Sir J. Knivet justice en bank le roy, mès nul endictment sur luy, per que les clerks luy fierent jurer que jammès ne serroit sorcier, et fuit deliveré del prison, et le teste et le livre arse à Touthil as costages le prison. *Year Book*, IV, p. 17.

[73] Archbishop of Canterbury, 1375–81 ; Lord Chancellor, 1380–1.

[74] Vol. IV, i, p. 93. See also the *Calendar of the Patent Rolls*, Henry IV, Vol. III, p. 112. It may be remembered that Henry IV's opponent Owen Glendower, " the great magician, damn'd Glendower," was traditionally a famous sorcerer skilled to " call spirits from the vasty deep."

[75] Rex dilecto et fideli suo Johanni Colepeper, ac dilecto sibi Roberto Passemer seruienti suo ad arma, salutem. Sciatis quod quibusdam certis de causis coram nobis et concilio nostro propositis, assignauimus uos conjunctim et diuisim ad Thomam Northfelde, sacræ paginæ professorem, ordinis prædicatorum, apud ciuitatem Wygorniæ commorantem, capiendum et arestandum, necnon ad omnimodo libros suos, tractantes materiam sortilegæ prauitatis, seu quascumque alias materias suspectas, scrutandum, capiendum seu arestandum, et ipsum Thomam, ac libros suos taliter suspectos, saluo et secure coram concilio nostro, omni celeritate possibili, adducendum, ad respondendum super hiis quæ sibi ex parte nostra obiicientur tunc ibidem, et ad faciendum ulterius et recipiendum quod per nos et dictum consilium nostrum consideratum fuerit in hac parte ; et ideo uobis mandamus quod circa præmissa diligenter intendatis, ac ea faciatis et exequamini in forma prædicta : Damus autem uniuersis et singulis uicecomitibus, maioribus, balliuis, constabulariis, ac aliis officiariis, ministris, ligeis et subditis nostris quibuscumque, tam infra libertates quam extra, tenore præsentium firmiter in mandatis quod uobis, seu alteri uestrum in executione præmissorum inten-dentes sint, consulentes, et auxiliantes, quotiens et quando per uos, seu alterum uestrum, ex parte nostra, fuerint rationabiliter præmuniti. In cuius, &c. Teste Rege apud Westmonasterium, septimo die Maii. Per concilium.

[76] A Mendicant Order which, after having for some time existed in Italy, appeared in England from the priory of S. Maria di Morella at Bologna in 1244 with official documents from Pope Innocent IV requesting leave to make foundations here. Their rule was that of S. Augustine ; their habit brown or black, afterwards changed to blue by Pius II. The first of their English houses was founded in 1245, and they settled in London in 1249. The Order, having dwindled to very few monasteries, was suppressed in 1636 by Alexander VII.

[77] Sir Harris Nicolas, *Proceedings and Ordinances of the Privy Council*, London, 1834–7, IV, p. 114.

[78] Rot. Parl., 1 Ric. III, printed in the *Rolls of Parliament*, Vol. VI, p. 240.

[79] It has been suggested by Mr. Archbold, the author of the article on Cardinal Morton in the *Dictionary of National Biography*, that the Cardinal perhaps wrote the history in Latin, and Blessed Thomas More turned it into English.

[80] Actually, of course, Anne Boleyn was merely a concubine.

[81] *Letters and Papers, Foreign and Domestic*, X, 199.

[82] *Letters and Papers*, VI, 1112.

[83] An earlier statute mentioned sorcery and witchcraft in connexion with medicine, but it was directed against quacks and irregular practitioners.

[84] *Acts of Privy Council*, n.s., VII, 6 and 22.

[85] *Calendar of State Papers, Domestic*, 1547–80, 142.

[86] British Museum, Add. MSS., 32,091, fol. 176.

[87] *Archæologia Cantiana*, Visitations of Canterbury, XXVI, 31.

[88] British Museum, Sloane MSS., 3,943, fol. 19.

[89] Kitchen of Llandaff and Thomas Stanley of Sodor and Man were the only two prelates found willing to change their religion. Of the expelled Bishops many were strictly imprisoned, others were held prisoners at large, three (Cuthbert Scott of Chester, Richard Tate of Worcester, Thomas Goldwell of S. Asaph) went abroad. *Zurich Letters*, 1st series, n. 33 and 35.

[90] He was also preacher to the malcontents at Basel.

[91] "I have at last returned to London," 2 November, 1559. *Zurich Letters*, I, 44, Parker Society, Cambridge, 1842.

[92] "Tanti est semel gustasse de missa ! Qui bibit inde furit : procul hinc discedite, queis est mentis cura bonæ : qui bibit inde furit : uident erepto illo palladio omnia ventura in periculum." *Zurich Letters*, IX. Candidly it was the Mass that mattered.

[93] *Zurich Letters*, IV, 20 March, 1559.

[94] Even Laurence Humphrey, his Puritan biographer, thought the terms of Jewel's challenge regarding the Fathers unwise. Bristow, *Motives*, ed. 1599, pp. 67–8.

[95] *Decem Rationes*, V, apud Simpson's *Edmund Campion*, 1907, p. 23.

[96] In *A True and Just Recorde of the Information, Examination, and Confession of all the Witches taken at St. Oses. . . . Written . . . by W. W.* (1582) we have : "there is a man of great cunning and knowledge come over lately unto our Queenes Maiestie, which hath advertised her what a companie and number of witches be within Englande." The reference is, no doubt, to Jewel.

[97] Strype, *Annals of the Reformation*, I, Pt. i, 11.

[98] Dekker, *Old Fortunatus*, 4to, 1600, the Prologue and Epilogue at Court.

[99] *Sub Nomine. Dic. Nat. Biography.*

[100] G. W. Prothero, *Statutes and Constitutional Documents*, 1558–1625, 3rd edition, 1906, pp. 78–9.

[101] *Acts of the Privy Council*, n.s., VII, 200–1.

[102] *Depositions . . . from . . . Durham* (Surtees Society), 99.

[103] The only original copy that can be traced is in the Lambeth Palace Library. It has been reprinted for the Philobiblion Society, London, 1864–5.

[104] *Wytches at Chensforde* (reprint), p. 24.

[105] *Ibid.*, pp. 20, 29.

[106] Alice Chandler was probably also hanged at the same time.

[107] *A Detection of damnable driftes, practised by three Witches arraigned at Chelmsforde in Essex at the last Assizes there holden, whiche were executed in Aprill*, 1579. Black-letter pamphlet, "London, for Edward White at the little North-dore of Paules."

[108] W. P. M. Kennedy, *Elizabethan Episcopal Administration*, 3 vols., Alcuin Club Collections, 1925.

[109] *The apprehension and confession of three notorious Witches arraigned and by Justice condemmde in the Countye of Essex the 5 day Julye last past*, 1589.

[110] Reginald Scot, *Discoverie of Witchcraft*, p. 542.

[111] *Acts Privy Council*, n. 3, XI, 292.

[112] *Ibid.*, XII, 21–3.

[113] *Ibid.*, XII, 29, 34.

[114] *Calendar of State Papers, Domestic*, 1581–90, 220.

[115] *Historical MSS. Comm. Reports*, IV, app. 366b.

[116] Cf. *Hudibras*, II, 3.

> Did not the Dev'l appear to *Martin*
> *Luther* in Germany for certain ?
>
> .   .   .   .   .
>
> Appear in divers Shapes to *Kelly*,
> And speak i' th' Nun of *Loudo'ns* belly ?
>
> .   .   .   .   .
>
> *Kelly* did all his feats upon
> The Devil's Looking-glass, a stone ;
> Where playing with him at bo-peep
> He solv'd all problems ne'er so deep.

[117] " She should have been executed, but that her spirit killed her in prison," says the account.

[118] Of this there are two copies—apparently the only exemplars known—in Lambeth Palace Library. It is superfluous to remark that all these pamphlets are of the last rarity, in some cases only one copy has been traced.

[119] Also known as Tissey. Tissey and Jack were males and could inflict death, being more powerful than Tyffin and Pygine, who were females, and only destroyed goods and cattle or punished with lighter ailments. In 1646 a Huntingdon witch, Elizabeth Werd of Great Catworth, gave a sister witch, Frances Moore, a white Cat, a familiar, named Tissy.

[120] *Discoverie of Witchcraft*, 1584, p. 543.

[121] 1593, 2nd edition 1603, reprinted from the Percy Society, 1842.

[122] Second wife of Sir Henry Cromwell, who was the grandfather of Oliver Cromwell.

[123] Mr. H. E. Norris has collected some thirty references to the Warboys witches in an elaborate and valuable bibliography. *Notes and Queries*, XII series, 1916, pp. 283 and 304.

[124] Edinburgh, 1597. Reprinted in London, 1603. In 1616 it appeared again as part of the collection of the King's *Workes* compiled by the Bishop of Winchester.

[125] " The Preface to the Reader."

[126] See Brinsley Nicholson's edition of the *Discoverie* (reprint, 1886), Introduction, xxxv.

[127] Nicholson thinks that he was himself a Justice of the Peace.

[128] There is a study by R. Binz ; Bonn, 1885.

[129] Mayhall, *Annals of Yorkshire*, London, 1878, I, 58. Also Edward Fairfax, *A Discourse of Witchcraft*, 1622.

[130] *The Most Cruell and Bloody Murther committed by an Innkeepers Wife called Annis Dell, and her Sonne George Dell, Foure Yeares since.* . . . *With the severall Witch-crafts and most damnable practices of one Johane Harrison and her Daughter, upon several persons men and women at Royston, who were all executed at Hartford the 4 of August last past* 1606.

[131] Glover, *History of Derby* (ed. Thos. Noble, 1833), Part I, Vol. ii, p. 613 ; also W. Andrews, *Bygone Derbyshire*, pp. 180–4.

[132] Thomas Potts, *Wonderfull Discoverie of Witches in the countie of Lancaster*, London, 1613. Alizon Device and Isabel Robey were actually indicted for causing illness, as also were John and Jane Bulcock. But the whole coven had conspired to murder.

[133] *The Witches of Northamptonshire*, 1612.

[134] Condemned 27 July. Potts, *Wonderfull Discoverie*.

[135] *A Booke of the Wytches Lately condemned and executed at Bedford*, 1612–13. Arbor, *Stationers' Register*, III, 234b.

[136] *Middlesex County Records*, II, lii, 95, 110, 217–18. She had previously been twice tried and acquitted.

[137] *Ibid.*, II, 108, 218.

[138] The three women were employed as cleaners in Belvoir Castle. Mother Flower was " a monstrous malicious woman full of oathes, curses, and imprecations irreligious." The two daughters made ample confession. They were said to have killed Henry, Lord Ross, son of the Earl of Rutland. Upon the Earl's monument in Bettesford Church, Leicestershire, it is recorded that he had " two Sons, both which died in their infancy by wicked practices and sorcery " (*Gentleman's Magazine*, LXXIV, Pt. 11, 909). There is a pamphlet *The Wonderful Discoverie of the Witchcrafts of Margaret and Phillip Flower, daughters of Joan Flower neere Bevor Castle : executed at Lincolne, March 11, 1618*. London, 1619.

[139] *The Wonderful Discoverie* . . . London, 1619.

[140] *The Wonderfull Discoverie of Elizabeth Sawyer* . . . *by Henry Goodcole*, 1621.

[141] *Hist. MSS. Comm. Reports*, XIII, Pt. 4, 136–7, 139–40, 147–8. The Lord Warden disputed the town's jurisdiction.

[142] *Middlesex County Records*, II, 116, 219.

[143] Alexander Roberts, *Treatise of Witchcraft*, London, 1616; also, Mackerell, *History and Antiquities of King's Lynn*, p. 233; see also *Calendar State Papers, Dom.*, 1611–18, 398, and William Kelly, *Royal Progresses in Leicester*, Leicester, 1855, Pt. II, 15.

[144] Robert Heyrick's letters from Leicester, 16 July and 15 October, 1616. Annual Register, 1800, p. 403.

[145] John Latimer. *Annals of Bristol in the Seventeenth Century*. Bristol, 1900, p. 91.

[146] British Museum. Sloane MSS., I, 954, 41–2.

[147] *Middlesex County Records*, II, 72, 73. She was again acquitted in 1625. *Ibid*, III, 2.

[148] *Church History of Britain*, V, 452 (chap. X, Sect. 4).

[149] *Miscellany*, 4–9.

[150] The authority is the famous narrative by Thomas Potts, *The Wonderfull Discoverie of Witches in the countie of Lancaster. With the Arraignment and Triall of Nineteene notorious Witches, at the Assizes and generall Gaole deliverie holden at the Castle of Lancaster, upon Munday, the seventeenth of August last, 1612. . . . By Thomas Potts, Esq.*, London, 1613. Reprinted by the Chetham Society, edited J. Crossley, 1845.

[151] Notestein, for no reason at all, suspects this plain and straightforward narrative which has the very impress of truth.

[152] Anne Redfearne, the daughter of old Chattox, never confessed.

[153] She had two familiars, Fancie and Tibbe. Three skulls with teeth were found in her possession. They had, of course, been used for a charm.

[154] This celebration of Holy Communion on Maundy Thursday is worth remarking.

[155] Jennet Device, a girl of nine years, was brought forward against her mother, " this odious witch, who was branded with a preposterous marke in Nature even from her birth, which was her left eye standing lower than the other, the one looking down, the other looking up."

[156] Baddeley, in his pamphlet *The Boy of Bilson* . . . London, 1622, says she was discharged after the inquiry; but Arthur Wilson asserts she was found guilty and condemned to death.

[157] Bishop of Chester, 1616; translated to Lichfield and Coventry, 1618; to Durham, 1632.

[158] The book had been written some four years earlier.

[159] E. Baines, *Lancaster*, 1868–70, II, 12.

[160] W. Boys, *Collections for an History of Sandwich in Kent*, Canterbury, 1792.

[161] MS. letter of 1685–6, *Gentleman's Magazine*, 1832, Pt. I, 405–10.

[162] Meric Casaubon, *Of Credulity and Incredulity*, London, 1668, pp. 170–1.

[163] John Aubrey, *Remaines of Gentilisme and Judaisme*, Folk-Lore Society, 61.

[164] *A Collection of Modern Relations*, London, 1693, 48–9.

[165] 4to, 1634.

[166] Overbury died 15 September, 1613. Sir Jervis Elwes, Franklin, and Mrs. Turner, the poisoners, were tried and executed between 19 October and 4 December, 1615. The Somerset trials took place in the following May. Dr. Forman had died.

[167] Richard Baxter in his *The Certainty of the Worlds of Spirits, fully evinced, by unquestionable Histories of Apparitions and Witch-crafts, Operations, Voices, etc.; . . . Written for the Conviction of Sadducees and Infidels*, 8vo, London, 1691 (*Term Catalogues*, Michaelmas-November), gives anecdotes of Dr. Lamb's sorceries.

[168] *Dr. Lamb's Darling, or Strange and Terrible News from Salisbury*, by James [Edmond ?] Bowen, Cleric, London, 1653; and *Doctor Lamb Revised, or Witchcraft condemn'd in Anne Bodenham* . . . by Edmond Bowen, London, 1653.

[169] The Royal Standard was raised at Nottingham, 22 August, 1642; Edgehill, 23 October, 1642.

[170] John Stearne, his colleague, was a bitter Calvinist. Hopkins also had a special commission from the Presbyterian Parliament, for there seems no reason to doubt Butler's definite statement :

> Has not this present Parl'ament
> A Ledger to the Devil sent
> Fully impower'd to treat about,
> Finding revolted Witches out ?—*Hudibras*, II, iii, 139–42.

[171] *The Discovery of Witches . . . by Matthew Hopkins, Witchfinder,* London, 1647.

[172] *A True Relation of the Arraignment of Eighteene Witches at St. Edmundsbury . . .* London, 1645.

[173] John Gaule's *Select Cases of Conscience Touching Witches,* London, 1646.

[174] Hopkins answers this accusation, which was doubtless true, in Query 9 of his *Discovery.*

[175] It was thought that everything unholy was repelled by water and refused to sink therein. Binsfeld, *De Confessione Maleficarum.* The Greeks believed in the cleansing power of " Waters at their priest-like task," and "Αλαδε μύσται was the cry of the hierophant to those about to celebrate Eleusinian rites. They plunged into the sea to attain ritual purity, for as Euripides says : Θάλασσα κλύζει πάντα τάνθρώπων κακά. (*Iphigenia in Tauris,* l. 1193.) One may compare the famous lines in *Macbeth*, II :

> Will all great Neptune's ocean wash this blood
> Clean from my hand ? No, this my hand will rather
> The multitudinous seas incarnadine,
> Making the green one red.

[176] *Dæmonologie*, III, 6. Actually the water ordeal, swimming a witch, was the Judgement of God, and applied for many crimes. It goes back to very early days, about the sixth or seventh century. It is prescribed in the code of S. Edward the Confessor, who ordained an oath with twelve compurgators, in cases of the relapsed thirty-six must be found a third time, " et si alias de latrocinio composuerit est ad iudicium aquæ."

[177] *De la Demonomanie des Sorciers,* IV, 4, Lyons, 1593, p. 417.

[178] Whose *A Confirmation and Discovery of Witch-craft,* London, 1648, is all-important for the Hopkins crusade.

[179] A Mr. Rivet, " who heard it from them that watched with him," gave Hutchinson this account.

[180] Samuel Clarke, *Lives of Sundry Eminent Persons . . .* London, 1683, p. 172.

[181] Stearne, *Confirmation and Discovery . . .* London, 1648, p. 14.

[182] A. G. Hollingsworth, *History of Stowmarket,* Ipswich, 1844, p. 170.

[183] Printed by Gaule at the opening of *Select Cases.*

[184] *Confirmation and Discovery . . .* London, 1648.

[185] J. T. Varden, *East Anglian Handbook for* 1885, p. 89.

[186] *Hudibras*, II, iii, ll. 139–54.

[187] William Robins (or Robinson), who at the capture of Basing House in 1645 was thus murdered by " Butcher " Harrison. See J. Wright, *Historia Histrionica,* 1699. Harrison, who signed the warrant for the execution of King Charles I, paid the penalty of his crimes on 13 October, 1660, when at Charing Cross he was " hanged, drawn, and quartered . . . at which there was great shouts of joy." Pepys, 13 October, 1660.

[188] P. Browne, *History of Norwich,* Norwich, 1814, p. 38.

[189] *The Divels Delusions,* 1649. Palmer gave information about a " whole colledge of witches."

[190] Thomas Widdrington's letter to Whitelocke. Whitelocke's *Memorials,* III, 99.

[191] Ralph Gardiner, *England's Grievance Discovered,* C. LIII, p. 108.

[192] *Ibid.,* p. 109.

[193] Laurence Eachard, *History of England,* folio, London, 1706, III, p. 181.

[194] *Hudibras . . . With Large Annotations . . . by Zachary Grey, LL.D.,* London, 1744, Vol. II, p. 11.

[195] *Middlesex County Records*, III, 284. *The Weekly Intelligencer*, 7 October, 1650.

[196] *Middlesex County Records*, III, 287. *The Witch of Wapping, A Declaration in Answer to several lying Pamphlets concerning the Witch of Wapping*, a stout defence of the accused. *French Intelligencer*, 6–13 April, 1652. *Mercurius Democritus*, 7–14 April, 1652. *Weekly Intelligencer*, 6–13 April, 1652. *Faithful Scout*, 9–16 April, 1652.

[197] Rug was the name of the familiar of Joyce Boanes, an Essex witch, who was examined by Starne in 1645. She confessed " she had two impes which came into the bed to her in the likeness of mouses, and that they sucked on this examinants body." T. B. Howell, *State Trials*, London, 1816, IV.

[198] *A Prodigious and Tragicall History of the Arraignment . . . of six Witches at Maidstone . . .* by " H. F. Gent," 1652.

[199] Baxter, *World of Spirits*, London, 1691, pp. 44, 45. " The now minister of the place " reported this trial.

[200] Richardson, *Table Book*, I, 286.

[201] *Mercurius Politicus*, 24 Nov.–2 Dec., 1653. R. and O. B. Peter, *The Histories of Launceston and Dunheved*, Plymouth, 1885, p. 285.

[202] *Middlesex County Records*, III, 217, 218, 289.

[203] F. Hutchinson, *Historical Essay concerning Witchcraft*, 1718 (enlarged edition, 1720).

[204] Glanvill, *Sadducismus Triumphatus*, 1681, II, 120–2.

[205] Notestein, *Witchcraft in England* (p. 219), absurdly says : " By 1653 the equilibrium of England had been restored. Cromwell's government was beginning to run smoothly." Ubi solitudinem faciunt pacem appellant.

[206] A MS. letter of 1685–6 printed in the *Gentleman's Magazine*, 1832, Part I, 405–10.

[207] P. Brown, *History of Norwich*, p. 39. Also Francis Bloomfield's *An Essay towards a Topographical History of the County of Norfolk*, London, 1805–10, III, 401.

[208] *Gentleman's Magazine*, 1856, Pt. I, 39, from a letter of J. Noake of Worcester, who used the Townshend MSS.

[209] *Hertfordshire County Sessions Rolls*, I, 137.

[210] Joseph Hunter, *Life of Heywood*, London, 1842, pp. 167–8, note. Oliver Heywood was a prominent Dissenter of the north of England.

[211] W. Welfitt (" Ciuis "), *Minutes of Canterbury*, Canterbury, 1801–2, X.

[212] It is interesting to note that Shadwell's *The Lancashire Witches*, which had been produced during the previous autumn, was published this year. In his preface *To the Reader* he remarks : " I have presented you a great part of the Doctrine of Witchcraft, believe it who will. For my Part, I am (as it is said of *Surly* in the *Alchymist*) somewhat costive of Belief " (*The Alchemist*, II, 3) :

> *Mammon.* I but come,
> To ha' you confute this gentleman.
> *Surly.* Who is,
> Indeed, sir, somewhat caustive of beliefe
> Toward your stone : would not be gull'd.

[213] Notestein, *Witchcraft in England*, p. 261, says of the evidence at this trial that it " was perhaps the absurdest ever used against even a witch." His industry in collecting data is most commendable, but his use of facts is extraordinarily uncritical. His mind has already been made up, and everything is wrested to square with these preconceived ideas, no small blemish in a historian.

[214] Glanvill, *Sadducismus Triumphatus*, II, 191–8.

[215] T. B. Howell, *State Trials*, London, 1810, VI, pp. 647–700.

[216] *A Full and True Relation of the Tryal, Condemnation, and Execution of Ann Foster . . . at the place of Execution at Northampton. With the Manner how she by her Malice and Witchcraft set all the Barns and Corn on Fire . . . and bewitched a whole Flock of Sheep.* London, 1674.

[217] T. B. Howell, *State Trials*, London, 1816, VIII, 1022.

[218] *Ibid.*, 1035.

[219] *Memoirs and Travels of Sir John Reresby*, London, 1812, p. 329.
[220] F. A. Inderwick, *Interregnum*, London, 1891.
[221] F. Hutchinson, *Historical Essay concerning Witchcraft.*
[222] W. Boys, *Collections for an History of Sandwich*, p. 718.
[223] London. No date. Printed for I.W. (probably John Wyatt of the Rose in S. Paul's Churchyard). The edition of 1700 was printed for J.M. (perhaps John Marshall).
[224] *The Witch-Cult in Western Europe*, p. 95 ; Bibliography, p. 285.
[225] *State Trials*, IV, 828.
[226] W. H. Bernard Saunders in his *Legends and Traditions of Huntingdon-shire*, 1888, entirely rejects the Hicks' case. He has an excellent summary of the arguments against such a trial. Chap. XIX, pp. 155–64, " Fabricated Executions for Witchcraft at Huntingdon." H. E. Norris has a valuable bibliographical note : " Witchcraft-Case of Mrs. Hicks." *Notes and Queries*, XII, Series 53, 30 December, 1916.
[227] *Witchcraft in England*, p. 382.
[228] 25 Henry VIII, c. 14.
[229] Stephen, *History of Criminal Law*, p. 477.
[230] Holinshed, *Chronicles*, pp. 1226, 1262.
[231] *Remarkable Trials*, 1765, II, p. 100.
[232] Lord Hallam's *Life of Tennyson*, c. I.
[233] *Confession . . . of Mary Saunders* [Monmouth], 1764.
[234] *Sussex Assize Records.*
[235] As printed by the Sussex Archæological Society, Vol. LII, p. 79.
[236] Hutchinson, *Historical Essay on Witchcraft*, pp. 44, 45.
[237] This and the next two cases are from Inderwick, *Interregnum.*
[238] *Spectator*, No. 117, 14 July, 1711.
[239] *An Account of the Tryal, Examination, and Condemnation of Jane Wonham.* One page.
[240] R. Clutterbuck, *History and Antiquities of the County of Hertford*, London, 1815–27, II, p. 461, note.
[241] A MS. in the British Museum, Sloane MSS., 3,943, continues the public discussion.
[242] *Leicestershire and Rutland Notes and Queries*, I, 247.
[243] British Museum, Add. MSS., 35,838, fol. 404 (Hardwicke Collection). Notestein has misread the MS. and gives an " Old woman, her son and daughter " as " Old woman Norton and daughter," which mistake occurs at least three times in his references. (*Witchcraft in England*, pp. 330, 333, 419.)
[244] Edited by Brinsley Nicholson, London, 1886.
[245] Second edition, 1603 ; reprinted for the Percy Society, 1842.
[246] Second edition, with appendix, 1655.
[247] Part I, Sec. 2, Mem. 1, Subs. 3.
[248] Johann Weyer, 1516–88. Lerchemer, Aug., *Bedenker von der Zauberen*, 4to, 1585. Biarmanus, Martin Biermann, *De magicis actionibus . . . Bodini*, *opposita disquisitio*, 4to, 1590. Ewichius, J. Ewick, *De sagorum . . . natura.* Hemingius, Nic. Hemmingius, *Admonitio de superstitionibus uitandis*, 8vo, 1575. Danæus, Lambert Daneau, Bremæ, 8vo, 1584, *De Sortiariis*, French translation, *Les Sorciers, s.l.* [Geneva ?], 12mo, 1574. Chytræus, David, *Explicatio Apocalypsis Ioannis*, 8vo, 1564. Zanchius, Hier., *De diuinatione . . . artificiosa*, 8vo, 1610. Aretius, Angelo Aretino, *Tractatus de Maleficiis*, folio, 1521. Delrio, Martin, S. J., 1551–1608. Sprenger, James, *Malleus Maleficarum*, c. 1495–9. Niderius, John, O.P., 1380–1438, *Formicarius.* Guatius, F. M. Guazzo, *Compendium Maleficarum*, 1608. Bartolus, a legal writer, *ob.* at Perugia, 1536. Bodin, Jean, 1520–96. Godelman, Johan Georg, *Disputatio de Magis*, 1584. Damhoderius, Iosse de Damhoudère, *La practique et enchiridion des causes criminelles.* Louvain, 4to, 1555. Paracelsus, 1493–1541. Erastus, Thomas, a doctor of Heidelberg, *De lamiis, Le povuoir des sorcières*, French translation (Geneva), 8vo, 1579. Scribanius, Gulielmus Adolphus, *De sagarum natura*, 1583. Camerarius, Philippe, a lawyer and councillor of Nuremberg, *Les méditations historiques*, French translation, Paris, 8vo, 1608.
[249] *Term Catalogues (Mercurius Librarius)*, Hilary (February), 1669.
[250] *Term Catalogues*, Easter (May), 1681.

[251] *Joseph Glanvill*, by H. S. Redgrove and I. M. L. Redgrove, 1921, an admirably compact little monograph, may be consulted with profit. There is a more elaborate study, *Joseph Glanvill*, by Ferris Greenslet, Columbia University Press, and New York, 1900.

[252] Even Lecky admits : " The *Sadducismus Triumphatus* . . . is probably the ablest book ever published in defence of the superstition," i.e. Witchcraft. *Rationalism in Europe*, Vol. I, c. 1.

[253] *Sadducismus Triumphatus* (3rd ed., London, 1700), Part I, pp. 7 and 8.

[254] *Ibid.*, p. 10.

[255] Glanvill very rightly refuses to trifle time in combating such a writer as Scot, whom he with reason dubs " ridiculous."

[256] " In octavo, Price, bound, 1s. 6d." *Term Catalogues*, Hilary (February), 1669.

[257] " In Folio. Price, bound, 10s." *Term Catalogues*, Trinity (5 July), 1677.

[258] *Displaying of Supposed Witchcraft*, p. 68. Notestein apparently approves this ineptitude.

[259] T. Charley's *News from the Invisible World*, " Impartially compiled from the Works of Baxter, Wesley, Simpson, and other Writers of Indisputable Veracity," is interesting. The writings of Dr. F. G. Lee, which specifically deal with the problems of Witchcraft, deserve honourable mention, especially *Glimpses of the Supernatural*, 2 vols., 1875 ; *More Glimpses of the World Unseen*, 1878 ; and *Glimpses in the Twilight*, 1885. Such works as *The History of Witches and Wizards* . . . by W.P. [1700 ?], giving short uncritical accounts of various trials, Julian Cox, Elizabeth Styles, the Bury St. Edmund's cases of 1682, the garbled narrative of the Boy of Bilson, and legends concerning Cornelius Agrippa, Dr. Faustus, have no value, save what lies in their great rarity and their amusingly crude woodcuts. *Witchcraft Detected and Prevented*, " By a Member of the School of Black Art, Italy," Peterhead and London, 1826, is written " more with a view to amuse than to be put in practice." The spells given range from : " To allay tempests," " To know if a wife encourage a gallant," " To know if water is mixed with wine," " How a person may render himself invisible," to " Infallible Negro remedy for rheumatism," " Edinburgh eye-water," the " Russian remedy for a vertigo," " Excellent worm powder," and other purely domestic remedies.

[260] In Ireland the law lasted until 1821. George Ives, *A History of Penal Methods*, p. 68.

[261] T. Wright, *Narratives of Sorcery and Magic*, London, 1851, II, pp. 326–8.

[262] The following letter " From Mr. Manning, Dissenting Teacher at Halstead, in Essex, to John Morley, Esq., Halstead," presents a strange circumstance, and may well be admitted in a foot-note here :

" HALSTEAD, *August* 2, 1732.

" SIR,—The narrative which I gave you in relation to witchcraft, and which you are pleased to lay your commands upon me to repeat, is as follows : There was one Master Collett, a smith by trade, of Haveningham, in the county of Suffolk, who, as 'twas customary with him, assisting the maide to churne, and not being able (as the phrase is) to make the butter come, threw a hot iron into the churn, under the notion of witchcraft in the case, upon which a poore labourer, then employed in carrying of dung in the yard, cried out in a terrible manner, ' They have killed me, they have killed me ; ' still keeping his hand upon his back, intimating where the pain was, and died upon the spot.

" Mr. Collett, with the rest of the servants then present, took off the poor man's clothes, and found to their great surprise, the mark of the iron that was heated and thrown into the churn, deeply impressed upon his back. This account I had from Mr. Collett's own mouth, who being a man of unblemished character, I verily believe to be matter of fact.—I am, sir, your obliged humble servant,   SAM. MANNING.

[263] *The Works of William Hogarth* . . . *Elucidated by Descriptions, Critical, Moral, and Historical*, by Thomas Clerk, London, 1810, Vol. I, p. 192, Plate liii.

[264] Which Clerk calls " Glanville's Book of Witches."

[265] This story is from Clarendon's *History of the Rebellion*. It was the subject of a common enough chap-book.

[266] This extraordinary impostor, in the year 1726, pretended that she bred rabbits, and even deceived two physicians, whereupon the affair was much debated. King George I sent down Sir William Manningham, one of the royal doctors, to investigate the matter, which was soon found to be a clever cheat.

[267] Ireland thinks this figure was intended for the Boy of Bilson. *Hogarth Illustrated*, II, p. 196.

[268] *Notes and Queries*, Vol. VI, November, 1853, p. 470. Quoting from the *Northampton Mercury of* 1785.

[269] Curate of Great Paxton, Little Paxton, and Toseland from about 1799 to 1825, and vicar, 1825. A M.I. in Great Paxton Church records that he " Died, Dec. 27, 1839, in the 59th year of his age." He wrote a large number of books, and many of his sermons were published.

[270] This sermon was reviewed in *The Monthly Repository*, Vol. III, No. xxxv, November, 1808.

[271] Charles Mackay, *Extraordinary Popular Delusions*, p. 187.

[272] *Ibid.*, pp. 187–8.

[273] *Hertford Reformer*, 23 June, 1838.

[274] Arthur Mee, *The Harrieses of Cwrt-y-Cadno*, an interesting brochure. Also Mary L. Lewes' valuable study *The Wizards of Cwrt-y-Cadno*, *Occult Review*, July, 1924, pp. 17–24.

[275] Charles Mackay, *Extraordinary Popular Delusions*, II, p. 189.

[276] *Witch Stories*, 2nd ed., 1883, p. 320.

[277] *The Times*, Tuesday, 24 March, 1857.

[278] *The Times*, Tuesday, 7 April, 1857. The letter is signed E. No names, merely one or two initials, and no place indications are given in the narrative which is of considerable length.

[279] *The Times*, Thursday, 24 September, 1863.

[280] Thomas Davidson, *Witchcraft*, article in *Chambers's Encyclopædia*, 1895, X, p. 699.

[281] C. Leland, *Etruscan Roman Remains*, London, 1892, p. 353. An old Italian woman, to whom an engraving from the *Folk-Lore Journal* of the " witch's ladder " was shown, recognized it as *la ghirlanda delle streghe*.

[282] *Daily Mirror*, Wednesday, 13 January, 1926.

[283] *Westminster Gazette*, Wednesday, 20 January, 1926. *Liverpool Post and Mercury*, 22 January, 1926. The Rev. Charles Kent, Rector of Merton, has courteously obliged me with a very ample letter on the subject.

[284] *Daily Mirror*, 22 February, 1923.

[285] *Daily Express*, 12 February, 1926.

CHAPTER III

SCOTLAND

IN no country did the witch-cult flourish more rankly, in no country did the belief persist more lately, in no country did the prosecution of sorcery rage fiercer and the fires blaze brighter than in Scotland. The lonely hills and wild untrod moors, the echoing glens and remote glades, seemed the very places for the hauntings of mysterious powers, influences which were, however, in popular lore always ranged on the side of evil, harbingers of death and destruction and hell. Even the realm of Færie, whose denizens were thought of elsewhere as being bright spirits friendly to humankind, lovely, gay, bounteous of goodly gifts, in Scotland becomes the Court of Elfame, a fearful country ruled over by the Devil, who is actually spoken of as a fairy-man, inhabited by malignant fiends, where the revels of elves and pretty pixies dancing their graceful rounds in the silvery moonlight, are a foul Sabbat of demons, hideous carlines and their dark familiars. It is, perhaps, no matter for surprise that under that quintessence of verjuice and venom, John Knox, whose loathsome slime fouled Caledonia from north to south and ate like a putrid sore through to the very heart of her children, an intenser gloom, a deeper despair, fell upon the unhappy land. The supremacy of the Devil seems an essential feature of Calvinistic teaching. How can anyone look for tranquillity or comfort, or ensue sweet communion with God, when his eyes are ever scorched and scarred by the red roar of the furnace of Hell, his ears ever stunned with the ceaseless howling of the damned who are eternally agonizing in the pit of Tophet ? Christ came to give the world love and peace ; Calvin and Knox strewed the cockle of hate and fear. And so in its dour fanaticism the Kirk proved a sterner judge and a more cruel executioner than even Boguet or De Lancre ; than Philip-Adolph von Ehrenberg, the burning Bishop of

Würzburg ; or Chancellor Carpzow, who sent no less than twenty thousand witches to the stake.

Even in the most distant and shadowy times of Scottish history the legend of Witchcraft has its part. When Corbreid Gald, that Galgacus of whom Tacitus[1] tells us, fought his gallant fight against Agricola upon the Grampian Hills (Mons Graupius) and was utterly crushed and overcome, " an eagle was seene almost a whole day, fleeing up and downe over the Scotish armie, even as though she had laboured herself wearie ; also an armed man was seen flieing about the armie, and suddenlie vanished away. There fell, in like manner, out of a dark cloud in the fields, through the which the armie should pass, divers kinds of birds that were spotted with blood."

Another early Celtic monarch, King Mogall, was suspected to have known through Witchcraft of that conspiracy against him to which he fell a victim in A.D. 169. In the reign of Natholocus, a witch dwelt in Iona, so celebrated for her skill, that the King, when compelled to withdraw from the attacks of his rebellious subjects, sent one of his trusty followers to inquire of her as to the issue of the war. " The witch, consulting with her spirits, declared in the end, how it should come shortlie to pass that the king should be murdered, not by his open enemies, but by the hands of one of his most familiar friends, in whom he had reposed an especiall trust. The messenger demanded by whose hands that should be ? ' Even by thine,' said she, ' as shall be well known within these few dayes.' The gentleman, hearing these words, railed against her verie bitterlie, bidding her go like an old witch, for he trusted to see her burnt before he should commit so villainous a deed. And, departing from her, he went by and by to signifie what answer he had received ; but before he came where the king lay, his mind was altered, so that, what for doubt on the one side, that if he should declare the truth as it was told him, the king might, happlie, conceive some great suspicion that it should follow by his meanes as she had declared, and thereupon put him to death first ; and for feare, on the other side, that if he keepe it secret, it might happen to be revealed by some other, and then he to run in as much danger of life as before. He determined with himself to work the surest way, and so coming to the king, he was led aside by him into his privie chamber, when all other being commanded to avoid, he declared how he had sped ; and then falling forthwith upon Natholocus with a dagger, he slew him outright."

There was no more uncompromising opponent of the foul mysteries of Druidism than the great and glorious S. Patrick, who was born at Kilpatrick, near Dumbarton, in A.D. 387. An old yet purely unhistorical tradition, although interesting as showing how long the memory of his struggle against these pagan sorceries survived, relates that the whole body of witches in Scotland assembled to endeavour to kill the Saint. Once when he was sailing upon the sea they hurled by their enchantments a huge rock at his vessel. It fell far short and in after days became the fortress of Dumbarton, whilst the Saint, whom they were powerless to harm, went on his way unscathed.

Among the laws attributed to King Kenneth I (d. 860), and which are doubtless very ancient, is one that ordains all warlocks and necromancers and such as invoke spirits " and use to seek upon them for helpe, let them be burnt to death."

The case of King Duffus, " the seventy-eighth King of Scotland " (A.D. 968), is related by many historians.[2] Whilst he " was about the setling of the Countrey, and punishing the Troublers of the Peace, he began to be sore afflicted in his Body with a new and unheard of Disease, no Causes of his Sickness appearing in the least." A rumour soon spread that the King's malady was due to Witchcraft. " This suspicion arose, from an unusual Sweating he was under, his Body pining and withering away by little and little and his strength failling day by day. And since all his Physicians had done their utmost, and yet no appearance of recovery it was supposed his case was extraordinary, therefore all men being vehemently intent upon the Event, news came to *Court* that *Night-meetings* were kept at *Farres* a Town in *Murray*, for taking away the life of the King." Donald, the Governor of Forres Castle, arrested a young wench who had been over-heard to threaten the King, and she confessed that her mother, a notorious sorceress, and a whole coven of devil-worshippers were slowly taking the life of Duffus, who would expire in a few days. That night a company of hags was surprised whilst roasting the King's image made of wax upon a long spit over a slow fire, reciting meanwhile certain mysterious words, and basting the figure with a poisonous brew. The whole gang was seized, and they declared that as the wax melted the body of the King would decay, whilst the muttered spells deprived him of the natural refreshment of sleep. The figure was stamped to dust ; the witches burned at Forres ; and King Duffus recovered both health and strength.

The encounter of Macbeth with the three witches, whom Holinshed in his *Chronicle* describes as " iij. women in straunge and ferly apparell, resembling creatures of an elder worlde," and again as " the weird sisters, that is (as ye would say) y[e] Goddesses of destinie, or els some Nimphes or Feiries," hardly calls for comment or description here.

On the 15 April, 1285, during the nuptial festivities of Alexander III and Joleteta, daughter of the Count de Dreux, at Jedburgh, a ghost or some strange spectre danced at a royal ball. The continuation of John Fordun's *Scotichronicon* by Abbot Walter Bower[3] says : " Insecutus est unus, de quo pene dubitari potuit utrum homo esset an phantasma ; qui ut umbra magis labi uidebatur, quam pedetentim transire." And Boece[4] has : " Effigies hominis mortui, carne nudatis eius ossibus, uisa est." Alexander died in less than a twelve-month from this date.

Many a fantastic legend has gathered about the name of Sir Michael Scott, who was born in the earlier part of the thirteenth century, probably about 1214. He is said to have lectured at Padua, celebrated for its occult schools, upon judicial astrology, and he also spent several years at Toledo and Salamanca, the former of which Universities was in particular reputed to be the head-quarters of magicians from all over Europe.[5] This great scholar is believed to have died in 1291, and was buried either at Holme-Cultram, in Cumberland, or in Melrose Abbey. All accounts agree that his books of occult lore were secretly interred with him, and some add that the undying lamp of the Rosicrucians for ever lights his tomb with its immortal glow. Dante placed Michael Scott in the fourth Bolgia of the Inferno, where sorcerers are punished :

> The next, who is so slender in the flanks,
> Was Michael Scott, who of a verity
> Of magical illusions knew the game.[6]

And Benvenuto da Imola (Rambaldi), a lecturer upon Dante at the University of Bologna in the fourteenth century, glosses : " Michael Scott the Magician practised divination at the court of Frederick II, and dedicated to him a book on natural history, which I have seen, and in which among other things he treats of Astrology, then deemed infallible."

A far more terrible figure is the Scotch Gilles de Rais, William, Lord Soulis, who sold himself to the Devil and seems to have trafficked in every abomination of black magic. The legend ran that he could summon the Demon whenever he chose to rap thrice on a certain iron chest, but he must never look in the direction of the spirit. Once, however, he forgot or ignored this proviso and saw a tall dark man wearing a red cap, crimsoned with the blood of human victims. His doom was sealed, but the compact was kept to the letter. Lord Soulis was protected by an evil charm against any injury from rope or steel ; cords could not bind nor sword pierce him. And so when he was seized by his enemies they rolled him up in sheets of lead and boiled him to death at a place called the Nine-Stane Rig.

> On a circle of stones they placed the pot,
>   On a circle of stones but barely nine ;
> They heated it red and fiery hot,
>   And the burnished brass did glimmer and shine.
> They rolled him up in a sheet of lead—
>   A sheet of lead for a funeral pall ;
> They plunged him into the cauldron red,
>   And melted him body, lead, bones and all.

Hermitage Castle,[7] one of the most famous of the Border keeps in the days of its splendour, was the scene of the demoniac orgies of Lord Soulis, and it is said to have sunk partially into the earth, unable to bear such an accumulation of crime. Once every seven years, the old wives tell, the tormented ghost of the wizard still keeps tryst with Red Cap in the chambers where he wrought his devilries.[8]

A contemporary account of the murder of King James I at Perth on the 20 February, 1436, gives some details of a curious prediction of the monarch's fate by an Irish prophetess or witch. " The kyng, sodanly avised, made a solempne fest of the Christynmes at Perth, which is clepid Sant John's Town, which is from Edenbourgh on that other side of the

Scottish see, the which is vulgarly clepid the Water of Lethe. Yn the myddis of the way, thare arose a woman of Yreland, that clepid herselfe as a suthsayer. The which anone as she saw the kyng, she cried with lowde voise, saying thus : ' My lord kyng, and ye pase this water, ye shall never turne agane on lyve.' The kyng heryng this, was astonyed of her wordis ; for bot a litile to fore he had red in a prophesie, that yn the selfe same yere the kyng of Scottes shuld be slayne ; and therwithall the kyng, as he rode, clepid to him one of his knyghtis, and gave hym in commandment to torne agane to speke with that woman, and ask of here what sheo wold, and what thyng sheo ment with her lowd crying ? And sheo began, and told hym as ye hafe hard of the kynge of Scottes yf he passed that water. As now the kynge askid her, how sheo knew that ? And sheo said, that Huthart told her so. ' Sire,' quod ho, ' men may calant ye tak non hede of yond woman's wordes, for sheo nys bot a drunkine fule, and wot not what sheo saith ' ; and so, with his folk, passid the water clepid the Scottishe see, towards Saynt Johnnes Towne." The chronicler relates some dreams ominous of James's murder, and afterwards proceeds : " Both afore soper, and long aftir ynto quarter of the nyght, in the which the Erle of Athetelles, and Robert Stward were aboute the kyng, where thay wer occupied att the playng of the chesse, att the tables, yn redying of romans, yn syngyng and pyping, yn harping, and in other honest solaces of grete pleasance and disport. Therwith came the said woman of Yreland, that clepid herself a dyvenourese, and entered the kynge's courte, till that sheo came streght to the kynge's chambur-dore, where sheo stood, and abode bycause that hit was shitte. And fast sheo knokyd, till at the last the usher opyned the dure, marvelyng of that woman's beyng there that tyme of the nyght, and askyng here what sheo wold ? ' Let me yn, sire,' quod sheo, ' for I haf sumwhat to say, and to tell unto the kyng ; for I am the same woman that noght long agone desired to haf spokyn with hym at the Lith, whan he should passe the Scottish see.' The usher went yn and told hym of this woman. ' Yea,' quod the kyng, ' let hir cume to-morrow ' ; bycause that he was occupied with suche disportes at that tyme, hym let not to entend her as thenne. The usher came agane to the chamber-dore, to the said woman,

and there he told hir that the kyng was besye in playing, and
bid her cum soon agane upon the morrow. ' Well,' said the
woman, ' hit shall repent yow all that ye wil not let me speke
nowe with the kyng.' Therat the usher lughe, and held her
bot a fule, chargyng her to go her way, and therwithall she
went thens." The Earl of Athole, one of the chief conspirators,
was afterwards, at his execution, crowned with a regal
diadem of red-hot iron, because, says Buchanan, certain
witches, for whom the county of Athole was always infamous,
had told him that he would be crowned a king in sight of all
the people. The historian adds,—"Idque uaticinium ita uel
impletum uel elusum est : ac certe tales predictiones frequenter huiusmodi sortiuntur euentus."

In Scotland as elsewhere political rancour was often mixed
with charges of witchcraft. In 1479 during the reign of
James III his brother the Earl of Mar was accused of practising
magic to shorten the King's life. Buchanan, indeed, attributes the hatred of James for his brother to a prophecy
uttered by certain witches, in whom that monarch greatly
trusted, or a prediction of Andrew, a Flemish astrologer high
in the royal favour, to the effect that in Scotland a lion should
be devoured by his whelps. Twelve mean women and several
wizards were burned at Edinburgh on a charge of having
employed diabolic arts in the service of Mar by roasting a
waxen effigy or puppet of the King.

About the same time many stories of incubi and succubi
seem to have circulated, and are referred to by the historians.
Thus Holinshed, drawing from Hector Boece, has the
following narrative : " There was in the countrie of Mar a
young gentlewoman of excellent beautie, and daughter unto
a nobleman there, refusing sundrie wealthie mariages offered
to her by her father, and other friends. At length she prooved
with child, and being rigorouslie compelled by her parents
to tell who was the father, she confessed that a certain young
man used nightly to come unto her, and kept her companie,
and sometimes in the day also, but how or from whence he
came, or by what meanes he went awaie, she was not able
to declare. Her parents, not greatlie crediting her words,
laid diligent watch, to understand what he was that had
defiled their house ; and within three days after, upon signification given by one of their maidens, that the fornicator was

at that very instant with their daughter, incontinentlie thereupon, making fast the doors, they enter the chamber with a great manie of torches and lights, where they find in their daughter's armes a foul monstrous thing, verie horrible to behold. Here a number coming hastilie in, to behold this evil favoured sight, amongst others, there was a priest of verie honest life, not ignorant (as was thought) in knowledge of holie scripture. This priest (all other being afraid), and some of them running their waies, began to recite the beginning of St. John's Gospell, and coming to these words, *Uerbum caro factum est,* suddenlie the wicked spirit, making a very sore and terrible roaring noise, flue his waies, taking the roofe of the chamber away with him, the hangings and coverings of the bed being also burnt therewith. The gentlewoman was yet preserved, and within three or four daies after was delivered of such a mishapen thing, as the like before had not beene seene, which the midwives and women, such as were present at her labour, to avoid the dishonour of her house, immediately burnt in a great fire, made in the chamber for the same intent."

During the troublous reign of James V (1513–1542), a daughter of a noble house, Janet Douglas, Lady Glamis, was sent to the stake on a charge of having attempted the King's life by poison and evil charms. The fact that she was sister of the Earl of Angus, widow of John Lyon Lord Glamis, and wife of Archibald Campbell of Hepneith, availed her no whit more than her courage and beauty. Found guilty, she was hurried from the bar of the assize to Castle Hill and burned alive as a traitress and a witch. The following record is from an abridgement of the Scotch Criminal Trials : " July 17, 1537.—Janeta Douglas, Domina de Glamis, convicted by the assize, viz. Earl of Athole, Earl of Buchan, Lord Maxwell, Master of Glencairne, Home of Coldinknows, Kirkpatrick of Kirkmichael, Crichton of Ravennis, Ker of Mersington, Earl of Cassillis, Lord Semple, Laird of Raith, Tower of Inverleith, Barclay of Mathers, Edmonston of that ilk, M'Lennan, tutor of Bomby. *Sententia Forisfacturæ.* It is fundin be the said assize, that Janet Douglas, Lady of Glamis, hes committed art and part of the treasonable consperation and magination of the slaughter and destruction of our sovereign Lord his most noble person by poyson, and for art and part of the treasonable assistance, supply, inter-communing, and fortifying of Archibald, sometime Earl of Angus, and George Douglas his brother, rebells and traitors, in a treasonable manner. For the whilk treasonable crimes the said Janet, Lady of Glamis, be forfaulted to our sovereign Lord, her life, lands, goods, moveable and immoveable, and that she shall be had to the Castle-hill of Edinburgh, and there burnt in ane fire to the dead as ane traitor ; and that I gif for doom."

Amongst other dames of high degree who were popularly charged with witchcraft, although never brought to trial, were Lady Buccleuch, who was supposed to have gained the consent of Queen Mary to Darnley's murder by her spells ;[9] Margaret, daughter of Malcolm, third Lord Fleming, Countess of Athole ; and the Countess of Huntley, whom Knox roundly accuses of being a patroness and encourager of sorcerers, and relying greatly upon " hir principall witch, called Jonet." It is not surprising that Knox himself was esteemed a warlock, and the story went that he had attempted to raise " some sanctis " in the churchyard of S. Andrews, where Satan, cornuted like a triple cuckold, leaped out, at which terrible sight the secretary of Knox went mad and presently died. But the dour old fellow was made of sterner stuff ; it may be familiarity had bred contempt. Nicol Burne, a secular priest, in his clever and conclusive *Disputation concerning the Controversit Headdis of Religion* (1580) says that Knox was vulgarly supposed to have employed philtres or some cunning charm to secure the affections of Lord Ochil-tree's daughter, " ane damosil of nobil blude, and he ane auld decrepit creatur of maist bais degree of onie that could be found in the countrey."

The ninth parliament of Queen Mary in 1563 passed an Act which decreed the punishment of death against all witches and consulters with witches. At once prosecutions followed. In 1572 at S. Andrews a notorious witch was burned, who, when a white cloth " like a collore craig with stringes whairon was mony knottis " (obviously *la ghirlanda delle strege*) was taken from her, gave way to utter despair, and cried : " Now I have no holp of myself," adding that she " cared not whether she went to heaven or hell."

In May, 1569, at S. Andrews " a notabil sorceres callit

Nicneven was condemnit to the death, and burnt." Nicneven is the name usually given to the Queen of the Fairies or, as it would be in Scotland, the Queen of Demons, and was probably bestowed on this witch because of her multifold crimes. About the same date " a Frenchman callit Paris, quha was ane of the designeris of the king's death, was hangit in St. Andro, and with him William Steward, lyoun king of armes, for divers pointes of witchcraft and necromancie."

On the 8 November, 1576, Bessie Dunlop of Lyne, in Ayrshire, as she was " make and hevye sair dule with hirself " since her husband and her bairn were ill and her cow had died, met " ane honest, wele, elderlie man, gray bairdit, and had ane gray coitt with Lumbart slevis of the auld fassoun ; ane pair of gray brekis and quhyte schankis gartanit abone the kne ; ane blak bonet on his heid, cloise behind and plane befoir, with silkin laissis drawin throw the lippis thairof ; and ane quhyte wand in his hand."[10]   This was Thomas Reid, who informed her he had been killed at the battle of Pinkie, 1547, and was now a dweller in Elfame, or Fairyland. He saluted her with " Gude day, Bessie." " God speid yow, gude man," says she. " Sancta Marie," says he, " Bessie, quhy makis thow sa grit dule and sair greting for ony wardlie thing ? " She told him her troubles and he comforted her. They met several times, and in the third occasion he endeavoured to persuade her to deny her baptism. That is to say this individual who gave himself out as Thomas Reid was obviously the Chief Officer of the Witches of the district, and was persuading her to join their company. Eventually she did so, and was introduced to the coven, " twelf persounes, aucht wemene and four men : The men wer clad in gentilmennis clething, and the wemene had all plaidis about thame, and wer verrie semelic lyke to se ; and Thome was with thame." Bessie Dunlop owing to Thomas Reid's directions and advice—" Sche culd do nathing, quhill sche had first spokin with Thom "—soon acquired a great reputation throughout the district as a " wise woman " and a midwife of extraordinary powers. This was enough to mark her out as a witch ; " confessit and fylit " (found guilty) she was " convict and brynt " on Castle Hill, Edinburgh.

On the 28 May, 1588, Alison Pearson, in Byre-hills, Fifeshire, was convicted of practising sorcery, and of invoking the foul fiend ; she acknowledged that she had been intimate with the Queen of Elfland for many years, and that she had many friends of her own kin in the Court of Fairy, with whom she had consorted some seven years. After being " wirreit (strangled) at ane staik " she was duly burned, " conuicta et combusta."

On the 22 June, 1590, Catharine Ross, Lady Foullis, was endited at the instance of the King's advocate, together with Hector Munro of Foullis, her own son-in-law, for witchcraft. The first article of accusation urged against her is " the making of two clay pictures, one for the destruction of the young Lady Balnagowan, and getting them enchanted, and shooting of elf-arrow heads at the said persons ; second, for making a stoupfull of poisoned aill for performance of your devillish malice, wherewith ye killed sundry ; third, sending a pigfull of poyson to the house where young Foullis was, the carrier whereof falling, and with the fall breaking the pig, and seeing the liquor, tasted it, and dyed immediately ; and the grasse which grows where it fell, no beast will eat of it ; fourth, for saying that ye would use all means that may be had of God in heaven, or the devill in hell, for destroying Marjory Campbell, the Lady Balnagowan, that the laird might marry the lady Foullis ; also hindering a commission that was granted for tryall of witches, and procuring a suspension thereof, which, if thou had been ane honest woman, thou would never have done." Curiously enough for Scotland both defendants were acquitted.

About a month later, Bessie Roy, nurreych (nurse) to the Leslies of Balquhain was " dilatit " as a notorious witch and " a common awa-taker of women's milk." Amongst other remarkable performances " once in the field, in the presence of sundry other servants, [she] drew a compas, made a hole in the midst of it ; then, by her conjurations, came forth a great worme, and crap over the circle ; then a small one, and also crap over ; then a great one, which sank again into the hole ; which enchantment she interpreted thus to them : The first great worm is the goodman, that he shall live long ; the second is a barne in the ladye's womb, (whereas nobody knew she was with barne,) and that the barne should live ; the last great worme was the goodwyfe, that should die of the birth ; all which came to pass as she said."

Notwithstanding all these circumstantial charges she was pronounced innocent.

In 1590 occurred one of the most extraordinary and notorious witch-trials in Scottish history, or indeed in the whole history of Witchcraft. Nearly seventy persons were more or less directly implicated.[11] The trouble seems to have begun with Geillis Duncan, the servant of Master David Seaton, the deputy-bailiff of Tranent, a small town in Haddington-shire, about ten miles from Edinburgh. Grave suspicion was aroused because she " vsed secretly to be absent and to lye foorth of her Maisters house euery other night :[12] this *Geillis Duncane* took in hand to help all such as were troubled or greeued with any kinde of sicknes or infirmitie : and in short space did perfourme manye matters most miraculous, which thinges forasmuch as she began to doe them vpon a sodaine, hauing neuer doon the like before, made her Maister and others to be in great admiracion, and wondred thereat : by meanes wherof the saide *Dauid Seaton* had his maide in some great suspition, that she did not those things by naturall and lawfull wayes, but rather supposed it to be doone by some extraordinary and vnlawfull meanes.

"Whervpon, her Maister began to growe very inquisitiue, and examined her which way and by what meanes she were able to perfourme matters of so great importance : whereat she gaue him no answere, neuerthelesse, her Maister to the intent that he might the better trye and finde out the trueth of the same, did with the helpe of others, torment her with the torture of the Pilliwinckes vpon her fingers, which is a greeuous torture, and binding or wrinching her head with a corde or roape, which is a most cruell torment also, yet would she not confesse any thing, whereupon they suspecting that she had beene marked by the Diuell (as commonly witches are) made dilligent search about her, and found the enemies marke to be in her fore crag or foreparte of her throate : which being found, she confessed that all her dooings was doone by the wicked allurements and inticements of the Diuell, and that she did them by witchcraft.

"After this her confession, she was committed to prison, where she continued for a season, where immediately she accused these persons following to be notorious witches, and caused them foorthwith to be apprehended one after an other, vidz. *Agnis Sampson* the eldest Witch of them al, dwelling in Haddington, *Agnes Tompson* of Edenborough, Doctor *Fian, alias Iohn Cunningham,* maister of the Schoole at Saltpans in Lowthian, of whose life and strange actes you shall heare more largely in the end of this discourse : these were by the saide *Geillis Duncane* accused, as also *George Motts* wife, dwelling in Saltpans, *Robert Griersonn,* skipper ; and *Iennet Bandilandis ;* with the Porter's wife of Seaton ; the Smith at the brigge Hallis ; with innumerable others in those parts, and dwelling in those bounds aforesaide : of whom some are alreadye executed ; the rest remaine in. prison, to receive the doome of Iudgement at the King's Maiesties will and pleasure.

" The said *Geillis Duncane* also caused *Ewphame Meealrean* to bee apprehended, who conspired and perfourmed the death of her Godfather, and who vsed her art vpon a gentleman being one of the Lords and Iustices of the Session, for bearing good will to her daughter : she also caused to be apprehended one *Barbara Naper,* for bewitching to death *Archibalde,* the last Earle of Angus, who languished to death by witchcraft, and yet the same was not suspected, but that he died of so straunge a disease as the Phisition knewe not how to cure or remedy the same : but of all other the saide witches, these two last before recited, were reputed for as ciuill honest women as anie that dwelled within the Citie of Edenbrough, before they were apprehended. Many other besides were taken, dwelling in Lieth, who are detayned in prison, vntill his Maiesties further will and pleasure be known : of whose wicked dooings you shall particularly heare, which was as followeth.

"This aforeaside *Agnis Sampson* which was the elder Witch, was taken and brought to Haliciud house before the Kings Maiestie and sundry other of the nobility of Scotland, where she was straitly examined, but all the perswasions which the Kings maiestie vsed to her with ye rest of his counsell, might not prouoke or induce her to confesse any thing, but stood stiffely in the deniall of all that was laide to her charge : whervpon they caused her to be conueied awaye to prison, there to receiue such torture as hath been lately prouided for witches in that country : and forasmuch as by due examination of witchcraft and witches in Scotland, it hath latelye

beene found that the Deuill dooth generallye marke them
with a priuie marke, by reason the Witches haue confessed
themselues, that the Diuell dooth lick them with his tung in
some priuy part of their bodie, before hee dooth receiue them
to be his seruants, which marke commonly is giuen them
vnder the haire in some part of their bodye, wherby it may
not easily be found out or seene, although they be searched :
and generally so long as the marke is not seene to those which
search them, so long the parties that hath the marke will
neuer confesse any thing. Therfore by special commaundement this *Agnis Sampson* had all her haire shauen of, in each
parte of her bodie, and her head thrawen with a rope according
to the custome of that Countrye, beeing a paine most greeuous,
which she continued almost an hower, during which time she
would not confesse any thing vntill the Diuels marke[13] was
found vpon her priuities, then she immediately confessed
whatsoeuer was demaunded of her, and iustifying those
persons aforesaid to be notorious witches.

"Item, the saide *Agnis Tompson* [i.e. Sampson] was after
brought againe before the Kings Maiestie and his Counsell,
and being examined of the meetings and detestable dealings
of those witches, she confessed that vpon the night of
Allhollon Euen last, she was accompanied aswell with the
persons aforesaide, as also with a great many other witches,
to the number of two hundreth : and that all they together
went by Sea each one in a Riddle or Ciue, and went in the
same very substantially with Flaggons of wine making merrie
and drinking by the waye in the same Riddles or Ciues, to
the Kerke of North Barrick in Lowthian, and that after they
had landed, tooke handes on the land and daunced this reill
or short daunce, singing all with one voice.

> *Commer, goe ye before, commer, goe ye,*
> *Gif ye will not goe before, commer let me.*

At which time shee confessed, that this *Geilles Duncane* did
goe before them, playing this reill or daunce vpon a small
Trump, called a Iewes Trump, vntill they entered into the
Kerk of north Barrick.

"These confessions made the King in a wonderful admiration, and sent for ye saide *Geillis Duncane*, who, vpon the
like Trump, did play the saide daunce before the Kings

Maiestie, who, in respect of the strangenes of these matters, tooke great delight to be present at their examinations.

"Item, the said *Agnis Tompson* confessed that the Diuell being then at North Barrick Kerke, attending their comming, in the habit or likenes of a man, and seeing that they tarried ouer long, hee at their comming enjoyned them all to a penance, which was, that they should kisse his Buttockes, in sign of duetye to him, which being put ouer the Pulpit barre, euerye one did as he had enjoyned them : and hauing made his vngodly exhortations, wherein he did greatlye inveighe against the King of Scotland, he receiued their oathes for their good and true seruice towards him, and departed : which doone, they returned to Sea, and so home againe."

It should be remarked that we have here well-nigh every circumstance of Witchcraft and the Sabbat orgies. The *osculum infame* as a token of service and submission is frequently alluded to in the witch-trials of all nations. It is specially mentioned by Guazzo in his *Compendium Maleficarum*,[14] by de Lancre, Bodin, Lambert Daneau in his *Dialogue of Witches* (1574 ; English translation, 1575), whence it is quoted by Reginald Scot, and other authorities. That a similar homage was paid to the Master was one of the charges brought against the Templars. Guillaume Edeline, who was tried in 1453, " confessa . . . de sa bonne et fraiche voulenté, avoir fait hommage audit ennemy en l'espèce et semblance d'ung monton, en le baisant par le fondement en signe de révérence et d'hommage."[15] The witches of Poitiers in 1574 " dansoyent à l'entour du bouc : puis vn chacun luy baisoit le derriere."[16] Jeanette d'Abadie in 1609 confessed that this degrading rite was continually repeated, after a renunciation of Christianity which " il luy faisoit renouueller toutes les fois qu'elle alloit au sabbat, puis elle l'alloit baiser au derriere."[17] It would be easy to give a very large number of other instances. Perhaps there is no ceremony which so frequently occurs.

Agnes Sampson, whose confession greatly interested King James, since he himself examined her in person, declared that the Devil hated the King, "by reason the King is the greatest enemy he hath in the worlde," a pretty piece of flattery and compliment. However, she proceeded to detail " sundrye thinges which were so miraculous and strange, as that his

Maiestie saide they were all extreame lyars." Whereupon she gave him a convincing token of her veracity, for " taking his Maiestie a little aside, she declared vnto him the verye woordes which passed betweene the Kings Maiestie and his Queene at Vpslo in Norway the first night of their marriage, with their answere eache to other : whereat the Kinges Maiestie wondered greatlye, and swore by the liuing God, that he beleeued that all the Diuels in hell could not haue discouered the same : acknowledging her woords to be most true, and therefore gaue the more credit to the rest which is before declared."

It is evident that an attempt was made upon the life of the King, and although the gangs did their best to bewitch him to death they were very ready to resort to poison, even if they brewed their venom with all manner of superstitious ceremonies. For Agnes Sampson further " confessed that she tooke a blacke Toade, and did hang the same vp by the heeles, three daies, and collected and gathered the venome as it dropped and fell from it in an Oister shell, and kept the same venome close couered, vntill she should obtaine any parte or peece of foule linnen cloth, that had appertained to the Kings Maiestie, as shirt, handkercher, napkin or any other thing which she practised to obtaine by meanes of one *Iohn Kers*, who being attendant in his Maiesties Chamber, desired him for olde acquaintance betweene them, to helpe her to one or a peece of such a cloth as is aforesaide, which thing the said *Iohn Kers* denyed to helpe her too, saying he could not help her to it. . . . And the saide *Agnis Tompson* [*Sampson*] by her depositions since her apprehension saith, that if shee had obtained any one peece of linnen cloth which the King had worne and fouled, she had bewitched him to death, and put him to such extraordinary paines as if he had beene lying vpon sharp thornes and endes of Needles." The witches also performed incantations to raise a storm that might wreck Queen Anne's ship on her voyage to Scotland. Among other ceremonies they took a cat and christened it, and bound various members of a corpse to the animal, which was afterwards cast into the sea near Leith. Nor did they forget to fashion a wax image of the King in order that as it was melted he might languish away and pine.

Upon the 31 October, All Hallows' Eve, the whole company

of witches assembled at the haunted church of North Berwick. Here they danced " endlang " round the kirk-yard, " and Gelie Duncan playit on ane trump, Johnne Fiene missellit [masked] led the ring ; Agnes Sampsoun and hir dochteris and all the rest following the said Barbara [Napier] to the nowmer of sevin scoir of persounes." In the church the Devil " start vp in the pulpett, lyke ane mekill blak man, haifand ane blak buik in his hand, callit on ewerie ane of thame, desyring thame all to be guid serwandis to him, and he sould be ane guid maister to thame." Agnes Sampson described the Devil as follows : " His body was hard lyk yrn, as they thoct that handled him ; his faice was terrible, his noise lyk the bek of an egle, gret bournyng eyn : his handis and legis were herry, with clawis vpon his handis and feit lyk the griffon." The meeting had been convened to discuss some way to harm and, if possible, kill the King.

The examination of John Fian, who was known as the Devil's Registrar or Secretary, is given in great detail in *Newes from Scotland*, and is full of interest.

" As touching the aforesaide Doctor *Fian, alias Iohn Cunningham*, the examination of his actes since his apprehension, declareth the great subtiltye of the diuell, and therfore maketh thinges to appeere the more miraculous : for being apprehended by the accusation of the saide *Geillis Duncane* aforesaide, who confessed he was their Regester, and that there was not one man suffered to come to the Diuels readinges but onlye he : the saide Doctor was taken and imprisoned, and vsed with the accustomed paine, prouided for those offences, inflicted vpon the rest as is aforesaide.

" First by thrawing of his head with a roape, wherat he would confesse nothing.

" Secondly, he was perswaded by faire means to confesse his follies, but that would preuaile as little.

" Lastly he was put to the most seuere and cruell paine in the world, called the bootes, who after he had receiued three strokes, being enquired if he would confesse his damnable acts and wicked life, his tung would not serue him to speak, in respect wherof the rest of the witches willed to search his tung, vnder which was found two pinnes thrust vp into the head, whereupon the VVitches did laye, *Now is the Charme stinted*, and shewed that those charmed Pinnes were

the cause he could not confesse any thing : then was he
immediatly released of the bootes, brought before the King,
his confession was taken, and his owne hand willingly set
ther-vnto, which contained as followeth.

" First, that at the generall meetinges of those witches, hee
was alwayes preasent : that he was Clarke to all those that
were in subiection to the Diuels seruice, bearing the name
of witches, that alwaye he did take their othes for their true
seruice to the Diuell, and that he wrot for them such matters
as the Diuell still pleased to commaund him.

" Item, he confessed that by his witchcrafte he did bewitch
a Gentleman dwelling neere to the Saltpans, where the said
Doctor kept Schoole, onely for being enamoured of a Gentlewoman whome he loued himselfe : by meanes of which his
Sorcerye, witchcraft and diuelish practises, he caused the
said Gentleman that once in xxiiij. howres he fell into a
lunacie and madnes, and so cotinued one whole hower together, and for the veritie of the same, he caused the Gentleman to be brought before the Kinges Maiestie, which was
vpon the xxiijj. day of December last, and being in Maiesties
Chamber, suddenly hee gaue a great scritch, and fell into a
madnes, sometime bending himselfe and sometime capring so
directly vp, that his heade did touch the seeling of the
Chamber, to the great admiration of his Maiestie, and others
then present : so that all the Gentlemen in the Chamber were
not able to hold him until they called in more helpe, who
together bound him hand and foot ; and suffering the saide
gentleman to lye still untill his furye were past, he, within
an hower, came againe to himselfe, when being demaunded
of the King's Maiestie, what he saw or did all that while
answered, that he had been in a sound sleepe.

" Item, The said Doctor did also confesse, that he had vsed
means sundry times to obtaine his purpose and wicked intent
of the same Gentlewoman, and seeing himselfe disappointed
of his intention, he determined, by all waies he might, to
obtaine the same, trusting by coniuring, witchcraft, and
Sorcery, to obtaine it in this manner.

" It happened this gentlewoman being unmarried, had a
brother who went to schoole with the said Doctor, and calling
his Scholler to him, demaunded if he did lye with his sister,
who answered he did, by meanes whereof he thought to

obtaine his purpose, and therefore secretlye promised to teach him without stripes, so he would obtain for him three haires of his sisters priuities at such time as he should spye best occasion for it : which the youth promised faithfullye to perfourme, and vowed speedily to put it in practise, taking a peece of coniured paper of his maister to lappe them in when he had gotten them : and therevpon the boye practised nightlye to obtaine his maisters purpose, especially when his sister was a sleepe.

" But God who knoweth the secrets of all harts, and reuealeth all wicked and vngodlye practises, would not suffer the intents of this diuilish Doctor to come to that purpose which he supposed it would, and therefore to declare that he was heauilye offended with his wicked entent, did so woorke by the Gentlewomans owne meanes, that in the ende the same was discouered and brought to light : for she being one night a sleepe, and her brother in bed with her, suddenlye cryed out to her mother, declaring that her Brother would not suffer her to sleepe, wherevpon her mother hauing a quick capacitie, did vehemently suspect Doctor *Fians* entention, by reason she was a witche of her selfe, and therefore presently arose, and was very inquisitiue of the boy to vnderstand his intent, and the better to know ye same, did beat him with sundry stripes, wherby he discouered the trueth vnto her.

" The Mother therefore being well practised in witchcrafte, did thinke it most conuenient to meete with the Doctor in his owne Arte, and therevpon tooke the paper from the boy, wherein hee should haue put the same haires, and went to a young Heyfer which neuer had borne Calfe nor gone to the Bull, and with a paire of sheeres, clipped off three haires from the vdder of the Cow, and wrapt them in the same paper, which she againe deliuered to the boy, then willing him to giue the same to his saide Maister, which he immediately did.

" The Schoolemaister so soone as he had receiued them, thinking them indeede to bee the Maides haires, went straight and wrought his arte vpon them : But the Doctor had no sooner doone his intent to them, but presentlye the Hayfer or Cow whose haires they were indeed, came vnto the doore of the Church wherein the Schoolemaister was, into the which the Hayfer went, and made towards the Schoolemaister, leaping and dauncing vpon him, and following him foorth of the church and to what place so euer he went, to the great admiration of all the townes men of Saltpans, and many other who did beholde the same.

" The reporte whereof made all men imagine that hee did woorke it by the Diuell, without whom it could neuer have beene so sufficientlye effected ; and thereupon the name of the said Doctor *Fian* (who was but a very yong man) began to growe so common among the people of Scotland, that he was secretlye nominated for a notable Coniurer.

" All which although in the beginning he denied, and would not confesse, yet having felt the pain of the bootes, (and the charme stinted, as aforesayd), he confessed all the aforesaid to be most true, without producing anie witnesses to justifie the same, & thervpon, before the kings maiesty, he subscribed the sayd confessions with his owne hande, which, for truth, remaineth vpon record in *Scotland.*

" After that the depositions and examinations of the sayd doctor *Fian, Alias Cuningham,* was taken, as alreadie is declared, with his own hand willingly set therevnto, hee was, by the master of the prison, committed to ward, and appointed to a chamber by himselfe, where, forsaking his wicked wayes, acknowledging his most vngodly lyfe, shewing that he had too much folowed the allurements and entisements of sathan, and fondly practised his conclusions by coniuring, witchcraft, inchantment, sorcerie, and such like, hee renounced the deuill and all his wicked workes, vowed to leade the life of a Christian, and seemed newly connected towards God.

" The morrow after, vpon conference had with him, he granted that the deuill had appeared unto him in the night before, appareled all in blacke, with a white wand in his hande, and that the deuill demaunded of him if hee would continue his faithfull seruice, according to his first oath and promise made to that effect. Whome (as hee then sayd) he vtterly renounced to his face, and sayde vnto him in this manner, *Auoide Satan, auoide,* for I haue listned too much vnto thee, and by the same thou hast vndone mee, in respect whereof I vtterly forsake thee. To whome the deuill answered, *That once ere thou die thou shalt bee mine.* And with that (as he sayde) the deuill brake the white wande, and immediatly vanished foorth of his sight.

" Thus all the daie this Doctor *Fian* continued verie

solitarie, and seemed to haue care of his owne soule, and would call vppon God, shewing himselfe penitent for his wicked life, neuerthelesse the same night hee founde such meanes, that hee stole the key of the prison doore and chamber in the which he was, which in the night hee opened and fled awaie to the Salt pans, where hee was alwayes resident, and first apprehended. Of whose sodaine departure when the Kings maiestie had intelligence, hee presently commanded diligent inquirie to bee made for his apprehension, and for the better effecting thereof, hee sent publike proclamations into all partes of his lande to the same effect. By meanes of whose hot and harde pursuite, he was agayn taken and brought to prison, and then being called before the kings highnes, hee was reexamined as well touching his departure, as also touching all that had before happened.

" But this Doctor, notwithstanding that his owne confession appeareth remaining in recorde vnder his owne handewriting, and the same therevnto fixed in the presence of the Kings maiestie, and sundrie of his Councell, yet did hee vtterly denie the same.

" Whereupon the kinges maiestie perceiving his stubbourne wilfulnesse, conceiued and imagined that in the time of his absence hee had entered into newe conference and league with the deuill, his master, and that hee had beene agayne newly marked, for the which he was narrowly searched, but it coulde not in anie wise be founde, yet, for more tryall of him to make him confesse, hee was commaunded to have a most straunge torment, which was done in this manner following.

" His nailes vpon all his fingers were riuen and pulled off with an instrument called in Scottish a *Turkas*, which in England wee call a payre of pincers, and vnder euerie nayle there was thrust in two needels ouer euen up to the heads. At all which tormentes notwithstanding the Doctor neuer shronke anie whit, neither woulde he then confesse it the sooner for all the tortures inflicted vpon him.

" Then was hee, with all conuenient speed, by commandement, conuaied againe to the torment of the bootes, wherein hee continued a long time, and did abide so many blowes in them, that his legges were crushte and beaten togeather as small as might bee, and the bones and flesh so brused, that the bloud and marrowe spouted forth in great abundance, whereby they were made vnseruiceable for euer. And notwithstanding al these grieuous paines and cruell torments hee would not confesse anie thing, so deepely had the deuill entered into his heart, that hee vtterly denied all that which he had before auouched, and woulde saie nothing therevnto but this, that what hee had done and sayde before, was onely done and sayde for feare of paynes which he had endured.

" Upon great consideration therefore taken by the Kings maiestie and his Councell, as well for the due execution of iustice vppon such detestable malefactors, as also for example sake, to remayne a terrour to all others heereafter, that shall attempt to deale in the lyke wicked and vngodlye actions, as witchcraft, sorcery, cuniuration, & such lyke, the sayde Doctor *Fian* was soone after araigned, condemned, and adiudged by the law to die, and then to bee burned according to the lawe of that lande, prouided in that behalfe. Wherevpon hee was put into a carte, and beeing first strangled, hee was immediatly put into a great fire, being readie prouided for that purpose, and there burned in the Castle hill of *Edenbrough* on a saterdaie in the ende of Ianuarie last past. 1591."

Agnes Sampson was also executed. Of the many other persons implicated Barbara Napier, a woman of good family, was acquitted, but Euphemia McCalyan, the daughter of Lord Cliftonhall, whose trial took place on the 9 June, 1591, was burned alive on 25 June. The Justiciary Record has the following : " Euphame Maccalzeane, (her father was ane advocate) spouse to Patrick Maccalzeane, *alias* Moscropt, for many treasonable conspiracies undertaken by witchcraft, to have destroyed the king's person by a pictur of wax, and have bereft his majesty of his life. *Item*, for enterprysing to kill her husband, that she might gett another goodman, and for drowning a boat betwixt Leith and Kinghorne, wherein were 60 persons lost ; convict of thir, and many other monstrous points, sentenced to be burnt quick to the death, and all hir lands and goods forfaulted."

I have dwelt upon this famous trial at length because it is obvious that here there was a deep-laid and widespread plot, and high treason is commingled with the sorcery. There can be no doubt that the whole body of witches combined

to attempt the life of the King by any possible means they
could. And as Charles Kirkpatrick Sharpe pointed out it is
certain that the brain which contrived and the hidden hand
which directed the conspiracy were those of Francis Stewart,
Earl of Bothwell, who was aiming at the throne. It was he,
probably, who played the rôle of the Devil in North Berwick
kirk. His connexion with the sorcerers seems to have been
common knowledge at the time, and in her confession Agnes
Sampson explicitly avowed that she made a wax image,
saying : " This is King James the sext, ordonit to be consumed at the instance of a noble man Francis Erle Bodowell."
And from the pulpit the Devil anxiously demanded to know
what effect the melting of the figure had, whilst some present
expressed their surprise that he could not harm the King.
Even in after life, when he was poor and exiled, Bothwell's
fame as an occulist persisted. Sandys, speaking of Calabria
in the year 1610, remarks : " Here a certaine *Calabrian*
hearing that I was an *English* man, came to me, and would
needs persuade me that I had insight in magicke : for that
Earle *Bothel* was my countryman, who liues at *Naples*, and
is in these parts famous for suspected negromancie."[18]

These trials, no doubt, gave King James the idea of writing
his *Dæmonologie, in Forme of a Dialogue, Diuided into three
Bookes,* Edinburgh, 1597. In " The Preface to the Reader "
the royal author without circumlocution or parade thus
explicitly states his purpose : *The fearefull aboundinge at this
time in this countrie, of these detestable slaues of the Deuill, the
Witches or enchaunters, hath moved me (beloued reader) to
dispatch in post, this following treatise of mine, not in any wise
(as I protest) to serue for a shew of my learning & ingine, but
onely (mooued of conscience) to preasse thereby, so farre as
I can, to resolue the doubting harts of many ; both that such
assaultes of Sathan are most certainly practized, & that the
instrumentes thereof, merits most severly to be punished : against
the damnable opinions of two principally in our age, wherof the
one called SCOT*[19] *an Englishman, is not ashamed in publike
print to deny, that ther can be such a thing as Witch-craft : and
so mainteines the old error of the Sadducees, in denying of
spirits. The other called VVIERVS,*[20] *a German Phisition,
sets out a publick apologie for al these craftes-folkes, whereby,
procuring for their impunitie, he plainely bewrayes himselfe to*

*haue bene one of that profession. And for to make this treatise
the more pleasaunt and facill, I haue put it in forme of a Dialogue, which I haue diuided into three bookes : The first speaking
of Magie in general, and Necromancie in special. The second
of Sorcerie and Witch-craft : and the thirde, conteines a discourse of all these kindes of spirits, & Spectres that appeares &
trobles persones : together with a conclusion of the whol work.
My intention in this labour, is only to proue two things, as
I haue alreadie said: the one, that such diuelish artes haue bene
and are. The other, what exact trial and seuere punishment
they merite.*

" Philomathes and Epistemon reason the matter," and it
must be confessed there is something very naïve in the
ingenuous efforts of the former to display the latter's erudition
and piety. No doubt several of the arguments are simple
words enough and not by any means convincing, nor do they
lose one jot of their artlessness by being couched in the
King's quaint speech, and again some of the talk is rank folly
and (quite unconsciously) profane to boot,[21] but these
reservations granted, we have a quota of clever pages and
here and there a shrewd hit. In many passages King James
has borrowed from the Continental demonologists, whom he
read with more diligence than acumen. For all his zeal and
dextrous learning one feels that there is something just a
little superficial in his grasp of the more scholarly writers and
theologians. And yet there is certainly a freshness in his
approach, and a brisk assurance in his methods, which are
not without their value and attraction. Perhaps we might
sum up the matter by saying that the treatise is able rather
than profound. It is rather " the small clack of Pistolet "
than " the rummishing shot of a Cannon." Upon his accession
to the throne of England the *Dæmonologie* at once became
authoritative, and there can be no doubt that the book had
a great influence and was used by officials as a text-book
on the subject.

It is curious to note that, in spite of himself, James I was
bound to confess the power of Catholic exorcisms, which he
attempts to explain away by some very lame evasion, and
with an uneasy shrug and a stammer that " such things are
' fashious and feckles to recite,' " he is glad to hasten on to
a description " of Spirites called the *Phairie*."

Under King James the prosecution of witches in Scotland increased apace, and it is notable how many persons of high degree were accused of consulting with hags and enchanters. On 24 June, 1596, John Stewart, Master of Orkney, and brother of the Earl, " was dilatit of consulting with umquhile Margaret Balfour, ane wich, for the destructionne of Patrik Erll of Orkney, be poysoning." In the dittay she is called " Alysoun Balfour, ane knawin notorious wich." After having been severely tortured she confessed all they desired, but when released she recanted, which availed her nothing. " The tyme of hir first deposition sche was tortorit, and severall tymes in the caspieclaws, and sindrie tymes taken out of them deid, and out of all remembrance either of guid or evill ; as lykewayes hir guidman being in the stokes, hir son torturit in the buits, and hir daughter put in the pilnie-winks, wherwith sche and they were swa kepit and tormentit, that pairtlie to eschew ane grittar torment and pownischment ; and upon promis of hir lyffe and guid deids be the said person, falslie agains hir saul and consciens sche mayd the confession, and na otherwayes ; for the qlk she askit the Lord mercy and forgivenes, and constantlie deitt yratt."

So Alison Balfour was burned on the Castle Hill, 16 December, 1594, whilst the Master of Orkney seems to have escaped all penalties.

In October, 1596, Alison Jollie was executed as a witch, and in the following month Christian Stewart was " strangled and burned " for casting a spell upon one Ruthven, whereof he died.

At Aberdeen one man and twenty-three women were sent to the stake within a few months on accumulated charges of Witchcraft. The archives faithfully detail the expenses for " peattis, tar barrelis, fir, and coallis " to which the town was put on account of these executions.

To catalogue, however briefly, the condemnations and executions year after year, month after month, would be a task tedious in its repetitions, distressful in its details, and superfluous in its result. A few typical cases, not one hundredth part of those on record, must be taken to exemplify the roll of death.

In March, 1607, Isobel Grierson was burnt and her ashes scattered in the wind, after being convicted of going one night into the house of Adam Clarke, in Prestonpans, in the likeness of his own cat, accompanied with a mighty rabble of cats, which, by their noise, dreadfully affrighted Adam, his wife, and maid-servant, the last of whom, the Devil, in the shape of a black man, dragged up and down by the hair of the head.

On 27 May, 1608, Beigis Tod, who had long been a frequenter of Sabbats, was burned at Lang Nydrie. In the same year the Earl of Mar informed the Privy Council that a number of women who had been arrested at Brechin and accused of sorcery, being put to " ane assize and convict albeit they persevered constant in their deniall to the end, yet they wes burnet *quick* after sic ane crewell maner that sum of thame deit in dispair, renunceand and blasphemand, and vtheris, half brunt, brak out of the fyre and wes cassin *quick* into it againe, quhill they war brunt to the deid." A goodly specimen of Calvinistic cruelty, and as horrible a tale, I think, as any to be met with in the annals of Witchcraft.

In 1616 Jonka Dyneis of Shetland, Katherine Jones, dochter of Shetland, Elspeth Reoch of Orkney, Agnes Scottie, Marable Couper, Agnes Yullock, and a large number of other women were sent to the stake in the north of Scotland.

In 1622 was executed Margaret Wallace of Glasgow, who long laid under suspicion on account of her consorting with Christian Grahame, a known and notorious witch. The chief charge seems to have been that they removed an ailment " from Margaret Muir, a bairne; to which end they went about 12 at night to a yard, and there used their devilish charms, whereby the disease was removed from the bairne."

Eight years later at Edinburgh there was executed on a very similar charge a warlock named Alexander Drummond, " indweller in the Kirktown of Auchterarder, as curing thereby of frenzies, the falling evil, persons mad, distracted, or possest with fearfull apparitions, as St. Antonie's fire, the sickness *noli-me-tangere*, cancers, worms, glengores, with other uncouth diseases, upon many persons ; also for burieng a quick ox for effectuating his sorcerie, and of pleuch-irons upon merches betwixt two lairds' lands, for curing of madness ; also for having a familiar spirit attending him neir this fifty yeiris. He confesses that such and such cures he did, but denies any incantation or charme therein. For verification of the dittay, produced his own depositiones, then the depositiones of an hundred of witnesses ; whereupon, convict and burnt."

" In the same year, Catharine Oswald, spouse to Robert Atchison, in Niddrie, was brought to triall for being *habite and repute* a witch, and defamed as such by Elizabeth Stevenson, *alias* Toppock, who was burnt for the crime, ' hersell an intimate ally of the said Catharine.' " And so Catharine Oswald was duly hanged, and her body burned.

In 1629 a notorious wizard, Alexander Hunter, or Hamilton, *alias* Hatteraik (which last name was given him by the Devil, it seems), was burned alive at Castle Hill. For many years he had been the chief gossip and abettor of all the worst witches in Scotland, and it is truly wonderful that he escaped his fate so long. His tale is told in *Relation XVII* of *Satan's Invisible World Discovered*, and Sinclar's account is so racy it may well be given in his own words :

" Anent *Hattaraik*, an Old Warlock.

" *This mans name was* Sandie Hunter, *who called himself* Sandie Hamilton, *and it seems was called* Hattaraik *by the* Devil, *and so by others as a nick-name. He was first a Neat-herd in* East-Lothian, *to a gentle-man there. He was much given to* Charming *and cureing of Men and Beasts, by* Words *and* Spels. *His* Charms *sometimes succeeded sometimes not. On a day, herding his kine upon a Hill side in the summer time, the* Devil *came to him in form of a* Mediciner, *and said,* Sandie, you have too long followed my trade, and never acknowledged me for your Master. You must now take on with me, and I will make you more perfect in your Calling. *Whereupon the man gave up himself to the* Devil, *and received his Mark with his new name. After this he grew very famous throw the Countrey for his* Charming *and cureing of diseases in Men and Beasts, and turned a vagrant fellow, like a jockie* [a Scottish wandering beggar], *gaining* Meal, Flesh, *and* Money *by his* Charms, *such was the ignorance of many at that time. Whatever House he came to, none durst refuse* Hattaraik *an alms, rather for his ill, than his good. One day he came to the* Yait* *of* Samuelstoun, *when some Friends after Dinner were going to Horse. A young Gentleman brother to the Lady seeing him, switcht him about the ears, saying, '* You *Warlok Cairle*, what have you to do here ? ' *Whereupon the fellow goes away grumbling, and was overheard*

* i.e. gate.

to say, you shall dear buy this ere it be long. This was Damnum
Minatum. *The young Gentle-man conveyed his Friends a far
way off, and come home that way again, where he supt. After
supper taking his horse and crossing* Tine-Water *to go home ;
he rides throw a shadowy piece of a* Haugh, *commonly called the*
Allers, *and the evening being some-what dark, he met with some
persons there that begat a dreadful consternation in him, which
for the most part, he would never reveal. This was* malum
secutum. *When he came home, the Servants observed terror and
fear in his Countenance. The next day he became distracted and
was bound for several days. His Sister, the Lady* Samuelstown,
hearing of it, was heard say, surely that knave *Hattaraik* is
the cause of his trouble. Call for him in all haste. *When he
had come to her,* Sandie, *says she,* what is this you have done
to my Brother *William ? I told him, says he,* I should make
him repent his striking of me at the yait lately. *She giving
the Rogue fair words, and promising him his Pock full of* Meal,
with Beaf, *and* Cheese, *perswaded the Fellow to cure him again.
He undertook the business, but I must first (says he) have one
of his Sarks, which was soon gotten. What Pranks he plaid
with it cannot be known. But within a short while the Gentleman
recovered his Health. When* Hattarraik *came to receive his
wadges, he told the Lady,* your Brother William shal quickly go
off the Countrey but shall never return. *She knowing the
Fellows Prophesies to hold true, caused her Brother make a
Disposition to her of all his Patrimony, to the defrauding of his
younger brother* George. *After that this* Warlock *had abused
the Countrey for a long time, he was at last apprehended at*
Dunbar, *and brought into* Edinburgh, *and burnt upon the*
Castle-hill." As pestilent a rogue, I doubt not, as any who
has robbed, threatened, blackmailed, and perhaps poisoned
his victims.

During the following decade trial follows trial, and in very
few cases were the accused acquitted. It is altogether
exceptional to find such a result as the verdict of " Not
guilty " which in 1634 was returned against Elizabeth
Bathgate, the wife of a maltster in Eimouth, whose dittay
contained eighteen damning articles. Sir George Horne of
Manderston made himself very conspicuous in the prosecution
of suspects, and upwards of twenty executions are attributed
to his private zeal. The prickers, too, men who hunted down

witches and searched them for the Devil's mark, that callous spot into which pins were thrust to test its sensibility, the guilty feeling no touch at all, were now very much to the fore. The expert offices of Mr. John Kincaid of Tranent were greatly in request, and he had a serious rival in Mr. John Balfour, of Corhouse, whose technical knowledge, however, does not appear on every occasion to have been rated as highly as his own valuation. Mr. John Dick was yet another pricker who showed exemplary zest in the pursuit of his profession.

The year 1643, in particular, seems to have been marked by a fiercer onslaught than ever before. Perhaps Puritanism was thus celebrating its unchecked power.

" About this time many witches are taken in Anstruther, Dysart, Culros, St. Andrews, and other parts on the coast side of Fife. They made strange confessions, and were burnt to the death."[22] One John Brugh, " a notorious warlock in the parachin of Fossoquhy, by the space of 36 years," was *wirriet at a stake and brunt*, 1643. The same year, Janet Barker, and Margaret Lauder, " indwellers and servands in Edinburgh, were convicted of witchcraft. They confessed that one Janet Cranstone, a notorious witch, introduced them to the devil, who promised, that they should be as trimlie cled as the best servands in Edinburgh."

Marion Cumlaquoy of Birsay was haled before the Orkney courts for bewitching crops and corn. She had been seen to turn herself three several times " withershins " in Robert Carstairs' house, and that year his barley was " blew and rottin." And so she went to the fire.

Janet Brown confessed amongst other iniquities that she had cast a spell upon James Hutton and Janet Scott, and her doom was sealed. Marion Peebles, a hideous hag, " a wicked, devilish, fearful, and abominable curser," had wrecked boats and drowned sailors to whom she bare " ane deadlie and veneficial malice." She cast her blear eyes upon a cow, and it " crappit togidder till no lyfe was leukit for her." Wretched was the fate of those who came under her malison. Her neighbours pined and languished, and were racked with aches and agues in every limb. But at length they took her, and justice sentenced her to be hanged, the body being burned.[23]

At Edinburgh Agnes Fynnie, a beldame of the vilest repute

who dwelt at the Potterrow Port, was prosecuted for witch-craft. Her dittay contained twenty heads, the last of which in fact sums up all the rest : " The 20*th* article is a generall, for beiring companie with the devill these 28 years bypast ; for consulting with him for laying on and taking off diseases, als weill on men as women and bestiall, which is nottourly known. *Item*, it is confest by hirself, that she has been commonlie called a rank witch these many years bygane, and has been sua diffamed, repute, and halden."

Agnes Fynnie was " brunt to the deid " and her ashes scattered to the four winds. Year after year the witch fires blazed redly upon Castle Hill, and the prosecution spread even more widely over the northern counties of Scotland, where the frightened justices abetted and spurred on by dour and fanatical ministers saw Satan at every turn.

In August, 1658, four women, " ane of them a maiden," were burnt on the Castle Hill ; and soon after five more from Dunbar ; and then again nine from Tranent, all confessing to commerce with the Devil.

In 1661 occurred the celebrated case of the Forfar witches, whose great Sabbats were held four times a year at Candlemas, Holy Cross Day, Lammas, and All Saints. Other meetings were more frequently held, particularly in Forfar churchyard at midnight, where, as Helen Guthrie confessed, " they daunced togither, and the ground under them was all fyre flauchter, and Andrew Watson hade his vsuale staff in his hand, altho he be a blind man yet he daunced alse nimblie as any of the companye, and made also great miriement by singing his old ballads, and that Isobell Shyrrie did sing her song called Tinkletum Tankletum ; and that the divill kist every one of the women." On another occasion they met at the house of a witch named Mary Rynd, " and sat doune together at the table, the divell being present at the head of it ; and some of them went to Johne Benny's house, he being a brewer, and brought ale from hence . . . and others of them went to Alexander Hieche's and brought aqua vitæ from thence, and thus made them selfes mirrie." It would seem that nearly thirty persons were implicated.

In 1662 we have the revelations of Issobell Gowdie, whose four depositions concerning the Auldearne witches were taken between the 13 April and the 27 May. Her whole confession,

which is very minute and circumstantial, was not forced
from her by any threats or torture but given voluntarily,
clearly, and with precision. There can be no doubt it is
substantially true, and we have the fullest details upon almost
every point of Witchcraft, the Sabbats, minor meetings,
adoration of the Devil, feastings, dances, sexual rites and
obscenities, the making of wax images, instruction in spells
and charms. It is unfortunate that it seems hardly possible
to identify the Grand Master, about whom these gangs of
witches had collected, but he was certainly an occultist who
had devoted much time and study to the black art, and who
insisted upon unswerving loyalty from his subjects.

One of the most astounding and terrible cases in the whole
annals of Scottish Witchcraft is that of Major Thomas Weir,
who was burned alive for his hideous crimes at the Gallowlie
between Edinburgh and Leith, on Monday, 11 April, 1670.[24]
The following account has been collected from various
authorities, of whom the most pertinent are contemporary,
and actually heard the confession of these monstrous doings,
whose horror dwelt as a long and lively tradition well within
the memory of the nineteenth century.

Thomas Weir, one of the most celebrated Wizards of
Scotland, was born near Lanark, in Clydesdale. Of his father,
or grandfather, mention is made in the *Memoirs of the
Somerville Family, written by James, eleventh Lord Somerville*
(edited, with illustrative notes, by Sir Walter Scott, and
published in 1815, 2 vols., 8vo), who, recording a proffer of
alliance tendered by Lockhart of Lee to Gilbert, ninth Lord
Somerville, whose daughter Lockhart wished to secure as a
wife to his eldest son, says, " It was supposed that Thomas
Weir of Kirktoune, Lee's own brother-in-law, was both the
traytor that betrayed, and the person that obstructed the
going on of this marriage." The proofs of Weir's treachery
respecting the marriage, and also the sale of Lord Somerville's
estate to the Earl of Marr, may be found in the second volume
of the Memoirs, pp. 73–77. Weir, the wizard, was a lieutenant
in the Puritanical army sent by the Scottish Covenanting
Estates in 1641, to assist in suppressing the Irish papists.[25]
He was also an eminent promoter of the " *Western Remonstrance,*" in the year 1650, and it is recorded, " To these
principles he stuck as close, as to the Devil himself ; insomuch

that when the government of the Church was restored, he avowedly renounced the communion of it, and endeavoured to widen the schism to the utmost of his power. He could not so much as endure to look upon an Orthodox Minister ; but when he met any of them in the street, he would pull his hat over his eyes in a Pharisaical kind of indignation and contempt."

In the years 1649–50 he had the great trust of the " Guards of the City of Edinburgh " committed unto him under the quality of *Major*, and from that time to the day of his infamous death, was always called by the name of *Major Weir*. " He behaved himself in this office with great cruelty and insolence towards the Loyal party, being very active in discovering and apprehending the Cavaliers, and bringing them to be arraigned and tried for their lives. He used to insult and triumph over them in their miseries, and persecute them with all manner of sarcasms and reproaches, when they were led out like victims to public execution. In particular, the barbarous villain treated the Heroic Marquess of Montrose, with all imaginable insolence and inhumanity, when he lay in prison, making his very calamities an argument, that God, as well as man, had forsaken him, and calling him *Dog, Atheist, Traytor, Apostate, Excommunicate Wretch*, and many more such intolerable names. This cruel manner after which he used to outrage the poor Royalists, passed among the people for extraordinary zeal ; and made them consider him as a singular worthy whom God had raised up to support the *Cause*. He studied the art of dissimulation, and Hypocrisie, always affecting a formal gravity and demureness in his looks and deportment, and employing a vast and tenacious memory which God had given him, in getting without Book such words, and phrases of the Holy Scriptures, as might serve best in all companies to make him pass for an Holy and gifted man. He had acquired a particular gracefulness in whining and sighing, above any of the sacred clan, and had learned to deliver himself upon all serious occasions in a far more ravishing accent than any of their Ministers could attain unto. By these and other Hypocritical arts he had got such a name for sanctity, and devotion, that happy was the man with whom he would converse, and blessed was the family in which he would vouchsafe to pray. For he pretended to pray only in the families of such as were Saints of the highest form ; insomuch, that the Brethren and Sisters of these precincts would strive who should have him to exercise in their houses, and of those that lived at a greater distance, some would come forty or fifty miles to have the happiness to hear him pray. He had indeed a wonderful fluency in extemporary Prayer, and what through Enthusiastical phrases, and what through Extasies, and raptures, into which he would appear transported, he made the amazed people presume he was acted by the spirit of God. Besides praying, he used to exhort, and bless the families in which he prayed ; but he never undertook to preach in them, for fear of invading the Ministerial Providence ; which certainly would have offended the *Kirk !* "

This base hypocrite professed wonderful sanctity ; he was known as one of the " Bowhead Saints," and used to pray in House-Conventicles ; though it appears, that he partially accommodated himself to the Prelatic rulers. According to a contemporary account, " His garb was still a cloak, and somewhat dark, and he never went without his staff. He was a tall black man, and ordinarily looked down to the ground ; *a grim countenance, and a big nose.* At length he became so notoriously regarded among the Presbyterian strict sect, that if four met together, be sure Major Weir was one. He had got himself the privilege, under a pretence of praying and exhortation, to go to their houses, and into their bed-chambers when he pleased ; and it was his practice to visit married women at such times especially as their husbands were from home. At private meetings he prayed to admiration, which made many of that stamp court his converse. Many resorted to his house to join with him, and hear him pray ; but it was observed that he could not officiate in any holy duty without the black staff, or rod, in his hand, and leaning upon it, which made those who heard him pray admire his flood in prayer, his ready extemporary expression, his heavenly gesture ; so that he was thought more angel than man, and was termed by some of the holy sisters ordinarily *Angelical Thomas !* " He never married ; but for many years he dwelt along with his sister, Jean Weir, in a house near to the Bow Head of Edinburgh. After this manner, and in this mighty reputation, he lived till the year 1670, which was the 70th year of his age. After a life characterized externally by all the graces of devotion, but polluted in secret by crimes of the most revolting nature, and which little needed the addition of wizardry to excite the horror of living men, Major Weir fell stricken, it would appear, with insanity, which affected his mind so much, that he was no longer able to endure the remorse of his awakened conscience ; but to ease the inquietudes of his guilty mind was forced to accuse himself, which he first of all did among those of his own party, and desired them to bring him to public justice to expiate for his abominable crimes. But they, considering what a confounding scandal, and dishonour the hypocrisy of such an eminent professor would reflect upon the whole sect, did with all possible care and industry strive to conceal the Major's condition, which they did for several months, till one of their own ministers, whom they esteemed more forward than wise, revealed the secret to Sir Andrew Ramsay, Lord Abbotshall, then Provost of Edinburgh, who judging human nature uncapable of such horrid crimes, as the minister told him the Major had confessed, concluded he was fallen into a phrenzy, or high degree of melancholy, and therefore courteously sent some physicians of his own perswasion and acquaintance to visit him, and physic him for his distempered brain. But the physicians returning to the Provost, assured him that the Major was in good health, and that he was free of hypochondriac distempers, and had as sound intellectuals as ever he had had, and that they believed his distemper was only an exulcerated conscience, which could not be eased till he was brought to condign punishment, as with cryings and roarings he desired to be. Afterwards, the Provost, for his further satisfaction, sent some Conventicle-Ministers to enquire into his condition, and make a report thereof ; who, finding it impossible to disguise the matter, which was now town-talk, told his Lordship that the Major was not affected with melancholy ; but that the terrors of God which were upon his soul, urged him to confess and accuse himself. The Provost thereupon began to conclude, that he had good grounds to take public notice of this affair ; and therefore, without further enquiry, sent the guards of the city to seize upon the Major and his sister Jean, who was involved in his confessions, and carry them both to the public gaol.

It is recorded—" When they were seized, she desired the guards to keep him from laying hold on a certain staff, which, she said, if he chanced to get into his hands he would certainly drive them all out of doors, notwithstanding all the resistance they could make." This magical staff was all of one piece, with a crooked head of thornwood. She said he received it of the Devil, and did many wonderful things with it, particularly that he used to lean upon it in his hypocritical prayers ; and after they were committed, she still desired it might be kept from him ; because if he were once master of it again, he would certainly grow obdurate, and retract the confession which he had so publicly made. She also confessed in prison, "·that she and her brother had made a compact with the Devil ; and that on the 7th of September, 1648, they were both transported from Edinburgh to Musselburgh, and back again, in a coach and six horses, which seemed all of fire, and that the Devil then told the Major of the defeat of our army at Preston in England ; which he confidently reported in most of its circumstances several days before the news had arrived here. This prediction did much increase the high opinion the people began to have of him, and served him to make them believe that, like Moses, he had been with God in the Mount, and had a spirit of prophecy, as well as of prayer. But as for herself, she said, she never received any other benefit by her commerce with the Devil, than a constant supply of an extraordinary quantity of yarn, which she was sure (she said) to find ready for her upon the spindle, whatever business she had been about."

When in the gaol they were visited by persons of all sorts and qualities, Clergymen, Laymen, Physicians, Lawyers, Conforming and Non-Conforming Ministers, who all flocked thither to see this monster, and discourse with him about his horrible crimes.

While the wretched man lay in prison, he made no scruple to disclose the particulars of his guilt, but refused to address himself to the Almighty for pardon. He acknowledged his hypocrisie, by which he had deluded men and mocked God, declaring that in all his life he had never prayed to God in private, nor had he any power to speak when he attempted to do it ; although he had such an extraordinary and charming utterance in his solemn conventicle-prayers. He also confessed that he never bowed his knee to God at his own, or other men's prayers ; and none of his own party can remember that at any devotion, even when he seemed most rapturous, they ever saw him kneel. . . . All the while he was in prison he lay under violent apprehension of the heavy wrath of God, which put him into that which is properly called despair ; a despair which made him hate God, and desist from duty to Him, and with which the damned souls in hell are reasonably supposed to be constantly affected. In this sense he was desperate, and therefore would admit neither *Church* nor *Conventicle-Ministers* to pray for him, or discourse with him about the infinite mercy of God, and the possibility of the forgiveness of his sins. Much less could he endure to be exhorted to repent, or be brought to entertain any thought of repentance, telling all the world, that he had sinned himself beyond all possibility of repentance, and pardon ; that he was already damned, that he was sure his condemnation to eternal burnings was already pronounced in heaven, and that the united prayers of all the saints in heaven and earth would be vain, and insignificant, if they were offered to God in his behalf. So that when some charitable ministers of the city, by name the present Bishop of Galloway, and present Dean of Edinburgh, were resolved to pray before him for his repentance, and pardon, against his consent, he was with much difficulty withheld from interrupting of them in their devotions, and the posture he put himself in when they began to pray, was to lye upon his bed in a most stupid manner, with his mouth wide open ; and when prayers were ended, being asked if he had heard them and attended to them, he told them, " They were very troublesome, and cruel to him, and that he neither heard their devotions, nor cared for it, nor could be the better for all the prayers that Men or Angels could offer up to heaven upon his account." It was his interest to believe there was no God ; and therefore to ease the torments of his mind, he attempted now and then to comfort, and flatter up himself into this absurd belief. For he was sometimes observed to speak very doubtfully about his existence ; in particularly to say, that if it were not for the terrors which he found tormenting him within, he should scarce believe there was a God.

Being with great tenderness and compassion besought by

one of the city ministers, that he would not so resolvedly destroy himself, by dispairing of God's mercy, which upon repentance had been granted to Murtherers, Adulterers, Sodomists, Bestialists, nay, to those that had denyed Christ ; he replyed in anger, " Trouble me no more with your beseeching of me to repent, for I know my sentence of damnation is already sealed in Heaven, and I feel myself so hardned within, that if I might obtain pardon of God, and all the Glories of Heaven for a single wish that I had not committed the sins, with the sence whereof I am so tormented, yet I could not prevail with myself to make that single wish. And were your soul in my soul's stead, you would find your exhortations impertinent, and troublesome, for I find nothing within me but blackness and darkness, Brimstone, and burning to the bottom of Hell."

They had not been long in prison before they were brought to Trial, which was on the 9th April, 1670. They were tried before the learned civilian Mr. William Murray, and Mr. John Prestoune, Advocates, who were made Judges by commission for that time. They were prosecuted by his Majesty's Advocate, Sir John Nisbett, and the Jury by whom they were tried was Gideon Shaw, Stationer ; James Penderer, Vintner ; James Thomson, Feltmaker ; Robert Brown, Stationer ; James Brown, Feltmaker ; Robert Johnston, Skinner ; John Clighorn, merchant ; with many more sufficient Citizens of Edinburgh. The Court being set, the Libel or Indictment against the Major was read. After setting forth his disgusting crimes, under four different heads, it proceeds thus : " It is no small aggravation, if anie can be, of so great wickedness and impietie, that being guiltie and conscious to himself of so great hyneous abominations, and being altogidder void of religione and fear of God, he hade the confidence, or rather impudence, to pretend to fear God in a singular and eminent way, and did make professione of strickness, pietie, and puritie, beyond others ; and did presume and tak upon you to pray publickly in many companies, and in the houses of youre friends, neighbours, and acquaintances ; and did affect, and hade the reputation and character of a pious and devot man, thereby endeavouring to conceale and palliate his villainies, and to abuse and impose upon the world, and to mocke God himself, as if his all-seeing eye could not see through the

slender veill of hypocrisie and formalitie, and could not discover and lay open to the view of the world so great and
flagitious lewdnes in its own colours, in which it does now
appear." It is stated that, " All which crimes particulariz'd
in manner aforesaid, he acknowledg'd judicially at the Bar."[26]
But " the Lord Advocate called for further probation." The
proof led against him, as to many points, was drawn from
his own confessions. The witnesses were "John Oliphant,
William Johnston, and Archibald Hamilton, Bailies, *i.e.*,
Alderman of Edinburgh; also Jean Weir, his sister, Anne
Simpson, Archibald Nisbett, Writer to the Signet, John
Alexander of Leith; and Maister John Sinclare, Minister at
Ormistoune,[27] aged fiftie years or thereby, married, sworne,
depones, that yesterday Major Weir having sent for him, and
that the Major told him he was to speak his conscience to
him, and make a frie confessione, and that the Major did
accordinglie confess unto him that he was guilty of Adulterie,
Incest, &c., and desired the deponer to pray for him as a
persone guiltie of the said grievous crymes ; and farder
declares, that after the Major was brought down out of the
Tolbuith, and the deponer being desired to retier with him
to the little roum before the Toune's Councill hous, he did
confess again, &c., and the deponer having asked him if he
had seen the Deivell, he answered, that any fealling he ever
hade of him was in the dark ; and this is treuth, &c." The
process being thus ended the jury did unanimously find the
Major guilty of Incest with his sister, and bestiality with a
Mare, and a Cow, and found him guilty of Adultery and
Fornication by a plurality of votes. Whereupon the deputed
Judges sentenced him to be strangled at a stake betwixt
Edinburgh and Leith, on Monday following, the 11th of April,
and his body to be burnt to ashes—a sentence executed at the
Galla-lee, where, however, it would seem, that this miserable
wretch was actually burned alive. This shameful circumstance is thus recorded, " That the body of this unclean Beast
gave manifest tokens of its impurity, as soon as it began to
be heated by the flames. In the flames along with him was
consumed his conjuring staff, carved with heads like those of
Satyrs, without which he could not pray, nor work many of
his other diabolical feats. Whatever incantation was in it,

the persons present own that it gave rare turnings, and was long a-burning, as also himself." [28]

The sum of the Libel against Jean Weir, his sister, " is reduceable to two heads. *First*, to the charge of incest, which she committed with her brother, and, *Secondly*, to the charge of Sorcery, and Witchcraft, but most especially of consulting Witches, Necromancers, and Devils ; and yet more particularly for keeping and conversing with a familiar spirit, while she lived at Dalkeith, which used to spin extraordinary quantities of yarn for her, in a shorter time than three or four women could have done the same." When the case came to trial, the proof against her, as to Witchcraft was chiefly her own confession ; for she declared, " That when she keeped a school at Dalkeith, and teached childering, ane tall woman came to the declarant's hous when the childering were there ; and that she had, as appeared to her, ane chyld upon her back, and one or two at her foot ; and that the said woman disyred that the declarant should imploy her to spick for her to the Queen of Farie, and strik and battle in her behalf with the said Queen, (which was her own words) ; and that the next day ane little woman came to the declarant, and did give her a piece of a tree, or the root of some herb or tree, as she thought, and told her that als long as she had the samen, she wold be able to doe what she should desyre ; and then the said woman did lay ane cloth upon the floor near the door, and caused the declarant set her foot upon the samen, and her hand upon the crown of her own head, and caused the declarant repeit these words thrice, viz., ' All my cross and trubles goe to the door with the ' ; which accordinglie she did ; and that she gave the woman all the silver she hade, being some few turners, and some meall ; and that after the said woman went away, the declarant did spin a verie short tyme, and that she did find more yearne upon her pirne, and good yearne, nor she thought could be spun in so short a tyme ; which did so affright the declarant, that she did set bye her wheile, and did shut the door, and did stay within her house for the space of twentie dayes or thereby, and was exceedinglie trubled, and weeped becaus she thought what she had done in manner forsaid was in effect the renuncing of her baptisme ; and being interrogate, If she knowes anything if her brother had any correspondence with the deivell ? declares that she hes been of a long tyme jealous of him that he hade, bot knows noe certaintie ; bot sex or seven years since or thereby, she and her brother having went to visit David Livingstone, wheill-wryht in Dalkeith, as they were in use to doe diverse tymes of befor, and her brother having desyred her to claw his back, she found upon his shoulder, as she thinks the right shoulder, a mark lyk that which they call the divell's mark ; and that when she found it she was affrighted." As for probation against Jean Weir, the Lord Advocate insisted on her own declaration, and all the depositions, in which as a party she was involved. All of which she judicially confessed in the face of the Court. The jury unanimously brought her in guilty of Incest with her brother. Whereupon the Judges condemned her to be hanged on the Tuesday following in the Grassmarket of Edinburgh.

In *Lamont's Diary*,[29] it is recorded, " 1670, Apr. 11. One Major Weyer, who lived in Edb. who had some allowance from the Towne, for waiting or otherways, being ane old man, about 75 or 76 yeirs of age, was brunt att the Gallo-lay, betwixt Leith and Ebd. for incest with his sister, beastialitie in laying with beasts, etc. He confest he had lyen with his sister, who was married to another, since she was 16 yeirs of age, and had layin with beasts divers tymes, etc. He was one that had a great profession, and keiped divers of the Conventicals att Edb. He wold not suffer the ministers to spake or pray for him (nether wold he seike God's mercy ; but when he was forced to doe it, he said, ' and now what better am I ? ') And Apr. 12, being Twesday, his sister [Jean] Weyer, being abowt or more then 60 yeirs of age, was hanged att Edb. She confest Incest, Witchcraft, etc. On the scafold she cast away hir mantell, hir gown tayle, and was purposed, as was sayde, to cast of all hir cloaths before all the multitude ; bot Baylie Oliphant, to whom the businese was intrusted, stoped the same, and commanded the execwtioner to doe his office. Bot whille he was abowt to throw hir ovir the leather, she smote the execwtioner on the cheike ; and hir hands not being tyed when she was throwen ovir, she labored to recover hir selfe, and put in hir head betwixt two of the steps of the leather, and keiped that powster for atyme, till she was put from itt. They dyed both impenitent persons, as was supposed be the standers by."

Another Account says, " As for Jane, this incarnate Devil's sister, she was very insensible of her great sins, and was so far from remorse of conscience for them, and despairing of the mercy of God, as he did, that she presumed too much upon it ; placing a great deal of confidence in her constant adherence to the Covenant, which she called *the cause and interest of Christ.* She confessed indeed as he did that her sins deserved a worse death than she was condemned to die ; but she never shewed herself in the least concerned for what might ensue after death. When she was upon the ladder she bespoke the people concerning her sins, her brother, his conjuring staff, and the Solemn League and Covenant, in the following words, ' I see a great croud of People come hither to day to behold a poor old miserable creatures death, but I trow there be few among you, who are weeping and mourning for the broken Covenant '; and having so spoken, she threw herself in greater hast off the ladder, than a person should have done, who was no better prepared for another world."[30]

In *Law's Memorials*,[31] it is recorded, "Aprile 12, 1670, was Thomas Weir, commonly called Major Weir, son of Thomas Weir of Kirktoun, put to death at Edinburgh, and brunt for incest with his sister, Jean Weir, laying in it about 40 yeirs ; (he himself was of age 70), for incest with his step-daughter, Margaret Burdoun ; for frequent adulteries with severalls and diverse persons, and other abominable things ; and, notwithstanding of all these flagittious and horrid sins, he was a dreadful Hypocrite and deceiver of God's People, in pretending to the fear of God in a singular and eminent way ; making profession of strickness in piety beyond others ; presuming to take upon him to pray publickly in many companies; and in the houses of his friends, neighbours, and acquaintances affecting the reputation and character of a pious and devout man. He died obduredly, without any sign of repentance, and would not hear any minister pray to and for him, telling, his condemnation was sealed, and that now since he was to goe to the devil he would not anger him. The said Jean Weir, his sister-German, was put to death at Edinburgh, and brunt for the same incest and witchcraft ; she also was under a profession of religion beyond others. The way how he was brought to confession was by torture of conscience ; he confessed that he never prayed in privat, but all his prayers were in public ; and, beside all his abomina- tions foresaid, he added this to all, that he did ly with his servant Woman, Bessie Weimis, in fornication for the space of 22 years. Thus did the holy justice of God eminently shyne furth in detecting such wreatched hypocrites."

It is certain that no story of Witchcraft or Necromancy, so many of which occurred near and in Edinburgh, made such a lasting impression on the public mind as that of Major Weir.

Robert Chambers, in his *Traditions of Edinburgh*, remarks, " The conclusion to which the humanity of the present age would come regarding Weir—that he was mad—is favoured by some circumstances. What chiefly countenances the idea, is the unequivocal lunacy of the sister. This miserable woman confessed to witchcraft, and related in a serious manner, many things which could not be true. The case of Weir and his sister immediately became a fruitful theme for the imaginations of the vulgar, and for upwards of a century after Major Weir's death, he continued to be the bugbear of the Bow, and his house remained uninhabited. His apparition was frequently seen at night, flitting, like a black and silent shadow about the street. His house, though known to be deserted by everything human, was sometimes observed at midnight to be full of lights, and heard to emit strange sounds as of dancing, howling, and, what is strangest of all, spinning. Some people occasionally saw the Major issue from the low close at midnight, mounted on a black horse without a head, and gallop off in a whirlwind of flame. Nay, sometimes the whole of the inhabitants of the Bow would be roused from their sleep at an early hour in the morning by the sound of a coach and six, first rattling up the Lawn-market, and then turning down the Bow, stopping at the head of the terrible close for a few minutes, and then rattling and thundering back again—being neither more nor less than Satan come in one of his best equipages to take home the Major and his sister, after they had spent a night's leave of absence in their terrestrial dwelling "; and that " Plebeian imaginations have since fructified regarding the staff, and crones will still seriously tell how it could run a message to a shop for any article which its proprietor wanted ; how it could answer the door when any one called upon its master; and that it used to be often seen running before him, in the capacity of a link-boy, as he walked down the Lawnmarket ! "

" About fifty years ago, when the shades of superstition began universally to give way in Scotland, Major Weir's house came to be regarded with less terror by the neighbours, and an attempt was made by the proprietor to find a person who should be bold enough to inhabit it. Such a person was procured in William Patullo, a poor man of dissipated habits, who, having been at one time a soldier and a traveller, had come to disregard in a great measur the superstitions of his native country, and was now glad to possess a house upon the low terms offered by the landlord at whatever risk. Upon its being known that Major Weir's house was about to be reinhabited, a great deal of curiosity was felt by people of all ranks as to the result of the experiment; for there was scarcely a native of the city who had not felt since his boyhood, an intense interest in all that concerned that awful fabric, and yet remembered the numerous terrible stories which he had heard respecting it. Even before entering upon his hazardous undertaking, William Patullo was looked upon with a flattering sort of interest, similar to that which we feel respecting a regiment on the march to active conflict. It was the hope of many that he would be the means of retrieving a valuable possession from the dominion of darkness. But Satan soon let them know that he does not tamely relinquish any of the outposts of his kingdom. On the very first night after Patullo and his spouse had taken up their abode in the house, as the worthy couple were lying awake in their bed, not unconscious of a certain degree of fear—a dim uncertain light proceeding from the gathered embers of their fire, and all being silent around them—they suddenly saw a form like that of a calf, which came forward to the bed, and, setting its fore-feet upon the stock, looked steadfastly at the unfortunate pair. When it had contemplated them thus for a few minutes, to their great relief it at length took itself away, and slowly retiring, gradually vanished from their sight. As might be expected, they deserted the house next morning; and for another half century no other attempt was made to embank this part of the world of light from the aggressions of the world of darkness."

In 1678 two old women of Prestonpans were burned, having accused before they went to their death seventeen others, of whom nine presently shared their fate.

During August of the same year " the devill had a great meeting of witches in Loudian, where, among others, was a warlock who formerly had been admitted to the ministrie in the presbyterian tymes, and when the bishops came in conformed with them. But being found flagitious and wicked was deposed by them, and now he turnes a preacher under the devill of hellish doctrine ; for the devill at this time preaches to his witches really (if I may so term it) the doctrine of the infernal pitt, viz. blasphemies against God and His Son Christ. Among other things, he told them that they were more happy in him than they could be in God ; him they saw, but God they could not see ; and in mocking of Christ and His holy ordinance of the sacrament of His supper, he gives the sacrament to them, bidding them eat it and drink it in remembrance of himself. This villan was assisting to Sathan in this action, and in preaching."[32] Another account adds that when the Devil " adventured to give them the communion or holy sacrament, the bread was like wafers, the drink was sometimes blood, sometimes black moss-water."[33] This travesty of a Protestant communion is certainly most curious, and perhaps it would not be too extravagant to suggest that it was introduced by somebody who knew of the Paris orgies and the Satanist's masses which were being carried on just at the same time. Fourteen years later we find the same thing in New England, so evidently the dark tradition was taken over the seas. The warlock parson was identified as Mr. Gideon Penman, a man of notoriously dissolute life, minister of Crighton. He was particularly active during the rites, " was in the rear in all their dances, and beat up all those that were slow."[34] His indignant denials and stout refutations of the charge seem to have been accepted by the court.

On 19 December, 1679, a coven of witches was discovered at Borrowstowness, of whom the chief was Annaple Thomson. They confessed to various sorceries, to sexual connexion with the Demon, to attendance at the Sabbat—" ye and ilk ane of yow was at ane metting with the devill and other witches at the croce of Murestaine, upon the thretten of October last, where yow all danced, and the devill acted the pyiper, and where yow indewored to have destroyed Andrew Mitchell, sone to John Mitchell, elder in Dean of Kinneil "[35]—and many other circumstances of witchcraft. Accordingly Annaple Thomson ; Margaret Pringle ; Margaret Hamilton (Mitchell) ; Margaret Hamilton, relict of James Pullwart ; Bessie Vickar ; and William Craw, " found guiltie be ane assyse of the abominable cryme of Witchcraft," were ordered to be taken to the west end of Borrowstowness, " the ordinar place of execution," betwixt two and four in the afternoon, and " there be wirried at a steack till they be dead, and thereafter to have their bodies burnt to ashes."

In 1697 occurred the trial and condemnation of the Renfrewshire witches. Christian Shaw, a girl about eleven years of age, the daughter of John Shaw of Bargarran, on the 17 August, 1696, saw the maidservant, Katherine Campbell, take a drink of milk from the can, and promptly threatened to tell her mother. The girl, vexed at being caught, turned on her smartly with a curse " that the devil might harle her soul through hell." A few days after, Agnes Naismith, a crone of ill repute, accosted Christian and asked her age, only to receive a pert reply. The next night the child was taken with fits and paroxysms of pain, her body now shaking as with palsy, now rigid and stiff in every joint. In her frenzies she cried out against Katherine Campbell and Agnes Naismith, and when she began to vomit strange substances such as crooked pins, small fowl-bones, sticks of candle-fir, filthy hay, gravel stones, lumps of candle-grease, and egg-shells—who could doubt she was bewitched ? By degrees a large number of persons were implicated, many of them of the lowest extraction, such as Elizabeth Anderson, a beggar's trull of seventeen, her cousin James Lindsay, aged fourteen, and gley'd Thomas his brother, not yet twelve, their grandmother Jean Fulton, Alexander Anderson, until at length no less than twenty were condemned, of whom five were burned on the 10 June, 1697, quick on the Gallow Green at Paisley.[36] One warlock, John Reid, hanged himself in prison, or, as the report went, had been strangled by the Devil lest he should reveal too many secrets of the infernal society. No doubt Christian Shaw was hysterical and epileptic, full of hallucinations and morbidities, but none the less it seems evident that there did actually exist at Bargarran a clandestine sect of Satanists, whose dark cult was unexpectedly exposed through the accident of this quarrel with Katherine Campbell, doubtless one of their number. Christian Shaw afterwards acquired a remarkable dexterity in spinning yarn, which she manufactured into thread ; and it was from her experiments, aided by a friend who had learned some technical secrets of the process when in Holland, that the famous Renfrewshire manufacture of thread originated. About the year 1718 she became the wife of Mr. Miller, minister at Kilmaurs Parish. He died in 1725, and was buried in Erskine Church, being greatly lamented by his flock.

The case of the Pittenweem witches in the year 1704 excited considerable interest. Peter Morton, a smith at Pittenweem, on 13 June, sent up a complaint to the Privy Council delating a certain Beattie Laing for having cast a spell upon him, whereby " he was seized with such a weakness in his limbs that he could hardly stand or walk." The local magistrates arrested the accused, who presently confessed her crime and implicated Janet Carset,[37] Lillie Wallace, and Nicolas Lawson, who " had framed a picture of wax," each one " having put their pin in the picture for torture." Isobel Adams, also, a young lass, " was in compact with the devil." The demon, or rather the Grand Master of the Satanists of that district, " appeared as a gentleman . . . she promised her service to him ; and he committed uncleanness with her (which she said no other had done before), and he put his mark in her flesh, which was very painful." All the witches were " prosecute by her Majesty's Advocate, 1704, but all set at liberty save one, who died in prison, in Pittenweem. Beattie Lang died undesired, in her bed, in St. Andrew's ; all the rest died miserable and violent deaths." Janet Corset, however, met a shocking fate. She had managed to escape from jail, but being caught and brought back to Pittenweem, the mob assailed her, and nobody attempting her rescue, she was hauled down to the beach, pelted with rubbish, swung in a rope betwixt a ship and the shore, and a heavy door being thrown upon her, over which stones were heaped, she was finally pressed to death.[38]

In the year 1705, we learn from the Parochial Register of Spott, that many witches were burnt on the top of Spott

Loan, and at the close of the year, two Inverness men, George and Lachlan Rattray, were executed, being found " guilty of the horrid crimes of mischievous charms, by witchcraft and malefice, sorcery or necromancy."

On 24 March, 1719, the Deputy-Sheriff of Caithness, with ample apology for his remissness, wrote from Thurso to lay the following information, a technical precognition, before the King's Advocate, Robert Dundas of Arniston, the celebrated lawyer, at Edinburgh : " In the month of December last, one William Montgomerie, mason, in Burnside of Scrabster, gave in a petition to the sheriff, representing that his house was severall times infested with cats to that degree, that he nor his family were in safety to reside there any longer, and particularly condescended, that upon the 28th of November last, and also five days thereafter, he had encountered with the said cats in his house, and with his sword, and some other weapons, had killed two of them, and, as he apprehended, had wounded some more of them ; and because ane woman in the neighbourhood contracted sickness immediately after these encounters, craved ane warrand from the sherrif to inspect the woman, but could not condescend in his petition upon the person ; and this representation seeming all the time to be very incredulous and fabulous, the sheriff had no manner of regard yrto. There was no farther thought of this affair from December, that the representation was not given in, intill the 12th of February last, that one Margaret Nin-Gilbert, in Owst, living about ane mile and ane half distant from Montgomery's house, was seen by some of her neighbours to drop at her own door one of her leggs from the midle, and she being under bad fame before for witchcraft, the legg, black and putrified, was brought to me ; and immediately thereafter I ordered her to be apprehended and incarcerated ; and she having been examined upon the 18th of February before me, and some ministers, and persons of reputation in the place, confessed her being in compact with the devil, and several others, as mentioned in her confession ; and particularly, that the time condescended upon by Montgomerie in his petition, she was bodily present in his house, though she appeared to him in the likeness of a catt, and that her leg was broke by a stroke received from him ; and condescended upon severall women who were present with her in Montgomerie's house that night, who were seized and continue imprisoned, except two, who dyed the night of the encounter with the catts in Montgomerie's house, or a few days thereafter."

When Mr. William Innes, minister of Thurso, had examined Margaret Nin-Gilbert, " In presence of Mr. John Munro, Minister of Halikirk, David Forbes, Bailzie of Thurso, Andrew Balfour, Merchand there, James Maky, William Munro, and Andrew Munro, Merchands there," the wretched crone freely confessed her compact with the devil, and implicated Margaret Olsone, Jannet Pyper, Helen Andrew, Margaret Callum, and old Mother M'Huistan as witches.

" *Nota*, That upon a vulgar report of witches having the devil's marks in their bodies, Margaret Olsone being tryed in the shoulders, where there were severall small spots, some read, some blewish, after a needle was driven in with great force almost to the eye, she felt it not. Mr. Inness, Mr. Oswald, ministers, and several honest women, and Bailzie Forbes, were witnesses to this. And further, that while the needle was in her shoulder, as foresaid, she said.—' Am not I ane honest woman now ? ' "

In January, 1720, great excitement ran like wildfire through the countryside owing to the alleged possession of Lord Torphichen's third son, who declared he had been forespoken by certain old women and a warlock living at Calder, the village near his father's mansion. The minister of the parish, and many others, quickly caught the infection ; a fast was proclaimed at Mid-Calder, and the sermon preached on that occasion, by Mr. John Wilkie, minister of the gospel at Uphall, was afterwards printed by desire of Lord Torphichen. At this discourse were present two of the confessing witches ; and Wilkie, in his Notice to the Reader, says that three more subsequently acknowledged their guilt. The piece is entitled : *A Sermon preached at Mid-Calder, on Thursday, January 14th, 1720. Being a Congregational Fast in that Place. James iv. 7 ;* [39] *by John Wilkie, Minister of the Gospel at Uphall.* Edinburgh, 1720, 12mo. Amongst others that ridiculous fantast, William Mitchell, the crazy Tincklarian Doctor, [40] *alias* White Smith, sallied forth from his shop in the West Bow of Edinburgh, in order to exorcise the evil spirits at Calder. He met with a cool enough reception from Lord Torphichen, who did not relish his house becoming the rendezvous of every fool in Scotland, but none the less he interrogated the supposed witches, and wrote an account of his proceedings which he published as folio broadside, *A Strange and Wonderful Discourse concerning the Witches and Warlocks in West Calder.* Although several of the accused were lodged in prison, and even confessed their guilt, the Crown Counsel refused to proceed to trial, whereon they were quietly released. In the course of a year or two the " witch-boy of Calder " was sent to sea, and by his gallantry obtained the command of an East Indiaman, from whose decks he had repulsed a party of the pirate Angria's buccaneers. He finally perished in a storm.

The last execution of a Scottish witch took place in June, 1722,[41] at Dornoch. Two poor Highland women, a mother and daughter, belonging to the parish of Loth, were brought before Captain David Ross of Littledean, Deputy-Sheriff of Sutherland, charged with Witchcraft and consorting with the Devil. The mother was accused of having used her daughter as her " horse and hattock," causing her to be shod by the Devil, so that she was ever after lame in both hands and feet, a deformity which was, rumour avers, afterwards entailed upon her son.[42] Captain David Ross, " in flagrant violation," comments Sir Walter Scott, " of the then established rules of jurisdiction "[43] pronounced the sentence of death. Stake and tar-barrel were provided at Dornoch in the early morning, and, it is said, that after being brought out to execution, the weather proving nippy and chill, the hag sat composedly warming herself by the bonny bright fire prepared to consume her, what time the other instruments of her horrid death were making ready.

To give even a tithe of the many stories concerning magic and witches which persisted in the eighteenth century and linger to-day is impossible. Two typical examples may, however, be pertinently cited. Captain Burt in his *Letters from the North of Scotland,* 1730, tells the first which he had from a minister. A certain laird, whose wine was disappearing mysteriously—through Witchcraft, as he suspected—went armed one night to the cellar, where he expected to find the nefarious gang at work. Closing the door carefully behind him, he found himself to his amaze surrounded by cats, but laying about him with his broadsword he very soon cleared the place. Some drops of blood upon the floor showed him that his weapon had claimed a victim. Next day the house of an old woman, locally notorious as a witch, was entered, and she was found in bed with one of her legs completely severed.

A similar story hails from the Lowlands. In 1752 Captain Archibald Douglas, accompanied by a sergeant, was on recruiting service in Jedburgh. This sergeant was intensely dissatisfied with his billet, which, he averred, was haunted. He had also learned that his landlord was gifted with second-sight, while the landlady was locally reputed to be a witch. Wearied by the man's incessant complaints, the captain resolved to spend the night with him and see if there was any truth in his story. About midnight a huge black cat seemed to fly into the room through the window. The officer promptly fired at it with his pistol and shot off one of its ears. With a scream it vanished. Next morning, on visiting the kitchen, he found the landlady lying senseless in a pool of blood which flowed from the side of her head. Removing her mutch he found that one of her ears had been shot away.

It is well known, that in the year 1736, the statutes against Witchcraft, Scottish as well as English, were repealed ; which gave so much offence to the *seceders* from the Established Church of Scotland, that in their annual Confession of National and Personal Sins, printed in an Act of their Associate Presbytery, at Edinburgh, 1743, are enumerated the Act of Queen Anne's Parliament for tolerating the Episcopal Religion in Scotland ; the Act for Adjourning the Court of Session during the Christmas Holydays ; as also the Penal Statutes against Witches having been repealed by Parliament, contrary to the express Law of God.

When we consider the long record of Scottish witch-trials and executions we may well bear in mind that although, no doubt, there were many innocent victims, many who fell a prey to hatred and revenge, on the other hand there were many who belonged to that dark and anarchical company which seeks to destroy all social order, to corrupt and to pollute, to replace Christianity by the worship of the Devil. Nor must we suppose that this is wholly a thing of the past. Methods change ; the object remains the same.

The belief in sorcery is still strong in the Highlands to-day, and many tales are yet whispered of the malefic powers of those who have sold themselves to Satan. In more than one remote hamlet is some canny shepherd or wrinkled beldame shunned and feared who two hundred years ago would have been fuel for the fire.

NOTES TO CHAPTER III

[1] *Agricola*, XXIX to XXXVIII.

[2] Buchanan, *Rerum Scoticarum Historia.* I have quoted from George Sinclar's *Invisible World Discovered*, Edinburgh, 1685, XIII.

[3] Or Bowmaker (d. 1449), Abbot of the monastery of Austin Canons at Inchcolm. Fordun (d. 1385 ?), a canon of Aberdeen Cathedral, carried his Annals to the death of David I in 1153. Abbot Bowen continued the record to the death of James I in 1437.

[4] Hector Boece (*c.* 1465–1536), Principal of King's College, Aberdeen, published in 1527 his *Scotorum historiœ a prima gentis origine* in seventeen books.

[5] See Gabriel Naudé, *Apologie pour les Grands Hommes soupçonnez de Magie*, Paris, 1625, pp. 81, 82. Also Buckle's *History of Civilization*, Vol. I, p. 334, note, and Simancas, *De Catholicis Institutionibus*, pp. 463–8.

[6] *Inferno*, XX, Longfellow's translation. To quote *The Lay of the Last Minstrel* would seem superfluous.

[7] Hermitage Castle, Hermitage, Liddesdale, some few miles from Riccarton Junction, Roxburgh.

> Haunted Hermitage,
> Where long by spells mysterious bound,
> They pace their round with lifeless smile,
> And shake with restless feet the guilty pile,
> Till sink the mouldering towers beneath the burdened ground.

[8] And still when seven years are o'er,
> Is heard the jarring sound,
> When hollow opes the charmed door,
> Of chamber underground.

[9] It is hardly necessary to point out that all charges connecting Queen Mary with Darnley's murder and Bothwell are entirely false. And although " aduersus eam hæretici debacchati sunt," as Benedict XIV says, in her case " nihil fortasse deerit quæ pro uero Martyrio sunt necessaria." *De Seruorum Dei Beatificatione et Beatorum Canonizatione*, III, xiii, 10, editio Secunda Romana, 1789, Vol. V, pp. 161–2.

[10] Robert Pitcairn, *Criminal Trials*, Edinburgh, 1833, I, ii, p. 51.

[11] Pitcairn gives the trials. I have also used, and freely quote from, the contemporary pamphlet, *Newes from Scotland, Declaring the Damnable life and death of Doctor Fian, a notable Sorcerer, who was burned at Edenbrough in Ianuary last*, 1591.

[12] She may have been a witch, but she was certainly a whore.

[13] Et quant aux marques, c'est bien chose certaine, & que les iuges voyent ordinairement, si elles ne sont bien cachees : comme i'ay sçeu d'vn gentilhomme de Valoys, qu'il y en a qui ont la marque entre les lebures, les autres soubs la Paupiere, comme escrit Daneau, les autres au fondement, quand ils craignent estre decouuers, & ordinairement sur l'espaule dextre & les femmes sur la cuisse, ou bien sous l'esselle, ou bien aux parties honteuses. Bodin, *De la Demonomanie*, II, 4.

[14] Milan, 1608. " Ad signum homagii eum [diabolum] podice osculantur." And Ludwig Elich in his *Dæmonomagia*, 1607, Quæstio 10, has : " Deinde quod homagii est indicium (honor sit auribus) ab eis ingerenda sunt oscula Dæmonis podici."

[15] Jean Chartier, *Chronique de Charles VII.*

[16] Bodin, *De la Demonomanie.*

[17] De Lancre, *Tableau*, p. 131.

[18] George Sandys, *Relation of a Journey*, London, 1632.

[19] Reginald Scot of Scots-Hall, Kent, whose *Discoverie of Witchcraft* was published in 1584.

[20] Johann Weyer, 1516–88, body-physician to Wilhelm IV, Duke of Jülich, Cleves, and Berg, to whom he dedicated his famous *De præstigiis et incantationibus et ueneficiis*, Basel, 1563.

[21] *E.g.* the conclusion of C.V. Book I.

[22] Spalding's *History*, Vol. II, p. 102.

[23] Samuel Hibbert, *Description of the Shetland Islands*, Edinburgh, 1822.

[24] This is the date given in Lamont's contemporary diary, and is doubtless correct. But Robert Law's *Memorialls* say Tuesday, 12 April, and a note in Sinclar has Thursday, 14 April.

[25] Weir had been an officer on the popular side in the civil war. In the Registers of the Estates, under March 3, 1647, reference is made to a supplication by Major Thomas Weir, in which he craved payment of 600 merks due to him by an Act of the Committee of Estates of date the 17th of December, 1644, and also payment of what might be due to him " for his service as Major in the Earl of Lanark's regiment by the space of twell months, and his service in Ireland as ane Captain-Lieutenant in Colonel Robert Home his regiment by the space of nineteen months " ; further asking " that the Parliament wald ordain John Acheson, Keeper of the Magazine, to re-deliver to the supplicant the band given by him to the said John upon the receipt of ane thousand weight of poulder, two thousand weight of match, and an thousand pound weight of ball, sent with the supplicant to Dumfries for furnishing that part of the country." The matter was given over to a committee.

[26] " He confessed crimes that it was possible for him to have committed, but he qualified his confession by answering ' that he thought himself guilty of the foresaid crimes, and could not deny them,' and I am convinced of the prisoner having been delirious at the time of his trial."—*Hugo Arnot's Criminal Trials*, 1536-1784. 4to, 1785.

[27] Brother to Professor George Sinclar of Glasgow.

[28] One of the female witnesses deponed as to what she saw him doing near " New-Mills," in the West Country, and " complained of him to Mr. John Nave, the Minister of New-Mills ; at whose instance he was brought back to the place by some soldiers, but was there dismissed for want of further probation ; and the woman that delated him for the fact near New Mills, was by order of the magistrates of Lanark whipped through the town by the hand of the common Hangman, *as a slanderer of such an eminent Holy Man !* "

[29] " The Chronicle of Fife : Being the Diary of Mr. John Lamont of Newton 1649-1671. Edited by Archibald Constable, 1810. New Edition, Edited by George Ritchie Kinloch, 1830." 4to.

[30] *Ravillac Redivivus, by Dr. George Hickes.* Sm. 4to, 1678.

[31] " Memorialls ; or, The Memorable things that fell out within this Island of Brittain from 1638 to 1684, by the Rev. Mr. Robert Law, Minister of Kirkpatrick. Edited from the MS., with a Prefatory Notice and Illustrative Notes, by Charles Kirkpatrick Sharpe, Edinburgh, 1818. 4to."

[32] Law's *Memorialls*, p. 145.

[33] Lord Fountainhall, *Decisions*, Edinburgh, 1759, I, 14.

[34] *Ibid.*

[35] *Scots Magazine*, 1814, p. 201.

[36] One account says that a gibbet and a fire were prepared, that the condemned persons were hanged for a few moments on the one and then cut down and cast into the flames.

[37] Whom Kirkpatrick Sharpe and others call Janet Cornfoot. But I have followed the *Additional Relations* appended to Sinclar.

[38] The best account is in the *Additional Relations* (II) to Sinclar : *Satan's Invisible World Discovered*, reprint, 1875, pp. 257–60.

[39] " Be subject therefore to God ; but resist the devil, and he will fly from you."

[40] 1672–1740. This silly body dubbed himself " The Tinchlarian Doctor, who cures Pans and old Lantrens."

[41] Burt, *Letters from the North of Scotland*, Vol. I, pp. 227–34, 271–7, speaks of a woman who was burned as a witch in 1727, but it is generally supposed he has misdated the Dornoch execution. Woodrow in his *Analecta* has some vague mention of executions in 1726, but as no details are given there is almost certainly some error.

[42] " And this son," says Sir Walter Scott, in 1830, " was living so lately as to receive the charity of the present Marchioness of Stafford, Countess of Sutherland in her own right."

[43] *Letters on Demonology and Witchcraft*, No. IX, 1830.

CHAPTER IV

NEW ENGLAND

IN 1606 King James the First granted all the American continent from 34 to 45 degrees, which he divided into two colonies, viz. the Southern, or Virginia, to certain merchants from London ; the Northern, or New-England, to certain merchants of Plymouth. By its charter from the same monarch, 3 November, 1620, which was generously renewed by King Charles I, 4 March, 1629, " The Governor and Company of the Massachusetts Bay in New England " possessed the entire sovereignty over all the territory thereby assigned to it. The principal undertakers were Puritans. Planters, and ministers of the same persuasion, together with servants, cattle, and all necessaries for beginning a colony, were soon sent over, albeit at a very great expense, and many discontented Genevans whose brabbles had made England too hot to hold them were glad to join the convoy.

On 30 April, 1629, the Company appointed Captain John Endicott, one of the original patentees, to be " Governor of the Plantation of the Massachusets Bay," to hold office, it was specified, for one year, but meanwhile it was resolved to transfer charter and company bodily to New England, when John Winthorp was elected Governor on 29 October, 1629, and, arriving in Salem on 12 June, 1630, he held his first court at Charlestown, 28 August.

From 1640 to 1660 the community became almost in every particular an independent commonwealth, and departing from their charter they made their own intolerant laws upon the true " Christian state " model. Moreover, although they had no power to judge and determine capital offences, they did not hesitate to give such a power to the judicatories they created, and as might have been expected, during the usurpation of Cromwell in England, they received every indulgence and encouragement.

Their meticulous meddlings, their interference with individual liberty, their peddling arrogance, and their penalties truly recall old Calvin, the block whence they were hewn. Thus we have recorded : " Captain Lovel admonished to take heed of light carriage. Daniel Clarke, found to be an immoderate drinker, was fined forty shillings. John Wedgewood, for being in the company of drunkards to be set in the stocks. Robert Shorthose, for swearing by the Blood of God, was sentenced to have his tongue put into a cleft stick, and to stand so for the space of half an hour."[1] It is not exceptional. Men who, although granted every laxity and given every allowance and loophole for long years, during which they were merely requested to conform to a few of the most elementary decencies of ecclesiastical order, one might almost say of the Christian religion, complained all the while of persecution and hard usage, stirring up unrest and disorder in every shire of England, utterly contemptuous of authority and decorum, and then when they have gained the upper hand, the supreme control in a lax colony of their own seeking and making, they prove the most relentless of tyrants, the harshest of taskmasters, grinding down their subjects and vexing them by mean regulations such as the fabled orgulousness of an imaginary Hildebrand or the legendary suspicion of a theatrical Louis XI would have spurned and disdained to impose. As one reads the earlier annals of Massachusetts one realizes that those treacherous fires which consumed the hapless Servetus, the smoke and stench of his roasting flesh, are not far in the background.

Owing the influx of Puritan influence from the Continent into England on the death of Queen Mary I a law had been passed in the fifth year of Elizabeth's reign by which Witchcraft was made a felony, in accordance with the statute under Henry VIII. The first Parliament of James I had been in session but eight days when steps were taken by the House of Lords with regard to strengthening the existing statute, and upon 9 June, 1604, about two months and a half after its introduction, the Bill passed its final reading in the Lords.[2] There are recorded many trials for Witchcraft during the latter years of Elizabeth, and after her death these showed a tendency to increase. In 1603 Mary Pannel, a Yorkshire witch, was executed ; and Lancashire, in particular, whence many of the influential Puritan emigrants hailed, was commonly known to be a very hotbed of sorcery which later exploded in two notable trials. [There can be no doubt that the settlers in New England were not only firm believers in every kind of Witchcraft, but well primed in every malevolent superstition that could commend itself to their verjuiced and tortured minds. They looked for the Devil round every corner, and saw Satan's hand in every mishap, in every accident.] The Devil, in fact, played a larger part in their theology than God. They were obsessed with hell and damnation ; their sky was cloudy and overset ; their horizon girded with predestination and the awful consciousness of sin. It is almost impossible to conceive the effect a new land, a strange mysterious bourne beyond the waves of the illimitable Atlantic, must have had upon the muddied morbid minds and tortured souls of these stern and stoic pioneers.

Cultivation had made but a slight encroachment on the wilderness. Directly he passed from the clearing or the village street, a man came to huge, dark, unexplored forests, which spread far over the distant hills, hung frowning above the lonely roads, and on every side seemed to encircle with unknown dangers the new and scattered settlements. Nothing could have been more impressive and more melancholy than the sombre stillness of those primitive woods, a silence only broken by the fluttering of unseen birds brushing through the foliage, the heavy fall of some rotted branch decayed from the parent tree, the sudden rustle of leaves at the stealthy stalking of some wild animal about to leap upon its prey, or the soft naked tread of savages who were fiercer still.

For the depths of the jungle were the abode of a mysterious race, the red men, of inhuman demeanour and unascertained origin. The aspect they wore, the horrid stories told of them, their devilries and cruelties, their barbaric rites, and, indeed, everything connected with them served to awaken fear, to bewilder the imagination, and drive minds already trembling and distraught to a very lunacy of terror and apprehension. What wonder then that common belief, encouraged not by their ministers alone, but sanctioned by the most learned scholars of that and the preceding ages, held the American Indians to be the bastards of demons and worshippers of the Devil, and their powwows, foul wizards mighty and malign ?

The hatred and vindictive hostility which the colonists bore to the name of Indian are scarcely a cause for wonder. Hardly a village where the marks of ruthless violence and bloody mischief could not be pointed out, hardly a settlement that had not been ravaged and burned, hardly a community that had not been plundered of cattle and goods, hardly a family which had not lost a member owing to the treachery, the malice, and swift sudden incursions of their tireless foe.

Thus in 1689, John Bishop and Nicholas Reed were killed by Indians at Salem; and in 1690 Godfrey Sheldon. In August, 1696, the marauders slew or captured fifteen persons at Billerica, leaving many houses ablaze. In October of the same year they descended on Newbury to carry off and tomahawk nine persons. In 1698 they raided Haverhill and wrought fearful destruction. On the night of the 3 July, 1706, a garrison at Dunstable was stormed, when Holyoke, Putnam and three other soldiers fell. These few scattered instances must serve for many. Some half a dozen cases may stand instead of a long catalogue of murderous forays. The menace was ever at the door.

Immediately upon the outbreak of the Civil War in England a fearful epidemic of sorcery swept the country, and this increased in virulence as Puritanism gradually got the upper hand. During the last six months of 1645, for example, the year of Naseby and Langport, nearly one hundred and fifty witches were put to death. It was then that Master Matthew Hopkins was in his full glory, slaughtering almost indiscriminately, striking his swashing blows to right and to left. Presbyterianism fanned the flame, and it is impossible that this crusade should not have been known, widely discussed and approved in the new American colony. It is hardly a coincidence that here the first suspicion of Witchcraft arose about the year 1645, at Springfield upon Connecticut river. Several persons, including two of the minister's children, were said to be possessed, but the evidence was not sufficient for a legal process, although great pains were taken to fasten the guilt upon certain suspected persons who were interrogated time after time but without result.

The first witch to be actually executed in New England was Alse Young, who was hanged in Connecticut, 26 May, 1647. On 15 June, 1648, Margaret Jones, a woman of

Charlestown, was put to death. " She was suspected partly because that after some angry words passing between her and her Neighbours, some mischief befel such Neighbours in their Creatures, or the like, partly because some things supposed to be bewitched or have a Charm upon them, being burned, she came to the fire and seemed concerned." She stoutly declared her innocence to the last. Shortly afterwards " H. Lake's wife of Dorchester," who had previously been a servant in the house of Master John Phillips, was executed. " And although Mr. Thompson, Minister at Braintree, took pains with her to bring her to repentance, she utterly denied her guilt of Witchcraft : yet justified God for bringing her to that punishment, inasmuch as when a single woman she had played the harlot, and being with child had used means to destroy the fruit of her body to conceal her sin and shame, and although she did not effect it, yet she was a murderer in the sight of God for her endeavours, and showed great penitency for that sin ; but owned nothing of the crime laid to her charge." A little later, in 1650, Mary Oliver confessed her guilt, and avowed herself a witch, as she had indeed been long commonly reputed, but there is no record of her execution. Another woman suffered at Cambridge ; and in 1651 Mary Parsons of Springfield was charged with having " used divers devilish practices by witchcraft to the hurt of the persons of Martha and Rebecca Moxon." The evidence did not convict her, but she was indicted for having killed her child, found guilty, and hanged.

It is evident that now men's minds were disturbed, and considerable alarm began to be generally felt, for on 13 May, 1651, the Court appointed a day of humiliation " throughout our jurisdiction in all the churches " to consider among other matters the extent to which " Satan prevails amongst us in respect of witchcrafts."

On 12 May, 1652, Hugh Parsons of Springfield was tried before the Court of Assistants, held at Boston, for Witchcraft, and " a jury of trials " found him guilty, but when the case came to the General Court that body decided " he was not legally guilty of witchcraft, and so not to die by law."

In September, 1652, John Bradstreet of Rowley was presented " for suspicion of having familiarity with the Devil. He said he had read in a book of magic." The case came before the Courts on 28 September, and they set " a fine of 20 shillings, or else to be whipped."

An important case was that of Mrs. Anne Hibbins, who was hanged on 19 June, 1656, " presently after the lecture at Boston . . . the marshal general taking with him a sufficient guard." This precaution was necessary, as she had always been held to be a very devout person and was highly respected. Many at the place of execution with tears openly bewailed her end which, however, she herself met with perfect calm. She is said to have been a sister of Richard Bellingham, at that very time deputy-governor, but if this were so it is difficult to understand why he did not interfere, especially as popular feeling would certainly have supported him.

In 1662, Ann Cole of Hartford in Connecticut, about thirty miles from Springfield, a young woman who lived next door to a Dutch family, was said to be possessed. In her fits she accused a woman named Greensmith of having forespoken her, and being examined by the magistrates and ministers persisted in her tale. Greensmith, who was already in prison on suspicion of Witchcraft, when questioned acknowledged the truth of what had been said. She avowed she had entertained a familiar with whom she had sexual connexion, that she had not as yet signed a contract with Satan, but that she had promised to do so shortly, and that she was to have had a high frolic at Christmas, which in Puritan eyes was probably as vile a crime as any. Increase Mather in his *Remarkable Providences* (Chap. V) has the following account of this case :

" Very remarkable was that Providence wherein Ann Cole of Hartford in New-England was concerned. She was, and is accounted, a person of real piety and integrity ; nevertheless, in the year 1662, then living in her father's house (who has likewise been esteemed a godly man), she was taken with very strange fits, wherein her tongue was improved by a dæmon to express things which she herself knew nothing of ; sometimes the discourse would hold for a considerable time ; the general purpose of which was, that such and such persons (who were named in the discourse which passed from her) were consulting how they might carry on mischievous designs against her and several others, mentioning sundry wayes they should take for that end, particularly that they would afflict her body, spoil her name, &c. The general answer made amongst the dæmons was, ' She runs to the rock.' This having continued some hours, the dæmons said, ' Let us confound her language, that she may tell no more tales.' She uttered matters unintelligible. And then the discourse passed into a Dutch tone (a Dutch family then lived in the town), and therein an account was given of some afflictions that had befallen divers ; amongst others, what had befallen a woman that lived next neighbour to the Dutch family, whose arms had been strangely pinched in the night, declaring by whom and for what cause that course had been taken with her. The Reverend Mr. Stone (then teacher of the church in Hartford) being by, when the discourse hapned, declared that he thought it impossible for one not familiarly acquainted with the Dutch (which Ann Cole had not in the least been) should so exactly imitate the Dutch tone in the pronunciation of English. Several worthy persons (viz. Mr. John Whiting, Mr. Samuel Hooker, and Mr. Joseph Haines) wrote the intelligible sayings expressed by Ann Cole, whilest she was thus amazingly handled. The event was, that one of the persons (whose name was Greensmith, being a lewd and ignorant woman, and then in prison on suspicion for witchcraft) mentioned in the discourse as active in the mischief done and designed, was by the magistrate sent for ; Mr. Whiting and Mr. Haines read what they had written, and the woman being astonished thereat, confessed those things to be true, and that she and other persons named in this preternatural discourse, had had familiarity with the devil. Being asked whether she had made an express covenant with him, she answered, she had not, only as she promised to go with him when he called, which accordingly she had sundry times done, and that the devil told her that at Christmas they would have a merry meeting, and then the covenant between them should be subscribed. The next day she was more particularly enquired of concerning her guilt respecting the crime she was accused with. She then acknowledged, that though when Mr. Haines began to read what he had taken down in writing, her rage was such that she could have torn him in pieces, and was as resolved as might be to deny her guilt (as she had done before), yet after he had read awhile, she was (to use her own expression) as if her flesh had been pulled from her bones, and so could not deny any longer : she likewise declared, that the devil first appeared to her in the form of a deer or fawn, skipping about her, wherewith she was not much affrighted, and that by degrees he became very familiar, and at last would talk with her ; moreover she said that the devil had frequently the carnal knowledge of her body ; and that the witches had meetings at a place not far from her house ; and that some appeared in one shape, and others in another ; and one came flying amongst them in the shape of a crow. Upon this confession, with other concurrent evidence, the woman was executed ; so likewise was her husband, though he did not acknowledge himself guilty. Other persons accused in the discourse made their escape. Thus doth the devil use to serve his clients. After the suspected witches were either executed or fled, Ann Cole was restored to health, and has continued well for many years, approving herself a serious Christian.

" There were some that had a mind to try whether the stories of witches not being able to sink under water were true ; and accordingly a man and woman, mentioned in Ann Cole's Dutch-toned discourse, had their hands and feet tyed, and so were cast into the water, and they both apparently swam after the manner of a buoy, part under, part above the water. A by-stander, imagining that any person bound in that posture would be so borne up, offered himself for trial ; but being in the like matter gently laid on the water, he immediately sunk right down. This was no legal evidence against the suspected persons, nor were they proceeded against on any such account ; however, doubting that an halter would choak them, though the waters would not, they very fairly took their flight, not having been seen in that part of the world since."

On 20 January, 1662, the woman Greensmith was hanged, two other witches apparently being executed at the same time.

In the autumn of 1671 a case of Witchcraft and possession occurred at Groton, and the Reverend Samuel Willard, the minister of the town, gave much attention and study to it. He wrote a long letter on the subject to Cotton Mather, who duly inserted it in his pedantic and inflated *Magnalia Christi Americana, or An Ecclesiastical History of New England,* folio, 1702, Book VI, c. vii, p. 67. The victim was one Elizabeth Knapp, who was born at Watertown, 21 April, 1655. She lived with her parents James and Elizabeth (Warren) Knapp, on the west side of Main Street. On Monday, 30 October, 1671, whilst sitting by the fire she suddenly fetched a great shriek and fell into convulsions, presently barking like a dog and bleating like a calf. Such an unusual phenomenon soon brought the pastor to examine her, and it was not long before he summed up the whole matter, especially as she abused and reviled him with the most scornful and opprobrious language.

She said that she saw a man's head and shoulders with a great white neckcloth look in through her window on the eve of Thanksgiving Day, 19 October, and she recognized this to be the Devil. She accused a neighbour of having bespoken her, but as this woman was known to all as most devout, Elizabeth Knapp changed her tactics and asserted that a demon had deceived her in this respect. " She is (I question not)," piously concludes Mr. Willard, concerning the sufferer, " a subject of hope and therefore all meanes ought to be used for her recoverye. Shee is a monum^t of divine severitye & the Lord grant y all y^t see or heare may feare & tremble : Amen."

Increase Mather in his *Remarkable Providences* (Chap. V) gives the following account of these notorious occurrences :

" Another thing which caused a noise in the countrey, and wherein Satan had undoubtedly a great influence, was that which hapned at Groton. There was a maid in that town (one Elizabeth Knap) who in the moneth of October, anno 1671, was taken after a very strange manner, sometimes weeping, sometimes laughing, sometimes roaring hideously, with violent motions and agitations of her body, crying out ' Money, money,' etc. In November following, her tongue for many hours together was drawn like a semicircle up to the roof of her mouth, not to be removed, though some tried with their fingers to do it. Six men were scarce able to hold her in some of her fits, but she would skip about the house yelling and looking with a most frightful aspect. December 17 : Her tongue was drawn out of her mouth to an extraordinary length ; and now a dæmon began manifestly to speak in her. Many words were uttered wherein are labial letters, without any motion of her lips, which was a clear demonstration that the voice was not her own. Sometimes words were spoken seeming to proceed out of her throat, when her mouth was shut : sometimes with her mouth wide open, without the use of any of the organs of speech. The things then uttered by the devil were chiefly railings and revilings of Mr. Willard (who was at that time a worthy and faithful pastor to the church in Groton). Also the dæmon belched forth most horrid and nefandous blasphemies, exalting himself above the Most High. After this she was taken speechless for some time. One thing more is worthy of remark concerning this miserable creature. She cried out in some of her fits, that a woman (one of her neighbours) appeared to her, and was the cause of her affliction. The person thus accused was a very sincere, holy woman, who did hereupon, with the advice of friends, visit the poor wretch ; and though she was in one of her fits, having her eyes shut, when the innocent person impeached by her came in, yet could she (so powerful were Satans operations upon her) declare who was there, and could tell the touch of that woman from any ones else. But the gracious party, thus accused and abused by a malicious devil, prayed earnestly with and for the possessed creature ; after which she confessed that Satan had deluded her, making her believe evil of her good neighbour without any cause. Nor did she after that complain of any apparition or disturbance from such an one. Yea, she said, that the devil had himself, in the likeness and shape of divers, tormented her, and then told her it was not he but they that did it."

In 1673 Eunice Cole of Hampton was tried, but although strongly suspected—it does not appear on what grounds—of copulation with the Devil, she was found legally not guilty.

The following year, 1674, Christopher Browne at a Court held at Salem, 24 November, acknowledged he had discoursed with one whom he took to be the Devil, " which came like a gentleman." But " his discourse seeming inconsistent with truth, the Court, giving him good counsel and caution, for the present dismiss him."

The following occurrences were noted by Increase Mather as particularly remarkable :

" As there have been several persons vexed with evil spirits, so divers houses have been wofully haunted by them. In the year 1679, the house of William Morse, in Newberry in New-England, was strangely disquieted by a dæmon. After those troubles began, he did, by the advice of friends, write down the particulars of those unusual accidents. And the account which he giveth thereof is as followeth :—

" On December 3, in the night time, he and his wife heard a noise upon the roof of their house, as if sticks and stones had been thrown against it with great violence ; whereupon he rose out of his bed, but could see nothing. Locking the doors fast, he returned to bed again. About midnight they heard an hog making a great noise in the house, so that the man rose again, and found a great hog in the house ; the door being shut, but upon the opening of the door it ran out.

" On December 8, in the morning, there were five great stones and bricks by an invisible hand thrown in at the west end of the house while the mans wife was making the bed ; the bedstead was lifted up from the floor, and the bedstaff flung out of the window, and a cat was hurled at her ; a long staff danced up and down the chimney ; a burnt brick, and a piece of a weather-board, were thrown in at the window. The man at his going to bed, put out his lamp, but in the morning found that the saveall of it was taken away, and yet it was unaccountably brought into its former place. On the same day the long staff, but now spoken of, was hang'd up by a line, and swung to and fro ; the man's wife laid it in the fire, but she could not hold it there, inasmuch as it would forcibly fly out ; yet after much ado, with joynt strength they made it to burn. A shingle flew from the window, though no body near it ; many sticks came in at the same place, only one of these was so scragged that it could enter the hole but a little way, whereupon the man pusht it out ; a great rail likewise was thrust in at the window, so as to break the glass.

" At another time an iron crook that was hanged on a nail, violently flew up and down ; also a chair flew about, and at last lighted on the table where victuals stood ready for them to eat, and was likely to spoil all, only by a nimble catching they saved some of their meal with the loss of the rest and the overturning of their table.

" People were sometimes barricado'd out of doors, when as yet there was nobody to do it ; and a chest was removed from place to place, no hand touching it. Their keys being tied together, one was taken from the rest, and the remaining two would fly about making a loud noise by knocking against

each other. But the greatest part of this devils feats were
his mischievous ones, wherein indeed he was sometimes antick
enough too, and therein the chief sufferers were, the man and
his wife, and his grand-son. The man especially had his share
in these diabolical molestations. For one while they could
not eat their suppers quietly, but had the ashes on the hearth
before their eyes thrown into their victuals, yea, and upon
their heads and clothes, insomuch that they were forced up
into their chamber, and yet they had no rest there ; for one
of the man's shoes being left below, it was filled with ashes
and coals, and thrown up after them. Their light was beaten
out, and, they being laid in their bed with their little boy
between them, a great stone (from the floor of the loft) weighing above three pounds was thrown upon the man's stomach,
and he turning it down upon the floor, it was once more
thrown upon him. A box and a board were likewise thrown
upon them all ; and a bag of hops was taken out of their
chest, therewith they were beaten, till some of the hops were
scattered on the floor, where the bag was then laid and left.

" In another evening, when they sat by the fire, the ashes
were so whirled at them, that they could neither eat their
meat nor endure the house. A peel struck the man in the
face. An apron hanging by the fire was flung upon it, and
singed before they could snatch it off. The man being at
prayer with his family, a beesom gave him a blow on his
head behind, and fell down before his face.

" On another day, when they were winnowing of barley,
some hard dirt was thrown in, hitting the man on the head,
and both the man and his wife on the back ; and when they
had made themselves clean, they essayed to fill their half-
bushel ; but the foul corn was in spite of them often cast in
amongst the clean, and the man, being divers times thus
abused, was forced to give over what he was about.

" On January 23 (in particular), the man had an iron pin
twice thrown at him, and his inkhorn was taken away from
him while he was writing ; and when by all his seeking it
he could not find it, at last he saw it drop out of the air,
down by the fire. A piece of leather was twice thrown at
him ; and a shoe was laid upon his shoulder, which he catching at, was suddenly rapt from him. An handful of ashes
was thrown at his face, and upon his clothes ; and the shoe

was then clapt upon his head, and upon it he clapt his hand,
holding it so fast, that somewhat unseen pulled him with it
backward on the floor.

" On the next day at night, as they were going to bed, a
lost ladder was thrown against the door, and their light put
out ; and when the man was a bed, he was beaten with an
heavy pair of leather breeches, and pull'd by the hair of his
head and beard, pinched and scratched, and his bed-board
was taken away from him. Yet more : in the next night,
when the man was likewise a bed, his bed-board did rise out
of its place, notwithstanding his putting forth all his strength
to keep it in ; one of his awls was brought out of the next
room into his bed, and did prick him ; the clothes wherewith
he hoped to save his head from blows, were violently pluckt
from thence. Within a night or two after, the man and his
wife received both of them a blow upon their heads, but it
was so dark that they could not see the stone which gave it.
The man had his cap pulled off from his head while he sat
by the fire.

" The night following they went to bed undressed, because
of their late disturbances, and the man, wife, boy, presently
felt themselves pricked, and upon search, found in the bed a
bodkin, a knitting-needle, and two sticks picked at both ends ;
he received also a great blow, as on his thigh, so on his face,
which fetched blood ; and while he was writing, a candlestick was twice thrown at him ; and a great piece of bark
fiercely smote him ; and a pail of water turned up without
hands.

" On the 28th of the mentioned moneth, frozen clods of
cow-dung were divers times thrown at the man out of the
house in which they were. His wife went to milk the cow,
and received a blow on her head ; and sitting down at her
milking work, had cow-dung divers times thrown into her
pail. The man tried to save the milk, by holding a piggin
side-wayes under the cowes belly ; but the dung would in
for all, and the milk was only made fit for hogs. On that
night, ashes were thrown into the porridge which they had
made ready for their supper, so as that they could not eat
it ; ashes were likewise often thrown into the man's eyes as
he sat by the fire ; and an iron hammer flying at him, gave
him a great blow on his back. The man's wife going into the

cellar for beer, a great iron peel flew and fell after her through the trap-door of the cellar ; and going afterwards on the same errand to the same place, the door shut down upon her, and the table came and lay upon the door, and the man was forced to remove it e'er his wife could be released from where she was. On the following day, while he was writing, a dish went out of its place, leapt into the pale, and cast water upon the man, his paper, his table, and disappointed his procedure in what he was about ; his cap jumpt off from his head, and on again, and the pot-lid leapt off from the pot into the kettle on the fire.

" February 2. While he and his boy were eating of cheese, the pieces which he cut were wrested from them, but they were afterwards found upon the table, under an apron and a pair of breeches ; and also from the fire arose little sticks and ashes, which flying upon the man and his boy, brought them into an uncomfortable pickle. But as for the boy, which the last passage spoke of, there remains much to be said concerning him and a principal sufferer in these afflictions : for on the 18th of December, he sitting by his grandfather, was hurried into great motions, and the man thereupon took him, and made him stand between his legs ; but the chair danced up and down, and had like to have cast both man and boy into the fire ; and the child was afterwards flung about in such a manner, as that they feared that his brains would have been beaten out ; and in the evening he was tossed as afore, and the man tried the project of holding him, but ineffectually. The lad was soon put to bed, and they presently heard an huge noise, and demanded what was the matter ? and he answered, that his bedstead leaped up and down ; and they (*i.e.* the man and his wife) went up, and at first found all quiet, but before they had been there long, they saw the board by his bed trembling by him, and the bed-clothes flying off him ; the latter they laid on immediately, but they were no sooner on than off ; so they took him out of his bed for quietness.

" December 29. The boy was violently thrown to and fro, only they carried him to the house of a doctor in the town, and there he was free from disturbances ; but returning home at night, his former trouble began, and the man taking him by the hand, they were both of them almost tript into the fire. They put him to bed and he was attended with the same iterated loss of his clothes, shaking off his bed-board, and noises that he had in his last conflict ; they took him up, designing to sit by the fire, but the doors clattered, and the chair was thrown at him ; wherefore they carried him to the doctors house, and so for that night all was well. The next morning he came home quiet ; but as they were doing some-what, he cried out that he was prickt on the back ; they looked, and found a three-tin'd fork sticking strangely there ; which being carried to the doctors house, not only the doctor himself said that it was his, but also the doctors servant affirmed it was seen at home after the boy was gone. The boys vexations continuing, they left him at the doctors, where he remained well till awhile after, and then he complained he was pricked ; they looked and found an iron spindle sticking below his back : he complained he was pricked still ; they looked, and found there a long iron, a bowl of a spoon, and a piece of a pansheard. They lay down by him on the bed, with the light burning, but he was twice thrown from them, and the second time thrown quite under the bed. In the morning the bed was tossed about, with such a creaking noise as was heard to the neighbours. In the afternoon their knives were, one after another, brought, and put into his back, but pulled out by the spectators ; only one knife, which was missing, seemed to the standers by to come out of his mouth. He was bidden to read ; his book was taken and thrown about several times, at last hitting the boys grandmother on the head. Another time he was thrust out of his chair, and rolled up and down, with outcries that all things were on fire ; yea, he was three times very dangerously thrown into the fire, and preserved by his friends with much ado. The boy also made, for a long time together, a noise like a dog, and like an hen with her chickens, and could not speak rationally.

" Particularly, on December 26, he barked like a dog, and clock't like an hen ; and after long distraining to speak, said, ' There's Powel, I am pinched.' His tongue likewise hung out of his mouth, so that it could by no means be forced in till his fit was over, and then he said 'twas forced out by Powel. He and the house also after this had rest till the 9th of January ; at which time the child, because of his intolerable ravings, lying between the man and his wife, was pulled out of bed, and knockt vehemently against the bedstead boards, in a manner very perillous and amazing. In the day-time he was carried away beyond all possibility of their finding him. His grandmother at last saw him creeping on one side, and drag'd him in, where he lay miserable lame ; but recovering his speech, he said, that he was carried above the doctors house, and that Powel carried him : and that the said Powel had him into the barn, throwing him against the cart-wheel there, and then thrusting him out at an hole ; and accordingly they found some of the remainders of the threshed barley, which was on the barn-floor, hanging to his clothes.

" At another time he fell into a swoon ; they forced somewhat refreshing into his mouth, and it was turned out as fast as they put it in ; e'er long he came to himself, and expressed some willingness to eat, but the meat would forcibly fly out of his mouth ; and when he was able to speak, he said Powel would not let him eat. Having found the boy to be best at a neighbours house, the man carried him to his daughters, three miles from his own. The boy was growing antick as he was on the journey, but before the end of it he made a grievous hollowing ; and when he lighted, he threw a great stone at a maid in the house, and fell on eating of ashes. Being at home afterwards, they had rest awhile : but on the 19th of January, in the morning he swooned, and coming to himself, he roared terribly, and did eat ashes, sticks, rug-yarn. The morning following, there was such a racket with the boy that the man and his wife took him to bed to them : a bed-staff[3] was thereupon thrown at them, and a chamber-pot with its contents was thrown upon them, and they were severely pinched. The man being about to rise, his clothes were divers times pulled from them, himself thrust out of his bed, and his pillow thrown after him. The lad also would have his clothes plucked off from him in these winter nights, and was wofully dogg'd with such fruits of devilish spite, till it pleased God to shorten the chain of the wicked dæmon.

" All this while the devil did not use to appear in any visible shape, only they would think they had hold of the hand that sometimes scratched them ; but it would give them the slip. And once the man was discernably beaten by a fist, and an hand got hold of his wrist, which he saw but could not catch ; and the likeness of a blackmore child did appear from under the rugg and blanket, where the man lay, and it would rise up, fall down, nod, and slip under the clothes, when they endeavoured to clasp it, never speaking anything.

" Neither were there many words spoken by Satan all this time ; only once, having put out their light, they heard a scraping on the boards, and then a piping and drumming on them, which was followed with a voice, singing, ' Revenge ! Revenge ! Sweet is revenge ! ' And they being well terrified with it, called upon God : the issue of which was, that suddenly, with a mournful note, there were six times over uttered such expressions as, ' Alas ! me knock no more ! me knock no more ! ' and now all ceased.

" The man does, moreover, affirm that a seaman (being a mate of a ship) coming often to visit him told him, that they wronged his wife who suspected her to be guilty of witchcraft ; and that the boy (his grandchild) was the cause of this trouble ; and that if he would let him have the boy one day, he would warrant him his house should be no more troubled as it had been. To which motion he consented. The mate came the next day betimes, and the boy was with him until night ; since which time his house, he saith, has not been molested with evil spirits.

" Thus far is the relation concerning the dæmon at William Morse his house in Newberry. The true reason of these strange disturbances is as yet not certainly known : some (as has been hinted) did suspect Morse's wife to be guilty of witchcraft.

" One of the neighbours took apples, which were brought out of that house, and put them into the fire ; upon which, they say, their houses were much disturbed. Another of the neighbours caused an horse-shoe to be nailed before the doors ; and as long as it remained so, they could not perswade the suspected person to go into the house ; but when the horse-shoe was gone, she presently visited them. I shall not here inlarge upon the vanity and superstition of those experiments, reserving that for another place ; all that I shall say at present is, that the dæmons, whom the blind Gentiles of old worshipped, told their servants, that such things as these would very much affect them ; yea, and that certain characters, signs, and charms, would render their power ineffectual ; and accordingly they would become subject, when their own

directions were obeyed. It is sport to the devils when they
see silly men thus deluded and made fools of by them. Others
were apt to think that a seaman, by some suspected to be a
conjurer, set the devil on work thus to disquiet Morse's
family ; or, it may be, some other thing, as yet kept hid in
the secrets of Providence, might be the true original of all
this trouble."

Increase Mather reminds his readers of the famous story
of the Drummer of Tedworth, with which happenings he
compares the troubling of the house at Newberry. Tedworth,
a small village in Wiltshire, was for awhile the most talked-of
spot in England, and a very Mecca for those interested in the
supernatural.[4] Among the visitors came Joseph Glanvill, who
spent a night there, and although none of the more striking
occurrences took place during his stay he was able to observe
sufficient to satisfy his own mind. King Charles sent Lord
Falmouth and the Queen the Earl of Chesterfield to investigate the matter, but they appear to have been somewhat
superficial in their examination, and as nothing marvellous
was exhibited for their benefit their report tended to discredit
the affair, a very shallow answer to the evidence of those
who had again and again witnessed the disturbances. The
phenomena which commenced in April, 1661, and appear to
have continued intermittently until April, 1663 (it is not
established that they then ceased), took the form mainly of
odd noises and the capricious movement of objects without
any apparent physical cause. The best account of this very
curious case is to be found in Glanvill, *Saducismus Triumphatus*,[5] of which Increase Mather gives the following convenient summary :

" Mr. Mompesson of Tedworth being in March, 1661, at
Ludgershall, and hearing a drum beat there, he demanded of
the bailiff of the town what it meant ; who told him, they
had for some dayes been troubled with an idle drummer, pretending authority and a pass under the hands of some gentlemen. Mr. Mompesson reading his pass, and knowing the hands
of those gentlemen whose names were pretended to be subscribed, discovered the cheat, and commanded the vagrant to
put off his drum, and ordered a constable to secure him ; but
not long after he got clear of the constable. In April following,
Mr. Mompesson's house was much disturbed with knockings

and with drummings ; for an hour together a dæmon would beat Round-heads and Cuckolds, the tattoo and several other points of war, as well as any drummer. On November 5, the dæmon made a great noise in the house, and caused some boards therein to move to and fro in the day time, when there was an whole room full of people present. At his departure, he left behind him a sulphurous smell, which was very offensive. The next night, chairs walked up and down the room ; the childrens shoes were hurled over their heads, The minister of the town being there, a bedstaff was thrown at him, and hit him on the leg, but without the least hurt. In the latter end of December, 1662, they heard a noise like the jingling of money, the occasion of which was thought to be, some words spoken the night before by one in the family, who said that fairies used to leave money behind them, and they wished it might be so now. In January, lights were seen in the house, which seemed blue and glimmering, and caused a great stiffness in the eyes of them that saw them. One in the room (by what authority I cannot tell) said ' Satan, if the drummer set thee a work, give three knocks and no more ' ; which was done accordingly. Once, when it was very sharp severe weather, the room was suddenly filled with a noisome smell, and was very hot, though without fire. This dæmon would play some nasty and many ludicrous foolish tricks. It would empty chamber-pots into the beds ; and fill porringers with ashes. Sometimes it would not suffer any light to be in the room, but would carry them away up the chimney. Mr. Mompesson coming one morning into his stable, found his horse on the ground, having one of his hinder legs in his mouth, and so fastened there that it was difficult for several men with a leaver to get it out. A smith, lodging in the house, heard a noise in the room as if one had been shoeing an horse, and somewhat come as it were with a pincers snipping at the smith's nose, most part of the night. The drummer was under vehement suspicion for a conjuror. He was condemned to transportation. All the time of his restraint and absence, the house was quiet."

The " idle drummer," whose name was William Drury, was, towards the end of 1662, arrested for stealing, and sentenced to deportation, but he managed to escape, in April, 1663, from the barge in which he was being conveyed. Whilst in gaol he was reported to have accused himself of being the cause of the disturbances at Tedworth, which fact came to the knowledge of Mr. Mompesson, who, learning that Drury had returned to his native village (Uscut, Wilts), caused him, a few days after his escape, to be apprehended for Witchcraft. According to a letter from Mr. Mompesson, printed in *Saducismus Triumphatus*, we learn that, whilst the Grand Jury found a true bill, the Petty Jury acquitted Drury ; and his actual connexion with the affair (apart from his supposed confession) appears to have been very slight.

The psychic phenomena at Newberry and at Tedworth belong to the type which are now generally known as poltergeist hauntings. The whole question is one of peculiar difficulty, as a number of material explanations, mice, rats, water pipes, hollow panels, the cracking of furniture under changed conditions of atmosphere, heat, cold, the pranks played by children or mischievous persons, at once suggest themselves and are suggested. But whilst all these may account for many things it is quite impossible that they should cover a tithe of the phenomena which have been investigated. That boys or girls may often be naturally clever at deception and tricks, I readily admit, but how can they possibly be such practised prestidigitators, such accomplished artists in the craft of hoax, that their performances have necessitated the close observation of trained investigators, of philosophers, shrewd lawyers, ecclesiastics of the highest rank, and not infrequently even of the lynx-eyed officers of the law ?

It may not be wholly impertinent very briefly to mention a few of the more prominent instances of poltergeist haunting. In 1695 the farm of Andrew Mackie, who lived at Ringcroft of Stocking, Kirkcudbrightshire, was pestered in this peculiar manner. The disturbances began one February evening, when various objects began to fly about as if of their own volition, and soon heavy showers of stones were thrown into the house, but by whom or whence could not be ascertained. A phantom was also seen, a lad about fourteen years old, red-faced, with yellow hair, dressed in hodden grey with a bonnet on his head. Ministers were then called in to watch and pray, but all the while hideous noises were heard, and on one occasion fire broke out simultaneously in the house in seven places. It was not until 1 May that the tormented family was left in peace.

Very famous are the Epworth phenomena, concerning which we have a number of letters dated from January to April, 1717, between young Samuel Wesley, who was then at school at Westminster, and his father, mother, sisters at home. We also possess an account written for his son Samuel by the elder Wesley, and a brief diary. Further, Mrs. Wesley and some others made a set of records, written August to September, 1726, at Epworth for John Wesley. It is hardly necessary to describe the Epworth phenomena in detail : " Loud mumblings followed above stairs and below ; a clatter among a number of bottles as if they had all at once been dashed to pieces ; footsteps as if of a man going up and down stairs at all hours of the night ; sounds like that of dancing in an empty room, the door of which was locked ; gobbling like a turkey-cock ; and, most frequently of all a knocking about the beds at night and in different parts of the house." It was noticed that the wind commonly rose after any of these demonstrations, and increased with it, whistling loudly round the house. The phenomena seem to have continued more or less during a period of four or five months, but were much more violent for the first month, gradually becoming less and less troublesome after this.[6]

In the celebrated case of the haunting of Willington Mill, which was at its height, 1835-47, the poltergeist disturbances were accompanied by spectral apparitions, and so it may be regarded as a complex haunting. Willington Mill stands upon what is locally known as Willington Gut, a sluggish stream that empties itself into the Tyne between Willington Quay and Wallsend. The mill itself is built upon the site of a cottage occupied more than two centuries ago by a notorious witch. The phenomena commenced when a Quaker, Mr. Unthank, was living at the mill. The noise of a mangle was heard going swiftly all night, when it was quite certain that there was no such machine on the premises. Mr. Unthank was succeeded by Mr. Proctor, likewise a member of the Society of Friends, and soon after he had settled a fearful uproar began late one night and persevered till dawn. Nobody in the house could sleep a wink. " Sometimes the noise was like a paviour at work with his rammer thumping on the floor till the whole building rattled again ; again it was like a donkey galloping round the room overhead ; at another time it was as if a shovelful of scrappy iron had been thrown upon the fireplace and fender. Heavy footsteps were heard ; there were continual rappings as if someone with a pencil was tabering upon the doors ; candlesticks were thrown about ; and pieces of furniture oscillated as though somebody were pushing them with a violent effort. These manifestations continued, though with less vigour and sporadically, for several decades, when it seemed as if the force were being exhausted. In 1891 the house, outwardly a wreck, had within been divided into cheap tenements. No disturbances were recorded for many years past."[7]

M. Tinel, the curé of Cideville, in 1851, had lodging with him in the presbytery two pupils, Gustave Lemonnier, aged twelve, and Brunel, aged fourteen. In the presence of these two lads loud rappings occurred, fire-irons left their places on the hearth, coverlets flew from beds, heavy desks moved briskly of their own accord across the room. At first the lads were suspected of some trickery, but a number of careful investigators bore witness that it was not possible for Lemonnier and Brunel to have anything to do with these phenomena. That was proved beyond all manner of doubt. At times the din caused by rappings and the falling of heavy bodies attracted the attention of persons in the street. The curé accused a shepherd named Thorel of causing the disturbances by Witchcraft, and the man summoned him for libel in the local Courts, which could find no explanation for these strange happenings. That the children were unconsciously mediumistic and therefore afforded an opportunity for the force to exhibit itself is not an improbable solution, but this is a very different matter from supposing they were conjurers of no ordinary ability and address, and indeed something more than mere conjurers.

Another very extraordinary case was that which occurred in the house of M. Joller, a lawyer of Lucerne from 1860–62. Joller, who was a man of high standing and a member of the Swiss House of Representatives, has told his own story in a pamphlet of some twenty pages which is now excessively rare. Manifestations commenced by rappings and knockings upon the walls and tables. A sound of sobbing was heard, and later the noise of spinning-wheels throughout the house, whilst the furniture began to move in an unaccountable fashion. M. Joller, who attributed the whole affair to rats, now dismissed their servant, as they suspected her of some trickery. The phenomena, however, continued until the unfortunate inmates of the house had no peace night nor day. A commission of inquiry, consisting of the President of the Court of Justice, Judge Schollberger, with several councillors and other persons of the highest integrity, came to visit the house, and were amazed at the confusion. Doors flew open and banged incessantly, sometimes being held fast when any person attempted to open them and suddenly released, whilst a perfect charivari of knocking and drumming sounded in every direction. No explanation was forthcoming in spite of the strictest search, and the place having become quite untenable, Joller was compelled to leave in October, 1862, and seek another home.

The Worksop phenomena occurred in a household of the lower middle class in 1883. A doctor and a policeman were called in, both of whom saw crockery fly from cupboards, cups leap into the air and fall to be smashed on the floor, a basin float through the air, turning over and over as it went, and many similar marvels. It was suggested that all this was the work of a servant, Eliza Rose, and she was dismissed, but it was remembered that the occurrences had commenced before she was in that employment. A number of persons inquired into the matter, but no pronouncement was ever definitely made.

In October, 1883, at Wood's Farm, near Wem, Shropshire, when the tenant, Mr. Hampson, his wife, two children, and two female servants, were about to have tea at four o'clock in the afternoon, a saucepan, as they declared, sprang off the fire and at the same moment, nobody being within reach of the table, the cloth was lifted and all the tea-things swept off crashing to the floor. Later pieces of burning coal were flung out of the fire, and the ornaments upon the mantelpiece fell to the ground.

In terror they called in their neighbours, a local farmer named Lea, who with the village constable, Bowen, witnessed the breaking and throwing about of crockery, and the hurling of platters and plates from dresser to ceiling. Everybody then quitted the house, and as they stood upon the lawn discussing the matter in deepest amazement a whole shower of articles was thrown out of the windows. Every endeavour was made to elucidate the mystery, but to no avail.[8]

During the year 1891 a small house in Mayor's Walks, Peterborough, was taken by a railway employe, named Rimes. From the time the family entered it the most extraordinary events were experienced, and the manifestations were such as eventually ended in the tenants being driven from the place. When the inmates were in bed the blankets and quilts were lifted and thrown in a heap by the bedside. Doors were shaken with the utmost violence ; on one occasion a door was actually splintered, although this was the only damage done. The most horrible noises were heard. One witness asserted that it seemed as if " a portion of the house was falling in with a crash " ; another described the din " as though a cart-load of bricks had been tipped up in the house." Once it seemed " as though a table laden with crockery had been overturned," and once " as if a sack of coals was being thrown down the stairs." Several witnesses agreed that " the noises were almost always preceded by a low humming sound, as if made by a rushing wind." Neither the residents, the neighbours, the police, nor a private detective could explain these occurrences.[9]

Professor Lombroso, the celebrated Italian criminologist, investigated some strange manifestations which took place in Turin, at number 6 Via Bava, in 1900. The house was a wine and spirit store, belonging to Signor Fumero. On the morning of 16 November, Signora Fumero and her assistant saw a bottle of wine which stood on the kitchen table slowly and deliberately turn over of its own accord. Other vessels proceeded to do the same, and the furniture, saucepans, and other cooking utensils began to move rapidly. Signora Fumero fainted with fright, and her husband who was absent was summoned by telegram. The phenomena continued, and it was particularly observed that when anyone entered the cellar used for storing bottles these hurtled together and broke. So great was the noise that the police intervened but utterly failed to cope with the unseen activities. Such un-pleasantness ensued that it was with difficulty Lombroso obtained permission to go down into the cellar and investigate.

" The cellar," he observed in the narrative of his experiences, " was at first in complete darkness, and I heard the noise of broken glasses and bottles rolling at my feet. The bottles were arranged in six compartments one above another. In the middle was a rough table on which I had six lighted candles placed, supposing that the spirit phenomena would cease in the bright light. But on the contrary I saw three empty bottles standing on the ground roll as though pushed by a finger, and break near the table. To obviate any possible trick, I carefully examined all the full bottles which were on the racks, and assured myself that there was no cord or string which could explain their movements. After a few minutes, first two, then four, then two other bottles on the second and third racks detached themselves and fell to the ground—not suddenly, but as though carried by someone. After their descent six of them broke on the floor already soaked with wine, while only two remained whole. Then at the moment of leaving the cellar, just as I was going out, I heard another bottle break."

Eventually the manifestations ceased when a boy employed in the shop was dismissed. It was conclusively proved that he could not have manipulated the phenomena, which often occurred when he was absent, but no doubt he possessed unusual mediumistic faculties which gave the power an opportunity to concentrate itself and cause the disturbance.[10]

Most curious molestations befell an old woman of Calabria, aged eighty, Signora Bruno, in December, 1904. She was persecuted by fire and by water, that is to say on one occasion a great quantity of water began to fall from the walls of her room on to her bed, and even on to her person, following her about all over the house. When this ceased, her dress began to burn, although she felt no sensation of heat whatsoever. Her bed and her clothes, though packed away in a trunk, and a quantity of hay in a loft also caught fire.[11]

During the summer of 1906 the farm of Monsieur and Madame Cointet at Neuville, Somme, was troubled by most mysterious occurrences, which seemed traceable to the unconscious mediumship of their grandson, a child of ten. The local gossips declared that he had been forespoken, and the boy himself constantly alleged that he saw an angry black dog which wanted to attack him. Once, when in company with several other persons, the child cried : " The brute has got hold of my clothes ! " and at the same moment the lad's trousers were rent in several places as by the fangs of some fierce animal. In the stables the cords by which the cattle were tethered, however cunningly tied, were loosed in an inexplicable manner. The kitchen utensils used to fly about the room as though hurled by invisible hands, and there was a general repetition of the phenomena already described as taking place at Ringcroft, Cideville, Wood's Farm, Peterborough, and other distressed localities.

Great prominence was given in the daily and weekly press to the disturbances at the village of Cheriton, near Folkestone, in 1917. These apparently commenced by the starting of work on an air-raid dug-out at Enbrock Manor, the residence of Mr. H. P. Jacques. Mr. Frederick Rolfe, a builder at Cheriton, was employed in connexion with the work required, and according to the *Weekly Dispatch* he gave the following account of his experiences :

" About six weeks ago I started work on the dug-out for Mr. Jacques, and during that time I have gone through experiences which you would hardly credit. All my life I have been dead against such things as spiritualism—dismissed them as impossible and absurd. What I have seen, however, through this remarkable period makes me realize that there is a hidden force which I cannot account for."

Mr. Rolfe said on one occasion a large stone from quite another part of the dug-out hit him on the crown of the head (the scar is still visible) ; on another occasion he received a severe blow on the hand (the wounds inflicted are also visible).

" The candles were repeatedly extinguished by air and a jet of sand accompanied by a sharp whiz, such as might be expected from a current of air blown through a peashooter.

" On several occasions pieces of rock, varying from 8 lb. to 20 lb., were hurled by some unseen foe from one position to another."

A boy named Penfold, who assisted, declared that he saw the stones lift themselves an inch and then drop again ; then about three inches and drop once more. Soon after, they would fly off by themselves to another position. There were bricks on the floor. These, too, lifted of themselves and shifted positions.

" Subsequently," Mr. Rolfe continued, " things became worse. Rocks and stones flew about, and so much so that an iron stove and iron pipe were smashed to pieces. Then, to crown all, a short hammer, such as bricklayers use, weighing about 4 lb., threw itself towards me. The boy Penfold then shouted, ' Look out, perhaps the sledge-hammer will come also.' Hardly had the lad uttered the words than the hammer, weighing with handle about 14 lb., flung itself at me from a considerable distance, as did also soon after a pickaxe.

" There were three chairs in the place, and one of these moved about in an alarming style. There were only myself and the boy in the place.

" There was a heap of stones in one corner of the place and, incredible as it may appear, these shifted themselves from one point to another."

No explanation appears to have been forthcoming of the cause of these phenomena, and it was found impossible to trace them to any normal agency.

All these cases are vouched for on irrefragable evidence, and it seems to me idle to question their substantial truth. I am not prepared to say that any one explanation will cover them ; in fact, I think it highly probable that results which as manifested are apparently very similar may proceed from entirely different causes.

More than one writer[12] has attributed the weird and awesome experiences which troubled the presbytery of S. Jean Baptiste Vianney[13] to these poltergeist hauntings, whereas they were in truth demoniac persecution. This commenced one night about nine o'clock when the holy curé was just about to retire to rest. He was already in his bedroom, and suddenly three terrific blows were struck upon the door of the house as if someone were battering it with an enormous club. He opened the window and cried " Who is there ? " but nobody was to be seen in the clear cold moonlight, not a footstep marked the expanse of spotless snow. Presently noises sounded on the staircase, and the Saint acknowledged that at the beginning of the visitations he felt as if he should die of terror in his bed, his teeth chattered, his blood froze, and his hair started like reeds on his scalp. Fearing at first that it might be some burglarious attempt to steal the church ornaments, since the Vicomte d'Ars had just presented the parish with new vestments, rich gilded candlesticks, jewelled reliquaries, and a magnificent monstrance, S. Jean Baptiste arranged for the village blacksmith to spend some nights in an adjoining room. This man, a powerful Hercules, who had armed himself with a gun and a flesher's whittle, declared that at midnight all the furniture flew about the room, and from the hubbub of crashes and wailings he thought the old presbytery was on the point of collapsing over his head. He called for lights, but when they searched nothing could be seen. Grappin, for this was the name the holy curé tauntingly gave the demon who attacked him, would pull the chairs to and fro screeching on the bare boards, disarrange all the crockery in the kitchen, drum upon the table or chimneypiece or water-jug, and at other times seem to be hammering nails into the floor, planing boards, or sawing planks as if a carpenter were busy in the house. At one time the curtains of the Saint's bed burst into flame when no candle or fire had been near them. These things were widely discussed in spite of the curé's efforts to keep them unknown, and on one occasion during a mission the clergy who had assembled began to rally him on the hauntings. It was agreed by all that this infernal mysticism was nothing in the world but mere hallucination, dreaming, and delusion ; and the curé himself was treated as a visionary and a hypochondriac. " Your presbytery," they laughed, " is nothing but an old barn without order or arrangement. The doors slam, the boards creak, the rats hold high carnival there, for they play their pranks night and day and you think you are persecuted by the Devil. Come, come, dear friend, behave like other people, eat more, and all this Satanic phantasmagoria will stop soon enough." And so all retired to their respective chambers with the happy indifference of philosophers, who if they believed in the Devil at all certainly absolved him from any interference in the affairs of the Curé d'Ars. But at midnight these hardy souls were awakened by the most hideous uproar. Doors open and shut with violence, windows rattle, shutters fly back, the very walls seem to shake and heave, footsteps rush up and down the staircase with terrific speed. The stranger priests dress all hurriedly shaking with fear. Every moment they expect the building to fall in ruin upon them. They hasten from their rooms, but are met by their host, who reassures

them in calm, collected tones. One of the missioners, l'Abbé
Chevalon, an old soldier of the Empire, when relating this
adventure said : " I made a promise to Our Lord never again
to jest about these stories of apparitions and nocturnal dis-.
turbances. It was more terrible than one could have believed.
As for the Curé d'Ars, I take him to be a saint."

S. Jean Baptiste Vianney endured this persecution for a
period of some thirty years. Towards the end of his life he
was left comparatively at rest, and during six months before
his death (4 August, 1859) there was a complete cessation of
the diabolic phenomena.[14]

In the fifth chapter of his *Remarkable Providences* Increase
Mather has some further particulars of poltergeist hauntings
in New England which are so curious as to warrant quotation
in full He writes :

" I proceed to give an account of some other things lately
hapning in New-England, which were undoubtedly præter-
natural, and not without diabolical operation. The last year
did afford several instances, not unlike unto those which have
been mentioned. For then Nicholas Desborough, of Hartford
in New-England, was strangely molested by stones, pieces of
earth, cobs of Indian corn, &c., falling upon and about him,
which sometimes came in through the door, sometimes
through the window, sometimes down the chimney ; at other
times they seemed to fall from the floor of the chamber, which
yet was very close ; sometimes he met with them in his shop,
the yard, the barn, and in the field at work. In the house,
such things hapned frequently, not only in the night but in
the day time, if the man himself was at home, but never when
his wife was at home alone. There was no great violence in
the motion, though several persons of the family, and others
also, were struck with the things that were thrown by an
invisible hand, yet they were not hurt thereby. Only the
man himself had once his arm somewhat pained by a blow
given him ; and at another time, blood was drawn from one
of his legs by a scratch given it. This molestation began soon
after a controversie arose between Desborough and another
person, about a chest of clothes which the other said that
Desborough did unrighteously retain : and so it continued
for some moneths (though with several intermissions), in the
latter end of the last year, when also the man's barn was

burned with the corn in it ; but by what means it came to pass is not known. Not long after, some to whom the matter was referred, ordered Desborough to restore the clothes to the person who complained of wrong ; since which he hath not been troubled as before. Some of the stones hurled were of considerable bigness ; one of them weighed four pounds, but generally the stones were not great, but very small ones. One time a piece of clay came down the chimney, falling on the table which stood at some distance from the chimney. The people of the house threw it on the hearth, where it lay a considerable time : they went to their supper, the piece of clay was lifted up by an invisible hand, and fell upon the table ; taking it up they found it hot, having lain so long before the fire, as to cause it to be hot.

" Another providence, no less remarkable than this last mentioned, hapned at Portsmouth in New-England, about the same time : concerning which I have received the following account from a worthy hand.

" On June 11, 1682, being the Lords Day, at night showers of stones were thrown both against the sides and roof of the house of George Walton : some of the people went abroad, found the gate at some distance from the house wrung off the hinges, and stones came thick about them, sometimes falling down by them, sometimes touching them without any hurt done to them ; though they seemed to come with great force, yet did no more but softly touch them ; stones flying about the room, the doors being shut ; the glass windows shattered to pieces by stones that seemed to come not from without but within, the lead of the glass casements, window-bars, &c., being driven forcibly outwards, and so standing bent. While the secretary was walking in the room, a great hammer came brushing along against the chamber floor that was over his head and fell down by him. A candlestick beaten off the table. They took up nine of the stones and marked them, and laid them on the table, some of them being as hot as if they came out of the fire ; but some of those mark't stones were found flying about again. In this manner, about four hours space that night. The secretary then went to bed, but a stone came and broke up his chamber-door ; being put to (not lockt), a brick was sent upon the like errand. The abovesaid stone the secretary lockt up in his chamber, but it was fetched out, and carried with great noise into the next chamber. The spit was carried up chimney, and came down with the point forward, and stuck in the back-log, and being removed by one of the company to one side of the chimney, was by an unseen hand thrown out at window. This trade was driven on the next day, and so from day to day ; now and then there would be some intermission, and then to it again. The stones were most frequent where the master of the house was, whether in the field or barn, &c. A black cat was seen once while the stones came, and was shot at, but she was too nimble for them. Some of the family say, that they once saw the appearance of an hand put forth at the hall window, throwing stones towards the entry, though there was no body in the hall the while : sometimes a dismal hollow whistling would be heard ; sometimes the noise of the trotting of an horse, and snorting, but nothing seen. The man went up the great bay in his boat to a farm he had there, and while haling wood or timber to the boat, he was disturbed by the stones as before at home. He carried a stirrup-iron from the house down to the boat, and there left it ; but while he was going up to the house, the iron came jingling after him through the woods, and returned to the house, and so again, and at last went away, and was heard of no more. Their anchor leaped overboard several times as they were going home, and stopt the boat. A cheese hath been taken out of the press and crumbled all over the floor. A piece of iron with which they weighed up the cheese-press, stuck into the wall, and a kittle hung up thereon. Several cocks of English hay, mowed near the house, were taken and hung upon trees ; and some made into small whisps, and put all up and down the kitchen, *cum multis aliis*, &c. After this manner have they been treated ever since at times ; it were endless to particularize. Of late, they thought the bitterness of death had been past, being quiet for sundry dayes and nights : but last week were some returnings again ; and this week (Aug. 2, 1682) as bad or worse than ever. The man is sorely hurt with some of the stones that came on him, and like to feel the effects of them for many dayes.' Thus far is that relation.

"I am moreover informed, that the dæmon was quiet all the last winter, but in the spring he began to play some ludicrous tricks, carrying away some axes that were locked up safe. This last summer he has not made such disturbances as formerly ; but of this no more at present.

" There have been strange and true reports concerning a woman now living near the Salmon Falls in Barwick (formerly called Kittery), unto whom evil spirits have sometimes visibly appeared ; and she has sometimes been sorely tormented by invisible hands : concerning all which an intelligent person has sent me the following narrative.

A brief Narrative of sundry Apparitions of Satan unto, and Assaults at sundry times and places upon, the person of Mary, the wife of Antonio Hortado, dwelling near the Salmon Falls. Taken from her own mouth, Aug. 13, 1683.

" ' In June, 1682 (the day forgotten), at evening, the said Mary heard a voice at the door of her dwelling, saying, " What do you here ? " About an hour after, standing at the door of her house, she had a blow on her eye that settled her head near to the door-post ; and two or three dayes after, a stone, as she judged about half a pound or a pound weight, was thrown along the house within into the chimney, and going to take it up it was gone ; all the family was in the house, and no hand appearing which might be instrumental in throwing the stone. About two hours after, a frying-pan then hanging in the chimney was heard to ring so loud, that not only those in the house heard it, but others also that lived on the other side of the river near an hundred rods distant or more. Whereupon the said Mary and her husband going in a cannoo over the river, they saw like the head of a man new-shorn, and the tail of a white cat, about two or three foot distance from each other, swimming over before the cannoo, but no body appeared to joyn head and tail together ; and they returning over the river in less than an hours time, the said apparition followed their cannoo back again, but disappeared at landing. A day or two after, the said Mary was stricken on her head (as she judged) with a stone, which caused a swelling and much soreness on her head, being then in the yard by her house ; and she presently entring into her house, was bitten on both arms black and blue, and one of her breasts scratched ; the impressions of the teeth being like mans teeth were plainly seen by many.

Whereupon deserting their house to sojourn at a neighbours on the other side of the river, there appeared to said Mary in the house of her sojourning, a woman clothed with a green safeguard, a short blue cloak, and a white cap, making a profer to strike her with a fire-brand, but struck her not. The day following, the same shape appeared to her, but now arrayed with a grey gown, white apron, and white head-clothes, in appearance laughing several times, but no voice heard. Since when, said Mary has been freed from those Satanical molestations.

" ' But the said Antonio being returned in March last with his family, to dwell again in his own house, and on his entrance there, hearing the noise of a man walking in his chamber, and seeing the boards buckle under his feet as he walked, though no man to be seen in the chamber (for they went on purpose to look), he returned with his family to dwell on the other side of the river ; yet planting his ground, though he forsook his house, he hath had five rods of good log-fence thrown down at once; the feeting of neat cattle plainly to be seen almost between every row of corn in the field, yet no cattle seen there, nor any damage done to his corn, not so much as any of the leaves of the corn cropt.' Thus far is that narrative.

" I am further informed, that some (who should have been wiser) advised the poor woman to stick the house round with bayes, as an effectual preservative against the power of evil spirits. This counsel was followed ; and as long as the bayes continued green, she had quiet ; but when they began to wither, they were all by an unseen hand carried away, and the woman again tormented.

" It is observable, that at the same time three houses in three several towns should be molested by dæmons, as has now been related."

The two Mathers, Increase and Cotton, as well by their writings, the *Remarkable Providences Illustrative of the Earlier Days of American Colonisation*, 1684, and the *Cases of Conscience : Concerning Evil Spirits Personating Men ; Witchcrafts Infallible Proofs of Guilt in such as are Accused of that Crime*, Boston, 1692, of the former, and *The Wonders of the Invisible World*, published at Boston in October, 1692, " Reprinted at *London*, for *John Dunton*, at the *Raven* in the *Poultry*," 1693, of Cotton Mather, as by their preachings, practice, and precepts perhaps did more than any others to fan into flame and keep alive the witch prosecutions of Salem, the most prominent episodes of the New England crusade, against sorcery. Some particular account, indeed, of these remarkable men is necessary. Increase Mather (1639–1723) was the youngest son of Richard Mather (1596–1669), a congregational divine of good, but impoverished, stock. Richard Mather was educated at Winwich grammar school, and in 1612 became the first master of a newly established school at Toxteth Park, Liverpool. A chapel was also built there, and when he had preached his first sermon on 30 November, 1619, he was ordained by Thomas Morton,[15] Bishop of Chester, a stout Protestant. For fifteen years he seems to have pursued his ministry with much zeal. In August, 1633, he was suspended by even the casual and weak-kneed Bishop Bridgeman,[16] Morton's successor, on the proven charge of having illegally disused the Church of England ceremonies, but some three months later at the intercession of powerful friends he was reinstated. Things continued, maugre this warning, in a very unsatisfactory state at Toxteth, and it was very clear that Mather held other than episcopalian views. In 1634 he was again suspended, as it transpired he had never worn a surplice, and the visitors of Dr. Richard Neile,[17] Archbishop of York, discovered other glaring irregularities and general lawlessness. In the following year Mather resolved to emigrate to New England, and upon receiving warm letters of encouragement from the Boston ministers John Cotton and Thomas Hooker, he left the port of Bristol with his family on 4 June, 1635, reached Boston harbour on Sunday, 16 August, and landed next day. After residing here for a few months he accepted a call from the congregation of Dorchester, Massachusetts, and became " teacher " of their community on 23 August, 1636. In this charge he remained till his death. He was soon to be an influential leader in the councils of New England congregationalism, and it was actually after presiding at one of these meetings, at Boston, 13–16 April, 1669, that he was seized with a violent attack of an old disorder, returning to Dorchester but to die there on 22 April following.

It will be seen that Increase Mather came of stern Puritan forbears. He was born at Dorchester, 1639, graduated M.A.

at Harvard in 1656, thereupon being immediately elected a
fellow of the College. In 1657 he visited England, and from
Lancashire proceeded to Dublin, where he entered Trinity
College, and was admitted M.A. in 1658. He seems to have
officiated at Great Torrington, Devonshire, until May, 1659,
when he was invited to Guernsey by Colonel Bingham, the
governor, who delighted in his long sermons. On the appointment of Sir Hugh Pollard, however, he left the island, and
rather than conform returned to New England, where he was
installed as minister of the New North Church, Boston, com-
mencing his functions on 27 May, 1664. His career was
certainly of great local importance, and he busied himself
very prominently in all civic and ecclesiastical affairs. Having
been rector of Harvard for some years, he was elected
President in 1684, which dignity he resigned in 1701 owing
to the requirement of residence. He remained in his Boston
charge until he had passed his eightieth year, and upon his
death, 23 August, 1723, he was honoured with a public
funeral.

His eldest son Cotton Mather, was born at Boston on
12 February, 1663, entered Harvard when but twelve years
old, and from May, 1684, as a minister at Boston and a busy
pragmatist he kept himself even more in the public eye than
his father. He died at Boston, 13 February, 1728.

The Salem troubles originated in the house of a very remarkable person, the Rev. Samuel Parris, the minister of
Salem Village, now the town of Danvers, adjoining the
present city of Salem. Samuel Parris, the son of Thomas
Parris, was born in London, 1653, but his father soon
emigrating to New England, he received his education at
Harvard, although he did not complete his scholastic course.
He left the University to engage in commerce, and was for
many years a merchant in the West Indies, his place of
residence being settled at Barbadoes. He is reported to have
shown the most grasping and avaricious spirit in all his
mercantile dealings and was notorious as an unduly sharp,
not to say an actually dishonest, hand at a shrewd bargain.
Later he came to Salem, where he engaged in the study of
divinity, making himself particular even among the fanatics
by his austere manners and excess of arid sanctimoniousness.
So high was he presently in favour with the bigots that on

29 April, 1689, he accepted " a call to the ministry," and was congregationally ordained on Monday, 19 November, of that year, succeeding after some interim Deodat Lawson.

The roll of the ministers of Salem at this period runs thus : First, James Bayley, who was followed in 1680 by George Burroughs. In 1683 Burroughs, being involved in various parochial quarrels, retired from his post, and the next year Deodat Lawson, consenting to some form of Congregational election, began his public ministry. Lawson is first heard of in New England in 1671. He seems to have been a man of talents and some learning, and his eloquence in the pulpit was universally admired. Whilst at Salem he lost both his wife and a daughter. In 1690 he married Deborah Allen, soon after accepting an appointment as " minister of the gospel " over the Second Society in Scituate, where he was living in August, 1693. In 1696 he went over to England, as his people believed for a short visit, but they found ere long that he had no intention of returning. Doubtless he was alive and in London when in 1704 his famous Salem Village Sermon was printed there. Samuel Parris followed Lawson, and exercised his ministerial functions for a term of seven years, being succeeded by the Rev. Joseph Green, whose tenure of office lasted no less than eighteen years, terminating on 26 November, 1715.

Almost immediately upon his induction in November, 1689, there was a sharp dispute between Samuel Parris and the authorities over a question of the arrangements pertaining to his salary. Matters, however, were composed, and the new minister forthwith began to exercise his disciplinary powers with a high hand. In the Parris household were several West Indian slaves brought by him from Barbadoes, of whom two, " John Indian " and " Tituba," were man and wife. These came from the Spanish settlements and were ignorant to a degree, being secretly addicted to savage practices, and well-versed in the voodoo lore of darkest superstition. During the long winter months of 1691 and 1692 a number of persons assembled evening after evening at Mr. Parris' house. Chief among these were Elizabeth Parris, a child of nine, the minister's daughter ; Abigail Williams, his niece, aged eleven, whose vanity bordered upon megalomania ; Anne Putnam, aged twelve, daughter of Sergeant Thomas Putnam, the parish clerk, a dour old infralapsarian ; Mary Walcot, an acutely hysterical subject of eighteen, who had lived for some time in the family of the Rev. George Burroughs, the daughter of Captain Walcot, deacon of the parish ; Mercy Lewis ; Elizabeth Hubbard, a neurotic green-sick wench of seventeen ; Elizabeth Booth and Susannah Sheldon, who were both a year older ; Mary Warren, a domestic servant of seventeen employed by John Proctor ; and Sarah Churchill, a maid in the house of George Jacobs. Three married women, Mrs. Anne Putnam, the wife of Serjeant Thomas Putnam ; Mrs. Pope ; and Mrs. Bibber, who lived at Wenham ; not unseldom put in an appearance, whilst a Mistress Goodell is spoken of as having attended only once or twice.

To while away the long dark nights when dusk had fallen and all was snow and bitter cold outside in the blackness, this young coterie used to invite Tituba into the room, and huddled round the blazing logs they would listen hour after hour to her grim tales of Indian wizardry, barbaric rites, and human sacrifice in the heart of the pathless forest where the hideous drone of the drums drowned the despairing cries of victims tortured and mangled before the monstrous bulk of some grinning shark-fanged god. She spoke of the ju-ju sorceries, of warlocks who by means of dancing, chants, and invocations were able to cast withering spells upon their enemies, who met evil spirits in secret communion and learned foul secrets of necromancy, who could blast with a look and send fever or consuming disease by a word. She told them of the powerful ones who could read the future in the palm of the hand, and picture what was to come in the smooth mirror of some unruffled loch or mountain mere. As they listened huddling in terror, fascinated by her mysterious gestures and flashing eyes what time she whispered in awesome accents the story of the Indian sabbat, little was wanting to persuade them that she, too, had her share in these evil orgies, that she knew the secrets of the spirits and the dark destroying angels. Sometimes even she would take their hands in her dusky fingers and effect to scan the future written in their palms. But more often she would dwell on the fate of those whom the witchmonger had cursed, those who drooped, and pined, and fell into an early grave, sickening with a sickness no herb could cure, no medicine allay.

It is hardly to be surprised at that the children well-nigh scared out of their wits began to imagine that some enemy had cast a malevolent charm upon them. All these morbid histories were their one topic of conversation by day, and haunted their dreams at night. Children are naturally imitative, and acting is ever their chiefest joy. [Soon it was noticed that Elizabeth Parris, Abigail Williams, and Ann Putnam were looking peaked and ill. " They would put themselves in odd postures, make antic gestures, and utter loud outcries and ridiculous, incoherent and unintelligible expressions." A physician, Dr. Griggs, who was called in, gravely shook his head and scented witchcraft. Forthwith Mr. Parris and the Putnams tried to mend the matter by prayer and fasting. Whole bevies of ministers were soon on the spot, and the whole township was ablaze. The Genevan divines uttered long orations and prayed lustily by the hour, exciting the three lasses to a perfect frenzy of rage, which was taken to be ample demonstration that the "afflicted children " —as henceforth the supposed victims were called—must indeed be under the influence of the Devil. They were vehemently exhorted to reveal the names of those who had injured them, whereupon falling into violent paroxysms they yelled " Good," " Osburn," " Tituba."]

Accordingly on the 29 February, 1692, warrants were duly issued against Sarah Good, Sarah Osburn, and the Indian woman, Tituba. The complainants in these cases were Joseph Hutchinson, Edward Putnam, Thomas Putnam, and Thomas Preston, all men of influence and unblemished character. Sarah Good and Sarah Osburn were two miserable hags who had been reduced to want and almost to beggary. Upon 1 March their examination took place before the principal magistrates of the district, John Hathorne and Jonathan Corwin, who sat in great state at the meeting-house, with a full complement of ministers. A vast crowd had assembled only a few of whom could be admitted, the rest thronging the courtyard and adjacent village street.

Sarah Good was first produced, and the proceedings commenced with the abrupt question : Sarah Good, what evil spirit have you familiarity with ? To which she answered : None.

Have you made no contracts with the Devil ?—No.

Why do you hurt these children ?—I do not hurt them, I scorn it.

Who do you employ then to do it ?—I employ nobody.

What creature do you employ then ?—No creature ; but I am falsely accused.

Why do you go away muttering from Mr. Parris his house ? —I did not mutter, but I thanked him for what he gave my child.

Have you made no contract with the Devil ?—No.

Hathorne desired the children, all of them to look upon her, and see if this were the person that hurt them ; and so they all did look upon her, and said this was one of the persons that did torment them. Presently they were all tormented.

Sarah Good, do you not see now what you have done ? Why do you not tell us the truth ? Why do you thus torment these poor children ?—I do not torment them.

Who do you employ then ?—I employ nobody. I scorn it.

How came they thus tormented ?—What do I know ? You bring others here, and now you charge me with it.

Why, who was it ?—I do not know, but it was some you brought into the meeting-house with you.

We brought you into the meeting-house.—But you brought in two more.

Who was it then that tormented the children ?—It was Osburn.

What was it you say when you go muttering away from persons' houses ?—If I must tell, I will tell.

Do tell us, then.—If I must tell, I will tell ; it is the Commandments. I may say my Commandments, I hope.

What commandment is it ?—If I must tell you I will tell ; it is a Psalm.

What Psalm ?

(After a long time she muttered over some part of a Psalm.)

Who do you serve ?—I serve God.

What God do you serve ?—The God that made heaven and earth (though she was not willing to mention the word " God "). Her answers were in a very wicked, spiteful manner, reflecting against the authority with base and abusive words ; and many lies she was taken in. It was here said that her husband had said that he was afraid that she either was a witch or would be one very quickly. The worshipful Mr. Hathorne asked him his reason why he had said so of her, whether he had ever seen anything by her. He answered, " No, not in this nature," but it was her bad carriage to him ; and indeed, said he, " I may say with tears, that she is an enemy to all good."

Sarah Osburn was next brought in, the examination being conducted upon much the same lines. She continually protested her innocence, and when informed that Sarah Good declared it was she who had hurt the children, her only reply was : " I do not know that the Devil goes about in my likeness to do any hurt."

It is noticeable that Increase Mather has actually discussed this very problem at some length in his treatise *Cases of Conscience Concerning Evil Spirits Personating Men,* originally printed at Boston, and reprinted at London " for *John Dunton* at the *Raven* in the *Poultrey*," 1693. Mather opens his tract with the question : " *Whether it is not Possible for the Devil to impose on the imagination of Persons Bewitched, and to cause them to Believe that an Innocent, Yea that a Pious person does torment them, when the Devil himself doth it ; or whether Satan may not appear in the Shape of an Innocent and Pious, as well as of a Nocent and Wicked Person, to Afflict such as suffer by Diabolical Molestations ?*

" The Answer to the Question must be Affirmative." He then proceeds to argue : " We find that the *Devil by the Instigation of the Witch at Endor appeared in the Likeness of the Prophet Samuel.*" A singularly unsafe statement since—to name but a few—Josephus, S. Justin, Origen, S. Ambrose, S. Augustine, Alonso Tostado, Suarez, Tommaso de Vio Gaetani, all hold the reality of the vision, that Samuel did indeed appear to Saul, and this certainly seems to be the correct interpretation of the passage.[18]

Sarah Osburn was committed to prison and heavily chained. From 7 March to 10 May she miserably languished in Boston jail, where she expired in durance, and so escaped the gallows tree.

Tituba the Indian played her rôle far more dextrously, and showed an appreciable amount of native cunning and craft. Clever enough clearly to see that mere denial of guilt and asseverations of innocence carried no weight at all she posed as a penitent, one who had been entangled for a while in the snares of sorcery, but had now shaken herself free, and was being persecuted and tormented by her former associates, the witches, to return to the Devil's allegiance. Her seeming struggles to persevere in the right path doubtless won her considerable favour in the eyes of the ministers and magistrates who cross-questioned her closely enough. So they ask :

Tituba, what evil spirit have you familiarity with ?—None.

Why do you hurt these children ?—I do not hurt them.

Who was it then ?—The Devil, for aught I know.

Did you never see the Devil ?—The Devil came to me and bid me serve him.

Who have you seen ?—Four women sometime hurt the children.

Who were they ?—Goody Osburn and Sarah Good, and I do not know who the others were. Sarah Good and Osburn would have me hurt the children, but I would not.

(She further said there was a tall man of Boston that she did see.)

When did you see them ?—Last night at Boston.

What did they say to you ?—They said, " Hurt the children."

And did you hurt them ?—No, there is four women and one man, they hurt the children and then they lay it all upon me ; and they tell me, if I will not hurt the children, they will hurt me.

But did you not hurt them ?—Yes, but I will hurt them no more.

Are you sorry that you did hurt them ?—Yes.

And why, then, do you hurt them ?—They say, " Hurt children, or we will do worse to you."

What have you seen ?—A man come to me and say, " Serve me."

What service ?—Hurt the children ; and last night there was an appearance that said, " Kill the children," and if I would not go on hurting the children they would do worse to me.

What is this appearance you see ?—Sometimes it is like a hog, and sometimes like a great dog.

(This appearance she saith she did see four times.)

What did it say to you ?—The black dog said, " Serve me," but I said, " I am afraid." He said if I do not he would do worse to me.

What did you say to it ?—" I will serve you no longer." Then he said he would hurt me ; and then he looks like a man, and threatens to hurt me. (She said that this man had a yellow bird that kept with him.) And he told me he had more pretty things that he would give me if I would serve him.

What were these pretty things ?—He did not show me them.

What else have you seen ?—Two cats ; a red cat and a black cat.

What did they say to you ?—They said, " Serve me."

When did you see them ?—Last night, and they said, " Serve me," and I said I would not.

What service ?—She said," Hurt the children."

Did you pinch Elizabeth Hubbard this morning ?—The man brought her to me and made me pinch her.

Why did you go to Thomas Putnam's last night and hurt his child ?—They pull and haul me, and make me go.

And what would they have you do ?—Kill her with a knife.

(Lieutenant Fuller and others said that at this time when the child saw these persons, and was tormented by them, that she did complain of a knife, and that they would have cut her head off with a knife.)

How did you go ?—We ride upon sticks and are there presently.

Do you go through the trees or over them ?—We see nothing, but are there presently.

Why did you not tell your master ?—I was afraid ; they said that they would cut off my head if I told.

Would you not have hurt others if you could ?—They said they would hurt others, but they could not.

What attendants hath Sarah Good ?—A yellow-bird, and she would have given me one.

What meat would she give it ?—It did suck her between her fingers.

Did you not hurt Mr. Curran's child ?—Goody Good and Goody Osburn told that they did hurt Mr. Curran's child, and would have had me hurt him too ; but I did not.

What hath Sarah Osburn ?—Yesterday, she had a thing like a woman, with two legs and wings.

(Abigail Williams, that lives with her uncle, Mr. Parris, said that she did see the same creature, and it turned into the shape of Goodie Osburn.)

What else have you seen with Osburn ?—Another thing, hairy, it goes upright like a man, it hath only two legs.

Did you not set Sarah Good upon Elizabeth Hubbard last Saturday ?—I did see her set a wolf upon her to afflict her.

(The persons with this maid did say that she did complain of a wolf. She further said that she saw a cat with Good at another time.)

What clothes did the man go in ?—He goes in black clothes ; a tall man with white hair, I think.

How doth the woman go ?—In a white hood and a black hood with a top-knot.

Do you see who it is that torments these children now ?—Yes, it is Goody Good, she hurts them in her own shape.

Who is it hurts them now ?—I am blind now ; I cannot see.

It appears that Tituba, as a penitent, was released without punishment, although doubtless in the charge of the Rev. Samuel Parris. The only further information we have concerning her is from a work by Robert Calef, *More Wonders of the Invisible World*, written in keen opposition to Cotton Mather and those who were conducting the witch-trials. Calef, a Boston merchant, was in no way personally interested in the crusade. He was a man of sceptical and unbelieving mind, whose incredulity went to the same extremes as the fanaticism of the Salem ministers and magistrates. He may perhaps be described as an American Reginald Scot, ready to accept the most far-fetched explanations of events not easily to be accounted for in an ordinary way. It is obvious that when he interviewed Tituba the cunning hag told him just what he wanted to hear, and he writes : " The account she since gives of it is, that her master did beat her, and otherwise abuse her, to make her confess and accuse (such as he called) her sister-witches ; and that whatsoever she said by way of confessing or accusing others was the effect of such usage."

On 19 March the Rev. Deodat Lawson, who was then

officiating as " minister of the gospel " at Scituate, visited Salem Village personally to investigate the extraordinary happenings which were so wofully perturbing his old parish, and he has left us so graphic an account of what he witnessed and heard that it is well worth reprinting this excessively rare tract in full.

A TRUE NARRATIVE of some Remarkable Passages relating to sundry Persons afflicted by *Witchcraft* at *Salem* Village in *New-England*, which happened from the 19*th.* of *March* to the 5*th.* of *April*, 1692.

COLLECTED BY DEODAT LAWSON.

ON the Nineteenth day of *March* last I went to *Salem* Village, and lodged at *Nathaniel Ingersol's* near to the Minister Mr. P.*'s* House, and presently after I came into my Lodging, Capt. *Walcut's* Daughter *Mary* came to Lieut. *Ingersol's* and spake to me ; but suddenly after, as she stood by the Door, was bitten, so that she cried out of her Wrist, and looking on it with a Candle, we saw apparently the marks of Teeth, both upper and lower set, on each side of her Wrist.

In the beginning of the Evening I went to give Mr. *P.* a Visit. When I was there, his Kinswoman, *Abigail Williams*, (about 12 Years of Age) had a grievous fit ; she was at first hurried with violence to and fro in the Room (though Mrs. *Ingersol* endeavoured to hold her) sometimes making as if she would fly, stretching up her Arms as high as she could, and crying, *Whish, Whish, Whish,* several times ; presently after she said, there was Goodw. *N.* and said, *Do you not see her? Why there she stands!* And she said, Goodw. *N.* offered her *THE BOOK,* but she was resolved she would not take it. saying often, *I wont, I wont, I wont take it, I do not know what Book it is : I am sure it is none of God's Book, it is the Devil's Book for ought I know.* After that, she ran to the Fire, and began to throw Fire-brands about the House, and run against the Back, as if she would run up Chimney, and, as they said, she had attempted to go into the Fire in other Fits.

On Lords Day, the Twentieth of *March,* there were sundry of the afflicted Persons at Meeting, as Mrs. *Pope,* and Goodwife *Bibber*, *Abigail Williams*, *Mary Walcut*, *Mary Lewes*, and Doctor *Grigg's* Maid. There was also at Meeting, Goodwife *C.* (who was afterward Examined on suspicion of being a *Witch:* They had several sore Fits in the time of Publick Worship, which did something interrupt me in my first Prayer, being so unusual. After *Psalm* was sung, *Abigail Williams* said to me, *Now stand up, and name your Text!* And after it was read, she said, *It is a long Text.* In the beginning of the Sermon, Mrs. *Pope*, a Woman afflicted, said to me, *Now there is enough of that.* And in the Afternoon, *Abigail Williams*, upon my referring to my *Doctrine*, said to me, *I know no Doctrine you had, If you did name one, I have forgot it.*

In Sermon time, when Goodwife *C.* was present in the Meeting-House, *Ab. W.* called out, *Look where Goodwife C. sits on the Beam suckling her Yellow Bird betwixt her fingers!* *Ann Putman*, another Girle afflicted, said, *There was a Yellow Bird sat on my Hat as it hung on the Pin in the Pulpit;* but those that were by, restrained her from speaking aloud about it.

On *Monday* the 21*st.* of *March*, the Magistrates of *Salem* appointed to come to Examination of Goodwife *C.* And about Twelve of the Clock they went into the Meeting-House, which was thronged with Spectators. Mr. *Noyes* began with a very pertinent and pathetical *Prayer;* and Goodwife *C.* being called to answer to what was alledged against her, she desired to go to *Prayer*, which was much wondred at, in the presence of so many hundred People : The Magistrates told her, they would not admit it ; they came not there to hear her Pray, but to Examine her, in what was Alledged against her. The Worshipful Mr. *Hathorne* asked her, *Why she afflicted those Children?* She said, she did not afflict them. He asked her, who did then ? She said, *I do not know; How should I know?* The Number of the Afflicted Persons were about that time Ten, *viz.* Four Married Women, Mrs. *Pope*, Mrs. *Putman*, Goodwife *Bibber*, and an Ancient Woman named *Goodall;* three Maids, *Mary Walcut*, *Mercy Lewes* at *Thomas Putman's*, and a Maid at Dr. *Griggs's;* there were three Girls from 9 to 12 Years of Age, each of them, or thereabouts, *viz.* *Elizabeth Parris*, *Abigail Williams*, and *Ann Putman;*

these were most of them at Goodwife *C.'s* Examination, and did vehemently Accuse her in the Assembly of Afflicting them, by *Biting, Pinching, Strangling, &c.* And that they in their Fits see her Likeness coming to them, and bringing a *Book* to them ; she said she had no *Book ;* they affirmed, she had a *Yellow Bird,* that used to suck betwixt her Fingers, and being asked about it, if she had any *Familiar Spirit,* that attended her ? she said, *She had no Familiarity with any such thing.* She was a *Gospel Woman :* Which Title she called her self by ; and the Afflicted Persons told her, Ah ! she was *A Gospel Witch. Ann Putman* did there affirm, that one day when Lieutenant *Fuller* was at Prayer at her Father's House, she saw the shape of Goodwife *C.* and she thought Goodwife *N.* Praying at the same time to the Devil ; she was not sure it was Goodwife *N.,* she thought it was ; but very sure she saw the shape of Goodwife *C.* The said *C.* said, they were poor distracted Children, and no heed to be given to what they said. Mr. *Hathorne* and Mr. *Noyes* replyed, It was the Judgment of all that were present, they were *Bewitched,* and only she the Accused Person said, they were *Distracted.* It was observed several times, that if she did but bite her under lip in time of Examination, the Persons afflicted were bitten on their Arms and Wrists, and produced the *Marks* before the Magistrates, Ministers, and others. And being watched for that, if she did but *Pinch* her Fingers, or *Grasp* one Hand hard in another, they were Pinched, and produced the *Marks* before the Magistrates, and Spectators. After that, it was observed, that if she did but lean her *Breast* against the Seat in the Meeting-House, (being the *Bar* at which she stood), they were afflicted. Particularly Mrs. *Pope* complained of grievous Torment in her *Bowels,* as if they were torn out. She vehemently accused the said *C.* as the Instrument, and first threw her Muff at her ; but that flying not home, she got off her *shoe,* and hit Goodwife *C.* on the Head with it. After these Postures were watched, if the said *C.* did but stir her Feet, they were afflicted in their *Feet,* and stamped fearfully. The afflicted Persons asked her, why she did not go to the Company of Witches which were before the Meeting-House Mustering ? Did she not hear the *Drum* beat ? They accused her of having Familiarity with the

Devil, in the time of Examination, in the shape of a *Black Man* whispering in her Ear ; they affirmed, that her *Yellow Bird* sucked betwixt her Fingers in the Assembly ; and Order being given to see if there were any sign, the Girl that saw it, said, it was too late now ; she had removed a *Pin*, and put it on her *Head ;* which was found *there* sticking upright.

They told her, she had Covenanted with the *Devil* for ten Years, six of them were gone, and four more to come. She was required by the Magistrates to answer that Question in the Catechism, *How many persons be there in the God-head ?* She answered it but oddly, yet was there no great thing to be gathered from it ; she denied all that was charged upon her, and said, *They could not prove a Witch ;* she was that Afternoon Committed to *Salem* Prison ; and after she was in Custody, she did not so appear to them, and afflict them as before.

On Wednesday the 23*d.* of *March*, I went to *Thomas Putman's*, on purpose to see his Wife : I found her lying on the Bed, having had a sore Fit a little before ; she spake to me, and said, she was glad to see me ; her Husband and she both desired me to Pray with her while she was sensible ; which I did, though the Apparition said, *I should not go to Prayer.* At the first beginning she attended ; but after a little time, was taken with a Fit ; yet continued silent, and seemed to be *Asleep :* When Prayer was done, her Husband going to her, found her in a *Fit ;* he took her off the Bed, to set her on his Knees, but at first she was so stiff, she could not be bended ; but she afterwards sat down, but quickly began to strive violently with her *Arms* and *Leggs ;* she then began to Complain of, and as it were to Converse Personally with, Goodwife N. saying, *Goodwife N. Be gone! Be gone! Be gone! are you not ashamed, a Woman of your Profession, to afflict a poor Creature so? What hurt did I ever do you in my life? You have but two Years to live, and then the Devil will torment your Soul; for this your Name is blotted out of God's Book, and it shall never be put in God's Book again; be gone for shame, are you not afraid of that which is coming upon you? I know, I know what will make you afraid; the wrath of an Angry God, I am sure that will make you afraid; be gone, do not torment* *me, I know what you would have* (we judged she meant, *her Soul*) *but it is out of your reach ; it is cloathed with the white Robes of Christ's Righteousness*. After this, she seemed to dispute with the Apparition about a particular *Text* of Scripture. The Apparition seemed to deny it ; (the Womans Eyes being fast closed all this time) she said, *She was sure there was such a Text*, and she would tell it ; and then the Shape would be gone, for, said she, *I am sure you cannot stand before that Text !* Then she was sorely Afflicted, her Mouth drawn on one side, and her Body strained for about a Minute, and then said, *I will tell, I will tell ; it is, it is, it is*, three or four times, and then was afflicted to hinder her from telling, at last she broke forth, and said, *It is the third Chapter of the Revelations*. I did something scruple the reading it, and did let my scruple appear, lest Satan should make any Superstitiously to improve the Word of the Eternal God. However, tho' not versed in these things, I judged I might do it this once for an Experiment. I began to *read*, and before I had read near through the first Verse, she opened her Eyes, and was well ; this Fit continued near half an hour. Her Husband and the Spectators told me, she had often been so relieved by reading Texts that she named, something pertinent to her Case ; as *Isa.* 40. 1. *Isa.* 49. 1. *Isa.* 50. 1. and several others.

On Thursday the Twenty-Fourth of *March*, (being in course the Lecture-Day at the Village,) Goodwife *N.* was brought before the Magistrates Mr. *Hathorne* and Mr. *Corwin*, about Ten of the Clock in the Forenoon, to be Examined in the Meeting-House, the Reverend Mr. *Hale* begun with Prayer, and the Warrant being read, she was required to give Answer, *Why she Afflicted those persons ?* She pleaded her own Innocency with earnestness. *Thomas Putman's* Wife, *Abigail Williams*, and *Thomas Putman's* Daughter, accused her that she appeared to them, and afflicted them in their Fits ; but some of the others said, that they had seen her, but knew not that ever she had hurt them ; amongst which was *Mary Walcut*, who was presently after she had so declared bitten, and cryed out of her in the Meeting-House, producing the *Marks* of *Teeth* on her wrist. It was so disposed, that I had not leisure to attend the whole time of Examination, but both Magistrates and Ministers told me, that the things alledged by the afflicted, and defences made by her, were much after the same manner as the former was. And her motions did produce like effects, as to *Biting, Pinching, Brusing, Tormenting*, at their *Breasts*, by her *Leaning*, and when bended back, were as if their Backs were broken. The afflicted Persons said, the *Black Man* whispered to her in the Assembly, and therefore she could not hear what the Magistrates said unto her. They said also, that she did then ride by the Meeting-House, behind the *Black Man Thomas Putman's* Wife had a grievous Fit in the time of Examination, to the very great imparing of her strength, and wasting of her spirits, insomuch as she could hardly move hand or foot when she was carried out. Others also were there grievously afflicted, so that there was once such a hideous scrietch and noise (which I heard as I walked at a little distance from the Meeting-House) as did amaze me, and some that were within, told me the whole Assembly was struck with Consternation, and they were afraid, that those that sate next to them were under the Influence of *Witchcraft*. This Woman also was that day committed to *Salem* Prison. The Magistrates and Ministers also did inform me, that they apprehended a Child of *Sarah G.* and examined it, being between 4 and 5 years of Age. And as to matter of Fact, they did unanimously affirm, that when this *Child* did but cast its Eye upon the afflicted Persons, they were tormented ; and they held her *Head*, and yet so many as her *Eye* could fix upon were afflicted. Which they did several times make careful Observation of : The afflicted complained, they had often been *Bitten* by this Child, and produced the marks of *a small set of teeth* accordingly ; this was also committed to *Salem* Prison, the Child looked *hail, and well* as other Children. I saw it at Lieut. *Ingersol's*. After the Commitment of Goodw. *N. Tho. Putman's* Wife was much better, and had no violent Fits at all from that 24*th.* of *March*, to the 5*th.* of *April*. Some others also said they had not seen her so frequently appear to them, to hurt them.

On the 25*th.* of *March* (as Capt. *Stephen Sewal*, of *Salem* did afterwards inform me) *Eliz. Paris* had sore Fits at his House, which much troubled *himself, and his Wife*, so as he told me they were almost discouraged. She related, that the great *Black Man* came to her, and told her, if she would be ruled by him, she should have whatsoever she desired, and go to a *Golden City.* She relating this to Mrs. *Sewal,* she told the Child, it was the *Devil,* and he was a *Lyar from the Beginning,* and bid her tell him so, if he came again : which she did accordingly, at the next coming to her, in her Fits.

On the 26*th.* of *March,* Mr. *Hathorn,* Mr. *Corwin,* and Mr. *Higison,* were at the Prison-Keeper's House to Examine the Child, and it told them there, it had a little *Snake* that used to suck on the lowest Joynt of its Fore-Finger ; and when they enquired where, pointing to other places, it told them, not there, but *there,* pointing on the lowest Joint of the Fore-Finger, where they observed a deep Red Spot, about the bigness of a *Flea-bite ;* they asked who gave it that *Snake ?* whether the great Black Man ? It said no, its Mother gave it.

The 31 of *March* there was a *Publick Fast* kept at *Salem* on account of these Afflicted Persons. And *Abigail Williams* said, that the Witches had a *Sacrament* that day at an house in the Village, and that they had *Red Bread* and *Red Drink.* The first of *April, Mercy Lewis, Thomas Putman's* Maid, in her Fit, said, they did eat *Red Bread,* like *Man's Flesh,* and would have had her eat some, but she would not ; but turned away her head, and spit at them, and said, *I will not Eat, I will not Drink, it is Blood, &c.,* she said, *That is not the Bread of Life ; that is not the Water of Life ; Christ gives the Bread of Life ; I will have none of it !* The first of *April* also *Mercy Lewis* aforesaid saw in her Fit a *White Man,* and was with him in a glorious Place, which had no *Candles* nor *Sun,* yet was full of Light and *Brightness ;* where was a great Multitude in White glittering Robes, and they Sung the Song in the fifth of *Revelation,* the 9th verse, and the 110 *Psalm,* and the 149 *Psalm ;* and said with her self, *How long shall I stay here ? let me be along with you :* She was loth to leave this place, and grieved that she could tarry no longer. This *white Man* hath appeared several times to some of them, and given them notice how long it should be before they had another Fit, which was sometimes a day, or day and half, or more or less, it hath fallen out accordingly.

The 3d of *April*, the Lord's-day, being Sacrament-day, at the Village, *Goodw. C.* upon Mr. *Parris's* naming his Text, *John* 6, 70. *One of them is a Devil*, the said *Goodw. C.* went immediately out of the Meeting-House, and flung the Door after her violently, to the amazement of the Congregation. She was afterwards seen by some in their Fits, who said, *O Goodw. C. I did not think to see you here!* (and being at their *Red Bread and drink*) said to her, *Is this a time to receive the Sacrament, you ran away on the Lord's-Day, and scorned to receive it in the Meeting-House, and, Is this a time to receive it? I wonder at you!* This is the sum of what I either saw my self, or did receive Information from persons of undoubted Reputation and Credit.

REMARKS OF THINGS MORE THAN ORDINARY ABOUT THE AFFLICTED PERSONS.

1. They are in their Fits tempted to be *Witches*, are shewed the List of the Names of others, and are tortured because they will not yeild to Subscribe, or meddle with, or touch the BOOK, and are promised to have present Relief if they would do it.

2. They did in the Assembly mutually *Cure* each other, even with a *Touch* of their Hand, when Strangled, and otherwise Tortured ; and would endeavour to get to their Afflicted, to relieve them.

3. They did also foretel when anothers Fit was a-coming, and would say, *Look to her!* she will have a Fit presently, which fell out accordingly, as many can bear witness, that heard and saw it.

4. That at the same time, when the *Accused* Person was present, the *Afflicted Persons* saw her Likeness in other places of the Meeting-House, sucking her *Familiar*, sometimes in one place and posture, and sometimes in another.

5. That their Motions in their Fits are *Preternatural*, both as to the manner, which is so strange as a well person could not Screw their Body into ; and as to the violence also it is preternatural, being much beyond the Ordinary force of the same person when they are in their right mind.

6. The *eyes* of some of them in their fits are exceeding fast closed, and if you ask a question they can give no answer, and I do believe they cannot hear at that time, yet

do they plainely converse with the Appearances, as if they did discourse with real persons.

7. They are utterly pressed against any persons *Praying* with them, and told by the Appearances, they shall not go to *Prayer*, so *Tho. Putman's* wife was told, *I should not Pray;* but she said, *I should:* and after I had done, reasoned with the *Appearance, Did not I say he should go to Prayer?*

8. The forementioned *Mary W.* being a little better at ease, the Afflicted persons said, *she had signed the Book;* and that was the reason she was better. Told me by *Edward Putman.*

REMARKS CONCERNING THE ACCUSED.

1. For introduction to the discovery of those that afflicted them, It is reported Mr. *Parris's* Indian Man, and Woman, made a Cake of *Rye Meal,* and the Childrens water, baked it in the Ashes, and gave it to a Dog, since which they have discovered, and seen particular persons hurting of them.

2. In Time of Examination, they seemed little affected, though all the Spectators were much grieved to see it.

3. *Natural* Actions in them produced *Preternatural* actions in the Afflicted, so that they are their own *Image* without any *Poppits* of Wax or otherwise.

4. That they are accused to have a Company about 23 or 24 and they did *Muster in Armes,* as it seemed to the Afflicted Persons.

5. Since they were confined, the Persons have not been so much Afflicted with their appearing to them, *Biteing,* or *Pinching* of them, &c.

6. They are reported by the Afflicted Persons to keep dayes of *Fast* and dayes of *Thanksgiving,* and *Sacraments;* Satan endeavours to Transforme himself to an *Angel of Light,* and to make his Kingdom and Administrations to resemble those of our Lord Jesus Christ.

7. Satan Rages Principally amongst the Visible Subjects of Christ's Kindgom and makes use (at least in appearance) of some of them to Afflict others; that *Christ's Kingdom may be divided against it self,* and so be weakened.

8. Several things used in *England* at Tryal of Witches, to the Number of 14 or 15 which are wont to pass instead

of, or in Concurrence with *Witnesses*, at least 6 or 7 of them are found in these accused : see *Keebles Statutes*.

9. Some of the most solid Afflicted Persons do affirme the same things concerning *seeing* the accused *out* of their Fitts as well as *in* them.

10. The Witches had a *Fast*, and told one of the Afflicted Girles, she must not *Eat*, because it was *Fast Day*, she said, she *would* : they told her they would *Choake* her then ; which when she did eat, was endeavoured.

In May, 1692, the whole countryside was swept by a panic of frenzied fear. The " afflicted children " were almost hourly convulsed, sometimes falling into an extreme sweat and agony, and " crying out " upon those who tormented them. All were aghast ; nobody knew who might not next be named as a witch, an accusation which meant haling to prison, and a trial concluding with almost certain condemnation. It seemed, as Hutchinson has put it, that the only " way to prevent accusation was to become an accuser." " The number of the afflicted increased every day and the number of the accused in proportion." None were so untiring in the persuit of witches as the Rev. Samuel Parris. He felt it his duty to labour night and day in the cause, and he never relaxed his efforts. With all his faults of character he was in this respect obviously a thoroughly sincere man, and he found an able and active second in the Rev. Nicholas Noyes of the First Church, Salem. The Rev. John Higginson and the Rev. Samuel Willard of the Old South Church, Boston, proved far more moderate in their judgements. In fact, Mr. Willard presumed to rebuke some of those who alleged that they had been bewitched, whereupon one of the " afflicted children " " cried out " upon him, but he was so universally beloved and respected that they promptly removed the girl from court, " and it was told about that she was mistaken in the person."

The Rev. John Hale of Beverly, too, although a firm believer, was by no means so zealous as many of his colleagues in the prosecutions, but Cotton Mather showed himself sufficient boutefeu to atone for the slackness of an hundred chicken-hearts and sceptics.

Although by no means the first person to be accused, the

first to be executed was Bridget Bishop. She had been thrice married, and was the mother of one child by her second husband, Thomas Oliver. The mistress of a hostelry, which stood on the high-road between Salem and Beverly, she was wont to deck her buxom person in "a black cap and a black hat, and a red paragon bodice, bordered and looped with different colours," which gave great offence to the Genevan housewives, who were clad in cinder-grey or subfuse brown and the "ornament of a meek and quiet spirit." Moreover, in her house there was actually a shovel-board for the entertainment of passing guests. Bridget Bishop was a woman of sharp tongue and heavy hand, both of which she very liberally employed against those who offended her, as many an idle ostler and slattern servant knew. Indeed, she had made enemies, and some five years before the panic began had actually been bruited as being a witch, although the charge came to nothing. Now, however, things had vastly changed, and when Deliverance Hobbs, who had once been a witch but was now penitent, cried out upon her, she was promptly arrested and brought to trial on 2 June, 1692. The following detailed account is given by Cotton Mather :—

THE TRYAL OF BRIDGET BISHOP, ALIAS
OLIVER, AT THE COURT OF OYER AND FERMINER, HELD AT SALEM, JUNE 2. 1692.

I.

SHE was indicted for Bewitching of several Persons in the Neighbourhood, the Indictment being drawn up, according to the *Form* in such Cases usual. And pleading, *Not Guilty*, there were brought in several persons, who had long undergone many kinds of Miseries, which were preternaturally inflicted, and generally ascribed unto an *horrible Witchcraft*. There was little occasion to prove the *Witchcraft*, it being evident and notorious to all beholders. Now to fix the *Witchcraft* on the Prisoner at the Bar, the first thing used, was the Testimony of the *Bewitched ;* whereof several testifi'd, That the *Shape* of the Prisoner did oftentimes very grievously Pinch them, Choak them, Bite them, and Afflict them ; urging them to write their Names in a *Book*, which the said Spectre called, *Ours*. One of them did further testifie, that it was the *Shape* of this Prisoner, with another, which one day took her from her Wheel, and carrying her to the River-side, threatened there to Drown her, if she did not Sign to the *Book* mentioned : which yet she refused.   Others of them did also testifie, that the said *Shape* did in her Threats brag to them that she had been the Death of sundry Persons, then by her named ; that she had *Ridden* a Man then likewise named.   Another testifi'd, the Apparition of *Ghosts* unto the Spectre of *Bishop*, crying out, *You Murdered us !* About the Truth whereof, there was in the Matter of Fact but too much suspicion.

II. It was testifi'd, That at the Examination of the Prisoner before the Magistrates, the Bewitched were ex-treamly tortured.   If she did but cast her Eyes on them, they were presently struck down ; and this in such a manner as there could be no Collusion in the Business.   But upon the Touch of her Hand upon them, when they lay in their Swoons, they would immediately Revive ; and not upon the Touch of any ones else.   Moreover, Upon some Special Actions of her Body, as the shaking of her Head, or the turning of her Eyes, they presently and painfully fell into the like postures.   And many of the like Accidents now fell out, while she was at the Bar.   One at the same time testifying, That she said, *She could not be troubled to see the afflicted thus tormented.*

III. There was Testimony likewise brought in, that a Man striking once at the place, where a bewitched person said, the *Shape* of this *Bishop* stood, the bewitched cried out, *That he had tore her Coat*, in the place then particularly specifi'd ; and the Woman's Coat was found to be Torn in that very place.

IV. One *Deliverance Hobbs*, who had confessed her being a Witch, was now tormented by the Spectres, for her Confession.   And she now testifi'd, That this *Bishop* tempted her to sign the *Book* again, and to deny what she had con-fess'd.   She affirm'd, That it was the Shape of this Prisoner, which whipped her with Iron Rods, to compel her thereunto. And she affirmed, that this *Bishop* was at a General Meeting of the Witches, in a Field at *Salem*-Village, and there partook of a Diabolical Sacrament in Bread and Wine then ad-ministred.

V. To render it further unquestionable, that the Prisoner at the Bar, was the Person truly charged in THIS *Witchcraft*, there were produced many Evidences of OTHER *Witchcrafts* by her perpetrated. For Instance, *John Cook* testifi'd, That about five or six Years ago, one Morning, about Sun-Rise, he was in his Chamber assaulted by the *Shape* of this Prisoner : which look'd on him, grinn'd at him, and very much hurt him with a Blow on the side of the Head : and that on the same day, about Noon, the same *Shape* walked in the Room where he was, and an Apple strangely flew out of his Hand, into the Lap of his Mother, six or eight Foot from him.

VI. *Samuel Gray* testifi'd, That about fourteen Years ago, he wak'd on a Night, and saw the Room where he lay full of Light ; and that he then saw plainly a Woman between the Cradle and the Bed-side, which look'd upon him. He rose, and it vanished ; tho' he found the Doors all fast. Looking out at the entry-door he saw the same Woman, in the same Garb again; and said, *In God's Name, what do you come for ?* He went to Bed, and had the same Woman again assaulting him. The Child in the Cradle gave a great Screech, and the Woman disappeared. It was long before the Child could be quieted ; and tho' it were a very likely thriving Child, yet from this time it pined away, and, after divers Months, died in a sad Condition. He knew not *Bishop*, nor her Name ; but when he saw her after this, he knew by her Countenance, and Apparel, and all Circumstances, that it was the Apparition of this *Bishop*, which had thus troubled him.

VII. *John Bly* and his Wife testifi'd, That he bought a Sow of *Edward Bishop*, the Husband of the Prisoner ; and was to pay the Price agreed, unto another person. This Prisoner being angry that she was thus hindred from fingring the Mony, quarrell'd with *Bly*. Soon after which, the Sow was taken with strange Fits ; Jumping, Leaping, and Knocking her Head against the Fence ; she seem'd Blind and Deaf, and would neither Eat nor be Suck'd. Whereupon a Neighbour said, she believed the Creature was *Over-looked ;* and sundry other Circumstances concurred, which made the Deponents believe that *Bishop* had bewitched it.

VIII. *Richard Coman* testifi'd, That eight Years ago, as he lay awake in his Bed, with a Light burning in the Room, he was annoy'd with the Apparition of this *Bishop*, and of two more that were strangers to him, who came and oppressed him so, that he could neither stir himself, nor wake any one else, and that he was the night after, molested again in the like manner ; the said *Bishop* taking him by the Throat, and pulling him almost out of the Bed. His Kinsman offered for this cause to lodge with him ; and that Night, as they were awake, discoursing together, this *Coman* was once more visited by the Guests which had formerly been so troublesom ; his Kinsman being at the same time struck speechless, and unable to move Hand or Foot. He had laid his Sword by him, which these unhappy Spectres did strive much to wrest from him ; only he held too fast for them. He then grew able to call the People of his House ; but altho' they heard him, yet they had not power to speak or stir ; until at last, one of the People crying out, *What's the matter ?* The Spectres all vanished.

IX. *Samuel Shattock* testify'd, That in the Year, 1680, this *Bridget Bishop* often came to his House upon such frivolous and foolish Errands, that they suspected she came indeed with a purpose of mischief. Presently, whereupon, his eldest Child, which was of as promising Health and Sense, as any Child of its Age, began to droop exceedingly ; and the oftner that *Bishop* came to the House, the worse grew the Child. As the Child would be standing at the Door, he would be thrown and bruised against the Stones, by an invisible Hand, and in like sort knock his Face against the sides of the House, and bruise it after a miserable manner. Afterwards this *Bishop* would bring him things to Dye, whereof he could not imagin any use ; and when she paid him a piece of Mony, the Purse and Mony were unaccountably conveyed out of a lock'd Box, and never seen any more. The Child was immediately, hereupon taken with terrible Fits, whereof his Friends thought he would have dyed : Indeed he did almost nothing but Cry and Sleep for several Months together ; and at length his Understanding was utterly taken away. Among other Symptoms of an Inchantment upon him, one was That there was a Board in the Garden, whereupon he would walk; and all the Invitations in the World could never fetch him off. About 17 or 18 years after, there came a Stranger to *Shattock's* House, who seeing the Child, said, *This poor Child is Bewitched; and you have a Neighbour living not for off, who is a Witch.* He added, *Your Neighbour has had a falling out with your Wife; and she said, in her heart, your Wife is a proud Woman, and she would bring down her Pride in this Child.* He then remembred, that *Bishop* had parted from his Wife in muttering and menacing Terms, a little before the Child was taken ill. The abovesaid Stranger would needs carry the bewitched Boy with him, to *Bishop's* House, on pretence of buying a pot of Cyder. The woman entertained him in furious manner; and flew also upon the Boy, scratching his Face till the Blood came; and saying, *Thou Rogue, what dost thou bring this Fellow here to plague me?* Now it seems the Man had said, before he went, That he would fetch Blood of *her.* Ever after the Boy was follow'd with grievous Fits, which the Doctors themselves generally ascribed unto *Witchcraft;* and wherein he would be thrown still into the *Fire* or the *Water,* if he were not constantly look'd after; and it was verily believed that *Bishop* was the cause of it.

X. *John Louder* testify'd, That upon some little Controversy with *Bishop* about her Fowls, going well to Bed, he did awake in the Night by Moonlight, and did see clearly the likeness of this Woman grievously oppressing him; in which miserable condition she held him, unable to help himself, till near Day. He told *Bishop* of this; but she deny'd it, and threatned him very much. Quickly after this, being at home on a Lords day, with the doors shut about him, he saw a black Pig approach him; at which, he going to kick, it vanished away. Immediately after, sitting down, he saw a black Thing jump in at the window, and come and stand before him. The Body was like that of a Monkey, the Feet like a Cocks, but the Face much like a Mans. He being so extreamly affrighted, that he could not speak; this Monster spoke to him, and said, *I am a Messenger sent unto you, for I understand that you are in some Trouble of Mind, and if you will be ruled by me, you shall want for nothing in this world.* Whereupon he endeavoured to clap his hands upon it; but he could feel no substance ; and it jumped out of the Window again ; but immediately came in by the Porch, tho' the Doors were shut, and said, *You had better take my Counsel !* He then struck at it with a stick, but struck only the Ground-sel, and broke the Stick : The Arm with which he struck was presently Disenabled, and it vanished away. He presently went out at the Back-door, and spied this *Bishop*, in her Orchard, going toward her House ; but he had not power to set one foot forward unto her. Whereupon, returning into the House, he was immediately accosted by the Monster he had seen before ; which Goblin was now going to fly at him ; whereat he cry'd out, *The whole armour of God be between me and you !* So it sprang back, and flew over the Apple-tree ; shaking many Apples off the Tree, in its flying over. At its leap, it flung Dirt with its feet against the Stomack of the Man ; whereon he was then struck Dumb, and so continued for three days together. Upon the producing of this Testimony, *Bishop* deny'd that she knew this Deponent : Yet their two Orchards joined ; and they had often had their little Quarrels for some years together.

XI. *William Stacy* testify'd, That receiving Mony of this *Bishop*, for work done by him ; he was gone but a matter of three Rods from her, and looking for his Mony, found it unaccountably gone from him. Some time after, *Bishop* asked him, whether his Father would grind her Grist for her ? He demanded why ? She reply'd, *Because Folks count me a Witch.* He answered, *No question but he will grind it for you.* Being then gone about six Rods from her, with a small Load in his Cart, suddenly the Off-wheel stump'd, and sunk down into an hole, upon plain Ground ; so that the Deponent was forced to get help for the recovering of the Wheel : But stepping back to look for the hole, which might give him this Disaster, there was none at all to be found. Some time after, he waked in the Night ; but it seem'd as light as day ; and he perfectly saw the shape of this *Bishop* in the Room troubling of him ; but upon her going out, all was dark again. He charg'd *Bishop* afterwards with it, and she deny'd it not ; but was very angry. Quickly after, this Deponent having been threatned by *Bishop*, as he was in a dark Night going to the Barn, he was very suddenly taken or lifted from the Ground, and thrown against a Stone-wall : After that, he was again Hoisted up and thrown down a Bank, at the end of his House. After this again, passing by this *Bishop*, his Horse with a small Load, striving to draw, all his Gears flew to pieces, and the Cart fell down ; and this Deponent going then to lift a Bag of Corn, of about two Bushels, could not budge it with all his Might.

Many other Pranks of this *Bishop's* this Deponent was ready to testify. He also testify'd, That he verily believ'd the said *Bishop* was the Instrument of his Daughter *Priscilla's* Death; of which suspicion, pregnant Reasons were assigned.

XII. To crown all, *John Bly* and *William Bly* testify'd, That being employ'd by *Bridget Bishop*, to help to take down the Cellar-wall of the old house wherein she formerly lived, they did in holes of the said old Wall, find several *Poppets*, made up of Rags and Hogs-bristles, with headless Pins in them, the Points being outward ; whereof she could give no account unto the Court, that was reasonable or tolerable.

XIII. One thing that made against the Prisoner was, her being evidently convicted of *gross Lying* in the Court, several times, while she was making her plea ; but besides this, a Jury of Women found a preternatural Teat upon her Body : But upon a second search, within 3 or 4 hours, there was no such thing to be seen. There was also an Account of other People whom this Woman had Afflicted ; and there might have been many more, if they had been enquired for ; but there was no need of them.

XIV. There was one very strange thing more, with which the Court was newly entertained. As this Woman was under a Guard, passing by the great and spacious Meeting-house of *Salem*, she gave a look towards the House : And immediately a *Dæmon* invisibly entring the Meeting-house, tore down a part of it ; so that tho' there was no Person to be seen there, yet the People, at the noise, running in, found a Board, which was strongly fastned with several Nails, transported unto another quarter of the House.

Bridget Bishop was hanged on 10 June.

On 29 June was tried Susanna Martin of Amesbury, a

widow, whom the " afflicted children " had continually seen tormenting and pinching them.

THE TRYAL OF SUSANNA MARTIN AT THE

COURT OF OYER AND TERMINER, HELD BY ADJOURN-MENT AT SALEM. JUNE 29. 1692.

I.

SUSANNA MARTIN, pleading *Not Guilty* to the Indictment of *Witchcraft*, brought in against her, there were produced the Evidences of many Persons very sensibly and grievously Bewitched ; who all complained of the Prisoner at the Bar, as the Person whom they believed the cause of their Miseries. And now, as well as in the other Trials, there was an extraordinary Endeavour by *Witchcrafts*, with Cruel and frequent Fits, to hinder the poor Sufferers from giving in their Complaints, which the Court was forced with much Patience to obtain, by much waiting and watching for it.

II. There was now also an account given of what passed at her first Examination before the Magistrates. The Cast of her *Eye*, then striking the afflicted People to the Ground, whether they saw that Cast or no ; there were these among other Passages between the Magistrates and the Examinate.

Magistrate. Pray, what ails these People ?

Martin. I don't know.

Magistrate. But what do you think ails them ?

Martin. I don't desire to spend my Judgment upon it.

Magistrate. Don't you think they are bewitch'd ?

Martin. No, I do not think they are.

Magistrate. Tell us your Thoughts about them then.

Martin. No, my thoughts are my own, when they are in, but when they are out they are anothers. Their Master——

Magistrate. Their Master ? who do you think is their Master ?

Martin. If they be dealing in the Black Art, you may know as well as I.

Magistrate. Well, what have you done towards this ?

Martin. Nothing at all.

Magistrate. Why, 'tis you or your Appearance.

Martin. I cannot help it.

Magistrate. Is it not *your* Master ? How comes your Appearance to hurt these ?

Martin. How do I know ? He that appeared in the Shape of *Samuel*, a glorified Saint, may appear in any ones Shape.

It was then also noted in her as in others like her, that if the Afflicted went to approach her, they were flung down to the Ground. And, when she was asked the reason of it, she said, *I cannot tell ; it may be, the Devil bears me more Malice than another.*

III. The Court accounted themselves alarum'd by these Things, to enquire further into the Conversation of the Prisoner ; and see what there might occur, to render these Accusations further credible. Whereupon, *John Allen* of *Salisbury*, testify'd, That he refusing, because of the weakness of his Oxen, to Cart some Staves at the request of this *Martin*, she was displeased at it ; and said, *It had been as good that he had ; for his Oxen should never do him much more Service.* Whereupon, this Deponent said, *Dost thou threaten me, thou old Witch ? I'l throw thee into the Brook :* Which to avoid, she flew over the Bridge, and escaped. But, as he was going home, one of his Oxen tired, so that he was forced to Unyoke him, that he might get him home. He then put his Oxen, with many more, upon *Salisbury* Beach, where Cattle did use to get *Flesh*. In a few days, all the Oxen upon the Beach were found by their Tracks, to have run unto the Mouth of *Merrimack-River*, and not returned ; but the next day they were found come ashore upon *Plum-Island.* They that sought them, used all imaginable gentleness, but they would still run away with a violence, that seemed wholly Diabolical, till they came near the mouth of *Merrimack-River ;* when they ran right into the Sea, swimming as far as they could be seen. One of them then swam back again, with a swiftness, amazing to the Beholders, who stood ready to receive him, and help up his tired Carcass : But the Beast ran furiously up into the Island, and from thence, thorough the Marshes, up into *Newbury* Town, and so up into the Woods ; and there after a while found near *Amesbury.* So that, of fourteen good Oxen, there was only this saved : The rest were all cast up, some in one place, and some in another, Drowned.

IV. *John Atkinson* testifi'd, That he exchanged a Cow with a Son of *Susanna Martin's*, whereat she muttered, and was unwilling he should have it. Going to receive this Cow, tho he Hamstring'd her, and Halter'd her, she, of a Tame Creature, grew so mad, that they could scarce get her along. She broke all the Ropes that were fastned unto her, and though she were ty'd fast unto a Tree, yet she made her escape, and gave them such further trouble, as they could ascribe to no cause but Witchcraft.

V. *Bernard Peache* testifi'd, That being in Bed, on the Lord's-day Night, he heard a scrabbling at the Window, whereat he then saw *Susanna Martin* come in, and jump down upon the Floor. She took hold of this Deponent's Feet, and drawing his Body up into an Heap, she lay upon him near Two Hours ; in all which time he could neither speak nor stir. At length, when he could begin to move, he laid hold on her Hand, and pulling it up to his Mouth, he bit three of her Fingers, as he judged, unto the Bone. Whereupon she went from the Chamber, down the Stairs, out at the Door. This Deponent thereupon called unto the People of the House, to advise them of what passed ; and he himself did follow her. The People saw her not ; but there being a Bucket at the Left-hand of the Door, ther was a drop of Blood found upon it ; and several more drops of Blood upon the Snow newly fallen abroad : There was likewise the print of her 2 Feet just without the Threshold ; but no more sign of any Footing further off.

At another time this Deponent was desired by the Prisoner, to come unto an Husking of Corn, at her House ; and she said, *If he did not come, it were better that he did !* He went not ; but the Night following, *Susanna Martin*, as he judged, and another came towards him. One of them said, *Here he is !* but he having a Quarter-staff, made a Blow at them. The Roof of the Barn, broke his Blow ; but following them to the Window, he made another Blow at them, and struck them down ; yet they got up, and got out, and he saw no more of them.

About this time, there was a Rumour about the Town, that *Martin* had a Broken Head ; but the Deponent could say nothing to that.

The said *Peache* also testifi'd the Bewitching the Cattle to Death, upon *Martin's* Discontents.

VI. *Robert Downer* testified, That this Prisoner being some Years ago prosecuted at Court for a Witch, he then said unto her, *He believed she was a Witch.* Whereat she being dissatisfied, said, *That some She-Devil would shortly fetch him away!* Which word were heard by others, as well as himself. The Night following, as he lay in his Bed, there came in at the Window, the likeness of a *Cat*, which flew upon him, took fast hold of his Throat, lay on him a considerable while, and almost killed him. At length he remembred what *Susanna Martin* had threatned the Day before; and with much striving he cried out, *Avoid, thou She-Devil! In the Name of God the Father, the Son, and the Holy Ghost, Avoid!* Whereupon it left him, leap'd on the Floor, and flew out at the Window.

And there also came in several Testimonies, that before ever *Downer* spoke a word of this Accident, *Susanna Martin* and her Family had related, *How this* Downer *had been handled!*

VII. *John Kembal* testified, that *Susanna Martin*, upon a Causeless Disgust, had threatned him, about a certain Cow of his, *That she should never do him any more Good:* and it came to pass accordingly. For soon after the Cow was found stark dead on the dry Ground, without any Distemper to be discerned upon her. Upon which he was followed with a strange Death upon more of his Cattle, whereof he lost in one Spring to the value of Thirty Pounds. But the said *John Kembal* had a further Testimony to give in against the Prisoner which was truly admirable.

Being desirous to furnish himself with a Dog, he applied himself to buy one of this *Martin*, who had a Bitch with Whelps in her House. But she not letting him have his choice, he said, he would supply himself then at one *Blezdels*. Having mark'd a Puppy, which he lik'd at *Blezdels*, he met *George Martin*, the Husband of the Prisoner, going by, who asked him, *Whether he would not have one of his Wife's Puppies?* and he answered, *No.* The same Day, one *Edmond Elliot*, being at *Martin's* House, heard *George Martin* relate, where this *Kembal* had been, and what he had said. Whereupon *Susanna Martin* replied, *If I live,*

I'll give him Puppies enough! Within a few days after, this *Kembal*, coming out of the Woods, there arose a little Black Cloud in the N.W. and *Kembal* immediately felt a force upon him, which made him not able to avoid running upon the stumps of Trees, that were before him, albeit he had a broad plain Cart-way, before him ; but tho' he had his Ax also on his Shoulder to endanger him in his Falls, he could not forbear going out of his way to tumble over them. When he came below the Meeting House, there appeared unto him, a little thing like a *Puppy*, of a Darkish Colour ; and it shot backwards and forwards between his Legs. He had the Courage to use all possible Endeavours of Cutting it with his Ax ; but he could not Hit it : the Puppy gave a jump from him, and went, as to him it seem'd, into the Ground. Going a little further, there appeared unto him a Black Puppy, somewhat bigger than the first, but as Black as a Cole. Its Motions were quicker than those of his Ax ; it flew at his Belly and away ; then at his Throat ; so, over his Shoulder one way, and then over his Shoulder another way. His Heart now began to fail him, and he thought the Dog would have tore his Throat out. But he recovered himself, and called upon God in his distress ; and naming the Name of JESUS CHRIST, it vanished away at once. The Deponent spoke not one Word of these Accidents, for fear of affrighting his Wife. But the next Morning, *Edmond Eliot*, going into *Martin's* House, this Woman asked him where *Kembal* was ? He replied, *At home, a Bed, for ought he knew*. She returned, *They say, he was frighted last Night*. Eliot asked, *With what ?* She answered, *With Puppies*. Eliot asked, *Where she heard of it, for he had heard nothing of it ?* She rejoined, *About the Town*. Altho' *Kembal* had mentioned the Matter to no Creature living.

VIII. *William Brown* testifi'd, That Heaven having blessed him with a most Pious and Prudent Wife, this Wife of his, one day met with *Susanna Martin ;* but when she approach'd just unto her, *Martin* vanished out of sight, and left her extreamly affrighted. After which time, the said *Martin* often appear'd unto her, giving her no little trouble ; and when she did come, she was visited with Birds, that sorely peck'd and prick'd her ; and sometimes a

Bunch, like a Pullet's Egg, would rise in her Throat, ready to choak her, till she cry'd out, *Witch, you shan't choak me!* While this good Woman was in this extremity, the Church appointed a Day of Prayer, on her behalf; whereupon her Trouble ceas'd; she saw not *Martin* as formerly; and the Church, instead of their Fast, gave Thanks for her Deliverance. But a considerable while after, she being Summoned to give in some Evidence at the Court, against this *Martin*, quickly thereupon, this *Martin* came behind her, while she was milking her Cow, and said unto her, *For thy defaming her at Court, I'll make thee the miserablest Creature in the World.* Soon after which, she fell into a strange kind of distemper, and became horribly frantick, and uncapable of any reasonable Action; the Physicians declaring, that her Distemper was preternatural, and that some Devil had certainly bewitched her; and in that condition she now remained.

IX. *Sarah Atkinson* testify'd, That *Susanna Martin* came from *Amesbury* to their House at *Newbury*, in an extraordinary Season, when it was not fit for any to Travel. She came (as she said, unto *Atkinson*) all that long way on Foot. She brag'd and shew'd how dry she was; nor could it be perceived that so much as the Soles of her Shoes were wet. *Atkinson* was amazed at it; and professed, that she should herself have been wet up to the knees, if she had then came so far; but *Martin* reply'd, *She scorn'd to be Drabbled!* It was noted, that this Testmony upon her Trial, cast her in a very singular Confusion.

X. *John Pressy* testify'd, That being one Evening very unaccountably Bewildred, near a Field of *Martins*, and several times, as one under an Enchantment, returning to the place he had left, at length he saw a marvellous Light, about the bigness of an Half-bushel, near two Rod, out of the way. He went, and struck it at with a Stick, and laid it on with all his might. He gave it near forty blows; and felt it a palpable substance. But going from it, his Heels were struck up, and he was laid with his Back on the Ground, sliding, as he thought, into a Pit; from whence he recover'd by taking hold on the Bush; altho' afterwards he could find no such Pit in the place. Having, after his Recovery, gone five or six Rod, he saw *Susanna Martin* standing on his Left-hand, as the Light had done before ; but they changed no words with one another. He could scarce find his House in his Return ; but at length he got home extreamly affrighted. The next day, it was upon Enquiry understood, that *Martin* was in a miserable condition by pains and hurts that were upon her.

It was further testify'd by this Deponent, That after he had given in some Evidence against *Susanna Martin*, many years ago, she gave him foul words about it ; and said, *He should never prosper more ;* particularly, *That he should never have more than two Cows ; that tho' he was never so likely to have more, yet he should never have them.* And that from that very day to this, namely for twenty years together, he could never exceed that number ; but some strange thing or other still prevented his having any more.

XI. *Jervis Ring* testify'd, That about seven years ago, he was oftentimes and grievously oppressed in the Night, but saw not who troubled him ; until at last he Lying perfectly Awake, plainly saw *Susanna Martin* approach him. She came to him, and forcibly bit him by the Finger ; so that the Print of the bite is now, so long after, to be seen upon him.

XII. But besides all of these Evidences, there was a most wonderful Account of one *Joseph Ring*, produced on this occasion.

This Man has been strangely carried about by *Dæmons*, from one *Witch-meeting* to another, for near two years together ; and for one quarter of this time, they have made him, and keep him Dumb, tho' he is now again able to speak. There was one *T. H.* who having, as 'tis judged, a design of engaging this *Joseph Ring* in a snare of Devillism, contrived a while, to bring this *Ring* two Shillings in Debt unto him.

Afterwards, this poor Man would be visited with unknown shapes, and this *T. H.* sometimes among them ; which would force him away with them, unto unknown Places, where he saw Meetings, Feastings, Dancings ; and after his return, wherein they hurried him along through the Air, he gave Demonstrations to the Neighbours, that he had indeed been so transported. When he was brought until these hellish Meetings, one of the first Things they still did unto him, was to give him a knock on the Back, whereupon he was ever as if bound with Chains, uncapable of stirring out of the place, till they should release him. He related, that there often came to him a Man, who presented him a *Book*, whereto he would have him set his Hand; promising to him, that he should then have even what he would; and presenting him with all the delectable Things, Persons, and Places, that he could imagin. But he refusing to subscribe, the business would end with dreadful Shapes, Noises and Screeches, which almost scared him out of his Wits. Once with the Book, there was a Pen offered him, and an Ink-horn with Liquor in it, that seemed like Blood : But he never toucht it.

This Man did now affirm, That he saw the Prisoner at several of those hellish Randezvouzes.

Note, this Woman was one of the most impudent, scurrilous, wicked Creatures in the World; and she did now throughout her whole Tryal, discover her self to be such an one. Yet when she was asked, what she had to say for her self ? Her chief Plea was, *That she had lead a most virtuous and holy Life.*

Upon the following day, 30 June, Elizabeth How of Topfield, who had been arrested on 28 May, was brought before the Court.

THE TRYAL OF ELIZABETH HOW, AT THE
COURT OF OYER AND TERMINER, HELD BY ADJOURNMENT AT SALEM, JUNE 30. 1692.

I.

Elizabeth How pleading *Not Guilty* to the Indictment of Witchcrafts, then charged upon her ; the Court, according to the usual Proceedings of the Courts in *England,* in such Cases, began with hearing the Depositions of several afflicted People, who were grievously tortured by sensible and evident *Witchcrafts,* and all complained of the Prisoner, as the cause of their Trouble. It was also found that the Sufferers were not able to bear her *Look,* as likewise, that in their greatest Swoons, they distinguished her *Touch* from other Peoples, being thereby raised out of them.

And there was other Testimony of People to whom the shape of this *How,* gave trouble nine or ten years ago.

II. It has been a most usual thing for the bewitched Persons, at the same time that the *Spectres* representing the *Witches,* troubled them, to be visited with Apparitions of *Ghosts,* pretending to have been Murdered by the *Witches* then represented. And sometimes the Confessions of the Witches afterwards acknowledged those very Murders, which these *Apparitions* charged upon them ; altho' they had never heard what Informations had been given by the Sufferers.

There were such Apparitions of Ghosts testified by some of the present Sufferers ; and the Ghosts affirmed, that this *How* had murdered them : Which things were *fear'd,* but not *prov'd.*

III. This *How* had made some Attempts of joyning to the Church at *Ipswich,* several years ago ; but she was denied an admission into that Holy Society, partly through a suspicion of Witchcraft, then urged against her. And there now came in Testimony, of preternatural Mischiefs, presently befalling some that had been Instrumental to debar her from the Communion whereupon she was intruding.

IV. There was a particular Deposition of *Joseph Stafford,* That his Wife had conceived an extream Aversion to this *How,* on the Reports of her Witchcrafts : But *How* one day, taking her by the Hand, and saying, *I believe you are not ignorant of the great Scandal that I lye under, by an evil Report raised upon me.* She immediately, unreasonably and unperswadeably, even like one Enchanted, began to take this Woman's part. *How* being soon after propounded, as desiring an Admission to the Table of the Lord, some of the pious Brethren were unsatisfy'd about her. The Elders appointed a Meeting to hear Matters objected against her ; and no Arguments in the World could hinder this Goodwife *Stafford* from going to the Lecture. She did indeed promise, with much ado, that she would not go to the Church-meeting, yet she could not refrain going thither also. *How's* Affairs there were so canvased, that she came off rather *Guilty* than *Cleared ;* nevertheless Goodwife *Stafford* could not forbear taking her by the Hand, and saying, *Tho' you are Condemned before Men, you are Justify'd before God.* She was quickly taken in a very strange manner, Ranting, Raving, Raging, and crying out, *Goody* How *must come into the Church; she is a precious Saint; and tho' she be condemned before Men, she is Justify'd before God.* So she continued for the space of two or three Hours; and then fell into a Trance. But coming to her self, she cry'd out, *Ha! I was mistaken;* and afterwards again repeated, *Ha! I was mistaken!* Being asked by a stander by, *Wherein?* she replyed, *I thought Goody How had been a precious Saint of God, but now I see she is a Witch: She has bewitched me, and my Child, and we shall never be well, till there be a Testimony for her, that she may be taken into the Church.* And *How* said afterwards, that she was very sorry to see *Stafford* at the Church-meeting mentioned. *Stafford*, after this, declared herself to be afflicted by the Shape of *How;* and from that Shape she endured many Miseries.

V. *John How*, Brother to the Husband of the Prisoner, testified, that he refusing to accompany the Prisoner unto her Examination, as was by her desired, immediately some of his Cattle were Bewitched to Death, leaping three or four foot high, turning about, speaking, falling, and dying at once; and going to cut off an Ear, for an use, that might as well perhaps have been omitted, the Hand wherein he held his Knife was taken very numb, and so it remained, and full of pain, for several Days, being not well at this very Time. And he suspected the Prisoner for the Author of it.

VI. *Nehemiah Abbot* testify'd, that unusual and mischievous Accidents would befal his Cattle, whenever he had any Difference with this Prisoner. Once, particularly, she wished his Ox choaked; and within a little while that Ox was choaked with a Turnep in his Throat. At another Time, refusing to lend his Horse, at the Request of her Daughter, the Horse was in a preternatural manner abused. And several other odd things of that kind were testified.

VII. There came in Testimony, that one Good-wife *Sherwin*, upon some Difference with *How*, was bewitched; and that she dyed, charging this *How* with having an Hand in her Death. And that other People had their Barrels of Drink unaccountably mischieved, spoil'd and spilt, upon their displeasing of her.

The things in themselves were trivial, but their being

such a Course of them, it made them the more considered. Among others, *Martha Wood*, gave her Testimony, That a little after her Father had been employed in gathering an account of *How's* Conversation, they once and again lost great quantities of Drink out of their Vessels, in such a manner, as they could ascribe to nothing but Witchcraft. As also, That *How* giving her some Apples, when she had eaten of them she was taken with a very strange kind of Amaze, insomuch that she knew not what she said or did.

VIII. There was likewise a Cluster of Depositions, That one *Isaac Cummings* refusing to lend his Mare unto the husband of this *How*, the Mare was within a day or two taken in a strange condition : The Beast seemed much abused, being bruised as if she had been running over the Rocks, and marked where the Bridle went, as if burnt with a red hot Bridle. Moreover, one using a Pipe of Tobacco for the Cure of the Beast, a blue Flame issued out of her, took hold of her Hair, and not only spread and burnt on her, but it also flew upwards towards the Roof of the Barn, and had like to have set the Barn on Fire : And the Mare dyed very suddenly.

IX. *Timothy Pearley* and his Wife, testify'd, Not only unaccountable Mischiefs befel their Cattle, upon their having of Differences with this Prisoner : but also that they had a Daughter destroyed by Witchcrafts ; which Daughter still charged *How* as the Cause of her Affliction. And it was noted, that she would be struck down whenever *How* were spoken of. She was often endeavoured to be thrown into the Fire, and into the Water, in her strange Fits : Tho' her Father had corrected her for charging *How* with bewitching her, yet (as was testified by others also) she said, She was sure of it, and must dye standing to it. Accordingly she charged *How* to the very Death ; and said, *Tho'* How *could afflict and torment her Body, yet she could not hurt her Soul :* And, *That the Truth of this matter would appear, when she would be dead and gone.*

X. *Francis Lane* testified, That being hired by the Husband of this *How* to get him a parcel of Posts and Rails, this *Lane* hired *John Pearly* to assist him. This Prisoner then told *Lane*, That she believed the Posts and Rails would not do, because *John Pearly* helped him : but that if he had got them alone, without *John Pearly's* help, they might have done well enough. When *James How* came to receive his Posts and Rails of *Lane*, *How* taking them up by the Ends, they, tho' good and sound, yet unaccountably broke off, so that *Lane* was forced to get thirty or forty more. And this Prisoner being informed of it, she said, She told him so before, because *Pearly* helped about them.

XI. Afterwards there came in the Confessions of several other (penitent) Witches, which affirmed this *How* to be one of those, who with them had been baptized by the Devil in the River, at *Newbury*-Falls : before which he made them there kneel down by the Brink of the River and worshiped him.

Accordingly on 19 July, five women, Sarah Good, who was one of the first to be accused with Sarah Osburn and the Indian Tituba, Sarah Wildes, of whom practically nothing is recorded, Susanna Martin, Elizabeth How, and Rebecca Nurse, were executed for witchcraft.

Rebecca Nurse was an aged matron of over seventy years of age, in failing health, and of blameless character. In fact, her reputation for piety was so great, and for so many years had she been highly esteemed in the community, that the jury brought in a verdict of " Not Guilty," upon which the mob broke out into the wildest clamour, yelling with horrid threats that they would pull the house about the judges' ears and tear the jurors to pieces. Benches were smashed, and missiles began to be thrown, when the acquittal was hurriedly withdrawn and sentence of death speedily pronounced. Moreover, as Hutchinson tells us, " Mr. Noyes, the Minister of Salem, a zealous prosecutor, excommunicated the poor old woman, and delivered her to Satan, to whom he supposed she had given herself formally many years before ; but her life and conversation had been such, that the remembrance thereof, in a short time after, wiped off all the reproach occasioned by the civil or ecclesiastical sentence against her."

The bodies of executed witches were not allowed to receive Christian burial, and were huddled with contumely into holes among the rocks of Gallows Hill where they suffered. But there always existed among her descendants a family tradition that the body of Rebecca Nurse was recovered by her devoted husband and sons, and tenderly buried near her old home. A pine grove covers the spot, and hard by has been erected a granite monument to record her end.

The most remarkable of all the Salem witch trials was undoubtedly that of the Rev. George Burroughs. He was a graduate of Harvard in the class of 1670, and after having preached in Maine for several years he became, in 1680, Pastor at Salem Village. Here his wife died, and seeing that his stipend had not been punctually paid him he was forced to run into debt for her funeral expenses, which caused such scandal in the community that he chose to retire in 1683 to Casco Bay. In 1692 he was a pastor at Wells, Maine. He was " cried out upon " by Abigail Hobbs, Abigail Williams, and particularly by Ann Putnam who told an extraordinary tale.

" The Deposition of Ann Putnam, who testifieth and saith, that, on the 8th day of May, at evening, I saw the apparition of Mr. George Burroughs, who grievously tortured me, and urged me to write in his book, which I refused. He then told me that his two first wives would appear to me presently, and tell me a great many lies, but I should not believe them.

" There immediately appeared to me the forms of two women in winding-sheets, and napkins about their heads, at which I was greatly affrighted ; and they turned their faces fowards Mr. Burroughs, and looked very red and angry, and told him that he had been a cruel man to them, and that their blood did cry for vengance against him ; and also told him that they should be clothed with white robes in Heaven, when he should be cast into hell ; and immediately he vanished away. And, as soon as he was gone, the two women turned their heads toward me, and looked as pale as a white wall ; and told me that they were Mr. Burroughs' two first wives, and that he had murdered them. And one of them told me that she was his first wife, and he stabbed her under the left arm and put a piece of sealing-wax on the wound. And she pulled aside the winding-sheet, and showed me the place ; and also told me that she was in the house where Mr. Parris now lives, when it was done.

" And the other told me that Mr. Burroughs and that wife

which he hath now, killed her in the vessel, as she was coming to see her friends, because they would have one another. And they both charged me that I should tell these things to the magistrates before Mr. Burroughs' face ; and, if he did not own them, they did not know but they should appear there. This morning also, Mrs. Lawson and her daughter Ann appeared to me, whom I knew, and told me Mr. Burroughs murdered them. This morning also appeared to me another woman in a winding-sheet and told me that she was Goodman Fuller's first wife, and Mr. Burroughs killed her because there was some difference between her husband and him."

On 30 April a warrant had been procured from Boston for the arrest of George Burroughs, " he being suspected of a confederacy with the Devil." Being found at the supper-table with his family when the marshal entered the house to execute the mandate, he was at once brought back in custody to Salem, whither they returned on 4 May. On 9 May a special session of magistrates was convened, William Stoughton coming from Dorchester and Captain Samuel Sewall from Boston to sit with Hathorne and Curwin that the proceedings might be carried out with fullest solemnity, Stoughton, indeed, being the temporary deputy-governor of the colony.

Burroughs was committed to jail, and on 5 August he was brought before a special court, appointed to investigate the crime of Witchcraft. Cotton Mather in his *The Wonders of the Invisible World* gives the following account of the proceedings :—

THE TRYAL OF G. B. AT A COURT OF OYER AND TERMINER,

HELD IN SALEM, 1692.

GLAD should I have been, if I had never known the Name of this Man : or never had this occasion to mention so much as the first Letters of his Name. But the Government requiring some Account of his Trial to be inserted in this Book, it becomes me with all Obedience to submit unto the Order.

I. This *G. B.* Was Indicted for Witch-craft, and in the prosecution of the Charge against him, he was Accused by

five or six of the Bewitched, as the Author of their Miseries ;
he was Accused by Eight of the Confessing Witches, as
being an head Actor at some of their Hellish Randezvouzes,
and one who had the promise of being a King in Satan's
Kingdom, now going to be Erected : He was accused by
Nine Persons for extraordinary Lifting, and such feats of
Strength as could not be done without a Diabolical Assistance.
And for other such things he was Accused, until about
thirty Testimonies were brought in against him ; nor were
these judg'd the half of what might have been considered for
his Conviction: However they were enough to fix the
Character of a Witch upon him according to the Rules of
Reasoning, by the Judicious *Gaule*, in that Case directed.

II. The Court being sensible, that the Testimonies of
the Parties Bewitched, use to have a Room among the
Suspicions or *Presumptions*, brought in against one Indicted for Witch-craft ; there were now heard the Testimonies of several Persons, who were most notoriously
Bewitched, and every day Tortured by Invisible Hands,
and these now all charged the Spectres of *G. B.* to have
a share in their Torments. At the Examination of this
G. B. the Bewitched People were grievously harrassed
with Preternatural Mischiefs, which could not possibly be
Dissembled ; and they still ascribe it unto the endeavours
of *G. B.* to Kill them. And now upon the Tryal of one
of the Bewitched Persons, testified, that in her Agonies, a
little black Hair'd Man came to her, saying his Name
was *B.* and bidding her set her hand to a Book which he
shewed unto her ; and bragging that he was a *Conjuror*,
above the ordinary Rank of Witches ; That he often Persecuted her with the offer of that Book, saying, *She should
be well, and need fear nobody, if she would but Sign it ;* But
he inflicted cruel Pains and Hurts upon her, because of
her denying so to do. The Testimonies of the other Sufferers
concurred with these ; and it was remarkable, that whereas
Biting was one of the ways which the Witches used for the
vexing of the Sufferers ; when they cry'd out of *G. B.*
Biting them, the print of the Teeth would be seen on the
Flesh of the Complainers, and just such a Set of Teeth as
G. B.'s would then appear upon them, which could be
distinguished from those of some other Mens. Others

of them testified, That in their Torments, *G. B.* tempted them to go unto a Sacrament, unto which they perceived him with a Sound of Trumpet, Summoning of other Witches, who quickly after the Sound, would come from all Quarters unto the Rendezvous. One of them falling into a kind of Trance, affirmed, that *G. B.* had carried her away into a very high Mountain, where he shewed her mighty and glorious Kingdoms, and said, *He would give them all to her if she would write in his Book ;* But she told him, *They were none of his to give ;* and refused the Motions ; enduring of much Misery for that refusal.

It cost the Court a wonderful deal of Trouble, to hear the Testimonies of the Sufferers ; for when they were going to give in their Depositions, they would for a long time be taken with Fits, that made them uncapable of saying any thing. The chief Judg asked the Prisoner, who he thought hindered these Witnesses from giving their *Testimonies ?* And he answered, *He supposed it was the Devil.* That Honourable Person replied, *How comes the Devil then to be so loath to have any Testimony borne against you ?* Which cast him into very great Confusion.

III. It has been a frequent thing for the Bewitched People to be entertained with Apparitions of *Ghosts* of Murdered People, at the same time that the *Spectres* of the Witches trouble them. These Ghosts do always affright the Beholders more than all the other spectral Representations ; and when they exhibit themselves, they cry out, of being Murthered by the Witch-crafts or other Violences of the Persons who are then in Spectre present. It is further considered, that once or twice, these *Apparitions* have been seen by others, at the very same time they have shewn themselves to the Bewitched ; and seldom have there been these *Apparitions*, but when something unusual or suspected, have attended the Death of the Party thus Appearing. Some that have been accused by these *Apparitions* accosting of the Bewitched People, who had never heard a word of any such Persons ever being in the World, have upon a fair Examination, freely and fully confessed the Murthers of those very Persons, altho' these also did not know how the Apparitions had complained of them. Accordingly several of the Bewitched, had given in their

Testimony, that they had been troubled with the Apparitions of two Women, who said, that they were *G. B.'s* two Wives, and that he had been the Death of them ; and that the Magistrates must be told of it, before whom if *B.* upon his Tryal denied it, they did not know but that they should appear again in Court. Now, *G. B.* had been Infamous for the Barbarous usage of his two late Wives, all the Country over. Moreover, it was testified, the Spectre of *G. B.* threatening of the Sufferers, told them, he had Killed (besides others) Mrs. *Lawson* and her Daughter *Ann.* And it was noted, that these were the Vertuous Wife and Daughter of one at whom this *G. B.* might have a prejudice for his being serviceable at *Salem Village,* from whence himself had in ill Terms removed some Years before : And that when they dy'd, which was long since, there were some odd Circumstances about them, which made some of the Attendants there suspect something of Witch-craft, tho none Imagined from what Quarter it should come.

Well, *G. B.* being now upon his Tryal, one of the Bewitched Persons was cast into Horror at the Ghost of *B.'s* two Deceased Wives then appearing before him, and crying for *Vengeance* against him. Hereupon several of the Bewitched Persons were successively called in, who all not knowing what the former had seen and said, concurred in their Horror of the Apparition, which they affirmed that he had before him. But he, tho much appalled, utterly deny'd that he discerned any thing of it ; nor was it any part of his *Conviction.*

IV. Judicious Writers have assigned it a great place in the Conviction of *Witches, when Persons are Impeached by other notorious Witches, to be as ill as themselves ; especially, if the Persons have been much noted for neglecting the Worship of God.* Now, as there might have been Testimonies enough of *G. B.'s* Antipathy to *Prayer,* and the other Ordinances of God, tho by his Profession, singularly Obliged thereunto ; so, there now came in against the Prisoner, the Testimonies of several Persons, who confessed their own having been horrible *Witches,* and ever since their Confessions, have been themselves terribly Tortured by the Devils and other Witches, even like the other Sufferers ; and therein undergone the Pains of many *Deaths* for their Confessions.

These now testified, that *G. B.* had been at Witch-meetings with them ; and that he was the Person who had Seduc'd, and Compell'd them into the snares of Witch-craft : **That** he promised them *Fine Cloaths* for doing it ; that he brought Poppets to them, and Thorns to stick into those Poppets, for the Afflicting of other People ; and that he exhorted them with the rest of the Crew, to Bewitch all *Salem Village,* but be sure to do it Gradually, if they would prevail in what they did.

When the *Lancashire Witches* were Condemn'd, I don't remember that there was any considerable further Evidence, than that of the Bewitched, and than that of some that confessed. We see so much already against *G. B.* But this being indeed not enough, there were other things to render what had been already produced *credible.*

V. A famous Divine recites this among the Convictions of a Witch ; *The Testimony of the party Bewitched, whether Pining or Dying ; together with the joint Oaths of sufficient Persons that have seen certain Prodigious Pranks or Feats wrought by the Party Accused.* Now, God had been pleased so to leave this *G. B.* that he had ensnared himself by several Instances, which he had formerly given of a Preternatural Strength, and which were now produced against him. He was a very Puny Man, yet he had often done things beyond the strength of a Giant. A Gun of about seven foot Barrel, and so heavy that strong Men could not steadily hold it out with both hands ; there were several Testimonies, given in by Persons of Credit and Honor that he made nothing of taking up such a Gun behind the Lock, with but one hand, and holding it out like a Pistol, at Arms-end. *G. B.* in his Vindication, was so foolish as to say, That *an* Indian *was there, and held it out at the same time :* Whereas none of the Spectators ever saw any such *Indian ;* but they supposed, the *Black Man* (as the Witches called the Devil ; and they generally say he resembles an *Indian*) might give him that Assistance. There was Evidence likewise brought in, that he made nothing of taking up whole Barrels fill'd with *Molasses* or *Cider,* in very disadvantageous Postures, and Carrying of them through the difficultest Places out of a Canoo to the Shore.

Yea, there were two Testimonies, that *G. B.* with only

putting the Fore Finger of his Right Hand into the Muzzle of an heavy Gun, a Fowling-piece of about six or seven foot Barrel, did lift up the Gun, and hold it out at Arms-end; a Gun which the Deponents thought strong Men could not with both hands lift up, and hold out at the But-end, as is usual. Indeed, one of these Witnesses was over-perswaded by some Persons, to be out of the way upon *G. B.'s* Tryal; but he came afterwards with Sorrow for his withdraw, and gave in his Testimony : Nor were either of these Witnesses made use of as Evidences in the Trial.

VI. There came in several Testimonies relating to the Domestick Affairs of *G. B.* which had a very hard Aspect upon him ; and not only prov'd him a very ill Man ; but also confirmed the belief of the Character, which had been already fastned on him.

'Twas testified, that keeping his two Successive Wives in a strange kind of Slavery, he would when he came home from abroad, pretend to tell the Talk which any had with them ; That he has brought them to the point of Death, by his harsh Dealings with his Wives, and then made the People about him, to promise that in case Death should happen, they would say nothing of it ; That he used all means to make his Wives Write, Sign, Seal, and Swear a Covenant, never to reveal any of his Secrets ; That his Wives had privately complained unto the Neighbours about frightful Apparitions of Evil Spirits, with which their House was sometimes infested ; and that many such things have been whispered among the Neighbourhood. There were also some other Testimonies relating to the Death of People whereby the Consciences of an Impartial Jury were convinced that *G. B.* had Bewitched the Persons mentioned in the Complaints. But I am forced to omit several passages, in this, as well as in all the succeeding Tryals, because the Scribes who took notice of them, have not supplyed me.

VII. One Mr. *Ruck*, Brother-in-Law to this *G. B.* testified, that *G. B.* and himself, and his Sister, who was *G. B.'s* Wife, going out for two or three Miles to gather Straw-berries, *Ruck* with his Sister, the Wife of *G. B.* Rode home very Softly, with *G. B.* on Foot in their Company, *G. B.* stept aside a little into the Bushes ; whereupon they halted and Halloo'd for him. He not answering, they went away homewards, with a quickened pace, without expectation of seeing him in a considerable while ; and yet when they were got near home, to their Astonishment, they found him on foot with them, having a Basket of Straw-berries. *G. B.* immediately then fell to Chiding his Wife, on the account of what she had been speaking to her Brother, of him, on the Road : which when they wondred at, he said, *He knew their thoughts.* *Ruck* being startled at that, made some reply, intimating, that the Devil himself did not know so far ; but *G. B.* answered, *My God makes known your Thoughts unto me.* The Prisoner now at the Bar had nothing to answer, unto what was thus witnessed against him, that was worth considering. Only he said, *Ruck and his Wife left a Man with him when they left him.* Which *Ruck* now affirm'd to be false ; and when the Court asked *G. B. What the Man's Name was ?* his Countenance was much altered ; nor could he say, who 'twas. But the Court began to think, that he then step'd aside, only that by the assistance of the *Black Man,* he might put on his *Invisibility,* and in that *Fascinating Mist,* gratifie his own Jealous Humour, to hear what they said of him. Which trick of rendering themselves *Invisible,* our Witches do in their Confessions pretend, that they sometimes are Masters of ; and it is the more credible, because there is Demonstration, that they often render many other things utterly *Invisible.*

VIII. *Faltring, faulty, unconstant, and contrary Answers upon judicial and deliberate Examination,* are counted some unlucky Symptons of Guilt, in all Crimes, especially in Witch-crafts. Now there never was a Prisoner more eminent for them, than *G. B.* both at his Examination and on his Trial. His *Tergiversations, Contradictions,* and *Falshoods* were very sensible : he had little to say, but that he had heard some things that he could not prove, Reflecting upon the Reputation of some of the Witnesses. Only he gave in a Paper to the Jury ; wherein, altho' he had many times before, granted, not only that there are *Witches,* but also, that the present Sufferings of the Country are the effects of *horrible Witchcrafts,* yet he now goes to evince it, *That there neither are nor ever were Witches, that having made a Compact with the Devil, can send a Devil to Torment other people at a distance.* This Paper was Transcribed out of *Ady ;* which the Court presently knew, as soon as they heard it. But he said, he had taken none of it out of any Book ; for which, his Evasion afterwards, was, That a Gentleman gave him the Discourse in a Manuscript, from whence he Transcribed it.

IX. The Jury brought him ín *Guilty :* But when he came to Die, he utterly deni'd the Fact, whereof he had been thus convicted.

Hutchinson, who had access to the same records, which have now perished, gives identical evidence with reference to the rites : " Richard Carrier affirmed to the jury that he saw Mr. George Burroughs at the witch meeting at the village and saw him administer the sacrament. Mary Lacy, senr. and her daughter Mary affirmed that Mr. George Burroughs was at the witch meetings with witch sacraments, and that she knows Mr. Burroughs to be of the company of witches."[19] John Hale also states : " This D. H. [Deliverance Hobbs] confessed she was at a Witch Meeting at Salem Village. . . . And the said *G. B.* preached to them, and such a Woman was their Deacon, and there they had a Sacrament."[20] Certainly all this was quite clear enough amply to justify Cotton Mather in his statement that the witches were wont to meet " in Hellish *Randezvouzes,* wherein the Confessors [penitent witches] do say, they have had their Diabolical Sacraments, imitating the *Baptism* and the *Supper* of our Lord."[21]

On 19 August George Burroughs was executed at Witchhill, and with him suffered four more, John Procter, George Jacobs, John Willard, and Martha Carrier.

John Procter was a native of Ipswich, and both he and his wife, Elizabeth, had lain in prison for some three months. Two weeks after he was put to death a child was born to Elizabeth Procter who was yet in hold. The fact of her pregnancy saved her life.

George Jacobs was a stout old patriarch who vigorously resisted the accusations, and roundly told the magistrates : " You tax me for a wizard ; you may as well tax me for a buzzard. I have done no harm," a speech which was probably not altogether to his advantage. He had been arrested on 10 May, and was much cried out upon by Mary Walcot.

Of John Willard little is known save that the afflicted children accused him of murder and sorcery. Brattle gives the following account of his demeanour at the gibbet : " Procter and Willard, whose whole management of themselves from the jail to the gallows, was very affecting, and melting to the hearts of some considerable spectators whom I could mention to you ; but they are executed, and so I leave them."

The trial of Martha Carrier is reported in detail by Cotton Mather, and presents some very extraordinary circumstances.

THE TRIAL OF MARTHA CARRIER, AT THE

COURT OF OYER AND TERMINER, HELD BY ADJOURNMENT AT SALEM, AUGUST 2. 1692.

I

MARTHA CARRIER was Indicted for the bewitching certain Persons, according to the Form usual in such Cases, pleading *Not Guilty*, to her Indictment; there were first brought in a considerable number of the bewitched Persons ; who not only made the Court sensible of an horrid Witchcraft committed upon them, but also deposed, That it was *Martha Carrier*, or her Shape, that grievously tormented them, by Biting, Pricking, Pinching and Choaking of them. It was further deposed, That while this *Carrier* was on her Examination, before the Magistrates, the Poor People were so tortured that every one expected their Death upon the very spot, but that upon the binding of *Carrier* they were eased. Moreover the Look of *Carrier* then laid the Afflicted People for dead ; and her Touch, if her Eye at the same time were off them, raised them again : Which Things were also now seen upon her Tryal. And it was testified, That upon the mention of some having their Necks twisted almost round, by the Shape of this *Carrier*, she replyed, *Its no matter though their necks had been twisted quite off.*

II. Before the Tryal of this Prisoner, several of her own children had frankly and fully confessed, not only that they were Witches themselves, but that this their Mother had made them so. This Confession they made with great Shews of Repentance, and with much Demonstration of Truth.

They related Place, Time, Occasion ; they gave an account of Journeys, Meetings and Mischiefs by them performed, and were very credible in what they said. Nevertheless, this evidence was not produced against the Prisoner at the Bar, inasmuch as there was other Evidence enough to proceed upon.

III. *Benjamin Abbot* gave his Testimony, That last *March* was a twelvemonth, this *Carrier* was very angry with him, upon laying out some Land, near her Husband's : Her Expressions in this Anger, were, That *she would stick as close to* Abbot *as the Bark stuck to the Tree ; and that he should repent of it afore seven years came to an End, so as Doctor* Prescot *should never cure him.* These Words were heard by others besides *Abbot* himself ; who also heard her say, *She would hold his Nose as close to the Grindstone as ever it was held since his Name was* Abbot. Presently after this, he was taken with a Swelling in his Foot, and then with a Pain in his Side, and exceedingly tormented. It bred into a Sore, which was lanced by Doctor *Prescot*, and several Gallons of Corruption ran out of it. For six Weeks it continued very bad, and then another Sore bred in the Groin, which was also launced by Doctor *Prescot.* Another Sore then bred in his Groin, which was likewise cut, and put him to very great Misery : He was brought unto Death's Door, and so remained until *Carrier* was taken, and carried away by the Constable, from which very day he began to mend, and so grew better every Day, and is well ever since.

Sarah Abbot also, his Wife, testified, That her Husband was not only all this while Afflicted in his Body, but also that strange extraordinary and unaccountable Calamities befel his Cattel ; their Death being such as they could guess at no Natural Reason for.

IV. *Allin Toothaker* testify'd, That *Richard*, the son of *Martha Carrier*, having some difference with him, pull'd him down by the Hair of the Head. When he Rose again, he was going to strike at *Richard Carrier ;* but fell down flat on his Back to the ground, and had not power to stir hand or foot, until he told *Carrier* he yielded ; and then he saw the shape of *Martha Carrier*, go off his breast.

This *Toothaker*, had Received a wound in the *Wars ;* and he now testify'd, that *Martha Carrier* told him, *He should never be Cured.* Just afore the Apprehending of *Carrier,* he could thrust a knitting Needle into his wound, four inches deep ; but presently after her being siezed, he was throughly healed.

He further testify'd, that when *Carrier* and he some times were at variance, she would clap her hands at him, and say, *He should get nothing by it ;* whereupon he several times lost his Cattle, by strange Deaths, whereof no natural causes could be given.

V. *John Rogger* also testifyed, That upon the threatning words of this malicious *Carrier,* his Cattle would be strangely bewitched ; as was more particularly then described.

VI. *Samuel Preston* testify'd, that about two years ago, having some difference with *Martha Carrier,* he lost a *Cow* in a strange Preternatural unusual manner ; and about a month after this, the said *Carrier,* having again some difference with him, she told him ; *He had lately lost a Cow, and it should not be long before he lost another ;* which accordingly came to pass ; for he had a thriving and well-kept *Cow,* which without any known cause quickly fell down and dy'd.

VII. *Phebe Chandler* testify'd, that about a Fortnight before the apprehension of *Martha Carrier,* on a Lordsday, while the Psalm was singing in the *Church,* this *Carrier* then took her by the shoulder and shaking her, asked her, *where she lived :* she made her no Answer, although as *Carrier,* who lived next door to her Fathers House, could not in reason but know who she was. Quickly after this, as she was at several times crossing the Fields, she heard a voice, that she took to be *Martha Carriers,* and it seem'd as if it was over her head. The voice told her, *she should within two or three days be poisoned.* Accordingly, within such a little time, one half of her right hand, became greatly swollen, and very painful ; as also part of her Face : whereof she can give no account how it came. It continued very bad for some dayes ; and several times since, she has had a great pain in her breast ; and been so seized on her leggs, that she has hardly been able to go. She added, that lately, going well to the House of God, *Richard,* the son of *Martha Carrier,* look'd very earnestly upon her, and immediately her hand, which had formerly been poisoned, as is abovesaid, began to pain her greatly, and she had a strange Burning at her stomach; but was then struck deaf, so that he could not hear any of the prayer, or singing, till the two or three last words of the Psalm.

VIII. One *Foster*, who confessed her own share in the Witchcraft for which the Prisoner stood indicted, affirm'd, that she had seen the prisoner at some of their *Witch-meetings*, and that it was this *Carrier*, who perswaded her to be a Witch. She confessed, that the Devil carry'd them on a pole, to a Witch-meeting; but the pole broke, and she hanging about *Carriers* neck, they both fell down, and she then received an hurt by the Fall, whereof she was not at this very time recovered.

IX. One *Lacy*, who likewise confessed her share in this Witchcraft, now testify'd, that she and the prisoner were once Bodily present at a *Witch-meeting* in *Salem Village;* and that she knew the prisoner to be a Witch, and to have been at a Diabolical sacrament, and that the prisoner was the undoing of her, and her Children, by enticing them into the snare of the Devil.

X. Another *Lacy*, who also confessed her share in this Witchcraft, now testify'd, that the prisoner was at the *Witch-meeting*, in *Salem Village*, where they had Bread and Wine Administered unto them.

XI. In the time of this prisoners Trial, one *Susanna Sheldon*, in open Court had her hands Unaccountably ty'd together with a wheel-band, so fast that without cutting, it could not be loosed: It was done by a *Spectre;* and the Sufferer affirm'd, it was the *Prisoners*.

Memorandum. This rampant Hag, *Martha Carrier*, was the person, of whom the Confessions of the Witches, and of her own children among the rest, agreed, That the Devil had promised her, she should be *Queen of Hell*.

On 9 September the Court condemned six persons, and eight days later nine more were sentenced to death.

As early as 19 March Martha Corey had been arrested under grave suspicion of Witchcraft. She was a woman constant in attendance at the meeting-house, and remarkable for her piety, facts which sadly militated against her when she was accused, since her devout profession was at once considered to be no more than a hypocritical mask of Christianity to hide her evil commerce with Satan and his agents. Her examination, in the handwriting of Mr. Parris, is of considerable length, and we find that she repeatedly asseverates that she is a " gospel woman," as when asked by the magistrates : " Tell us what you know of this matter," she replied : " Why, I am a gospel woman, and do you think I can have to do with witchcraft too ? " Whereupon the afflicted children broke in : " There is a man whispering in her ear," and Hathorne promptly queried : " What did he say to you ? " " We must not believe all that these distracted children say," was her reply. " Cannot you tell what that man whispered ? " they urged. " I saw nobody." " But did you hear ? " they pressed. " No," she answered curtly enough. " Here was extreme agony of the afflicted." She was further accused of covenanting with a familiar, a bird that was visible to the children, and the Rev. Nicholas Noyes roundly declared : " I believe it is apparent she practiseth witchcraft in the congregation ; there is no need of images."

Martha Corey had more than once flatly declared her disbelief in Witchcraft, but her husband, Giles Corey, a passionate robust old man of fourscore, who followed the proceedings with the most intense zeal, bordering upon fanaticism, was so enraged at his wife's attitude that he let drop some angry expressions, which were carefully noted and remembered to her hurt. Even when called upon to give evidence he made several entirely damaging statements, and then perhaps realizing the folly of his vehemence, that he was in effect sending his wife to the gallows, he ceased abruptly and refused to utter another word. Whereupon he was arrested for contumacy, upon which charge sorcery was quickly clapped. On 19 April his examination took place, and from the scanty papers which can be traced he seems to have been labouring under the greatest distress of mind. The only papers relating to him, on file as having been sworn to before the Grand Jury, are a few brief depositions. If he had actually been put on trial, no doubt we should have ample documents. Besides his own vindictive course towards his wife, two of his four sons-in-law had turned against her. One (Crosby) had testified to her undoing, and another

(Parker) had allowed his name to be used as an adverse witness. Giles Corey, then, made a will, or more properly a deed, by which he gave all his property to his " beloved sons-in-law William Cleeves of Beverly and John Moulton of Salem "; a clearly writ document, duly signed and witnessed. He knew now that if brought to trial his death was certain, and he realized that conviction and execution, owing to the concomitant attainder, might invalidate all attempts of his to convey his excellent property. Whereas if he should not be brought to trial and condemnation his deed must legally stand and nothing could break or defeat its effect. Accordingly he made up his mind not to be tried. When called into Court to answer to the indictment found by the Grand Jury, he did not plead " Guilty " or " Not Guilty," but vouchsafed no reply. This rendered it technically impossible to bring him to trial, and the authorities did not hesitate to apply to the prisoner who refused to plead the horrid penalties prescribed by law. Having been called upon thrice, if he yet remained mute of malice, the accused was sent to a low dark cell, where he was stretched almost naked upon the stone floor, and loaded with a mass of heavy iron, daily increasing in weight, until such time as, if he persisted in his obstinacy, his life was slowly crushed from his body. A few crumbs of black bread and a sip of bracken water on alternate days were all the sustenance that justice allowed. This was the *peine forte et dure*. Giles Corey's pressing to death was on 19 September, and tradition tells that it took place in the open field near the jail, somewhere between Howard-street burial ground and Brown Street. In order that the spiritual weapons should not rust the Rev. Nathaniel Noyes, as soon as it was known that the prisoner refused to plead, solemnly declared him excommunicate, whilst on 11 September, the Assembly voted the excommunication of Martha Corey for Witchcraft, clear and proven, sentence being pronounced by the Rev. Samuel Parris on 14 September.

A well-known antiquarian who was living at Salem as recently as 1891, heard from his grandmother (who died in 1862, aged ninety-two) the anecdote told by her grandmother, whose mother was an eye-witness of the scene she described ; she was living at the time in Essex Street, where the Perley block now stands, and related, that as the tumbril bearing the dead body of Giles Corey passed her door, she saw a man push back with his cane the blackened tongue of the unfortunate wretch, which had been forced from his mouth by the agonizing pressure of his doom.

On 22 September Martha Corey was executed at Gallows Hill, together with Mary Easty, Alice Parker, Ann Pudeator, Margaret Scott, Wilmot Reed, Samuel Wardwell, and Mary Parker. As they were launched from the gibbet Mr. Noyes, who stood by, pointed to their bodies and exclaimed in stentorian tones : " Alas ! What a sad sight it is to see eight firebrands of hell hanging there ! "

Mary Easty, the sister[22] of Rebecca Nurse, was aged fifty-eight years, and the mother of seven children. She had first been accused and examined in April, but was released from prison on 18 May. Immediately, however, Mercy Lewis fell into the wildest fits and convulsions to the horror and alarm of all the neighbours, whilst the afflicted children kept crying out that it was Goodwife Easty tormenting her. This continued until Mistress Easty was arrested and once more laid in bonds.

Of Alice Parker little is recorded save that she was the wife of a sailor with whom she had incessant quarrels as he loved to frequent the tavern. Her husband was wont to call her hard names in his cups, and on one occasion she followed him scolding lustily as far as Westgate's ale-house, where she heartily abused him before all the company. When the host remonstrated with her he also got a smart lick with the rough side of her tongue, and at the trial he recited this volley of abuse, adding that a few nights later whilst on his way home in the dark he encountered a number of shadowy animals with gleaming eyes who sprang upon and cowered in his path so that he had many a sorry tumble and only reached his door half-dead with terror and mightily bruised. Mr. Noyes, also, who visited Alice Parker when she was sick, affirmed that " discoursing with her about witchcraft, whether she were not guilty, she answered, ' If she were as free from other sins as from witchcraft, she would not ask of the Lord mercy.' " This reply, which is in truth somewhat impious, was held by the ministers to be damning to the last degree.

The story of the rest runs upon much the same lines. They were suddenly cried out upon by the children, suspicion was aroused which soon in the magistrates' minds grew into certainty, arrest and judgement inevitably followed. Some few persons managed to escape. Philip English and his wife [23] were figures of no small prominence. They owned houses, land, a wharf, and a whole fleet of sailing-vessels. Mary English was first arrested,[24] and a few days after her husband was sent to join her in Boston prison. Owing probably to large bribes they were enabled secretly to escape from Massachusetts, whither they did not return for some years, when the prosecutions were over and done.

After Dudley Bradstreet, the magistrate of Andover, had committed some forty persons to jail he refused to order any more arrests. The consequence was that he and his wife were accused of sorcery and had to fly for their lives.

The last executions which took place were those on 22 September, 1692. None the less the jails throughout the whole district were crowded with suspects. The prisons of Salem, Boston, Cambridge, and Ipswich were full to excess, and it became almost impossible to receive any more accused. When the prosecutions seemed at their zenith, by an extra-ordinary circumstance the crusade came suddenly to an end with startling abruptness. The first check was the accusation in October of Mrs. Hale, the wife of the Rev. John Hale, minister of the First Church in Beverly. But the acknow-ledged and distinguished virtues of this lady, her solid piety and a thousand charities, had made her so beloved by the people and had so idolized her in their hearts, that not at all the crying out of the afflicted children could sully or shake their confidence. From that moment the power of the accusers was destroyed. The whole community rose in defence of Mrs. Hale and roundly declared that the children were perjurers and liars.

Just at this juncture Sir William Phips, the Governor of the Colony, stepped in and forbade the Special Courts of Oyer and Terminer to try any more cases of Witchcraft. He further ordered that no spectral testimony was henceforth to be received as evidence. Obviously it was now impossible to obtain another conviction. Mr. Samuel Parris, Judge Stoughton, Cotton Mather, and Mr. Noyes were aghast. The afflicted children promptly cried out upon the Governor's lady and declared she was a leader among the witches, but some very drastic measures effectually closed their mouths once and for all. The ministers were reduced to silence, and the magistrates shook in their shoes, for they had received something more than a hint that they might be called to a strict account of their proceedings. In May, 1693, Sir William Phips discharged all prisoners, and nearly two hundred persons were set at liberty.

Judge Stoughton in sore displeasure had already retired from public life. " In January, 1692–3, word was brought in that a reprieve was sent to Salem, and had prevented the execution of seven of those that were condemned, which so moved the chief judge that he said to this effect : ' We were in a way to have cleared the land of them ; who it is that obstructs the cause of justice I know not ; the Lord be merciful to the County ! ' and so went off the bench, and came no more into that Court."

Judge Sewall, on the other hand, feeling that many innocent persons had suffered, observed annually for the rest of his life a day of fasting and prayer in private, and in public on the " day of the general fast " stood up before the whole congregation of the chapel where he worshipped, and made a general acknowledgement of his errors, requesting all present to join with him in earnest supplication for the forgiveness of their sins, particularly their misguidance in this matter.

The efforts of Mr. Parris to stem the tide which had so suddenly and irresistibly turned against him aroused bitter feelings among his parishioners. It was remembered that from his house flew the sparks which were kindled into a fatal flame, and month after month the controversies into which he plunged with vigour if not even recklessness grew more and more acute. On 14 July, 1696, his wife died, and he was pressed by many influential persons to retire from his charge. This he obstinately refused to do until the authorities urged him in a way that allowed no option, whereupon in sore vexation he removed to Newton, and next to Concord. In November, 1697, he began to preach at Stow, his stipend being forty pounds a year, half in money and half in kind. Later he officiated at Dunstable, and finally at Sudbury, where he died 27 February, 1720.

In 1710 his daughter Elizabeth had married Benjamin

Barnes of Concord. Two other daughters married in Sudbury. His elder son Noyes, who graduated at Harvard in 1721, became deranged and was supported by the town. Samuel, the younger, was for many years deacon of the church at Sudbury, where he died on 22 November, 1792, aged ninety-one.

Samuel Parris was succeeded at Salem by the Rev. Joseph Green, under whom the excommunication of Martha Corey for Witchcraft, voted on 11 September, 1692, and pronounce, by Parris on 14 September, was rescinded. In March, 1712, the similar sentences against Rebecca Nurse and Giles Corey were annulled.

The parents of Ann Putnam, Serjeant Thomas Putnam and Mrs. Ann Putnam, who had played a prominent part in the prosecutions, died in 1699, when she was nineteen years old, leaving to her charge several younger brothers and sisters. Her health, however, soon began to fail her. She was obviously morbid and hysterical from the first, and on 26 August, 1706, when she had lain sick and ill for many months, there was read out in her presence before the whole congregation at the meeting-house a public confession, attested by the Rev. Joseph Green, which she had herself for the greater ease of her conscience carefully written out and signed. This ran as follows :—

The Confession of Anne Putnam, when she was received to Communion in 1706.

" I desire to be humbled before God for that sad and humbling providence that befell my father's family in the year about '92 ; that I being then in my childhood, should, by such providence of God be made an instrument for the accusing of several persons of a grievous crime, whereby their lives were taken away from them, whom now I have just grounds and good reason to believe they were innocent persons ; and that it was a great delusion of Satan that deceived me in that sad time, whereby I justly fear I have been instrumental, with others, though ignorantly and unwittingly, to bring upon myself and this land the guilt of innocent blood ; though what was said or done by me against any person I can truly and uprightly say, before God and man, I did it not out of any anger, malice or ill-will to any person, for I had no such thing against one of them; but what I did was ignorantly, being deluded by Satan. And particularly, as I was a chief instrument of accusing of Goodwife Nurse and her two sisters, I desire to lie in the dust, and to be humbled for it, in that I was a cause, with others, of so sad a calamity to them and their families; for which cause I desire to lie in the dust, and earnestly beg forgiveness of God, and from all those unto whom I have given just cause of sorrow and offence, whose relations were taken away or accused."

Anne Putnam died some ten years later, in 1716, at the age of thirty-six. Her will is dated 20 May, 1716, and was presented in probate on the following 29 June.

So sudden and complete a cessation of the witch crusade in Salem is certainly remarkable, but the events which abruptly checked the prosecutions and changed public opinion are manifest and entirely logical and clear in their effect.

It is worth remark that superstitions yet covertly lingered among the community, for on the 5 and 7 September, 1746, the Rev. Peter Clark, solemnly warned and rebuked the people of Salem for clandestinely resorting to a " reputed witch or fortune-teller."

There can be no doubt that the diseased imaginings of the neurotic children and young girls, who used to meet at the Parris' house, set aflame by the wild tales of the Indian Tituba, fancies and fantasies which quickly ripened into acute hysteria and neurosis accompanied by grave functional disorders, were the origin of the terrible panic that gave rise to such wholesale accusations and condemnations. The community was already predisposed to black superstitious terrors by the stern rigours and hell-fire teaching of its Genevan gospel, and consequently that it should be swept by crowd-fear, a well-known and generally recognized psychic phenomenon, seemed inevitable. It is plain that terrible sufferings resulted, and much innocent blood was shed.

We have the official acknowledgement of Judge Sewall; the public confession of Anne Putnam. It seems certain that Rebecca Nurse, Mary Easty, old George Jacobs, suffered wrongfully. The few historians of Salem Witchcraft—

Charles Wentworth Upham in his monumental *History of Salem Witchcraft*; Caroline Upham in her *Salem Witchcraft in Outline*, Salem, 1891 ; as again Longfellow in poetry and Lowell in prose—have poured forth pity and sentiment upon those who fell victims. All this is very proper, and very just, no doubt. We also have the contemporary sceptic Robert Calef, who, determined neither to see nor hear anything save what he was already resolved to see and hear, explains and rationalizes apace in the bad old materialistic way at the expense of truth and accuracy.

The question remains to be asked whether there did not secretly exist in New England a coven of witches, who were partially, at least, discovered by the accident of the general prosecution wherein so many guiltless became involved. And the answer, I think, must be in the affirmative. It is most certain from the testimony of Deliverance Hobbs that she had belonged to such a coven, of which the evidence against the Rev. George Burroughs, Bridget Bishop, and Martha Carrier, proves them to have been members. There is a considerable amount of exaggeration, as we should expect, but when every allowance has been made a few salient facts with regard to this Devil's Society are clear.

Their place of meeting was " upon a plain grassy place, by which was a Cart path and sandy ground in the path, in which were the tracks of Horses feet."[25] Initiation was by a form of baptism. Mary Osgood, wife of Captain Osgood, went " to five mile pond, where she was baptized by the devil, who dipped her face in the water, and made her renounce her former baptism, and told her she must be his, soul and body for ever, and that she must serve him, which she promised to do. She says, the renouncing her first baptism was after her dipping."[26] The same Mary Osgood met the Devil as a black man who presented a book ; and Mary Lacy of the Salem coven described him as a black man in a high-crowned hat. It seems probable that this office of the " Devil " was filled by the Rev. George Burroughs, for he was "head Actor at some of their Hellish Randezvouzes "[27] ; and also " He was the person who had Seduc'd and Compell'd them into the snares of Witchcraft."[28] That a minister, and one who was actually the pastor of Salem, should have secretly been a high official among the witches is no matter for surprise. The case, indeed, can be repeatedly paralleled. Mr. Gideon Penman (1678), who had once been minister at Crighton in Scotland, used to frequent the Sabbats, where the Devil spoke of him as, " Mr. Gideon, my chaplain."[29] He was most notorious, for " the devil had a great meeting of witches in Loudian [Lothian], where, among others, was a warlock [Penman] who formerly had been admitted to the ministrie in the presbyterian tymes, and when the bishops came in, conformed with them. But being found flagitious and wicked, was deposed by them, and now he turnes a preacher under the devill of hellish doctrine ; for the devill at this tyme preaches to his witches really (if I may so term it) the doctrine of the infernall pitt, viz., blasphemies against God and His Son Christ. Among other things, he told them that they were more happy in him than they could be in God ; him they saw, but God they could not see ; and in mockrie of Christ and His holy ordinance of the Sacrament of His Supper, he gives the sacrament to them, bidding them eat it, and to drink it in remembrance of himself. This villan was assisting to Sathan in this action, and in preaching."[30] Lord Fountainhall describing the same assembly of witches relates that the Devil " adventured to give them the communion or holy sacrament, the bread was like wafers, the drink was sometimes blood, sometimes black moss-water. He preached and most blasphemously mocked them, if they offered to trust in God who left them miserable in the world, and neither He nor His Son Jesus Christ ever appeared to them when they called upon Him, as he had, who would not cheat them."[31]

It will be remembered that Deliverance Hobbs, who acknowledged she had been a witch, confessed that " she was at a Witch Meeting at Salem Village. . . . And the said *G. B.* preached to them, and such a Woman was their Deacon, and there they had a Sacrament." Abigail Williams also related how " the Witches had a *Sacrament* that day at an house in the Village, and that they had *Red Bread* and *Red Drink*." According to Madeleine Bavent, the Host at the mass of blasphemies was red—L'hostie ressemblait aux nôtres ; cependant elle me paraissait toujours rougeâtre et sans image[32]—and there are many references to the red wine of the chalice. The Abbé Guibourg even mixed fresh blood in the chalice. There can be no doubt that at Salem the traditional rites of the hideous black worship were precisely observed, allowing, of course, that it was a Protestant Communion and not Holy Mass which was the model of their hellish liturgy. These practices must have been carefully handed down and taught to the New England representatives of the witch society.

It is impossible that the several witnesses should have so exactly invented the details of these old occult ceremonies and the ancient cryptic rites from their own imaginations. They had obviously been present more than once at the witch sacrament, and assisted at the Sabbat orgy. That a coven of witches did indeed exist in Salem is proved beyond all question, and it is, I think, equally certain that George Burroughs was the grand-master, Bridget Bishop and Martha Carrier, high officials. Whether any other of those whom justice seized and hanged upon the accusation of the afflicted children were members of the coven seems wholly uncertain. We have not sufficient evidence to decide. On the other hand, it is plain that the majority at least of those who were executed died upon a false charge, and that they had no knowledge at all of the sorceries which were so secretly practised in their midst. The existence of this coven at Salem has not, I believe, been before recognized. It throws fresh light upon many of the proceedings, whilst in no way absolving the magistrates and ministers from the guilt of having shed much innocent blood.

The story of Witchcraft in America is, so to speak, singularly concise and compact. That there should be indiscriminate prosecution was inevitable. The Genevan ministers had neither the spiritual nor the practical knowledge necessary to deal with so dark and difficult a task. Naturally they blundered woefully and abundantly. As in England, their mistakes have provided the sceptic and the materialist with many a text for trite moralizing and meditation upon the ignorance of our forefathers.

At the beginning of the eighteenth century Witchcraft was little in evidence in the New World. The venom, however, only lay perdu, and waited its time, as is shown by the fact that in 1848 it burst forth with new vigour and force under the guise of Spiritism in the Fox family at Hydesville,

Catherine and Margaretta Fox are universally regarded as the originators of the modern manifestations of Spiritism, and it is not without significance that in November, 1850, whilst Margaretta Fox was staying at West Troy in the house of a Mr. Bouton, an angry and outraged crowd surrounded the place uttering threats and imprecations against the " unholy witch-woman within."[33] Deplorable indeed as is the violence of such demonstrations, and altogether to be condemned, these people had exactly hit upon and were vociferating the truth.

NOTES TO CHAPTER IV

[1] T. Hutchinson, *History of Massachusetts*, 2 vols., 1764–7, Boston, I, p. 436.

[2] *Calendar State Papers, Domestic*, 1603–10, 117.

[3] A staff or stick used in some way about a bed. Dr. Johnson has : " A wooden pin stuck anciently on sides of the bed-stead to hold the cloaths from slipping on either side." It may also be explained as a staff used to smooth down the sheets and bedclothes. Or ; the stout sticks or staves laid (loose) across the bed-stocks in old wooden bedsteads to support the bedding (precursors of the modern laths). In Scotland these were called *bed-rungs*, in some parts of England *bed-sticks*. The bed-staff often served as an improvised weapon. There are innumerable allusions. E.g. Brome, *The City Wit*, 8vo, 1653, IV, 3, where Crasy says to Josina : " Bastinado him soundly," and she replies : " If I do not make him an example . . . say there is no virtue in Cudgels and Bedstaves." In Shadwell's comedy, *The Virtuoso*, 4to, 1676, the coxcomb Sir Samuel Harty uses the phrase (I, 1) " in the twinkling of a Bedstaff," and explains the words as " a witty way I have of expressing my self."

[4] Pepys, Monday, 15 June, 1663, writes : " Both at and after dinner we had great discourses of the nature and power of spirits, and whether they can animate dead bodies ; in all which my Lord Sandwich is very scepticall. He says the greatest warrants that ever he had to believe any, is the present appearing of the Devil in Wiltshire, much of late talked of, and, they say, very true ; but my Lord observes, that though he do answer to any tune that you will play to him upon another drum, yet one tune he tried to play and could not ; which makes him suspect the whole ; and I think it is a good argument." Surely rather superficial on the other hand. In Shadwell's comedy *The Humourists*, produced in the winter of 1670, 4to, 1671, Act IV, Drybob says : " If this be the Devil that touch'd me, I don't like his sly Tricks to fright a Man thus ; 'would he would be as civil as the *Wiltshire* Devil was ; and beat a Drum, to give a Man notice where he is, that I might avoid him."

[5] Two or three details concerning the matter which are omitted by Glanvill will be found in the report of the case published in *Mercurius Publicus. Comprising the Sum of all Affairs now in agitation in England, Scotland, and Ireland.* . . . From Thursday, April 16th, to Thursday, April 23rd, 1663 ; and *The Kingdoms Intelligencer of The Affairs now in Agitation in England, Scotland, and Ireland.* . . . From Monday, April 20th, to Monday, April 27th, 1663. It may be remembered that Addison's comedy, *The Drummer, or, The Haunted House*, produced at Drury Lane in March, 1715–6, which I have seen acted with good applause and have enjoyed more on the boards than in the reading, was largely founded upon the story of Tedworth. The play was published anonymously in 1716, and later reissued with a long preface by Steele in 1722. Although at first not wholly successful it won its way into popular favour. During the eighteenth century it was frequently translated

into foreign languages, by Destouches as *Le Tambour Nocturne* in *Nouveau Recueil Choisi*, 1733, Vol. V, not acted until 1762 ; by Descazeaux Desgranges as *La Prétendue Veuve ou l'Epoux Magicien*, 1736 ; J. C. Gottsched as *Das Gespenst mit der Trummel* in *Die deutsche Schaubühne*, 1742, Vol. II ; and by L. A. V. Gottsched under the same title, *Ein Lutspiel des Herrn Addisons nach dem Französischen des Herrn Destouches übersetzt*, in *Neue Sammlung von Schauspielen*, 1764, Vol. V.

⁶ *The Epworth Phenomena*, to which are appended certain psychic experiences recorded by John Wesley in the pages of his *Journal*. Collected by Dudley Wright, London, 1917.

⁷ W. T. Stead, *Real Ghost Stories*, 1897. Reprinted from the Christmas and New Year's numbers of *The Review of Reviews*, 1891–2, Part II, c. 11, " Willington Mill."

⁸ *Daily Telegraph*, 5 November, 1883.

⁹ *The Peterborough Advertiser* for January, 1892, and the *Echo*, January, 1892, have independent accounts.

¹⁰ The journal *Annales des Sciences Psychiques* quotes from a Turin paper of November, 1900.

¹¹ *La Tribuna*, 5 and 21 March, 1905.

¹² E.g. Ralph Shirley, Editor of *The Occult Review*, in his *Notes for the Month*, January, 1918, *The Poltergeist*, a thoughtful study of a difficult and baffling subject.

¹³ Canonized, Whit Sunday, 31 May, 1925.

¹⁴ *Le Curé d'Ars, par l'Abbé Alfred Monnin*, 2 vols., Paris, 1861 ; 19th ed. Paris, 1907 ; translated London, 1862. Also *The Life of the Blessed Curé d'Ars, From the French of the Abbé Alfred Monnin*, with a Preface by Henry Edward Manning, Cardinal Archbishop of Westminster, N.D. (c. 1890). *Le Bienhereux Jean Vianney*, par Joseph Vianney, English translation, 1906. *Béatification du Bienhereux Jean Vianney*, Belley, 1907. *Le Curé d'Ars*, Mello, in *Le Siècle*, Paris, 1905. There is a recent translation (1924) of the Abbé Monnin's great work, with a supplementary chapter upon the Beatification and Canonization of S. Jean Baptiste Vianney, by Father B. Wolferstan, S.J.

¹⁵ Thomas Morton, 1564–1659, Bishop successively of Chester, Lichfield and of Durham. Amongst his many works, some of which are bitterly polemical such as the futile *Encounter against M. Parsons*, London, 4to, 1610 ; an ungracious *Causa Regia . . . aduersus R. Bellarminum*, 1620 ; the scurrilous *Antidotum aduersus Ecclesiæ Romanæ de merito proprie dicto ex condigno uenenum*, Cambridge, 4to, 1637 ; is *A Defence of the Innocence of the Three Ceremonies of the Church of England, viz., the Surplice, Crosse after Baptisme, and Kneeling at the Receiving of the Blessed Sacrament*, London, 4to, 1609.

¹⁶ John Bridgeman, 1577–1652, appointed Bishop of Chester 15 March, 1619, and instituted on 9 May. His scandalous leniency in dealing with Nonconformists and Puritans brought a sharp and well-deserved rebuke from his Metropolitan of Canterbury, after which he seems to have awakened to his duty for a while. In 1620 he suspended Thomas Paget, a few years later John Angier, and in 1631 Samuel Eaton of Wirral, all notorious and stubborn dissentients.

¹⁷ Richard Neile, 1562–1640, Archbishop of York, having previously held in succession the sees of Rochester, Lichfield and Coventry, Durham, and Winchester. He was a close ally of Archbishop Laud, but no bigot, although a strict disciplinarian owing to the anarchical state in which he found the Northern Province. He was an organizer rather than a scholar.

¹⁸ *Ecclesiasticus*, xlvi. 23, is convincing on the point. However, it is only fair to say that S. Basil (*In Isaiam*, VIII, 218) and S. Gregory of Nyssa (*De pythonissa ad Theodos. episc. Epistola*) hold that it was the Devil who in the phantom guise of Samuel deceived Saul.

¹⁹ *History of Massachusetts Bay*, 1828, II, p. 55.

²⁰ G. L. Burr, *Narratives of the Witchcraft Cases*, 1914, p. 417.

²¹ *The Wonders of the Invisible World*, " An Hortatory and Necessary Address."

[22] Another sister, Sarah Cloyse, was accused and committed for trial.
[23] She was the daughter of Richard Hollingsworth, and inherited his wealth.
[24] The Rev. William Bentley, D.D., in his *Description of Salem*, gives full details of this incident, and has a considerable account of the English family.
[25] G. L. Burr, *Narratives of the Witchcraft Cases*, p. 418.
[26] T. B. Howell, VI, p. 660. J. Hutchinson, *History of Massachusetts Bay*, II, p. 31.
[27] Cotton Mather, *Wonders of the Invisible World*, " The Tryal of G. B. I."
[28] J. Hutchinson, *ibid.*, II, pp. 37 *sqq.*
[29] Lord Fountainhall, *Decisions*, Edinburgh, 1759, I, p. 14.
[30] Robert Law, *Memorialls* (ed. Sharpe), Edinburgh, 1818, p. 145.
[31] Fountainhall, *Decisions*, I, p. 14.
[32] Görres, *La Mystique Divine* ; French translation by Charles Sainte-Foi, Deuxième ed., Paris, 1862, V, p. 230.
[33] *History of Modern Spiritualism*, 4th Edition, New York, 1870, p. 88.

CHAPTER V

FRANCE

THE Gauls were from very early times notorious in the ancient world for their sorceries and superstitions. Justin tells us that when Brennus was invading Macedonia and Greece in 280 B.C., and during the following year had even penetrated to Delphi, his expedition was made under the conduct of the sacred birds, that is to say, no important step was taken unless the omens had first been consulted and found favourable, for—adds the historian—the Gauls are more skilled than all other nations in the arts of augury and divination.[1] Cæsar, also, remarks upon the native superstitions and the human sacrifices which were offered by the Druids, without whom it was not lawful to perform these horrid rites.[2] Pomponius Mela, again, the geographer, writing a century later, speaks of the Gauls as proud and superstitious, a people upon whose altars formerly bled human victims, whose wise men, the Druids, instruct their disciples in astrology, the will of the Heavens, and teach them occult lore in secret caves or in the very heart of some thick forest where is their sanctuary.[3]

A certain class of Druids, known as the *Ovates* or magicians, made prophecy, oneirocriticism, and the reading of omen their special province, and it was their duty to foretell the future by the inspection of the entrails at a solemn sacrifice, or by the winged flight of birds across the sky. Upon the Isle of Sein (in the department of Finisterre) was a famous oracle, whose responses were interpreted by nine Druidesses, vestals, called *Gallicenæ*, who were believed to have the power of raising storms and quelling tempests, of changing themselves into the shape of any animal, of healing all manners of disease, of predicting man's destiny.[4]

It was at the commencement of the fifth century that the Franks began to occupy Gaul, and the most ancient document of Frankish legislation, the Salic Law (*Lex salica*),[5] was reduced to a written form, revised and finally sanctioned, under Clovis (born 466 A.D.), who succeeded his father, Childeric, as King of the Salic Franks in 481, was baptized by S. Remigius of Reims on Christmas-day, 496, and died at Paris, 27 November, 511. As was the custom, the Salic Law inflicts various fines for Witchcraft of which all had a most wholesome dread.[6] Seventy-two sous and half a golden coin for launching a mortal curse or fashioning the witch's-knot ; the same for defaming a man as a wizard or accusing anyone of having assisted at the Sabbat ; one hundred and eighty-seven sous for branding a woman as a witch, unless proof were forthcoming ; two hundred sous for any witch convicted of having feasted upon human flesh.

The Ripuarian laws ordained that the magician should be mulcted in *wehrgeld,* that is to say he must give ample pecuniary compensation for any harm to limb or to property which he had done. In doubtful cases he might clear himself by a solemn oath with six compurgators, men of substance.[7]

The code of the Visigoths, which was to some extent founded on Roman law, punished the wizard who had killed any person by spell or incantation with death ; Witchcraft, not proven to have taken life, was rewarded with scourging or slavery. The formularies show us the belief of the Visigoths in the sixth and seventh when they were still masters of the southern provinces of Gaul : " Workers of evil and those who raise tempests, those who are said to destroy the vines or harvest by their incantations, those who by the invocation of devils trouble their neighbours or who sacrifice at night to the Demon whom in their wickedness they call upon with impious prayers ; any such person being found guilty by the judge shall receive two hundred lashes in public ; his head shall be ignominiously shaven and he shall be paraded through ten villages near the place where he dwells that his disgrace may serve as a meet example and a deterrent to others."[8]

Ecclesiastical sentence was also launched against the witch. The offender, if a person of quality, was to be publicly excommunicated and thrust out from the Church. If of humbler rank or a slave he was to be beaten, that haply by blows he might learn wisdom.[9]

The Council of Elusa (Eauze) in 555, the fortieth year of the reign of King Childebert I and Clotaire, prescribed scourging for serfs who bewitched drinking-horns. The Council of Narbonne, thirty-four years later, spoke of sorcerers as *carages*, augurs, and complained that the South was overrun by these diviners, who privily introduced themselves into houses and by their skill and address were gaining a foothold on all sides. The Bishops ordered that they shall be denounced, when, after meet punishment they will be sold as slaves.

In 578 Queen Fredegonde lost one of her sons, who died of dysentery, upon which the courtiers promptly accused the general Mummol, whom she hated, of having killed the Prince by witchcraft. It was reported that he consulted secretly with several beldames of ill repute. These were at once arrested and under torture confessed that they had long been witches, that the Prince had been killed to preserve Mummol's own life as it was written one of the two must perish. Some were burned at the stake, others drowned, others broken on the wheel. Mummol was arrested, and put to the question. Even in the midst of the most exquisite agonies he uttered no incriminating word. They tore his nails from hands and feet with hot pincers and lacerated the tenderest parts of the human frame, but he endured all in silence. At last, when his head was about to be severed from his body, the Queen with cruel mercy granted him life. Accordingly he was placed in a rude cart to be conveyed to Bordeaux, but on the way he expired, either owing to his sufferings, or perhaps swiftly assassinated at the royal command.

The sudden loss of two other children of Chilperic and Fredegonde at once gave ground for new accusations of sorcery, in which were implicated Clovis, the son of the King by a former wife, this Prince's mistress, and her mother, who when placed on the rack avowed her complicity with Clovis, that their Witchcraft had caused the deaths, and indeed everything she was asked. The infamous Fredegonde promptly obtained her husband's consent to the execution of Clovis, who was poignarded, it being given out that he had taken his own life. His paramour was secretly put away, and her mother, who when released from the torture had immediately denied all that was wrung from her by pain, was burned alive, precautions being taken that she should be rendered incapable of uttering a word. This series of crimes, although alleged to be justice done to murderers and magicians, had in fact a deep political motive. For Frede-gonde, for all her pretended zeal against sorcerers, was always surrounded by a pack of witches, in whose powers she trusted for supernatural protection. And so, a few years before, when King Sigebert defeated Chilperic, and gaining possession of Paris was on his way to invest his foe at Tournai whither the vanquished monarch fled from the capital, Fredegonde had sent two of her servants, armed with charmed knives named *scramasax* whose venomed blades were consecrated to the Demon, and these fellows, on some pretext gaining audience of Sigebert at Vitri, stabbed him there in 575.[10]

Among the black calumnies which have stained the memory of Fredegonde's rival, Brunehaut (Brunehilde), who was horribly executed in 613, are charges of Witchcraft, especially that of eunuchizing by a malefic spell her grandson Thierry II, so that he was unable to consummate his marriage with Ermenberge. This sterile charm, *nouer l'aiguillette*, was always regarded with a particular abhorrence, and the accusation of its employment occurs again and again in the witch-trials.[11]

It will be seen that the first dynasty of French kings was continually legislating against witches, and Childeric III in 742 appeals to the Bishops to help him suppress all kinds of divination, sacrifices to demons, human sacrifices, which were still covertly offered, impious worship of the dead, any communication with spirits, the brewing of love-philtres and any other devilish charms and ritual.[12]

Briefly to summarize it may be said that during the Merovingian period the law punished the practice of magic by heavy fines, such as were usual in the case of other grave offences ; the Church strongly opposed her authority and influence to sorcery or indeed any similar superstitions ; from time to time accusations of Witchcraft were brought by and against persons in high places, and the death-penalty with torture was then almost invariably inflicted, but it is strongly to be suspected that such prosecutions were largely political.

A Council of Soissons in 744, whilst Pepin le Bref was still Mayor of the Palace and had not yet assumed the royal title,[13] strictly charges the Bishops to be on the watch against any creeping in of sorcery mingled with pagan rites, such observances as might yet prevail in country districts and open the door to an influx of evil. Under Charlemagne a law was passed forbidding any consultation of wizards, any interpretation of dreams or taking of omens ; enchanters, diviners, mediums, those who brew philtres, evokers of storm or hail, those who tie the witches' knot, are to be shunned. Let them amend their ways or they will be cast into a close prison. Fairy trees, pagan monoliths, haunted wells, the rendezvous of witches, are to be destroyed and demolished utterly.[14]

In view of later ages the code of Charlemagne, imprisonment and a season for repentance, seems exceptionally mild, but this attitude towards magic was very short-lived. Evidently at first under the Carlovingians the full horror and blasphemy of Witchcraft were not realized. But in the days of Louis le Debonnaire (le Pieux), son of Charlemagne and Hildegarde, who succeeded his father in 814, very serious consideration was devoted to the alarming spread of sorcery. King Louis himself, being eminent for his holiness of life, regarded these matters more deeply perhaps than the men of action and conquest whose thoughts were, perhaps, elsewhere. A Council of Paris in 829 addressed a very solemn appeal to this sovereign to assist by the secular arm the Church in the crusade against Witchcraft. As it has been well said[15] that to some extent the provisions of all future French ordinances are contained in this canon it is undoubtedly worth detailed examination. The Fathers formally rehearse various Biblical ordinances dealing with the necromancer and the witch, and continue to say that there yet exist certain offscourings of heathendom, magicians, diviners, sorcerers, poisoners, false seers, enchanters, and interpreters of dreams, whom the Divine Law ordains shall be punished with the last severity. For it is written : " A man, or woman, in whom there is a pythonical or divining spirit, dying let them die " (Lev. xx. 27), and again, " Wizards thou shalt not suffer to live " (Exodus, xxii. 18). It is certain, and indeed common knowledge, that by enchantments and demoniacal charms the brains of many men have been so disordered by love-philtres,

medicined food, amulets, that they have run mad, ignorant
of their own shame. Witches can raise tempests with their
incantations, send the hail-storm, foretell future events,
carry off fruit and milk from one to give it to another, and
accomplish the strangest prodigies. Wherefore the guilty,
when found, be they men or women, must be sharply and
cogently punished by the Prince of the land, seeing that they
have arrived at such a point of wickedness as to transfer their
allegiance to Satan.[16]

The civil power once invoked was not slow to act, and
recognizing, as the Statute says, that it was the duty of
Kings to slay the wicked, *Regis ministerium est impios de
terra perdere*, death was adjudged the punishment of the
sorcerer and witch, and not merely of the prime agents alone
but, by a far-sweeping enactment, of all who consulted or
visited them. So ordains a Capitulary of Charles the Bald,
promulgated at Kiersy-sur-Oise in 873. " We have learned,"
he says, " that warlocks and witches have established themselves in divers places within this our realm, that their evil
charms have devoted many to sickness and even to death,
and since, as the Saints have written, it is the duty of Kings
to slay the wicked, not to suffer wizards and poisoners to
live, we enjoin therefore that all and any such shall be sought
out and taken. If they be found guilty, whether men or
whether women, let them die the death as law and justice
demand. And not only the principals in this abomination,
but also those who consort with or consult them, shall pay
the penalty in order that the very memory of so heinous a
crime may be utterly abolished and uprooted from our land."[17]
In cases where the accused avowed innocence, and the
evidence was not conclusive, resort was had to the Judgement
of God, an ordeal already in practice and by Charles the Bald
to be applied in witch-trials as a test. There were very many
methods of the Judgement of God, but in the case of Witchcraft the ordeal by water was most popular and considered
the most convincing. It was, of course, granted for any
crime, but ere long this particular test became specialized,
so to speak. Before the immersion of the accused the water,
whether an artificial reservoir, a pool, a running stream, was
solemnly blessed by a priest.[18]

The usual ordeals were also allowed, for example that of the hot iron, when the accused picked up and even held for a few moments a bar of red-hot metal. His hand was then swathed in bandages which were sealed, and if on the third day there was no trace of burning he was innocent. Much the same kind of proof was required in the ordeal of boiling water, when the arm had to be plunged in a steaming caldron suspended over a fire, and a ring or some other object recovered from the bottom of the vessel. If the arm was whole in three days' time and showed no scalding then had the suspect proved that he was free from guilt. There were several Judgements of God of the same nature, such as the solemn oaths upon Holy Relics, the walking barefoot with the eyes blindfolded among red-hot ploughshares set at uneven distances,[19] the going through the heart of blazing pyres of wood whereby the Vallombrosian S. Peter Igneus won his triumph,[20] and, most long-lived of all, the single combat or duel.[21]

The chronicles of the tenth century are full of the accounts of miraculous happenings, and an epidemic terror seemed to seize Christendom since numbers of fanatical preachers appeared in France and Italy loudly proclaiming that the thousand years prophesied in the *Apocalypse* of S. John as the term of the world's duration were about to expire, that Antichrist was at hand and the Son of Man would shortly appear in the clouds to judge the ungodly and the righteous.

The Church strove to stem these superstitions, which none the less spread rapidly among the deluded people. The scene of the last judgement was expected to be at Jerusalem and as the year 1000 drew nigh the number of pilgrims proceeding eastward to await the coming of the Lord in that city was so great as to be compared to a desolating invasion. Most of the wayfarers had sold all their possessions before leaving Europe, and were supporting themselves on the proceeds. Buildings were allowed to fall into decay. It was thought idle to repair these when the end of time was so near. Many even deliberately pulled down their houses, as shelters for which they had no further use. Persons of all ranks of life and every calling, forsaking the one his castle, the other his plough, leaving arms, counting-house, merchandise, tillage, vineyards, made their way in mighty companies to the Holy City, singing psalms as they went, their eyes fixed in ecstasy upon the heavens,

which every moment they expected to see open revealing the
Son of God in all His glory.

During the thousandth year the pilgrims increased, and for
the most part they were stricken with abject terror as with
a plague. A thunderstorm flung them all on their knees in
mid-March. They shuddered as they heard the crash and roll
of the elements, looking with blanched faces to see the graves
yawn and the dead arise. At Jerusalem itself the scenes of
confusion baffled all description. However slight an alarm,
and the whole Christian population rushed into the streets, to
weep and lament, to intone penitential hymns and canticles,
and pray with increasing fervour. Enthusiasts kept up the
flame of frenzy. It was firmly believed that the powers of
evil were having full fling before their final subjection, and the
legends of demons abound. In many countries the legislation
against witches became more and more severe,—thus as early
as the reign of Ramiro I, King of Aragon (842–50), several
Jewish astrologers were burned alive, and, in Westphalia in
914 a whole coven of witches was sent to the stake,[22]—so
although documentary evidence as to trials for sorcery under
the later Carlovingians is singularly scanty, this is perhaps
because the people, frantic with superstitious fears, may
often have taken the law into their own hands.

That the forces of evil should particularly trouble the
strongholds, the monasteries, was only to be expected, and
when we have liberally discounted such exaggerations as
there may be, enough remains to prove very extraordinary
and very hideous manifestations endeavouring to destroy
the peace of the cloister. Blessed Peter the Venerable (1092–
1156) has several accounts of diabolic invasions of Cluny,
when cases of actual possession occurred among the monks.
He also speaks of a certain Count of Mâcon who acquired most
evil notoriety as a magician, and who, the peasants believed,
was eventually carried off by the Demon. S. Bernard, the
glory of Clairvaux (1090–1153), was famous for the power
of his exorcisms, and healed many who were afflicted.

In 1022, during the reign of Robert the Good, a band of
Manichees was discovered at Orleans and sent to the stake
for their sorceries. They used to meet on certain nights in a
lonely and deserted house, whither they repaired each with a
lantern in his hand. There after certain loathsome ceremonies

they chanted a litany invoking Satan and other devils under obscene and abominable names, extinguishing meanwhile the lights they carried, and giving themselves over to the most revolting debaucheries. Sometimes they sacrificed a child, making a paste of the blood and portions of the flesh, which they moulded into wafers to serve in their blasphemous parodies of Holy Mass. It was in vain that learned priests and doctors strove to convert them as they lay in prison. Unhappily certain clerics were of the number of these wretches, and among them, it is said, one Stephen who had formerly been the confessor of Queen Constance.[23]

On Holy Saturday, 1066, Evrard, Archbishop of Treves, expired suddenly at the very Font of his Cathedral, as clad in full pontificals he was solemnly baptizing the catechumens according to the rite of that day. It was whispered that a number of witches had fashioned a wax figure of the prelate, which they had bribed an apostate priest to baptize by the Bishop's name, and having stuck it full of pins melted it at a slow fire, so that he died as the last drops ran away.[24] Bernard, Duke of Gascony, was supposed to have been slain by a similar spell in 1013, and in 1173 Stephen, Archbishop of Bourges, was alleged to have fallen a victim to the same sorcery.[25]

It is hardly surprising to find that Berengarius of Tours (*circa* 999–1088), who seems to have held very many erroneous beliefs concerning such matters as the spiritual power, marriage, the baptism of children,[26] although his most notorious heresy attacked the Holy Eucharist, was reputed to be a sorcerer,[27] and strange stories were told of his necromantic powers, traditional stories indeed, some of which we recognize when repeated in connexion with Cornelius Agrippa. So early was heresy regarded as involving Witchcraft.

In 1030 we hear the whisper of a scandal concerning a great prelate, Poppo (1016–47), son of Margrave Leopold of Austria and Archbishop of Treves. He is said to have become madly enamoured of a religious, but when a pair of buskins she had worked for him were worn by another ecclesiastic he also was devoured with passion for the same nun. Suspicion being aroused it was found that a potent charm was sewn in the silk lining of her gift. This was burned, and the offending sister expelled from her convent, which shortly afterwards was given over to a congregation of monks. In 1074 the citizens of Cologne hurled from their city walls a witch, who was found guilty of having driven certain persons lunatic by her spells and drugs.

In France itself during the twelfth and thirteen centuries the witch-trials are very few, and in truth they are far from numerous in other countries, which is largely to be attributed to the unsettled state of Europe, the quarrels of kings, campaigns, the Crusades. During the reign of Alexander III (1159–81) a priest of the Venetian diocese of Aquileia in Grado (Venice) was accused of having consulted an astrologer and with him invoked a demon to declare where was hidden some precious vessel which had been stolen from his church. The Patriarch of Aquileia deprived the offender of all exercise of sacerdotal power *in perpetuum*, but the Supreme Pontiff, although denouncing the sortilege and evocation as a heinous sin, changed the sentence to suspension for a period of two years.[28]

It was commonly bruited that witches had ensorcelled Ingeburga, sister of Canute VI, King of Denmark, a lady whom Philip Augustus of France married in 1193, but only almost immediately to repudiate, a measure approved by an assembly of complaisant Bishops and barons, and sternly forbidden by Innocent III, who therefor in 1198 placed France under an interdict.[29]

Frederick II in his Constitution of 1224 lays down that heretics convicted by an ecclesiastical court shall, on imperial authority, be put to death by fire, *auctoritate nostra ignis iudicio concremandos*, and in 1230, his son, Henry, afterwards Henry VI, decreed that all sorcerers must likewise suffer death. Heresy and sorcery were looked upon as one and the same crime so far as prohibition and punishment extended.

Gregory IX by his Bulls of 13, 20, and 22 April, 1233,[30] solemnly and officially established the Order of Preachers as the Pontifical Inquisitors for all dioceses of France to check the anarchy and ravages of the heretics. The office of Inquisitor was not, however, by any means confined to the one Order, for we often meet with Franciscan delegates, Cistercians, Canons Regular, as also secular priests.[31]

The Inquisitors at once began to take cognizance of Witchcraft, and indeed it was impossible that they should not have

done so seeing that sorcery and heresy were essentially intermingled. Thus a hag of the sect of the Cathari, who belonged
to Mont-Aimé in the Champagne district, was arrested with
a whole gang of her co-religionists by Robert le Bougre, a.
Bulgarian (Catharist) convert to Christianity, and subsequently a Dominican. The accused were charged with
having employed the aid of demons as well as with their
particular heresy, and this crone seems to have been the
officer of the coven. On 29 May, 1239, about one hundred and
eighty persons whose trial had begun and concluded within a
week were consigned to the flames at Montwimer. Complaints,
however, were lodged protesting against so summary a
process ; Robert was recalled to Rome, deposed from his
office, and confined within a monastery for life.[32]

At Toulouse, the hot-bed of Catharan evil, in 1275 an
Inquisitor, Hugues de Baniols, gave judicial sentence of death
by fire on Angèle de la Barthe, a beldame of some sixty years,
who confessed to having had intercourse with an evil spirit
from which conjunction she brought forth a monster whom
she nourished with the flesh of infants, slain by her or dug up
from their graves in remote churchyards.[33]

It must be remembered that all the great contemporary
Schoolmen, Blessed Albertus Magnus, S. Thomas Aquinas,
S. Bonaventura, the Venerable Duns Scotus, and many names
of lesser, but yet no inglorious, fame, admitted the possibility
of carnal intercourse between demons and human beings.
This is also accepted by Suarez ; the Salamanca theologians ;
S. Alphonsus de Liguori, Charles-René Billuart, o.p. ; Dom
Dominic Schram, o.s.b. ; Benedict XIV, and by such later
writers as Görres, Bizouard (*Rapports de l'homme avec le
démon*), Gougenot de Mousseaux (*Les hauts phénomènes de
la magie*).

It was at the beginning of the fourteenth century that all
Christendom, from Great Britain to Cyprus, was convulsed
by the tragic catastrophe of the Knights Templars, than
which, it has been said, history knows no more formidable
trial, nor has the final verdict been given even to-day.

Immediately after the deliverance of Jerusalem, the
Crusaders, considering their vows fulfilled, returned in a body
to their homes. But the defence of this precarious conquest,
surrounded as it was by Mohammedan neighbours, remained.

Accordingly in 1118 two French Knights, Hugues de Payens and Geoffroy de St. Omer founded a monastic-military Order to defend the Christian kingdom and to protect poor pilgrims visiting the Holy Land. Nine companions bound themselves by perpetual vows in the presence of the Patriarch of Jerusalem, and Baldwin II accepting their services, assigned them a portion of his palace adjoining the Temple, whence their title, " Pauvres Chevaliers du Temple." Hugues de Payens shortly afterwards travelled to Europe to obtain recruits, and before long an immense number of novices responded to his enthusiasm. At the Council of Troyes (1128) the Knights Templars adopted the Rule of S. Benedict, as recently reformed with great vigour by the Cistercians. They undertook not only the three solemn vows, besides the crusader's vow, but also the austere regulations concerning the chapel, the refectory, and the dormitory. They further adopted the white Cistercian habit adding thereto a red cross. The newly formed Order comprised four ranks of brethren : the *Knights*, equipped like the heavy cavalry of the Middle Ages ; the *Serjeants*, who formed the light cavalry ; the *Farmers*, entrusted with the administration of temporals ; and the *Chaplains*, who alone were priests ministering to the spiritual needs of the brethren. The Order, combining the two absorbing passions of the Middle Ages, religious fervour and chivalry, rapidly grew in popularity. Ecclesiastical and lay authorities heaped favours upon the Templars ; the Popes took them under their immediate protection, exempting them from all other jurisdiction, episcopal or secular ; their estates were free from all taxation, assimilated to church land ; their monasteries, chapels, and cemeteries could not be placed under an interdict. Before long the Templars had com-manderies in every State. In France they formed no less than eleven bailiwicks, subdivided into more than forty-two commanderies. The Order, in spite of the articles of the original rule requiring a probationary period, began to make immediate use of recruits. All that was demanded from a new member was blind obedience, he had to declare himself for ever " serf et esclave de la maison." To prove his sincerity he was subjected to a secret test, the nature of which was never officially declared. The Knights were largely drawn from the ranks of the higher nobility many of whom brought vast possessions to the general coffers, and before many years had passed the Order, which began in simplest poverty, was wealthy almost beyond imagination. To it belonged at one time more than nine thousand estates, the accumulated revenues of which in common with hoards of other treasure were laid up in the Temples at London and Paris. Princes, also, and private individuals deposited their personal property, owing to the solid credit of such bankers. In Paris the royal treasure was kept in the Temple. It is hardly to be wondered at that as time went on the Order, having no superior save the distant authority of the Pope and enjoying financial power equal to that of any temporal sovereign, began to make its influence felt throughout Europe and assumed the direction of the Kingdom of Jerusalem, at best an unstable monarchy and insecure, which after many chances and changes finally came to an end in 1291. Excessive pride is an accusation so continually and so generally brought against the Templars that the truth of the charges can hardly be doubted, whilst popular proverbs of the day such as " to drink like a Templar " and " Avoid the Templar's kiss," although perhaps no evidence in themselves, show that the Order was at least acquiring the common repute of intemperance and luxury. After the Christian power had been expelled from Palestine, the Grand Master of the Temple, Jacques de Molay (1244–1314) fixed his residence at Cyprus where he kept almost imperial state, and it seemed as though the Order would form a kind of independent and international aristocratic republic.

It is now necessary briefly to inquire into the peculiar doctrines and cult of the Templars, who were asserted by their opponents to be secretly Mohammedans, if not devil-worshippers, and addicted to the darkest vices. It is, I think, idle to deny that the charges made against the Order were in the main well founded, but it must also be acknowledged that the degree of culpability varied in different branches, and the majority of members of certain preceptories may have been to some extent ignorant of these transgressions against faith and morals, the secret and genuine doctrine of the Templars not having been communicated to them in its entirety. Certain preceptories were, in fact, possibly only novice-houses (although not known as such save to the higher officials), the sojourn of neophytes and those members whom it was not thought fit to initiate further into the ultimate mysteries.

It must be borne in mind that the Christians in Palestine at the time of the Crusades were often affected by their contact and intercourse with the religious systems of the East, notably with Gnostic bodies professing a distorted form of Christianity, as also by their constant intermingling with their Mohammedan neighbours. Nor in the case of these quasi-Christian sects was there any such antagonism between themselves and the Mohammedans as is usually supposed ; in fact, they often borrowed ideas from the Saracens and the Turk.

The Templars had been formed in this atmosphere, and the intimacy of their associations with the Assassins and with other sects which carried on a form of the ancient Gnostic tradition under the veneer of Mohammedanism is fully established. The Templars, in fact, were Gnostic heretics, dualists, whose beliefs had developed on the lines of the Luciferians. They worshipped not only a Supreme Deity, the Creator of Spirit and all good, yet who was, however, supposed to be unapproachable by man and inaccessible to human understanding, but they also acknowledged another Deity, the author of Matter and all evil, and him they adored with mystic and peculiar ceremonies.

This lower God was the eldest son of the higher God. Being at variance with his Father he, the First Born, is driven from Heaven and creates for himself the world and man. But the Templars followed the Luciferian doctrine even to the extreme of blasphemy, and looked upon the earthly and visible Christ, who was born at Bethlehem and died on Mount Calvary, as an evil-doer and an impostor, and in accordance with this notion, at the full initiation of new members into the Order, Christ was denounced as a false prophet, and the candidate was called upon to demonstrate his belief that Christ suffered not for the salvation of man but on account of His own wickedness.

The Templars took as their Patrons S. John Baptist and S. John the Evangelist, and although the S. John from which they originally derived their title was undoubtedly S. John the Almoner,[34] the assumption of the two Patrons throws a flood of light upon their secrets. For it is known that the Templars were very closely connected with the sect of the Nabatheans, Nasoræans, Mandæans, Sabians, or Johannites as they were indifferently called, and there is even a tradition that the Patriarch Theocletes, the sixty-seventh successor of the Apostle S. John, transmitted in 1118 his powers as Grand Pontiff to Hugues de Payens, whom he appointed to follow him.[35]

The Mandæans inhabited, and still inhabit, the district round Bassorah. They hold or held that there are Three Primæval Æons, one of which, Máná Rábbá, the Great Spirit of Glory, called into existence Hayyé Kadmáyé, or Primal Life, the God whom they adore. S. John Baptist, the true prophet, was an incarnation of Hibil (Abel), who was himself an incarnation of Mandá d' Hayye ($\gamma\nu\hat{\omega}\sigma\iota\varsigma\ \tau\hat{\eta}\varsigma\ \zeta\omega\hat{\eta}\varsigma$), who was an emanation from Hayyé Kadmáyé. Yishu M'Shíhá, the Jesus of the Christians, was the false Messiah, and an impostor: His Crucifixion was brought about by the true Messiah, Anúsh 'Uthra, the younger brother of Hibil.

Here then we have a very clear and sufficient reason for the adoption of S. John Baptist as one of the Patrons of the Templars.

The Order was also very intimately associated with the Assassins and the Ishmaelites, whose successors the Druzes still inhabit the Lebanon, the Hauran, and other districts near Damascus. Their present name is derived as a plural from Dorazy, who was a Persian at the court of El Hakim in Egypt, about 1015, but the real founder of the sect was another Persian, Hamzeh Ibn Ahmed El Hady, who preached that the mad Fatimite caliph, El Hakim, was an incarnation of God. After this monarch had been murdered Hamzeh wrote a treatise to prove that he had only disappeared for a while to test the faith of his followers, and the ultimate return of El Hakim is a fundamental of the modern Druze creed. The prophet of El Hakim, the Deity, is Hamzah-ben-Ali, who is identical with S. John Baptist. The Druzes recognize three Apostles of Truth, "the Feet of Wisdom," S. John the Evangelist, S. Mark, S. Matthew. They are also spoken of as heavenly powers, and have passed through many incarnations. The Gospel of S. John is regarded as the gospel of the "true Messiah," and held in high esteem. It is, of course, wrested and perverted to square with their nightmare Gnosticism, for the Druzes hold that there was a distinction between Jesus, the Son of Joseph, and Christ. Christ instructed Jesus, but Jesus disobeyed Christ and was in consequence crucified. It would be impertinent to follow them through all the wild mazes of their fantasies, but the prominence given to S. John the Evangelist must have particularly brought this Saint under the notice of the Templars, and there can be no doubt, I think, that here we have the explanation why S. John the Evangelist was recognized as Co-Patron of the Order with S. John Baptist.[36] In view of the scanty material at our disposal it would be futile to attempt to demonstrate the full and direct connexion in belief between the Templars, the Mandæans, and the Assassins (Druzes), and obviously a large quantity of evidence has been deliberately destroyed, but we can at least say that everything points to such a reciprocality, and it is this corrivation which explains as nothing else the whole history of the Order, its rise, its grandeur, and its fall.

These two bodies, the Assassins, or followers of the Sheikh or Old Man of the Mountains, and the Mandæans or Christians of S. John, with whom the Templars were in close connexion, were not Mohammedans but Gnostic sects. The Assassins actually paid tribute to the Templars, and it is notorious that the Order murdered the emissaries sent in 1172 by Hassin to Amaury I, King of Jerusalem (1162–74). These envoys had been commissioned to open negotiations for Hassin and all his followers to embrace Christianity, with the proviso that thereby they were released from the tribute which they paid to the Templars. That the Templars, presumably doughty champions of the Faith, should so strongly have objected to the conversion of the Assassins is extremely significant. It is not impossible that the Assassins were in some way subordinate to the Mandæans, and the tradition that the Patriarch Theocletes had invested the Grand Master of the Templars with his rights and powers, would seem to be borne out by the fact that the Assassins were thus paying tribute to the Supreme Head.

Philip IV of France, surnamed Le Bel, the son of Philip III and Isabel of Aragon, was born at Fontainebleau in 1268, and died there 29 November, 1314. He became King 5 October,

1285, and was consecrated at Reims on the feast of the Epiphany, 6 January, 1286. He has been accused of being a free-thinker, which he most certainly was not ; for he was religious, and even made pilgrimages. Yet his attitude towards ecclesiastical authority was often very reprehensible, and as King he deemed himself above all justice, human or divine. He was, in fine, an absolutist in the fullest and most unfortunate sense of the word. In his proceedings against the Templars his motives have been pronounced as avarice and hypocrisy, but this judgement seems altogether too sweeping. The fact is men do not act from single, but from mixed motives, and such was the case with Philip Le Bel. He regarded with suspicion, no doubt, the fortresses and strongholds which the Templars had scattered here and there up and down his realm, castles which were very able to give shelter to malcontent nobles and which might be found impregnable in war ; he looked with a wishful, perhaps a greedy, eye upon the vast riches of the Order, wealth whose influence might make many a throne tremble and fall. There is no doubt he was afraid of the Order, and fear is a bloody counsellor of kings. None the less, it would seem that he was profoundly shocked and horrified at the revelations concerning their dark mysteries, which secretly filtered through to him. Towards the end of the year 1304 or very early in 1305, Philip's minister, the legist Guillaume de Nogaret, an unscrupulous politician, which is the worst that can be said of any man, arrested several Templars, who were conveyed to Corbeil and strictly questioned, perhaps with torture when they made the most incriminating confessions. Accordingly, when King Philip attended the coronation of Clement V (Bertrand de Got) at Lyons, 14 November, 1305, he hinted to the Pontiff something of the disorders he had learned. At first Clement could not believe the charges, as is shown by his kindly reception of Jacques de Molay, who had been summoned to a conference at Poitiers in order to consider a union between the Templars and the Hospitallers, a plan which the former rejected with scorn and contemptuous pride. On 14 May, 1307, Philip Le Bel visited the Pope, who was now suffering from the painful languor which accompanies chronic ill-health and was continually in the hands of his physicians. With eager insistence the impetuous monarch

pressed Clement to investigate the accusations brought
against the Templars, and when the Grand-Master himself,
becoming aware of the scandals that were being bruited
abroad, loudly demanded an inquiry, the sick Pontiff, beyond
measure weary and distracted by their importunities, reluctant to believe the possibility of such depths of evil, ordered
that the requisite steps should be taken by a Bull of 24
August, 1307.

Guillaume Imbert, the Grand Inquisitor for France, a man
of iron strength and will, next began to move in the matter.
The Templars were suspected of heresy and sorcery and these
crimes fell within the cognizance of the Holy Office, but Frère
Imbert demanded the assistance of the civil power. Letters
were ready on the 14 September, and on 22 September, 1307,
at Maubuisson Philip made Nogaret Keeper of the Seal, and
the same day the Royal Council issued a warrant for the
arrest of the Templars. But everything must be wholly secure
for making a decisive move, and accordingly it was not until
the morning of Friday, 13 October, that Jacques de Molay
and his assistant knights were arrested, whilst at the same
time the Templars in Paris were taken and flung into prison.
The chroniclers tell us that at the same hour on the same day
all the Templars in France were seized, and although there is
some exaggeration here there can be no doubt that the blow
fell with instantaneous severity far and wide, so that on
Monday, 16 October, King Philip was able to dispatch letters
to all the sovereigns of Europe, detailing the crimes of the
Order and inciting them to follow his example. [37]

The exact source whence the immediate denunciation of
the Templars came is uncertain. [38] Rumour spoke of a
Templar who lay at Toulouse under sentence of death
and who, unloading his bosom of no ordinary guilt, confessed in bitter despair the foul orgies and hideous ceremonies to a fellow-prisoner named Squin de Florian, or
Esquins de Floriac. This man demanded to be led to the
King, to whom he told the whole story, whereupon Philip
privately incarcerated and questioned other of the religious,
obtaining ample proof of their crimes. Another tradition
runs to the effect that the Prior of Montfaucon in the diocese
of Toulouse revealed the abominations of the brotherhood.
A third account relates that Jean de Banbellant, a *Farmer*

belonging to the diocese of Soissons, abandoned the Order in 1305, and informed the Inquisitor of Poissy of the heresies and sorceries in which he had once participated.[39] On the other hand, from the letters of Kind Edward II dated 30 October and 20 November, 1307, to the Seneschal of Agen it would appear that the earliest revelations were made in that town.

The charges may be grouped under five heads :—

1. The trampling upon, spitting at, and defiling the Crucifix by the new initiate ; with which is coupled the obscene kiss.
2. The adoration of an Idol having the form of a human head.
3. The omission of the words of Consecration at Holy Mass.
4. The granting of absolution by laymen.
5. The practice of sodomy.

It is true that some writers brush aside the accusations with a disgustful contempt and aver that they were completely disproved during the trials. Any such view it is in face of the overwhelming evidence impossible to maintain, and unprejudiced scholars have no doubt that the charges were substantially established. It may be that many members were not admitted into the foul mysteries of the advanced initiates, who formed the backbone of the Order and were both in act and creed Gnostics devoted to the utmost licentiousness and blasphemy.

The first accusation has been variously explained. One priest declared that it was a trial of the candidate's firmness to see if he would renounce Christianity if captured by the Saracens. This is ridiculous, for we have no record of any novice who rejected the test, and refused to trample the Cross of his Saviour. Almost equally futile is the argument that by this act of contempt the novice evinced his detestation for the Cross as the instrument of Christ's sufferings. The true explanation is that the Templars held the Mandæan heresy, regarding Our Lord as an impostor, and thus the maltreatment of the Cross showed their abhorrence of Him Who had suffered thereon, an act of Satanism which can be paralleled in the profanities of the Black Mass. This is borne out by the fact that upon each Good Friday in an excess of foul sacrilege they were wont to urinate upon the Rood. This is borne out by the evidence of Galcerand de Teus in the Sicilian trial at Santa Maria, and of Etienne Trobati before Clement V and a commission of Cardinals.

Moreover, at his initiation the candidate stripped himself stark naked,[40] gave to and received from his Preceptor the *osculum obscœnum* and submitted to the most infamous complaisances. Unnatural vice is an accusation which it is easy to bring and wellnigh impossible to disprove. It was, moreover, in the mediæval mind closely connected with heresy. Already had the heretic Bulgarians given the English and French languages a word that it is shameful to pronounce and most odious to hear. The evidence, however, with regard to the Templars hardly admits of doubt.[41]

There have been many descriptions of the idol which the Templars worshipped. In the original trials it is simply stated to be a Head : " Quod erat de metallo et habebat faciem quasi humanam, capillos nigros et crispos et non recordatur quod habuerat barbam."[42] The Chronicle of St. Denis describes it as a stuffed human Head : " Un viel pel d'omme embasmée et de toile polie." There were, of course, many of these Heads. England alone possessed four specimens ; one concealed in the sacristy of the London Temple ; one at Byteleshame ; one at Bruer, near Lincoln ; and one beyond the Humber. The knight Bernard von Parma, when tried in Tuscany, confessed that the general belief was this Head was powerful to save and to enrich, and it was the source of all the wealth and prosperity of the Order. To this Head, which seems to have been beardless, the name *Baphomet* was given. The nomenclature Nicolai[43] well suggests is composed of the words βαφὴ μῆτις (or μήτιος),[44] which may be Englished as " Absorption into Wisdom," and hence the Head represented the Deity. Now the Cabbalists represented God *in abstracto* by a Head without a beard, and there can be no doubt that the Head worshipped by the Templars to them represented Deity.[45]

The omission of the words of Consecration at Holy Mass may be due to the use by the Templars not of the Western Rite but of an Eastern Liturgy. In all Eastern Liturgies occurs the prayer in which, after the words of Consecration, the celebrant prays that God may send down His Holy

Spirit to change this bread and wine into the Body and Blood of His Son. This is known as the Epiklesis, ἐπίκλησις, *inuocatio*. All Orthodox theologians now believe that the Epiklesis, and not the words of Institution, is the essential form (or at least the essential complement) of the Sacrament. Some even go so far as to say that the Epiklesis alone conse-crates,[46] so presumably the words of Institution might be omitted without affecting the validity of the Sacrament, although the greater number require the words of Institution as well. A few minor Liturgies indeed do not recite the words of Institution, and therefore they have been held invalid. All of these are forms which were used by heretical sects, and it seems certain that the form employed by the Templars belonged to this family. The explanation that the Templars omitted the words of Institution because in common with many Gnostics they entirely rejected the idea of there being any virtue in the Sacraments is very improbable.

It is undoubted that lay members of the Order gave absolution after confession, and this is by no means merely to be understood of the monastic *culpa*, or public acknow-ledgement of faults against rule. Herr Dr. Prutz, in view of the formula of absolution quoted in more than one of the trials, concludes that this practice links the Templars very closely with the Katharists, and with those bodies which specifically denied the Divinity of Christ.

There was also a book of secret doctrines and instructions, apart from the Statutes of the Order, which was only delivered to certain of the brethren.[47] In every case of examination it appears either from the personal knowledge of the examinee, or from statements which he had received at first hand from other initiates, that such a volume with occult rules and regulations actually existed. The nature and scope of these mysterious writings will probably never be known, for it is almost certain that all copies were destroyed.[48] It has been acutely suggested that some concealed reference to these documents may be found in the various compositions which form the cycle of the legends of the Holy Grail.[49]

Various extravagant stories which were popularly spread in connexion with the Templars, that a monstrous black cat presided at their Chapters and was worshipped, that demons accompanied them as familiars, that every year the Devil took toll of the Order and carried off a Templar of high degree, we may, of course, discount and disregard, although they show the general repute in which the Brethren were held.

At first the various monarchs to whom King Philip had addressed his letters were slow to move, they awaited the lead of the Holy See. The Duke of Brabant and the King of Sicily, it is true, did not hesitate, and possibly they had some individual information which strengthened their hands. At Paris one hundred and seventy-four Templars were interrogated, and Clement V, thinking that things were moving too fast, by a Bull of suspension[50] temporally deprived Bishops and Inquisitors of their power to try these cases. None the less the prisons were full. And in a short while the Pope, having gathered further details, issued a second Bull, 22 November, 1307, *Pastoralis præeminentiæ*, in which he bade all sovereigns follow the example of the French King. He had himself interrogated high dignitaries of the Order who confessed unspeakable sorceries and heresies, especially the trampling upon and defilement of the Cross.

The Pontiff reserved the final decision to the Apostolic Chair, and on 29 and 30 June, 1 and 2 July, 1308, seventy-two Templars were interrogated by a committee of six cardinals, presided over by the Pope in person, when the accused frankly and freely admitted their guilt in every particular. Horrified as he was, Clement did not move quickly. He deliberated, sifted the evidence, conducted fresh inquiries, the result of which merely confirmed the truth of what had been avowed, but it was not until the 30 December that he launched a Bull declaring the Templars apostates and impure, forbidding any to comfort, harbour, succour, or protect them.

The trials of the Templars in various countries of Europe, in the cities and provinces of France, extended over a period of more than five years, and those writers who mistakenly seek to establish the innocence of the Order emphasize the unfortunate and cruel fact that the accused were subjected to torture, as though indeed this were something novel and unaccustomed in similar proceedings at that date. It is not to be denied that torture was repeatedly and rigorously employed in the case of the Templars, and many of their confessions were wrung from them by this means. On the other hand, many acknowledged their guilt without being put to the question, although perhaps through fear of it. Yet the mysteries which were revealed in France, in Italy, in England, and elsewhere, by the Brethren are all so consistent in their details, so correspondingly exact, and so circumstantial, that it is impossible any false tales or feigned accounts or fictions should thus precisely agree on all points and in all particulars. There were, of course, those of the Orders who knew nothing of the sorcery and occult obscenities, and naturally they could not tell that of which they were ignorant. But the initiates who were examined all agreed in the story of their culpability, and the five charges we have enumerated cannot but be looked upon as fully established.

The ancient Roman code was accustomed from the earliest times to employ torture not as a punishment, but simply as a regular means of extracting the truth from the accused. The appeal to the Judgement of God, Ordeals, " dropped out of practical usage during the thirteenth century . . . unhappily to be succeeded by a dreadful revival of torture all over Europe, where it was in full blast in the fourteenth century . . . the custom spread to the lay courts towards the end of the thirteenth century."[51] In 1252 Innocent IV (1243–54), a stern Pontiff who was dealing with treachery, anarchy, rebellion, and problems of overwhelming difficulty, allowed torture to be introduced into the trials of heretics. It is clear that the employment of torture in the prosecutions of the Templars was no more than following the wont and custom of the day.

To summarize, however briefly, the many interrogations during the long and complicated trials would be impertinent, but it is necessary to point out that two phases must be carefully and continuously distinguished ; the royal commission and the papal commission. The latter, which followed in the process, was extended to all the Christian countries of Europe, and even to the Orient. Canonical penances were imposed upon the guilty, and only those who repeatedly lapsed were handed over to the secular arm. Thus on 12 May, 1310, fifty-four Templars who had confessed to Satanism and recanted, persisting in the face of all evidence in their denials and refusing to be reconciled were condemned to the flames and executed the same day. Eight days later four more Knights were sent to the stake, and the dead body of a high officer, Jean de Thuro, some time Treasurer of the Temple, was cast upon the pyre.

On 22 March, 1312, by his Bull *Uox in excelso* Clement V officially notified Christendom that the Order of the Knights-Templars was found to be so corrupt and so rotten with heresy, the whole question having been debated at the Council of Vienne (Dauphiné), it must be dissolved and was thereby declared suppressed. The members who were found guiltless were allowed to join another Order, or return to the secular state if they would, in which case an ample pension for life was assigned each individual. The possessions of the Order were for the most part granted to the Hospitallers, and these were to be applied to their original use, the defence of the Holy Places in Palestine. The Pope reserved to his own judgement the cases of the Grand-Master, Jacques de Molay, and three Preceptors of the highest rank. These had already confessed their guilt, and the Holy Father delegated a special tribunal composed of three cardinals, the Archbishop of Sens, and other prelates to reconcile them to the Church, after which they were to be removed to lifelong imprisonment. On 19 March, 1314, before an immense crowd which had gathered in the square facing Notre-Dame at Paris, the four religious were set upon a platform, their former declarations read aloud, and a formal public abjuration of their heresies demanded. When this had been made, absolution was given. But Jacques de Molay suddenly calling for silence delivered a long harangue in which he theatrically declared that he, his companions, and the whole Order were innocent of all the charges made against them. Geoffrey de Charnay, Preceptor of Normandy, loudly seconded his words. Their judges amazed at this recantation ordered them back to custody that the new situation might be debated calmly and at leisure. But when the news was brought to the King, Philip, furious with rage, gave instant orders that Molay and Charnay should die that very day. Without the knowledge, much less with the consent, of the ecclesiastical commission, the two Templars protesting their innocence to the last, were burned at the stake before the gates of the royal palace. It is said that their brave demeanour greatly impressed those who had assembled to witness their punishment, and it is no doubt this constancy which has led many writers to defend the Order in spite of the crushing evidence of their Satanism and esoteric debaucheries.[52] Many men have died well in a bad cause.

The reign of Philip le Bel was marked by many other trials for sorcery. In 1308 Guichard, Bishop of Troyes, was arrested, chiefly at the secret instigation of Nogaret, upon a charge of having poisoned Queen Joanna of Navarre and the proceedings were unduly protracted until 1313, for when no traces of poison could be found the Bishop was accused of having bewitched the Queen to death. A hermit of St.-Flairt de Villemaur came forward with an extraordinary tale. The Prelate had fashioned, it was alleged, a wax figure to obtain the love of the royal lady and when this had no effect he threw it into the fire so that she languished and died. He had brewed venom from asps and adders, from toads and spiders ; he held continual consultations with a demon who appeared robed as a Black Monk but with horns upon his forehead. Margueronne de Bellevillette, herself in evil repute as a witch, had caught sight of a dark shadowy winged figure of awe conversing with the Bishop. Detail was heaped upon detail, murder, the seduction of nuns, necromancy, false-coining, and every crime human wit could invent. One Noffodès, who was afterwards hanged for a felony and at the foot of the gallows attested the Bishop's innocence, showed himself particularly active and fertile in invention. In 1313 the Prelate was transferred to Avignon, examined by Pope Clement V himself, honourably acquitted, and dispatched on an apostolic mission to Bosnia.[53]

After the death of Philip IV the enemies of his minister, Enguerrand de Marigny, who had taken no insignificant part against the Templars, openly accused the favourite of sorcery, and caused him to be thrown into prison. His wife, Alips de Mons, and his sister, la dame de Canteleu, were tried as accomplices. The usual story of the fabrication of waxen puppets was related, and a magician, Jacques Dulot, who had modelled these was seized. Mad with terror this poor wretch took his life in jail, and on 30 April, 1315, Enguerrand de Marigny was hanged upon the highest gibbet at Mont-faucon.

In 1321 a panic spread throughout France owing to the reported discovery of a vast and hideous conspiracy among the lepers to poison and contaminate all the wells and pure water in France. A lazar confessed that certain sorcerers had distributed a distillation of human blood and urine commixed with three unknown herbs, made up into a paste with which was mingled the Blessed Sacrament stolen from churches. This was all ground to powder to fill large numbers of little bags and purses one of which thrown into water would pollute the whole stream.

A woman, scarred with the fearful disease, was found to have secreted among her garments a little packet sewn in linen, which when cut open was seen to contain the head of a snake, the legs of a toad, and strands of human hair, cemented together with a black and noisome gum. From border to border France thrilled with horror and alarm, and King Philip V at once commanded that all the guilty should be burned alive on the charges of murder and sacrilege. A number of Jews, who were said to have instigated these abominations, perished at the stake ; in Languedoc, where the alarm chiefly prevailed, no less than six hundred lepers were in one day thrown into the flames, and at Paris almost as many more.

Upon the accession of Pope John XXII (Jacques d'Euse), who was enthroned 5 September, 1315, a Bull deposed Hugues Géraud, Bishop of Cahors, who was sentenced to perpetual imprisonment and the confiscation of all his possessions for crimes which are not specified in the official documents. Two men had been arrested at the gates of Avignon, and in their luggage was found poisons, noxious herbs, arsenic, quicksilver, dried toads, lizards, the tails of rats, spiders, the hair of a hanged malefactor, vervain, marjoram, mint, and many other compounds for philtres, and above all wax figures of the Pope, cunningly hidden among the crumb of large loaves. Their confession involved many ecclesiastical dignitaries, including the Bishop of Cahors ; Gaillard de Pressac, Bishop of Toulouse ; and Bernard Gasc, Bishop *in partibus* of Ganos, three bitter opponents of the reigning Pontiff. There can be no doubt from the evidence that a widespread conspiracy was on foot to destroy Pope John, and had wizardy failed the knife or a medicated dram would have been employed. During the trials, the papal nephew, Jacques de Via, Cardinal-Vicar of Avignon, suddenly died, and the prisoners were lost. Hugues Géraud in particular was degraded, and delivered over to the secular arm to be burned alive for sorcery, which sentence was carried out in 1317.[54]

Of the Bulls of Pope John XXII directed against witches a detailed account will be given later. The French trials began to multiply apace, and it must suffice merely to indicate one or two of the most important of these. In 1329 the Carmelite Pierre Ricordi, after investigations which had lasted several years, was condemned to perpetual imprisonment by Henri de Chimay, Inquisitor of Carcassone. In order to obtain the love of certain women the friar had fashioned under the invocation of demons figures of wax moulded with his own blood and saliva, and the blood of toads. The puppet, consecrate to the Devil by magic rites, was then buried under the threshold of the house where the woman, of whom he was amorous, lived, and unless she yielded to his desires she was tormented in evil dreams and uncouth happenings, spectres and voices. He avowed that thus he had corrupted three honest housewives. When he had attained his ends, he sacrificed in thanksgiving to Satan. To shield the honour of the Order sentence was privately passed upon the offender by a special court which sat in the episcopal palace at Pamiers.[55]

In 1330 eleven witches were at Carcassone delivered to the secular arm for punishment of death. Three shepherds, Jean, Pierre, and Barthélemy Andrius, were convicted of killing cattle and flocks by evil spells ; eight women had forespoken children, composed philtres, fashioned amulets, and openly practised divination ; of these one confessed to frequent attendance at the Sabbat.[56]

During the whole reign, indeed, of Philip VI (de Valois), 1328–58, the Inquisition dealt with a very large number of witchcraft trials, many of the accused being first delated for heresy, and upon examination found to be versed in necromancy and the black art. Thus in 1335 at Toulouse a solemn *auto-da-fè* of no less than sixty-three persons was held. Two witches, Anne-Marie de Georgel and Catherine Delort, had made ample acknowledgement of their diabolic

pacts and commerce. They confessed that they habitually
attended the Sabbat which was held, especially on a Friday
night, sometimes in the vicinity of Pech-David, sometimes
in the forest of Bouconne, or again in the low-level country
stretching between Toulouse and Montauban. There they
adored the Demon who was present under the form of a huge
black goat, they had had sexual connexion with him in this
shape as well as having been enjoyed by the foul warlocks
who frequented these assemblies ; they offered infants, stolen
from the cradle, to the Master of these orgies ; they ate too
of the Devil's banquets whereat no salt was served. Catherine
Delort had taken the lives of her two aunts, whose property
she was to inherit, by melting from time to time wax images
slowly before a fire ; so that these women sickened and
languished as the wax flowed away. Both Anne-Marie de
Georgel and Catherine Delort held that the Devil was equal
in power to God ; that their Master reigned on earth, God
only in Heaven ; that over the earth and all that therein is
the Devil is lord. This shows that they were Gnostic heretics,
Manichees, and they belonged, no doubt, to a secret society
of these witches at whose nocturnal meetings the abominations they described took place. And indeed they were
not far wrong in deeming such assemblies the Devil's
Sabbat.[57]

At Carcassone in 1335 the Inquisitor Jean Duprat was
inquiring into the cases of Paul Vignier, Armande Robert,
Matheline Faure, Pierrille Roland, and others who had
boasted of their assistance at a Sabbat held on Mont Alaric.

André Cicéron, a shepherd, in order to confect a charm
had parodied the Sacrifice of Holy Mass. He celebrated the
Mass in a complete state of nudity, asserting that Adam had
thus offered the Eucharist. Two other rustics, Catala and
Paul Rodier, were found guilty of having poisoned various
wells, as also of sacrificing a black cock one midnight where
three ways met in order to bring another war upon the
district. All three were burned alive.[58]

In 1340 a priest, Lucas de Lafond, of Grenade in the
diocese of Toulouse, was condemned to perpetual imprisonment. An ignorant girl, whom he had seduced, bore witness
that he had celebrated Mass in honour of Satan, and was in
the habit of employing holy water, Paschal wax, incense,

and even the Blessed Sacrament Itself as the ingredients of his charms.

In the space of thirty years, 1320–50, the Inquisition at Carcassone heard no fewer than four hundred cases and at least two hundred witches were burned, whilst the Holy Office at Toulouse during the same period presided over some six hundred cases and sent four hundred witches to the stake.[59]

In 1352 eight warlocks were burned at Carcassone; in 1357 no less than thirty-one; whilst from 1387–1400 the Inquisitors of that town, Durand Salranch and Bouit Liestel, delivered over sixty-seven persons, convicted of Witchcraft and of various forms of Gnostic heresy, to the secular arm to be punished according to the law.

Similar proceedings were taking place all over France, in Switzerland, Germany, and many other countries. The problems of Witchcraft were soon to exercise the pens of the legists, and during the fifteenth century no inconsiderable number of technical and highly specialized treatises began to appear. The *De Superstitionibus*, written in 1405, of Nicolas de Jauer, Master in Theology of Prague, has never been printed, but the very many manuscript copies which exist prove that the work had a large circulation and was widely consulted. The Most Christian Doctor, Jean le Charlier de Gerson (1363–1429); Henry of Gorcum, O.P., a famous commentator on S. Thomas; Alonso Tostado (*circa* 1400–55) the Biblical exegete; Juan de Torquemada (Turrecremata), O.P. (*ob.* 1468), Cardinal-Bishop of Sabina and Master of the Sacred Palace; John of Mechlin, Professor of Theology at Cologne; Ambrose of Vignate, an acute jurisconsult; and very many other scholars of immense learning and equal piety wrote at length upon the vexed subject of sorcery.

Especially remarkable is the *Formicarius*,[60] a treatise on the philosophical, theological, and social questions of the day, composed at the Council of Basle during the years 1435–37, by John Nider, Prior of the Convent of Strict Observance at Basle, and attending the Council in the capacity of theologian and legate. Born in Swabia, 1380, Nider took the Dominican habit at Colmar, and soon won a great reputation as a preacher throughout Germany. Elected Prior of the Nuremberg house in 1427 he made himself felt as a just but not harsh reformer, and such were his tact and persuasive moderation that at the instance of Cardinal Julian he made several embassies to the Hussites. After the dissolution of the Council of Basle by Pope Eugenius IV in 1436 Nider resumed his theological lectures at Vienna, and was twice elected Dean of the University before his death at Colmar, 13 August, 1438. The *Formicarius* is valuable because the author frequently quotes actual trials for Witch-craft and the evidence submitted to him by his colleagues, the Inquisitors at Berne or at Autun. Accordingly we have recorded a number of facts concerning the prosecution of witches in the Swiss districts and Rhineland during the first quarter of the fifteenth century. Nider allows that in many cases the demoniacal experiences were subjective, and he gives it as his opinion that the voyage to the Sabbat was sometimes a trance or hallucination.

The Sabbat largely occupies the pen of the Savoyard demonologist who composed *circa* 1450 the famous *Tractatus in Errores Gazariorum*. The writer was doubtless an official who had taken part in trials, since he cites the very words of the accused. He very justly makes no great distinction between the Gazariens, the Cathari, the Vaudois, and sorcerers. There may be subtle technicalities wherein they slightly varied, but all were tarred with the same brush, and broadly their Gnosticism was the same, Satanism. Here we have the Sabbat described in full detail from the confessions of those who had assisted, the orgies, the unspeakable profanities, the bestial turpitudes, the rank obscenity, which go to make up that pandemonium.

About 1450 also Jean Vinet, O.P., Inquisitor at Carcassone, composed his *Tractatus contra inuocatores dæmonum*, which yet may only be found in manuscript. Herein the possibility of carnal connexion with the Devil or some evil entity is discussed, and the writer concludes that the confessions of those who had declared themselves guilty of this abomination must not lightly be disregarded.

The *Flagellum Dæmonum Fascinariorum* (1458) of Nicolas Jacquier. O.P. (*ob.* 1472) holds a very important place in the library of the demonologists, and whilst many of Jacquier's pages have been elaborated and illustrated by numbers of new and carefully observed examples, only the most erudite have actually added to his exposition any details which are substantially unrecorded there. He speaks with knowledge, for example, of the blasphemy of the Black Mass, of the Devil's Mark, of the adoration of Satan, the aerial voyage to the Sabbat, the dreams and subjective illusions of wizards. Moreover, he recognizes the essential link between heresy and Witchcraft, so intermingled and unified that to separate them is impossible, for is not Witchcraft the worship of the Devil, the heresy of heresies ?[61]

Of lesser note is the *Flagellum Maleficorum* (*circa* 1462), which was several times reprinted, of Pierre Mamor, a native of Limousin, Canon of Saintes and Rector of the University of Poitiers (*circa* 1460). A *Liber contra artem magicam* (*circa* 1475) of Jean Vincent, Prior of Moustiers-en-Lay, La Vendée, remains in manuscript. He is inclined to explain the Sabbat as, though sometimes a real experience, frequently dreamed in a trance, induced and prolonged by evil charms. It is interesting to find some mention of lycanthropy in this treatise.

But perhaps the most celebrated of all works upon Witchcraft is the *Malleus Malleficarum* of James Sprenger and Henry Kramer, the Dominican Inquisitors who were appointed by Innocent VIII to cleanse Bavaria and Saxony from sorcerers. This great treatise, which may not unfittingly be described as a Manual for the use of judges at witch-trials, was based upon their own personal notes and actual experiences, although perhaps suggested by the *Directorium inquisitorum* of Nicolas Eymeric, O.P.,[62] Inquisitor-General of Aragon, which had been compiled as early as 1376, and seems to be the only one of all Eymeric's voluminous writings that is printed.[63] The first edition of the *Malleus* appeared at Frankfort without a date, but it was issued not earlier than 1485[64] and not later than 1489.[65] Giving, as it does, a most full and detailed account of the methods of procedure, the infliction of torture, the examination of witnesses, the sifting of evidence, the *Malleus Maleficarum* is a most valuable historical document.[66]

To attempt any complete list of the witch-trials in France during the fifteenth century is a task which, however interesting, space will not here allow. In Languedoc the activities of the Inquisition extended over a wide area. The records of Hugues de Verdun, Grand Inquisitor of Toulouse, are largely missing, but with Raymond de Tilhol (1430), his successor, they become more regular. In the year 1432 we find that, although one hundred and twelve persons were found guilty of heresy and magic, only sixteen were executed. In 1433 there were eight sentences of death. Nor does the toll appear to have been greater towards the end of the century, for in 1484 Antoine de Clède, an Inquisitor, passed sentence on eleven sorcerers, but only two—and those aggravated cases— a shepherd and a woman, went to the stake.

At Carcassonne in 1410 Géraud Gassendi was accused of debauching married women and young maidens by the aid of evil charms and the help of the Devil. He had stolen certain threads of gold from the festal cloak of Our Lady in the Church of the Martyrs S. Nazarius and S. Celsus to weave into his shirt, and he had evoked seven demons in the wood of Bogoyran. The result of the trial is unknown. In 1412 several young men of Carcassonne were found guilty of sorcery and sodomy and handed over by the Inquisitor Pierre de Morelegio to the secular magistrates by whom they were burned. In 1423 several warlocks were condemned to the flames, and in 1435 great scandal was caused by the prosecution of Etienne de Vals, a canon of Montréal, on multiplied charges of divination and necromancy.

In 1453 during an epidemic at Marmande, at the height of the mortality a hag named Jeanne Canay, long reputed a witch, was seized, and in a few days some dozen of her accomplices were likewise thrown into prison. Torture was freely employed ; the rack extorted detailed confessions ; and five wretched creatures who avowed they had spread the infection were burned. Two expired during the question. The members of the local tribunal, which seems to have grossly exceeded its powers, being called to a sharp account by Charles VIII, who took cognizance of the affair, escaped with no light fines and reprimand.

In the Bibliothèque Nationale of Paris may be found a manuscript (Mst. Latin, 3446, f. 58–62), a confession made before the Inquisition of Lyons, possibly the actual screed taken down in court. Throughout that district wizards were known as " Vaudois," so deeply rooted is the traditional connexion between heresy and sorcery, and their Sabbat was the " Synagogue." The various details comprise the appearance of the Devil in the form of a man ; the riding upon a besom or stick ; anointing the body with hellish unguents ; the obscene ritual of the Sabbat ; the horrible desecration of the Blessed Sacrament, defiled and given to toads ; urination into a stolen chalice which had recently been used at Holy Mass ; magic powders distributed, by sprinkling which on men and cattle diseases would be spread ; blasphemies and obscenities beyond imagination. Here also we have a rare and interesting detail, the visits by witches to wine-cellars and the broaching of mighty tuns for Satan's bacchanalia.[67]

During the visitations of Frère Ponce Feugeyron, a Franciscan, who was commissioned by Alexander V in 1409, a number of sorcerers were interrogated and discovered hideous abominations. During their assemblies they had adored the Master of the Sabbat, who appeared as a tall dark man, with the most disgusting ceremonies ; they trampled under foot the Crucifix and defiled the Sacred Host with nameless profanities and vileness ; periodically they bound themselves by horrid oaths never to reveal the mysteries of darkness.

In 1438 Pierre Vallin of Tour du Pin was executed for having delivered his daughter to the embraces of one of the Masters of the Sabbat from the results of whose lust and violence she expired ; in 1462 at Chamonix, seven women and several men were condemned to the stake by the secular arm. Of these one, Jean Greland, who had on many occasions stolen the Blessed Sacrament, thrown It into the gutter and stamped It in the mud, was compelled to kiss three times a cross painted on the earth in the very spot he had dared his sacrilege, his right foot was struck off by the executioner, and he was flung into the blazing pyre.

In the archives of l'Isère there exists a contemporary record of about one hundred and ten women and fifty-seven men who were executed for sorcery, some being burned, others drowned, between the years 1428 and 1447.

At Cambrai in 1460 a sorcerer named Jennin was haled before the Bishop's tribunal. Upon his arrest he endeavoured to stab himself with a knife, but was prevented, and when interrogated confessed to having entertained a familiar for many years, by whose help he pretended to foretell, or foretold, future events. He had also abandoned himself to every impurity, and had achieved no small reputation as a confectioner of love-philtres and evil amulets. He was condemned to make public confession of his heresy and sorceries, to renounce the demon, and to perform some just and exemplary penance. But, as on his return from the scene of the public *auto-da-fè*, he not only tore his sackcloth robe but broke and dashed to the ground the crucifix he was carrying, he was considered to have merited the doom of a relapsed heretic, was brought to trial, and two days after burned at the stake.[68]

Among the most resounding trials of the fifteenth century must be accounted those of the Vaudois at Arras in 1459. These wretches whose heresies and sorceries were the scandal of the province had long been grievously suspected of robbing the tabernacles and using the Hosts to mingle with their hell-broths and devilish unguents.

It happened that in 1459 whilst Jean Jouffrey, the Bishop of Arras, was absent in Rome, the Dominican Inquisitor, Pierre le Broussart, arrested at Douai a woman of evil life named Deniselle Grenière, upon the denouncement of an old warlock, who had been burned at Langres. When she was examined by the Vicar of the episcopal court and the doyen of the Chapter, Jacques du Boys, she implicated four hags and an old villain named Jean Lavite. So abominable were the charges, so hideous their confessions that all five were executed, being brought to the pyre their heads adorned with paper mitres, on which were painted the devils they had worshipped and served. Next the Inquisitor laid his hands upon a large number of persons of every degree who had been delated as seen at the local Sabbat, whereupon many more fled, some to the court of the Duke of Burgundy, some actually to Rome. Panic reigned throughout the country-side, and the Duke, Philippe le Bon, ordered a Council to be held at Brussels to consider the whole question. The ecclesiastical dignitaries of Arras, the Inquisitors, and many doctors of Louvain, were convened to discuss every aspect of the outbreak of " vaulderie " as the commixture of heresy and witchcraft was called. But now the Parliament of Paris interfered and ordered the release of the accused ; the Archbishop of Reims and the bishops of Amiens and Paris refused to hear charges of sorcery and dismissed all cases brought before them ; the chapter of Arras was in a sad plight, nor was their dismay lightened when their bishop returned from Rome to undo all their proceedings, to declare the whole process illegal and worse, to set free all who had been imprisoned upon suspicion of Witchcraft.[69]

There occurred in 1491 a case of possession in a convent, a singularly rare happening at so early a date, although unhappily far more common some hundred and thirty years later. Among the Augustinian nuns of the Reform at Quesnoy-le-Comte, near Cambrai, was a young, ardent, and emotional sister, named Jeanne Potier. Although always of most exemplary character and strictest observance she was suddenly seized with a burning passion for the confessor, who upon understanding the situation at once withdrew from the place, his duties being undertaken by a venerable religious of extraordinary sanctity and wisdom. But the nympho-maniac burst out into the wildest ravings ; she shrieked blasphemies and obscenities ; sang bawdy songs such as it was humanly impossible she should ever have heard ; displayed the utmost lubricity in gesture and imagination ; evinced an almost supernatural strength when it was attempted to restrain her ; and, what was worse, in some mysterious way communicated her malady to other religious, until the peaceful cloister became a very bedlam of riot and impurity. Monks and friars came from all parts to exorcize the demons who were thus afflicting the house, and who gave their names as Tahu, Gron, and Gorgias. At length the Bishop of Cambrai, Monsignor Henry de Bughes, visited the convent with much state and ceremony. On the Second Sunday after Easter he assisted at High Mass, and solemnly blessed the whole cloister. He then proceeded to exorcize the possessed nuns, and having expelled the diabolic influences ordered Sister Jeanne Potier to be kept in strictest seclusion until she had shown unmistakable signs of recovery. Order was thus restored to those walls where pandemonium had reigned for no less than seven months.[70]

So immense a literature has gathered round the name of S. Joan of Arc that it is impossible here even to touch upon her long and intricate trial in any useful or satisfactory detail. I will merely content myself with drawing attention to Father Herbert Thurston's ample and complete refutation[71] of the ignoble fatuities, so seriously yet so idly, put forward by Miss M. A. Murray in her *The Witch-Cult in Western Europe* (pp. 270–6). It will hardly be believed that, obsessed with her figment of an ancient religion which she terms the " Dianic cult," Miss Murray not merely declares S. Joan to have been a member of this " Dianic cult " but " actually the Incarnate God." The monstrous extravagance of such imaginings. which it is superfluous to add have not a very shadow of foundation in fact, almost renders it impossible to treat them as worthy of any consideration. They fall owing to their own nightmare impossibility. Even the two Saints who appeared from Heaven to S. Joan, S. Katherine of Alexandria and S. Margaret of Antioch, are witches. Naturally in the ages of faith, when nomenclature was limited, the names of these two popular Virgin Martyrs occur again and again, even as their pictures or statues were found in every church however poor and humble. Through the centuries of witch-trials we find that many of the accused bore one of these two names—even as there were many who were called Mary at the font in honour of Our Blessed Lady— and this is enough for Miss Murray to write of the two Saints in the most fantastic strain. The fact that as S. Joan lay in prison S. Katherine appeared to her gives occasion for the wild suggestion that some female impersonated S. Katherine and obtained access to the dungeon by a secret passage. The whole thing is more than incredible, it is irrational. Yet it is instructive, as showing the lengths to which writers will go who wish to avoid the natural and true explanation.[72]

There is no part of France more conservative and more devout than Brittany. Here happily linger yet the old traditions, the old courtesies, and the old homely Saints, elsewhere wellnigh forgotten. And so at the little gothic Chapel of Notre-Dame-du-Haut, near Moncontour, they still pray to S. Mamert, who cures gastric disorders ; to Saint Livertin, who with S. Urlou, heals migraine ; to S. Houarniaule, who makes cowards brave ; and S. Meen, who chases away rheumatism and sciatica. S. Cornelius, S. Nicodemus, S. Herbot, and S. Thégonnec, watch over flocks and cattle ; S. Eloi protects the horses ; until recently S. Hervé was invoked to guard the wayfarer from wolves, of which one who attacked a peasant was killed not longer than some forty years ago. The village maidens still stick pins into the statue of S. Guirec at Ploumanac'h to remind him to bring them a husband soon ; S. Trémeur carries his head in his hand ; mothers hang tiny shirts and caps before the shrine of S. Languy at Plougastel-Daoulas if their children are languishing from any ailment or slow of wit ; in the little village church of Guimilau their patron, the murdered prince, S. Guimilau has his altar, rich with carven figures and fruit and foliage, all dight with colour and gold, albeit the legend grow faint with years.

Brittany has her wonderful faith, most precious of all her possessions. And, as may be supposed, a land so ancient, so alive to the sense of the supernatural, has also its occult lore and whispered tales of sorcery. Menhirs and dolmens, great monolithic circles like Carnac and Kergouen, recall the memories of the Druids. Heloïse, who loved Abelard, is still spoken of in Brittany as a " druidess," and there exists a strange ballad which extols her magic powers. Folk-lore says that the fairies built the Druid monuments.

Well within the last century certain villages and hamlets were tainted with an evil reputation for sorcery as the dwelling-places of necromancers and enchanters. Breton proverb speaks of the witches of Fougères, of Trèves, of Concoret, of Lézat.

The demonology of Brittany is unique, and finds in cottage and in lonely farm more than a half-credence yet. At the dead of night a harshly creaking wain may be heard on the silent road. It halts before some door. A soul quits the doomed house and the cart passes on its way. It is the Ankou, the spirit of death, who travels in the darkness, calling to those who are about to die, summoning them to take their place beside her. It is said that in some churches a figure of the Ankou may be seen, a grisly skeleton.

The Mourioche is a demon of hideous malignity, who appears in the shape of some four-footed beast, most often a year-old colt. Woe to the wight who mounts him deeming that he is some ordinary steed ! That ride will end in the pit of hell. Around Morlaix the peasants fear the Teurst. He is black and shadowy, but terrible, like the Highland Ourisk, who haunts moors and glens. The Teursta Poulict is invariably seen in the form of a pig or cat, or some domestic animal.

Among the ancient dolmens, relics of a vanished race, lurks the Nain. He is dark as an Ethiop, with dishevelled locks, a cruel countenance wherein his eyes gleam red as carbuncles with the fire of the damned ; his voice is harsh and horrible, he has the legs and hoofs of the goat. In the pale starlight he treads an uncouth measure around the ancient stones to the screech and drone of some mysterious cornemuse. The Nains are the inventors of a cabalistic alphabet, the characters of which are engraved on several of the megalithic monuments of Morbihan, and particularly those of Gavr'inis. He who can decipher the magic screed will be able to tell where hidden treasure is to be found in any part of the country.

Inferior demons, the Crions, Courils, and Gorics, haunt the cellars of ancient castles and châteaux. Here gold is hidden away, a vast store. Thus the Gorics watch the secret hoards, whose resting-place no man knows, in the depths of the Castle of Morlaix.

The Korrigan is a succubus of infernal beauty. Her golden tresses, red lips, and sparkling eyes, the beauty of hell, can entrap the heart of the most constant swain, and her embrace will draw him for love of her to vow his soul to Satan.

Brittany teems with legends of witches and their foul deeds, some exaggerated, some wholly imaginary, no doubt, but some fearfully true. And of these latter there is no more hideous tale than the history of Gilles de Rais.

Gilles de Rais was born about 1404 in the château of Machecoul, which lies on the borders of Brittany and Anjou. His father, Guy de Laval II, died towards the end of October, 1415 ; and his mother, Marie de Craon, marrying the Sieur d'Estouville, handed him and his brother Réné de Rais to the lax guardianship of his grandfather, Jean de Craon, lord of Champtocé and La Suze " homme viel et ancien et de moult grand âge." On the 30 of November, 1420, when he was at the most seventeen years of age, Gilles de Rais married Catherine de Thouars, by which union he became one of the wealthiest, perhaps the wealthiest, noble in Europe.

At this time the state of France seemed desperate. The English were swarming over a country already decimated by massacres and ravaged by plague. As far as Orleans had the invaders penetrated, leaving burning villages, blood, famine, disease, and destruction on every side. Charles VII, the Dauphin, disowned by his parents, his father mad, his mother a whore, derided as a bastard, his authority mocked, his courage failing, held some kind of court at Chinon, where in profligacy and debauch he endeavoured to forget. But from time to time he roused himself to issue a piteous appeal and it was in 1425 that Gilles de Rais came to the help of this puppet king, lending him huge sums of money, raising an army, " bon et hardy capitaine," the old chronicler says. It was then that S. Joan appeared upon the scene to save France, and the King entrusted her to Gilles de Rais, who was ever at her side,[73] her comrade, her protector, fighting in all her battles, remaining with her all day under the very walls of Paris when she was wounded. The abbé Bossard has proved that in his wardship he was absolutely loyal and true to S. Joan. He was already saturated with the most exalted mysticism, and there is no doubt that he believed firmly in the divine mission of the Saint in whose cause he fought so gallantly and so royally. He saw her fulfil all that she promised to accomplish, and when King Charles was crowned at Reims Gilles de Rais was created a Marshal of France, enjoying the honour of bearing the King's arms on his escutcheon.

In 1426, however, weary of both court and camps, he has retired to his castle of Tiffauges, where we find that he kept a truly imperial state. The details of luxury and magnificence outvie the chronicles of Sultan and Cæsar. He retained a bodyguard of more than two hundred men, no mere common soldiers, but knights, captains, squires, pages of high degree, each one of whom wore brocade or velvet and had his own retinue. The pomp of his chapel, which resembled a collegiate church, where High Mass was sung every day and the Office recited with full ceremonial and ritual observance, seemed that of a metropolitan basilica. At Tiffauges resided a prelatical establishment, the doyen, vicars, treasurers, canons, priests, and deacons, clerks, scholars, singers, a regular choir-school of sweetest voices. The rochets, amices, albs, corporals, lavabos, and altar cloths were of finest linen. The vestments glittered with gold and jewels ; we hear of

tunicles of emerald-green silk woven with threads of gold ;
of heavy copes, crimson and violet, sewn with seed pearls ;
of great canopies of yellow damask and white ; of dalmatics
of amber-coloured silk and blue and silver ; of chasubles
figured with the Nativity and the Passion of Christ, the
Annunciation and the Assumption of the Mother of God ;
of scarlet cloth to hang the chapel on festal days ; of dossal
tapestries woven with the Legends of the Saints that decked
the chancel upon Easter, Pentecost, Christtide, Lady Day in
harvest, Hallowmas, and the Patrons of the place. Upon the
altar stood huge candlesticks of massy gold ; gold were the
patens, the chalices, ciboria, the basons and lavers, the pax
and the reliquaries, of which the chiefest, that of Saint
Honoré, blazed with gems, treasure of incalculable value,
wrought by a cunning craftsman who lived and fashioned
these things in the castle itself.

Moreover Gilles de Rais kept open house ; day and night
his board groaned beneath the weight of baked meats and
roast, huge baskets of white bread, pasties, mortreux,
manchets and collops, to feed not only his officers but those
travellers who should pass that way. He himself loved rare
spiced food and rich wines of Cyprus or from the East wherein
a gout of amber had been dissolved.

He was a bibliophile to boot, and stored in mighty chests
his precious manuscripts, which were painted for him by a
famous illuminator named Thomas, who clothed them in
velvets and gay Oriental stuffs from Cairo and Damascus.
He was especially fond of the works of Ovid, of Valerius
Maximus, and above all the Histories of Suetonius, his copy
of which was bound in red leather with a golden lock and
clasp.

It is obvious that even the revenues of a kingdom could not
sustain such a superfluity of extravagance, and gradually
manors and meadows and parks and forests began to be sold,
until in 1436 his family, alarmed for their inheritance,
petitioned King Charles who " sûr du mauvais gouvernement
du sire de Rais " by an order in Council forbad him to
dispose of any property whatsoever.

For a long while Gilles de Rais had experimented in
alchemy and sought the philosopher's stone, and now he
began the quest in real earnest under the guidance of a

famous occultist of the day, Gilles de Sillé, a priest of St. Malo.
Vast sums were expended ; gold and silver melted in crucible
and retort ; but without result. One of the Marshal's
chaplains, Eustache Blanchet, set out for Italy to discover
some master of the craft, but in the meantime Gilles de Rais
seems to have determined to have resource to demoniac
powers to assist him. He applied to Jean de la Rivière, a
sorcerer who had just come from Poitiers, but spells and
incantations proved unavailing. A second warlock, named
Du Mesnil, persuaded Gilles to sign with his blood a parchment swearing to give the Devil all he demanded " hormis sa
vie et son âme," and in order to strengthen the evocation the
Office of the Damned was chanted in the chapel at midnight
upon the Feast of All Saints.

Shortly afterwards Blanchet returned from Italy bringing
with him Francesco Prelati, a Florentine priest. Prelati,
who was a scholar and a man of extraordinary charm, soon
gained complete ascendancy over Gilles de Rais, and then
began that hideous series of murders, blasphemies, and
abominations, which seem to have exhausted the foulest
depths of black magic. Satan, declared the wizard, must be
propitiated by blood, the blood of children. He would thus
show himself favourable and heap riches upon his devoted
servants. The name of the first victim of Gilles de Rais is
unknown. It appears to have been a young boy, who was
enticed one evening to the castle, and when in a secret
chamber the erotomaniac had satiated his lust upon this
unhappy child, they suddenly strangled their outraged prey,
and cutting the heart from the warm body offered the young
limbs that yet quivered and writhed with agony to the Demon
whom they invoked with the most horrible oaths and adjura-
tions. Presently Prelati wrapped the corpse in linen, and
under cover of darkness buried it in consecrated ground, a
cemetry hard by a chapel of S. Vincent of Saragossa. The
blood was preserved in phials and with it on virgin vellum
were written a grimoire and the liturgy of Satan.

It is useless to reiterate these hideous scenes of Sadism and
sacrilege ; to describe the Black Masses which were celebrated
in the castles ; to enumerate the rapes, tortures, and murders.
From 1432 to 1440 the orgy continued, and children disappeared from all directions into the monster's den. Endless

lists of boys and girls were read out at the trial : Lost, at
Rochebernart, the son of the widow Peronne, a boy who was
going to school " et apprenait moult bien " ; Lost, at Saint-
Etienne de Montluc, the son of Guillaume Brice, a poor man ;
Lost, at Machecoul, the son of Georget le Barbier ; Lost, at
Thouaye, the son of Mathelin Thouars, " était ledit enfant de
l'âge d'environ douze ans " ; and so the records continue,
until it is believed that more than eight hundred victims
perished. Their bodies were burned, or thrown into the vaults
and latrines of the castle. Night after night de Rais gloated
fondly over anguish and death, for as he himself said : " J'étais
plus content de jouir des tortures, des larmes, de l'effroi et du
sang que de tout autre plaiser." But his sleep was troubled
with fearful dreams. He built a college at Machecoul, and
dedicated it to the Holy Innocents. He spoke often of
retiring to a cloister ; of walking barefoot to Jerusalem,
begging his bread as he went.

All the while it seemed as though John V, Duke of
Brittany, who was buying the Marshal's lands and houses
cheaply enough, refrained from interfering whilst he could
replenish his coffers and swell his possessions. The sad
murmurs of the peasantry hardly reached his indifferent ears.
But there was one power which, upon complaint, could and
did move with relentless force. Jean de Malestroit, Bishop
of Nantes, a prelate of the highest probity and sincerest
piety, at length heard rumours of these foul businesses.
A month sufficed to make inquiry ; a band of armed men
marched against Tiffauges, whilst a second expedition
invested Machecoul whither Gilles de Rais had fled in deadly
fear. Resistance was useless ; escape impossible ; on the 14
September the wretched murderer, Prelati, and those of his
followers who had not abandoned him at the first sign of
danger were arrested, loaded with chains, and cast into
prison. The ecclesiastical proceedings lasted a month and
eight days ; the civil proceedings forty-eight hours. Bishop
Jean de Malestroit himself presided over the court, with the
Bishops of Mans, Saint-Brieuc, and Saint-Lô as his assessors.
Pierre de l'Hospital, Chancellor of Brittany, watched the case
on behalf of the lay authorities. But perhaps the most
pregnant figure was he who sat by the side of the president ;
a simple friar in the black and white habit of S. Dominic,

Jean Blouyn, delegate of the Holy Inquisition for the city and diocese of Nantes.

The Promoter, Guillaume Chapeiron, a learned jurist, rector of S. Nicolas at Nantes, read an appalling list of crimes. Gilles de Rais was accused of the violation and murder of children, of witchcraft and Satanism which involved blackest heresy, and the prosecution demanded his instant excommunication as an evoker of demons, a sodomite, and apostate, a heretic relapsed. The prisoner replied to these charges with blasphemy and foul railings. He refused to offer any defence. Then the Bishop of Nantes and the Inquisitor declared him contumacious, and solemnly cast him out of the bosom mercy of Mother Church.

On the third day the scene was changed. Gilles was now entirely broken in spirit ; he hardly seemed the same man as the haughty noble who with sullen port had hurled defiance at the judges ; bent, bowed, wrinkled, trembling and tearful, his fevered eyes blazing in his ashen face, he had veritably aged twenty years. When adjured to make full and ample confession, a recital which was not to be " dubia, uaga, generalis, illatiua, iocosa," but plain and pertinent, with downcast glances and clasped hands that shook as with palsy, in the midst of that crowded court he began the horrid chronicle of his deeds. And as the dark tale poured forth in his dull monotonous voice, emotionless and dead, the hush grew more and more intense, whilst cheeks blanched with terror, and even the billsmen, sturdy soldiers steeped in rapine and war, would fain have stopped their ears to shut out the chronicle of hell. Without faltering, without pause, he told the details of his murders, his rapes of tender youth who sobbed and struggled mad with fear and shame, he gloated upon the ease with which the sharp knife sank into their white throats, his orgasm as the red stream gushed out warm and slab. He shook his long lean fingers as if scattering the drops in some. horrible asperges of crime. He spared no horror of his sadism, unmasquing his bestial appetites which reverenced not even the dead. The bishops signed themselves with unsteady hands, and Jean de Malestroit, arising, took a veil and for modesty sake covered the face of the Crucifix that hung above his throne. At length the raucous accents died away and with a piercing shriek the baron cried :

" O my God, my Redeemer, mercy, mercy, and forgiveness !
And do you the fathers and mothers of those so piteously
slain, pray for me ! " A vast sound of weeping shook the
hall ; great tears rolled silently down the cheeks of even the
Bishops who sat in judgement and doom. But Jean Blouyn,
who had heard all motionless with unwinking eyes and
unchanged look, made a solemn gesture. The Promoter
arose. The crimes were manifest, clear, and amply confessed,
he said, the next step was to pronounce sentence. The
Tribunal appointed the morrow. The first sentence was
passed by the Bishop of Nantes conjointly with the Inquisitor.
By them Gilles de Rais was declared guilty of Witchcraft,
Satanism, heresy, and apostacy, and handed over to the Civil
Arm to receive the punishment due to such deeds. The
second sentence, pronounced by the Bishop alone, declared
the prisoner convicted of sodomy, sacrilege, and violation of
ecclesiastical rights. Then upon the frantic prayers and
abasement of the unhappy wretch the ban of excommunication was lifted, but he was handed over to the secular court,
who sentenced him to death, on multiplied charges of murder,
as well as for the aforesaid crimes. Until his execution, which
took place on 26 October, 1440, he spent the hours in trans-
ports of prayer and aspiration ; the murderer, the sadist, the
demoniac, had disappeared ; the mystic, the devotee, the
erstwhile companion of S. Joan alone remained. At eleven
o'clock on the fatal day he was led with his two companions,
Henri Griart and Etienne Corrillaut, from prison in funereal
procession to the Place de la Biesse, where had been piled
huge stacks of brushwood and tar over which towered high
gibbets. " We have sinned, all three of us," were his last
words to his comrades, " but as soon as our souls have left our
bodies we shall all see God in His Glory in Paradise." The
prisoners, at the express desire of the Marshal, were simultaneously executed. They were launched from the gibbets,
and in a few moments the red flames blazed beneath. But
when the heat had severed the rope by which Gilles was suspended, certain noble ladies caused the body to be drawn from
the fire. The remaining bodies were wholly consumed, the
ashes being scattered to the winds. The corpse of the
Marshal, however, was honourably interred in the Carmelite
church hard by the scene of execution. Thus perished one of

the most extraordinary figures in the whole history of witchcraft.[74]

Throughout the sixteenth century the prosecution of witches increased steadily in zest and bitterness on every hand in France, and this vigour is especially noticeable from the time when the Inquisition began to delegate its jurisdiction in these matters to the civil courts, who dealt with delinquents and suspects with a severity that almost amounted to cruelty. It must be remembered, however, that authority and order were faced with a terrible problem and menace, a band of malefactors, devoted to Satan and versed in every phase of wickedness, adepts at poisoning and secret murder, whose one aim was to spread anarchy, ruin, and death, the kingdom of their master.

In 1519 a very horrible case was heard before Louis Bruni (or Brun), a Franciscan, Vicar of the Grand Inquisitor for Dauphiné. Catherine Peyretonne was tried on multiplied charges of sorcery. She confessed to constant attendance at the Sabbat, where she had indulged in every possible sexual excess with the demon. She had stolen and killed infants from the cradle to satisfy a hideous cannibalism, and sacrificed them to her familiar, Barrabam. She had adored the Devil with most filthy ceremonies, and vowed herself to evil. It is curious to note that she speaks of the blue flames at the nocturnal meetings of witches, a fact that points to the burning of sulphur, and also of the black candles which were distributed to those present. As a criminal of no ordinary guilt she was sent quick to the stake, and executed at Montpezat on the 9 October.[75]

At Besançon in 1521 some curious cases of lycanthropy were investigated by the Inquisitor. Two shepherds, Michel Verdung and Pierre Burgot, made a detailed acknowledgement of their crimes. Even if they had not assumed the shape they had been filled with all the desires of wolves, even to coupling with females of that kind. Burgot confessed that he had on several occasions met a tall dark man, who declared himself to be a servant of the lord of hell, evidently the official for the witches throughout the district. Before this man he knelt and renounced God, Our Blessed Lady, the Saints, his baptism ; swearing, moreover, never again to recite the *Credo*. He then kissed the stranger's left hand,

which was black and cold as that of a corpse. It may indeed
have actually been a dead hand held from beneath a disguise
cloak. In company with Verdung, who seems to have
initiated him into these abominations, Burgot attended the
local Sabbat, where he was assigned a familiar named Moyset.
A long tale of murders followed. Both Verdung and Burgot
swore that they had killed and devoured five persons, including a little girl of four years old and a child aged nine.[76]
They were burned alive at Poligny, and about the same time
a third were-wolf, Philibert Montôt, was executed.

During the reign of Francis I (1515–47) a great sensation
was caused by an outbreak of demoniac possession at the
convent of St.-Pierre at Lyons. The cloister was solemnly
exorcised by a Bishop assisted by three priests. Before finally
leaving the building, the demon who had especially haunted
the dormitory, took refuge by the obsession of a nun, Sister
Alexis de Thesieux, to the great terror of the religious.
Owing, however, to the powerful prayers of the exorcists she
was presently delivered.[77]

The witches who were sent to the stake for the most part
were accused of the Gnostic heresy as well as sorcery. Thus
a warlock, who ate meat on a Friday without a dispensation,
was burned in 1539. A woman, who had committed
bestiality with a dog, her familiar, was executed in 1540
at Toulouse. In the same year the Norman Parliament
burned in the old Market-Place at Rouen two shepherds of
Tosny, a hamlet near Gisors, by name Delarue and Morin,
who had confessed their Satanism and witchcrafts to the
hurt of man and beast.

In the days of Henri II (1547–59) the punishment of
witches began to be more drastically and more systematically prosecuted by the civil arm. Seven sorcerers were
burned at Nantes in 1549, one of the chief articles against
them being that they had composed a grimoire, which they
intended to take to the witches of Norcia for evil consecration.[78] They seem to have had the power of throwing themselves at will into mediumistic trances during which they
supposed they had attended the Sabbat, the revolting details
of which they described with extraordinary exactitude. In
1549, also, the Vicar of St. Jean at Lyons [79] was condemned
to the stake as a sorcerer.

In 1556 a witch was put to death at Bièvres, a village some two leagues from Laon. She confessed that she had had carnal connexion with a demon who served her for many years. She was condemned to be strangled and burned, but by the bungling of the executioner she was consumed alive.

Under Charles IX (1560–74) the trials begin to be even more frequent, and fuller details are forthcoming. In 1564 at Poitiers three warlocks and a witch confessed that they had worshipped a monstrous goat, whom they obscenely kissed offering each a candle in sign of homage. They had danced, back to back, at the Sabbat, around the throne of Satan who played upon a flute or pipe of shrill and hideous note. All were summarily put to death. Apres auoir esté accusés, & cõueincus de plusiers malefices, ils furent tous bruslez.[80]

At Laon, Nicole Aubry, the wife of a tailor of Vervins, declared herself possessed. She declared that she was surrounded by the shadowy forms of demons who threatened her, and at last she fell into a cataleptic state, and when roused spoke in a harsh rough voice entirely unlike her own. The Bishop of Laon himself interviewed and afterwards exorcised her ; she answered in a trance-like state questions put to her in Hebrew and Greek in the tongues they were asked ; she resolved theological difficulties, and above all acknowledged the truth of Christ's Body in the Most Holy Sacrament ; she had intimate knowledge of affairs passing at a distance as was several times proved by the event.

The Prince de Condé, who had just apostatized to Protestantism, was so confounded and enraged that he flung her into prison, but Charles IX promptly released her from so unjust a durance, and compensated her husband with a handsome bounty.[81]

In 1571 or 1574 was executed on the Place de Grève at Paris, a sorcerer named Trois-Echelles. The extraordinary feats he accomplished had long excited suspicion, and when interrogated he confessed before the King, the Marshals de Montmorency, De Retz, and the Sieur du Mazille, the royal physician, that he had sold himself to the Devil by whose aid he·performed these sorceries. He described at great length the saturnalia of the fiends, the sacrifices which they offered up, the debaucheries they committed with the young and handsome witches, and the various modes of preparing the infernal unguent for blighting cattle. He said he had upwards of twelve hundred accomplices in the crime of Witchcraft in various parts of France, whom he named to the King, and many of whom were afterwards arrested and suffered execution.[82]

At Dôle, in 1573, Gilles Garnier, a native of Lyons, was indicted for being a *loup-garou*, or man-wolf, and for prowling in that shape about the country at night to devour little children. The indictment against him, as read by Henri Camus, doctor of laws and counsellor of the King, was to the effect that he, Gilles Garnier, had seized upon a little girl, twelve years of age, whom he drew into a vineyard and there killed, partly with his teeth and partly with his hands, seeming like wolf's paws ; that from thence he trailed her bleeding body along the ground with his teeth into the wood of La Serre, where he ate the greatest portion of her at one meal, and carried the remainder home to his wife ; that upon another occasion, eight days before the festival of All Saints, he was seen to seize another child in his teeth, and would have devoured her had she not been rescued by the country people, and that the said child died a few days afterwards of the injuries he had inflicted ; that fifteen days after the same festival of All Saints, being again in the shape of a wolf, he devoured a boy thirteen years of age, having previously torn off his leg and thigh with his teeth, and hid them away for his breakfast on the morrow. He was furthermore indicted for giving way to the same diabolical and unnatural propensities even in his shape of a man ; and that he had strangled a boy in a wood with the intention of eating him, which crime he would have effected—" nonobstant qu'il fust iour de uendredy "— if he had not been seen by the neighbours and prevented.

Gilles Garnier was put to the rack after fifty witnesses had deposed against him. He confessed everything that was laid to his charge. He was thereupon brought back into the presence of his judges, when Dr. Camus, in the name of the parliament of Dôle, pronounced the following sentence :—

" Seeing that Gilles Garnier has, by the testimony of credible witnesses, and by his own spontaneous confession, been proven guilty of the abominable crimes of lycanthropy and witchcraft, this court condemns him, the said Gilles, to be this day taken in a cart from this spot to the place of execution, accompanied by the executioner (*maître exécuteur de la haute justice*), where he, by the said executioner, shall be tied to a stake and burned alive, and that his ashes be then scattered to the winds. The court further condemns him, the said Gilles, to the costs of this prosecution.

" Given at Dôle, this 18th day of January, 1573."

In 1574 was hanged at Paris a sorcerer who denounced more than one hundred and fifty persons, of whom several were executed being found guilty of having committed horrible profanations upon the Host. " Mais ceux qui furent pendus furent conuaincus d'auoir plusiers fois vsé de l'hostie consacree en leurs sorcelleries."[83] In the same year was also executed a gentleman who was discovered to have a waxen image the heart of which was pierced by a long bodkin stained with blood.

The same long record of trials continues under Henry III (1574–89), most decadent of monarchs, who spent his days between the caresses of his curled minions and penitential processions of bleeding flagellants to avert the wrath of Heaven. It were tedious and useless to recapitulate condemnation after condemnation. In 1576 Marguerite Pajot was executed at Tonnerre. She had for years attended the Sabbat, caused men to languish and cattle to die, and even slain an accomplice, a wizard who refused for some reason to lend her a Relic of the Wood of the True Cross to employ in her sorceries. In the following year the court of Cœuvres burned Catherine Dorée, who had sacrificed her baby to the Devil who appeared to her as a tall dark man magnificently attired. In 1574 at Valéry-en-Savoie eighty witches perished in one bonfire. One of these wretches confessed that she had been an *eryge*, a heretic practising magic, for upwards of thirty years.

In 1578, Jeanne Harvilliers of Verberie, near Compiègne, was convicted of causing deaths and misfortunes by enchantment. She confessed that she was witch-born, and that her mother had offered her to Satan from the womb. From the time she was twelve years old a stranger, whom she understood to be the Devil, had debauched her. " Et qu'au mesme instant elle eut copulation charnellement auec le Diable, continuant depuis l'aage de douze ans, iusques à cinquante ou enuiron, qu'elle fut prise."[84] It came out in the process of the trial that her mother had been burned as a witch, and the daughter soon met the same fate.

The trial of this woman has an especial interest as it suggested to Jean Bodin his erudite and comprehensive work *De la Demonomanie des Sorciers*, which, first published at Paris, 4to, 1580, ran into several editions : 4to, Paris, 1581 and 1582 ; 8vo, Anvers, 1586 ; " Reueu, corrigé et augmenté," 4to, Paris, 1587 ; " De noueau reueu," 8vo, Anvers, 1593 ; 8vo, Lyon, 1593 ; 16mo, Paris, 1598 ; 12mo, Paris, 1598 ; " Quatriesme édition," 8vo, Lyon, 1598 ; " Edition dernière," 12mo, Rouen, 1604.

Jean Bodin, born at Angers in 1520, died at Laon in 1596. He studied law at Toulouse, and yet unknown at forty years of age visited Paris. Here he soon attracted attention by his legal writings, many of which, however, are very unsound in principle and dangerous. In 1576 he was chosen a deputy of the Third Estate (*tiers état*) to the States-General of Blois, and fourteen years later (1590) he is Attorney-General at Laon. He was a man of shifty and ever-shifting ideas, and his political writings betray an anti-Catholic temper, although he ever clung to the Catholic religion, and was actually buried in the Franciscan Church at Laon. Brunetière assigns Bodin a place in French literature beside Henri Estienne and Amyot.

Throughout France execution now followed execution. In 1583 a were-wolf was burned alive at Orleans ; and in the same year a woman, named Jeanne Bonnet, suffered at Boissy-en-Ferez for having given herself to the embrace of a familiar. Three years later, Marie Martin of Neuf-ville-le-Roi was discovered to be marked with the devil's claw. She confessed she entertained a demon, Cerberus, who escorted her to the Sabbat, but could not save her from the gallows. At Paris a priest, named Sèchelle, was burned on the Place de Grève for sorcery ; and a few months after one Dominic Mirot and his mother-in-law, Marguerite, met the same fate.

It is now fairly well established that the assassination of Henry III on 1 August, 1589, was largely the outcome of constant reports which were assiduously circulating throughout the north of France accusing him of Satanism. The murder of the Cardinal of Lorraine on 23 December, 1588, and the subsequent denunciation of the King from Parisian pulpits as a heretic, deposed, excommunicate, had inflamed popular feeling from rebellion to the highest pitch of civil war, but the charges of devil-worship seem to have determined his death. How far such rumours were well founded it is impossible to say. A contemporary pamphlet of fifteen pages, octavo, *Les sorceleries de Henry de Valois, et les oblations qu'il faisoit au diable dans le bois de Vincennes. Auec la figure des démons, d'argent doré ausquels il faisoit offrandes ; et lesquels se voyent encores en ceste ville*, published at Paris by Didier Millot in 1589,[85] accuses him of having practised Satanism almost openly with D'Epernon and other favourites, and arraigns his homosexuality and sorceries in sternest condemnation. It is said that in a grove of the forest of Vincennes two silver statues of satyrs, each about four feet high, were discovered. Opposite them stood a golden cross in the midst of which was set a splinter of wood, presumed to be a Relic of the True Cross. The tanned skin of a child inscribed with magical characters lay beside the images. Another pamphlet, *Remonstrances à Henry de Valois sur les choses horribles envoyées par un enfant de Paris*, 1589, gives fantastic stories of schools for magic being held at the Louvre, and accuses the King of maintaining a familiar, named Terragon, to whose embraces he compelled a public prostitute to submit herself. Whether Henry III dabbled in occult arts or no, and the evidence is, it must be remembered, violently prejudiced, inimical, and partizan, it was well known at the time that prominent Leaguers attempted the King's death by fashioning his image in wax, and piercing it with long pins to the heart. But the knife of Jacques Clément proved more efficacious than their bodkins and needles.

During the reign of Henry IV (1589–1610) there are the same lengthy and detailed records, year after year, of witch-trials and executions. In 1597 a certain Chamouillard was hanged and burned for having by his charms rendered a young demoiselle de la Barrière sterile and unable to perform the marriage act ;[86] and in the same year Jean Belon, the rector of St.-Pierre des Lampes, in the diocese of Bourges, was put to death for using evil enchantments. At Riom Vidal de la Porte was condemned as a *nœur de l'aiguillette*,[87] by whose spells not only youths, but even dogs, cats, and other animals were rendered impotent. At Angers a were-wolf, Jacques

Roulet, who had been discovered devouring the flesh of a child he had just strangled, was burned alive. He accused his brother and his cousin of also being addicted lycanthropy.

Pierre Aupetit, Vicar of Pageas, a village near Chalu in the province of Limousin, who was sent to the stake at Bordeaux in 1598, made a long and detailed confession. He acknowledged that he had attended Sabbats for twenty years past, generally in the landes of Mathegoutte or at Puy-de-Dôme. He had frequently celebrated the black mass in honour of Satan, who taught him to pronounce in a mocking tone the words "Beelzebub! Beelzebub!" after the consecration. He confected and used a certain poison, a black powder, by means of which he had killed several persons, notably one Jean Maume and a man named Pichin. He also administered aphrodisiacs to young girls, of whom he had bebauched a large number.

Bordeaux and Rouen seem to have been two great centres of witch executions during this period and the archives of both cities teem with accounts of condemnations to the stake.

In 1598 a great sensation was caused at Paris by a girl some twenty years old, Marthe Brossier, the daughter of a weaver, who declared herself possessed. The Bishop of Orleans who had examined her declared the case a fraud. When she was sprinkled with ordinary water she fell into convulsions thinking it to be holy water, and on one occasion an adroit priest read a passage from Petronius which by her screams and frantic gestures she obviously believed to be the *Ritual*. When the family, however, appeared in the capital these facts were, of course, carefully kept concealed, and Henri de Gondi, Bishop of Paris, appointed five physicians to examine the girl, who was also exorcised at Ste-Geneviève by the Capuchins. The whole case seemed exceedingly doubtful, and the patient began to show even more extraordinary signs of possession. It may well be that although she began with imposture her state predisposed her to actual demoniac obsession, of which unmistakable symptoms showed themselves. The affair made a great noise; the Parliament interfered and directed that the girl and her father should be sent to Romartin and kept under surveillance. However, Alexander de la Rochefoucauld, abbé of St.-Martin, apparently convinced of their sincerity, protected them, until by his championship he came in collision with the King, and considerable trouble ensued. It would seem that, as I have suggested above, we have in the case of Marthe Brossier, an admixture of conscious fraud, hysteria, no doubt, and something which goes deeper.[88]

The title of the following pamphlet, 12mo, no date but 1610, tells its own tale : *Discours prodigieux et espouuantable du Thresorier & Baquier du Diable & son fils ; qui ont esté brusles à Vesouz en la Frache Comté le 18 Januier 1610. Apres auoir confessé vne infinité de malefices et sorcelleries par eux comises. Ensemble le moyen comme ils furent descouuers. Auec la copie de l'Arrest du Parlement de Dole. Lyon. Iean Doret.* Mansfredo Dorlady, and Fernando, his son, were denounced by Georges Roulet as holding the unique position of bankers to the Devil. He swore that he had been presented with a draft for money by a tall dark man who, as he after-wards discovered, was none other than Satan, and that it was immediately honoured by the house of Dorlady. He was closely interrogated, and persisted in his tale, adding a quantity of extraordinary details concerning a toad, which was believed to be a familiar. Dorlady and his son were arrested, confessed under torture, and were burned at Vesoul, 18 January, 1610.

It may be well briefly to consider here three figures of prime importance in the history of French Witchcraft, Nicolas Remy, Henri Boguet, and Pierre de Lancre.

Born at Charmes in 1530 Nicolas Remy,[89] after having filled various legal positions of importance, in 1575 was appointed secretary to Duke Charles III of Lorraine, and in the following year a member of the supreme judicial court of Nancy. His business was not only concerned with trials in the bailiwick of Nancy itself, but it was also his duty to examine into, confirm or dismiss, any appeals which were made from the other courts throughout Lorraine, and it was owing to his activities in this function that he gained the reputation of the scourge of witches. During the fifteen years (1576–91) he held this office he pronounced or ratified about nine hundred capital sentences against sorcerers, that is to say some sixty a year, an average of more than one a week. In 1591 he became procurator-general, and as such was armed with almost unlimited powers of control

over all the courts of justice in the whole duchy. Not only
did he encourage the magistrates to exercise the utmost
vigilance in the pursuit, and the most unrelenting severity in
their condemnation, of witches, but he himself journeyed up
and down the province examining suspects, searching out
even the most remote villages and hamlets, and inquiring
into all cases of witchcraft with tireless energy. Remy died in
1612. He was a man of considerable learning, and among
his compositions are several historical works of value,
especially a *History of Lorraine.* But the most famous of his
productions is his *Demonolatry,* a vast collection of trials and
examinations of witches, with amplest details upon the
Sabbat, their enchantments, magic practices, spells and
harms, culled from hundreds of confessions. It is, indeed,
a terrible, and in some sense an awe-inspiring, volume.
*Nicolai Remigii, Sereniss. ducis Lotharingiæ a consiliis
interioribus et in eius ditione lotharingica cognitoris publici*
DÆMONOLATRIÆ *libri tres, ex iudiciis capitalibus nongentorum
plus minus hominum, qui sortilegii crimen intra annos
quindecim in Lotharingia capite luerunt.*[90]

At the same time as Remy was prosecuting his crusade
in Lorraine, Henri Boguet, president of the tribunal of Saint-
Claude, in the province of Burgundy, was displaying an
equal activity and no less severity in his pursuit of witches
throughout the district of the Jura. It has been calculated
that he ordered at least six hundred executions, many of
these being upon charges of lycanthropy.

By 1590 Boguet had published his famous *Discours des
Sorciers avec six advis en faiet de Sorcelerie et une instruction
pour un Juge en semblable matière,*[91] a book which ran into
at least eleven editions. In spite of this it is, however, very
rare owing to the fact that Boguet's family and heirs bought
up every copy they could find to destroy them. The
Instruction is dedicated to " M. Romanet, juge à Salins,"
and consists of ninety-one articles. The merest suspicion of
sorcery is enough to insure the arrest of the accused, who
must be most carefully watched by the magistrate. Should
the prisoner not shed a tear, should he fix his eyes on the
ground, should he mutter to himself, above all should he
utter any oath or blasphemy, there is a strong presumption
of guilt. It is well for a clerk to be concealed behind a curtain,

who may take down an exact record of the interrogations. Wise physicians should search the prisoner to discover the Devil's mark. Boguet does not approve of the custom of some judges who promise release after a full confession and then do not hesitate to break their word. Any witness may be admitted, even a child. The fitting punishment is the stake. Witches may be strangled and their dead bodies consumed to ashes, but it is fitting that were-wolves, as specially heinous offenders, be burned alive. No doubt the learned Daniel Romanet was vastly edified by this treatise, the provisions of which he probably put into practice. Boguet died in 1619.

In 1603 a certain Seigneur de Saint-Pé complained to the Parliament of Bordeaux of the fearful increase of witches, who even held their Sabbat not far from his manor, whereupon orders were given that two judges should form a commission extraordinary to visit the whole district of Bayonne and Labourd, a locality which was terribly infected. The two councillors who went out on this special circuit were Jean d'Espagnet and Pierre de Lancre. The writings of the latter not only give us a full account of the trials and examinations, but the amplest possible details upon the Sabbat and every abomination of Witchcraft. It must be remembered that De Lancre was a scholar, a patron and follower of the fine arts, a writer of no inconsiderable power and precision, a clear-headed shrewd observer of men and manners. The works of De Lancre are as follows : *Tableau de l'inconstance et instabilité de toutes choses, où il est monstré, qu'en Dieu seul gist la vraye Constance à laquelle l'homme sage doit viser.* . . . *Seconde édition. Paris. La vefue Abel L'Angelier.* 4to, 1610 and 1611, a treatise afterwards revised and expanded as *Tableav de l'inconstance des mavvais anges et démons, ov il est amplement traicté des sorciers et de la sorcelerie. Livre très vtile et nécessaire, non seulement aux Iuges, mais à tous ceux qui viuent soubs les loix chrestiennes. Avec vn discours contenant la procedure faicte par les Inquisiteurs d'Espagne et de Nauarre à 53 magiciens, apostats, Iuifs, et sorciers, en la ville de Logrogne en Castille, le 9 nouembre, 1610. En laquelle on voit combien l'exercice de la iustice en France est plus iuridiquement traicté et auec de plus belles formes qu'en tous austres empires, royaumes, républiques et estats. Paris, Barjon,* 4to, 1612.[92] Ten years later De Lancre published

L'incredvlité et mescréance dv sortilege plainement convaincve. Ov il est amplement et cvrievsement traicté de la verité ou illusion du sortilege, de la fascination, de l'attouchement, du scopelisme, de la diuination, de la ligature ou liaison magique, des apparitions, et d'vne infinité d'autres rares et nouueaux subjects. Paris, Nic. Bvon., 4to. A very rare and little-known, but most important work of De Lancre is his *Du Sortilège, ou il est traicté s'il est plus expédient de supprimer et tenir soubs silence les abominations et maléfices des sorciers que les publier et manifester,* 1627, 4to. These writings are of the greatest value, and I have largely relied upon them in my account of the Sabbat and other evil practices of the witches in the sixteenth and seventeenth centuries. De Lancre sent to the stake a large number of sorcerers,[93] and his drastic measures went far to stamp out the evil. He found St. Jean de Luz a centre for the witchcrafts of a wide district and here the execution fires blazed brightly. Actually the last person burned for sorcery in this town seems to have been a Portuguese woman of rank, who was discovered to have secreted the Host for magical purposes. While her case was being investigated before the Bishop of Bayonne in the crypt of the church, a mob of terrified fishermen, on the eve of starting for Newfoundland, burst in, tore her out of the church, and dragged her to the market-place where they flung her into a huge pyre which had been previously kindled. They averred they dare not set sail if so foul a blasphemy were not summarily expiated. The Bishop's *procés-verbal* of the happenings is still extant in the archives of the Mairie.[94]

The tale of those executed by De Lancre is uncertain, but during the years 1609–10 so many witches were sent to Bordeaux for punishment that the prisons were found insufficient to contain the multitude of guilty. De Lancre died at Paris about the year 1630.

The seventeenth century in France is especially remarkable for the number of cases in which convents became the scenes of Witchcraft and demoniac possession. It seemed as though the forces of evil were launching their whole strength against the houses of prayer and contemplation, boldly storming the very citadels of God. As early as 1551 the religious of the convent of Uvertet in the province of Hoorn in Holland were seized with a mysterious malady which was shrewdly suspected to have no natural origin. In a house of Bridgettines near Xante the sisters imagined themselves transformed into various animals and with loud shrieks imitated the bleating of sheep, the squealing of pigs, the lowing of cows, and other strange bestial sounds. The cloisters of Hessimont near Nieumeghe were haunted by a low sweet music which stirred the heart to passionate longings and an agony of sensual desire. About 1560 the nuns of a convent of Nazareth at Cologne were suspected by the episcopal visitor to be obsessed. Upon examination they avowed that the convent was the resort of incubi with whom they indulged in the most unbridled licentiousness. It was, in fact, proved that many of them had been deflowered, but their paramours were never traced. The ecclesiastical authorities, sore grieved and alarmed, treated the guilty with the utmost severity. At Hensberg, in the duchy of Cleves, the sisters complained of having seen men, who glided along the corridors noiselessly and vanished like shadows, in the actual clausura where no man could possibly be.

The Order of Ursulines, founded under episcopal approbation by S. Angela de Merici in 1535, for the purpose of educating young girls, spread through Italy, Germany, and France with extraordinary rapidity. Already in 1544, when approved by Paul III, several centres of great importance were established, and two large and influential Congregations, the Congregation of Paris and the Congregation of Bordeaux, had been organized in France alone. In 1574, moreover, Françoise de Bermond had opened a house at Avignon, and some twenty years later a convent was instituted at Aix, which became famous as the school attended by all maidens of good birth throughout the district, many of whom were attracted to the religious life and after their own period of tutelage, taking the vows required by the Order,[95] remained on to instruct and train new-comers. Among these was Madeleine de Mandol, youngest daughter of Antoine Demandols de la Palud and Françoise Glandevès-Gréoulx, his lady, who had sent their child at a tender age to the Ursulines of Marseilles, whence later she had been transferred to the house at Aix. The director of this convent, a priest of an intensely mystical turn of mind, was a converted Huguenot, Father Romillon. During the year 1609 he took note that Sister Madeleine, and another nun, Louise Capel, who seems to have been one of the few inmates not of aristocratic birth, were attacked by a strange disorder, which did not yield to any natural remedies. So hideous were their convulsions, so extravagant their gestures, that the good priest determined to exorcise them, which he accordingly did in the sacristy of the chapel, so that no scandal might be given. The two patients fell into the most terrible paroxysms as the words of the ritual were pronounced ; their cries and screams filled the assistants with horror ; now they yelled in piercing tones, now howled with a deep gruff clamour that could hardly be believed to issue from the throats of two frail women. Madeleine at length fell into a comatose trance and averred that she was possessed by Beelzebub, Leviathan, Verrine, and many other devils, to whom she had succumbed owing to the incantations of a priest of Marseilles, Louis Gaufridi.[96] She further alleged that he had debauched when she was but a child of nine years, and that she had been compelled by him to nameless infamy and debauch.

Louis Gaufridi was born at Beauvezer, a village of Colmars, situate on the right bank of the river Verdon, in 1572. He was educated by his uncle, Christophe Gaufridi, a priest of Pouvrières, from whose care he passed to Marseilles, where he distinguished himself by his eagerness for study and a memory unusually retentive and adroit. It would seem that these qualities, to which must be added a handsome face and elegant manners, recommended to the notice of M. de Demandols, who possessed estates which were bordered by the Verdon. Soon after his ordination he was appointed vicar of Accoules (Marseilles), and here he had opportunity for constant intercourse with Madeleine de la Palud, who was his penitent, and whom he sacrilegiously violated whilst she was yet a child.

When after some eighteen months Father Romillon found himself unable to free the two nuns, he appealed to the saintly Sebastian Michaelis,[97] a Dominician of great learning and authority, who was then at St.-Maximin. By his advice the sisters were brought to the sacred grotto, La Sainte-Baume, hallowed by the tears and penances of S. Mary Magdalen, and there exorcised by Father Francis Domptius, O.P., who was reputed to be well skilled in these matters.

Again and again the possessed launched the same accusations against Gaufridi ; there were the same scenes of hideously unnatural agitation and violence, twisted limbs, staring eyes, blanched faces, champing mouths that dripped with foam and poured forth fetid blasphemies and obscenities beyond all human imagining.

To relate the horrible story in all its details were super-fluous. On the 5 February, 1611, Father Michaelis, who came to Aix to preach a Lenten course in the Cathedral, submitted his depositions to the civil authorities and demanded the arrest of Gaufridi as a sorcerer, an apostate, a heretic soiled with nameless crimes. This relegated the affair to Guillaume Du Vair (ob. 1621), who although a priest, had been appointed by Henry IV as Intendant-General of Marseilles, and a little later had established himself at Aix with the powers and pomp of a viceroy. A man of bitter and acrid temper his justice became cruelty, his government a tyranny. Even his apologist Sapey is bound to acknowledge that his despotic rule caused him to be hated, and many memoirs of the time speak of him with loathing and contempt. Proud in his bearing, little in his ideas, rough in his speech, unhappy in his temper, he met with a tart rebuff from Richelieu, who publicly accosted him with : " Sir, no man has ever entered upon the office you hold with fairer opportunities ; no man has acquitted himself therein with greater discredit."

On the 19 February, 1611, a commission was issued to one de Séguiran, a councillor, to arrest Louis Gaufridi, accused of rape, seduction, magic, sorcery, blasphemy, and other heinous and abominable offences.

Madeleine de la Palud was interrogated during three days, 21, 22, 23 February, by President Thoron when she made the amplest confession concerning witchcrafts of every kind, especially the Sabbat at which she had frequently assisted. There she had worshipped the Prince of the Synagogue (for so the coven was called), a man, Lucifer's lieutenant, in effect Gaufridi himself. All present renounced the Holy Trinity, their baptism, and the Catholic Faith. A banquet was spread at several tables, some of which were piled with goodly viands and wine ; upon others was served the roast flesh of newly slain infants. Lewd dances were performed, and bawdy songs sung. Each day of the week had its own sexual observances, proceeding to the most infamous conjunctions. The black mass in honour of Satan was celebrated, sometimes by Gaufridi, sometimes by some other wretch, the Host being often thrown to a dog, and the Sacred Blood being scattered over the vile crew who shouted : " Sanguis eius super nos et super filios nostros." Upon one occasion a dog who had been led in to devour the consecrated Species, stretched out his paws in adoration before God's Body and bowed his head, nor could kicks and blows compel him to stir. Several broke in floods of tears and began to bewail their sins, after which it was decreed that in future the Host should be defiled and trodden under foot, but that no dogs should be admitted. There seems no reason to doubt that this confession is substantially true, and that these foul rites had been for several years practised by a gang of infamous wretches under conditions of all but inviolable secrecy.

Gaufridi, who was thrown into prison on the 20 February, made a complete avowal of his iniquities, his sorceries and seductions of religious. It is true that he was tortured according to the usage of the day, but none the less his story seems to be proven in every particular, and not merely wrung from him by the torments of the question. It was published under fifty-three articles in a rare pamphlet, *Confession faicte par messire Loys Gaufridi, prestre en l'église des Accoules de Marseille, prince des magiciens depuis Constantinople jusqu'à Paris, à deux pères capuchins du couvent d'Aix, la veille de Pâques, le onzième avril mil six cent onze. A Aix, par Jean Tholozan, imprimeur du roi et de la dicte Ville*. MVCXI.

On 30 April, Gaufridi was publicly degraded from all ecclesiastical order by Monsignor Turicella, a Florentine, erstwhile confessor to Maria de' Medici, now Bishop of Marseilles, and delivered over to secular justice. About five o'clock in the afternoon he was burned at the stake before an immense concourse of people.

Madeleine de la Palud and Louise Capel were both expelled from the convent by the Ursulines. Of the latter nothing more is known, but the principal actress in these scandals was reduced to penury and was seen to beg her bread in the streets. In after years she apparently inherited her father's estates, for she bestowed de la Palud upon the discalced Trinitarians as a suitable site for a church and monastery.

In 1653 she was accused of having cast an evil spell upon Madeleine Houdol, but she managed to clear herself, although according to one account she was condemned to perpetual imprisonment. This would appear to have been an easy relegation to a convent or some institution, and there is a tradition that she was alive as late as 1669.[98]

There was an extraordinary sequel to the scandals and sorceries of Aix when some two years after three Bridgittines of the convent of S. Bridget of Sweden at Lille, Sisters Francoise Bolonnais, Catherine Fournier, and Imbert, declared themselves to be possessed. They fell into violent paroxysms, vomited strange substances, spoke in divers tongues normally unknown to them, Hebrew, Greek, English, Spanish, and in short gave every sign of Satanic disease. In their convulsions they accused a nun, Marie de Sains, who until then had been accounted a saint far advanced on the mystic way, of having cast an evil spell upon them. When interrogated she denied any such complicity with demons, but none the less she was put under cloistral restraint and carefully watched. Presently Father Sebastian Michaelis and Father Domptius, the two Dominican exorcists, arrived at Lille, and proceeded to examine closely into the affair. Marie de Sains was closely questioned by these experts, and before long she made the most astounding confessions. She swore that she had dedicated herself body and soul, her will, every wish and movement to the powers of hell. She had confected charms to cause sickness and delirium, and these she had secretly fastened to the habits of the nuns, in the straw of their pallets, in some corner of their cells. It was these which caused the possession of the three Sisters, as well as the diabolic attacks on Sister Vandermotte, Sister Launoy, and Sister Peronne, who were now on the verge of madness. The formula for these amulets of evil power had been invented by none other than Louis Gaufridi, who had taught her how to fashion them at the Sabbat. They were composed of the Sacred Host and the Precious Blood, commingled into a paste with a powder made from human and animal bones, the skulls of infants, hair, nails, flesh, the liver, brain, and spleen of an executed murderer, and the semen of a sorcerer. She further avowed that she had slain a number of young children, many of whom she had cut open alive to offer their agonized and writhing limbs as a sacrifice to the Devil. Some she had suffocated ; others she had put to death in exquisite torments. Several she had crucified in mockery of the Cross of Calvary. She added the most obscene details concerning the debaucheries of the Sabbat, where she had abandoned herself to every species of lewdness, defiling her body with the demons, with goats and dogs. What is even more surprising she uttered long dissertations upon the coming of Anti-Christ and expounded the more obscure prophecies of the Apocalypse. The Man of Sin was the offspring of a witch and a demon, he was baptized by Gaufridi, and ere long would be manifested upon earth. In hideous mimicry of the mission of S. John Baptist, he also would be distinguished by a precursor, the son of Gaufridi and Madeleine de la Palud. The wretched woman was discovered to be pregnant, and she acknowledged she had already given birth to two children, the father of the first being a warlock who had deflowered her during the orgies of the Sabbat, the father of the second Gaufridi. Another sister, named Didyme, and a novice, Simonne Dourlet, were intimately concerned in these abominations. Frantic and extravagant as much of the confession of Marie de Sains was ; in some details, humanly speaking, impossible ; it was established beyond all doubt that a very substantial amount of fact underlay her ravings. She had for many years managed to creep out of the convent secretly at night, helped by her accomplices and sometimes accompanied by them. She was wont to resort to a den of Satanists, where the lubric scenes she rehearsed in such detail were actually transacted. Her brain was obviously unsettled by her debaucheries, but even at this distance of time it is possible to disentangle to some extent the false from the true in her story. We know that the witches had a very ample knowledge of toxicants and drugs, and a subtly administered potion would account for the sickness and distractions of the sisters, whom she probably feared and hated as having some suspicion or even knowledge of her clandestine excursions.

The Bishop of Mechlin, who caused the case to be examined by a conclave of divines, physicians, and lawyers, declared that such blasphemies and depravity were incredible indeed, but yet he was convinced that much of her confession was only too terribly true. Marie de Sains was condemned by the ecclesiastical court to perpetual imprisonment in the dungeons of Tournai.[99]

The case of the possessions at Loudun has often been told, and famous as it is hardly offers any new details which call for a lengthy investigation. In 1617 Urbain Grandier, a young and gallant priest, good-looking, witty, elegant and eloquent in the pulpit, was appointed vicar of Saint-Pierre du Marché at Loudun. His fascinating exterior, gracious manners, and silvery tongue found him many friends, whilst an overweening pride and intellectual contemptuousness of his colleagues made him not a few enemies. He was vulnerable too ; stories of his amours began soon to circulate. His intrigue with Philippe Trincant, daughter of the procureur of the King at Loudun, resulted in the birth of a child. His relations with several of his penitents were extremely improper, and a young girl Madeleine de Brou, whom he had seduced, was so openly his mistress that considerable scandal ensued to the great chagrin of certain holy Carmelites and Capuchins, belonging to the houses of those orders at Loudun. With fatal imprudence in 1617 Grandier also gave offence to Richelieu, Bishop of Luçon, and at that time in retirement at the priory of Coussay owing to his disfavour with Louis XIII. One account tells us that Grandier refused to allow the Bishop due precedence in a solemn procession ; another story has it that somewhat later he published a satire, *La cordonnière de Loudun*, attacking the mighty minister ; however that may be, upon his return to power Richelieu neither forgot nor forgave. In 1630 the opponents of Grandier laid a complaint before Louis de la Rocheposay, Bishop of Poitiers, accusing him of immorality, and after an inquiry a penance was imposed, and the guilty priest was inhibited *a rebus diuinis* for five years in the diocese and in Loudun itself *in perpetuum*. The following year, however, Henri de Soublis, Archbishop of Bordeaux, quashed the whole proceedings.

Reports were now current that several of the Sisters of the Ursuline convent at Loudun were possessed. The superior, Sister Jeanne des Anges (in the world Madame de Beleiel), had been seized with a succession of alarming fits which shortly communicated themselves to other religious. It was whispered that phantoms had been seen in the cloister, and strangely hollow voices heard to mutter and gibber during the

still night watches. The director of the nuns, Mignon, called
in several Carmelite Fathers to help him in exorcising the
afflicted, and presently they had resource to the vicar of
Saint-Jacques at Chinon, Pierre Barrè, a priest of austere
and severely simple life. After long preparation the superior
and a lay sister Jeanne Dumagnoux were exorcised according
to the ritual. The superior at the first words fell into fearful
paroxysms, her face seemed to alter to that of a grinning
fiend, a circumstance which filled the bystanders with no
ordinary fear ; her tongue, black and swollen, was thrust
from her parched and cracking lips ; her skin dripped with
sweat ; her limbs which seemed endued with an unnatural
elasticity writhed and twisted in all directions ; her body
balloonered to an immense size ; whilst a harsh mocking
voice growled out that two devils, Asmodeus and Zabulon,
possessed her. Again and again were the exorcisms renewed,
and the patients began loudly to accuse Grandier of having
bewitched them. After a while two magistrates, Messire
Guillaume Cerisay de la Guerinière, seneschal of the district,
and Messire Louis Chauvet, lieutenant civil, attended to take
the depositions of the possessed. The proceedings now
dragged on for several months and made a great noise.
Grandier was warned of his peril, but seemed to despise the
danger. Several new exorcists were summoned, notably
Father Lactance, a well-known Franciscan of spotless
integrity, and Father Tranquille of Saint-Rémi, a Capuchin.
The possessed nuns were exorcised in the church, which was
crowded with people, and reiterated their charges against
Grandier, who had, they asserted, entered into a close
compact with the lords of hell. It so happened that the
all-powerful Jean de Laubardemont was at Loudun to
superintend the destruction of the castle of that town. He
issued orders for the arrest of Grandier, who was accordingly
thrown into prison on the 30 November, 1633. The evidence
of the exorcists, the Carmelites and Capuchins, was carefully
taken ; the court examined the sisters again and again ;
divines and physicians attended the exorcisms and watched
the possessed Ursulines night and day ; Grandier, at whose
house a heretical document of the most incriminating nature
was discovered, was interrogated with unwearied patience.
The surgeon Mannouri was charged to search the prisoner

for the Devil's mark, and reported that he had found two places on his body insensible to any probe, although a needle had been inserted some inches into the flesh. At length, on the 18 August, 1634, the tribunal condemned Grandier to the stake. The unfortunate wretch was declared to have been " duly tried and convicted of the crime of magic, of injuries and possessions practised upon the persons of several Ursuline nuns of this town of Loudun, as well as upon other seculars," whereupon after having made public confession of his faults " before the principal door of the church of Saint-Pierre du Marché, and before that of Sainte-Ursule of this town " he was to be taken " to the public place of Sainte-Croix, and fastened to a stake upon a scaffold, which shall be erected upon the said place, and there to be burnt alive, together with all the compacts and magical characters used by him, as well as the manuscript book composed by him against the celibacy of priests ; and his ashes scattered to the wind."

Before this sentence was carried out Grandier was put to the question, ordinary and extraordinary. He was then conveyed to the various churches, where the public acts of reparation were to be performed in a low cart, and thence to the place of execution. All this was done on the same day, the sentence having been pronounced as early as five o'clock, and the burning being accomplished about four in the afternoon. It is noteworthy that the possession of the nuns did not cease at Grandier's death, but that they were tormented for several years more. The famous Jesuit, Jean-Joseph Surin (1600–65), celebrated as a mystical director, a true saint—" consumed with spirituality," is Bossuet's phrase—was sent to Loudun to exorcise the harassed Ursulines. He was so horrified at the terrible sacrileges intended for three desecrated Hosts that a physical breakdown of health and a long-continued psychic obsession resulted, but with heroic charity he persevered in his task and after three years, in 1637, the unhappy victims were freed. From that time sister Jeanne des Anges, who had been so grievously tormented, was rewarded with heavenly consolations and died a holy death in 1665.[100]

Throughout the whole history of Witchcraft there is no history so infamous as that of Madeleine Bavent, Mathurin

Picard, and Thomas Boullé. Nowhere have I read so hideous a confession. The details are so utterly abominable that even the soul of a priest steeped in the fires of the confessional, whom no human aberration can shock or surprise, shudders and sickens at the dark mass of turpitudes which are as the stench and vomit of the pit of hell.

In 1616 at Louviers, a busy little old-world town of Normandy situate on the river Eure, some seven-and-twenty miles from Rouen, was founded the convent of S. Louis IX and S. Elizabeth of Hungary, for a community of Regular Tertiaries of the Third Franciscan Order. Their first director was an old priest named David, shortly to be succeeded by Mathurin Picard, the vicar of Mesnil-Jourdain, whose curate, Thomas Boullé, assisted him, and upon his death in 1642 was installed with full responsibility in his room. By some unhappy fate—it was more than mere chance without design—all three were adherents of the Manichees, concealing their Satanism under a guise of orthodox sanctity. From the commencement they set to work to corrupt the hapless religious whose faithful pastors and guardians they should have been, and instead of lifting their souls to heaven they dragged them down to the nethermost inferno. As early as 1634 there were indications that something was seriously amiss. Two or three Sisters were seized with fits of an abnormal nature, now standing rigid in some paralytic trance, now foaming on the ground in an epilepsy and writhing as some boneless contortionist of the circus arena. Matters, however, seem to have been hushed up for a while, although the infamous Picard ran some danger of being exposed. He was, in truth, the Chief Officer and Grand-Master of all the witches and devil-worshippers throughout the district. Having seduced and entirely subjected to his will an unfortunate nun, Madeleine Bavent, he used her as his instrument, his associate, and intermediary. There can be no doubt, I think, that Picard must have possessed extraordinary hypnotic powers, and Madeleine Bavent is probably not to be accounted morally responsible for the orgy of crime into which she was plunged. The details are known from the confession which she wrote in prison at the instance of the Abbé de Marets, an Oratorian, who helped and counselled her in those hours of penitence and remorse. Several nights a week she was awakened just before Matins, that is to say about midnight, by one of the nuns, and conducted to the Sabbat. It is clear that Picard had provided himself with false keys so that he could gain admission to any part of the cloister at any hour. She declared that she never used any ointment or recited any spell, but that she was conveyed to the Sabbat by the power of Picard without knowing how she arrived there, obviously in a state of trance. The exact place where the Sabbat took place she could not identify, but it was presumably in some house not far from the convent. It was a long and narrow room, lighted by flares and the candles upon the Devil's altar which had been erected there. This certainly suggests a cellar. A number of persons dressed as priests were present, and some in grotesque masking habits, half-animal, half-human. She never assisted at any adoration of the demon in the form of a he-goat, and the rites were seldom followed by a banquet. The Black Mass of Satan was continually said at the altar. The host appeared to be of a red colour, and communion was given to the worshippers. The liturgy was read from a book of blasphemies, which was also carried in procession. It contained the most hideous maledictions against all things sacred and divine, and seems to have been a manuscript rather than a printed book. There was also a register or roll of the Satanists in which her name had been inscribed by David. This was kept with the utmost care and Madeleine was never told the names of any who were present. She recognized four religious from her own house, Catherine of the Cross, Catherine of S. Geneviève, Elizabeth of the Nativity, and Anne Barré, also Thomas Boullé and several other priests whom she knew only by sight, probably as having served the convent chapel. Prominent among the assistants were an elderly man with iron-grey hair, who was generally richly dressed in a purple velvet suit, and a matron, said to be Mother Frances of the Cross (in the world Simonne Gangain), a co-foundress of the Louviers convent, who ordinarily resided at Paris. It is impossible to relate certain abominations and unnatural defilements of the Blessed Sacrament which these evil priests practised. The details are frankly too monstrous for reproduction.[101] The wretched woman further related : " On the Good Friday night of one year Picard and Boullé brought with them four Hosts ; two of these they put in their own mouths, and the other two into Mother Simonne's mouth and mine; then they exchanged theirs for ours in order to cement for ever the union and connexion between us. One night, after the book of blasphemies had been carried in procession, a little crucifix was brought in and large Hosts were nailed to the hands and feet of the figure of Christ, and each one present stabbed the Hosts with a sharp knife. There fell two or three drops of blood, which were gathered up carefully and preserved with the Hosts to confect a charm." " I cannot but believe," she cried in tones of utter despair, " that this is a renewal of the Crucifixion of Our Lord." On one occasion a priest brought a Host to burn it; and another time a priest brought a chalice half-filled with the Precious Blood, which they poured out over the floor. One Holy Saturday a woman handed over to these men-devils her newly born child. The babe was crucified on a rough cross, its little hands and feet being fastened to the wood with nails which pierced large Hosts. Two men, who had ventured to the Sabbat out of curiosity, filled with horror at the spectacle refused to take part in the orgies of lust and murder. They were not allowed to leave the house alive. Picard used to delight to subject the miserable Madeleine to the most infamous sexual connexions, to prostitute her publicly before the fiendish assembly. In fine, the pages of de Sade contain nothing fouler than the confessions of this wretched woman; the most cruel and obscene episodes of *Justine* or *Juliette* pale before the sworn statement of this demoniac nun.

Mathurin Picard died in 1642, and was buried in the chapel of the Franciscans, near the choir grille. No doubt Boullé, who succeeded him, could not maintain the same magnetic influence over the Sisters as their late director, and the master-mind removed conscience began to make itself heard. Several religious sickened of a strange malady, and were driven almost to madness by their guilt and the pangs of remorse. They uttered piercing cries, accusing themselves of hideous crimes. Fear fell upon them, and before long some twenty inmates of the house were in the last stages of nervous disorder, broken in spirit and body. The thing could not be hid, and early in 1643 the Bishop of Evreux, Monsignor François Péricard, determined to begin a thorough investigation. He was assisted by several Capuchin fathers of great tact and experience. The nuns soon made the most alarming confessions, mortally implicating Madeleine Bavent, who they seem to have regarded as the chief instrument of their undoing, the dead Picard, the living Boullé. The good Bishop did not delay to promulgate his sentence. Madeleine Bavent was to be degraded from religion and imprisoned for life ; the body of Picard was no longer to be suffered to remain in consecrated earth, but to be disinterred and flung with contumely into a ditch, le Puits Cronier, which lay outside the boundaries of the town ; Boullé was pronounced worthy of death. This judgement was delivered on 12 March, 1643, and before a few months were out Monsignor Péricard, heart-broken at the insults offered to the Most Holy Sacrament, had sunk into an untimely grave. Secular justice stepped in, and the accused were transferred to Rouen. Delay followed delay, and procrastination procrastination, until after four years a final condemnation was issued by the supreme courts. On 21 August, 1647, Thomas Boullé, after having humbly begged pardon of God and the King before the principal door of Rouen Cathedral, was degraded from all ecclesiastical order, and burned alive in the market-square. The corpse of Picard was flung into the same fire. Madeleine Bavent remained in close confinement, and ended her days forgotten in a dungeon. At first she revolted against her doom, and attempted suicide, wounding her throat with a knife she had concealed and thrusting it into her side. She also swallowed glass, and would have starved herself to death. In time a deep resignation succeeded, but there is no further record of her fate.[102]

The reign of Louis XIII, 1610–43, is signalized by no decrease in the number of witch-trials, and executions were numerous. In 1610 the Parliament of Bordeaux sent to the flames four Spanish witches, old gipsies, three men and one woman, who were accused of commerce with evil spirits, of having ridden through the air on magic besoms, of destroying persons, cattle, and the fruits of the earth by their malefic craft. They were denounced by a priest upon whom they had endeavoured to cast a spell.[103] In 1615–16 took place an important series of trials at Orleans when a gang of no less than twenty-one devil-worshippers was discovered. The whole facts are related at length by De Lancre. Three managed to fly, but the rest were first strangled and then burned. For many years they had secretly attended Sabbats, at which the Black Mass with all its abominations, followed by an unspeakable riot of lust and blasphemy, was continually celebrated. An old villain of seventy-seven, named Silvain Névillon, confessed that on one occasion no less than two hundred persons, many of whom were masqued, had assembled for these orgies. In 1618 the Provost of Londinières hanged eight wretches who were found guilty of attending the Sabbat and adoring Satan there. In fact, the archives of Rouen, Orleans, Bordeaux and other great cities contain an almost innumerable list of trials and condemnation, whilst in their proportion the smaller towns and even villages are no whit behind in their holocausts and hangings.

When Concini, Maréchal d'Ancre, had been shot dead on 24 April, 1617, by the King's gentlemen, and Louis XIII declared himself of age to govern France without the help of his mother, Marie de' Medici, the Louvre was cleared of a whole pack of parasites, sorcerers, astrologers, charlatans in medicine and magic, and Leonora Galigaï, the Maréchal's widow and the Queen's favourite, was brought to trial on accumulated charges of Witchcraft and Satanism. Three grimoires and a large number of strange periapts and amulets were discovered in her apartments, as well as several waxen images stuck full of black pins. It was proved that she habitually consulted diviners and empirics, especially relying upon the prediction of the Florentine, Cosmo Ruggieri, who more than forty years before had been vehemently suspected of poisoning Charles IX. She was condemned to death, and beheaded on Saturday, 8 July, 1617, at the Place de Grève, the body afterwards being consumed in a huge bonfire. Political animus, no doubt, sealed her doom, but it seems quite plain that she was guilty of the crimes laid to her charge.[104]

In 1620 at Nancy a doctor named Poiret was burned being accused of having debauched and bewitched an honourable gentlewoman Marie-Elisabeth de Ranfaing. His accomplice, Anne Boulay, who had escaped to Paris, was captured there, and brought back to Nancy where she suffered the same fate. A special commission of four-and-twenty judges tried the case.[105]

Eight years later Desbordes, an attendant upon Charles IV, Duke of Lorraine, was arrested at the instance of his master upon a suspicion of having hastened the death of the Princess Christina, mother of the Duke, by a deftly mixed potion. Desbordes was greatly feared on account of various marvellous feats he is supposed to have performed, such as causing the figures worked in the arras to leave their station and dance in the midst of the room. It seems probable that he was able to hypnotize the company who witnessed this fantastic round, and other stories point to the fact that he was a clever prestidigitator. In any case his juggleries cost him dear, for being found guilty of sacrilege and magic, he was sent to the stake.[106]

In 1631 at Nancy Melchior de la Vallée was burned as a sorcerer.[107]

About the year 1650, in the reign of Louis XIV, another case of conventual possession occurred. A house of Ursulines at Auxonne was afflicted with a demoniac malady, and two old peasant women were accused of having bewitched the Sisters and their chaplains. The charges were so ill-sustained and the evidence so flimsy that it was impossible for the court to condemn them. They were recommended, however, to leave the district, a verdict which threw the populace into such a state of fury that seizing the hapless prisoners they beat one to death with clubs and stones, and cast the other into the Saône where she was drowned.

In 1669–70 two brothers Ernoul and Charles Barneville lodged a complaint with the Parliament of Rouen concerning the increase of witches in the district of Coutances, Carentan, and Haye du Puits. At once a number of witnesses came eagerly forward and no less than five hundred persons, amongst whom appear the names of a hundred priests, were involved. Two young girls, one seventeen and the other a year older, swore that a boy of eight had taken them to the Sabbat. When examined on the 16 May, 1669, he acknowledged the truth of the accusation. Jeanne de Boulanger made a solemn declaration that one evening she had seen many persons in a remote place dancing naked and performing lewd rites. Another witness Michel Marais had caught sight of several companies who were dancing in a state of nudity. The same story was related by many others, especially by Isaac Marais, who sleeping in a lonely hut in the forest, was awakened by a strange music and peeping through a chink saw a procession of naked persons of both sexes, each one of whom held a black candle burning with a sulphurous blue flame. Jean le Cousteur described the Black Mass at the Sabbat, which was chanted by a priest named Marin, the deacon being Jacques le Gastelois, and the sub-deacon Semion, the base-born child of a trull named Marguerite. Six months and more were spent in searching inquiries, and at length twelve wretches were condemned to immediate execution, and the capital sentence on four-and-thirty was only deferred until after the first burnings. An appeal, however, was made to the King, and Louis after hearing the case commuted the sentences to perpetual banishment. The Parliament, amazed and dumbfounded, protested vigor-ously and addressed the following weighty remonstrance to the monarch who had thus clipped their claws.

" SIRE,—Emboldened by the authority which Your Majesty has committed into our hands in the Province of Normandy, to try and punish offences, and more particularly those offences of the nature of witchcraft, which tend to the destruction of religion and the ruin of nations, We, Your Parliament, remonstrate humbly with Your Majesty upon certain cases of this kind which have been lately brought before us. We cannot permit the letter addressed by Your Majesty's command to the Attorney-General of this district, for the reprieve of certain persons condemned to death for witchcraft, and for the staying of proceedings in several other cases, to remain unnoticed, and without remarking upon the consequences which may ensue. There is also a letter from Your Secretary of State, declaring Your Majesty's intention to commute the punishment of these criminals into one of perpetual banishment, and to submit to the opinion of the Procureur-General, and of the most learned members of the Parliament of Paris, whether, in the matter of witchcraft, the jurisprudence of the Parliament of Rouen is to be followed in preference to that of the Parliament of Paris, and of the other Parliaments of the kingdom which judge differently.
" Although by the ordinances of the Kings your predeces-sors, Parliaments have been forbidden to pay any attention

to *lettres de cachet ;* We, nevertheless, from the knowledge
which We have, in common with the whole kingdom, of the
care bestowed by Your Majesty for the good of your subjects,
and from the submission and obedience to your commandments which We have always manifested, have stayed all
proceedings, in conformity to your orders ; hoping that Your
Majesty, considering the importance of the crime of witchcraft, and the consequences likely to ensue from its impunity,
will be graciously pleased to grant us once more your
permission to continue the trials, and execute judgement
upon those found guilty. And as, since We received the letter
of your Secretary of State, we have also been made acquainted
with the determination of Your Majesty, not only to commute
the sentence of death passed upon these witches into one of
perpetual banishment from the province, but to re-establish
them in the possession of their goods and chattels, and of their
good fame and character, Your Parliament have thought it
their duty, on occasion of these crimes, the greatest which men
can commit, to make you acquainted with the general and
uniform feelings of the people of this Province with regard to
them ; it being, moreover, a question in which are concerned
the glory of God and the relief of your suffering subjects, who
groan under their fears from the threats and menaces of this
sort of persons, and who feel the effects of them every day in
the mortal and extraordinary maladies which attack them,
and the surprising damage and loss of their possessions.

" Your Majesty knows well that there is no crime so
opposed to the commands of God as witchcraft, which
destroys the very foundation of religion, and draws strange
abominations after it. It is for this reason, Sire, that the
Scriptures pronounce the punishment of death against
offenders, and that the Church and the holy Fathers have
fulminated their anathemas, and that canonical decisions
have one and all decreed the most severe punishments, to
deter from this crime : and that the Church of France,
animated by the piety of the Kings Your predecessors, has
expressed so great a horror at it, that, not judging the
punishment of perpetual imprisonment, the highest it has the
power to inflict, sufficiently severe, it has left such criminals
to be dealt with by the secular power.

" It has been the general feeling of all nations that such

criminals ought to be condemned to death, and all the ancients were of the same opinion. The law of the ' Twelve Tables,' which was the principal of the Roman laws, ordains the same punishment. All jurisconsults agreed in it, as well as the constitutions of the Emperors, and more especially those of Constantine and Theodosius, who, enlightened by the Gospel, not only renewed the same punishment, but also deprived, expressly, all persons found guilty of witchcraft of the right of appeal, and declared them to be unworthy of a Prince's mercy. And Charles VIII., Sire, inspired by the same sentiments, passed that fine and severe ordinance (*cette belle et sévère ordonnance*), which enjoined the Judges to punish witches according to the exigencies of the case, under a penalty of being themselves fined or imprisoned, or dismissed from their office ; and decreed, at the same time, that all persons who refused to denounce a witch, should be punished as accomplices ; and that all, on the contrary, who gave evidence against one should be rewarded.

" From these considerations, Sire, and in the execution of so holy an ordinance, your Parliaments, by their decrees, proportion their punishments to the guilt of the offenders ; and your Parliament of Normandy has never, until the present time, found that its practice was different from that of other courts ; for all the books which treat upon this matter cite an infinite number of decrees condemning witches to be burnt, or broken on the wheel, or to other punishments. The following are examples :—In the time of Chilperic,[108] as may be seen in Gregory of Tours, b. vi. c. 35 of his *History of France*,[109] all the decrees of the Parliament of Paris passed according to, and in conformity with, this ancient juris-prudence of the kingdom, cited by Imbert, in his *Judicial Practice ;* all those cited by Monstrelet, in 1459, against the witches of Artois ; the decrees of the same parliament, of the 13 of October 1573, against Mary le Fief, native of Saumur ; of the 21 of October 1596, against the Sieur de Beaumont, who pleaded, in his defence, that he had only sought the aid of the devil for the purpose of unbewitching the afflicted and of curing diseases ; of the 4 of July 1606, against Francis du Bose ; of the 20 of July 1582, against Abel de la Rue, native of Coulommiers ; of the 2 of October 1593, against Rousseau and his daughter ; of 1608, against another Rousseau and

one Peley, for witchcraft and adoration of the Devil at the
Sabbat, under the figure of a he-goat, as confessed by them ;
the decree of 4 of February 1615, against Leclerc, who
appealed from the sentence of the Parliament of Orleans, and
who was condemned for having attended the Sabbat, and
confessed, as well as two of his accomplices, who died in
prison, that he had adored the Devil, renounced his baptism
and his faith in God, danced the witches' dance, and offered
up unholy sacrifices ; the decrees of the 6 of May 1616,
against a man named Leger, on a similar accusation ; the
pardon granted by Charles IX. to Trois Echelles, upon
condition of revealing his accomplices, but afterwards
revoked for renewed sorcery on his part ; the decree of the
Parliament of Paris, cited by Mornac in 1595 ; the judgements
passed in consequence of the commission given by Henry IV.
to the Sieur de l'Ancre, councillor of the Parliament of
Bourdeaux ; of the 20 of March 1619, against Etienne
Audibert ; those passed by the chamber of Nerac, on the 26
of June 1620, against several witches ; those passed by the
Parliament of Toulouse in 1577, as cited by Gregory
Tolosanus,[110] against four hundred persons accused of this
crime, and who were all marked with the sign of the devil.
Besides all these, we might recal to your majesty's recollec-
tion the various decrees of the Parliament of Provence,
especially in the case of Gaufredi in 1611 ; the decrees of the
Parliament of Dijon, and those of the Parliament of Rennes,
following the example of the condemnation of the Marshal de
Rais, who was burned in 1441, for the crime of witchcraft, in
presence of the Duke of Brittany ;—all these examples, Sire,
prove that the accusation of witchcraft has always been
punished with death by the parliaments of Your kingdom,
and justify the uniformity of their practice.

" These, Sire, are the motives upon which Your Parliament
of Normandy has acted in decreeing the punishment of death
against the persons lately brought before it for this crime.
If it has happened that, on any occasion, these Parliaments,
and the Parliament of Normandy among the rest, have
condemned the guilty to a less punishment than that of death,
it was for the reason that their guilt was not of the deepest
dye : Your Majesty, and the Kings Your predecessors,
having left full liberty to the various tribunals to whom they

delegated the administration of justice, to decree such punishment as was warranted by the evidence brought before them.

" After so many authorities, and punishments ordained by human and divine laws, We humbly supplicate Your Majesty to reflect once more upon the extraordinary results which proceed from the malevolence of this sort of people ; on the deaths from unknown diseases, which are often the consequence of their menaces, on the loss of the goods and chattels of Your subjects, on the proofs of guilt continually afforded by the insensibility of the marks upon the accused, on the sudden transportation of bodies from one place to another, on the sacrifices and nocturnal assemblies, and other facts, corroborated by the testimony of ancient and modern authors, and verified by so many eye-witnesses, composed partly of accomplices, and partly of people who had no interest in the trials beyond the love of truth, and confirmed, moreover, by the confessions of the accused parties themselves ; and that, Sire, with so much agreement and conformity between the different cases, that the most ignorant persons convicted of this crime have spoken to the same circumstances, and in nearly the same words, as the most celebrated authors who have written about it, all of which may be easily proved to Your Majesty's satisfaction by the records of various trials before Your Parliaments.

" These, Sire, are truths so intimately bound up with the principles of our religion, that, extraordinary although they be, no person has been able to this time to call them in question. If some have cited, in opposition to these truths, the pretended canon of the Council of Ancyra, and a passage from S. Augustine, in a treatise upon the *Spirit and the Soul*, it has been without foundation ; and it would be easy to convince Your Majesty that neither the one nor the other ought to be accounted of any authority ; and besides that the Canon, in this sense, would be contrary to the opinion of all succeeding Councils of the Church, Cardinal Baronius and all learned commentators agree that it is not to be found in any old edition. In effect, in those editions wherein it is found, it is in another language, and is in direct contradiction to the twenty-third Canon of the same Council, which condemns sorcery, according to all preceding constitutions. Even supposing that this Canon was really promulgated by the Council of Ancyra, we must observe that it was issued in the second century, when the principal attention of the Church was directed to the destruction of paganism. For this reason, it condemns that class of women who said they could pass through the air, and over immense regions, with Diana and Herodias, and enjoins all preachers to teach the falsehood of such an opinion, in order to deter people from the worship of these false divinities ; but it does not question the power of the Devil over the human body, which is, in fact, proved by the holy Gospel of Jesus Christ Himself. And with regard, Sire, to the pretended passage of S. Augustine, every body knows that it was not written by him, because the writer, whoever he was, cites Boethius,[111] who died more than eighty years after the time of S. Augustine. Besides, there is still more convincing proof in the fact, that the same Father establishes the truth of witchcraft in all his writings, and more particularly in his *City of God ;* and in his first volume, question the 25th, wherein he states that sorcery is a communion between man and the Devil, which all good Christians ought to look upon with horror.

" Taking all these things into consideration, Sire, the officers of Your Parliament hope, from the justice of Your Majesty, that you will be graciously pleased to receive the humble remonstrances they have taken the liberty to make. They are compelled, for the acquittal of their own consciences and in discharge of their duty, to make known to Your Majesty, that the decrees they passed against the sorcerers and witches brought before them were passed after a mature deliberation on the part of all the judges present, and that nothing has been done therein which is not conformable to the universal jurisprudence of the kingdom, and for the general welfare of Your Majesty's subjects, of whom there is not one who can say that he is secure from the malevolence of such criminals. We therefore supplicate Your Majesty to suffer us to carry into effect the sentences we passed, and to proceed with the trial of the other persons accused of the same crime ; and that the piety of Your Majesty will not suffer to be introduced during Your reign an opinion contrary to the principles of that Holy Religion for which You have always employed so gloriously both Your Cares and Your Arms."

The only response returned to this appeal was a stern injunction that the prosecutions were immediately to be suspended, and the Parliament dared not disobey. In 1682 Louis XIV published various directions with regard to the witch-trials, which were not only extremely significant, but of the utmost importance in practice. Magicians and fortune-tellers are to be punished as rogues and charlatans ; severe penalties are incurred by those who endeavour to work spells or operate enchantments by the abuse of prayers or litanies ; death is the portion of those who to evil superstitions add any sacrilege for the sake of necromancy or evocation of spirits. In fine, the edict is directed against common cheats, against blasphemers and Satanists,[112] against poisoners and murderers who cloak their villainies under a masque of magic. Until the passing of this statute, and indeed for some years later, the witch-fires still blazed brightly throughout France. Thus in 1684 at Rouen several men and women were hanged and then burned for making a pact with the Devil, and in the following year a priest, accused of sorcery, was sent to the stake and suffered in the Market Place. In 1699, however, the Parliament of Rouen commuted the sentence of death pronounced by the magistrates of Valognes upon a certain Marie Bucaille, to perpetual banishment. This woman, who had for a long while so duped the people of Valognes that they venerated her as a Saint, had feigned to enjoy visions, pretended she was marked with the stigmata, boasted that she could work miracles, essayed to heal the sick by the imposition of hands. She was, in fact, an associate of a band of Satanists whose Sabbats at Cherbourg she frequently attended.

By a warrant of 18 December, 1691, confirming the sentence of the magistrates of Passy delivered on the previous 26 October, the Parliament of Paris sent three shepherds of la Brie, Bras de Fer, Jardin, and Petit-Pierre, to the stake. They were at first accused of killing flocks and herds by evil spells, but it was soon discovered that they used a paste or some arsenical extract compounded with other toxicants. They even succeeded in poisoning an accomplice, Etienne Hocque, whilst he lodged in jail.[113]

In 1696 ten men and women, belonging to a village near Auxerre, whose lives were made utterly miserable by accusations of sorcery and the fear and hatred of their neighbours, demanded to be put to the water-ordeal. They were accordingly swum in the River Senin, near the Abbey of Pontigny. To their infinite confusion only two sank, the rest floating upon the stream. A century before they would have been burned without question or delay, but the local magistrates did not dare proceed against them, and things continued as before save that the terror they inspired was intensified a hundredfold.[114]

Three years later at St. Florentin, in Burgundy, a poor wretch who was popularly suspected of Witchcraft insisted upon undergoing the same test. When lowered into a pond he did not sink, which the onlookers took to be proof positive of his guilt. However, the magistrates refused to punish him, and the parish priest gave him an excellent character. All this availed nothing, for nobody throughout the whole province would give him even a day's work, and he was obliged to tramp to some other part of France.[115]

It will be seen that trials for sorcery were rapidly on the wane; the people believed as firmly as their fathers, but in face of the known attitude of the King magistrates were reluctant to punish and refused to condemn.

It is, perhaps, not impertinent to note that the last culprit burned at Paris for heresy suffered in 1663, when a certain Simon Morin, a native of Aumale in Normandy, was sent to the stake. Morin preached that he was Christ Incarnate, that to him all power had been given by God, and that his followers, those who possessed the true light, were incapable of sinning. These Illuminati practised the most infamous debaucheries under the pretext of religious assemblies, and it was shown that Morin was insatiable in his lusts and corruptions. A wealthy widow, named Malherbe, who had joined the sect, confessed the usual catalogue of filth and folly. She had had sexual connexion with the Devil, had attended the Sabbat, banqueted with demons, entertained imps and familiars. The Parliament of Paris ordered her to be branded with the fleur-de-lys and banished from the city.

But all these trials and processes were as nothing in comparison with the hideous scandals which were unveiled before the Chambre Ardente in 1679–82. This court, which was instituted in 1679 by the King with special powers to deal with the cases of poisoning that seemed so terribly on the increase, sat at the Arsenal in a hall whose windows were curtained with black, and therefore necessitating the constant use of lighted candles, whence it took its name. At the earliest investigations, conducted by La Reynie, chief lieutenant of police, a whole gang of poisoners and sorcerers was discovered, and as the inquiry was pursued it soon became evident that not only persons of low degree but nobles of the highest rank and proudest families in France were wofully implicated. Venomed philtres had been brewed, black masses said, necromancy practised, plots laid for the deaths of court favourite and political foe, the Devil propitiated and adored, and all these abominations seemed to centre round two figures of the blackest underworld of Paris, the abbé Guibourg and la Voisin.

Catherine Deshayes, widow of Antoine Montvoisin, and commonly known as la Voisin, had long been known to the criminal and the curious as midwife, bawd, and witch. In the secret chambers of her house in the rue Beauregard she told fortunes by cards, by the grounds of coffee, by the magic crystal, just as any Bond Street seer of to-day. But for a heavier fee she would inspect the entrails of beasts, she would evoke the dead, and for yet more gold you might be admitted to the hideous mysteries of Satan's eucharist. Gold too would buy a flask of clear liquid, a few drops of which was a sure dormitive for the jealous husband, the rival who had lived too long. She was assisted in her profession by numerous satellites ; her lovers, Romani, a handsome young Italian boy ; a lusty Norman named Lesage. A wanton hermaphrodite, exotic and perverse, la Trianon, dwelt in the house, to which also some curious old women, whose calling no one rightly knew, la Caillet, la Lepère, la Desportes, la Thomas, were daily visitors. The two executioners of Paris, M. Guillaume and M. Larivière contended for la Voisin's favours, bringing her gallant presents of the limbs and fat of murderers on the gibbet or wheel, whence she made tall black tapers for her secret ceremonies. It is no exaggeration to say that all Paris from duchess to drab, from marshal to muck-man, thronged to la Voisin's doors. Thither came the Duchess de Bouillon ; the Duchess de Lusignan ; the Duchess de Vivonne to devote herself and the babe in her womb to

Satan; the Duchess de Vitry; the Comtesse de Soissons (Olympe Mancini); the Comtesse de Rouse and Madame de Polignac, both burning to be raised to the royal bed and seeking the death of Louise de la Vallière; the Comtesse de Rouse; the Comtesse de Montmorency-Boutteville; the Princess de Tingry, seeking love-philtres and erotic charms; Madame de Baucé to buy a hand of glory and a toad; Madame de Gand and Madame d'Argenton; Madame de Chapelain; Madame Baron, seeking a draught to render impotent a priest who was unfaithful to her charms; Madame de Dreux, wishing to procure abortion; in brief all the fair and utterly corrupt aristocracy of France, and above all the greatest lady in the realm, greater than the Queen, the imperial Athénais de Montespan. Nor were men lacking: the Marquis de Feuquières; the chevalier de Varnens; the comte de Longueval; the Duke de Luxembourg, who asked to have speech with the Devil; a mysterious figure who was, they whispered, the Duke of Buckingham; and a whole troop of Colbert's enemies demanding spells to insure his speedy death.

The abbé Guibourg, the illegitimate son of Henri de Montmorency, was a man of some sixty years, who is described as tall and heavy-limbed with a malign and sensual face. It was he who celebrated innumerable Satanic masses at the instance of Madame de Montespan in order to secure her supreme power and eternal fidelity on the part of the King. A long black velvet pall was spread over the altar, and upon this the royal mistress laid herself in a state of perfect nudity. Six black candles were lit, the celebrant robed himself in a chasuble embroidered with esoteric characters wrought in silver, the gold paten and chalice were placed upon the naked belly of the living altar to whose warm flesh the priest pressed his lips each time the missal directed him to kiss the place of sacrifice, uel extra uel intra corporale. All was silent save for the low monotonous murmur of the blasphemous liturgy. The Host was consecrated, and then the Precious Blood. An assistant crept forward bearing an infant in her arms. The child was held over the altar, a sharp gash across the neck, a stifled cry, and warm drops fell into the chalice and streamed upon the white figure beneath. The corpse was handed to la Voisin, who flung it callously into an oven fashioned for that purpose which glowed white-hot in its fierceness.[116] It was proved that a regular traffic had been carried on for years with beggar-women and the lowest prostitutes, who sold their children for this purpose. At her trial la Voisin confessed that no less than two thousand five hundred babies had been disposed of in this manner, for the black mass was continually being celebrated, not only by Guibourg but by other priests. Many ladies of the court had served as an altar, whilst not infrequently some bulker from the street was called in to fill that function. Madame de Montespan was generally attended on these occasions by her confidante, Madame de la Desoeillets. Guibourg celebrated three masses in this way upon the naked body of Madame de Montespan. At the first the following conjuration was used : " Astaroth, Asmodeus, princes of friendship and love, I invoke you to accept the sacrifice, this child that I offer you, for the things I ask of you. They are that the friendship and love of the King and the Dauphin may be assured to me, that I may be honoured by all the princes and princesses of the Court, that the King deny me nothing I ask whether it be for my relatives or for any of my household."

On another occasion an erotic charm was confected in the following manner : Guibourg " a fait chez la Voisin, revêtu d'aube, d'étole et de manipule, une conjuration en présence de la Des Oeillets, qui prétendait faire un charme pour le [Roi][117] et qui était accompagnée d'un homme[118] qui liu donna la conjuration, et comme il était nécessaire d'avoir du sperme des deux sexes, Des Oeillets ayant ses mois n'en put donner mais versa dans le calice de ses menstrues et l'homme qui l'accompagnait, ayant passé dans la ruelle du lit avec liu Guibourg, versa de son sperme dans le calice. Sur le tout, la Des Oeillets et l'homme mirent chacun d'une poudre de sang de chauve-souris et de la farine pour donner un corps plus ferme à toute la composition et a pris qu'il eut récité la conjuration il tira le tout du calice qui fut mis dans un petit vaisseau que la Des Oeillets ou l'homme emporta."[119]

Not the least sad circumstance that came to light during the investigation of these orgies of Witchcraft was the large number of priests implicated. Amongst others concerned were : Abbé Brigallier, almoner to the Grand Mademoiselle ;

Abbé Bouchot, director of the convent of La Saussaye; Abbé Dulong, a canon of Notre Dame; Abbé Dulaurens, assistant priest at Saint-Leu; Abbé Dubourquet; Abbé Seysson; Abbé Dussis; Abbé Lempérier; Abbé Olivier, who consecrated a stone altar in a brothel; Abbé Cotton, who offered in sacrifice to the Devil a child baptized with the *Oleum Infirmorum* (the oil used for the Sacrament of Extreme Unction) and then strangled; Abbé Lepreux; Abbé Davot, assistant priest at Notre Dame de Bonne-Nouvelle, whose custom it was to lay under the corporal a piece of paper inscribed with the name of a person who should be brought to love, or, if hated, damned to die, a practice eagerly pursued to-day—if a priest may be found; Abbé Mariette, vicar of St.-Séverin; Abbé Rebours; Abbé Le Franc; Abbé Lemeignan, curate of St.-Eustache, who offered infants stolen from the cradle to Satan; Abbé Tournet; Father Gérard, a Capuchin; Father Gabriel; and, above all, Guibourg himself, any one of whose mistresses, la Fleurette, la Chaufrein, and la Jeanneton, the hangman's niece, would always serve him as an altar for his foul rites. A certain Jean Baptiste Sébault, of the diocese of Bourges, who was lodging in Paris at the house of a doctor, named Chamillon, seduced Marianne Chamillon, his host's daughter, a girl of twenty-two, and continually brought her to the black mass. The Abbé Guignard celebrated a Satanic mass in a cellar, and was served by Sébault in a state of complete nudity. An aphrodisiac was brewed at this orgy.

It is curious to note that the witches frequented the church of Ste.-Ursule de Montmarte, where a statue of S. Ursula was greatly venerated, as well as a picture representing the appearance of Our Lord after His Resurrection to S. Mary Magdalene, which was honoured under the title *Rabboni*.[120] They also worshipped at the church of the Holy Ghost, Place de Grève, where three novenas of masses, the first said in honour of God the Holy Ghost, the second in honour of S. Antony of Padua, and the third in honour of the Augustinian S. Nicolas of Tolentino, were considered to be an infallible means to obtain any object desired, whatsoever it might be.

The scandals when this whole terrible affair came to light were terrific. More than two hundred and forty-six persons

were deeply implicated in these abominations, and many of
these who had taken part were among the noblest names of
France. It was necessary that certain reports and dossiers
should disappear, and the King very properly forbade the
Court to follow up various inquiries which he indicated,—the
names of Madame de Montespan and the Comtesse de
Soissons, for example, must be completely safeguarded.
It appears that the lives of Louis XIV, the Dauphin, Colbert,
Louise de la Vallière, the Duchess de Fontanges, had been in
imminent danger. La Voisin was condemned to death and
burned at the stake on the 22 February, 1680. Several
persons died in prison ; others again committed suicide in
agonies of shame at the thought of a trial ; thirty-six who
had been found guilty of murder, chiefly by poisoning, were
executed ; five were sent to the galleys ; twenty-three
perpetually banished ; one hundred and forty-seven sentenced
to long or shorter terms of imprisonment at various towns
throughout the kingdom.

The authority for the confessions and trials is François
Ravaisson's amply detailed and great work, *Archives de la
Bastille. Documents inédits.*[121] This is truly a mine of
documents of first-hand importance. I have briefly summar-
ized in the following conspectus the most striking of
these :

Volume IV. A shepherd, Grand-Etienne, essays to kill
Louis XVI by Witchcraft ; Mme de Montespan employs
magical spell against Mlle de La Vallière ; a priest of
St-Séverin is imprisoned as a magician.

Volume V. Mme Baron veut faire *nouer l'aiguillette* à un
abbé ; Mme de Baucé buys a toad and a hand of glory from
la Voisin ; Bosse, *alias* Belamour, writes a billet in order to
go to the Sabbat ; la duchesse de Bouillon, le marquis de
Feuquières, le duc de Luxembourg desire to converse with
the Devil ; Coeuret, *alias* Dubuisson, *alias* Lesage, practise
magic with l'abbé Davot : Gérard, a Capuchin, le chevalier
de Bernières, l'abbé Olivier, le chevalier de Varnens, perform
magical rites ; la Leroux, a witch, employs charms.

Volume VI. Mme Relout, a butcher's wife, Filastre, *alias*
La Boissière, Mme de Montespan, Pajot, l'abbé Guibourg
make pacts with Satan ; l'abbé Cotton, l'abbé Davot, l'abbé
Dulaurens, le P. Gabriel, a religious of Picpus, l'abbé Gérard,

l'abbé Rebours, l'abbé Tournet, l'abbé Lepreux celebrate black masses, des messes sur le ventre ou consacrent des couleuvres ; Debray, Decennes, l'abbé Cotton, l'abbé Le Franc, l'abbé Lemperier, l'abbé Mariette, employ charms, conjure, and practise black magic ; l'abbé Cotton offers to the Devil a child baptised with the oil of Extreme Unction and then strangled ; another sacrifice of a child to the Devil ; la Duchesse de Vivonne devotes herself and her child to the Devil ; l'abbé Lemaignan sacrifices children to the Devil ; Monsignol desires to devote a child to Satan ; Mme de Montespan se fait dire des messes sur le ventre, ainsi que Mme de Gand, Mme d'Argenton et d'autres dames de la cour ; witchcraft and charms of la Bergeret, a fortune-teller, of the Duchesse de Bouillon, of Lesage, of Mme Chapelain, of la David, a witch, and of several priests, of the relations of Fouquet, of la Petit, a fortune-teller, of the vicomtesse de Polignac, of de Regnard, called " le Grand-Auteur," of the Marquise de Roure, and of others to kill Louis XIV ; Mme de Montespan is present at the strangling of a child offered to Satan : the porter of the hospice " des Quinze-Vingts " has a black mass celebrated ; abbé Olivier set up a stone altar in a bawdy-house ; candles made of the fat of a criminal who has been hanged ; pacts against Colbert ; abortion by la Voisin ; Marre, an Italian sorcerer ; Mabile celebrates the sacrifice of the Death's Head ; the Duchesse de Lusignan performs blasphemous rites in a wood ; la Morand devotes herself to the Devil.

Volume VII. Sacrifice of a child given to Satan ; Conjuration by Perceval ; le sousdiacre Sebaud fait dire des messes sur le ventre de sa maîtresse.

Volume VIII. Conjurations and magic rites practised by the Comte de Longueval.

Volume X. La Berthemet, la Fenouillet, are eager to give themselves to Satan who will have naught of them ; Mme de Grancey, Destouches, ask for money from the Devil ; le capitaine Bederode, Picault, Tirmont, Davou, wizards ; la Créancier, la Ducatel, la Dumouty, la Loysel, la Manneville, la Randon, la Siamoise, la Sivry, la Fleury, witches or fortune-tellers ; M. de Feuquières wishes to make a compact with Satan ; Protain, a schoolmaster, writes a pact.

Volume XI. Aulmont, Lavaute, Lebègue, Siriaque,

Saint-Vidal, wizards ; La Chesnau, la Delprade, la Devaux, la Pigeon, la Rochefort, la Rousseau, witches.

Volume XII. La Dequien, la Doublet, la Duchesse, la Rancine, witches.

Volume XIII. The baron de Cerlach, wizard, raises the Devil ; Loroux, Morin, wizards ; la Fouconnier, la Feugère, la Gallet, la Norcy, witches.

Volume XIV. Duprat writes out grimoires ; Forcassy, a warlock.

Volume XV. Prince Camille and Dubuisson evoke the Devil on the plain of Montrouge ; the Comtesse de Montboissier asks fifteen millions and the Duc d'Ollone fourteen millions from the Devil ; d'Olonne pays 113 livres for a magic goat skin.

Towards the end of the reign of Louis XIV persons accused of sorcery no longer went to the stake but to the Salpêtrière. This was the punishment of a woman named d'Amour, a celebrated fortune-teller, as also of three notorious pretenders to occult arts, la Créancier, la Ducatel, la Loysel. One Picault, who boasted that he was a magician of no mean power, and a schoolmaster, named Protain, who had written out in a fair hand a contract with the Devil, were dealt with in the same way. A man and his wife named Barot who were arrested on charges of sorcery were sent, the husband into the army, the woman to la Salpêtrière. The warlock Bourdeaux was imprisoned at Bicêtre. Many other such instances might be given.[122]

The last execution in France seems to have been that of a man who was condemned to death in 1718 by the Parliament of Bordeaux upon a charge of having by his spells rendered a citizen impotent in the marriage-bed, his bride barren, and otherwise afflicting the whole household.

In 1702 much talk was caused by the case of a young girl, who had been overlooked, and for eleven years, since 1691, had been possessed of a devil that was dumb. It will be remembered that this affliction was known of old in Palestine, since on one occasion Our Lord " was casting out a devil and the same was dumb ; and when he had cast out the devil the dumb spoke "[123] (Et erat eiiciens dæmonium, et illud erat mutum. Et cum eiecisset dæmonium, locutus est mutus. S. Luke xi. 14). She was taken on a pilgrimage to the tomb of King James II, who died at Saint-Germain-en-Laye, 16 September, 1701, a sanctuary where already miracles had been worked. After fervent prayer and an invocation of the holy exile the girl was cured and spoke, and as in the Gospels " the multitudes were in admiration at it " (admiratæ sunt turbæ). King James, always profoundly religious, in his later years advanced to true sanctity. Such was his sinlessness that his Confessor stated, after nine years of spiritual service, that it was very rare to find, in the most virtuous souls of Christendom, intentions more pure, a vigilance more close, or a greater delicacy of conscience as to the smallest imperfections. In view of this saintly life and the stupendous sacrifice that the King made for the Catholic Faith it is not surprising that his Canonization should have occupied the attention of the Holy See. It appears, indeed, that he would certainly have been raised to the Altars of the Church towards the end of the eighteenth century had not the crushing catastrophe of the French Revolution come wellnigh to obliterate from men's minds all reverence and all thought of sentiment for the past.

In 1720 at Bully a number of young girls declared themselves possessed. When exorcised by the abbé d'Esquinnemare they shrieked out in their convulsions that a poor worker, Laurent Gaudouët, was the magician who had caused the mischief. The affair made a great noise, and Gaudouët lodged a formal complaint of defamation of character before the local magistrates. The Parliament of Rouen, than which no tribunal had been more active in the prosecution of witches, interfered. The sufferers were brought to Rouen, and to their surprise imprisoned in the Conciergerie. Here they were kept under a strict discipline for several months, at the end of which time they were glad to return home and remain unknown.[124]

Four years later at Landes, in the diocese of Bayeux, a child of ten, the daughter of a petty noble, Claudine Le Vaillant de Léaupartie, on the eve of her First Communion, suddenly fell into fierce paroxysms, insulted her parents, uttered the most astounding obscenities, and when prayer was made on her behalf blasphemed like a maniac. As she had hitherto been distinguished by her meekness and piety, great alarm was felt. Abbé Hurtin, the parish-priest, by permission of the

Bishop of Bayeux, exorcised her, and she was for a while lodged with the nuns of the Bon-Sauveur convent at St.-Lô. In a few months she seemed perfectly healed, and was able to make her first communion, when she returned to her father's house.

Eight years after another of the family, a younger daughter, was taken with a mysterious malady. In a day or two Claudine showed even stronger symptoms of the same attack. A third sister succumbed ; the disease manifested itself in a servant-maid, two nuns at Bayeux, the housekeeper of the parish-priest at Landes, and a simple village girl. All were thrown into hideous convulsions ; they foamed at the mouth ; struck and bit any who attempted to hold them ; fell writhing to the ground ; yelled and cursed all sacred things ; blasphemed God, Our Lady, and the Blessed Sacrament with such filthy opprobrium that all who heard were petrified with horror and amaze. The abbé Hurtin after several exorcisms petitioned for the help of some priest skilled in these matters. The Bishop promptly sent several learned divines, amongst whom was the saintly superior-general of the Eudists.[125] Two friars even came from Paris, and a number of doctors debated upon the disease in all its bearings. They decided that no natural explanation could be given of the phenomena, and in 1735 the Sorbonne, when consulted, after minutest inquiry declared that it was a true instance of demoniac possession. Eventually the unhappy victims were separately confined in various convents of the stricter observances throughout the kingdom, and it is said that most, if not all, recovered in the course of years.[126]

Although the case is very famous, and caused at the time almost unprecedented talk and scandal, it is not necessary to do more than touch very briefly upon the *affaire* Cadière-Girard. Marie Catherine Cadière was born at Toulon on the 12 November, 1709. Her father having died during her infancy, she was brought up in the utmost seclusion by her widowed mother. The whole family was deeply, not to say fanatically, religious ; of her three brothers the eldest had married, the second, Etienne Thomas, became a Dominican, the third, François, a secular priest. Unfortunately Catherine was of a highly neuropathic disposition, and suffered from a morbidly sensual complex, which was aggravated by the circumstances of her education and home. In April, 1728, Father Jean-Baptiste Girard, a learned and eloquent member of the Society of Jesus, was appointed rector of the seminary of Toulon. The fame of his preaching had preceded him, and when he occupied a pulpit the church was thronged by crowds which hung upon his persuasive words. His confessional, also, was besieged by penitents, and under his direction a number of pious persons, of whom one was Catherine Cadière, formed themselves into a society or gild living under a rule and aiming at a more perfect life. From time to time they met in a chapel or some convenient place, when after certain devotions Father Girard gave addresses upon the mystical state. He seems to have thought at first that he had to do with elect souls, who might become as S. Teresa or S. Catherine of Siena and tread the paths of the ecstatic S. Maria Maddalena de' Pazzi or that Visitation nun to whom Jesus revealed the love of His Most Sacred Heart. In any case his only faults were over-enthusiasm and a little lack of discretion. But before long he rectified these errors and perceiving that his devotees were unfitted for the higher things, he led them along the well-worn simple ways of prayer and good works. This was not to the taste of la Cadière and she soon became hysterical and unhappy. Acting upon Father Girard's advice she made a retreat at the convent of Ste-Claire d'Ollioules, which so far from calming her but increased her pithiatism and melancholy. She fell into ecstasies, professed to have visions, conversed with the Saints, and above all was seen to be marked with the stigmata. Louis, Bishop of Toulon, himself visited the convent, bade her return to her home, and requested an aged and experienced religious, Father Nicolas of S. Joseph, prior of the discalced Carmelites at Toulon, to inquire into the matter. Catherine Cadière now told a most extraordinary tale. She averred that Father Girard had bewitched her, that he had violated her chastity, and when she feared she had conceived he compelled her to drink a draught which would procure abortion. She accused him of propagating the doctrines of Molinos,[127] that whosoever was filled with heavenly love rose above the trammels of the body, which was a mere envelope, and could indulge sinlessly in any fleshly lust or perversion without harm or hurt to the soul. She gave the most disgusting details of her intercourse with him, alleging that he was wont to compel her to undress and then amid circumstances of the greatest indecency to inflict a severe discipline upon her naked body, and having wakened his desires by this amorous flagellation to proceed to the commission of the sexual act. Father Nicolas, who was entirely deceived by this story reported the complaint to the Bishop, and meanwhile the relatives of la Cadière carried the matter to the civil courts of Toulon. The most resounding scandals ensued, and it is hardly too much to say that the South of France was thrown into a fever of excitement and unrest. The case was discussed on every hand, and in 1731 the Parliament of Aix, upon an express order from the King, made a searching investigation into the whole matter. There were long and vehement disagreements ; endless discussions and debate. It was obvious from the first that the girl's story was utterly and entirely false. But the enemies of the Jesuits had massed their forces to heap discredit upon the Society, and by the most underhand means and lying methods they were straining every nerve to bring about the disgrace of Father Girard. Jansenists and anti-clericals moved earth and hell to effect his ruin. This, how-ever, was beyond their power, and in 1731 Father Girard, after a long canonical investigation, was solemnly declared innocent in every particular and much maligned. The nymphomanic la Cadière was sent to her home, and vanishes into obscurity.[128]

Thus gradually prosecutions for Witchcraft ceased in France. The so-called Philosophers who deny the super-natural inevitably mocked at the idea of any such power. Diderot, indeed, hesitates to go too far,[129] but Condillac[130] and Voltaire[131] are wholly sceptical, whilst the Encyclo-pædists under the word " Sorcellerie " sum up their ignorance in the following phrase : " Opération magique honteuse ou ridicule, attribuée stupidement par la superstition à l'invocation et au pouvoir des démons."

During the eighteenth century the practise of magic and the black art was common throughout France, nor were these dark superstitions found only amid the peasantry and in remoter provinces. Barbier's *Journal*,[132] for instance, relates that the Duc de Richelieu was much suspected of studying " sorcery and every kind of occult science." A story was noised to the effect that he had formed too close an intimacy with an Austrian noble whose tastes lay in the same direction. Two Capuchins were found to say Mass, at which the devotees assisted, in the old deserted chapel of a lone country-house. After this the Duke and his friend defiled the Hosts, in the hope that thereupon Satan would appear to crown the blasphemy.

Saint-Simon remarks that the Regent, Philippe d'Orléans, was notoriously addicted to goety. D'Alméras in an important monograph writes : " Necromancers, old wizards who brewed philtres and confected charms, *denoueurs d'aiguilette*, fortune-tellers by cards, diviners of every kind, says a historian who has delved deeply into the secrets of the eighteenth century, swarmed in certain obscure districts of Paris, covens which the police could not track, but which were soon found by those who required their aid. The alchemists, of whom there were great numbers, were ensconced in the faubourg St. Marceau."[133]

Extraordinary and fearful stories were bruited concerning the mysterious occultists who from time to time loomed so largely before the public : Albert Aluys, the Comte de Saint-Germain, Cagliostro, Louis Claude de Saint Martin, Martinès de Pasqually, Franz Anton Mesmer, and many of lesser note, many who were mere charlatans and vulgar adventurers. Cabalistic romances, *Le Comte de Gabalis*, *Le Sylphe Amoureux*, *Les Ondins*, *L'Amant Salamandre*, Laffichard's *La Salamandre*, Venice, 1744 ; *Le diable amoureux*, 1776, of Cazotte, whose fantasies more than one reader took seriously, deeming the author a skilled magician ; the abbé Bordelon's *Histoire de M. Oufle*, Paris, 1789. Such works as Saint-André's *Lettres au sujet de la magie*, the *Traité sur la Magie*, 1732 ; of Antoine-Louis Daguis, Pierre Le Brun's *Histoire critique des pratiques superstitieuses*, 1732 ; Lenglet-Dusfresnoy's *Philosophie-hermetique*, 1744, *La Clef du Sanctuaire philosophique*, 1781, of Madame Sabine Stuart de Chevalier, were devoured with feverish eagerness by all classes of society.[134]

The eighth volume of the *Bibliothèque Ecclesiastique*, 8 vols., Paris, 1771, of the Abbé Claude-Marie Guyon, is nothing else than a veritable enchiridion of magic. Especially addressed to priests, the author announces that his book is

" a compendium of all that it is fitting to know upon the subject of judicial astrology, the power of demons, and such communion as they may hold with man, upon various branches of Magic, enchantments, mediæval sorceries, omens, the casting of lots, amulets and talismans, dreams, divination, and all ways in which man has essayed to read the future. It is a manual of these sciences, a work which is not misplaced in, but rather indispensible to, a priest's library."[135] Daguis in his *Traité de la magie* (1732, p. 127) had indeed affirmed that a belief in the possibility of Witchcraft is " an article of faith which cannot be denied without falling into heresy."

There is, perhaps, scarcely any fact which more clearly brings home to us the prevalence of the black art in the eighteenth century than a consideration of the vast numbers of grimoires and books of goetic theurgy which poured from the press and were scattered in every direction. *Les Secrets du Petit Albert* (*Alberti Parui Lucii libellus de mirabilibus Naturæ arcanis*) which tells how to confect philtres, fashion talismans, employ the hand of glory, discover treasure, and many a foul spell, was edited in 1758 ; *Les Secrets du Grand Albert* (which has nothing to do with the great Dominican doctor), in 1729, to be reprinted 1791, 1793. An *Albert Moderne* appeared in 1769. The grimoire miscalled Pope Leo's was printed in 1749 ; *La Véritable magie noire* in 1750. In 1727 Levassau translated the *Occulta Philosophia* of Cornelius Agrippa, whose *Œuvres magiques* were published by the firm of Beringo, whose bookshop at Lyons was famous throughout France. Many of these works have the imprint Rome, which is, of course, incorrect and a mere guise. The *Clauicula Salomonis* was actually issued at the expense of M. de Bachelay, a farmer-general, who died in 1766.

In France Satanism, although largely driven underground, persisted throughout the eighteenth century. As might be expected, there are revolting pictures of the black mass in the lewd pages of de Sade. In *Justine*,[136] such a mass celebrated in a cloister is described in filthy detail. When Juliette[137] is initiated into the " Society of the Friends of Crime " the Host and Crucifix are desecrated. Again, a little later, two Satanic orgies are exhibited, when the High altar is the scene of every defilement.[138] By a stroke of unparalleled impudence and malice the very quintessence of blasphemy is attained, when the holy and suffering Pius VI is made to take part in these abominations.[139]   In the country districts, moreover, the belief in witches and their malice had hardly waned.   Jules Garinet in his *Histoire de la Magic en France*, Paris, 8vo, 1818, cites more than twenty cases of alleged sorcery which were brought before the courts owing to the assault on the witch by peasants or some such matter between 1805 and 1818.   None present any features of special interest, although in 1818 no less than three tribunals were occupied with trials resulting from this belief.   Upon the night of the execution of King Louis XVI, 21 January, 1793, a number of French Satanists formed themselves into a definite society to prosecute their ends and propagate their worship of evil.   In this they were very active, and the Abbé Fiard, who in his *La France trompée par les magiciens et démonolâtres du dix-huitème siècle. Fait demontré par des faits*, Paris, 1803, gives a truly appalling picture of their blasphemies and sacrilege, was so heart-broken by the abominations practised on every side and which seemed almost on the increase that he prophesied the coming of Antichrist must be near at hand.   As early as 1818 these Satanists had an active branch in the department of Lot-et-Garonne, and in 1843 it was proved that during some twenty-five years of their existence they had defiled and mutilated no less than three thousand three hundred and twenty Hosts.   In 1855, in 1874, and again in 1878 it was discovered that professional Host-stealers were at work in Paris.   In 1865 hideous scandals disturbed the dioceses of Lens and Auxerre, the department of the Yonne, and in fact all France.   A nun, named Cantianille, of the convent of Mont-Saint Sulpice at Auxerre had been corrupted in her fifteenth year by an apostate priest who vowed her to the Devil.   This priest himself had been initiated into Satanism by a cleric who had taken part in the founding of the evil Society at Paris, 21 January, 1793.   The scenes which took place in the cloister recalls the demoniac frenzies and obscenities of Madeleine de la Palud and Madeleine Bavent. Cantianille was exorcised by the Abbé Thorey, and in her convulsions confessed such defilements of the Host, such blasphemies, and fetid lewdness that the Bishop incontinently banished her from his diocese.   Rome took cognizance of the affair, but the Bishop, literally brokenhearted at the terrible things he had heard and seen, resigned his see to withdraw to Fontainebleau, where after two years of utter seclusion and ceaseless prayer, he died slain by the wickedness of the world.

Satanism yet has its votaries and is extensively practised. It is a matter of notoriety that in 1924 two ciboria, containing one hundred consecrated Hosts, were carried off by an old woman from the cathedral of Notre Dame in circumstances which clearly indicate that the holy vessels were not the objects of the larceny. During recent years similar depredations have increased in an extraordinary manner, and have occurred throughout all France. No less than thirteen churches belonging to the one diocese of Orleans were despoiled within a twelvemonth, whilst not long since the Archbishop of Lyons, Cardinal Maurin, issued special instructions to his clergy with regard to the safe custody of the tabernacles. The departments of Aude, Isère, Tarn, Gard, Nièvre, Loiret, Yonne, Haute-Garonne, Somme, Le Nord, and the Dauphiny, have all been the scene of similar outrages. In 1895 a particularly revolting instance of defilement of the Host occurred in the Island of Mauritius. Rome, Salerno, Naples, Florence, Lyons, London, Brussels, Bruges, and many other towns have all suffered from the abominations. Even as I write these words news comes from The Hague concerning a sacrilege which undoubtedly points to Satanism. The ciborium with the Sacred Host was stolen out of the tabernacle of the church at Amsterdamsche Veld. The golden ciborium was afterwards discovered thrown into a muddy ditch on the moors hard by the town. In order to prevent any possible repetition of this outrage orders of watchers have enrolled themselves, who will remain all night before the Blessed Sacrament, and guard the altar at any time when such profanation might be attempted.[140]

It is very well known that the terrible picture of the black mass drawn by Huysmans in his sombre romance *Là-Bas* is true in every detail.[141] A considerable amount of information as to occult practices was given the writer by the Abbé J.-A. Boullan, editor of a small review, *Les Annales de la Sainteté*, who lived at Lyons, lodging with an architect, M. Misme, in the rue de la Martinière. Two mediums,

Madame Laure and Madame Thibaut, resided in the same house. Boullan did not hesitate to accuse his personal enemies of black magic and sorcery. A lengthy correspondence was exchanged between Boullan and Huysmans, from 6 February, 1890, to the 4 January, 1893. Huysmans, however, burned nearly all these letters. Under the date 10 February, 1890, Boullan wrote from Lyons : " Je puis mettre à votre disposition les documents pour établir que le satanisme est vivant de nos jours, et comment et sous quelle forme. . . . Au sein du clergé, le satanisme contemporain est plus cultivé, plus savant qu'au Moyen âge ; il se pratique à Rome et surtout à Paris, Lyon, Châlons, pour la France, et à Bruges, pour la Belgique." The Abbé particularly detested the Marquis Stanislas de Guaita, Joséphin Peladan, and Oswald Wirth, whom he frequently stigmatized as adepts in Witchcraft and baleful spells. Perhaps it should be mentioned in passing that the orthodoxy of Boullan was very much suspect. There was some gossip of strange masses performed in secret, the sacrifice of the New Carmel as it was called, by which enchantments were dissolved, a mysterious liturgy whose priest wore at the sacrifice a long robe of vermilion silk girt about the loins with a blue and white cord. Over this he donned a cloak of white samite, and on his finger was the consecrated ring. The mass was not the Oblation of Calvary but the Eucharist of Glory, in some sense the Mass of Heaven, when the Paraclete reigns over all. There is little wonder that his ecclesiastical superiors looked askance at Abbé Boullan.

The Abbé died suddenly on the 3 January, 1893, and six days later, in the *Gil Blas*, Jules Bois commented upon this " mysterious decease," which, he asserted, was brought about by the spells of the Rosicrucians and in particular by Stanislas de Guaita. On the following day in an interview which appeared in the *Figaro* Huysmans confirmed these statements, which Jules Bois reiterated on the 11 January in the columns of the *Gil Blas*. Stanislas de Guaita, who was then living in the Avenue Trudaine, protested against such imputations in the *Figaro* of the 12 January. Jules Bois replied on the following day in the *Gil Blas* openly averring that de Guaita had caused Boullan's death. On the 15 January de Guaita addressed a most indignant letter to the

Gil Blas in which he said that his seconds were calling upon Huysmans and Jules Bois. No duel with the former took place, but the latter met de Guaita on the 19 January. Two shots were fired on either side, but both parties left the field untouched.[142]

Towards the end of February, 1922, a young farm-hand, named Barbeau, was arrested at the hamlet of St.-Georges de Pointindoux, in the heart of the Vendée country, and charged with having murdered a farmer's son, called Chaillot, who when returning home late one night was shot dead on his father's doorstep. For some weeks the police vainly sought a clue to the crime, but at last it appeared that a bitter enmity existed between the Chaillot family and some neighbours, Archambaud. Once they were close friends, but recently Archambaud's cattle had been thinned by disease, and it was openly suggested that old Chaillot had cast a spell upon them. Then Archambaud's nephew, the prisoner Barbeau, assaulted Chaillot's son. Immediately after Barbeau fell ill of mysterious internal pains. The doctor attributed these to a kick from a horse, but his rustic friends loath to be so prosaic at once scented Witchcraft. Barbeau fired the shots that night to rid himself of the man, who he believed could bewitch him to death, and several witnesses assert that they frequently heard him say the deceased was killing him inchmeal.[143]

Cases such as these, though rare, are not unique, and they form a very certain and real link with the old days of Trois Echelles, and the shepherds of the sixteenth and seventeenth centuries on the one hand, and on the other with the Satanism of Gilles de Rais, Picard, the Abbé Guibourg, and the infamous la Voisin.

Stories of the *loup-garou* are yet told in many parts of France, and in more than one village there is hated and feared some man, or old hag it may be, who is commonly believed to prowl the neighbourhood forests on a winter's night in the shape of a great grey ravening wolf. It is also believed that demons will adopt this form to scare the chance traveller and drive children to maddening terror.

In the Sologne some years ago, Monsieur l'Abbé Grélot, curé of Selles-sur-Cher, was carrying the Host to a dying man in the late gloaming, when he found a wolf walking beside him. He was both amazed and greatly alarmed since wolves were unknown in the Sologne, but pursued his way, aware of the power of the Blessed Saviour whose Body he bore, though as darkness deepened the glare of red and green lights in the animal's eyes gleamed yet more ferociously.

In November, 1925, a curious case of supposed lycanthrophy occurred in Alsace when the *garde-champêtre*, or village policeman, of Uttenheim, near Strasburg, was tried for shooting dead a boy, who had mischievously worked upon his belief that he was haunted by animals with human faces. He knew that the boy was playing tricks upon him, but declared his conviction that, by means of sorcery, the lad had acquired the power of turning himself into the forms of other animals—the were-wolf, in fact—and the whole village believed him.

A few weeks later occult circles in Paris were greatly excited by the case of a certain Madame Picquart, a medium, who was convicted of having stolen various articles from a house where she was employed as a daily dressmaker. After vehemently denying that she took them, she then pretended that she must have done so under the influence of a spell cast upon her by some enemy, and many kindly spiritualists believed the story, and appeared as witnesses in support of the appeal which she made against her conviction, but which resulted in merely confirming it.

This, however, was nothing in comparison with the extraordinary scandals arising from the fierce fanaticism of a strange sect, which had established itself at Bordeaux, under the direction of an ignorant concierge " Mother Marie Mesmin." In 1906 Madame Mesmin brought back from Lourdes a life-sized plaster statue of Our Lady, which was placed in the porter's lodge she occupied. It was shortly afterwards bruited that tears were observed to fall from the eyes of the figure, and a miracle was promptly proclaimed. According to M. Parentel, a bank-clerk, the figure " shed tears in sufficient quantity for us to collect them in vases in order to heal the sick." In some three years no less than three hundred worshippers of the Weeping Virgin formed themselves into a society under the patronage of " Our Lady of Tears," and transferred the statue to an Oratory. Rumours of these extravagances reached the ears of Cardinal

Andrieu, Archbishop of Bordeaux, and His Eminence, who
though seriously concerned was unwilling at first to use harsh
measures, dispatched two priests to convey the statue to a
Franciscan convent in order that by this removal the cult
might forthwith cease. The adorers however refused to
listen to authority and were enraged at being deprived of
their miracles. A large oil painting depicting the original
statue was promptly installed in their sanctuary, as also a
figure of the Infant Christ, which, it is claimed, gives forth
sweet perfumes when persons kneel before it in prayer. It
stands upon an altarino amid masses of artificial flowers, ever
fragrant (they declare) with the scent of lilies and roses. The
Cardinal forthwith condemned this cult in uncompromising
terms, and formally forbad any Catholic to visit the Oratory
or to communicate with members of the sect. None the less
two priests, Monsignor Sapounghi, a Syrian, Archimandrite
and Vicar-General of Sidon, and the Abbé Lebret, were found
willing to assist Madame Mesmin in the direction of her
new society.

In 1914 Monsignor Sapounghi was lodging in the house
of Madame Mesmin, who declared that not only had he made
immodest proposals to her but also endeavoured to obtain
possession of the fees she received from the votaries of her
miraculous statue and cult. Scandal ensued, and Monsignor
Sapounghi retired to Nantes. As soon as the priest had left
Bordeaux, Madame Mesmin asserted that she was the prey
of his " satanic machinations." An invisible moth used to
bite her, leaving one of its invisible teeth in an invisible wound.
She was the continual victim of abnormal seizures and attacks
of uncontrolled nymphomania. She solemnly swore that
Monsignor Sapounghi " was wont to celebrate black masses,
putting toad's blood in the chalice which he consecrated
upon the breast of a life-sized doll, nude, and perfectly
modelled in every particular." Several persons gave entire
credit to this story. Four men, M. Cardon, Chief Inspector
of the Bordeaux Police, a stockbroker, the conductor of
an orchestra, and another, heard Mass very devoutly, prayed
" that our hands may not become criminal," and took a
journey to Nantes, where Monsignor Sapounghi taught
mathematics in a school, when having armed themselves
with whips they stripped and handcuffed their victim to

thrash him with savage violence leaving him covered with blood and half-dead. He was indeed obliged to keep his bed for a month. At the very same moment Madame Mesmin in Bordeaux was for ever relieved of her terrible sufferings and temptations, and recreated with floods of heavenly peace and joy.[144] The avengers of Madame Mesmin carried off with them a skull, a book of curses, and a waxen statue. The four assailants, on their return to Bordeaux, were prosecuted and sentenced to three months' imprisonment, with the benefit of the First Offenders Act. The judgement contains the quaint phrase : " Whereas in the present state of science it is not certain that Mme Mesmin has been the victim of spells."

Throughout the Great War, Madame Mesmin distributed sacred medals to soldiers, and her followers declared that these rendered the wearers immune from enemy bullets, bombs, and shells, but nothing much was heard of the devotees of this strange cult until January, 1926, when a sensational outrage filled the columns of the world's newspapers with the most startling headlines and special articles. The Abbé Desnoyers, parish priest of Bombon, near Melun, noticed on Sunday morning 3 January, the Feast of the Holy Name of Jesus, the presence of twelve strangers, two men and ten women, among his congregation. At the close of Mass when he had retired to the sacristy and was unvesting the two men advanced towards the door with such threatening gestures that the priest's old servant, a woman of seventy, turned the key in the lock. The intruders, however, suddenly seized her, took the key from her by force, and placed a gag in her mouth so that she should not scream. They then opened the door, and, after throwing a handful of pepper in the cure's face, bound and gagged him. He was thrown on the floor, and his gown was pulled up over his head. Each of the flagellants then inflicted twenty-five blows with a discipline. In order to hit harder the men took off their coats. After the first fifty strokes the priest's under-garments were all torn, and from his waist to his knees he was soon covered with blood. At each blow the flagellants cried out : " Take that, Satan, and that, and that." When the flagellation had lasted for more than a quarter of an hour, they released the gag from his mouth, and asked if he would withdraw the evil spells he had cast upon their " sainted mother." " I withdraw them," gasped the priest. " Withdraw them in the name of God," came the command enforced by a stinging blow. " I withdraw them in the name of God," cried the priest, who was in a fainting condition. At this juncture the *gendarmerie* arrived, led by the old servant woman, and arrested all the participants, who, however, showed no compunction or regret for their behaviour. The astonished gendarmes were amazed to hear the assailants all claim the honour of responsibility : " We have performed a divine mission, and are sent by God to drive the devil out of this priest," they said, and then, folding their arms, they chanted the Magnificat.

The unfortunate victim was carried to his room, and a doctor hastily summoned. As soon as he had sufficiently recovered Abbé Desnoyers at once wrote an account of the assault to the Bishop of Meaux, in which letter the following passage occurs :

" If the brigadier of *gendarmerie* had not intervened, I should have been dead in five minutes. My body was cruelly bound in four places. Like my patron Saint Paul I was scourged—at least three hundred stripes were inflicted upon me—and I was tightly gagged, one gag over my nostrils, one over, or rather in, my mouth, the third around my neck, the last being formed of handkerchiefs tied together, which could be tightened like a tourniquet. My flagellation lasted twenty minutes, and, half-choked, I ceased to offer any resistance. I was attacked by three handfuls of pepper thrown into my face by my aggressors, who took off my shoes, and had brought with them everything in readiness to burn the soles of my feet and cut out my tongue. I did not belong to the group of Our Lady of Tears, but I have had correspondence with some of its members, who displayed great piety. Mme Marie Mesmin has frequently claimed that she saw visions of the Blessed Virgin, and of M. Robert, a captain in Syria. She saw the latter with a halo of light around his head. This led me to conclude that I was dealing with mystics and fanatics."

On Saturday, 23 January, the assailants appeared before the magistrates at Melun. The two men had been kept in custody, but the women were released on bail. These fanatics were Maurice Lourdin, 27 ; Albert Froger, 39, chief accountant of an important navigation company ; Mmes Aline Senan, 53, and Heloise Berton, 75, of independent means ; Mme Robert, 49, widow of a French army officer, and her daughter Anne Marie, 17 ; Mme Meline Charles, 70, dressmaker ; Mme Culpain, 60, charwoman ; Mme Gilberte Burr, 47, a supervising clerk ; Mme Marie Betts, 51, proprietress of a steam laundry ; Mme Marie Vigneau, 61, one of her ironers ; and Mme Berthe Lagardère, 50, in domestic service. The report in *The Times* (25 Jan., 1926) (From Our Own Correspondent, Paris, 24 January) may be quoted at length :

" The prisoners arrived at Melun yesterday, wearing as a protection against photography black veils and spectacles, which they were with difficulty persuaded to remove while giving evidence. The younger of the men, a street sweeper, aged 27, when confronted with the Abbé, had no hesitation in identifying him as Satan himself. The Abbé had, he said, sent diseases to Bordeaux from Bombon by means of birds, which flew over Mme Mesmin's gardens, and their droppings gave rise to fungi of obscene shapes, which emitted such appalling odours that those who breathed them were smitten with horrible diseases. He himself had contracted a disease in this unusual fashion. Mme Mesmin had a boil and her eyes were bloodshot. He added, unofficially, that the Abbé Desnoyers was one of the greatest sorcerers of the age. He was even more powerful than the Syrian Archimandrite who had persecuted Mme Mesmin six years ago. He could cause the death of anyone he liked in 24 hours, with or without suffering. A priest sold to the Devil was all-powerful. He had at his disposal dolls into which one stuck pins in order to injure one's enemies, and his were the spells which were transmitted by means of birds.

" The other man said that he inferred that the Abbé had put a spell upon him from the fact that he had lost " phosphates." He had thrown pepper in the Abbé's eyes and had flogged him with a scourge which he had used himself for 15 months. Neither of the men expressed regret for his offence.

" Mme Robert, a widow, said that since she and her daughter had known the Abbé they had suffered from giddiness at night. Her deceased husband had written that

he was afraid that the Abbé would put a spell on them. She
regretted what he had done because it had brought the
Virgin Mary into the case.

" Mme Berton, aged 75, described how, when the statue
of the Virgin wept, they caught the tears in a glass. This
never overflowed—a fact which was to be regarded as
miraculous. [It will be remembered that an ecclesiastical
investigation showed the tears to be of ordinary water.] Mme
Mesmin had cried out between midnight and two in the
morning : ' The Abbé Desnoyers is killing me ; get rid of
him.'

" Mlle Culpain gave corroborative evidence, and added
that Mme Mesmin had found the Abbé's fingers round her
throat and bore the marks of blows which he had sent her
from afar.

" At the request of counsel, the Magistrate said that he
would consider whether Mme Mesmin would be charged with
inciting to violence. There the matter remains for the
moment, except that the accused are also charged with
assaulting the Abbé's servant and her niece."

As might be expected the affair gave occasion for some
ribald songs and lewd ballads which were hawked for a few
pence about the streets. Sightseers flocked to Bordeaux, and
Mother Marie Mesmin, who is described as " a stout, red-
faced woman of 50 with flashing black eyes and a big black
wig," exploited the situation to the full. She may consider
herself happy that she did not live in the days of Boguet and
De Lancre.

In the same issue of *The Times* we are told :

" Several other cases of sorcery have been reported
recently. The latest has occurred at Cieurac, in the Lot,
where the house of a couple aged respectively 91 and 88
has been bewitched by an old woman to whom, on July 14,
1924, they refused lodging. The furniture dashes about
the room, candles and lamps go out without apparent reason,
doors open of their own accord, buckets of water and heaps of
fodder place themselves before the cattle, and the other day
a cauldron of water in which a pig was to be scalded, when
placed over a big fire, showed no rise of temperature until
the pig-butcher swore terribly, at which it boiled immediately."

Such instances of belief in black magic and enchantment are indeed remarkable. It is in vain that France tries to be materialistic and sceptical, she will never lose her hold upon the supernatural, and if tyranny try to wrest her from things divine, in her yearning she will embrace the supernatural run to seed.

NOTES TO CHAPTER V.

[1] *Historiæ*, XXIV, 4. ". . . ducibus auibus (nam augurandi studio Galli præter ceteros callent)." The *History* of Marcus Junianus Justinus is an epitome, executed in the age of the Antonines, of the *History of the World* written in forty-four books by Pompeius Trogus who flourished under Augustus.

[2] *De Bello gallico*, VI, 16. " Natio est omnis Gallorum admodum dedita religionibus, atque ob eam causam, qui sunt adfecti grauioribus morbis quique in prœliis periculisque uersantur, aut pro uictimis homines immolant aut se immolaturos uouent administrisque ad ea sacrificia druidibus utuntur, quod, pro uita hominis nisi hominis uita reddatur, non posse deorum immortalium numen placari arbitrantur, publiceque eiusdem generis habent instituta sacrificia."

[3] *De Situ Orbis*, III, 2. " Gentes superbæ, superstitiosæ, aliquando etiam immanes adeo, ut hominem optimam et gratissimam diis uictimam cæderent. . . . Habent tamen et facundiam suam, magistrosque sapientiæ druidas. Hi terræ mundique magnitudinem et formam, motus cœli ac siderum, et, quid dii uelint, scire profitentur. Docent multa nobilissimos gentis clam et diu iucenis annis, aut in specu, aut in abditis saltibus."

[4] *Ibid.*, III, 6. " Sena in Britannico mari, Osismicis aduersa littoribus, Gallici numinis oraculo insignis est ; cuius antistites perpetua uirginitate sanctæ, numero nouem esse traduntur ; Gallicenas uocant, putantque ingeniis singularibus præditas, maria ac uentos conciliare carminibus, seque in quæ uelint animalia uertere, sanare quæ apud alios insanabilia sunt, scire uentura et prædicare : sed non nisi deditas nauigantibus, et in id Cantum, ut se consulerent profectis."

[5] *Lex Salica*, tit. 22, 77. *Recueil des historiens de la Gaule*, IV, pp. 136, 138.

[6] S. Gregory of Tours, *Historia Francorum*, IV, 29 ; V, 14, 40 ; VI, 35.

[7] *Lex Ripuariorum*, tit. 83. *Recueil* . . . IV, p. 251.

[8] *Lex Wisigothorum*, Lib. VI, tit. 2, 1. 3. It is curious to note that certain judges in doubtful cases had resource to augury to decide the right. The law places these practices on the same level as inquiries of a diviner concerning the health of the Prince or any of the royal stock.

[9] C. J. Hefele, *Conciliengeschichte*, 2nd ed., 9 vols, 8vo, Fribourg-im-Brisgau, 1890, *sqq.*, p. 9, Sec. 284. " De incantatoribus uolens (?), qui instinctu diaboli cornua præcantare dicuntur, si superiores forte personæ sint, a liminibus excommunicatione pellantur ecclesiæ, humiliores uero personæ uel serui, correpti ad iudicium fustigentur, ut si se timore Dei corrigi forte dissimulant, uelut scriptum est uerberibus corrigantur."

[10] S. Gregory of Tours, *Historia Francorum*, IV, l. 11.

[11] Beaumont and Fletcher in their fine drama *The Tragedy of Thierry, King of France, and his brother Theoderet*, 4to, 1621, have for theatrical purposes effectively made Brunehaut a monster of evil. This, of course, is absolutely unhistorical. A play called *Brunhowlte* is mentioned by Henslowe in 1597, and a *Brunhowlle* in 1598.

[12] Philip Fabre, s.J., *Sacrosancta concilia* . . . 18 vols., folio, 1671, Vol, col. 1535.

[13] He was proclaimed King at Soissons in 751.

[14] *Capitulare incerti anni*, XL. *Recueil des historiens*, V, p. 691 : " Ut nemo sit qui ariolos suscitetur, uel somnia obseruat, uel ad auguria intendat : nec

sunt malefici, nec incantatores, nec phitones, nec cauculatores, nec tempestarii, uel obligatores. Et ubicumque sunt emendentur uel damnentur." Ch. XLI. " Ut obseruationes, quos stulti faciunt ad arbores uel petras uel fontes, ubicumque inueniuntur, tollantur et destinantur." The exact force of *damnentur*, let them be cast into a close prison, is made clear by a *Capitulare* of the year 805 : " Sed tali moderatione fiat eadem districtio ne uitam perdant, sed ut saluentur in carcere afflicti, usque dum, Deo inspirante, spondeant emendationem peccatorum." *Recueil des historiens*, V, p. 674. The *obligatores* make witches' knots or witches' ladders, *la ghirlanda delle streghe ;* these are woven to-day in England and Italy ; they are also *noueurs d'aiguillette.* There are also other Capitularies of Charlemagne which forbid superstitious practices, each Bishop is admonished to investigate and extirpate any heathen observances and to be zealous in cleansing his diocese of " diuinosque et sortilegos, aut auguria, phylacteria, incantationes, uel omnes spurcitias gentilium." *Capitulare anno* 769, ch. vii. Also *Capitulare anno* 789, ch. iv. " Ut nullus in psalterio uel in euangelio uel in aliis rebus sortire præsumat nec diuinationes aliquas obseruare." This allusion to the mode of divination by a book (usually the Bible or Vergil, *Uergilianæ sortes*), is extremely interesting. The practice preserves even to-day. See further on these capitularies, Soldan, *Geschichte der Hexenprozesse* . . . Stuttgard, 1880.

[15] De Cauzons, *La Magie et la Sorcellerie en France*, Paris, II, p. 118.

[16] " Extant et alia perniciosissima mala quæ ex ritu gentilium remansisse dubium non est, ut sunt magi, harioli, sortilegi, uenefici, diuini, incantatores, somniatorum coniectores, quos diuina lex irretractabiliter puniri iubet." The scriptural texts are quoted. " Dubium etenim non est, sicut multis est notum quod aquibusdam præstigiis atque diabolicis illusionibus, ita mentes quorumdam inficiantur poculis amatoriis, cibi, phylacteriis, ut in insaniam versi a plerisque iudicentur, dum proprias non sentiunt contumelias. Ferunt enim suis maleficiis aera posse conturbare, et grandinem inmittere, futura prædicere, fructus et lac aufere, aliisque dare et innumera a talibus fieri dicuntur. Qui ut fuerint huius modi comperti, uiri seu feminæ, in tantum disciplina et uigore principis acrius corrigendi sunt, in quantum manifestius ausu nefando et temerario seruire diabolo non metuunt." *Concil. Parisiensis liber III*, c. 2 ; Labbe, *Concilia*, VII, col. 1658 ; Soldan, *Geschichte der Hexenprozesse* . . . p. 130.

[17] Et quia audiuimus quod malefici homines et sortiariæ per plena loca in nostro regno insurgunt quorum maleficiis iam multi homines infirmati et plures mortui sunt ; quoniam, sicut sancti Dei homines scripserunt, Regis ministerium est impios de terra perdere, maleficos et uenefices non sinere uiuere, expresse præcipimus . . . ut tales perquirantur et comprehendantur. Et si iam inde comprobati masculi, uel comprobatæ feminæ sunt, sicut lex et iustitia docet, disperdantur. Et non solum tales istius mali auctores, sed et conscii ac complices illorum, siue masculorum siue feminarum, disperdantur, ut una cum eis scientia tanti mali de terra nostra pereat. *Capitulaire de Hiersy-sur-Oise*, 873 A.D., VII ; *Recueil* . . . Vol. VII, p. 686. Ficker, *Die gestezliche Einführung der Todesstrafe für Hetzerei (Mittheitungen des Instituts für œsterreichische Geschichtsforschung*, 1880), p. 181, allows that death by burning was a punishment for sorcerers common among the Franks and Saxons in very early times, although in cases not considered capital other penalties were, of course, inflicted.

[18] Grimm, *Deutsche Rechtsalterthum*, 3rd ed., 1881, p. 923, Formulas of adjuration : Martène, *De Antiquis Ecclesiæ ritibus, Ordo*, III, VII, VIII, IX, XVI : *Recueil des historiens*, Vol. VI, p. 448. Dom J. Mabillon, *Uetera Analecta*, Paris, 1675, *sqq.*, 4 vols., Vol. I, p. 47. Conrad of Ursperg, *Conradi Urspergensis Chronicon*, anno 1126, in Vol. II of the *Collectio judiciorum* . . . of Charles du Plessis d'Argentré, Bishop of Tulle, 3 vols., folio, Paris, 1728. Goldast, *Collectio constitutionum imperii*, Frankfort, 2 vols., folio, 1613, Vol. II, p. 48. C. J. Hefele, *Conciliengeschichte*, 2nd ed., 1890, etc., p. 56. Hingmar, *De diuortio Lotharii, Recueil* . . . Vol. VII, p. 292. L. Tanon, *Histoire des justices* . . . Paris, 1883, p. 310. *Historia Vizeliacensis monasterii*, lib. iv, *Recueil* . . . Vol. XII, p. 343. In England the swimming ordeal is prescribed

in the ecclesiastical code of S. Edward the Confessor. In the seventeenth century many persons thought that witches flung into the water would swim because the demons with whom they had commerce and who possessed them were by nature fiery. This ancient ordeal was soon appropriated to test the witch only, and there are cases of it being put in practice as late as 1863 in a rural district of Norfolk, and possibly it was essayed on occasion even later.

[19] The holy Queen Emma, the mother of S. Edward the Confessor, proved her innocence of the charges of sacrilege and incontinence by walking unhurt over nine red-hot plough-shares laid in S. Swithun's Church at Winchester. So also S. Cunegunda, *ob.* 1040, feast 3 March, when calumniated appealed to God's judgement and walked without harm over burning plough-shares, as she is seen in a print by Hans Burgmair.

[20] Over the Florentine simoniacs. S. Peter Igneus is often termed Blessed, but in the Vallombrosian Proper, *Officia Propria Sanctorum Ordinis et Congregationis Uallis Umbrosæ*, Florence, 1892, we have : " Die VIII Februarii. In Festo *S. Petri Ignei*, Ord. N. Cardinalis Episcopi Albanensis, et Confessoris. Dup. 2, Cl. cum Octaua (nisi in Quadragesima)." The antiphon to the Magnificat at First Vespers is : " Excussit Dominus flammam ignis, et fecit medium eius quasi uentum roris flantem." The whole office contains many beautiful allusions to the Ordeal.

[21] Agobard, Archbishop of Lyons (*ob.* 840) wrote a *Liber aduersus . . . impia certamina*, and the Council of Valence, 855, prohibited the combat, reiterating the anathema of the Council of Worms twenty-six years before. Stephen V (885–91) forbade the ordeal, and Alexander II (1061–73) specifically condemned the hot iron, the cold or boiling water. Celestine III (1191–98) interdicted the duel, and Innocent III (1198–1216) would no longer suffer ecclesiastical assistance at ordeals of any nature whatsoever.

[22] Soldan, *Geschichte der Hexenprozesse*, Stuttgart, 1880.

[23] Acts of the Council of Orleans in the *Recueil des historiens de la France*, Vol. X, p. 538.

[24] *Gesta Pontificum Treuirensium ; Recueil des historiens*, XI, p. 194.

[25] Guillaume Godeau, a monk of S. Martial, *Chronicon* (1193), in the *Recueil des historiens*, XIII, p. 677.

[26] Bernard of Constance, *De Berengerii hærisiarchæ damnatione multiplici.* Migne, *Patres Latini*, Vol. CXLVIII, 1456 ; and Guitmond, *De Corporis et Sanguinis Christi ueritate in Eucharistia*, *P.L.*, Vol. CXLIX, 1429, 1480.

[27] Aubry or Alberie, a monk of Trois Fontaines, *Chronicle (Recueil des historiens de la France*, XI, p. 354).

[28] *Decretales Gregorii IX*, l.v, tit. 21, c. 2.

[29] Rigordus, *De Gestis Philippi Augusti (Recueil des historiens* . . . XVII, p. 38).

[30] " Nos considerantes quod dicti fratres prædicatores tam contra profligandas hæreses quam contra pestes alias mortiferas extirpandas se dedicauerunt euangelizationi uerbi Dei, et quod uos diuersis occupationum turbinibus agitati uix ualetis inter mundantium sollicitudinem angustias respirare. . . ." Bull of Gregory IX to the Archbishops, Bishops, and all Prelates of France, 13 April, 1233. John II Rumigney Prince Bishop of Li\`ge, had introduced the Dominicans in his diocese in 1229, reserving the old rights of the episcopal courts ; Peter Amélius, Archbishop of Narbonne (1226–45) had called upon Fra Ferrier, o.p., to act as inquisitor throughout his province, so the Papal edict to a large extent merely confirmed and sanctioned an existing state of affairs.

[31] See the roll of Inquisitors given by C. Donais, *Documents pour servir à l'histoire de l'Inquisition dans le Languedoc*, 2 vols., Paris, 1900, and by Dr. Paul Fredericq at the beginning of Vols. I and III of his *Corpus documentorum Inquisitionis hæreticæ prauitatis neerlandicæ*, 5 vols, Gand, 1889, *sqq.*

[32] Aubey de Trois Fontaines, *Recueil des historiens* . . . Vol. XXI, pp. 618 and 624.

[33] Vaisette, *Histoire du Languedoc*, édition Privat, IX, p. 39. In connexion with this extraordinary tale it may not be impertinent to record in brief the title of an old chap-book (*c.* 1709) : " The Miracle of Miracles. Being a full and

true Account of *Sarah Smith*, Daughter of *John Symons*, a Farmer, who lately was an Inhabitant of Darken Parish in Essex, that was brought to Bed of a Strange Monster, the Body of it like a Fish with Scales thereon, it had no Legs but a pair of great Claws. . . . Which eat and fed for some time which Monster has surprised many Thousand people that came there to see it . . . it was by Command of the Magistrates knock'd on the Head, and several Surgeons were there to dissect it. Also you have a Funeral Sermon on the Woman who brought it forth, a very Wicked Liver, and disobedient to her Parents, and one that was Mightily given to Wishing, Cursing, and Swearing. . . . This strange and unheard of Monster was brought into the World in May last, and if any doubt the truth thereof, it will be certify'd by the Minister and Church-Wardens of the said Parish of Darkins in Essex as aforesaid.''

[34] Joannes Eleemosynarius, or Joannes Misericors, Patriarch of Alexandria (606–616), born at Amathus in Cyprus, c. 550, and died in that island 616. His body was brought to Constantinople, and thence to Ofen by King Matthias Corvinus of Hungary. In 1530 it was translated to Toll, near Presburg, and finally, in 1632, to Presburg Cathedral, where it is venerated to-day. He is commemorated by the Catholic Church on 23 January, by the Greeks on 12 November. He was inexhaustible in his charities, continually practising the profoundest humility.

[35] Fabré Palaprat, *Recherches Historiques sur les Templiers*, Paris, 1835. The existence of Theocletes is historically at least exceedingly doubtful. That he was a successor of the Apostle S. John is, of course, absurd. But none the less, Hugues de Payens certainly absorbed some occult teaching, and perhaps some propagandist commission, from the Mandæan priests.

[36] The Druze catechism, a French translation of which is given by M. B. De Bock in his *Essai sur l'Histoire du Sabéism*, Paris, 1788, is illuminating, and there seems no reason to suspect its authenticity.

[37] Havemann, *Geschichte des Ausgangs des Tempelherrenordens*, Stuttgard, 1846, p. 211. Lettres de Thibaut de Bar, Bishop of Liège, and of John II of Brabant. Fredericq, *op. cit.*, II, n. 35, Letter to King Jayme II of Aragon. Villanueva, *Viage literario*, V, p. 176. Schottmüller, *Der Untergang des Templerorden*, Vol. I, p. 369.

[38] As early as the year 1238 Gregory IX had declared that he suspected the Templars of heresy ; in 1265 Clement IV contemplated a searching examination of the Order, which in 1272 the Council of Salsburg impeached as sadly in need of drastic reform.

[39] Michelet, *Procès des Templiers*, I, p. 553.

[40] Here we probably have some connexion with the Adamite heresy, whose adherents condemned marriage as unknown in Eden and celebrated their rites in a state of nudity. They date perhaps from the second century. They were seemingly an offshoot of the Carpocratian Gnostics who professed a sensual mysticism and complete emancipation from the moral law. In the thirteenth century these excesses were revived in the Netherlands by the Brethren and Sisters of the Free Spirit, and in an even grosser form in the fourteenth by the Beghards in Germany, a sect practically exterminated in 1421. Owing to the edict of toleration by Joseph II these practices reappeared in Bohemia after 1781, and the Adamites actually had to be suppressed by force in 1849. In April, 1925, investigations were made into an extraordinary religious cult at Oroville, California. (*The Sunday Express*, 26 April, 1925 ; from New York correspondent, 25 April.) Anna Rhodes, the high priestess of the sect declared : '' I am Eve, my husband is Adam. We are reincarnated. I was named a disciple of God to purge my brother and others by fire.'' Nude dances were performed, and the fire ceremony consisted of branding on the naked flesh. It appeared that in consequence of this branding a devotee, Herman Schalow, died, possibly from shock or exposure, and District Attorney William Rothe ordered an inquiry. Anna Rhodes asserted that her home at Biggs, thirteen miles from Oroville, was the original Garden of Eden, re-created by divine dispensation. A naked orgy took place in the Rhodes farmyard round a huge bonfire, and Frank Rhodes, Mrs. Rhodes' son, related that the blood of animals was used in wild sacrificial ceremonies of the most bestial

kind, on one occasion a live lamb being burned. It is clear that these ceremonies recall the Adamite abominations.

[41] Dr. Havelock Ellis writes : " At the beginning of the fourteenth century,
sodomy was still regarded as very prevalent. At that time it was especially
associated with the Templars, who, it has been supposed, brought it from the
East. Such a supposition, however, is not required to account for the existence
of homosexuality in France." *Studies in the Psychology of Sex*, Vol. II. *Sexual
Inversion*, 3rd ed., Philadelphia, 1915, p. 36.

[42] Loiseleur, *La doctrine secrète des Templiers*, 1872, p. 192.

[43] *Beschuldigungen gegen den Tempelherrenorden*, Berlin, 1782.

[44] βαφή (βάπτω), a *dipping* of red-hot iron into water, *the temper produced
thereby*. τὴν βαφὴ ἀφιᾶσιν ὥσπερ σίδηρος, εἰρηνην ἄγοντες. Aristotle, *Politics*, VII,
14. Æschylus, *Agamemnon*, 239, κρόκου βαφάς, the saffron-*dyed* robe.

[45] According to some accounts the Head of the Templars was bearded. The
Cabbalists represented the creative God by a bearded head. C. W. Heckethorn.
Secret Societies, London, 1897, Vol. I, p. 160. The suggestion that *Baphomet*
is a corruption of Mahomet is obvious, but almost certainly mistaken. See also
Joseph de Hamner, *Memoires sur deux coffrets gnostiques du Moyen-Age du
cabinet de M. le duc de Blacas*, Paris, Dondey-Dupré, 4to, 1832. The author
believed that in these boxes he had found the various Cabbalistic symbols of
the worship of Baphomet. J. Collin de Plancy says that one of the Heads,
gilded, which had been seized in a Templar's fortress at the time of the
dissolution of the Order was long preserved at Marseilles. *Dictionnaire Infernal*
Paris, 1863, sixième édition, p. 656 ; article *Tête de Bophomet*.

[46] Peter Mogilas ; Kimmel, *Monumenta fidei eccl. orient.*, Jena, 1850, I,
p. 180.

[47] " Quod habebat quendam librum paruulum, quem bene ostendebat, de
statutis ordinis, sed alium Secretiorem habebat, quem pro toto mundo non
ostendebat." Michelet, *Procès des Templiers*, I, p. 175.

[48] The pretended discovery in 1877 of these secret statutes by Dr. Merzdorf,
head librarian of the Grand Duchy of Oldenburg, is entirely untrustworthy.

[49] In the *Titurel* of Albrecht von Scharfenburg, the Graal Knights, and
distinctly spoken of as Templars. Many Troubadours and Minniesingers
spread Gnostic doctrines throughout Europe under the allegories of Graal
legends. It is significant that the Graal cycle never found any favour with
the Church.

[50] It has not been preserved.

[51] George Ives, *A History of Penal Methods*, Chap. I, p. 24, and n. 9.

[52] A whole literature of research and debate has gathered round the
Templars. It must suffice to specify a few works : Pierre Messie (Pedro
Mexia), gentil-homme de Seuile, *Les diverses leçons de Pierre Messie*, Paris,
12mo, 1556. Pierre Du Puy, *Traité concernant l'histoire de France*, 4to, 1654
(*La Condamnation des Templiers*) ; *Histoire de l'abolition de l'ordre des
Templiers*, Paris, 12 mo, 1779. K. Anton, *Versuch einer Geschichte des Tempel-
herren Ordens*, 1781. F.-J. M. Raynouard, *Monuments historiques relatifs à la
condemnation des Chevaliers du Temple*, 8vo, 1813. Joseph de Hamner,
Mémories sur deux coffrets gnostiques du Moyen-Age, Paris, 4to, 1832. Fabré
Palaprat, *Recherches historiques sur les Templiers*, 1835. C. H. Maillard de
Chambrea, *Règle et statuts secrets des Templiers*, Paris, 8vo, 1841. Havemann,
Geschichte des Ausgangs des Tempelherrenordens, 1846. Jules Loiseleur, *La
doctrine secrète des Templiers*, 8vo, 1872. Dr. Hans Prutz, *Geheimlehre und
Geheimsstatuten des Tempelherren-Ordens*, 1879. H. Gaidoz, *Note sur une
statuette en bronze représentant un homme assis, les jambes croisées*, *Revue
Archéologique*, Nouvelle série, 22. année, Vol. XLI, p. 36. The statue is phallic,
and connected with the Templars' secret cult. Schottmüller, *Der Untergang
des Templerordens*, 1887. E. Rey, *Etude sur les Templiers*, 8vo, 1891. Gmelin,
Schuld oder Unschuld des Templerordens, 1893.

[53] Guillaume de Nangis, *Recueil des historiens*, XX, p. 608. *Chroniques de
St. Denis*, *Recueil*, XX, p. 690. Girard de Frachet, *Recueil*, XXI, p. 31.
Jean de Saint-Victor, *Recueil*, XXXI, pp. 644, 652, 655. Rigault, *Le procès
de Guichard, évêque de Troyes*, Paris, 1896.

[54] Bernard Gui, *Recueil des historiens*, XXI, p. 727. Abbé Albi, *Autour de Jean XXII, Hugues Géraud, évêque de Cahors*, Cahors, 1904. Langlois, *Revue de Paris*, 1 February, 1906, pp. 532, 533.

[55] Doat, Bibliothèque Nationale MSS., XXVII, 150, Paris, 1829, III, p. 212.

[56] Lamothe-Langon, *Histoire de l'Inquisition en France*.

[57] Extracts from the archives of the Toulouse Inquisition. Lamothe-Langon, III, p. 235.

[58] *Ibid.*, III, p. 226 *sqq.*

[59] *Ibid.*, III, p. 226.

[60] I have used the edition, 5 vols., Douai, 1605.

[61] It may be noted that Jacquier recommends extreme caution in accepting denunciations for Witchcraft.

[62] Born at Gerona, *c.* 1320, and died there 4 January, 1399. Eymeric, " prædicator ueridicus, inquisitor intrepidus, doctor egregius," attacked with much vigour and pertinacity the philosophy of Blessed Ramón Lull, Doctor Illuminatus, and the Lullists, on which account he was temporarily banished by King John I of Aragon. Quétif and Echard, *Scriptores Ordinis Prædicatorum* (Paris, 1719), I, 709–19, give the titles of thirty-five of Eymeric's works, contained in eleven MSS. volumes.

[63] Barcelona, 1503; and many subsequent editions of which the best is that printed at Rome, 1578, with a copious commentary by Francesco Peña, the famous Spanish canonist.

[64] The first Bull of Innocent VIII was issued 5 December, 1484.

[65] I have, with constant reference to the *editio princeps*, generally used the excellent reprint in four volumes, 1669, to which have been appended many other authoritative treatises on Witchcraft.

[66] Certain writers have made themselves very merry concerning Sprenger's etymologies, but this is impertinent matter.

[67] Compare the brilliant description in *The Ingoldsby Legends, The Witches' Frolic*.

[68] " Deux jours après fut condamné à être ars et fut son corps ramené en poudre." *Memoires de Jacques du Clercq*, edited by the Baron de Reiffenberg, 4 vols., Brussels, 1823, Vol. III, pp. 29, 30.

[69] Tanon, *Histoire des tribunaux d'Inquisition en France*, p. 125. Limborch, *Historia Inquisitionis*, Lib. I, c. xxiii.

[70] Chroniques de Jean Molinet, édition Buchon, Vol. IV, p. 147.

[71] *The Month*, January, 1922.

[72] It may not here be impertinent perhaps to record my admiration of the chapel and altar of S. Joan in Rouen Cathedral. It is a sanctuary in which one lingers with devotion, and which one leaves with regret.

[73] With admirable ingenuity and inconsequence Miss Murray (*Witch-Cult in Western Europe*, pp. 276–9) hails Gilles de Rais also as an " Incarnate God— or at any rate a candidate for that honour," whatever this latter phrase may mean. Both S. Joan and Gilles de Rais were " Devils," that is to say " Incarnate Gods," presumably because each rode a black war-horse ! Folk-lore has run mad.

[74] Boissard et Maulde, *Gilles de Rais, dit Barbe bleue*, Paris, 1886. De la Borderie, *Histoire de Bretagne*, Vol. IV, p. 248 *sqq.* Jean Chartier, *Histoire de Charles VII*, anno 1440. Monstrelet, *Chroniques*, édition de Buchon, Paris, 1875, II, c. 248. Charles Duplessis d'Argentré, *Collectio iudiciorum . . .* 3 vols., folio, Paris, 1728, Vol. I, 2, c. 27. It is often said that the local traditions of Gilles de Rais gave rise to the story of Blue Beard, Perrault's *Barbe-Bleue*, but it seems more probable that this story is founded on the legend of an old Breton King, Cômor, who ruled in the sixth century, and the remains of whose castle are yet shown.

[75] Baissac, *Les Grands jours de la Sorcellerie*, Paris, 1889, p. 339.

[76] It is undoubted that some such epidemic mania did prevail at the time. In recent months (May, 1925) there have been an extraordinary number of cases of the violation and murder of children, e.g. George Jeffrey, a lad of fifteen years and seven months, who killed Joan Annett, ten years old, on 24 April, 1925.

[77] Adrien de Montalembert, *Aumosnier du Roy François I.* " La merveil-leuse histoire de lesprit qui depuis nagueres s'est apparu au monastère des religieuses de Saint Pierre de Lyon, laquelle est plaine de grant admiration." Colophon : *Nouuellement imprime a paris en la rue Saint Jaques a l'enseigne du chasteau rouge, pres les Mathurins (chez Guillaume de Bossozel).* Acheue le XVᵉ iour doctobre lan mil cinq cens xxviij.

[78] Norcia was infamous as a centre of Witchcraft. Cellini tells us of the priest who was minded to consecrate a book of spells among the Norcian mountains. Cf. Folengo, *Maccaronea XXI* : " Qualiter ad stagnum Nursæ sacrare quadernos."

[79] Always the hot-bed of strange heresies. Here (rue de La Martinière) lived the esoteric abbé J.-A. Boullan (*ob.* 3 January, 1893), whom Huysmans has introduced into *Là-Bas* as Dr. Johannès. "Lyon est aussi le refuge du mysticisme, le havre des idées préternaturelles et des droits douteux . . . c'est là que les envoûtements sévissent, car à la Guillotière, on fait maléficier, pour un louis, les gens ! " *Là-Bas*, XX.

[80] Bodin, *De la Démonomanie des sorciers*, II, v.

[81] Iehan Boulæse, prêtre, professeur des Saintes Lettres Hébraiques, pauvre perpétuel du Collège de Montaigut. *Le manuel de l'admirable victoire du corps de Dieu sur l'esprit maling Beelzebub, obtenue à Leon*, 1566, Paris, D. Du Val., 1575, 16mo. Also the same author's *L'abbrégée histoire du grand miracle par nostre Sauueur et Seigneur Iesvs-Christ en la Saincte Hostie du Sacrament de l'Autel, fait à Laon*, 1588, Paris, Belot, 1573, 16mo. 16 leaves.

[82] Bodin, *De la Demonomanie*, III, v. "Confessa deuant le Roy . . . la façon du transport des sorciers, des dances, des sacrifices faicts à Satan, des paillardises auec les Diables en figure d'hommes & de femmes : & que chacun prenoit des poudres pour faire mourir hommes, bestes, et fruits."

[83] Bodin, *De la Demonomanie*, IV, 1.

[84] Baudrillat, *Jean Bodin et son temps*, Paris, 1853. Brunetière, *Trois artisans de l'idéal classique* in *Revue des deux mondes*, 1 March, 1907.

[85] It has been reprinted in Cimber and Danjou, *Archives curieuses de l'Histoire de France*, Vol. XII, as also in L'Estoile's *Journal de Henri III*, Vol. III (pp. 369 *sqq.*) of the edition of 1744. See also the Leber Catalogue, II, No. 4037 ; Brunet's *Manual*, V, 457 ; and the Ouvaroff Catalogue, No. 1736.

[86] Collin de Plancy, *Dictionnaire Infernal*, 6th ed., 1863, p. 154, *sub. v.* Chamouillard.

[87] *Le Petit Albert. Le solide trésor des secrets merveilleux de la magie naturelle et cabalistique*, of which there are numberless editions, many being mere chap-books, gives stupid formulas how to perform this charm and how to dissolve it.

[88] *Discours veritable sur le fait de Marthe Brossier, de Romorantin, prétendue démoniaque.* [By a physician named Marescot.] Paris, Mamert Patisson, 8vo, 1599 (Tallemant des Reaux wrongly attributes this book to Mgr. Le Boutellier, Archbishop of Tours). This should be checked by the work of the saintly Cardinal de Berulle, *Traité des énergumènes, suivi d'un discours sur la possession de Marthe Brossier, contre les calomnies d'un médecin de Paris*, Troyes, 8vo, 1599. Written as by Léon d'Alexis, it was reprinted under the real name of the author at Paris, 8vo, 1631, in which year there were two several editions, Cottereau and Fiacre Dehors. All copies of the *Discours* which I have been able to examine end abruptly at page 56.

[89] Ch. Pfister, *Nicolas Remy et la sorcellerie en Lorraine, Revue historique*, 32 year, Vol. 93, March-April, 1907, p. 225 *sqq.* ; May-June, 1907, p. 43.

[90] I have used the quarto edition, Lyons, 1595, The *Dæmonolatria* was reprinted at Hamburg as late as 1693.

[91] This date I owe to Yve-Plessis, who is scrupulously exact. He gives the 8vo 1590 edition of Lyons (Rigaud) as the third edition. The 8vo Lyons edition (Iean Pillehotte), 1602, is quoted by most authorities, e.g. Collin de Plassey, Theodore de Cauzons, as *editio princeps*. But James I in his *Dæmonologie*, Edinburgh, 1597, quotes from and translates Boguet, to whom he is greatly but silently indebted, as in the passage concerning legal witnesses : " But in my opinion, since in a mater of treason against the Prince, barnes or

wiues, or neuer so diffamed persons, may of our law serue for sufficient witnesses and proofes. I thinke surely that by a far greater reason, such witnesses may be sufficient in matters of high treason against God : For who but Witches can be prooues, and so witnesses of the doings of Witches." I have failed to trace the exact date of the first edition of the *Discours*, and the whole bibliography is exceedingly difficult. We have : " Seconde édition augmentée," Lyons, Pillehotte, 8vo, 1603 ; other editions, Paris, Binet, 8vo, 1603 ; Rouen, Le Mesgissier, 12mo, 1603 ; Lyons, Pillehotte, 8vo, 1605 ; Rouen, Osmont, 12mo, 1606 ; Rouen, de Beauvais, 12mo, 1606; Lyons, Pillehotte, 8vo, 1607. There is another " Seconde ?dition," Lyons, Rigaud, 8vo, 1608 ; " Troisièsme édition," Lyons, Rigaud, 8vo, 1610 ; Lyons, Pillehotte, 8vo, 1611.

[92] Other editions, Paris, Abel Langelier, 4to, 1612 ; Paris, Nic. Buon, 4to, 1612 ; " Reueu corrigé et augmenté," Paris, Nic. Buon, 4to, 1613. Some copies, which are very rare and much sought after by bibliophiles, contain an illustration depicting the orgies of the Sabbat, engraved by the Polish artist J. Ziarnko.

[93] *La chasse aux sorcieres dans le Labourd* (1609), *Etude historique*, by J. Bernou, Agen, Calvet et Célérie, 8vo, 1897, is wholly based on de Lancre. An engraving from Goya is given as a frontispiece.

[94] Wentworth Webster, *Basque Legends*, 2nd ed., 1879, p. 65.

[95] In some Ursuline communities solemn vows are taken, and papal enclosure is in force. In some houses the vows, though perpetual, are simple. To-day many large and important communities still retain their independent organization.

[96] The name is variously spelled in documents and contemporary printed accounts of the trial : Gaufridy, Gaufredi, Gofridi, Jaufredi, Gauffridi, Godefroy, Jauffret, Jouffroy.

[97] Born at Saint-Zacharie, near Sainte-Baume, in 1543, he took the habit of S. Dominic at an early age and filled many high and important positions in the Order. He promoted various reforms in the province of Southern France, and was in high favour with Pope S. Pius V. He had the gift of prophecy, and his cause having been introduced he is declared Venerable by the Holy See.

[98] A considerable literature has grown up round Madeleine de la Palud and there are many valuable monographs and detached studies. The contemporary *Histoire admirable de la possession et conversion d'une pénitente séduite par un Magicien la faisant sorcière* . . . by Father Sebastian Michaelis, 8vo, 1612, which ran into some eight editions, Paris, Douai, Lyons, 1613, 1614, and later, is, of course, of prime importance. Raoul Gineste, *Les Grandes Victimes de l'Hystérie, Louis Gauffridi* . . . *et Magdeleine de la Palud*, Paris (no date, c. 1900), contains much valuable material but is ill-arranged, and must be used with great caution. The work of Ven. Sebastian Michaelis was translated into English, London, 1613, *Admirable Historie of the Possession and Conversion of a Penitent Woman*.

[99] Our chief authority is the contemporary work of J. Lenormant de Chisemont, [I] *Histoire veritable, mémorable de ce qvi c'est passé sovs l'exorcisme de trois filles possédées ès pais de Flandre, en la descouuerte et confession de Marie de Sains, soy disant Princesse de la Magie ; et Simone Dourlet complice, et autres. Ou il est avssi traité de la police du Sabbat, et secrets de la Synagogue des magiciens et magiciennes. De l'Antichrist et de la fin du monde. [II] De la vocation des magiciens et magiciennes par le ministère des démons : et particvlièrement des chefs de la magi a sçauoir de Magdeleine de la Palud, Marie de Sains, Louys Gaufridy, Simone Dourlet, etc. . . . Item de la vocation accomplie par l'entremise de la seule authorité ecclesiastique à sçauoir de Didyme, Maberthe, Loyse, etc. Auec Trois petits tractez. Paris, De Varennes et Nicolas Bvon*, 1623, 3 parts in two volumes, 8vo. The second volume, unknown to Brunet, and bearing (as above) a different title from Volume I is of the last rarity. One may also consult *Les confessions de Didyme, sorciére pénitente, avec les choses qu'elle a déposées touchant la synagogue de Satan ; Plus les instances que cette complice (qui depuis est rechûtée) a faites pour rendre nulles ses premières confessions : Veritable récit de tout ce qui s'est passé en*

cette affaire, Paris, 1623, 8vo. A valuable work is *Historia de tribus energumenis in partibus Belgii, scilicet Magdalenæ de Palud, Mariæ de Sains*. Paris, 8vo, 1623.

[100] Urbain Grandier and the Loudun possessions have been the subject of a whole library of works. These range from contemporary records such as *Interrogatoire de maistre Urbain Grandier, prêtre* . . . Paris, 8vo, 1634, and *Arrest de condemnation de mort contre Maistre Vrbain Grandier, prestre* . . . Paris, 8vo, 1634, to Dr. G. Legué's *Urbain Grandier et les possédées de Loudun*, Paris, 8vo, 1880, and *Sœur Jeanne des Anges* . . . *Autobiographie d'une hysterique possédée* (with a preface by Charcot), Paris, 1886, and second edition, 1888. I have myself studied fifty-four separate monographs and studies, which list does not include incidental essays and chapters in other works. However graphic, such a narrative as that of Alexandre Dumas in *Crimes Célèbres* (1839–41) is utterly unreliable and has no more historical basis than the Dumas and Maquet drama *Urbain Grandier*, Paris, 1850. Many of the monographs deliberately suppress the facts that the possession did not cease upon Grandier's execution. In fact, most of these works must be used with caution.

[101] Görres, *La Mystique Divine*, French translation by Charles Sainte-Foi, 2nd ed. 1862, Vol. V, p. 232.

[102] It were wellnigh impossible to enumerate the vast number of books and pamphlets, over forty of which I have consulted, that deal with the Louviers scandals. Perhaps the most famous is that of the theologian Desmarets : *Histoire de Magdelaine Bavent, Religieuse du Monastère de Saint-Louis de Louviers, auec sa confession generale & testamentaire, ou elle declare les abominations, impietez & sacrileges qu'elle a pratiqué & veu pratiquer tant dans ledit Monastère qu'au Sabbat & les personnes qu'elle y a remarquées. Ensemble l'Arrest donné contre Mathurin Picard, Thomas Boullé, & ladite Bavent. tous conuaincus du crime de Magie. Dediée à Madame la Duchesse d'Orléans. Paris, Iacques le Gentil*, 4to, 1652. Reprinted twice in the same year, as also at Rouen, 1878. A certain physician named Yvelin, who showed himself sceptical, published an *Examen*, Paris, 4to (18 pp.), 1643, but several writers gave a complete and unanswerable reply to his objections. Görres has an excellent account of Madeleine Bavent.

[103] *Discours prodigieux et epouuentable de trois Espagnols & une Espagnole, magiciens et sorciers qui se faisoient porter par les diables de ville en ville* . . . *Ensemble l'arrest prononcé contr'eux par la tour de parlement de Bordeaux*, 1610. Paris, 8vo (15 pp.), 1625.

[104] I have examined some fifteen contemporary accounts. Naturally there was a whole crop of satires, pamphlets, and pasquils on the occasion, and ephemeral writings such as *La Magicienne Estrangère*, a tragedy, by " un bon François," Rouen, 8vo, 1617.

[105] Le Sieur Pichard, *Admirable Vertu des saints exorcismes sur les princes d'enfer, possédant réellement vertueuse Dam^{selle} Elisabeth de Ranfaing*, Nancy, 12mo, 1622.

[106] Collin de Plancy, *Dictionnaire Infernal*, 6me édition, Paris, 1863, p. 205.

[107] *Mémoires de la société d'archéologie lorraine*, 3e série, Vol. X, Nancy, 1882, p. 257 *sqq.*

[108] Son of Clotaire I, King of Soissons or Neustria, 562–83.

[109] S. Gregory of Tours, 538–39 to 593–94. The fifth and sixth books of his famous *Historia Francorum* treat of events which took place between 575–84, and were written in 585.

[110] Pierre Grégoire, a famous lawyer, originally of Toulouse, and then of Pont-à-Mousson. The citation is from his *Syntagma iuris uniuersi atque legum pene omnium gentium et rerum publicarum*, 3a pars, l. xxxiv, c. 2.

[111] S. Augustine, born 13 November, 354 ; died 28 August, 430. S. Severinus Boethius, whose local cult at Pavia was confirmed by the Sacred Congregation of Rites in 1883, born 480, died 524–25.

[112] But Satanism and Witchcraft are essentially the same thing.

[113] E. Gilbert, *Sorciers et magiciens*, Moulins, 12mo, 1895. Dom Calmet, *Traité sur les Apparitions*, Paris, 1751, Vol. I, pp. 72, 74 *sqq.*

[114] Lebrun, *Histoire des pratiques superstitieuses.*

[115] *Idem.*

[116] " Il avait acheté un écu l'enfant qui fut sacrifié à cette messe qui lui fut présenté par une grande fille et ayant tiré du sang de l'enfant qu'il piqua à la gorge avec un canif, il en versa dans le calice, après quoi l'enfant fut retiré et emporté dans un autre lieu, dont ensuite on lui rapporter le cœur et les entrailles pour en faire une deuxieme [oblation]." François Ravaisson, *Archives de la Bastille.*

[117] Said to be Louis XIV or Charles II. But this purely conjectural, and the assertion of Madame de la Desoeillet's was probably quite untrue.

[118] " On a pensé que cet homme mystérieux devait être lord Buckingham. Il semblerait ici que la Desoeillet travaillant pour Louis XIV, auquel on avait fait prendre aussi bien qu'à Charles II d'Angleterre ce mélange ignoble." Docteurs Caufyenon et Jaf, *Les Messes Noires,* Paris, 1905, p. 125. But surely this is mere guess-work.

[119] F. Ravaisson, *Archives* . . . 1679–81, p. 336.

[120] Jesus saith to her : Mary. She, turning, saith to him : Rabboni (which is to say, Master), S. John's Gospel, xx. 16.

[121] Paris. A. Durand et Pedone Lauriel, 1866–84, 17 vols., 8vo. S. Caleb, *Les Véritables et les Fausses Messes Noires,* c. xiv (*Messes Noires sous Louis XIV*) ; Roland Brévannes, *L'Orgie Satanique à travers les Siècles,* Paris, 1904, Troisième partie, c. 11 (*La Messe Noire sous Louis XIV*) and c. iii (*Madame de Montespan chez la Voisin*) ; and Docteurs Cauffeynon et Jaf, *Les Messes Noires,* Paris, 1905, c. ix, give excellent summaries of the witch-cult under Louis XIV.

[122] Ravaisson, *Archives de la Bastille,* X.

[123] Cf. *S. Matthew* ix. 32, and xii. 22.

[124] A. Floquet, *Histoire du Parlement de Normandie.* Rouen, Edouard Frère, 1840–42, 7 vols., 8vo, Vol. V, p. 374.

[125] The Eudists, or Society of Jesus and Mary, instituted at Caen, France, 25 March, 1643, by Saint Jean Eudes, is an ecclesiastical body for the education of priests in seminaries and the giving of missions. The Eudists direct many colleges in Belgium, Spain, South America, Canada, and the West Indies. The majority of Fathers, however, is still resident in France.

[126] Calmeil, *De la Folie,* II, p. 401. A somewhat prejudiced account.

[127] Miguel de Molinos, 1640–96, the founder of Quietism, taught interior annihilation and the complete disregard of bodily acts in attaining a perfect purity of soul. Hence followed the most lascivious practices. Innocent XI, in the Bull *Cœlestis Pastor,* 2 November, 1687, condemns as heretical, suspect, erroneous, and scandalous, sixty-eight propositions which Molinos admitted to be his, although not all are to be found in *La Guida Spirituale,* Rome, 1675. September 3, 1687, Molinos was sentenced to perpetual imprisonment of a greatly mitigated nature.

[128] Even now ignorant and contemptible party-writers retail these incidents and assert the truth of la Cadière's story in order to attack the Society of Jesus. Books and pamphlets to which the scandals gave rise are very numerous. I have examined some eighty of these. Many are violently partizan libels such as : *Factum pour Marie Catherine Cadière contre le Père J.-B. Girard, jésuite, où ce religieux est accusé de l'avoir portée par un abominable Quiétisme, aux plus criminels excès de l'impudicité, et d'avoir, sous la voile de la plus haute spiritualité, jetté dans les mêmes excès six autres dévotes, qui, comme elle, s'étoient mises sous sa direction.* La Haye, Scheurlear, 8vo, 1731. Of course not the slightest credence must be given to the vomit of Jansenist venom and spite. A good work is Pazerpy-Thorame's *Démonstration des impostures sacrilèges des accusateurs du P. Girard . . . et de l'innocence de ce père.* Aix, *s.d.* [1731], folio. As we might expect, we also find obscenities inspired by the anti-clericals : *La sainte d'Ollioules ou éclaircissements sur le rapport mystérieux entre le P. Girard et la demoiselle Cadière,* Paris, 1738, editions of which containing the lewd pictures are very rare. *Les Amours en estampe du P. Girard et de la Belle Marie Cadière,* 1740, consists of a series of thirty-two bawdy engravings. *Les Amours de Sainfroid, jésuite, et d'Eulalie, fille dévote.*

Histoire véritable. Suivie de quelques nouvelles. A la Haye, 1729, is a con-
temporary piece of pornography. Above all we have the infamous *Thérèse
Philosophe, ou Memoires pour servir à l'Histoire de D. Dirrag et de Mademoiselle
Eradice* (anagrams of Girard and Cadière), 2 vols. La Haye, about 1748, with
twenty-four indecent illustrations. The book has been frequently reprinted,
e.g. in 1783, 1785 (twice), 1796, 1797, 1869, 1882, etc. The author was De
Montigny, although the Marquis de Sade attributed it to the Marquis Jean-
Baptiste de Boyer d'Argens. A ballad-opera, *The Wanton Jesuit; or, Innocence
Seduced,* performed at the little theatre in the Haymarket and published,
8vo, 1731, is worthless. In *de Nouveau Tarquin, Comédie en trois Actes,* 1730–1,
ascribed to J. J. Bel, Girard is also vilely traduced. This is a lewd little burletta
"assaissoné de salet.'s & de boufonneries . . . des fades turlupinades & les
plus sales équivoques y tiennent lieu de sel."

[129] Diderot, *Œuvres,* 22 vols., 8vo, Paris, 1821, Vol. XV, *Dictionnaire,* under
Divination ; Vol. XVII, *Ligature.*

[130] Condillac, *Œuvres,* 16 vols., 8vo, Paris, 1822, Vol. II, *Traité des systèmes,*
c. v, pp. 46, 53, 65.

[131] *Dictionnaire philosophique,* under *Démoniaque ; Magie.*

[132] *Journal historique et anecdotique,* E.-J.-F. Barbier, Paris, 1847.

[133] Henri d'Alméras, *Cagliostro,* Paris, 1904, p. 113.

[134] An excellent and detailed study is *La Croyance à la Magie au XVIIIe
Siècle en France dans les Contes, Romans, et Traités,* by Constantin Bila, Paris,
1925. See also V. Delaporte, *Du merveilleux dans la littérature francaise,* Paris,
1891.

[135] *Bibliothèque Ecclesiastique,* VIII, p. 90.

[136] *Justine ou les Malheurs de la Vertu,* 4 vols., 1797, Londres (Paris), II,
p. 239. The first edition of *Justine* is two volumes, 1791.

[137] *La Nouvelle Justine ou les Malheurs de la vertu, suivi de l'Histoire de
Juliette sa sœur, ou les Prospérités du vice,* Hollande (Paris, Bertrandet or
Didot ?), 1797, 10 vols., 18mo, Volume III, p. 35. There are several reprints of
this edition which should have a frontispiece and one hundred and four
engravings. Generally only one hundred illustrations are found, or even a
lesser number. One of the latest impressions is Brussels, 1875. The first
edition of *Juliette* (as distinct from *Justine*) is in four volumes, 8vo, 1796 ;
there is also an edition of six volumes, 18mo, 1797.

[138] *Ibid.,* III, 147.

[139] *Ibid.,* V, 1.

[140] *The Universe,* 22 May, 1925.

[141] *Là-Bas* ran through the *Echo de Paris,* and was published in book form
by Tresse et Stock, 1891. It caused an enormous sensation. Dr. Johannes is
the Abbé Boullan ; Gevingey, Ledos ; Docre, Rocca. Madame Chantelouve
is a real person. " Maman " Thibaut is sketched in Huysman's later work as
Madame Bavoil. *The Satanist,* a fine novel by Mrs. Hugh Fraser and J. I.
Stahlmann, gives a sad picture of diabolism in Italy. Mrs. Hugh Fraser wrote
to me : " The incidents of the story all have their foundation in fact, so far as
Satan-worship, its adherents and its victims are concerned. Would that it
were not so ! "

[142] Joanny Bricaud. André du Fresnois withdrew from circulation his
interesting study, *Une étape de la conversion de J.-K. Huysmans,* and a series
of articles by Henry Céard and Jean de Caldain, *Huysmans intime,* which were
being published in the *Revue hebdomadaire* in 1908, ceased most abruptly.

[143] *The Evening News,* Thursday, 2 March, 1922.

[144] *Daily Sketch,* Monday, 5 January, 1920.

CHAPTER VI

GERMANY

THE conversion of Germany to Christianity was very slow, for here the Church had a most difficult problem to solve, namely, to replace the primitive and seemingly natural conception of life by an entirely different one which appeared strange to the people, who for a long while regarded the new ideas not only with mistrust, but also with a certain contempt especially hard to eradicate and overcome. Their acceptance of the Christian teaching and name was at first purely mechanical, although when later it became a true and inner conviction few nations during the Middle Ages contributed more to the greatness of the Catholic Church.

In the actual conversion of this country much credit is due to the Irish and Scotch missionaries, but the real founders of Christianity in Germany are the Anglo-Saxons, and above all the glorious Apostle S. Boniface (Winfrid, Wynfrith), the pride and joy of the Benedictine family. S. Columbanus, who laboured in Swabia, was the first to come to the Continent, about 583; S. Fridolin founded Sachingen; Pirminius established the monastery of Reichenau in 724; whilst about 613 S. Gallus founded the Abbey of S. Gall, for many centuries one of the chief monastic houses in Europe. The cause of Christianity was spread in Bavaria by S. Rupert of Worms, at the beginning of the seventh century;[1] by S. Corbinian (d. 730) and S. Emmeram (d. 715). The chief missionary of the faith to the Franks was the Scotchman S. Kilian, at the end of the seventh century; the Frisians received Christianity through S. Willibrod, Bishop of Utrecht, who died at Echternach in Luxemburg, 7 November, 739.

On 15 May, 719, Pope S. Gregory II gave S. Boniface a solemn and official mandate "to go forth and preach the truths of both Testaments" unto "the wild nations of Germany," that is to say the heathens in Germany to the

465

right of the Rhine. The holy missionary when travelling through Bavaria found S. Rupert's labours had brought forth good fruit in a number of convents and sanctuaries, whilst Alamannia was equally flourishing. Thuringia, however, which at Rome was still assumed to be Christian had fallen back into the grossest heathendom. Duke Gotzbert, and his son Duke Hethan II, both converts of S. Kilian, and zealous promoters of the Faith, had been murdered. Their rebellious subjects forthwith lapsed into what was at best a mixture of Christianity and their old paganism. Moreover in 716 King Radbod, who had gained possession of all Frisia, drove out S. Willibrod and destroyed most of the churches, replacing them by temples and altars to the idols. This persecution, waged with hideous cruelty, lasted three years, for the tyrant perished miserably in 719, but its effects endured for more than a century. After a while S. Boniface was recalled to Rome when S. Gregory II on 30 November, 722 (723) consecrated him a regional Bishop, sending letters to his diocesans in Thuringia and Hessia enjoining canonical obedience to their new superior. When S. Boniface revisited Upper Hessia he discovered that even during his short absence a large number had drifted back into paganism, a loss which seems to some extent to have been the fault of the clergy, many of whom, ill-taught and irregularly appointed, were equally ready to say Mass for the Christians or offer sacrifices to the idols for the heathen. Naturally this caused the holy Bishop intense anxiety and suffering, as may be seen in his letters to England. In order to show the heathen how utterly powerless were the gods in whom they placed their trust, at Geismar, near Fritzlar, S. Boniface with his own hands felled an ancient oak, sacred to the Lord of Thunder, and as the strokes of the axe rang loud upon the gnarled bark of the wizard tree the pagan throng stood confounded and amazed when no bolt from the sky, no swift red levin destroyed this bold defier of mighty Thor. Many were converted upon the spot, and it has been said without exaggeration that the fall of this old oak marked the fall of heathenism in Germany. With the wood S. Boniface built a chapel, dedicated to the first Pope, the Prince of the Apostles. Not long after he passed on to Eschwege where he overthrew and ground to powder the

demoniacal statue of Stuffo, a fearful idol. Naturally the
forces of evil were all the more enraged by the victories of
the Saint, and their malice blazed forth with murderous fury,
when after years of glorious labour he journeyed to the
Frisians and gained many converts to the East of the Zuider
Zee. On 5 June, 755, a vast concourse of catechumens had
gathered for the Sacrament of Confirmation at Dokkum on
the River Borne. Suddenly an armed host of heathens burst
upon them with hideous shouts and yells, and scattering the
unprotected candidates in all directions they massacred the
Saint and fifty-two of his companions. When the Christians
had rallied the body covered with wounds was conveyed to
Utrecht, whence it was soon brought to Mainz, and in after
years translated to the Abbey of Fulda.[2]

As late as the end of the tenth century primitive paganism
prevailed among the Prussian tribes, who inhabited the
territory about the Gulf of Danzig, for it was at this period
that they were visited by S. Adalbert, Bishop of Prague, who
had been driven from his see[3] at the command of King
Boleslas, the tyrant being unable longer to endure the holy
prelate's stern reproach for the murder of his two brothers
through whose blood he mounted the throne. The heroic
Saint made his way athwart the untracked forests and
marshes where the cold Vistula flows to the very source of
the river, and by his preaching to the inhabitants of the
town of Dantzig vast numbers were converted, receiving
Holy Baptism at his hands. *Baptizabantur hominum multæ
catervæ.* Crowds upon crowds were baptized, says **Pagi** in
his valuable annotations to the *Annales* of the Venerable
Cesare Baronius. This almost miraculous conversion of the
whole country-side was the affair of a few weeks at most—
many authorities assign only ten days—and the wrath of the
heathen wizards and priests knew no bounds. They plotted
his destruction, and the Bishop was assassinated by some
temple servant who pierced him through with a mighty lance.
The feast of S. Adalbert is celebrated on 23 April, and he is
generally venerated as the Apostle of Prussia. Immediately
after his death, Bruno, a monk of the Aventine monastery at
Rome, who in the world had been the Count de Querfurt,
set out with a small band to continue the martyr's good
work. In 1009, however, he fell into the hands of the savage

pagans, and was butchered together with eighteen of his companions. For nearly two centuries the Prussians lapsed into darkness[4] until they were evangelized by a number of Cistercians, chief amongst whom were Abbot Godfrey of the Polish province, Dom Christian, and Dom Philip, whose work was blessed and encouraged by the great pontiff, Innocent III.

Very different from the gods of sunlit Greece, the nurse of poetry and all arts, were the dark cruel gods of the northern nations. Not least amongst these, worshipped at midnight in the haunted glades of the cold snowy forests, adored with foul mystic rites beneath the black shadows of immemorial fir and pine, was Kurche the lord of the pathless woodland, who symbolized in some sort the blind pitiless forces of nature. The word *Hexe*, which in German signifies a witch, occurs in old authors under a double form *hagedisse* or *hagetisse* in Low German, and *hagezisse* or *hagezussa* in the purer dialects. Now the Hagedisses were the nymphs of the forest, who may be compared with the Greek Dryades and Hamadryades ; the Alseides ;[5] the Huleoroi,[6] watchers of the wood ; the Auloniades,[7] dwellers in the glen ; the Napaiæ, who lurk amid the brakes ; not kindly maidens to whom simple rustics pour libation of milk and oil, but those strange visions which if mortal see he is bereft of his senses and driven frantic, and becomes νυμφόληπτος, nympholept ; lymphatus or lymphaticus[8] in Latin phrase. " Nympholepsy," writes Robert Chandler in his *Travels in Greece* (1775), " is characterized as a phrensy, which arose from having beheld them [the nymphs]."

The Hagedisses are near akin also to the Valkyries. The Valkyries sped through the clouds on their courses swift as air from whose flowing manes are scattered both dew and hail. It was they who fertilized the wide champaign. So in legend did the witch ride athwart the storm-evoking wind and tempest. She could fill with plenty the garners of those who propitiated her, albeit evil were her gifts. In some parts of Germany to-day the peasants term sorcerers *Valriderske*, which was one of the names of the Valkyries. *Wünschelwip*, a word used in precisely similar fashion, has also been preserved. The Valkyries took part in the banquets of Odin. When the coven of witches assembled at the Blocksberg or Brockula they shared in the devil's carousals and adored

Satan as Wotan or Donar was worshipped of old. An ancient tradition averred that young girls who had never lost their maidenhead and were of an Amazon spirit could under certain conditions join the band of Valkyries, being admitted to swell the train of Frigg or Freya when as Holda,—euphemistically called the Good Lady,[9]—or in more northern climes as Huldra and Holla, she rode abroad o' nights charioted upon the whirlwind and the gale. Hence the name *Hollenfahrt*, Holla's ride, was popularly given to the voyage of witches hastening to their Sabbat orgies.

It is clear that in Germany mediæval Witchcraft absorbed at least in the popular imagination a number of dark traditions that had lingered on from pagan days. It must, however, be most carefully emphasized that this is by no means any continuance of or any sort of link with some hypothetical old religion, such as that for which the writer of a recent study in anthropology has evolved the title " the Dianic cult,"[10] postulating a secret organization which in fact is merest fable and moonshine. Very often the lees of black heathendom envenomed the true Faith. Many a heresy was spawned in Germany, and where heresy flourishes witchcraft is not far behind. *Crescit cum magia hæresis et cum hæresi magia*. Heresy grows alongside Witchcraft, and Witchcraft alongside heresy, wrote the learned theologian Thomas Stapleton, in a Louvain thesis[11] of 1549. Germany (Mid-Europe) seems to have been especially troubled with frantic sects and painful schisms. Many of these were speedily suppressed, but others did infinite mischief before they could be completely crushed. In 1051 a number of Cathari were hanged at Goslar by order of and in the presence of the Emperor Henry III. Early in the twelfth century, S. Norbert, Bishop of Magdeburg (*d.* 6 June, 1134), was combating the foul heresies and anarchy which Tanchelin had shamelessly propagated and practised ; in 1114 a number of heretics who had been provisionally placed in prison by the Bishop of Strasburg were, during that prelate's absence, forcibly seized upon by the crowd who feared clerical lenience, dragged out of the town, and burned alive ;[12] a similar event happened at Cologne in 1143. In 1184, Lucius III and Frederick Barbarossa held a conference at Verona, the result of which was the publication on 4 November of the famous

Bull *Ad abolendam*, anathematizing the Cathari, Paterini, the Poor Men of Lyons, Arnaldists, and other wretches. Rules were laid down for the examination of suspects, the visitation of infected areas, and the ample co-operation of civil authority. The Emperor, also, officially placed heretics under the imperial ban.[13] Ten years later, Henry, Bishop of Worms, is proceeding against heretics with a necessary severity, as directed by the Emperor Henry VI.[14] Less than half a century after Frederick II extended the penalty of death at the stake for obstinate heresy into the Empire, introducing this measure into the Sachenspiegel and Schwabenspiegel of Germany. On 20 November, 1220, a first constitution was published for Lombardy ; in March, 1224, this was reiterated and reinforced, capital punishment being prescribed ; and the amended law was finally promulgated throughout the Empire in 1238.[15] This constitution has been ascribed to the influence of Albert, Archbishop of Magdeburg, who was horrified by the spread of the most abominable ideas and revolutionary theories, which seriously threatened the peace and prosperity of his people. Some writers have blamed Frederick for his sanction of the extreme penalty. This is foolish and short-sighted to a degree. He was merely giving legal recognition to an actual practice, and the time for tolerance had passed.

This catena of repression and legislation clearly demonstrates that the fires of revolt were simmering all the while. In Bohemia the subversive anarchy of such boutfeus as Conrad Waldhäuser, John Militz Kremsier, and the rationalistic Matthias of Janow, burst out into full flood with John Hus and Jerome of Prague, culminating with the atrocious wars of Ziska and Prokop, pointing the way to the heresiarch Luther.

A clause of great importance occurs in the articles of peace signed between the King of the Romans, Henry, son of Frederick II, and the nobles of the Empire in 1230. It prescribes that "heretics, sorcerers, and evildoers, when found guilty of the crimes laid to their charge, shall receive the punishment due to the offence as the judge may ordain."[16] Three years before, Gregory IX had delegated powers extraordinary to that remarkable man Conrad of Marburg, who was enjoined to uproot the tares of heresy. Conrad of

Marburg seems to have been a secular priest, at least he is so described by the Thuringian court chaplain Berthold and by Cæsarius of Heisterbach, and therefore he was neither a Dominican, as Hausrath states, nor a Franciscan, as is asserted by Henke and others. Contemporary chroniclers describe him as a man of great ability, deep theological learning, burning eloquence, zealous in the defence of the Faith, and a severe ascetic. In 1225 Conrad became the spiritual director and confessor of the landgravine of Thuringia, S. Elizabeth, whom he led in the highest paths of perfection, so that she was canonized at Pentecost, 1235, less than four years after her death, 17 November, 1231.

On 11 October, 1231, Pope Gregory directed a bull to Conrad, who was thereby relieved of some more onerous duties in order that he might devote his attention to the inroads of the Luciferians,[17] an abominable sect, whose covens, as it was alleged, actually saw the Demon under a human form and worshipped him with foul ceremonies at their midnight assemblies. They were, in fact, Satanists who devoted themselves to the most monstrous profanations, and stopped at nothing to spread their devilish doctrines. Small wonder that Conrad proceeded against them with exemplary severity, and delivered the guilty to legal punishment, the stake. Plots, however, were incontinently laid against him and snares multiplied, until on 30 July, 1233, both he and his companion, a holy Franciscan named Gerhard Lutzelholb, were assassinated as they returned to Marburg. He is fittingly buried in the exquisite Gothic fane of S. Elizabeth, not far from the shrine of his spiritual daughter " die liebe Frau," where the old stone steps are worn hollow by the knees of pilgrims.

The Satanists seldom failed to perform their bad work with untiring energy, sowing evil and anarchy on every side, as was only too clearly evident from the revolt of the Stedingers, who had long been secretly corrupted by sorcerers and heretics. The Stedingers (a word meaning those living about the shore) were a tribe of Frisian peasants who in past years proved wellnigh the despair of missionaries on account of their bitter resistance to both Christianity and culture and their obstinate perseverance in cruel pagan superstitions and darkness. Even in the thirteenth century their profession of faith seems to have been at best lukewarm, and we are hardly surprised to learn that ignorance and rudeness made them an easy prey to the emissaries of the pestilential sects who now began to ravage and infest Europe. The Satanists taught the Stedingers anarchy, and in 1204 they broke out into open rebellion against the Archbishop of Bremen, Hartwich II, an enlightened and generous prelate. His successor Gerhard II (1219–57) was a man of sterner mould, and unable to endure their insolence and violence he sent a levy of troops against them. His army, however, was defeated in 1229, whereupon the Stedingers elated with their victory overran the whole country-side, burning and plundering on every side. In particular were churches and monasteries the objects of their attack ; the flame and smoke of reverend sanctuaries and hallowed houses of prayer mounted to heaven in ceaseless clouds amid the roar of crashing roofs and falling walls ; neither age nor sex was spared ; priest and nun were put to the sword amid cruel scenes of fearful blasphemy and the desecration of a thousand altars. A synod held at Bremen, 17 March, 1230, in addition to these acts of violence and outrage, accuses the rebels of the most hideous profanities and the open practice of sorcery, wherefor they were sternly excommunicated, a discipline which but served to spur the Stedingers on to fresh atrocities, whilst Gregory IX commissioned the Bishop of Lübeck aided by certain zealous Dominicans to use his best endeavours to quell the revolt by an appeal to reason and sanity. A little later, however, the Pontiff learned the full extent of the evil, and the remorselessness of the ruffians with whom authority had to deal ere law and order might be restored. Frederick II placed the Stedingers under the ban of the Empire. Anarchy was growing apace. The strong castle of Slutterberg, near Delmenhorst, had been razed to the ground by a fearful horde of marauders, and Count Burckhardt of Oldenburg, its lord, was slain whilst bravely fighting in defence of his property. Vast multitudes of lubber kerns, ferocious levellers, savage desperadoes and brigands, the vilest rascality, swarmed like locusts over the land. With them went a train of sorcerers and sibyls, who prophesied their ultimate triumph throughout the world, and spurred them on to every deed of violence and licentiousness,

The Archbishop of Bremen was greatly alarmed, and applied to Pope Gregory for counsel and aid. The successor of Peter, who had also learned the details of the catastrophe— for it was little less—from other trustworthy sources, no longer stayed his hand. A crusade against the Stedingers was preached in all that part of Germany. The supreme Pontiff wrote instantly to all the Bishops and leaders of the faithful an exhortation to arm, to root out from the land those abominable witches and wizards. " The Stedingers," said his Holiness, " seduced by the Devil, have abjured all the laws of God and man, slandered the Church, insulted the holy Sacraments, consulted witches to raise evil spirits, shed blood like water, taken the lives of priests, and concocted an infernal scheme to propagate the worship of the Devil, whom they adore under the name of Asmodi. The Devil appears to them in different shapes,—sometimes as a goose or a duck, and at others in the figure of a pale black-eyed youth, with a melancholy aspect, whose embrace fills their hearts with eternal hatred against the holy Church of Christ. This Devil presides as their Sabbats, when they all kiss him and dance around him. He then envelopes them in total darkness, and they all, male and female, give themselves up to the grossest and most disgusting debauchery."

Bishop Otto II of Münster, a mighty temporal prince as well as powerful prelate, Bishop Engelbert of Osnabrück, Bishop Peter of Ratzeburg who was suzerain of Butin, together with the Bishops of Lubeck and Minden, the Duke of Brabant, the Counts of Holland, Cleves, of the Mark, of Oldenburg, of Egmond, and of Diest, and many other nobles, assembled an army of no less than forty thousand men, who under the conduct of the Duke of Brabant, marched against the Stedingers. The rebels, who had become a mere disorderly rout, rallied their troops with the wild energy of madness and despair. They were crushed, however, on 27 May, 1234, eight thousand being left dead upon the field. The rest were scattered, and when sharp justice was meted out to those who still resisted, the revolt so strangely commingled with heresy and Witchcraft was at an end. On 24 August, 1236, Pope Gregory directed that they should be relieved from the excommunication after due penance had been performed and satisfaction given,

Witchcraft was, indeed, so closely identified with heresy that during the thirteenth and fourteenth centuries in Germany this crime was tried by the Papal inquisitors, of whom the zealous Conrad of Marburg is one of the earliest and most renowned. At the same time a Dominican, Conrad Dorso or Tors,[18] with a colleague John, made a visitation of several disturbed districts, and purged them of the more notorious criminals. After the publication of the Clementines[19] in 1312 new efforts were made to suppress various anarchical and nihilistic bodies, bent on disrupting human society, such as the Beghards and Bogomiles, but the good work seems to have been organized and carried on by the episcopal courts rather than by papal Inquisitors. The secular arm dealt with the few cases of Witchcraft when heresy was only a secondary or accidental charge, and fire was the penalty which had been juridically appointed for this offence by the secular codes known as the " Sachsenspiegel " (1225), and the " Schwabenspiegel " (1275). It was not in truth until 1367 that Blessed Urban V (Guillaume de Grimoard) stabilized the Inquisition throughout Germany by the appointment of two Dominican delegates. There was certainly need of organized repression, for the scandals of the Adamites had become very gross, a shameless communism being openly taught and naked debauchery elevated to a cult and a religion. It is curious to note that these practices still survive, since in the *Daily Express* of Tuesday, 9 June, 1925, under the headings " The Society of Eden Fined," " Nude Sect Seeks a New Paradise," the correspondent from Geneva is quoted as follows :

" A queer sect, which calls itself the ' Society of Eden,' has been founded at Rapperswil, near Zurich. The members believe in the simple life of Adam and Eve.

" The sect consists of a score of persons of both sexes and of various nationalities, among them being a countess and a retired general. They declare that they are tired of the conventions of modern life with its useless ceremonies. Their only garment is a shirt, worn to the knees, but even this garment is discarded during prayer-meetings, which take place in a forest twice a week.

" The inhabitants, shocked to see nude men and women walking and singing hymns among the trees near the road, informed the police, who arrested the band. They were made to put on their shirts, and were taken to the police-station, where their names and addresses—'The Earth'—were registered.

The simple lifers appeared before the tribunal on a charge of outrage against public morals, and the Public Prosecutor demanded imprisonment and a heavy fine. The magistrates, however, took a more lenient view, and fined them £2 each, warning them that if they ' continued to play at Adam and Eve in public ' they would be sent to prison.

The Society of Eden is now looking for another forest, in another canton."

In Germany, at Magdeburg, Erfurt, Mühlhausen, and other cities, Kerlinger, to whom Blessed Urban had committed jurisdiction extraordinary, displayed unusual energy, driving the Sectaries out of the northern and central provinces, restoring peace, seemly order, and prosperity.

About the year 1400 numerous prosecutions for Witchcraft were instituted at Berne in Switzerland by Peter de Gruyères, a secular judge. Several witches from Simmenthal were sent to the stake. In 1399 a woman was exiled by the Bâle courts for five years upon an accusation of having cast a charm upon her neighbours, whilst at Berlin during the same year the Supreme Court with greater severity burned a witch for sorceries, manifest and abominable.

In 1420 and during the following decade the Dominican Inquisitor Ulrich de Torrente condemned at Neuchâtel and at Fribourg a number of hags and secret poisoners who were charged with black magic ; some years later, in 1439, Hanchemand le Mazelier, a Satanist, and four other wretches, his accomplices, were seized at Neuchâtel. They confessed to devil-worship, sorcery, and bestiality, crimes which sealed their fate.[20] In the records the name *Vaudois* is given to these miserable creatures, since in France about this period *vauderie* is a term often used to designate Witchcraft, whence is derived the word voodoo, the use of and belief in sorcery prevalent among West Indian and American creoles and negroes. There was, undoubtedly, a close connexion between the sorcerers and that secret body, the followers of Peter Waldes. Throughout the whole district of Constance, Lucerne, Bâle, Zurich, Neuchâtel, there are almost unbroken records of executions for Witchcraft. Many such are chronicled in detail for 1437, 1438, 1440, 1442, 1444, 1454, 1457, 1458, 1462, 1477, 1482, and 1493. In 1447 a whole coven of witches was discovered at Heidelburg to the great alarm of the townsfolk who insisted upon the law being carried out without let or relaxation.

The archives of Metz and contemporary documents repeat a long and monotonous tale of executions. In 1482 at Monthureux and at Senones three men and one woman were burned; in 1488 a sorcerer died in prison at Metz; on the 17 June of that year three witches were executed at Mairange; on the 25 June two more; the following day three at Chastel; on the first of July two were committed to the flames at Metz together with the corpse of a crone who had expired in bonds; a witch was burned at Salney on 3 July; on the twelfth two more at the same village; on the nineteenth three notorious sibyls; and the same day a warlock was put to death at Brieg. On 19 August two women were burned at Juxey; four days later at Thionville two men and three women were executed for necromancy; on the 2 September a woman shared their fate at Metz; on 15 September a crazy beldame suffered at Vigey; yet another at Juxey on the 22nd of that month.[21] The list might be indefinitely and tediously prolonged. Metz, it must be borne in mind, was a fief of the Empire, and throughout all the Rhine towns, Strasburg, Cologne, Mainz, the same persecution raged, bonfires blazed almost daily in their market-places and squares.

On 9 December, 1484, Pope Innocent VIII (Giovanni Battista Cibo) issued in the first year of his pontificate the famous Bull *Summis desiderantes affectibus,* in which he details the fearful growth of Witchcraft, especially in the archdioceses of Mainz (Archbishop Berthold of Henneberg); Cologne (Archbishop Hermann IV of Hesse); Salzburg (Archbishop Leonhard of Keutschach); Bremen (Archbishop Meinrich von Schwarzburg); and Trèves (Archbishop John II, Margrave of Baden). The Pontiff speaks of incantations, charms, necromancy, black magic, communion with devils, sexual commerce with incubi and succubi, and a thousand other abominations. Fearful crimes were openly committed, and to such a height had the mischief grown that fresh powers were granted to the two Dominican Inquisitors,

Henry Krämer[22] and James Sprenger, bidding them not
shrink from the most drastic penalties if no gentler measures
could eradicate the evil thing. The Bull was published on
23 July, 1485, by George Gosler, Prince-Bishop of Brixen,
and on 14 October of the same year the campaign was
initiated in his diocese. In 1486, by a rescript dated from
Brussels on 6 November, the Emperor Maximilian I took
the Inquisitors under his very singular and especial protection,
bidding all and each of his subjects to lend them help, aid,
and assistance in the prosecution of their mission. In 1487
the Faculty of Theology at Cologne warmly approved and
humbly received the Bull.

The prosecutions in the German Tyrol were commenced by
Henry Krämer himself at the express desire of the Archduke
Sigismund, who upon his departure for Germany loaded him
with presents and the highest tokens of a prince's esteem.
Krämer very shortly, indeed, rejoined his colleague James
Sprenger with whom he worked diligently at the *Malleus
Maleficarum*. In 1495 he occupied the Chair of Theology
at the University of Salzburg, and later he was sent by
Alexander VI into Bohemia and Moravia officially to visit
those provinces, and to report upon the progress of the
Faith. He is the author of several works, amongst which is an
important monograph attacking the Vaudois, *Clypeus sanctæ
Romanæ Ecclesiæ defensionis*.

The *Malleus Maleficarum*, the first edition of which was
published at Cologne in 1489, is an exhaustive treatise
detailing and regulating the procedure to be followed in witch-
trials. As introductory matter, we have the " Apologia
Auctoris " and the Apostolic Bull *Summis desiderantes
affectibus*. The treatise is divided into three parts, of which
the First contains eighteen chapters ; the Second, sixteen,
with nine supplementary chapters discussing the precautions
(*remedia*) to be taken against Witchcraft ; the Third, sixteen
chapters, with a supplement of nineteen chapters.[23] The
earlier chapters of Part I propose the Catholic doctrine as to
witches ; Chapter I discussing whether it be orthodox to
maintain that there are witches, and whether the contrary
opinion be heretical. The question of incubi and succubi is
bruited, whether procreation by such connexion be possible.
In Chapter VI we find : " Why are women more often given

to sorcery than men ? " which was also posed and answered by James I. Chapter VII seeks to know whether witches can for hire induce love or hate, and Chapter VIII takes up a point in the Bull to the effect that witches may hinder human generation and render impotent the sexual act. Chapter XII has a rubric : " What are we to think concerning men who are sometimes devoured by wolves, and children who are thus snatched from their cradles. May not this not unseldom be wrought by black magic ? " It is set forth that witches can slay babes in the womb and procure abortion, their sin is greater than that of the rebel angels or that of our first parents who fell, therefore as the offscouring and scum of humanity they deserve the heaviest punishments.

In Part II (Chapter IV) is argued how witches are carried *localiter* from place to place ; how the incubus copulates with the witch (Chapter V), an abomination which was continually confessed in the trials, and we soon proceed to the cognate subject, " Of the way in which the Sacraments of the Church are vilely abused by witches practising their vile art. And of the way in which they let and hinder generation." Chapter VII announces *De modo quo mēbra uirilia auferre solent ;* Chapter VIII, How witches may seem to metamorphose men into beasts. Chapter XIII tells of the mischiefs which midwives who are sorceresses may do, by slaying children, or worser yet by offering them to Satan in horrid sacrifice. The devilish raising of tempests with thunder, lightning, and hail to destroy the earth's produce is narrated, and we proceed to the Remedies against Magic and the black art, such as the Exorcisms of the Church, and in what manner those afflicted by sorcery are to be exorcized (Capitulum VI, Remediorum).

Part III concentrates upon the method of dealing with the evil and the form of the legal punishment of witches *in foro ecclesiastico.* In fullest detail is prescribed how the process shall be commenced ; the numbers and respectability of the witnesses ; how they are to be examined ; what questions shall be put to them ; the arrest and imprisonment of the accused ; of the lawyers to be briefed ; of the interrogatory of the accused and of the use of torture during the trial, when the accused is to be adjured to confess " by the bitter Tears which Our Lord Jesus Christ shed upon the Cross for the salvation of the world, and by the burning tears of the Most Glorious Virgin, Saint Mary, His Mother, which when evening was come She shed over His Most Precious Wounds." These pages have very full instructions with regard to the many cases which may arise, how heretics who are penitent but relapsed should be dealt with and judged ; the punishment of heretics who are impenitent and relapsed, vaunting their crimes ; of those who flee from justice or contumaciously refuse to appear ; *insuper etiam super maleficas obstetrices et maleficos sagittarios.*

Meagre and superficial as it is, yet from this baldest outline it will be seen that the *Malleus Maleficarum* is a document of the first importance, both from a historical and a social point of view. There are, it may be, some obvious errors, but it is a work of enormous erudition, and its influence was felt far and wide throughout Europe. It is hardly too much to say that nearly all succeeding demonologists owe a vast debt to Krämer and Sprenger. Even those to whom in a later day the pages of this encyclopædic manual seem most fantastic, most unreal, will be bound to acknowledge the profundity of the exposition, the tireless care and exactest pains with which a subject wellnigh infinite is pursued and clearly tracked in all its ramifications and subtlest intricacies. Some may not grant the premises, some may not approve, but surely no man can scorn or contemn so zealous an earnestness, so serious and grave a labour.

Germany is the home of one of the most famous figures in the annals of Witchcraft, for there are few, if any, modern legends which have so impressed themselves upon the popular imagination of Europe as deeply as the story of Faust. The origin and development of the early traditions seem fairly clear. Faust was an historical personage who lived in Germany during the first half of the sixteenth century, and explicit mention of whom by contemporaries can be traced from 1507 until about 1540. He was born at Knittlingen in Würtemberg, or, according to others, at Roda near Weimar. His parents were poor, but the legacy of a rich uncle enabled him to study medicine at Cracow, where he began to dabble in magic. John Trithemius (1462–1516), the famous scholar and Benedictine abbot of Spanheim, in a letter dated 20 August, 1507, speaks of him as having been at

Gelnhaussen in the previous year, and subsequently as having visited Würtzburg and Kreuznach. He is called Georgius Sabellicus, *Faustus iunior*. He is described as a vagabond, boastful and insufferably braggart, travelling up and down the country-side under pompous and exotic names, for ever proclaiming his skill in necromancy, astrology, magic, chiromancy, agromancy, pyromancy, hydromancy, and all goetic arts, blasphemously declaring that by his crafts he could reproduce as often as he would the very miracles of Christ. At Kreuznach Faust was employed by Franz von Sickingen to lecture and teach, but he soon rendered himself so odious by his debaucheries that he was compelled incontinently to flee the town. In 1509 one Johann Faust, who may not improbably be the same individual, took the degree of Bachelor of Divinity at Heidelberg. The distinguished humanist, Konrad Mutianus Rufus (1471–1526), canon of Gotha, in a letter of 1513 to Henri Urbain, speaks with contempt of the charlatanry of one Georgius Faust at Erfurt. This was, no doubt, the same vagabond scholar, and in 1516 he was at Maulbronn ; in 1525 (according to tradition) he dwelt in Leipzig ; in 1528 Dr. George Faust of Heidelberg was expelled on a charge of suspected sorcery from Ingolstadt. The famous physician, Philip Begardi of Worms, in his *Index Sanitatis* (1539) speaks of Faust as a fellow who was for several years notorious as an impudent quack and wandering empiric, one who gave himself out as *philosophus philosophorum* and was highly acclaimed by his dupes as a mighty magician whose cures and marvels were certainly due to supernatural powers. Begardi had not himself seen the necromancer, but he had spoken with many who had been most egregiously swindled by this clever chouse. A somewhat ambiguous passage in the narrative is interpreted as signifying that Faust was just dead ; in any case we know that he was no longer alive in 1544. The Protestant divine, Johann Gast, in the second volume of his *Conuiuialium Sermonum Liber* (1544) speaks of having supped with Faust at Basel, when he was attended by a dog and a black horse that were obviously demons, and there is a further account of the sudden and violent end of the warlock, who was found dead one morning with a twisted neck, his countenance black, horribly distorted, and swollen. Although as often as five times turned Christianly upwards, the corpse lay constantly on its face on the bier.

In 1561 Conrad Gesner of Zurich mentions Faust as a wandering scholar of no mean powers, long since dead. Manlius, a pupil of Melanchthon, in his *Locorum Communium Collectanea*, 1562, relates that his preceptor knew Faust, who was a native of Kundling, and describes him " a most filthy beast, the midden of numberless devils " (*turpissima bestia, et cloaca multorum diabolorum*). He continues to tell of his magical studies at Cracow, his sorceries performed throughout all Germany, and how at last Satan carried him to eternal bale. The famous physician of Cleves, Johann Weyer, in his *De Præstigiis Dæmonum* (1561) speaks of Faust as a profligate and profane wretch ; according to Widman Luther discoursed of Faust and his familiars ; Count Froben Christoph von Zimmern in his *Chronik* twice alludes to Faust who was strangled one night at a hostelry by his demons. In the *Christliche Bedenken und Erinnerung von Zauberei* (1585) of the Protestant theologian Augustin Lereheimer of Steinfelden details are given of Faust's life ; two of the seventeen tracts in *Theatrum de Ueneficis* (1586), the Jesuit scholar Martin Delrio in his *Disquisitionum Magicarum Libri Sex* (1624), and Philip Camerarius in his *Opera Horarum Subcisiuarum* (1658) all testify to the story. The man was beyond all question a notorious and defamed foist, a lewd boaster of his bad proficiency in malefic arts, a subtle diviner and nigromant, so small wonder that when he came by his death at a wayside house in mysterious circumstances rumour at once bruited of a strange fierce storm one black night wherein the Devil had borne him away amid thunder-claps and levin, whence immediately arose the story of a dark compact and conveyance with Satan.

The first literary version of the Faust legend was the Volksbuch, published by Johann Spies at Frankfurt in 1587, under the title *Historia von Dr. Johann Fausten, dem Weitbeschreiten Zauberer und Schwartzkünstler*, etc., the preface to which is a treatise upon the damnable consequences of magic and commerce with the Devil. The book is divided into three parts of unequal length. All the incidents which since have been so often used and related are to be found here. We have the meeting of Faust with the fiend who

gives his name as Mephistophiles ; the signing of a contract
with blood ; Faust's voyages to Paris, Naples, Venice,
Rome, and other cities ; the evocation of Alexander the
Great to satisfy the emperor's request ; the presenting of
fresh grapes and apples at a banquet in a snowy January ;
the raising of Helen of Troy, whom he uses as his succubus
and who bears him a son ; the fearful end of the wizard,
whose limbs are scattered far and wide by howling demons,
whilst Helen and her child disappear, and the famulus Wagner
succeeds to his master's estate.

It is unnecessary to detail the immense popularity of this
work, of which as many as four impressions were printed
before the end of 1588, a second and corrected edition being
issued by Spies himself in that year. A low German rendering
at once appeared, and before 1589 a close, if somewhat
abbreviated, English translation. Danish, Dutch, Flemish,
and French versions followed fast. Abridgements began to
swarm from the press as also enlarged editions and rewritings.
At Hamburg in 1599 was printed Widman's version, a later
recension of which by the Nuremberg physician, Johann Nicol
Pützer (1674),[24] is interesting as containing a shadowy hint
of Goethe's Gretchen in the citizen's fair daughter whom
Faust wishes to marry, but which the demon will not permit
him to do.

Not even the chap-books, however, spread the legend of
Faust so widely and so inspired the popular imagination as
the dramatic versions of the tale. One of the greatest, as one
of the earliest, of these is Marlowe's mighty play *The Tragical
History of D. Faustus*. Written, it is generally believed, in
1588, it was received with unbounded applause, and wellnigh
a century later Phillips notes in 1675, " Of all that *Marlowe*
hath written for the stage, his *Doctor Faustus* hath made the
greatest noise." Marlowe follows Spies' narrative with some
exactness. In the forms which have come down to us,
however, there intermingle with scenes of impassioned
grandeur and awful doom episodes characterized by the
most witless lamblack buffoonery, as also offensive matter
even more out of place than mere clowning, the low and
farcical picture of the Pope and the friars, an unnecessary
and entirely displeasing indecorum reproducing only too
faithfully the atmosphere of the anti-Catholic Volksbuch.[25]

The marvellous lines in which Faust hails Helen's beauty are well known, and Lamb justly remarked : " What has Margaret to do with Faust ? Marlowe, after the original story, makes Faust possess Helen of Greece." It is interesting to note that William Prynne in his noisome *Histriomastix* (1633) retails an idle story that on one occasion the Devil himself " appeared on the stage at the Belsavage Playhouse in Queen Elizabeth's days " while this tragedy was being performed, " the truth of which I have heard from many now alive who well remember it," says the rabid old canter.[26]

English companies were playing *Dr. Faustus* at Grätz in 1608, at Dresden in 1626, and in many other continental cities during the seventeenth century. These performances may well have given rise to the numberless motions when puppetry enacted the Faust drama throughout the length and breadth of Germany.[27] " The marionette fable of *Faust*," says Goethe, " murmured with many voices in my soul." His great masterpiece had been thought out as early as 1774, but the first part was not published till 1808, the second part in 1831.

It were impertinent and wellnigh impossible to attempt to mention even merely by name the many dramas which have the Faust legend as their theme. Indeed, the Faust literature is so vast that Karl Engel's *Zusammenstellung der Faust- schriften* (Oldenburg, 1885) contains 2714 numbers.[28] Lessing had projected two versions of the story, one which followed the original legend, the other eliminating any supernatural element, but of these only a few fragments remain. Klinger worked the subject into a romance, *Fausts Leben, Thaten, und Hollenfahrt* (1791) ;[29] a libretto was written for Spohr's opera in 1814 by Bernard ; the following year Klingemann published his unequal tragedy ; Lenau's epico-dramatic *Faust* appeared in 1836 ; and Heine's ballet *Der Doctor Faust, ein Tanzpoem* in 1851.

The historical figure of Faust is extremely significant. To some extent the literature which has thus magnificently grown up about his name has obscured his individuality. We are apt to think of the Faust of Marlowe or of Goethe rather than of the vagabond warlock whose ill repute so deeply impressed his contemporaries, who was, beyond all doubt, a student of black magic, an adept in evil, possessed of malefic and occult powers.

Cornelius Agrippa von Nettesheim, who was born at Cologne the city of the great Dominican doctor, Blessed Albertus Magnus, on 14 November, 1486, was early reputed to be a skilled magician, even whilst he was yet a mere youth of two-and-twenty and serving the Emperor Maximilian as his confidential secretary. It was shortly after his marriage that he addressed himself to his grand design the writing of the *De Occulta Philosophia* in three books, a work every page of which is informed and influenced by the Cabalistic mysteries. The third part, in particular, treats of divine names and their influences, Angels and Devils, sacred characters and figures, and the evocation of spirits. The last chapters tell of rites, forms, incense, their use and purposes. Although the three volumes were not published in their entirety until after Agrippa's death, manuscript copies had been made of various sections and passed from hand to hand. These naturally caused no small stir, and considerable suspicion began to attach to the writer. In 1518, at the age of thirty-two, he was named advocate and orator to the free town of Metz, but so distasteful did the appointment prove and so strenuously did the Dominican and Franciscan fathers oppose him that he was compelled to abandon his post and retire to his native Cologne. Dark tales began to dog his footsteps, and although it is very certain that many harmless incidents and ordinary accidents were magnified into happenings supernatural and mysterious, more than once he was openly proclaimed as " heretic and magician," and I suspect that the charge went little, if at all, beyond the truth. He was hunted from city to city, from state to state, and when he died in obscure and almost unknown circumstances, although it is clear that he was in full communion with the Catholic Church at the end, the reputation of a notorious wizard clung, and has clung, through the years to his name.

With the secession of Martin Luther and Huldreich Zwingli from Catholic unity, the cockering of human fraility and men's worst passions, the anarchy of belief and practice, a terrible wave of fanaticism swept throughout Germany. The Lutheran princes for their own political purposes fostered the spread of the new doctrines, interpreting them as they pleased, and presently conflicts between the adherents of the various sects, which were almost daily breaking up into fresh bodies and subtle subdivisions, began to increase confusion tenfold. If men professed religion it was not from love of God but for fear of the Devil, who had a finger in every pie.

A horror of sorcery and Witchcraft filled every heart. Unrest and disquietude scorched the land like a fierce flame ; fear, vague ill-defined shadowy fear, drove the people to a frenzy of cruel prosecution. It will be sufficiently instructive to take one typical case. The little town of Waldsee on the ·Steinach in Wurtemberg has some two thousand inhabitants, and during the sixteenth century it probably held no greater tale of souls. The following list of executions, which is by no means complete, is terribly significant :[30]

1518. Elsa Pæffin and Elsa Khünlin, found guilty of sorcery, were condemned to be burned.

1518. The wife of Simon Thausser was condemned to the stake on the same charge.

1528. Ursula Wachin of Waldsee burned for Witchcraft.

1531. Elsbet Müllerin of Waldsee condemned to be burned as a witch.

1581. Three beggar women, Eva Schwarz, Anna Beuchel, and Elsbeth Scharber, all of Waldsee, sentenced to be burned as notorious witches.

1581. Appollonia Buckh, sentenced to be burned for the same crime.

1581, 6 July. Madlen Isolin, Maria Rosch, Brigida Wunsil, Catharina Einseler, and Anna Flieger, all of Waldsee, were condemned to death and burned on multiplied charges of sorcery.

Another document, relating to the same town, records :

Hans Deiner burned as a warlock. (The year is not stated.)

Simon Thausser, whose wife had been executed in 1518, burned at the stake as a sorcerer.

Joachim Hezensohn, who confessed to copulation with a succubus, was beheaded on the Friday following *Lætare* (the fourth Sunday of Lent), 1557.

Barbara Echtinger, found guilty of magical practices, on the Friday after Bartlemas (24 August), 1545, was condemned to perpetual imprisonment.

Maria Reich, Trauben Wirth, Waldburg Lachenmayer, and Anna Treher, all four of Waldsee, were found guilty of repeated acts of sorcery and condemned to be burned, 5 July, 1585.

Margaret Rohrfelder, Barbara Ulmer, and a fearful hag Ursula Sailler, were sent to the stake 24 August, 1585.

Felicitas Schneider, Anna Erb, Ursula Schultheiss, all three of Waldsee, were burned as obstinate witches, 9 March, 1586.

Anna Hoyd of Waldsee, a known witch, burned 24 November, 1586.

Catharina Rauffains, Ursula Isel, Ursula Stadelmann, all three of Waldsee, were found guilty of diabolic sorcery and sent to the stake, 7 November, 1586.

Agatha Weiss, Anna Dormar, Christina Mayer, all of Waldsee, burned as witches, 9 October, 1586.

Anna Kleiss of Waldsee sent to the stake for sorcery, 30 October, 1586.

Ursula Fray and Catharina Kless of Waldsee, condemned to be burned for known and proven sorceries, 12 June, 1587.

Barbara Huebmeyer, Appela Huebmeyer, and Anna Schelling of Waldsee, were burned as witches, 11 September, 1589.

Margrett Fray and Agata Birenseng, both of Waldsee, were condemned to be burned at the stake for demonolatry and practising the black art, 25 June, 1594.

This brief catalogue, in which there are many lacunæ, refers only to one small town. Similar prosecutions were raging with ever fiercer intensity throughout the whole land. The chronicler of Treves records : " In the year 1586 the diocese of Treves was so scoured and purged of sorcerers and witches that in two villages only two women were left alive."[31] The commissary Claude de Musicl made the following entry in his judicial register : " From 18 January, 1587, to the 18 November, 1593, there were executed for witchcraft in the diocese of Treves three hundred and sixty-eight persons of both sexes ; this does not include the number of sorcerers who were burned at Treves itself, or in the vicinity of the city."[32] The Archbishop John VII von Schönenberg (1581–99) was a prelate of unblemished reputation and admirable piety, but the ravages of Protestantism had little inclined him to temper justice with mercy.

In 1589 at Quedlinburg in Saxony, a town of some 12,000 inhabitants, one hundred and thirty-three wretches, found guilty of Satanism, were burned in one day.[33]

At Bamberg, the Prince-Bishop, Gottfried von Aschhausen, 1609–22, horrified at the blasphemies with which the devil-mongers almost openly vaunted their foul mystery, initiated the prosecutions. This excellent prelate in 1612 invited the Jesuit fathers to the diocese and put them in charge of ecclesiastical seminary, appointing them also as cathedral preachers. A widespread spiritual revival was the result. His successor, Bishop John George II Fuchs von Dornheim, 1623–33, showed equal zeal. His saintly coadjutor, Freidrich Fœrner, Bishop *in partibus* of Hebron, to whose pen we owe an important treatise, *Panoplia armaturæ Dei, Conciones contra omnes superstitiones et præstigias diaboli*, Ingolstad, 1626, ably seconded his efforts. To the horror of the Bishops it was found that the diocese was permeated by bands of devil-worshippers who had for years been spreading their damnable doctrines in secret, corrupting whole families and districts. A special court was convened to deal with the situation. Six doctors *utriusque iuris* Vasold, Schwarzconz, Einwag, Eppenauer, Harsen, and Neusesser, sat with several minor colleagues under episcopal presidency. The sternest measures were necessary. A gigantic conspiracy was on foot and had been maturing for years. The chancellor of the Bishop, Doctor George Haan, Ursula his wife, their daughter Maria Ursula, and their son Doctor George Adam Haan, were discovered to be deeply implicated, and sent ruthlessly to the stake. Five rich burghers of Bamberg, John Junius,[34] George Neudecker, Daniel Bayer, Jacob Dittmayer, Albert Ritcher ; several senators ; even a few priests, amongst whom was Michael Kœtzner, chaplain of S. Martin's, shared the same fate. Frenzied with rage at the discovery of their fell designs, some of these wretches had the audacity to accuse Bishop Fœrner himself of complicity in their abominations, an impudence which but recoiled on their own heads as such malice filled the Prince-Bishop John George II with almost ungovernable rage. The prosecutions concluded in 1631, and the following year Bamberg fell into the hands of the Swedes. In 1633 the Prince-Bishop died in Carinthia far away from his see, but Franz von Hatzfeld, his lawful successor, was not able to take possession of the cathedral until 1635. More than nine hundred executions for Witchcraft are officially chronicled between 1627 and 1631. The following contemporary record only gives one hundred and fifty-six, but it is valuable as showing how deeply the virus had infected the body of the state.

A list of witches who suffered death by the headman's sword and whose bodies were then burned at Würzburg.[35]

First execution, four persons :
The woman Liebler. Old widow Ancker. The woman Gutbrod. The woman Hœcker.

Second execution, four persons :
Old mother Beutler. Two women, strangers. Old mother Schenck.

Third execution, five persons :
A man named Tungersleber, a fiddler. A woman named Kuler. An old bawd named Stier. The woman Bürsten-Binderin. The woman Goldschmidt.

Fourth execution, five persons :
The wife of a burgomaster, Siegmund Glaser. The woman Brickmann. A midwife named Schickelte. (It is said that she was responsible for much sorcery throughout the district.) Old mother Rum. A stranger, a man.

Fifth execution, eight persons :
Lutz, a well-known merchant. A merchant named Rutscher. The wife of the Intendant of the Provostry of the Cathedral. Old mother Hof Seiler. A woman named Steinbach. The wife of a Senator named Bannach. A woman named Zuickel Babel. An old woman.

Sixth execution, six persons :
The Intendant of the Council, by name Gering. Old

mother Canzler. A woman named Schneider. The cook of M. Mengerdœrfer. A stranger. A stranger, a woman.

Seventh execution, seven persons :
A young girl, a stranger, aged twelve. A stranger. A stranger, a woman. A stranger, a lawyer. Three women, strangers. At the same time was executed in the market-place a soldier who had allowed some prisoners to escape.

Eight execution, seven persons :
The Senator Bannach. The Intendant of the Provostry of the Cathedral. A stranger. A man named Schleipner. A woman, a milliner who sold masks. Two women, strangers.

Ninth execution, five persons :
A wheelwright named Wunth. A stranger. A woman named Bentz. Her daughter. A woman named Eyering.

Tenth execution, three persons :
Steinacher, one of the wealthiest citizens. Two strangers, a man and a woman.

Eleventh execution, four persons :
A vicar of the Cathedral named Schwerdt. The wife of the Intendant of Rensacker. A woman named Stiecher. A man named Silberhans, a fiddler.

Twelfth execution, two persons :
Two women, strangers.

Thirteenth execution, four persons :
Old Hof-Schmidt. An old woman. A little girl of nine or ten years old. Her younger sister.

Fourteenth execution, two persons :
The mother of these two girls. Lieber's daughter, aged twenty-four.

Fifteenth execution, two persons :
A boy of twelve years old in one of the lower forms of the school. A woman who kept a pie shop.

Sixteenth execution, six persons :
A page of Ratzenstein was executed this morning at six o'clock in the courtyard of the Town Hall, where his body remained all day in a barrow. The next day it was burnt with the following : A boy, ten years old; the two

daughters of the aforesaid Intendant and their maid; a woman named Seiler.

Seventeenth execution, four persons :
The host of the Golden Orchard at Baumgarten. A boy eleven years old. An apothecary's wife, and her daughter who lived at the Sign of The Stag. A woman named Harfner hanged herself in the prison.

Eighteenth execution, six persons :
A tanner named Batsch. A boy of twelve years old. Another boy of the same age. The daughter of D. Jung. A girl of fifteen. A stranger, a woman.

Nineteenth execution, six persons :
A page of Rotenhan was executed at six o'clock in the courtyard of the Town Hall, and his body burned on the following day. The wife of Secretary Schellhar. Another woman. A boy, ten years old. Another boy, twelve years old. A baker's wife named Bügler was burned alive.

Twentieth execution, six persons :
A girl named Gabel Babelin, said to be the loveliest lass in Würzburg. A young student, who was an excellent musician, *uocaliter et instrumentaliter.* Two choir boys belonging to the new Cathedral aged twelve. The daughter of an upholsterer named Babel. The ferryman's wife.

Twenty-first execution, six persons :
The Master of the hospital of Dietrich. A man named Stoffel Holzmann. A boy fourteen years old. The young son of Senator Stolzberger. Two seminarists.

Twenty-second execution, six persons :
A cooper named Stürmer. A stranger, a boy. The wife of Senator Stolzberger. His granddaughter. A washerwoman. A stranger, a woman.

Twenty-third execution, nine persons :
The son of David Crots, a boy aged twelve. The two young sons of the Prince's cook, the eldest was fourteen, the younger twelve years old. Melchior Hammelmann, parish priest of Hach. Nicodemus Hirsch, canon of the Cathedral. Christopher Berger, a vicar of the Cathedral. A seminarist. An officer of the Court of Brennerbach and a seminarist were burnt alive.

Twenty-fourth execution, seven persons :
Two boys belonging to the hospital. A rich cooper.
Laurence Stüber, vicar of the Cathedral. Martha Rosslein.
[Two names are missing here.]

Twenty-fifth execution, six persons :
Frederick Basser, a vicar of the Cathedral Chapter.
Stab, parish priest of Hach. Lambrecht, a canon of the
Cathedral. The wife of Gallus Haus. A boy, a stranger.
A woman named Schelmerey Krämerin.

Twenty-sixth execution, seven persons :
David Hans, canon of the Cathedral. The Senator
Weydenbusch. The wife of the host of the Golden Orchard
at Baumgarten. An old woman. The young daughter of
Valkenberger was executed privately and the body burnt
in its coffin. The young son of an Officer of the Council.
Wagner, a vicar of the Cathedral Chapter, was burnt alive.

Twenty-seventh execution, seven persons :
A butcher named Kilian Hans. The ferryman. A boy,
a stranger. A woman, a stranger. The son of a woman
named Hafner of Hach. Michael Wagner of Hach. Knor
of Hach.

Twenty-eighth execution, which took place after Candlemas,
1629, six persons :
A woman, who kept a pie shop, called Knertz. Babel
Schutz. A young blind girl. Schwartz, a canon of Hach.
Ehling. Bernard Mark, of the Cathedral Chapter, was
burnt alive.

Twenty-ninth execution, seven persons :
Viertel Beck. Klingen Wirth. The steward of Mergel-
sheim. A woman named Beck of Ochsenthor. A woman
of rank named Edelfrau. A doctor of theology, by name
Meyer, of Hach, and a canon were executed at five o'clock
in the morning ; their bodies were burnt. A gentleman of
rank, the Chevalier Fleischbaum. Paul Vaecker of Breit-
Hüt. Since then there have been two other executions,
16 February, 1629.

To this list is appended a memorandum : " Since which
date there have also been very many other executions."

Such a catalogue, it is true, at first glance seems horrible to a degree, but it must be remembered that these frequent executions only serve to show how deeply gangrened was this unfortunate and unhappy district. The Satanists had secretly pursued their evil crusade with an energy and determination worthy of a better cause. They corrupted old and young, rich and poor, vagabond minstrel, comfortable burgers, princely aristocrat alike ; nay, even priests were drawn into the toils of hell. The poison of social anarchy and demoniac revolution must be purged with drastic measures if the whole body were not to become infect and not utterly, to stink in the nostrils of God and man. It is sad, indeed, to read of children who were thus early tainted by evil. Yet such cases persist throughout the ages. In Chile the priests sadly complain of the perversion of the school-children. A Lazarist Father of Santiago relates that not many years ago some of the Catholic Indians saw a young white boy, not more than fifteen years old, nail a Host to a tree in the suburbs of the town, and stab It again and again until they realized what was happening and rushed forward to stop him. The Satanists of South America get hold of boys and girls of twelve and less and make them swear to blaspheme, never to enter a church, to devote themselves to Satan.

All eminent historians speak of the Prince-Bishop John George II as a " humane and pious man " (Doctor Leitschuh). a prince who often interfered on the side of mercy and who was mild in his judgements.[36] Perhaps the saddest and most woeful of all the tragedies of Würzburg was the awful blow which struck so nearly at this gracious Prelate himself, the discovery that Satanism had perverted those of his own household, his very kith and kin.

Of the princely pages the chief favourite with the Bishop was young Ernest von Ehrenberg,[37] who merited his cousin's favour not so much by reason of his comeliness, his courage, his vigour, as by the eminent qualities of his mind, his talents, and an unfeigned piety. It was noticed, however, that he lapsed from his first fervour into indifference—a common enough fault with youth—from indifference into a strange contempt for holy things, seldom was he seen at Holy Mass, never did he seek the confessional, he plunged into wildest debauchery and sought the harlot and the sot as his boon-companions. His speech was foul with obscenities and studied blasphemy. The Jesuit Fathers were perplexed and alarmed, this was no question of a young profligate given to lewdness from his earliest years, but a youth whose devotion had been admirable, his honour unblemished, falling suddenly into foul courses and worse.

Certain of the witches under examination swore that Ernest von Ehrenberg was a frequent assistant at the Sabbat, that he was not the least conspicuous in their orgies. The Prince-Bishop, broken-hearted, bade the good Fathers watch the suspected lad carefully, and if convinced of the truth of these accusations bring him back to the right path. This they did, and when taxed with his crimes the boy broke down and in tears confessed that he had been diabolically seduced by an old lady of the court, a known and notorious witch. He vowed amendment, and the Fathers joyfully absolved him. His penitence, however, proved false. Again and again he was caught slipping out of the palace at night to join the demon's orgies ; scapulars and medals he burned ; the Host he unspeakably profaned ; his attendance at Mass and the Offices of the Church was mere hypocrisy ; " if he spent his days with God, he passed his nights with the Devil." Some holy Capuchins, priests of the most eminent piety, learned, deeply versed in scholastic and mystical theology, were sought to turn the errant boy. He received their ministrations and counsel with hideous profanities and foul abuse. At length they admitted that they were unable to influence him, and the Prince-Bishop delivered him to the Council who pronounced a sentence of death. The Jesuit Fathers endeavoured to prepare him for his doom. On the day fixed for the execution he was led into a hall draped with black in the centre of which upon a scaffold some six feet high, hung with scarlet, was the block scattered with sawdust and a linen shroud. As the masked headsman placed his hand upon the unhappy youth the poor wretch swooned for fear. The judges, who were present, instantly stopped the procedure and sent to the Prince-Bishop begging him to sign a pardon. The Jesuit Father, who accompanied the lad, exhorted him to penitence, but suddenly he was met with a string of foulest profanity. He recoiled in horror, and when the incident was related to the Prelate, turning away with a bitter sob he exclaimed in broken accents : " Alas ! Alas ! Justice must then have its course." The archers closed round the raving youth who was led into a smaller chamber, and there struggling, shouting, blaspheming, as he was, the executioner took off his head with a sudden sweep of the sword. " He fell," writes the good Father who relates the terrible scene, " he fell without a sign or word of penitence, he fell calling not upon God but the Devil. Christ grant that he has not fallen into eternal bale ! "

During the seventeenth century similar crusades against witches and Satanism were prosecuted throughout Germany with the utmost vigour. A few examples will save the monotony of recounting all. In Mainz between 1626 and 1629, at Miltenberg, a town of 3000 souls, there were fifty-six executions for sorcery ; at Burgstadt, which numbers some 2000, seventy-seven ; at the little village of Eichenbühel, nineteen ; at the hamlets of Berndit, Buttan, Ebenheit, Wenschdorf, Heinbach, seven apiece ; at the even smaller hamlets of Prozelten and Amorbach, four apiece. Throughout the bailly of Miltenberg the number of burnings in three years was one hundred and sixty-eight.

The Prince-Elector of Mainz, John Philip von Schoenborn, who reigned from 1647–73, was one of the first to check the prosecution of witches in Germany. He had been a Canon of Würzburg, and as such had assisted at innumerable executions. He was, however, chiefly guided in his policy by the Jesuit Freidrich von Spee. Von Spee was born at Kaiserswirth on the Rhine, 25 February, 1591, and died at Treves 7 August, 1635. He distinguished himself by his vast scholarship and occupied the professorial chair of theology at many Universities. The work by which he is best remembered is the *Cautio Criminalis,* written in admirable Latin, and it is in effect an arraignment of the witch-trials. He does not by any means, as has been erroneously stated, ask for the complete suppression of such trials, but he does advocate measures of reform, such as a new German imperial law on the subject, and it was his bold pleading which gradually brought about the abolition of witch trials upon any save the gravest and most weighty evidence. The treatise, which might perhaps be counted a little lax in some respects, was printed at Rinteln in 1631 without Spee's name or permission, although he was doubtless generally

known as the author. The General of the Jesuits, Mutius
Vitelleschi, with some reason mildly rebuked Spee inasmuch
as he had not attempted to suppress the treatise, and the
Provincial of the Order on the Lower Rhine demanded certain
explanations. Yet no charge of heterodoxy can be brought
against the book, although it can hardly be commended
without a certain reserve. [38]

In the diocese of Cologne the witch prosecutions were
numerous. One of the most famous cases was that of
Catherine de Henott, who was burned alive in 1627. She
was accused, amongst other abominations, of having
bewitched a convent of Poor Clares, renowned for their piety.
That she was a Satanist the Jesuit Fathers seem to have had
no doubt. [39] One of the fiercest opponents of sorcery in this
district was Franz Buirmann, who brought a large number
of malefactors to the stake.

At Zuckmantel in 1551 it was found necessary to employ
no less than eight executioners. In 1654 at the same place
were burned one hundred and two Satanists, upon whom the
most hideous outrages had been proved.

It has been said that from 1590 to 1600 in the Duchy of
Brunswick an average of ten wretches were burned daily, so
that before the principal gate of the town there seemed to be a
veritable forest of charred stakes. "All over Germany," wrote
von Spee, "pyres are blazing, the flames of execution are red."

It were useless to give long catalogues of the Satanists who
perished thus throughout every province and dukedom of
Germany. At Nœrdlingen, for example, a little town in
Swabia, from 1690 to 1694 thirty-five women and one man
were burned upon the charge of black magic. In Alsace the
witches were executed in batches of three, four, seven, and
eight. In one year, 1678, at Salzburg no less than ninety
were sent to the stake.

A very famous case which occupied the tribunal of Lienz
for a full year was that of Emerenziana Pichler of Defereggen,
who with two of her children, the one aged fourteen, the other
twelve, was condemned for manifold, manifest, and proven
acts of sorcery in September, 1680. The mother was executed
on the 25th of that month, the two boys a couple of days
later, on the feast of SS. Cosmas and Damian.

On 23 July, 1738, thirteen persons were burned alive at

Szegedin in Hungary as vampires and warlocks. There were seven women and six men. As late as 1746 a woman was executed in the same town for Witchcraft,[40] and the place of her punishment is yet preserved in the district called *Boszorkány sziget*, the Island of Enchanters.

In the village of Lindheim, Wetterau, in the Grand Duchy of Hesse, there stands on the banks of the Nidder some hundred paces from the parish church a round tower of great antiquity, isolated and detached as were many of these mediæval fastnesses. A roof of slates which covered it in the sixteenth century no longer exists. It is a huge heavy mass of stone, windowless, with but one entrance, a door eighteen feet from the ground reached only by an exterior flight of steps, to-day crumbled, broken and insecure. The interior, says Horst, is supremely horrible, and so deep is the gloom and depression, which never lift, that it is impossible to gaze into the shadows without a shudder. About five yards apart are constructed in the actual thickness of the walls several square niches three or four feet in size, which run straight down to the very base of the building. When Horst first examined the place early in the nineteenth century he saw fifteen feet high, firmly mortared in the blackened walls of these grim recesses, handcuffs and leg-irons attached there by chains but a few inches in length such as would effectually impede and prevent any movement. It is believed that the unhappy wretches condemned to death for sorcery were thus fastened in helpless agony suspended several feet from the ground, until led forth to their doom. Local tradition even asserts that warlocks and witches were actually burned or rather calcined alive as they hung there. This is supported, if not actually proven, by the fact that there may be traced at the foot of the tower on the north side a door, now blocked up with more recent masonry than the rest, the use of which can hardly otherwise be explained. Moreover, at the bottom of the tower, amid the broken slates of the roof and the weed-grown rubbish which had collected there, was found a quantity of charred faggots and brushwood. At regular intervals, five feet from the ground, are a series of machicolations or squints " contrived to let smoke escape and by the passage of air to fan the flames."

To-day the Tower of Lindheim stands in a lovely park,

its old walls surrounded on all sides by parterres of gaily coloured flowers. When the ground was dug in order that the lawns might be turfed and the beds laid out there was found buried at the foot of the stair a vast quantity of human bones, amongst which were five or six skulls, and these as well as other mortal fragments had unmistakably been scorched and consumed by fire. " I myself saw and examined these bones," says Horst. " There can be no doubt that they were the remains of persons who had been burned, if not actually within the Tower itself, at least directly under the walls." It appears almost certain that those condemned to die were fixed in the recesses and horribly consumed. A more recent writer than Horst, Otto Glaubrecht, tells us that the nicked chains are blackened with fire, and the squints even now bear the traces of soot and smoke. The Tower, which bears the name of The Witch-Tower, is to-day almost exactly as George-Conrad Horst described it. Several parts which seemed dangerous have been strengthened and made secure, but otherwise it is unchanged. This building and the pleasaunce around belonged to the famous novelist Sacher-Masoch.

The earliest records of witch-trials at Lindheim have not been exactly preserved. We know[41] that in 1630 three women, one of whom, la Pombanne, was the wife of a Conrad Lorsch, were beheaded and their bodies burned in 1631. From 1650 to 1653 the whole country-side was panic-stricken by a prosecution for sorcery which involved a large number of individuals, and several, both men and women, were imprisoned in the Tower and burned alive, doubtless within the walls. Details of these processes are not now extant, but we have the fullest documents relating to the trials of 1662–63, when the district was groaning under the cruelties of a certain George Ludwig Geiss, an old soldier who had taken part in the Thirty Years War, and who even during that period of bloody anarchy had distinguished himself by his ferocity and savage deeds. Geiss was acting with full powers of life and death as mayor and judge for the Baron Herman Oynhausen, an absentee. Oynhausen himself was answerable to the over-lord Johann Hartmann von Rosenbach, doyen of the Würzburg canonical chapter. Geiss, a most formidable ruffian, joined with himself four fellows of low estate and brutal manners, a weaver and three peasants, none of whom could write nor read. Andrew Krieger, the weaver, soon became notorious for his rapacity, and the rustic Conrad Euler, his colleague, was known to be completely ignorant, avaricious, revengeful, and cruel. On 17 August, 1662, Geiss wrote to Oynhausen that he had arrested six persons, and that the land should have no rest until the whole tribe of sorcerers was stamped out and destroyed. A little lower in the same letter he relates the arrest of five other miserable wretches, among them being the King of the Sabbat (probably the local Devil), and the Queen of the Witches. That Lindheim was polluted with Satanism admits of no doubt, but it is also true that the whole prosecution was carried on in a most illegal and improper manner by base fellows whose motives were not above suspicion so eagerly did they confiscate the goods of the accused, and who showed themselves monsters of cruelty in the conduct of the assize. The Queen of the Witches was justly condemned. She died blaspheming and cursing God. Before long, however, it was evident that Geiss was ordering the arrests of those whose properties he coveted, persons who were demonstrably innocent of the crimes laid to their charge. A general revulsion of popular feeling ensued, particularly when Johan Schüler, a wealthy miller of good report, and his wife were seized and imprisoned in the Tower. After a few days Schüler escaped from durance. Several of his friends banded together to deliver him. An opening was made in the old slate roof and a blacksmith descending by a rope-ladder released the prisoner from his chains on the night of 18 February, 1663. His wife who was afraid to follow him they were obliged to leave behind, but he himself succeeded in making his way to Würzburg, where he interested Hartmann von Rosenbach in his case. Geiss was furious at the escape and revenged himself by the summary execution of the unfortunate Madame Schüler who was burned alive, perhaps in one of the recesses of the Tower, on 23 February with scarcely the empty formality of a trial. Hartmann von Rosenbach meanwhile had directed a letter to Oynhausen bidding him look well into the proceedings instituted by Geiss, to whom Oynhausen wrote in hot haste. An even weightier authority now slowly began to move. Schüler,

whom the fearful death of his wife had plunged into bitterest
sorrow, swore by Heaven and Earth to avenge her fate. At
his instructions Dr. Maurice William von Gulchen, one of the
foremost lawyers of the day, addressed a cogent memorial to
the Supreme Imperial Court of Speyer, detailing the cruelties
and iniquities of Geiss and his satellites. At Lindheim the
disaffection made itself felt by something like a popular
rising. Twelve persons who had been imprisoned in the
Tower, amongst whom were two women condemned to death
on the following day, were hastily released during the first
week of March, and when Andrew Krieger ventured to arrest
a woman named Horn her husband Matthew Horn set upon
him and thrashed him so unmercifully in the market square
that the puisne judge fled howling with a broken arm.
A hostile crowd collected and chased him to his house where
he lay concealed behind shuttered windows and barricaded
door quaking with fear in instant terror of death. The
prisoners who had been set free made their way to Speyer,
and suddenly appeared before the Supreme Tribunal clamour-
ing for redress. When the judges saw this wretched band,
whose pale haggard faces, attenuated forms, crippled legs,
and feeble gait showed only too plainly the hardships they
had endured, an official mandate was conveyed to Geiss
prohibiting any further prosecutions. His rage was terrible
and in his frenzy he at first refused to obey, replying in the
most insolent terms by a justification of his cruelties.
Immediately, however, the Baron Oynhausen in order to
ingratiate himself with the higher authorities dismissed him
from his offices and deprived him of all his power. It was
just at this juncture that a violent death overtook him. It
is said that whilst he was riding hard in pursuit of a suspected
witch who had escaped his clutches his horse, which he had
spurred to leap a wide ditch, some half a league from Lindheim, threw him heavily breaking his neck. Thereafter the
spot was known as the Devil's Ditch.

As has been remarked above, there can be little doubt that
Satanism had actually penetrated to Lindheim, but this
unhappily gave an opportunity for a knot of lawless and
brutal ruffians to terrorize the country-side with their
cupidity and blackmail amid circumstances of the most
hideous cruelty and lust.

Two or three years before the Lindheim prosecutions a famous case of Witchcraft had been widely talked of in Germany. On 8 November, 1658, George Eve, a recent member of the commune of Wehlitz (Wahlitz), a small village on the river Ehle about three miles from Gommern,[42] lodged with the magistrates an accusation of sorcery against Elizabeth Brose, the wife of a neighbouring shepherd. When she was summoned before the tribunal this woman unfolded a curious tale. She said that a little against the harvest her two daughters, the one eleven, the other a mere child of two and a half years, were occupied in a remote spot on the banks of the Ehle, not far from Eve's cottage, the elder washing linen and keeping a watchful eye on her sister's baby games. Eve's wife, Anna, passed near, and when she spied them assailed them with horrid curses, calling them " toads of the devil's begetting," and adding, " May Satan twist your arms and legs for you ! " She then spat thrice upon the younger girl. A little after the child fell sick, and in her bed were continually found animals not unlike huge meat-flies the presence of which could not be explained. But a few days passed ere she expired in strange convulsions. When Anna Eve was interrogated upon these strange happenings she could only give most rambling and inconclusive answers. She stammered that she had never recognized the children, that one day in summer she had stretched out some linen to dry on the bank of the stream, and that when she saw some boys and girls playing at a distance she may have scolded them as once they had muddied a newly washed kerchief and smock which were bleaching in the sun. The tribunal was ill content with her halting equivocations, and on 14 February, 1659, further inquiries were instituted. It is true that a number of peasants came forward to testify in the favour of Anna Eve, but there is ample warrant to suppose they were influenced by fear. On the other hand, the local minister, owing to his strong suspicion of black magic wrought by the woman Eve, had felt obliged to refuse her Holy Communion, probably lest she should not swallow the bread but convey it away in order to desecrate it. Two women, also, by name Richter and Volkholzen, averred that they had seen unearthly sights when one dark evening out of curiosity they awesomely peeped through the uncurtained lattice of Eve's lone hut.

There can be no doubt that the village thought as their pastor believed, although he may have hesitated plainly to deliver his verdict. It was found, moreover, upon inquiry that both Eve and his wife, who were resident at Wehlitz not above a year, had continually changed their abode, gipsy-fashion, sojourning now here, now there, leaving no very good reputation in their tracks.

Viewing all the circumstances it is hardly surprising that the judicial Court of Leipzig, to whom the plaint and the matters which arose from it were referred, summoned Anna Eve before a full bench of magistrates and submitted her to a formal interrogatory. When asked if she thought that Brose's child had been bewitched she showed considerable confusion and gave evasive quibbling answers. It was declared upon oath by several witnesses that in a quarrel she called Elizabeth Brose " a devil's whore," and she had been overheard saying to the frightened child who died, " You young bastard, I have bewitched you and that devil's whore, your mother." Although known to be a foul-mouthed wretch she indignantly denied having used such expressions. Various other questions were put to which she replied in a taunting manner, and, indeed, the deposition mentions that all the while she smiled contemptuously at the bench, and it would seem even jeered them, out of senseless bravado, one supposes, or relying upon some dark power to deliver her from their hands. Such a demeanour was little calculated to ingratiate her with her judges, and when other accusers came forward to give evidence of dark and secret practices, she was according to the legal procedure of the day put to the torture, albeit only in a lesser degree, in order to extract an avowal of her guilt. To detail the trial were useless, suffice she defied every effort to make her speak. Moreover, she did not even utter a groan or shed a tear. This alone would have been enough to convict her, for it was universally held that witches were unable to weep. Boguet in his *Discours des Sorciers*[43] expressly states : " Common experience shows us that witches are unable to shed a tear. Sprenger, Grilland, and Bodin all agree that if the accused does not weep there is strong presumption she is a sorceress."[44]

So unprecedented was her behaviour that the sworn tormentor drew up a special report which was read with much astonishment. It was even shown that she had slept whilst on the rack. The tribunal then decided to proceed to the extraordinary question, and accordingly on 4 November, at four o'clock in the morning, the Chief Justice Ernst Friedrich Heinitz, Judge Moritz Arntz, and the two senior Clerks of the Assize, Hans Polch and Ditmar Arnoldt, caused the prisoner to be brought to the Hall of the Halbadiers in the Castle of Gommern. Here she endured the question ordinary and extraordinary, always mute and obstinate, until just as the clock was striking eight the unfortunate woman expired without shedding a tear or uttering a sigh. It should be mentioned that her husband seemed obviously relieved when her death was reported to him. A messenger brought him into court at ten o'clock, just two hours after the event. He acknowledged frankly that his marriage had been unhappy, and that he often suspected his wife of some evil craft into which he was afraid to inquire lest she should kill him. When he was dismissed he went away, says the official report, " with a smiling face and lissom step." The corpse was buried in some unfrequented distant spot on the moors before dawn, 11 November, 1660. It is difficult, perhaps impossible, to unravel all the intricacies of such a trial, such accusations and evidences, at the present date of time. So far as we may securely judge it appears that Anna Eve was indeed a Satanist, something more than a dabbler in occult and forbidden things, and reading between the lines it becomes plain that she was a poisoner to boot. Many witches had studied deeply the qualities of nocent plants and herbs ; old secrets of toxic lore were handed down in that dark society from generation to generation. Some tempting morsel, some cate or comfit wherein venom had been deftly mingled, proffered to the little girl playing by the water's edge, quickly eaten as children will, and certain death would follow, a mysterious sickness attended by such symptoms as the documents describe. In poison we may surely find full often a key to the doom of many a forespoken wight, one who has been blasted by the witches' eye or the witches' ban.

A passage in *Lettres Historiques*,[45] published at The Hague in 1698, tells as that on 26 March of that year eight youths, not one of whom had passed the age of fifteen or sixteen, and a girl of twelve who confessed to having fornicated eight times with the Devil, all frequent assistants at the Sabbat, were burned upon multiplied and proven charges of Satanism at Burghausen in Bavaria. Here we have another terrible instance of the cunning and vile craft of demonolaters who are ever particularly anxious to corrupt and seduce the young to swell their accursed society.

On 13 December, 1714, King Frederick William I ordered that throughout the realm of Prussia a full report of any case of sorcery which incurred the penalty of death must be submitted in writing to himself and that no such execution might take place unless the warrant bore the royal signature. Seven years later a country woman who was accused of sorcery at Nau was acquitted, and the King openly informed the magistrates that no more charges of this kind were to be heard. At Berlin there happened a much-talked-of case in 1728. A young girl swore that she had seen and made a close compact with the demon. The court, under the King's direction, decided that she was a subject for the hospital, and ordered her to be detained in the asylum at Spandau.

In Austria, however, Joseph I renewed in 1707 the old laws having reference to Witchcraft, adding none the less some important regulations which forbade the use of torture save in the rarest instances. In the Trentino two executions took place in 1716 and 1717. At Szegedin an especially baneful gang of Satanists was discovered in 1728. Six sorcerers and seven witches were burned alive. In 1730 an official of the same town, who had secretly leagued with them and was perpetuating their hideous craft, went to the stake. Three warlocks suffered at Karpfen in 1744 ; two years after three more at Mühlbach in Saxony ; and in 1752 an old midwife of most evil repute at Maros Vasarheli.

About 1732 a veritable epidemic of vampirism terrorized Hungary, Moravia, Poland, and Serbia.[46] It was reported that in many villages shadowy figures haunted the churchyards and even penetrated into houses sucking the blood of their victims who were mysteriously thrown into an hypnotic sleep. At Medreïga in Hungary the graves of a man named Arnold Paul and a girl Stanoske were opened. The corpses were discovered to be fat and well-nourished, of a ruddy hue as though blooming with health. A sharp stake was driven through the heart of each, the heads severed, and the coffins burned with the bodies. As is well known, a belief in vampirism is yet widely prevalent in Eastern Europe. At Sujos in Serbia, as late as 1910, the body of an old woman was dug up, pierced with a yard, and burned. She had been universally regarded as a witch during her lifetime, and the peasants feared she would return as a vampire to maraud the village.[47]

One of the most interesting of the witch-trials in Germany is also one of the latest.

At the distance of a league from Würzburg, down the river Main, there may be seen an ancient and imposing pile which in the good old days of the Prince-Bishops was a convent of Premonstratensian nuns.[48] This was known as Unterzell ; whilst a little higher, a yet more extensive and wealthier house, stood the Abbey of Oberzell, the home of the Premonstratensian canons, to one of whom, Father Oswald Loschert, who was an actual eye-witness of and intimately concerned in the whole proceedings, we owe the most reliable and fullest account of those dark and mysterious occurrences which he so succinctly and impartially relates in his report addressed to the Empress Maria-Theresa. This great princess, who was deeply religious, expressed herself as keenly interested in the terrible series of events. The monograph bears the following title : *Die wahrhafte und umständliche Nachricht von dem Zufalle, so das jungfräuliche Kloster Unterzell nächst Würzburg betroffen verfasset im Jahr* 1749.[49]

The Order of Prémontré was founded by S. Norbert in 1120 at Prémontré near Laon, France. At first there was no fixed rule, but after a while the Saint unfolded to his companions the plan of a regular organization. It was then that S. Augustine of Hippo appeared to him and in a vision delivered the old canonical code, to which S. Norbert added fastings, penances, and other mortifications together with some pious customs and venerable practices peculiar to the Benedictine family, whereby the new foundation (1121) became, as it were, monastico-canonical.

The five particular ends of the Order are : *Laus Dei in choro,* the singing of the Divine Office in choir ; *Zelus animarum,* zeal for the salvation of souls ; *Spiritus iugis pœnitentiæ,* the spirit of habitual mortification ; *Cultus Eucharisticus,* a special devotion to the Blessed Sacrament ; *Cultus*

Marianus, a special devotion to Our Lady, and in particular to her Immaculate Conception.

The first Order is comprised of priests and clerics; the second of nuns, who being strictly enclosed work for the salvation of souls by their prayers and penances, rising for Matins at midnight and spending much time in contemplation, thus co-operating with the missionary efforts and active administrations of the Fathers. The third Order consists of lay folk, whose duties are in the world, but who wear a small white scapular and have certain prayers to recite. After the death of S. Norbert this institution was imitated by other founders, notably by S. Francis, S. Dominic, and the holy Servites. The nuns wear a white habit, white scapular, white shoes, as the canons, save that the white biretta is replaced by the black veil.

Blessed Ricwera, widow of Raymond de Castro, was S. Norbert's first spiritual daughter. Her example was followed by Ermengardis, Countess of Roussi; by Agnes, Countess of Braim; by Fredesindis, the foundress of Mount S. Martin; by Guda, Countess of Bonneburg; by Beatrix, Viscountess of Amiens; by Anastasia, Duchess of Pomerania; by Hadnigis, Countess of Cleves, and her daughter Gertrude; by Adelia of Montmorency, daughter of Burchard, Constable of France; and by very many more. Though the rule was most austere it is said that in less than fifteen years there were ten thousand cloistered virgins and widows in the Norbertine convents of Europe. The especial glories of the second Order are S. Gertrude, daughter of S. Elizabeth of Hungary (feast 13 August); B. Bronislava (feast 30 August); B. Petronilla (13 July), and B. Poncia (16 May), the wife and daughter of S. Gilbert the Abbot.

Prior to the destruction of the monasteries under Henry VIII there were in England two houses of Premonstratensian nuns, at Irford, near Market Rasen, Lincolnshire, and at Broadholme, near Tuxford, Notts. There are now convents in Holland, France, Belgium, Spain, Poland, Switzerland, and elsewhere.

During the seventeenth and eighteenth centuries the Canonesses were far more numerous than in less fervent and decadent days, when the evil of war and tyranny expelled so many from their homes, burning to the ground spots hallowed for centuries by prayer and penance, or else defiling them to secular uses.

It was towards the end of the year 1746 that Sister Cecilia, a professed nun of the Convent of Unterzell, was attacked by a mysterious and unaccountable malady. At first an obscure nervous complaint was suggested and appropriate measures for the relief of the patient were commenced. However, other symptoms soon appeared. The sufferer was seized by painful cramps in every member, her body swelled as if from dropsy, the muscles contracted and were again suddenly relaxed so as to cause her intense agony, hallucinations of the senses, sight, hearing, touch, succeeded and developed into actual delirium. Although the senior nuns took every precaution that the details of Sister Cecilia's illness should not be known, and although the infirmary was isolated under even stricter regulations than usual, before long strange stories began to be whispered among the community. Shadowy figures had been seen at night in the corridors; mocking laughter was heard which suddenly died away in a awesome silence;[50] the cries of animals, a porcine grunting, the deep baffing of huge hounds, the angry miauling of cats, sounded in the refectory, but when the doors were hastily opened the room was empty and still; and, as so often in poltergeist hauntings, articles of furniture moved here and there, seemingly of their own volition, chairs being overthrown without any visible agency, whilst a huge oak chest no two men could shift was overturned with a loud crash that rang through the vaulted cloisters. An atmosphere of indefinable terror possessed the place. Other and unseen inhabitants, not of this earth nor from heaven, had occupied those hallowed walls.

Cecilia Pistorini, the sick religious, was originally from Hamburg, the descendant of an Italian family which had long been settled there. During her novitiate at Unterzell she was distinguished by her fervour and piety, but, as is not unusual in these cases, in order to test her constancy her solemn profession had been deliberately deferred. Whilst the question was under discussion by the Mothers it was remarked that the Sub-Prioress Maria-Renata Sænger showed a most determined and even violent opposition to the young novice, even voting for her dismissal from the convent. In order that they should make no mistake, to assure themselves that her zeal for the cloister was no mere romantic enthusiasm, her superiors, says Father Loschert, legitimately " made her submit to hard, not to say harsh, trials of her patience, which gave her ample opportunity of practising the virtue of humility. It was noticed that prominent among the Mothers who advocated this strict probation was Renata who, when possession or some demoniac malice came to be suspected in Sister Cecilia's illness, openly declared that there were neither witches nor occultists, that possession was a fable—rationalistic arguments many Satanists use as a wicked blind to compass their ends—and that Sister Cecilia was an hysterical subject who had brought about her own sickness, for which she deserved to be punished rather than consoled." As Görres says : " Renata distinguished herself throughout the whole community by the hatred she displayed towards Sister Cecilia." So here we have a nun of high position in the convent who not only expresses herself in scoffing and atheistical language but shows herself full of malice and rancour which she is ready to visit in every possible way upon a simple and pious girl, a novice of the Order. It might seem that Renata had some presentiment that through this humble Sister, who was eventually admitted to take solemn vows in 1745, her own evil life would be dragged to the light of day.

Suddenly as the religious were reciting their office in Choir several of the nuns collapsed in their stalls uttering raucous cries and even piercing yells. They shook from head to foot as if with an ague, their bodies were convulsed, they rained blows upon invisible enemies who assailed them, they foamed at the mouth, wrestled, and struggled with a more than human strength. It was wellnigh impossible to stifle the scandals of some years' continuance any longer. Yet with praiseworthy anxiety for the good name of her house and tenderest love for her little flock whom the wolf had so foully ravaged, the Prioress, awful suspicions gnawing at her heart, heroically endeavoured to bear the burthen without complaint, without appeal. At length, however, the whole business was inevitably and immediately exposed. One of the elder sisters was stricken with a mortal disease. Upon her death-bed she revealed to her confessor, a Canon of Oberzell, that the illness which had sapped her life was the result of the secret machinations of the Sub-Prioress, whom for a number of years she had recognized as a Satanist, an adept in black magic, a worker of enchantments and noxious spells. The dying woman attested that Renata by the employment of certain herbs and drugs had contrived to affect four choir nuns and a lay sister with lingering complaints. There can be little doubt, in fact, that the Sub-Prioress was a skilled poisoner, versed in the horrid crafts of the Roman witch Hieronyma Spara, her companion La Graziosa, and the infamous Toffania, whose *acqua tofana* dispersed half over Europe under the name of " Oil of S. Nicolas of Bari " was regulated so that the victims would die in a week, a month, a year, according to the strength and doses.[51]

At first the confessor, appalled at these monstrous accusations, refused to give credit to the tale ; he remonstrated with his penitent, reminded her that she lay on a bed of death, and adjured her by that living God Whose judgement she was so soon to endure to speak the truth, the just truth only concerning these dark matters. The aged nun in most solemn tones reiterated all she had revealed, nay more, she declared that she must tell her story in the presence of witnesses so that it should not be for ever lost under the seal of Sacramental Confession. Accordingly when the Host was brought into her chamber, then in the very presence of her Maker, before the numerous persons who had assembled there, she repeated every detail already whispered to the priest, openly denouncing Renata as author of these hideous crimes, and invoking God, Whom she was about to receive as Viaticum, to attest her sincerity and faith. The scene must have been intensely dramatic in its impressiveness and terror. The failing woman is stretched upon her pallet in the humble room, her wrinkled cheeks and trembling veined hands almost as pale as the snowy counterpane over which they feebly strayed or the spotless pillows which propped her high ; strange broken accents fall hesitatingly and slow from her parched gasping lips, words at which the sisters kneeling all round blanch and quiver with fear what time the star-capped tapers shake in their grasp ; tempered by the fire of a thousand confessions the grave priest in his white robe and flowing surplice of goffered lawn down which hangs the purple stole, a narrow splash of colour, stands silent by the bed ; in the centre of all, upon a table covered with damask and fair linen, ablaze with wax flambeaux is the golden ciborium scintillating in the candlelight, the ciborium whereon are fixed the dim-mantled eyes of the expiring nun.

" Even yet," says Father Loschert, " the community was loth openly to accuse the Sub-Prioress to denounce her to the authorities. They preferred to suffer in patience rather than allow themselves to be persuaded that a religious, at any rate a person wearing the religious habit, could be guilty of such abominations. However, the demon declared by the mouth of a possessed nun that he seized Renata even in her mother's womb, that she was his slave and a cursed thing."

Maria Renata Sænger von Mossau was born at Munich about 1680, and she had commenced her postulancy with the Premonstratensians of Unterzell at the age of nineteen. It afterwards came to light that she had been devoted to Satan when only seven years old, a ceremony repeated with binding oaths two years later. An old woman had instructed her in occult lore and magic, and no doubt in the art of poisoning as well. At eleven she had lent herself to the foul desires of a man of high estate, and at thirteen she was engaged in a disgusting intrigue with two lewd officers. A little later she was baptized with the Devil's baptism by a woman of ill life, one of her father's household, a Satanist, who introduced her to that horrid society. A woman of rank, whose name was not revealed, became her mistress in the most intimate arcana of goetic lore, and it was finally under this tutelage that she became a skilled chemist, a very Locusta in her knowledge of herbs and venomed drugs. She entered the convent only to sow dissension and evil in the very strongholds of God's kingdom, to debauch and torment souls essaying the perfect life. She was, indeed, as Joannes Scherr says, " no ordinary woman," a virago as strong for evil as some have been strong for good. For fifty years had she hidden her abnormal wickedness under a cloak of cunningest hypocrisy. None so regular as she at office, in chapter, at refectory ; none so devout in choir ; none so attentive, so punctual, so reserved. She seemed the very model of a good religious. It was this masquerade which had gained her the position of Sub-Prioress. She would even have been elected Prioress, had not an indefinable something, not a suspicion, not a suggestion, but yet a vague shadow of mistrust hindered the community from appointing her to that all-important office.

This was providential, as I believe in the exactest sense of the word. From the very first hour she had entered the convent Renata had secretly been in touch with the Satanists of Würzburg ; sometimes before, sometimes after Matins she had stolen out to their assemblies ; they had supplied her with poisonous roots and *acqua tofana*, with magical screeds and amulets, of which not a few, including the witches' unguent, were found concealed in her room. Indeed, the continual visits to the Convent of an old beldame who sought to hold long conferences with Renata in private gave rise to gossip. It seems certain that by their aid she had procured duplicate keys to the doors, both exterior and interior. Impressions could easily be obtained with a little soft wax, and then the thing were done. Father Loschert relates that in her youth Renata almost nightly frequented the local Sabbat, that the Grand Master of the Satanists of Würzburg had welcomed her there, that in the presence of all that accursed society she renounced Almighty God and His Blessed Mother, that her name Maria whereat Satan trembles and is afraid was changed to Ema, under which nomenclature she was inscribed in the Black Book, that she was marked on the back with the brand of hell. As I have said elsewhere, although the rôle of Devil at such Sabbats was often undertaken by the chief officer, the leader of the Satanists, in any particular locality, I have no doubt that there was on occasion an actual manifestation of the materialized evil power, who was adored by his worshippers with filthy blasphemies and mysterious rites.

Immediately after the death-bed revelations of the aged nun, who had denounced Renata, special prayers, novenas and tredicinas, mortifications, rigid fasts, litanies, penetential psalms, were ordered for the community. The Blessed Sacrament was solemnly exposed and the *Miserere* sung in choir to obtain grace and guidance during those dark and troubled days. On Christmas Day the almoner of the convent, a pious and discreet priest, determined to proceed

to the solemn exorcism of the afflicted nuns. For three days
he continued his efforts, and the morning of Holy Innocents,
certain of whose Relics were shown for the veneration of the
religious, a terrible scene took place. All were in chapel, the
almoner had begun the formula of exorcism when the
possessed women fell into frenzied convulsions. They rolled
on the ground howling and snapping like mad curs. Hideous
blasphemies mingled with their raucous yells. At length they
shrieked out: " Our time is come ! Our time is come !
We cannot longer lie hid ! " As in the days of our Divine
Lord the demons were speaking through the mouths of their
miserable victims.

Diabolic possession was proven. " Nobody," says Father
Loschert, " could from this moment doubt but that the six
nuns were possessed by the Devil; one could only in all
humility wonder that Heaven had permitted so terrible a
curse to fall upon a convent where day and night the occupa-
tion of all was the praise of God and prayer. This hour,
however, had been ordained by Providence to expose that
foul witch who hid her sorceries beneath the holy habit, to
expel her from that fair community to which in spirit and
in truth she had never belonged."

Another solemn exorcism of the afflicted sisters took place
in full choir. The evil spirits when adjured revealed their
names in the kingdom of darkness—fantastic, hideously
grotesque labels—Datas Calvo, Dusacrus, Nataschurus,
Nabascurus, Aatalphus, Elephatan. Renata was present,
and it is said that in horror at her stony silence, the contemptuous smile that curled her lip, her flashing eyes, the
Prioress and the nuns, even the priest himself, shrank from
the blast of malice and hate that seemed to encompass her
and dart malevolently from such hellish fury.

As may be well supposed Renata concentrated her rage
upon the almoner, who had been so largely instrumental in
discovering the Satanist.

The Lord Abbot of Oberzell forthwith made a formal
visitation of the convent, in the course of which he ordered
Renata to be confined in a room apart, straitly charging that
she should be allowed no communication with the rest of
the community. This quick move filled her with apprehension, as well it might, and when she was immediately

put under restraint before she had the opportunity of returning to her own room, she began to lose her stoic attitude and
to show signs of distress. She earnestly pleaded to be
allowed to furnish herself with certain books of devotion,
a mere subterfuge as shortly appeared. "She asked that
she might go to her room," reports Father Loschert, "in
order to get a few articles of pious use, but this was a flimsy
pretext, and it was soon evident that she was anxious to
destroy various unhallowed objects she had concealed there,
ingredients for her spells and sorceries. Leave was denied."
On the other hand grave suspicions were aroused by her
pertinacity and manifest uneasiness. Several learned priests
made a thorough examination of the chamber, and there they
found not only noxious herbs and phials containing potions
and lotions, which when analysed by skilled chemists were
discovered to be swift poisons, but also a number of pots of
ill-savoured ointment, the witches' unguent, and above all
a yellow robe curiously embroidered with cabalistic sigils
and signs, which, as she afterwards confessed, Renata wore
at the conclaves of Satanists she was wont secretly to
frequent. It will not be impertinent to note that Weyer has
preserved for us three formulæ of " witch " ointment :

1. Du persil, de l'eau de l'Aconite, des feuilles de Peuple,
   et de la suye.
   (Parsley or rather hemlock, water of aconite, poplar
   leaves, and soot.)
2. De la Berle, de l'Acorum vulgaire, de la Quintefeuille,
   du sang de chauvesouris, de la Morelle endormante,
   et de l'huyle.
   (Water hemlock, sweet flag, cinquefoil, bat's blood,
   deadly nightshade, and oil.)
3. De graisse d'enfant, de sue d'Ache, d'Aconite, de
   Quintefeuille, de Morelle, et de suye.
   (Baby's fat, juice of cowbane, aconite, cinquefoil,
   deadly nightshade, and soot.)

" These prescriptions," says Professor A. J. Clark, " show
that the society of witches had a very considerable knowledge of the art of poisoning."[52]

As Renata continued to display such a violent animosity
toward the almoner of Unterzell it was resolved that a

confessor extraordinary should be applied for, whose ministrations and ghostly counsel might prevail upon her to relieve her guilty soul by a frank and free acknowledgement of her crimes. This is strictly in accordance with the provision of the Council of Trent : " Præter ordinarium autem confessorem alius extraordinarius ab Episcopo et aliis superioribus bis aut ter in anno offeratur qui omnium confessiones audire debeat." Sessio XXV. cap. 10. (In addition to the ordinary confessor, another priest, a confessor extraordinary may be provided by the Bishop or other superiors twice or thrice a year, and he shall then hear the confessions of the Community.) The Prince-Bishop of Würzburg, when formal application was made, at once authorized a confessor extraordinary to visit the convent, and with the approbation of his Abbot, Dom Maurus, a learned and experienced director, a Benedictine of the Würzburg monastery, undertook the task. There were many religious houses in the city, Augustinians, Franciscans, Dominicans, Jesuits, and others, but of them all the Benedictine family was reputed to be the most scholarly, the most deeply versed in things mystical, true monks, true contemplatives, not mingling with the world, but wholly devoted to the interior life, walking in heavenly places. Dom Maurus enjoyed the reputation of a Saint ; his knowledge of the spiritual life, his gentleness, his charity, had won him not only the love but also the reverence of the whole district. At his first interview with the unhappy Renata his holy admonitions so touched her heart, that she unburdened her conscience of the load of guilt and poured forth a tale of blackest infamy. This she related openly, not under the sacramental seal, and later her long and terrible confession was reduced to thirteen heads : (1) She acknowledged that she was a Satanist ; (2) that she had made a covenant with the Demon, changing her name Maria, as especially hateful to Satan, to Ema, under which title she had been entered on the local roll of witches ; (3) that she was marked on her body with the Devil's character ; (4) that at night she frequently rubbed her body with the witches' ointment, and attended the Sabbat, wearing the yellow robe which had been discovered in her room ; (5) that at these assemblies she had abjured God, Our Blessed Lady, the Sacraments ; (6) that she had had carnal intercourse with a Demon and with Satanists at the Sabbat ; (7) that she had enticed three persons outside the convent to join the hellish society ; (8) that she was accompanied by a familiar, a rat ; (9) that she attempted to cast spells upon the almoner of the convent and the Lord Abbot of Oberzell, but in this instance she had failed ; (10) that by her enchantments [and, doubtless, by her poisons] she had caused six persons in the house and several persons not of the house to fall ill of wasting diseases, that she had stricken several with paralysis and other ailments ; (11) that she was responsible for the diabolic possession of six nuns ; (12) that she had ensorceled Father Gregory of the monastery of Ebrach and Father Nicolas Venino of Ilmstadt ; (13) that at her communions she was wont not to swallow the Sacred Host but to keep It, and then to throw It into the fish-ponds or on a midden, or again down the latrines, or not unseldom to carry It to her secret rendezvous when the company would stab and pierce It with bodkins and needles in their insensate hatred of God. It was, in truth, this last and most horrible confession which sealed her doom.

The unhappy woman showed every sign of a sincere and complete penitence, but the evil she had wrought could not be so soon undone. The afflicted nuns were still tortured and tormented by the devils, for as was divinely said in days of old : " Hoc genus in nullo potest exire, nisi in oratione et ieiunio." (This kind can go out by nothing, but by prayer and fasting.) The Prince-Bishop, to whom a full report was addressed, now ordered the transference of Renata to the fortress of Marienberg where she was kept under strict ward. Her religious habit was taken away and she was dressed in a dark robe of secular fashion. Several pious priests visited her and spent long hours in exhortation and prayer, and " although they knew she had been a hardened and infamous malefactor, nevertheless they believed that she had truly repented of her crimes, since she gave such unmistakable signs of contrition and a change of heart." The unclean spirits, furious at their prey being thus snatched from them, raved more madly and foully from the mouths of the possessed, tearing and rending their poor victims in hideous convulsions and paroxysms of frenzy.

An ecclesiastical tribunal sat to judge the case. The

assessors were two priests of tempered experience and probity, of whom one was Father Loschert; two Jesuit fathers; Dom Maurus and the almoner of the convent. After long deliberations, which lasted several weeks, Renata was condemned as guilty of sorcery, heresy, apostasy, and of having defiled the Host in the Manichæan manner. She was degraded from religion and handed over to the secular courts. " After a new inquiry, a report was submitted to His Highness the Prince-Bishop [23 May, 1749] and the prisoner was condemned to be burned for her crimes ; this punishment, however, Monsignor, in consideration of the extreme youth of the accused when she was first seduced to the heinous sin of Witchcraft mitigated to death by the headsman's sword within the precincts of the prison, and that her body should afterwards be publicly burned upon a great pyre." Renata heard her sentence calmly, accepting it without a murmur as the just penalty of her crimes.

On 21 June, 1749, between the hours of eight o'clock and nine, the prisoner was carried in a chair to the place of execution, a bastion of the castle. She wore a long black dress, a white apron, a white gorget, and a coif of black and white. Two priests, Dom Maurus, her confessor, and the almoner of the prison, Father Gaar, S.J., walked by her side, to comfort and exhort her in this extremity. An eye-witness, who was officially present as the representative of a civic corporation, relates that she showed a truly perfect and humble resignation at the last, and the executioner most dextrously severed her neck with one swift sudden sweep of his sword.

The body was then conveyed by two serjeants, " night watchmen," to the other side of the Main, and there on a hill locally dubbed " Sorcerers' Square," perpetuating the fact that a century and a half before numbers of witches had perished at the stake on that spot, it was consumed in an immense fire of faggots, brushwood, and tar-barrels, which had been built up the preceding day. A vast crowd had assembled to witness the event, and Father Gaar, mounting a movable pulpit, first addressed the throng in an eloquent and admirably reasoned discourse. He impressed upon his hearers that sorcery although a rare was none the less a very real offence, that unclean spirits might yet possess and torment persons even as in the days of Our Lord, that the Devil even now " tamquam leo rugiens circuit, quærens quem deuoret," " as a roaring lion, goeth about seeking whom he may devour."

The whole account of Maria Renata Sænger is recorded with the utmost clarity without passion, without partiality. There are ample documents, and the train of events is perfectly simple and logical. It is obvious that she was a Satanist, who had early been introduced into that dark society, that for years she was trained in all their evil secrets, and that at last discovery came almost by an accident.

There can be no doubt that these hideous doctrines were assiduously propagated. Two years after the Würzburg scandals Anna Bayerin was executed at Salzburg for unspeakable outrages upon the Host which she had retained at Communion, and defiled according to the Satanist tradition.

From 1736 until 1779 the whole district of Limburg, parts of Lorraine, and the province of Treves, were infested by a vast secret society known as the " Buxen." Their organization was singularly complete. Their custom was to meet after nightfall in some lonely spot and to commence proceedings by the celebration of Black Mass when Hosts, which were stolen from the tabernacle, were grossly desecrated. This was the time when recruits were initiated into the gang. It is said that their foul ceremonies were generally conducted in one of three ruined sanctuaries, that of S. Rose near Sittardt, of S. Leonard near Roldyck, and a chapel at Oermond on the Maas. Afterwards they sallied forth and raided farms, country houses, and even villages. If they passed a church on their way they invariably burst open the doors, robbed the tabernacle, and gutted the whole building, leaving it in flames. A state of anarchy and terrorization prevailed. At length in the Roldyck district stern measures were taken. Permanent gallows were set up in many places, some hamlets had two gibbets apiece. Breaking on the wheel and burning alive soon became the fate of any of the gang who were captured, and the court records of Falkenburg show that between 1772 and 1774 over one hundred Buxen were thus executed. Leopold Leeuwerk, who was dubbed their chaplain, a Satanist, was caught at last, and the most infamous of their leaders, Abraham Nathan, a renegade

Jew, was put to death at Haeck, on the moor of Graed, 24 September, 1772.

The last official trial and execution for Witchcraft in Germany was that of Anna Maria Schwaegel, the daughter of an artisan at Lachen. Being in service with a well-to-do family of the town she was seized with an inordinate passion for a fellow-servant, the coachman, a smart young Lothario, who deliberately set himself out to win her affections. He gave himself out to be a Lutheran, and insisted as a preliminary to their marriage that she should renounce the Catholic Faith to join his sect. So besotted was she that the unhappy girl obeyed her paramour's behest only to discover she was being trifled with and abused. The man had no intention of making her his wife, in fact he wedded another. In despair Anna Maria fled from the place, and half-distracted by what had occurred she wandered blindly to and fro, a beggar, until one day she was found by the wayside in the last extremity of wretchedness, starving, clad in a few miserable rags, and so taken to an asylum at Laneggen, between Kempten and Immensadt in Bavaria. It was noticed that here she seemed always uneasy, always afraid. In time she related her adventures to other inmates of the home and one day she revealed her secret. She told them how she had lapsed from the Church to become a Lutheran, and she added that her lover beneath the pretext of this form of belief was in reality a Satanist, that she attended the Sabbat with him, and there committed unspeakable abominations at his behest. " It was the Devil under the form of this coachman, who betrayed me," was her constant cry. This exclamation makes the event amply clear. As I read the story, the coachman was the Grand Master, the Devil, that is to say, of the local Satanists.

The Superior of the home, Madame Anna Maria Kuhstaller, a sincerely pious if somewhat rigid *dévote*, could not fail to hear the tale, and in her first impulse of horror she informed the magistrates of Kempten of what had happened. On 20 February Anna Maria Schwaegel was arrested and carried to Kempten, where she was lodged in custody. When interrogated she not only maintained her story, but added many new and conclusive facts. She had twice made an express compact with the Demon, she had assisted at the

Sabbat many times, and defiled herself with foulest profanations and blasphemies. On 11 April, 1775, three judges— Treichlinger, Feiger, and Leiner—passed sentence of death, which was forthwith submitted to the Prince-Bishop, who after reading the culprit's confession, wrote on the parchment with his own hand *Fiat iustitia, Honorius,* Prince-Bishop. There was some discussion amongst the lawyers whether the punishment should be the stake, *pœna ignis,* the traditional method, or the ax, *pœna gladii,* conformably to article 109 of the penal code of Charles V. It was decided that the headsman should be called upon to do his office.

The last regularly official trial and execution for Witchcraft in Western Europe was that of Anna Goeldi who suffered at Glaris, a Protestant district of Switzerland, 17 June, 1782. This woman was accused by a doctor named Tschudi of having cast evil spells upon his little son, who had fallen into a decline. Possibly there was some suspicion of poison, the witch's readiest weapon to strike her foe. Anna Goeldi was hanged.

Probably the last trial and judicial execution for Witchcraft in Europe was that of two fearful hags, notorious and rampant Satanists, who were burned at the stake in Poland in 1793.[53]

That Satanism survived, and although driven underground was strong in Germany during the nineteenth century, is hardly to be doubted. In the twentieth century it has wellnigh been flaunted by debauchs and decadents, more than one sounding scandal being the result of their effrontery. In December, 1919, the authorities broke up a gang of Devil worshippers at Berlin. The police, who were more than a hundred strong, surprised the demonists at their orgies in the Café Kerkau. The whole assembly, which numbered wellnigh five hundred persons, offered a brief resistance, only to be coerced at the revolver's point. Most of the company were in a state of stark nudity, and there was evidence that no foulness of the Sabbat had been forgotten. All were conveyed to durance in covered motor-lorries, and it is said that several persons of high standing were gravely implicated.[54]

In November, 1925, a boy at Uttenheim near Strasburg was shot by the village policeman as being a werewolf, and

the whole country-side who had gone in terror of the dead
lad firmly believed that he continually affected that transformation to ravage their flocks and folds.

There are few European countries which so teem with
legend and superstition as Germany. The Rhine is the river
of the undine and the lorelei ; along its banks are countless
haunted castles, in the romantic woods innumerable phantoms
and unearthly visitants. The Brocken was the rendezvous
of witches the whole world over ; in the Hartz Mountains
you may meet the Black Huntsman ; and amid the glades of
the Black Forest the werewolf yet prowls for his prey. Old
beliefs, old customs linger still. On Walpurgis night in many
parts of Bavaria and among the Germans of Bohemia the
country folk will yet expel the witches, or, at least, such was
the invariable practice until some twenty or thirty years ago.
In the Böhmerwald Mountains, which divide Bavaria from
Bohemia, all the young fellows in the village assemble on
some height, especially at a crossroad, and lustily crack huge
whips with all their strength. Where the noise of the whip
is heard the witch can do no harm. In other places the
herdsmen wind their horns meanwhile, and the long loud
notes will effectually keep the hags at bay. In Voigtland,
a mountainous region of Central Germany bordering on the
Frankenwald range, the witch is still hated and feared.
For on certain days, Walpurgis night, S. Thomas' Eve,
Midsummer, the sorceress will make her way into a neighbour's house and try to borrow some trifle or else filch it
unobserved. Misfortune will fall on that homestead when
they have succeeded in their quest. On these days, too, the
cattle are protected from their blasting spells by the sign of
the most Holy Cross chalked upon the byres, and bunches of
sweet herbs hung around, marjoram and gillyflowers, which
the foul crew loathe and warily shun.

In Bohemia the peasantry on Walpurgis night strew
brambles and thorns on the house lintels and around the
cowsheds and pens to keep far those who are riding aloft in the
darkness and gloom. Huge bonfires are lit and effigies of
witches consumed therein. At a certain hour all the horns
and musical instruments, in fact anything capable of making
a noise, are sounded and clanged throughout the village.
The witches are hurrying from the chimneys on their way to

the Sabbat and the din will drive them faster and further on their course.

The Silesian rustics also dread Walpurgis night. The housewife carefully removes her utensils from the fireplace and hides her broom, the goodman locks up his pitchfork and his rake, lest haply the witch should seize them and in an instant be astride hey ! for the Sabbat, hey ! for the worship of hell, the orgy of bane and bale.

NOTES TO CHAPTER VI

[1] S. Rupert is by authorities said to have died on Easter Sunday, 27 March, 718. Other writers reject this date, and speak of the fifth and beginning of the sixth centuries as the age of his missionary work. The latest research, however, inclines to the seventh, or even as above, to the eighth century.

[2] There are important relics at Louvain, Mechlin, Prague, Bruges, and Erfurt. A considerable portion of an arm is at Eichfeld. On 11 June, 1874, Pope Pius IX extended the feast of S. Boniface to the entire world.

[3] Baronius, 997.

[4] The inhabitants of Livonia twice fell back from Christianity to paganism. In 1201 Albrecht founded the city of Riga, of which he became Bishop, and reclaimed the people by a crusade. In 1202 he established the famous Order of Knights of the Sword.

[5] *Grove-nymphs*, Apollonius Rhodius, I, 1066.

[6] *Ibid.*, I, 1227.

[7] *Orphica*, 50.

[8] Lympha = νύμφη.

[9] Cf. the Greek *Eumenides* for Erinyes. Sophocles, *Œdipus at Colonus*, 128.

[10] Miss M. A. Murray, *The Witch-Cult in Western Europe*, pp. 11, 12, etc.

[11] *Cur magia pariter cum hæresi creuerit.*

[12] Havet, *L'Hérésie et le Bras Séculier au Moyen Age*, *Œuvres* (Paris, 1896), II, pp. 117–81.

[13] See the provisions of the Bull *Ad abolendam*. Also Mansi, *Sacrorum conciliorum noua . . . collectio*, Venice, 1769, Vol. XX, pp. 476 *sqq.* And Frédéricq, *Corpus documentorum Inquisitionis . . .*, Ghent, 1889, *sqq.*, I, 56. And Havet, *op. cit.*

[14] Lami, *Lezioni d'antichità Toscana*, Florence, 1766, II, pp. 484 and 523.

[15] *Monumenta Germaniæ historica*, ed. G. A. Pertz, II, p. 252.

[16] *Monumenta Germaniæ historica*, Leges, II, p. 268.

[17] Michael, *Geschichte des deutschen Volken*, II, p. 266.

[18] Some authors write that he was a lay-brother, but this does not seem credible. In fact, there is a good deal of obscurity in the records. The commission handed offenders over to the secular courts for punishment. The chronicler of Worms notes that the proceedings were authoritatively approved by Henry, King of the Romans, and by many other princes. *Annales breu. Worm. ; Monumenta German. Script.*, XVIII, pp. 38 *sqq.*

[19] A number of canons issued in 1312 by the Council of Vienna under Pope Clement V. The Bull *Multorum querela* was incorporated in the decrees of this Council. P. Frédéricq, *Corpus documentorum . . .* (Ghent, 1889–1906), Vol. I, No. 170.

[20] Charloz, *Les sorcières neuchâteloises*. Jeanneret, *Les sorciers dans le pays de Neuchâtel*.

[21] Diary of Johan Aubrion, a solid burgess of Metz (1461–1512), cited by Hansen, *Geschichte des Hexenwahns*.

[22] Who often appears as Henry *Institor* the Latinized version of his surname.

[23] I have used the edition of 1494. *Liber Malleus maleficarū a suo editore nuncupatus Impressus per me Joannen Koelhoff incola Ciuitatis sancte Colonien. Anno saluti* MCCCC, xciiij *in vigilia sanet. Katherine Regine ac Vginis martyris finem accepit feliciter.* The Vigil of S. Catharine is 24 November. The book consists of one hundred and eight folios.

[24] A new edition by A. von Neller, Stuttgart, 1880.

[25] By an almost inconceivable breach of good taste these banalities were preserved in a recent performance of Marlowe's play (1925).

[26] For a theatrical history of *Faust* in England see my *History of Witchcraft,* c. vii.

[27] They were seldom printed, and usually largely extemporized, keeping at the same time fairly closely to the original theme. See the Ulm piece and others in Vol. V of Scheible's *Kloster* (1847) ; also the puppet versions edited by W. Hamm (1850) ; O. Schade (1856) ; K. Engel (1874) ; Bielschowsky (1882) ; Kralih and Winter (1885).

[28] Dr. Ernest Faligan's *Histoire de la Légende de Faust,* 1888, has a valuable "index bibliographique."

[29] Translated into English by George Barrow, 1826. G. W. M. Reynolds has a lurid romance, *Faust,* with its sequel, *Wagner, the Wehr-Wolf.*

[30] Carl Haas, *Hexenprocesse,* pp. 84 *et sqq.*

[31] *Gesta Treuirorum,* 189. Hontheim, *Diplomatische trierische Geschichte,* Vol. I, p. 877.

[32] *Kleiner Beitrag zur Geschichte des Hexenwesens im* 16 *Jahrhundert,* Trier, 1830, p. 7.

[33] This seems correct, although a late account, Voigt, *Berliner Monatschrift von 1781* (April), says "one year."

[34] His youngest daughter Anna Maria, a Sepulchrine nun, has left a few fragments of a diary. Under the year 1627 she speaks of the condemnation of the Satanists.

[35] Hauber, *Bibliotheca magica.*

[36] M. J. Diefenbach, *Der Hexenwahn,* p. 124, n.

[37] *Historia tragica adolescentis prœnobilis Ernesti ab Ernberg.*

[38] For a good bibliography of von Spee see the Introduction to the *Trutznachtigall,* a collection of some fifty to sixty sacred lyrics, by Weinrich, 1907.

[39] See the *Gazette de Cologne,* 3 January, 1875.

[40] Kohl, *Reise in Ungarn,* Dresden, 1842.

[41] Otto Glaubrecht, *Die Schreckensjahre von Lindheim,* Stuttgart, 1886.

[42] A small town of some 2000 souls about seven miles from Magdeburg.

[43] *Premier avis,* No. LX.

[44] Esquirol gives tearlessness as a symptom in some forms of insanity. See E. K. Hunt's translation of *Mental Maladies,* p. 245, Philadelphia, 1845.

[45] May, 1698, pp. 535, 536, La Haye, 1698.

[46] *Traité sur les Apparitions des Esprits et sur les Vampires, ou les Revenans de Hongrie, de Moraire, &c.,* Dom Augustin Calmet, 2 vols., Paris, 1751. See especially Vol. II, c. 14.

[47] *Le Matin,* 4 January, 1910.

[48] Now desecrated and turned into a Palace of Industry.

[49] Amongst other cognate matter we have : *Christliche Anred nächst dem Scheiterhaufen, worauff der deichnam Mariae Renatae, einer durchs Schwert hingerichteten Zauberin den* 21ten *Jun. A.* 1749, *ausser der Stadt Würzburg, verbrennet worden, an ein zalreich versammeltes Volk gettan. . . .* Von P. Georgio Gaar, s.j., *Aktenmaessiger Bericht von der zu Unterzell bei Würzburg vorgefallenen erschrecklichen Begebenheit puncto Maleficiorum et Magiæ,* in the *Zauber bibliothek* of Horst, Vol. I, pp. 205 *sqq. Der letzte Hexenprocess in Deutschland,* Pirna, 1849. *Die letzte Reichshexe* in *Hammerschläge und Historien,* by J. Scherr, Vol. II. Görres in his *Die christliche Mystik* has a very reliable account of the Maria Renata case.

[50] A detailed examination of these phenomena would repay study. They may be closely paralleled by much of the thaumaturgy of modern spiritism,

and by many supernormal happenings which are described in the writings of authoritative investigators.

[51] La Spara and La Graziosa were executed in Rome under Alexander VII, 1655–67.   The hag Toffania at the age of threescore and ten was overtaken by justice at Naples, and strangled in 1719.   Hahnemann says that her poison was compounded of arsenical neutral salts.   Garelli, physician to the Emperor of Austria, considered it to have been crystallized arsenic, dissolved in a large quantity of water by decoction, with the addition (for some unexplained purpose) of the herb *cymbalaria.*

[52] See Appendix V, p. 279, to Miss M. A. Murray's *The Witch-Cult in Western Europe.*

[53] It is worth recording that the burning alive of five witches by the Alcade Ignacio Castello of San Jacobo in Mexico on 20 August, 1877, " with consent of the whole population," is merest fiction.   See *Stimmen aus Maria-Laach,* XXXII, 1887, p. 378.

[54] *Daily Express,* 9 December, 1919.

CHAPTER VII

ITALY

ALTHOUGH, doubtless, the deadly poison had been in secret filtering through from the East for many years, it was not until early in the eleventh century that the Gnostic heresy began to show itself openly in Italy. The various sects, all of debased Manichæan origin, Paulicians, Bogomiles, Kathari, Paterini, Vaudois, Albigenses, Tartarins, Beghards, Pauvres de Lyon, or what not, were clandestinely devoted to Satanism, adepts in the most lewd and abominable rites glorifying the principles of anarchy and evil, fanatics whose active propaganda soon fanned to flame the dying embers of sorcery and revivified every foul superstition which the Church had wellnigh stamped out, but which yet lingered in remote districts amongst the fearful and ignorant peasantry.

That profound scholar Mons. Aroux[1] suggests that this invasion of the West was made by two routes, one of which was by sea through the trading relations existing between Provence and the East; France and Spain being reached in this manner. The other route was through Bulgaria, the sectaries overrunning Moldavia, Pannonia, Moravia, Bohemia, and Dalmatia, thus entering Italy. Lombardy, where these two streams would converge, naturally became the headquarters of the organization. Those corrupt Oriental philosophies which, mingled with a distorted form of Christianity, were carried westward by the Crusaders, certain of whom had become gravely infected, now began to corrode whole sections of society and a further impetus was given to the movement by the foundation in 1118 of the Order of the Templars whose ranks were from the very beginning tainted with Dualism, and who assiduously propagated a secret doctrine closely akin to the arcana of the Gnostic bodies that vermiculated Europe.

This work was carried on very secretly and with infinite

precautions, so that for many years at least the inroads made by heresy and magic were hardly suspected.

In 1080 Pope S. Gregory VII writing to King Harold of Denmark restrains that monarch's zeal, and forbids him to condemn witches to death without the clearest proofs of their guilt, a mere accusation of having raised storms or blighted standing corn and invoked pestilences must be at once set aside. As yet then heresy is not overtly interlocked with necromancy and malignant spells.

The most important and, of course, supremely authoritative series of documents dealing with the conduct of witch-trials in Italy and elsewhere are the Papal Bulls. In 1233 Pope Gregory IX (Ugolino, Count of Segni) addressed a Bull to the famous Conrad of Marburg bidding him proceed against the Luciferians, who addressed homage and prayers to the Demon, but it may fairly be said the first Bull which directly reviews the situation was issued 13 December, 1258, by Pope Alexander IV (Rinaldo Conti). Addressing the Franciscan inquisitors[2] this prudent and holy pontiff ruled that they must carefully refrain from any intervention in charges of sorcery unless there be some clear presumption of heretical belief and practice, "manifeste hæresim saperent." But it is obvious that the two things were now so intermingled that one could hardly exist without the other. It was, at any rate, at Toulouse, a hot-bed of Katharan infection, that in 1274 the earliest example occurs of a witch being burned after judicial sentence of an inquisitor ; a malignant hag named Angèle de la Barthe was there condemned by the learned and clement Hugues de Baniols. Amongst other abominations she confessed to having murdered a number of infants whose flesh she and her fellows devoured. This wretch also boasted of having had commerce with the Demon, and of being a constant attendant at the Sabbat.[3] On 10 January, 1260, Alexander IV directed a similar Bull to the Dominicans.

At the opening of the fourteenth century occurred the scandals connected with Walter Langton, Bishop of Lichfield and treasurer of Edward I, who was accused of magical practices upon the most circumstantial evidence—eye-witnesses coming forward and swearing they had seen him pay homage to Satan—but who succeeded in clearing himself with the compurgators. Boniface VIII (Benedetto Gaetani), the greatest jurist and acutest diplomat of his age, issued a weighty and considered Bull on the occasion, dated 8 June, 1303, which commences thus : " Dudum ad audientiam nostram peruenit, quod uenerabilis frater noster W. Couentrensis et Lichefeldensis episcopus erat in regno Angliæ et alibi publice defamatus quod diabolo homagium fecerat et eum fuerat osculatus in tergo eique locutus multotiens. . . ." It will be remarked that the details of the charges are set forth clearly and in explicit terms.

The next Papal Bull is of prime importance. It is dated 27 February, 1318, and addressed from Avignon by John XXII (Jacques d'Euse) to Bartholomew, Bishop of Fréjus,[4] Prior Pierre Tisserand of the Monastery of S. Antoninus of Pamiers, and Pierre de Champs, Archdeacon of the Cathedral Church of Clermont. The Holy Father gives these three prelates complete and ample inquisitorial powers to proceed against nine persons, eight clerics (of whom one Giovanni di Ansanto was a physician) and a certain Innocent, who belonged to the household of no less a prelate than Peter of Savoy, Archbishop of Lyons, and is described as " barbitonsor," barber, a position of considerable confidence and trust. A barber in the service of so great a noble would at least have had a fair knowledge of drugs and medicine, and have been " grounded in astronomye " and " magik naturel." The accused seem to have studied the black art deeply in all its branches. They had collected a large number of grimoires and books of spells ; used enchantments to afflict their enemies with diseases and death ; consecrated puppets, mirrors, and rings for purposes of divination ; evoked the fiend after fencing themselves in pentacles and magic circles which they traced ; inquired of the future from demons and discarnate intelligences ; nourished familiars[5] ; paid divine honours to the powers of hell, from whom they hoped for all temporal good, a distinctly Manichæan belief. These renegades seem to have been indiscreet enough publicly to boast that by certain words and mystic runes they had the power to cure a man of any sickness, nay, actually to prolong life, and contrariwise to visit any who molested them with sudden and immediate destruction, a vaunt which for a long while successfully secured their immunity from any active interference on the part of the civil authorities. The evidence was overwhelming and the scandal grew day by day until it reached the ears of the Vicar of Christ who was not slow to deal with the matter. The Bishop of Fréjus and his co-inquisitors are recommended, nay commanded, to deal with the affair at once, without favour and without advertisement, to hear all witnesses indifferently, to find out all who are implicated in these malpractices, summarily to punish the guilty. The Pope remarks with no little acumen that they will undoubtedly find heresy mingled with sorcery, " præsertim cum labem sapiant hereticæ prauitatis."

The text of this important Bull is as follows :

[John XXII] to Our Venerable Brother Bartholomew, Bishop of Fréjus, and to Our beloved son Pierre Tisserand, Doctor of law, Prior of the Monastery of S. Antoninus of Pamiers in the diocese of Rodez, and to Pierre de Champs, Professor of civil law, Archdeacon of the church of Clermont, Our chaplains. The Roman Pontiff, Whose particular duty and care it is to watch over the safety of souls, must needs be most instant in correcting His sons, when they are straying from the Faith, for assuredly nothing is more certain than that naught availeth to salvation, unless it be firmly rooted in the Faith. Now there hath newly come to Our ears a report which is worthy of all credence and which is bruited abroad by common talk, namely that John de Lemorici ; James said to be of Brabant ; Giovanni di Ansanto, a physician ; Radulph Penchadau ; Walter Laflamene ; Guglielmo Marini ; Conrad a German ; to whom was erstwhile joined one Thomas said to be a German likewise ; all being clerics, as well as Innocent, the barber and leech of Our Venerable Brother, Peter, Archbishop of Lyons, of whom some are dwelling in Our own court, disdaining to follow the precept of the Apostle and be wise unto salvation, but rather being curious with inordinate desires and intoxicated with the folly of overweening vanity, these, We say, have entangled and enmeshed themselves in the dark toils of nigromancy, geomancy, and other magic arts, possessing writings and books that treat of these arts, which inasmuch as they are the arts of devils born of a baleful and hated correspondence between men and the evil angels, must be

avoided by every Christian and reprobated from the heart
with every circumstance of contumely, yet these wretches
having consecrated certain mirrors and images according
to their accursed ceremonies not unseldom make use of such
objects and taking their place in circles they frequently
invoke evil spirits, that they may by this means do a mischief
to men's health, either by slaying them owing to the blighting
curse of some spell or by shortening their days and wasting
them with disease. On occasion, moreover, they enclose in
mirrors, circles, or rings, devils, who may answer their
inquiries concerning the past and the future, seeking from
these hellish communications to predict the future, which is
known to God alone, wherefore they eagerly practise divination and soothsaying, and in most evil wise do they defile
themselves by connexion with succubi. When they have
evoked these foul spirits they essay many a curious experiment in every branch of diabolic lore. They further make
bold to declare that by no medicine, food, or draught, but
merely by the power of some formula they can shorten or
prolong a man's days or at will slay him, and contrariwise if
such be their good pleasure they will heal him of any sickness.
This do they maintain they have not infrequently performed.
Wherefore abandoning their Creator and placing their trust in
this sort of devilish cantrips, and foully deeming that evil
spirits are worthy of service and of divine honours, they
presume and dare to worship them with all outward show
of reverence and adoration even as idolators and heathen use.
The aforesaid clerics, then, and the barber, each several one
and all of them, as also others who yet live at Our court, are
said to have committed these enormities again and again,
to the imminent peril of not only their own souls but of
many another soul to boot. So vile and pestilent a superstition, whose evil and reprobate adherents the common
consent of society holds as enemies to general order and,
indeed, the foes of humanity, We neither can nor will wink
at, especially since it is polluted with the taint of heretical
pravity, and accordingly in regard to all the aforesaid
matters owing to Our great zeal for the Faith, whose interests
must be everywhere diligently safeguarded, We direct that
the Inquisition proceed against the clerics, the barber, and
all whose names are herein rehearsed, nor shall it be any let

that the aforesaid Thomas is dead, for in a business of such black and heinous crimes, the memory even of a man who is dead must be assailed, since in some way his infamy, if clear proven, may yet be lawfully punished. Wherefore to you, to each one severally, and to all, in whose sound judgement We place entire trust under Our Lord God, by the authority of these presents we commit this weighty charge, solemnly requiring you that whensoever ye may find the aforesaid clerics and barber and others who reside at Our court, who have been publicly defamed as reputed to be evilly and criminally concerned in all these vile businesses or aught cognate to them, ye by the aid of any fitting and proper persons shall forthwith and presently without noise or disturbance attach their persons, and no appeal being allowed, according to course of justice, having the fear of God alone before your eyes ye shall with exactest carefulness proceed to inquire into the truth of the accusations, and when the inquiry has been duly made ye shall deliver sentence according to the course of law.   By the tenor of these presents unto you, to each one severally and to all, We grant and give full and amplest powers, so that each one of you, whatsoever be his rank and estate, may commence a process when and wheresoever he will, and that another may continue and conclude the said process, and ye shall summon whomsoever ye will as witnesses to places convenient to yourselves, just as and so often as seemeth expedient to you, and these shall be called upon, required to attend, and personally cited to appear.   And if there be any recalcitrant or disobedient they shall be forcibly constrained and compelled by ecclesiastical censures and Our Apostolic authority, if it be expedient for the judging of the aforesaid crimes or any questions relevant and pertinent.   All this notwithstanding the two decisions arrived at in the general council, notwithstanding also any other constitutions delivered by Our predecessors the Roman Pontiffs.   Given at Avignon. 27 February [1318].[6]

On the 22 August, 1320, John XXII addressed a Bull from Avignon upon the subject of Witchcraft[7] to the Dominican Cardinal of S. Sabina, William de Laudun, Bishop of Carcassone and Toulouse, to which was added in 1326 the Constitution *Super illius specula*.   Four years later, 4

November, 1330, the same Pope issued a Bull *Sano nouiter intellecto* to Bernard de Farges, Archbishop of Narbonne, and his suffragans. The whole of that district had been honeycombed by the sect of the Albigenses of whom Innocent III justly remarked : " They are worse than the Saracens." Strictly speaking, Albigensianism was not even a Christian heresy, but an extra-Christian religion deeply involved with Oriental magic and blasphemous parodies of Holy Mass ; in a word, Satanism. When the adherents of this cult had gained sufficient power in a district they did not hesitate to spread their doctrines by fire and sword. The holy Cistercian S. Peter of Castelnau, whom they martyred in 1208, and S. Camelia, put to death by the same ruffians, are both honoured in the Proper of Carcassone. Other similar cases might be cited. The dregs of the heresy were finally driven underground, but they reappear in the form of Witchcraft and the black art.

On the 12 April, 1331, John XXII addressed his Bull *Uiros maleficos humani generis* to Bishop Hugh II of Paris. This document is particularly directed against Hercaudus, a Benedictine abbot of the diocese of Autun, who was reported to have attempted by spells the life of Philip VI. The fearful spread of sorcery throughout Europe greatly exercised the third of the Avignon Popes, the Cisterican Benedict XII.[8] A profound patristic scholar, a learned theologian, a subtle disputant, he took a keen and active part in the settlement of the problems of his day, than which none seemed more formidable than the increase of Witchcraft and its kindred abominations. The list of the Bulls dealing with demonism which begins less than two years after his accession to the throne, is both lengthy and important. On 13 April, 1336, the Supreme Pontiff writes to Bishop William of Paris, concerning William Altafex, an English warlock, " nigromanticum de Anglia " ; and during that summer no less than three papal letters followed to various chapters, 17 June, 9 August, 17 August. On 9 August various guilty persons were mentioned individually : one Fra Peter Thomas, a sorcerer ; Bertrand of Narbonne, a relapsed heretic ; Gerald, a cleric ; Rostagno, accused of necromancy ; a woman named Decelma, and others. On 21 December, 1336, a brief was dispatched to Gaston de Foix recommending renewed civil vigilance throughout the territory of Narbonne, whilst on the same date no less than four other briefs were indited, one of which to the Bishop of Tarbes gives ample evidence of the Pope's solicitude and preoccupation with this business. Scarcely a month later, 18 January, 1337, a bull is addressed to William Lombard, a canon of Mirepoix, a famous scholar, and we have Bulls of 12 June and 13 June, *Dudum ad audientiam nostram perducto,* in the same year. On 29 October, 1337, appeared the Bull *Ad ausus nefarios improborum et malignantium reprimendos,* directing more drastic measures to stem the flood of anarchy and diabolism, injunctions which were repeated on 7 April, *Non absque horrore detestando percepimus,* in the following spring. On 3 December, 1339, a similar Bull was issued to the Cistercian Durand,[9] Abbot of Bolbona (Mirepoix).

We have one Bull from Gregory XI (Pierre Roger de Beaufort), "the best of the Avignon popes," says Höfler, dated from Avignon 14 August, 1374, two years previously to his departure for Rome; one Bull of the Franciscan Alexander V (Petros Filargis), a man "of the highest knowledge," dated from Pisa, 30 August, 1409, two months after his election to the throne of Peter;[10] one Bull of Martin V (Oddone Colonna) from Constance, 3 February, 1318.[11] Eugenius IV (Gabriello Condulmaro), the great Venetian scholar and noble patron of Humanism, published four Bulls with reference to Witchcraft. The first, 24 February, 1434, is addressed from Florence to a Franciscan inquisitor, Pontius Fougeyron; the second appeared in 1437 : *Ad nostrum non sine graui mentis amaritudine peruenit auditum;* the third 23 March, 1440, was issued from Florence ; and the last, 17 July, 1445, from Rome. Nicholas V (Tommaso Parentucalli), "a name never to be mentioned without reverence by every lover of letters," indicted a Bull on 1 August, 1451, to the Inquisitor Hugo Niger, O.P. ; Callixtus III (Alfonso de Borja), "a man of lofty ideals, of boundless courage, energy, and perseverance," published a Bull, dated from Rome, 19 October, 1457 ; and Pius II (Enea Silvio de' Piccolimini) a Bull from Mantua on 17 December, 1459, fifteen months after his election.

The vigilant and vigorous Sixtus IV (Francesco della Rovere) soon took active measures to crush the Waldenses whose practices and doctrines menaced the stability of society, and in his reign we have three Bulls directly attacking sorcery, which he identifies with heresy, 17 June, 1473 ; 1 April, 1478 ; and 21 October, 1483.

Important, weighty, and supremely authoritative as it is, the Bull *Summis desiderantes affectibus* of Pope Innocent VIII has been dwelt on in the past by most writers with exaggerated emphasis, as though it were unique, the very *fons et origo* indeed of the witch-trials throughout Europe, and it is, moreover, even yet generally alluded to by modern historians and by scholars of no mean standing too in terms which show that they consider it an extraordinary and unparalleled document, responsible for the outbreak of a campaign against witches which soon grew to be a universal, terrific, and almost indiscriminate persecution. Such views are purely illusory, for in truth the Bull of Pope Innocent was, as may be very clearly seen, merely one of many ordinances dealing with a demoniac pestilence that wellnigh threatened to overwhelm the world's civilization.

Innocent VIII is so important a figure in the history of Witchcraft that it will not, perhaps, be impertinent to give a brief impartial account of this great Pontiff, than whom few have been more ignorantly and more evilly maligned.

Giovanni Battista Cibó was born at Genoa in 1432. The son of a Roman senator Aran Cibó and Teodorina a lady of the house de' Mari, his youth was devoted to the Humanities, and early he gained great reputation as one of the most elegant and correct Latinists of the day. Having taken Holy Orders he entered the family of Cardinal Calandrini, and in 1467 was created Bishop of Savona, which see he exchanged for Molfetta in 1472, being raised to the Sacred College in the following year. At the conclave of 1484 the choice fell upon this distinguished and scholarly cardinal, who in honour of his famous countryman Innocent IV (Sinibaldo de' Fieschi) ascended the throne of Peter as Innocent VIII. The chief concern of the new Vicar of Christ, whose kindliness of heart won golden opinions on every side, was the promotion of peace amongst the princes of Europe. Many difficulties and obstacles lay in the path of the Pontiff who, in the true spirit of his Master, so pathetically endeavoured to unite Christendom, his charge, against their common enemy, the Turk, the hater of the Cross. Secular ambitions and royal jealousies intervened. But the Pope had at least the compensation of witnessing the fall of Granada in 1491, the crowning glory of the reconquest of Spain from the Moors, whereby Ferdinand won the proud title of "Catholic Majesty." Innocent VIII was deeply spiritual. He issued an appeal for a crusade against the abominable Waldenses ; he strenuously opposed the pestilential Hussites in Bohemia ; and it was he who forbade under penalty of excommunication (December, 1486) the reading of the nine hundred theses, which Pico della Mirandola had publicly posted in Rome. This was an eminently proper precaution, and shows the zeal of the Holy Father for purity in religion, since several learned theologians had declared that at least thirteen of these propositions were gravely heretical, and great scandal ensued. As a matter of fact it is doubtful whether they were worse than nonsensical, and the mere unskilled posing of insoluble problems. Pico had printed his theses, *Conclusiones philosophicæ, cabalisticæ, et theologicæ* (Romæ, 1486, folio), a strange farrago, but the book was prohibited and the author condemned.[12] The Pope canonized Margrave Leopold of Austria (6 January, 1485), and on 31 May, 1492, he solemnly received at Rome the Holy Lance[13] which Sultan Bajazet at last surrendered to Christendom.[14] Worn-out with anxiety, and proclaiming always his heart's desire for peace, the Vicar of Christ presently sank into a swift decline, which terminated during the summer heat, on 25 July, 1492, when he passed away as if in sleep. His body was set upon a magnificent catafalque in S. Peter's, and they buried him there, on the fifth of August, not inaptly writing upon his tomb "*Ego autem in Innocentia mea ingressus sum.*"[15]

Many historians have conspired to blacken the character of this noble and admirable Pope. A narrative must be, if not more interesting, at least more exciting when confected from the lurid pages of Infessura and Burchard, than if merely drawn from the less melodramatic true unvarnished story. During his youth, before he had taken Holy Orders, Giovanni Ballista Cibó became the father of two illegitimate children, Franceschetto and Theodorina. Burchard overtly describes Franceschetto as, " Filius Papæ, etiam bastardus,

prout Domina Theodorina." Both children, as was natural
and just, were provided for well ; in 1487 his father married
Franceschettò, an amiable and pleasing youth, to Maddalena,
the daughter of Lorenzo de' Medici, whilst Theodorina was
bestowed upon a Roman noble of good estate. Admitting
the fact that his earlier years were not stainless, after that
surely there is no very great harm in all this ; indeed it shows
the affection and kindly thought of the father. Yet we have
quoted the exaggerated statements of Egidio di Viterbo[16]—
to whom Leo X was to give the Red Hat—" Primus
[Innocentius] pontificum filios filiasque palam ostentauit,
primus eorum apertas fecit nuptias, primus domesticos
hymenæos celebrauit." And the unworthy epigrams of
Michaele Marullo of Constantinople,[17] no mean poet it must
be confessed, are dragged from their oblivion to complete
the tale. Our own King James II was in his youth con-
fessedly lax and the Duke of Berwick was acknowledged to
be his son. But King James died a saint at Saint Germains.
It is highly indecorous to retail these scandals concerning
the Supreme Pontiff, and it is something worse than indecorous to repeat obscure gossip which has no basis in fact.

Innocent VIII, in spite of his few faults, was a Pope of
fine intelligence and great heart. His mildness and quiet
sweet manners especially impressed his intimates. Roscoe,
perhaps, hardly does him justice,[18] although the verdict of
that admirable historian may be read and pondered with
profit when the simian chatter of more recent writers is
happily forgotten.

A Bull proceeding from such a Pontiff bears no wonted
weight. The full text of the famous ordinance is as follows :

Innocent, Bishop, Servant of the servants of God, for an
eternal remembrance.

Desiring with the most heartfelt anxiety, even as Our
Apostleship requires, that the Catholic Faith should especially
in this Our day increase and flourish everywhere, and that all
heretical depravity should be driven far from the frontiers
and bournes of the Faithful, We very gladly proclaim and
even restate those particular means and methods whereby
Our pious desire may obtain its wished effect, since when all
errors are uprooted by Our diligent avocation as by the hoe

of a provident husbandman, a zeal for, and the regular observance of, Our holy Faith will be all the more strongly impressed upon the hearts of the faithful.

It has indeed lately come to Our ears, not without afflicting Us with bitter sorrow, that in some parts of Northern Germany, as well as in the provinces, townships, territories, districts, and dioceses of Mainz, Cologne, Treves, Salzburg, and Bremen, many persons of both sexes unmindful of their own salvation and straying from the Catholic Faith, have abandoned themselves to devils, incubi and succubi, and by their incantations, spells, conjurations, and other accursed charms and crafts, enormities and horrid offences, have slain infants yet in the mother's womb as also the offspring of cattle, have blasted the produce of the earth, the grapes of the vine, the fruits of trees, nay, men and women, beasts of burthen, herd-beasts, as well as animals of other kinds, vineyards, orchards, meadows, pasture-land, corn, wheat, and all other cereals ; these wretches furthermore afflict and torment men and women, beasts of burthen, herd-beasts, as well as animals of other kinds, with terrible and piteous pains and sore diseases, both internal and external ; they hinder men from performing the sexual act and women from conceiving, whence husbands cannot know their wives nor wives receive their husbands ; over and above this, they blasphemously renounce that Faith which is theirs by the Sacrament of Baptism, and at the instigation of the Enemy of Mankind they do not shrink from committing and perpetrating the foulest abominations and filthiest excesses to the deadly peril of their own souls, whereby they outrage the Divine Majesty and are a cause of scandal and danger to very many. And although Our dear sons Henry Krämer and James Sprenger, Professors of theology, of the Order of Friars Preachers, have been by Letters Apostolic delegated as Inquisitors of these heretical pravities, and still are Inquisitors, the first in the aforesaid parts of Northern Germany, wherein are included those aforesaid townships, districts, dioceses, and other specified localities, and the second in certain territories which lie along the borders of the Rhine, nevertheless not a few clerics and lay folk of those countries, seeking too curiously to know more than concerns them, since in the aforesaid delegatory letters there is no express and specific mention by name of these provinces, townships, dioceses, and districts, and further since the two delegates themselves and the abominations they are to encounter are not designated in detailed and particular fashion, these persons are not ashamed to contend with the most unblushing effrontery that these enormities are not practised in those provinces, and consequently the aforesaid Inquisitors have no legal right to exercise their powers of inquisition in the provinces, townships, dioceses, districts, and territories, which have been rehearsed, and that the Inquisitors may not proceed to punish, imprison, and penalize criminals convicted of the heinous offences and many wickednesses which have been set forth. Accordingly in the aforesaid provinces, townships, dioceses, and districts, the abominations and enormities in question remained unpunished not without open danger to the souls of many and peril of eternal damnation.

Wherefore We, as is Our duty, being wholly desirous of removing all hindrances and obstacles by which the good work of the Inquisitors may be let and tarded, as also of applying potent remedies to prevent the disease of heresy and other turpitudes diffusing their poison to the destruction of many innocent souls since Our zeal for the Faith especially incites us, lest that the provinces, townships, dioceses, districts, and territories of Germany, which We have specified, be deprived of the benefits of the Holy Office thereto assigned, by the tenour of these presents in virtue of Our Apostolic authority We decree and enjoin that the aforesaid Inquisitors be empowered to proceed to the just correction, imprisonment, and punishment of any persons, without let or hindrance, in every way as if the provinces, townships, dioceses, districts, territories, yea, even the persons and their crimes in this kind were named and particularly designated in Our letters. Moreover, for greater surety We extend these letters deputing this authority to cover all the aforesaid provinces, townships, dioceses, districts, and territories, persons, and crimes newly rehearsed, and We grant permission to the aforesaid Inquisitors, to one separately or to both, as also to Our dear son John Gremper, priest of the diocese of Constance, Master of Arts, their notary, or to any other public notary, who shall be by them, or by one of them, temporarily delegated to those provinces, townships, dioceses, districts, and aforesaid territories, to proceed, according to the regulations of the Inquisition, against any persons of whatsoever rank and high estate, correcting, mulcting, imprisoning, punishing, as their crimes merit, those whom they have found guilty, the penalty being adapted to the offence. Moreover they shall enjoy a full and perfect faculty of expounding and preaching the word of God to the faithful, so often as opportunity may offer and it may seem good to them, in each and every parish church of the said provinces, and they shall freely and lawfully perform any rites or execute any business which may appear advisable in the aforesaid cases. By Our supreme authority We grant them anew full and complete faculties.

At the same time by Letters Apostolic We require Our venerable Brother, the Bishop of Strasburg [Albrecht von Bayern, 1478–1506], that he himself shall announce, or by some other or others cause to be announced the burthen of Our Bull, which he shall solemnly publish when and so often as he deems it necessary, or when he shall be requested so to do by the Inquisitors or by one of them. Nor shall he suffer them in disobedience to the tenor of these presents to be molested or hindered by any authority whatsoever, but he shall threaten all who endeavour to hinder or harass the Inquisitors, all who oppose them, all rebels, of whatsoever rank, estate, position, pre-eminence, dignity, or any condition they may be, or whatsoever privilege of exemption they may claim, with excommunication, suspension, interdict, and yet more terrible penalties, censures, and punishment, as may seem good to him, and that without any right of appeal, and if he will he may by Our authority aggravate and renew these penalties as often as he list, calling in, if so please him, the help of the secular arm.

Non obstantibus . . . Let no man therefore . . . But if any dare to do so, which God forbid, let him know that upon him will fall the wrath of Almighty God, and of the Blessed Apostles Peter and Paul.

Given at Rome, at S. Peter's, on the 9 December of the Year of the Incarnation of Our Lord one thousand four hundred and eighty-four, in the first Year of Our Pontificate.[19]

On 18 June, 1485, Innocent VIII again recommended the Inquisitors Henry Krämer and James Sprenger to Berthold,

Archbishop of Mainz, in the Bull which commences *Pro causa fidei et summi dei honore cupientes negotium inquisitionis heretice prauitatis*, words of the deepest significance as showing that in the judgement of the Pope, at any rate, sorcery and heresy were one. On the same date a similar Bull was sent to the Archduke Sigismund of Austria in which Abbot John of Wingarten in the diocese of Constance is warmly praised for his zeal. The Abbot himself was addressed in a brief issued the same day. " It hath been told Us with what zeal thou dost undertake the defence of the Faith against heretics, and with what kindliness and help thou dost aid the Inquisitors. Most highly do We commend thy devotion, the piety and sincerity of thy heart. Thou dost indeed perform the part of a good and orthodox Prelate." [20]

On 30 September, 1486, Innocent VIII issued a Bull to Paolo Zane, Bishop of Brescia, and Antonio di Brescia, O.P., the Inquisitor for Lombardy, and this again emphasizes the heresy which is so inevitably commingled with sorcery ; " contra nonnullos utriusque sexus hæreticos, ut accepimus, quos culpabiles ut hæreticos impœnitentes repertos pœna debita iuris puniendos condemnauit," a most striking phrase (Certain heretics of both sexes, as we are informed, whom as guilty and impenitent heretics the just laws rightly condemned.)

Alexander VI (Roderigo Borja) on 31 January, 1500, repeats almost the same phrases with even added stress : " multos nequissimi hostis uenenis infectos contra catholicam ueritatem in uerba blasphemiæ prorumpere et in praua hæreticorum dogmata impudenter . . . insurgere " and " quamplurimi illarum regionum in damnatas Waldensium hæreses prolabuntur." Nothing could be plainer. In 1501 the Pope sums up the evils of Witchcraft very concisely in a brief [21] to the Lombard Inquisitor Fra Angelo of Verona, O.P., when he writes : " Inasmuch as We have been informed that in the province of Lombardy various persons of both sexes use and practise various magical arts and devilish abominations, and by their poisons and other spells have committed many heinous crimes, destroying both men and beasts and blasting fruitful fields and spreading horrid heresies so that great scandal is given, We are determined in accordance with the solemn duty of executing Our Apostolic office bestowed upon us from on high, to crush—With the help of Almighty God—all such enormities, to put an end to these heresies and scandals."[22] A noble and truly magnificent exordium.

In a brief to Giorgio de' Casali, O.P., Inquisitor at Cremona, Julius II (Giuliano della Rovere) speaks of " personæ utriusque sexus . . . certam sectam facientes, fidem . . . abnegantes, . . . ecclesiasticis et præsertim eucharistiæ sacramentis abutentes, diabolum in suum dominum et patronum assumentes eique obedientiam et reuerentiam exhibentes." In this there is more than a hint of the abominations of the Black Mass, to which, perhaps, the Pontiff was unwilling to refer more plainly. The date of this document does not appear, but it may be approximated by several references in the Dominican registers to Giorgio de' Casali. " 1502, April 25, Brescia. Ciuitas Placentina et Cremonensis cum suis diocesebus separantur a ciuitate Papiensi et diocesi quoad officium inquisitionis, et magister Georgius de Casali instituitur inquisitor in ciuitate Placentina et Cremonensi." And in the Register of the Generals under 19 June, 1512, Rome, we have : " M. Georgius de Casali instituitur inquisitor super Bergomo, Cremona, Crema, et Brixia cum eorum districtibus."

The Mæcenas of Renaissance Humanism, Leo X (Giovanni de' Medici), on 15 February, 1521, issued a long and weighty Bull to the Bishops and Inquisitors of the Venetian republic, of Bergamo and Brescia, in which the Pontiff with dignity and restraint denounces " quoddam hominum genus perniciosissimum ac damnatissimum labe hæretica, per quam suscepto renunciabatur baptismatis sacramento, dominum abnegabat et Satanæ, cuius consilio seducebantur, corpora et animas conferebant." Of these " quot redire ad ecclesiæ unitatem uellent, clementer suscipiendi," but those who obstinately persist in their misdeeds must suffer the penalties enacted " contra maleficos et sortilegos ac a fide apostantes, prout criminis postulauerit qualitas."

In the same strain sadly writes the holy and ascetic Adrian VI (Adrian Dedel) addressing Modesto Vincentino, the Dominican Inquisitor of Como. The Bull was issued on 20 July, 1523, and the long-considered sentences throb with the anxiety and agony that were wellnigh breaking that fatherly heart. " Præsertim eucharistiæ sacramentis abutentes," what a cry of sorrow can be heard in those four words ! The full text of this ordinance, a document of great importance in the history of Witchcraft, runs as follows :

To Our beloved Son Modesto Vincentino, of the Order of Preachers.

Yet a little while ago, as thou didst so clearly make known to Us, Our predecessor Pope Julius II of happy memory, learned, to his bitter sorrow and sore grief, from George de' Casali, Professor of the Order of Friars Preachers and accredited Inquisitor in the diocese of Cremona to punish heretical pravity, that in certain parts of Lombardy and especially in those districts in which the said George was accredited Inquisitor, there were found to be many persons of both sexes, who forgetful of their own souls' salvation and straying far from the Catholic Faith, made a certain sect, utterly denying the Faith which they received in Holy Baptism, spurning beneath their feet the Holy Cross and treating it with vilest contumely, above all abusing the Divine Sacrament of the Altar, taking the Devil to be their Lord and Master, promising him worship and obedience, and with accursed incantations, charms, sortilege, and other foul magic rites ever doing grave harm and hurt to men, animals, and the fruit of the earth, ensuing and wreaking numberless other abominations, enormities, and heinous crimes at the instigation of the Devil as aforesaid, to the deadly peril of their own souls, giving offence to the Divine Majesty of God, affording also an ill example and grave scandal to many. Yet when (as the aforesaid George declared) the Inquisitor, George de' Casali, in the course of his duties in the said districts to which he was accredited, would have proceeded against these wretches, some there were, clerics as well as lay folk of these parts, who seeking to know more than was their business most rashly and naughtily presumed to affirm that such offences did not fall under the jurisdiction of the Inquisitor George, attempting moreover to stir up hatred against him among the populace and to hinder his efforts, which indeed they did then hinder, wherefore the aforesaid persons who practised blasphemies and impieties remained unpunished and by their examples and precepts they kept continually inducing others to use like abominations which caused no small mischief and shame to the Faith, danger to immortal souls, and scandal to very many. Our predecessor accordingly being altogether loath that the execution of the Inquisitor's office should be hindered in any way at all and thuswise the poisonous taint of vile heresy be more widely spread, enjoined and commanded by a Brief addressed to the said George, that as Inquisitor he should take full cognizance of such infamies which fell within his jurisdiction and that he should exercise and employ to their uttermost his inquisitorial powers against all and sundry of whatsoever estate or rank they might happen to be, and that it was his duty, full power being assigned to him, to correct and punish the offences of all whom he might find guilty of the aforesaid enormities, the charges being heard by him and the Vicars of the local Ordinary, whensoever they wished to sit as assessors, and the judgements being delivered as is decreed in the case of other heretics according to the canon and civil law. Any persons who dared oppose this procedure were to be punished by ecclesiastical censures and other legal remedies. But those, who in regard to these matters lent him advice, help, or favour, Our predecessor decreed should gain and enjoy the same indulgences as those who bear the Cross against other heretics then gained and enjoyed according to the Apostolic indult conceded to them, as is more amply set forth in the particular Brief. To this We append a further declaration, that not only do impieties and crimes of this kind against the Catholic Faith and the Christian Religion come under the jurisdiction of the Inquisitor at Cremona, but in all other districts and dioceses they now come under the jurisdiction of the other Inquisitors of the Lombard congregation of the said Order. For inasmuch as they are the same offences they shall meet with the same treatment and punishment according to the tenor of the same letters. Wherefore thou, who art, as thou dost show Us, the accredited Inquisitor of these crimes in the city of Como, hast, in thine own name as in the names of all other Inquisitors of heresy of this Order and Congregation wheresoever they be stationed or accredited, humbly made supplication that We would vouchsafe to extend unto you the aforesaid letter with certain additions and other provisions now conveniently to be made. We there-

fore lending a gracious ear to this thine prayer, by Our
Apostolic authority and by these presents extend the aforesaid
letter with all that is contained therein in every clause and
proviso to thee as also to the other Inquisitors of the Order
and Congregation, as well those who are now accredited as
those who shall be accredited at some future date to all
perpetuity, as if the letter were directed and delivered to thee
and to each several person of the aforesaid Inquisitors. This
letter, then, with all the benefits thereby conferred We
concede to thee and to them. Notwithstanding any hindrance, let, or bar, which Our predecessor Julius in the aforesaid letter was minded should not hinder, let, or bar, and
notwithstanding aught else whatsoever to the contrary. And
because it would be indeed a hard task to convey the present
letter to the several places, where perchance it might be
necessary that the provisions thereof should be recognized
and accepted, it is Our good pleasure and We decree by Our
Apostolic authority that when it has been transcribed by the
hand of any public notary and signed and sealed with the
seal of some member of the Curia or some Dignitary of the
Church as a token of surety, should such need arise, the same
respect is thereto to be shown as would be shown to these
presents were they published or posted.

Given at Rome, at S. Peter's, under the Fisherman's Ring,
20 July, 1523, in the first year of Our Pontificate.[23]

With complete conviction is the heresy of Witchcraft
recognized in a brief of Clement VII (Giulio de' Medici)
addressed on 19 January, 1524, to the Governor of Bologna,
Bishop Altobello Averoldo di Pola (1497–1531), which recommends the Parmesan Inquisitor, Fra Jeronimo of Faenza, O.P.,
and in unmistakable phrase speaks " de hæresi strigatus "
being directed against " quosdam infectes prædicta hæresi."
Upon this the learned Bartolomeo de Spina in his *Quæstio
de strigibus* comments : " Assuredly Our Most Holy Lord
would not have indited this brief nor would he have issued
these injunctions, if such persons, witches to wit, who are
declared to be heretics, were not in very truth heretics, or if
these enormities that they use and practise, on account of
which they are judged to be heretics, were but empty
illusions of the Devil."[24] We have also a later brief of

Clement VII in 1526, where his injunctions are reiterated and reinforced.

Many of the banditti who infested the Campagna during the middle years of the sixteenth century were addicted to black magic, and a document[25] which describes the times of Gregory XIII (Ugo Buoncompagni, elected Pope 13 May, 1572, died 1585) tells us how gangs of outlaws " non semel sacra supellectile e templis direpta, augustissimam et sacratissimam eucharistiam in siluas et latibula asportarunt, qua ad magica flagitia et execrementa abuterentur." Two centuries later, the Buxen, an immense secret society which from 1736 until 1779 terrorized last districts of Germany and Brabant by plunder and brigandage combined Satanism with wholesale robbery and murder. They used to meet after nightfall to attend a Black Mass, which was generally celebrated at one of three ruined chapels, Saint Rose, near Sittardt ; another at Saint Leonart, near Roldyck ; another at Oermond, by the Maas. It is said these wretches never passed a church without breaking in to desecrate and defile the Tabernacle.

Among the most important of the Papal pronouncements upon the subject of Witchcraft is the long and weighty Constitution, *Cœli et Terræ Creator Deus*,[26] issued on 5 January, 1586, by that great and extraordinarily able ruler Sixtus V (Felice Peretti, O.F.M.), against those who practise the Art of Judicial Astrology, and any other kind of divination, as well as those who read and retain treatises dealing with such matters. The Pontiff dwells at some length upon the evils which arise from the credulous consultations of fortune-tellers and astrologers, aptly quoting the divine words, " Non est uestrum scire tempora uel momenta, quæ Pater posuit in sua potestate." He points out that the future cannot be foretold by man, and all such prognostications are " false and vain, merely published and promulgated by the cunning of wicked men and the deceits of devils, from whose work, counsel, or aid, all divination is derived. . . . For, indeed, what knowledge they possess is not from any divination nor from any true insight into the future, but ariseth from the shrewder wisdom of their spiritual nature, and is acquired in certain other ways not clear to man's intelligence, which is less perspicacious. Wherefore there can be no doubt at all that in the inquiry after and foretelling of future events and happenings which may chance, the work of the Devil is most deceitfully and intimately concerned, so that by his craft and wiles he may turn wretched men away from the path of salvation, and entangle them in the snares of perdition." Wherefore all professed occultists who cast nativities " such most especially are Astrologers, those who were once called Mathematicians [*Mathematici* in its technical sense[27]], Genethliacs, Horoscopers, and Planetaries " are to be utterly avoided and eschewed. Various methods of divination are in some detail enumerated to be condemned : " For many, not without some secret correspondence with the Demon, or at least by some tacit pact, use and practise Geomancy, Hydromancy, Aeromancy, Pyromancy, Onomancy, Cheiromancy, Necromancy, and other spells and magic arts, nay they do not hesitate to employ such unlawful methods of divining as by small dice, by grains of wheat, by beans which are thrown in a certain way, [i.e. by astragalomancy, by krithomancy, by kuamomancy]. And some there are also who enter into communion with the Dead and compact themselves with Hell ; who further busy themselves with accursed sciences that they may discover treasures, or that they may ensue and commit other enormities, even though they must needs then expressly bind themselves by a bond to the Devil's slavery at the dire hazard of their souls, and these wretches will employ the most abhorred charms of black magic, the properties of sorcery, and poisons too ; they draw circles and trace the dark characters of the pit. They evoke and consult demons from whom answers are sought and obtained ; they offer prayers to them and incense, or the smoke of noxious herbs, or fumigations with impious sacrifices ; they light candles in their honour ; they most blasphemously abuse sacred things, to wit the Sacraments, or Sacramentals ; they worship them with latria, genuflections, and other ceremonies of profane adoration ; they venerate and reverence them ; they make or cause to be made rings, or mirrors, or small phials, in order that they may (as they suppose) enchain or enclose herein evil spirits from whom they will demand and obtain answers to their questionings." The Inquisitors are straitly charged and directed to search out and deal with all offenders, " even although in many of the aforesaid cases they have hitherto either not taken measures against the offenders, or were unable to take measures " ; whilst the ordinaries are to assist especially by suppressing and destroying grimoires, " all books and every book, volume, and pamphlet of this kind, treating of Judicial Astrology, Geomancy, Hydromancy, Pyromancy, Onomancy, Cheiromancy, Necromancy, Goety, or in which are described or contained fortune-telling, poisons, augurisms, auspicies, abominable incantations, and devilish superstitions."[28] Care is to be taken that no works of value dealing with medicine, navigation, the natural sciences, and the like are mistakenly attacked under this rule.

Among the latest Papal ordinances directed against Witch-craft is the famous Constitution *Omnipotentis Dei* issued by Gregory XV (Alessandro Ludovisi) on 20 March, 1623. A changed point of view is clearly shown. It will be seen that former punishments are lessened ; the death penalty is decreed only for those who were proved to have entered into a formal compact with the Devil, and to have committed homicide by infernal assistance. Since the Great Schism of the sixteenth-century sorcery, although a frequent con-comitant of, was not at all necessarily coincident with heresy as had been the position in earlier days. Had such continued to be the case the Pontiff would not have hesitated to declare it, for he was ready to take drastic measures against the Huguenots, and in his own just phrase Geneva was " non solo come piena di uomini appestati ma come catedra di pesti-lenza."[29] With holy zeal he urged Louis XIII and the Duke of Savoy " di domare in ribellati heretici." From every point of view, then, the Constitution is of exceptional interest.

The Constitution of our Most Holy Lord Gregory the Fifteenth against those who practise the Black Art or Witchcrafts.

Gregory Pope XV. *Ad perpetuam rei memoriam.*

We, who although all unworthy, fulfil here on earth the office of Almighty God Our Saviour, Who, in order to free man from the snares of the Devil, vouchsafed to suffer upon the Cross, according to the duties incumbent upon Us and to Us entrusted from above by Our Apostolic servage, are instant with the utmost zeal and care to accomplish Our task, to wit the defence of the Lord's flock redeemed with an inestimable price against the malice and deceits of Satan, by employing the divine resource of this same authority which Heaven has bestowed, whensoever and whereas we deem it may be necessary and healthful in the Lord. For of a truth there are some who, wholly forgetful of their own estate, and of the solemn promises of them made, when they were enrolled in the flock of Christ by the Sacred lavacre of spiritual regeneration, have not shrunk from wholly giving themselves up to Satan, whose wiles, wickednesses, abominations, and evil works they renounced, nay, more, following in the footsteps of their Master, who never ceases to lay snares for men by that mortal hate with which he harrieth mankind, they do not fear to hurt their neighbour in many a way, and assuredly to damn their own souls. Wherefore, in order that such heinous enormities may be abhorred of all Christian folk, we decree that such flagrancy be punished with sad and severe penalties. Accordingly by Our Own proper Motion, and of certain knowledge, and mature consideration, as also from the fulness of Our Apostolic Power, by the tenor of these presents, We decree, We ordain and command, that if it be proven that anyone has made a compact with the Devil, and by apostasizing from the Faith, either by the black art or by charms, hath so harmed any single person or several persons, that owing to the black art or to charms death ensued, even if it be the first offence, he shall be delivered to the secular Courts to meet the just punishment of his crimes ; And more, if anyone apostasizing in similar manner, hath made a compact with the Devil, as afore rehearsed, and hath practised any magic art or spell, whereby, albeit death did not ensue, yet there did follow sickness, divorcements, sexual impotence, or some serious harm to cattle, fruits, or crops of any kind, he shall be duly incarcerated and strictly held in durance, or confined for life in the prisons of the Inquisition wheresoever the Holy Office is established. If anyone hath cognizance of any such criminals he is bound to declare them to the Bishop or to the Inquisitor. And these notwithstanding any constitutions, or Apostolic ordinances, or other statutes, or anything of whatever sort to the contrary. We also require that these presents shall be transcribed, as also printed, and subscribed by the hand of a Public Notary, and sealed with the seal of an Ecclesiastical dignitary, and that they shall then have the same weight everywhere as these presents carry if they are exposed or published. These presents, after they have been affixed to the doors of the Basilicas of S. John Lateran and of the Prince of the Apostles in Vatican, as also upon the Column in the Campo di Fiori, shall bind and law all and single whom they may concern, and all persons shall be held to have knowledge of and be acquainted with their contents. Given at Rome at S. Peter's under the Fisherman's Ring, upon the 20 March, MDCXXIII, in the Third Year of Our Pontificate.

S. Cardinal of S. Susanna.[30]

[Rome: From the Printing Offices of the Apostolic Chamber, M.D.C.XXIII.]

It has sometimes been stated by scholars[31] that this Constitution, *Omnipotentis Dei*, of Gregory XV was the last Papal enactment against Witchcraft, but this is incorrect, for on 1 April, 1631, Urban VIII (Maffeo Barberini) issued his Constitution *Inscrutabilis iudiciorum Dei altitudo*[32] " Contra Astrologos Iudicianos, qui de statu Reipublicæ Christianæ, uel Sedis Apostolicæ, seu uita Romani Pontificis, aut eius consanguineorum Iudicia facere, necnon eos qui illos desuper consulere præsumpserint." The Pontiff reiterates the measures promulgated by Sixtus V, and adds that any person of any rank whatsoever, even be he count or duke, who consults fortune-tellers concerning affairs of state, particularly the length of time Christ's reigning Vicar may live, is *ipso facto* excommunicate, and upon conviction will be condemned to death with confiscation of all his goods. The penalties are insisted upon with solemn emphasis and in some detail.

As the German witches were supposed to hold high Sabbat amid the Hartz Mountains, on the Brocken or Blocksberg, whilst the Swedish covens assembled at their Blockula, the French favoured Puy-de-Dôme, and the English the Wrekin or Malking Tower, so an old walnut tree of dense shade and mighty girth near Benevento was reputed to be the general rendezvous of all the witches in Italy, where they forgathered for the *treguenda*. It is certain that from very early times

dark beliefs became associated with walnut trees, which were
considered of ill-omen for a traveller to catch sight of unless
the spell was broken by pelting them with stones. And so
Ovid in his poem *Nux* commences

> Nux ego iuncta uiæ, quum sim sine crimine uitæ
> A populo saxis prætereunte petor.

The *Nux* was, perhaps, suggested by an epigram, formerly
attributed to Plato, which may be found in the Greek
Anthology :[33]

> Εἰνοδίην καρύην με παρερχομένοις ἐφύτευσαν
> Παισὶ, λιθοβλήτου παίγνιον εὐστοχόιης.

The last line is significant :

> Δυσδαίμων ἐπ' ἐμὴν ὕβριν ἐκαρποφόρουν.

Pope Paschal II (Rainerius, O.S.B., 1099–1118) ordered a
large walnut tree which stood in the Piazza del Popolo to be
hewn down and burned owing to the gross superstitions to
which it had given rise. There is a pamphlet by Peter of
Piperno, *De Nuce Maga Beneuentana*, which gives in some
detail the history of and many legends connected with the
wizard walnut tree of Benevento. He mentions the curious
fact that the nuts were triangular in shape : " qua tragu-
laribus lineis emittebat." The original, or at least a very
ancient, walnut tree was destroyed by S. Barbatus (663).
Here was worshipped with mysterious rites in Lombard times
a golden serpent. This the Saint melted in a crucible and of
the metal he made a sacred paten which was preserved up
till the time of the French invasion in 1799. The tree was
replanted in the eighth century, and during a local trial for
sorcery in 1519 a witch named Violanta confessed that in the
company of other Satanists she had performed certain
ceremonies under this tree. A witness, Alberto Alutario, who
passed the place late at night, testified that he had seen a
numerous assembly of persons there. They were all carrying
lanthorns or tapers.

Dom Piccini in his *Ottava della Notte* has the following
lines, thus translated by C. G. Leland :

> In Benevento a nut-tree stands
> And thither by night from many lands,
> Over the waters and on the wind,
> Came witches flying of every kind,

On goats, and boars, and bears, and cats,
Some upon broomsticks, some like bats,
Howling, hurtling, hurrying, all
Come to the tree at the master's call.

A current Neapolitan proverb says :

Sott' acqua e sotta viento
Sott' e nuce 'e Veneviento.

The Papal Bulls and briefs of the fifteenth century are fre-quently and repeatedly directed to the Inquisitors of the dio-ceses of Como, Bergamo, and Brescia, since in Northern Italy Witchcraft was chiefly localized among the Lombard valleys of the Alps. This was notorious, and is often alluded to by Italian writers. Thus Bandello (III, 52) speaks of : " Val Camonica, ove si dice essere di molte streghe. It was Lombardy where, as we have seen, the two floods of Manichæan heresy from the East converged and commingled as they swept into Europe, and for centuries the unfortunate province became a pullulating nursery of Satanism and every monstrous evil. The Italian *strega* was as loathsome as the vilest of the foul Northern sisterhood, nay, she was, if possible, even more dangerous, since she studied deeply the properties of simples and poisonous plants, the chemistry of drugs and abortives, and when sorcery and maledictions failed venom was employed to complete the work. Heretics, poisoners, quack-vendors, blackmailers, bawds, these hags and their accomplices strove to make a hell upon earth, and small wonder then that the tribunals, both ecclesiastical and civil, strove to stamp out the pestilence with relentless severity.

During the fifteenth century the prosecution of witches throughout the North of Italy was pursued with unrelent-ing severity. Agnes Arizonelli, of Val Leventina, St. Gothard, confessed that she had invoked the Devil, worshipped him under the form of a black goat, and used spells to devastate fields by storm and hail (1432). In 1455 a witch was burned at Locarno at the command of the Count of Locarno. In the same year the Inquisitor at Brescia appealed to the Venetians to help him in his campaign against the Satanists of Val Camonica, who defiled the Blessed Sacrament and adored the Demon as God, offering human sacrifices of infants. In the following thirty years we find continual witch-burnings in Lombardy and Piedmont ; in 1472 three women were sent to the stake at Forno-Rivara ; two at Levone in 1474 ; five at Forno in 1475 ; whilst larger centres show an increasing number of condemnations.

There is no grimmer portrayal of Italian Witchcraft to be found than that depicted by the fantastical Girolamo Folengo (Merlinus Cocaius), and the fact that his poems are composed in Maccaronic verse makes the details only more ghastly and more shameful. It is impossible to question their truth, the sincerity and serious intention of the writer. " There is," says John Addington Symonds, " no mistaking the veri- similitude of the picture he drew. All the uncleanliness of a diseased imagination, all the extravagances of wanton desire, all the consequences of domestic unchastity—incest, in- fanticide, secret assassination, concealment of births—are traced to this one cause and identified by him with witch- craft."[34]

Folengo, who was born in 1491 at Cipada, a village of the Mantuan district, after some wild and reckless years of undergraduate life at Bologna, entered in December, 1507, a Benedictine monastery of the Cassinese Congregation, which title had been adopted only three years before by the Congre- gation of S. Justina of Padua. In 1509 Folengo was professed at the abbey of S. Euphemia at Brescia, when he changed his name Girolamo to Teofilo, and it is by this latter he is most generally known. In 1515 he broke his vows, flying from the cloister, and for the next eleven years he seems to have led a wandering and, as might have been expected, an unhappy life,[35] until in a spirit of deep penitence he resumed his habit, to die at last in December, 1544, at the house of S. Croce di Campere, near Padua.

The *Maccaronea*[36] first appeared at Venice in 1519, and the *Orlandino*,[37] a burlesque of Boiardo and Ariosto, in 1526. The first is a mock epic, written in an extraordinary jargon where plebeian Italian and the Mantuan dialect to boot are mingled with the classic and mediæval Latin of sonorous hexameters. It tells the adventures of Baldus, son of the peerless Paladin Guido and of the Princess Baldovina, daughter of the King of France. In *Maccaronea* XXI Baldus makes his way to the court of Gulfora, Reine du Sabbat, the

Scotch Queen of Elphin, or Elfhame, Scortum Luciferi. He has already denounced her in trenchant terms :

> Olim quarundam uetularum parua striarum
> Turba dabat pœnas meritis incensa casottis,
> Sed modo non tantum confectæ tempore uecchiæ
> Gattas, Montones, Capras, Porcosque caualcant,
> Uerum Magnates plures, Dominique togati,
> Et qui dant populis in sacro iura senatu
> Se sub Gulforea statuunt ditione regendos.
> Obseruant zobias,[38] ungunt sua membra cirottis,
> Quos ego sæpe cauas tueor transire per istas,
> Namque suam properant ad cortezare[39] Madonnam,
> Gulfora quæ dicta est, reliquarum prima striarum,
> Scortaque Luciferi, tot certe digna casottis,[40]
> Quot lapides terræ, Maris undæ, sidera cœli.[41]

It is very significant to find here more than a hint that whilst wretched old beldames, malicious, doting, miserably poor, were burned wholesale as witches, often the sorcerers of high rank escaped untouched and undetected. It is only fair to say that the authorities, both ecclesiastical and civil, knew no distinctions when punishing this sorcery.

Baldus having a magic stone " scondificam " penetrates unseen into the most secret chambers of the infernal palace where Gulfora holds her Sabbat. Here he finds a crowd of witches compounding foul philtres in hell's laboratory :

> Taxum, cambrossen, squillas, Aconita, cicutas.
> Electuaris complentur bissola mille,
> Compositis, heu heu, nigro de puluere mortis :
> De spuma zatti[42] de ladri carne picati,
> De pulmone asini, uirda de pelle Ranocchi,
> De lue matricis, de Infantis sanguine cœci.
> De Cadaueribus tumulorum, deque sagina
> Uirginulæ, de felle bouis, de lacte sigorum,
> De sudore patris proprii, de proh scelus ! alba
> Paschalis ceræ candelis[43], deque sacrato
> Chrismate, de Christi dono Baptismatis unda.

Folengo refuses to give further details :

> Pingunt mixturas cum sacris mille profanas,
> Quas uti componant, describere sorte ualerem,
> Sed metuo, errores si quando reprehendere uellem,
> Errorum fierem præceptor.

It is interesting to compare Jean Bodin's sharp chiding of John Weyer, whom he sternly reproves for having copied

into the *De Præstigiis Dæmonum* a number of charms and
spells, the mischief of which might thus be propagated.

The loathsome ingredients, yew, privet, aconite, hemlock,
the venom of a toad, the flesh of a brigand's parboiled limbs,
the skin of a green frog, the blood of an infant, dust from a
grave, and the rest, can be paralleled over and over again in
the confessions of the witches and from the pages of the
demonologists. The " slips of yew," " root of hemlock,"
" swelter'd venom." " lizard's leg," " toe of frog," " finger of
birth-strangled babe " of the cauldron in *Macbeth* at once
leap to the memory.

Baldus finds books of spells and grimoires in Gulfora's
bower :

> Librazzos aperit, uel apertos lectitat omnes,
> Nil nisi lethales considerat esse recettas.
> Quomodo Garzones[44] faturentur, amare negantes,
> Quomodo adulterium uxoris uir noscere possit.
> Quomodo uirgineæ cogantur amare puellæ.
> Quomodo non tumeat mulier cornando Maritum.
> Quomodo si tumuit, Fantinum mingit abortum.
> Quomodo uix natos uitient sua fascina puttos.
> Quomodo deficient odiati membra mariti.
> Quomodo de birlo mentem, de corpore uitam
> Eiusdem tollant, ualeant ut pascere Mœchos.
> Fœtentes ibi sunt, ranzæ,[45] uecchiæque striazzæ,
> Quæ uadunt, redeunt portantes Bissola[46] circum.

This catalogue of erotic enchantments is very striking,
more particularly when we remember that in Italy the witch
was continually resorted to for some charm or elixir to cause
love or hate, and that any mad overwhelming passion, any
sudden sexual obsession was immediately attributed to magic
and supernatural influences. Thus in the long confession of
her amours with Gianpaolo Osio Virginia Maria de Leyva, a
nun of the convent of S. Margherita at Monza, acknowledged
that she had first entertained his addresses in the year 1599
or 1600, and as soon as she admitted him into the cloister he
made her take a little jewel in her mouth. This was a white
load-stone, blessed by the confessor of the convent, Paolo
Arrigone, who was privy to the intrigue, and it was declared
to be a powerful love-charm. That Virginia believed she was
bewitched is obvious from her own words : " Some diabolical
force compelled me to go to the window overlooking his

garden." She endeavoured to struggle against the influence of her seducer. " But the sorceries with which I was surrounded, prevailed. In my bed were found the bones of the dead, hooks of iron, and many other things of which the nuns were well informed."[47] In 1582–83 when Vittoria Accoramboni was separated from the Duke of Bracciano and living in enforced retirement at Gubbio, her brother Marcello clung ever at his master's side to keep alive the flame should it seem to cool, and gossip freely chattered of a mysterious Greek sibyl whom he had hired with much gold to brew those potions and possets which foster desire.

In Galfora's domain there was a school of Witchcraft where Baldus saw hideous beldames instructing young damsels in all the lore of hell.

> Est locus alter ibi ter centum brachia longus,
> Quo docet heu quantas ! uecchiarum turma puellas
> Sunt ibi Dongellas scarcossæ[48] mille docentes,
> Suntque Pedantrices in despensare Triacas,
> Et pedagogarum dant ritus more tenendos :
> Qualiter obsequio[49] Ueneris sua uota sequantur,
> Qualiter Infantes tenerini membra[50] smedullent,
> Qualiter ungantur, moueantque tonitrua cœli.
> Qualiter et segetes, et uites grandine tollant.
> Qualiter in uarias formas sua corpora mutent.
> Qualiter efficiant[51] quod amantis forma diabli est.
> Qualiter et Christum renegent, Christique batesmum.
> Qualiter alliciant Pretos, sibi tradere sanctam
> Eucharistiam, aut alicuius membra Beati.
> Qualiter, ah facinus ! Crucifixum stercore turpent.

Even to-day a dark superstition lingers in Romagna Toscana that Witchcraft runs in families, and that the secrets of sorcery are perpetuated by word of mouth, the young being carefully instructed and drilled in this horrid business by their older relatives. The fact that the newly made witches learned spells and runes from those who had been long initiated is alluded to in the trials of all countries. During the investigation of the Lancastrian cases under James I it was acknowledged by the accused that " old Demdike." consistently brought up her children and grandchildren to be witches, and had been their daily monitress in evil. Elizabeth Device, her daughter; Alison, James, and Jennet Device, her grandchildren; all testified against her. Nor was Elizabeth Device slow to carry on the tradition, for Thomas Potts apostrophizes her in the following trenchant terms : " O barbarous and inhumane monster beyond example ; so farre from sensible understanding of thy owne miserie as to bring thy owne naturall children into mischiefe and bondage, and thyselfe to be a witnesse vpone the gallowes, to see thy owne children, by thy deuillish instructions, hatcht vp in villanie and witchcraft, to suffer with thee, euen in the beginning of their time a shamefull and untimely death ! "[52] In some instances it seems to have been the Chief Officer of the district, whose business it was to prime new adherents in the art and practice of sorcery. " He *deliuers* unto his *Proselite*, and so to the rest, *the Rules of his Art*, instructing them in the manner of *hurting* and *helping*, and acquainting them with such *medicines* and *poysons* as are vsuall herevnto."[53]

Every detail of this vile poem which Folengo recites is to be found again and again in the trials of every country and every age. We might almost think his lines a paraphrase of the Decretal Epistle of Pope Adrian VI who denounced the witches " as a Sect deviating from the Catholic Faith, deny-ing their Baptism, and showing Contempt of the Ecclesiastical Sacraments, treading Crosses under their Feet, and, taking the Devil for their Lord, destroying the Fruits of the Earth by their Enchantments, Sorceries, and Superstitions."[54] The horrible profanation of the Host, of which Folengo speaks, points to the blasphemies of the Black Mass, and the defilement of the Crucifix is akin to the mysteries of the Templars.

All the foulness and stench of the Sabbat froths and foments before Galfora's throne :

> Turpia dico, iocis lasciuis, atque pruritu,
> Turpia nequitiis blandis, luxaque petulco,
> Turpia mollitie, Uenerisque libidine, scortis,
> Pellicibus, tandem quicquid patet esse Lupanar.

Obscene forms of Incubi and Succubas mingle with the throng :

> Leggiadros iuunenes, bellos, facieque uenustos,
> Stringatos, agiles, quos iudicat esse Diablos,
> Humanum piliasse caput, moresque decentes.
> Conspicit innumeras circum scherzare puellas.

Their eyes glowing with bestial lust the witches adorn them-selves for demoniac accouplements. They bathe their arms and necks with milk-white fucus, they trick their lashes with kohl, they carmine their lips, and spread maquillage upon their cheeks,

Incrispantque comas propter placuisse Diablis.

I have dwelt thus long and in such detail upon Folengo's poem and quoted thus freely his bizarre hexameters because I feel that here we have a contemporary picture of a rank social evil supplied with photographic exactitude by a closely observant and uncompromising realist.[55] It is, in fine, a most valuable document, every detail of which can be authenticated and paralleled with the evidence of a thousand trials.

Although Witchcraft was extensively practised throughou the length and breadth of Italy we have not the almost excessive wealth of material for an intensive study of Witch-craft such as we meet with in England during the century 1560–1660, in Scotland, and in France. This is not to say that there are not very many records of exceptional interest and importance, and it is scarcely hazardous to suppose that many more must lie unexamined and unedited in the libraries of noble houses and the archives of the great cities.

During the sixteenth century the Inquisition was very busy throughout the northern provinces of Italy, a veritable hotbed of Witchcraft. In 1510 Silvester Mazzolini (1460–1523) (Prierias), the famous Dominican, burned sixty witches on various charges of sorcery ; about the same time Bernard of Como proved so zealous in his pursuit of these criminals, that the ignorant rustics, living in the villages to the north of Milan, who were too often in collusion with the accused, threatened to rise in revolt.[56] In the diocese of Como, Bartolomeo de Spina was assisted by ten colleagues, and he records that in one year, 1523, no less than a hundred witches were sent to the stake.[57] The official records of Val Camonica from 1518 to 1521 contain over a thousand names ; of these at least sixty-four were executed, whilst a crowd of fugitives found an asylum in cities further south, where they spread their evil practices and enchantments. In 1588 Cardinal Valieri, Bishop of Verona, in a pastoral letter bewails the prevalence of sorcerers ; whilst Bononio, Bishop of Como, drew up a whole procedure for the examination of witches, whom he orders to be interrogated and punished by the episcopal courts over which he himself presided.

It is now fully established that the Roman Academy founded by Pomponius Lætus contained an inner circle whose initiates were Satanists meeting in the obscurity of the Catacombs for devil worship and demonolatry. Giulio, the natural son of a nobleman of the Sansevino house, was born in Calabria in 1425. When very young he presented himself in Rome, where he became a favourite pupil of the irreligious Lorenzo Valla. Pomponius devoted his energies to the enthusiastic study of antiquity, an excellent pursuit, but unfortunately this led to sheer paganism and before long he was a contemner of Christianity and an avowed enemy of Christ. A number of kindred souls gathered round him ; an Accademia was formed, and meetings were regularly held. Outwardly they seemed innocent enough. There was no harm in celebrating the festival of the Pallia—the anniversary of the foundation of Rome. There was actual good in perform-ing the comedies of Plautus.[58] But these were only a cloak to blind. Paul II (Pietro Barbo), shrewdest of pontiffs, then occupied the Chair of S. Peter (1464-71). He was a Humanist, a Patron of Universities, a collector of works of ancient art, an elegant and accomplished Latinist, deeply interested in the new invention of printing. Yet he suppressed the Accademia, and years after a prominent member thereof, Bartolomeo Platina, completest of liars, wrote a calumnious biography of the Pope. Pomponius, Platina, and their fellows were imprisoned upon charges—only too well-founded—of conspiring against the life of the Pontiff. The tales of torture are mere nonsense. Sixtus IV, large-hearted, trustful, and generous, upon his accession (1471) released the culprits from S. Angelo. It would appear that in future they mainly held aloof from politics, but that they studied magic and celebrated Black Masses is undeniable. Until the last, Pomponius, who died in 1498, desired to be buried in an ancient sarcophagus on the Appian Way. His wishes were not agreed to, for he was interred in Aracoeli. Sentimental writers—I will not say historians—delight to draw a picture of the old man, lantern in hand, descending from his modest house upon the Esquiline[59] to the lecture-room, where, however early the hour, however inclement the weather, crowds of eager students await him. And at night amid the gloom of the Catacombs or in some dark cellar of his ill-omened villa the warlock defiles the Host, or in hideous mockery offers the Sacrifice of the Mass to the Powers of Darkness and Destruction.

However curious, it must be allowed that save for the spirited narration the necromantic episode in Cellini's *Memoirs* is not very remarkable and offers no new features. A Sicilian priest, a wizard ; Cellini ; Vincenzio Romoli ; and a man from Pistoia, who was versed in the black art, repair to the Colosseum. Circles are drawn upon the ground, and perfumes are burned, when after about an hour and a half " several legions of devils " seem to appear. Cellini asks that he may be brought into the company of Angelica, a light o' love who had gone off to Sicily and left him in the lurch. No answer is returned ; the spirits vanish ; but the priest declares that they may look for better success the next night, when they must further bring with them a lad of spotless purity, a virgin. On the following evening the same cere-monies are repeated, Cellini having with him his apprentice about twelve years old. The wizard furnishes a pentacle of great virtue which is held over the boy's head. Tremendous invocations and conjurations in Hebrew, Greek, and Latin follow. Devils are seen, and in answer to Cellini's demand some vague prophecy is uttered. Thousands of ghosts appear in every part of the Colosseum to the intense alarm of the experimenters, who have to remain within their magic circle until the church bells ring for prime. As dawn breaks they set out for home all keeping very close together ; and even then, so the boy avers, a couple of demons follow them at a distance, leaping and skipping, and playing strange pranks. The priest further endeavoured to persuade Cellini to assist him in the consecration of a book of spells, whispering in his ear that the best place to perform the operation would be among the mountains of Norcia, where the peasants were not ignorant of the black art and might even lend valuable aid in the ceremony. It so happened, however, that in spite of constant entreaties Cellini, who was not altogether unwilling to essay the adventure, was prevented from taking part. Norcia, be it noted, was one of the great centres of Italian sorcery ; and among the remoter Apennines many a pagan superstition lingered until late centuries.[60]

Throughout the sixteenth and seventeenth centuries Italy was overrun with dabblers in magic, who, like this Sicilian priest, made almost open boast of their commerce with spirits. They cast nativities; drew horoscopes; practised cheiromancy; fashioned talismans; interpreted dreams; sought the philosopher's stone; augured by stereomancy, theriomancy, and the flight of birds; foretold days lucky and unlucky; played Pandarus; brewed philtres; confected a ceruse; mixed a lotion; were half herbalist and half physician, half astrologer and half witch. If now and again one of the fraternity was unfortunate and found himself lodged in the dungeons of the Holy Office, they were at least generally tolerated, and often secured favour in the highest places of the land. So Diego Hurtado de Mendoza, the famous diplomat and politician, who represented Charles V at the Council of Trent, writing to the Emperor a description of Rome during the pontificate (1534–49) of Paul III (Alessandro Farnese), says : " Es venido la cosa a que ay muy pocos cardenales, que concierten negocios, aunque sea para comprar una carga de leña, sino es o por medio de algun astrologo o hechizero." As might have been expected under such conditions there at once sprang into existence a swarm of idle charlatans, pimps and quacks, of whom the best were impostors, the worst poisoners, ready for any infamous job that filled their pockets, often mere rogues who traded on the folly of their employers, but sometimes fantasts who believed to some extent at any rate in their own powers and pretensions and were only a little less credulous than their dupes. These are figures which continually appear in contemporary literature, in the dramatists and novellieri ; thus we have Ariosto's *Il Negromante,* della Porta's *L'Astrologo,* Grazzini's *La Strega,* and the same author's novel of Zoroastro, *La Seconda Cena,* IV.[61] But it sometimes happened that these mountebanks overreached themselves. There is a story related in an Italian diary of the seventeenth century[62] concerning a fellow who donned some strange habit and arrived at Rome in a painted carriage drawn by two large black dogs. Great curiosity was aroused, which he further inflamed by having the incredible folly to report that these were two familiars, who conducted him at lightning speed whithersoever he wished to go. Just then an express courier happened to arrive from Milan—perhaps a confederate —and he asserted that he had left the conjurer in that city, only to recognize him in the Piazza del Popolo and to learn that he had been several days established in a lodging there. The pleasant public interest gave way to an ugly fear. The wizard was promptly arrested, and before many weeks executed on a charge of sorcery. That such condemnations were rare[63] is, I think, obvious from the fact that the incident finds mention in a record of only fifty leaves which covers no less than twelve reigns, a period of seventy-seven years.

In 1633 a far more resounding scandal amazed and horrified Rome. A mysterious astrologer had some few years before prophesied to Giacinto Centini, nephew of the Cardinal d' Ascoli, that his uncle would succeed Urban VIII in the Chair of S. Peter. The impulsive and ambitious young man soon tired of waiting, and rashly resolved to hasten the event. He first applied to Fra Pietro da Palermo, an Augustinian Eremite, than whom, it was whispered, there were few more deeply skilled in the mysteries of the Holy Kabbalah and necromantic lore. This sage declared that the Pope still had many years to live, although the Cardinal d' Ascoli would certainly be elected at the next conclave. He hinted that it was in his power to shorten Urban's days, a suggestion Giacinto Centini eagerly embraced. The aid of a certain Fra Cherubino, a Friar Minor of Ancona, and a master of goetic science, was called in, as well as that of yet another occult adept, Fra Domenico da Fermo, O.S.A. The four accomplices at once set to work to destroy the Pope by their spells. They caused a knife to be secretly forged after the model of the Key of Solomon, and this was engraved with hermetic characters. A clean virgin was employed to spin hemp into a thread. They then repaired to a secret room in Giacinto's palace, where Fra Pietro solemnly celebrated the Black Mass. A circle was next drawn with the mystic thread, a fire lighted in the centre, and before the blaze a wax figure of Pope Urban, stabbed through and through with the knife, was slowly melted until utterly consumed. The friars had informed Giacinto that a demon would infallibly appear and announce the Pontiff's sudden decease. All their ceremonies and invocations, however, were vain, and at last Fra Pietro explained the failure by asserting that some treacherous

murder had been committed in the palace, and this prevented
the operation of their magic. A few days later they repeated
their rites, but this time in a remote vineyard, at midnight,
under the canopy of heaven. And yet no Satanic vision was
vouchsafed, no demon issued from the darkness. Now
Fra Pietro attributed their non-success to the score of foul
weather and angry elements. So far from being chagrined
at these disappointments Giacinto only urged him on with
greater eagerness, and when the wizard announced that he
knew a sure and deadly spell of awful power, which needed
the assistance of seven priests to confect the charm, and of
these one must be stabbed to the heart at the moment of
consummation so that the warm reeking drops of blood might
more swiftly wing the curse, without hesitation the head-
strong youth instructed his servants to search him out seven
priests who would lend themselves to these dark superstitions.
Such a quest could but attract attention and give rise to
inconvenient talk. Meanwhile Giacinto, who seems to have
been a hysterical neuropath, incapable of holding his tongue
on the subject of his obsession, kept throwing out hints, and
something more than hints, to his friends, promising he would
make them all cardinals, when he should in a little time
become the Papal nephew. Little wonder that the Holy
Office descended rous upon the persons implicated in the
conspiracy, and that when they were brought to trial the
most damning evidence of their guilt was speedily established.
The end of it all was that Giacinto lost his head upon the
scaffold, Fra Pietro and Fra Cherubino were burned alive for
sorcery and high treason, Fra Domenico went to the galleys
for life. Several other men who were more or less involved in
the process received punishments of considerable severity.
Incredible as the folly of Giacinto may seem, psychologically
it is not merely possible but not even rare. On the other
hand, the only explanation of the conduct of the friars,
the fact that at the peril of their lives they confided their
hideous secrets to a young man whom they must have known
to be a tattler and a braggart coxcomb, would appear to lie
in a firm conviction of the reality of their own occult powers,
a belief that they could save and shield themselves from any
harm, and defy human justice.[64]

During the sixteenth and seventeenth centuries fearful

pestilences devastated Savoy, Lombardy, and the North of Italy. In 1524 the mortality in Milan and the country-side was reckoned at 140,000 ; at Venice in 1575–77 no less than 50,000 perished ; whilst in 1630–31 nearly 47,000 were carried off within a space of sixteen months in the city, to which if we add the number of those who died in the lagoons a total of wellnigh 95,000 is reached. On these occasions Venice celebrated her deliverance by the votive offerings of the churches of Il Redentore, built by Palladio in 1577, and of S. Maria della Salute, built by Baldassare Longhena in 1632. At Milan in 1629–30 sixty thousand victims were swept away, whilst many of the neighbouring villages literally lost all their inhabitants. In 1598 whole districts of Piedmont were scourged with the utmost virulence of the plague. In May, 1599, it was calculated that less than four thousand persons could be found in Turin. The streets were piled with unburied corpses, the palaces were strewn with rotting bodies of the dead, whilst the survivors only thought of debauchery and plunder, often to be struck down in the midst of their riot and marauding. The history of these visitations is ghastly in the extreme, and the details reported by cold and exact chroniclers make reading of almost unexampled horror and loathliness.

It was probably first at Milan during the sickness of 1598 the belief awoke in the popular mind that the disease had been introduced and was being actively disseminated by sorcerers. Two strangers of suspicious habit were arrested and presently confessed that they had come from Geneva for this express purpose. They were condemned to death, and a few weeks later two other poisoners were burned. At Turin in 1600 four men were executed on the same charge. They indicated a wood where they said they had buried a purulent liquid intended to be used for smearing doors and walls. The spot was searched and some jars were discovered. Other wretches avowed that they had at the Devil's instigation collected the pus from the sores of plague-stricken corpses, and kept it in phials. The Demon secured their own safety, but any person whom they touched, be it ever so lightly, with the foul matter was infected and inevitably perished. Such vessels as they described were found secreted in their houses.

The name given to these diabolical malefactors was *Untori*, the Smearers, and the plague of Milan in 1629–30 was known as " La Peste degli Untori." It is singular to note that this pestilence was foretold a year before it broke out, since a large comet which appeared in 1628 was announced by the astrologers to portend a terrible mortality. Other prophecies were current, especially an ancient distich which said that in 1630 the Demon would endeavour to poison all Milan. It was remarked one morning in April, when owing to the warm dry weather the disease was raging, that many of the doors and walls were stained with a curious daub, as if a sponge, saturated with the thick matter from the pustules and sores of the sick had been pressed against them. Frantic alarm spread rapidly, and the pestilence fearfully increased. The witches were supposed to go about the city smearing benches, the handles of doors, furniture, chairs, confessionals, choir-stalls, even fruit, flowers, and food with the deadly stuff. They scattered magic powders in a circle on the pavement. To set a foot in one of these meant certain destruction. Hundreds of such *untori* were seized and condemned by the magistrates. In particular one Mora, half-barber, half-alchemist, who had long lain under the suspicion of necromancy, was arrested on this charge. Various mysterious ungents were found secreted in his house, and the physicians upon analysis declared these to be rank poison. He was racked, and at length confessed all his accusers desired. He had smeared houses and every article of touch with venom of the plague, he was in league with the Devil to infect all Milan. He named several persons as his accomplices, and these were instantly executed as the vilest of criminals.

About the same time a wild enthusiast, who came forward at the height of the scourge, told a long and circumstantial story to the effect that he had actually been tempted by the Demon to smear all the houses and walls of Milan with a pestiferous salve, and thousands at once believed his tale. It was said that a band of warlocks had taken a house in the city, and that there they concocted their drugs, and met in midnight Sabbat to debate on the progress of the plague, and make plans for its furtherance and increase. So convinced were the citizens of the truth of this report, that repeated search was officially made for the mysterous abode, but all in vain.[65]

The evidence for the *untori* is so overwhelming that it seems certain there were at least some few moral maniacs who, crazed by despair or by their brooding upon death and corruption, yielded to a spell of fearful malignity and endeavoured to spread the contagion. Certainly such persons by influencing the overwrought and sickly imaginations of their fellows could do incalculable harm, and appreciably extend the sphere of the pestilence by frightening others into the very disease. It is obvious, however, that many innocent persons must have been not only falsely accused but have perished miserably through accident or, it may be, an enemy's revengful design.

Throughout Piedmont and Lombardy, especially in the Alpine valleys and the villages of the Tyrol, the witch prosecutions were actively promoted and pursued during the greater part of the seventeenth century. Even in these districts, however, the records of trials are far less common and less complete than those of France and England at a corresponding period.

For the virus of heresy had infected deeply—and it was, we may remind ourselves the degraded Manichæan heresy, with whose dark doctrines and foul practice Satanism is inextricably mingled. The Inquisitors, who had jurisdiction in the northern cities, often went in fear of their lives. The zealous Michele Ghislieri, afterwards Pope S. Pius V, an untiring opponent of sorcerers and witches, upon entering the city of Como was more than once received with volleys of stones. To save his life he not infrequently had to escape in disguise, and conceal himself in the remote cottage of some faithful rustic. Nay more, at Bergamo a mob actually stormed the monastery of S. Dominic and released a warlock named Giorgio Mondaga, who had been incarcerated there. " In Bergamo li fu levato per forza dalle prigioni del monastero di San Domenico, dove allora si solevano mettere i rei, un principale heretico, nominato Giorgio Mondaga, con gran pericolo suo e de' frati."[66]

It is known to have been a great grief to S. Carlo Borromeo that his diocese was so corrupted by demonolatry. On one occasion, it is said, that when he passed through certain villages of the Val Camonica, highly suspect as being the haunt of necromancers, the Saint in silent rebuke kept his

eyes turned upon the ground, and did not move a hand to
bless the peasantry who had assembled to watch his progress.
On one occasion he received the submission and confessions
of no less than one hundred and thirty sorcerers of Mesolcina,
a valley of the Grisons. In 1583 several witches of this
district were burned, including a priest Domenico Quattrino,
of Rovereto, convicted by the testimony of eleven independent witnesses of having attended the Sabbat dressed in
chasuble, stole, and maniple, of having carnal intercourse
with a notorious whore suspect of magic and poisoning, and
of having used the Holy Oils to confect a charm.

Cardinal Federico Borromeo, the cousin and successor of
S. Carlos, a prelate of great learning and rare intelligence
and Archbishop of Milan from 1595 to 1631, was well known
for his zeal against witches and did much to suppress magical
superstitions in his diocese.

It is comparatively seldom that we hear of trials for
sorcery in other provinces of Italy, and pamphlets which
were so common at that time both in France and England
are not often to be met. Such a one, however, is the following : " Histoire admirable et prodigieuse d'un Enchanteur
Italien lequel fut bruslé tous vif en la ville de Pezaro le 26
octobre dernier avec un asne duquel il se servoit en ses
sortileges ; ensemble les charmes, philtres et compositions
par lui faites sur la personne de la Signore Alinda pour
l'émouvoir à son amour. Paris, *Jean de Bordeaulx*, 1614."
8vo.

A typical case of Witchcraft, and one which owing to its
prominence and the meticulous investigations of the authorities has luckily been reported in full, attracted considerable
attention in the winter of 1646 and the following spring.
It will, moreover, be found to present so many factors and
features, which occur again and again in the contemporary
trials of wellnigh every European country, that it may
profitably be dealt with in some detail.

A certain old woman of Castelnovo, Maria Salvatori,
nicknamed " la Mercuria," who had long been suspected of
sorcery, was arrested on 26 October, 1646, and formally
examined. At first the two principal charges, sufficiently
damning in themselves, seem to have been that at her
communions she did not swallow the Sacred Host, but kept

It in her mouth to spit It out secretly and reserve It for some abominable purpose, and also that by her ecbolic spells she had caused the young Marchesa Bevilacqua to miscarry in childbirth. She was again interrogated on 3 November and put to the torture of the cord when she accused Domenica, the widow of a certain Tomaso Camelli, and Domenica's daughter, Lucia, the wife of Antonio Caveden, both of whom dwelt at the hamlet of Villa, of being rank witches. She also avowed she had taken a Host from her mouth to give to Lucia Caveden, who thereby confected a charm which caused the abortion of the Marchioness. She added that she had also bewitched Cristoforo Sparamani, the son of Cecilia Sparamani, and that a certain Delaito Cavaleri was a necromancer and a worshipper of Satan. A further interrogation followed on 15 November, as a result of which the court, consisting of Paride Madernino, delegate in all criminal and civil cases in the districts of Castelnovo and Castellano, and his assessor Giovanni Ropele, doctor utriusque iuris, promptly gave orders to Giuseppe Coriziano, " bargello di questa turia," to arrest Domenica and Lucia. This was done, and on Saturday, 24 November, 1646, at Nogaredo, the proceedings against the witches were formally opened. " Processus Criminalis pro destructione lamiarum." On 27 November Domenica Camelli was questioned by the judges, but they got little enough out of her. Two days following Lucia Caveden was brought before the tribunal. She vehemently declared that the charges were all malice ; the hag Salvatori was her enemy ; and with many cries she called Heaven to witness her innocence, repeatedly exclaiming " per grazia del Signor Iddio no son una stria ! " But the next day she proved less firm and implicated yet another woman, Domenica Gratiadei, who was immediately thrown into prison, a number of suspicious objects being found in her house when it was closely searched by the officers. Certain pots of a dark unguent and a mysterious powder being produced in court, Lucia Caveden confessed that these were for the destruction of human life and cattle. Seeing that the game was up Domenica Gratiadei, upon being put to the torture, soon laid bare all the secrets of the infernal sisterhood. She had made this unguent with which she anointed herself to attend the Sabbat " trasformata in gatto," she had cast the evil eye on Cristofero Sparamani, she had renounced her baptism, defiled the Blessed Sacrament, adored Satan with divine honours. The judges were filled with horror, and trembled at the hideous tale of diabolism these women poured forth. Cecilia Sparamani, a plain honest woman, was next summoned as a witness and told how her son fell into fits of no ordinary kind. The doctors had acknowledged their skill baffled, and in spite of the prayers of two Capuchin fathers and the exorcisms of Monsignore the Bishop of Brondolo, this preternatural sickness still persisted. She informed the court that as soon as summer came and the roads were passable she intended to take the boy to the shrine of S. Antony at Padua, to whom she had a special devotion.

On 18 December, 1646, Benvenuta, the daughter of Domenica Gratiadei, made a startling confession. She declared that she had been taken by her mother " as if in a dream " to a place where there was dancing and singing, where she had been welcomed by a large number of revellers, and especially by a young man, who having kissed and fondled her awhile afterwards had connexion with her. This was, her mother averred, Satan himself. When closely questioned as to these proceedings the girl could only reply : " Tutto mi sembra, come ho detto, un sogno : e parevami che sempre vi fosse il diavolo in forma di quel giovene." It would seem from these very striking and significant words that the girl was a hypnotic subject, entirely under her mother's control, and that on these occasions she passed into a semi-trance state. The case dragged on throughout the months of January and February, 1647. There were interminable interrogations, and a large number of persons were gradually implicated.

On 2 January 1647, Domenica Gratiadei gave a detailed description of the Sabbats she had attended. She and an old warlock named Santo Peterlino always led the coven. " The rest followed in the shape of cats ; but the Devil went first of all." They enjoyed banquets, dances, plays, music, songs, and afterwards all worshipped Satan, presenting him with Hosts which they kept from their last communion. Before attending the Sabbat she anointed herself with an unguent made of " the Blessed Sacrament, the blood of certain small animals, Holy Water, the fat of dead babies " which was mixed with horrible imprecations and blasphemies to confect the charm.

On 10 January, a strange figure, Maddalena Andrei, nick-named " La Filosofa," first appears in the case. She confessed that she had assisted in the making of the ointment and had also adored the Devil who frequently appeared to her, " brave, like a gallant captain, dressed all in red." On 9 March, when Giuseppe Goriziano entered the cell of La Filosofa to summon her to court he found her lying dead upon the floor. The common people believed that she had been carried off by Satan, especially as the Archpriest of Villa, Don Giovanni Bragliardi, shrewdly suspecting that the unhappy woman had committed suicide, refused her sepulture in consecrated ground.

This long and complicated Witchcraft-trial at length came to an end in April, 1647. The court was thronged with an excited yet hushed crowd, when the judge Paride Madernino and his assessors the Counts of Lodrone and Castel-Romano delivered the sentences. Domenica Camelli, Lucia Caveden, Domenica Gratiadei, Catterina Baroni, Zinevra Chemola, Isabella and Polonia Gratiadei, and Valentina Andrei were condemned to death. Maria Salvatori, "la Mercuria," and Maddalena Andrei, " la Filosofa " had expired in prison. The condemned were beheaded and their bodies burned. It would seem, however, that Isabella and Polonia Gratiadei and Valentina Andrei managed to escape and could not be traced. The execution of the rest took place on 14 April, 1647, when Leonard Oberrdorfer the common hangman carried out the judicial sentence.

The chief witches here naturally fall into four groups each constituted of one old and one young woman, Domenica Camelli and Lucia her daughter ; Domenica Gratiadei and Benvenuta her daughter ; Isabella Gratiadei and Polonia her daughter ; Maddalena Andrei and her daughter Valentina. The chief of the coven was undoubtedly Domenica Gratiadei, whose vile confessions, a mixture of most horrid blasphemies and lewdest obscenity, convince her of being a wretch wholly devoted to evil, and an active propagandist of the Satanic cult. It was she who had debauched her own daughter to " the Devil," that young man whose name and individuality do not appear, but who may be guessed to have been a noble of the district, using the witches for his own ends and, presumably, supplying them with money to carry out his dark designs. That the whole gang frequently attended the Sabbat, at which he was not unseldom present, there can, I think, be no question. The horrid circumstance confessed by the beldame Salvatori, that at her communions she did not consume the Sacred Host, but impiously retained It in her mouth to eject It secretly for use as some profane charm, occurs also during the trial of Silvain Nevillon at Orleans in June, 1614. " Dit aussi auoir veu des Sorciers & Sorcieres qui apportoient des Hosties au Sabbat, lesquelles elles auoient gardi lors qu'on leur auoit baillé à communier à l'Eglise, & que le Diable faisoit des gestes comme en depitant sur icelles Hosties, desquelles ou faisoit de la poudre, & quelque fois ou les mettoit dans l'eau, & que le Diable estoit fort ayse quand ou luy apportoit lesdites Hosties."[67] In France (1652) a witch was " interrogée sy le diable ne luy avoit conseillé de cracher la Sainte Hostie hors de sa bouche, ou bien ne la point recepvoir, dist que non, mais bien que le diable l'at une fois battue fort parce qu'elle l'avoit receu."[68] In an old Basque legend, *The Witches at Akhelarre* (*The Sabbat*),[69] a lady is very ill. A witch is overheard to say that the sick woman " as she was going out of the church, let the holy wafer fall on the ground, and a toad had picked it up ; and this toad is still near the door, under a stone, with the bread in his mouth. And again, this same witch saw that, until they took away this bread out of the toad's mouth, this lady will not be cured."[70] James Device, who was one of the Lancashire witches executed in 1613, confessed " that upon Sheare Thursday was two yeares, his Grand-Mother Elizabeth Sothernes, alias Dembdike, did bid him this Examinate goe to the Church to receive the Communion (the next day after being Good Friday) and then not to eate the Bread the Minister gaue him, but to bring it and deliuer it to such a thing as should meet him on his way homewards." Some little distance from the church " a thing in the shape of a Hare." crossed his path, and he understood this to be the animal that awaited the bread, which, however, he had already swallowed.[71] A similar practice is said to have prevailed in certain Welsh districts.

There is a story of two old women who about a hundred years ago attended the morning service at Llanddewi Brefi Church, and received Holy Communion. They kept the bread in their mouths, and forthwith went out into the churchyard. They then walked round the building nine times, and at the ninth time the Demon came out of the old wall in the shape of a frog, to whom they gave the bread from their mouths. Thus they were supposed to be selling themselves to Satan, and become witches. An old man in North Pembrokeshire used to boast that he had obtained the power of bewitching by making a pretence at eating the bread of his First Communion, whilst in reality he pocketed it. When he left the church there met him at the gate a dog to which he gave the bread, thus selling his soul to the Evil One, and thenceforth he possessed magic and malignant powers.[72]

The Satanist of to-day will often attend Holy Mass and receive Communion in order to retain the Sacred Host, which he defiles at his abominable rites. It is almost impossible for a priest to prevent this, as one may not refuse to give Holy Communion save under the most exceptional conditions. One morning, not many years ago, there was found in a remote corner of a London church a Host, soft and moistened as from lying upon a human tongue. Two or three Low Masses had been said and Communion given to perhaps some forty or more persons. The Host had evidently been removed from the mouth with the intention of secreting It, and It must have slipped to the pavement from the handkerchief or hand in which It was being conveyed to the pocket. In 1855 there was discovered at Paris an association of Satanists who communicated daily in order to gain possession of the Host by quickly passing It from their mouths. They were dispersed by the efforts of Monseigneur Sibour, the Archbishop, who on 3 January, 1857, was assassinated by an excommunicate priest named Verger. It has been suggested that this apostate may have been secretly connected with these miscreants. In 1874 a similar abominable sacrilege came to light, and Monseigneur Guibert, the Archbishop, found no little difficulty in suppressing them, as the wretches involved used to present themselves at the altar on different mornings in distant churches of the city and the suburbs.

It is not unknown that the Tabernacle itself should be

violated, and from time to time it would seem as though a regular gang of Host-stealers systematically sets to work. More than one London church has been robbed in this manner, and there are instances of churches in the country being profaned in precisely the same way. The particulars make it certain that no ordinary theft was intended. The gold ciborium, studded with jewels, was left overthrown upon the altar, but the Contents had gone.

The pots of unguent found concealed in the house of Domenica Gratiadei are none other than that " flying ointment " with which sorcerers were frequently wont to besmear themselves before they proceeded to the Sabbat. It makes a constant figure in the trials, and Weyer gives us the exact formulæ for its composition. The ingredients, according to the hag Gratiadei, were : "the Blessed Sacrament, the blood of certain small animals, Holy Water, the fat of dead babies." Weyer has three prescriptions : (1) Du pusil, de l'eau de l'Aconite, des feuilles de Peuple, et de la suye ; (2) De la Berle de l'Acorum vulgaire, de la Quintefeuille, du sang du chauvesouris, de la Morelle endormante, et de l'huyle ; (3) De grasisse d'enfant, de sue d'Ache, d'Aconite, de Quintefeuille, de Morelle, et de suye. It will be noticed that in numbers two and three the blood of bats and baby's fat severally occur.

The transformation into cats or the cat disguise is so common as to be proverbial everywhere. At a witch-trial in Guernsey in 1563 Martin Tulouff confessed that he had assisted at a Sabbat " là ou ly avoet chinq ou vi chatz, d'ou il y en avoet ung qui estoet noir, qui menoit la dance, . . . q̄ ledit Chat estoet le diable." During the winter of 1718, one William Montgomerie, of Barnside near Thurso, a mason, complained to the acting-sheriff " that his house was severall times infested with cats to that degree that he nor his family were in safety to reside there." On one dark November evening armed with a dirk and an ax he had rushed out into his yard and dispersed a gathering, as is seemed, of all the grimalkins in Scotland. Two he had killed, of one he had half sliced off the leg, and several others he had sorely wounded. In the morning no bodies and no traces of blood were to be found. Suspicion was aroused, and a crone named Margaret Nin-Gilbert, who had long borne a very evil reputation, was discovered in bed with her leg bleeding and broken. The sheriff and local ministers at once made official inquiry into the matter. " Being interrogat, If she was in the house of William Montgomerie, mason in the Burnside of Scrabster, especially on that night, the —— day of ——, when that house was dreadfully infested with severall cats, to that degree that W.M. foresaid was obliged to use sword, durk, and ax in beating and fraying away those catts ? Confessed, That she was bodily present yr, and that the said M. had broke her legg either by the durk or ax, which legg has fallen off from the other part of her body ; and that she was in the likeness of a feltered catt, night forsaid, in the said house : and that Margaret Olsone was there likeness of a catt also." This late Caithness trial is certainly one of the most curious instances of the cat superstition.

The confessions of Benvenuta Gratiadei ; her attendance at the Sabbat, sometimes, no doubt, an experience on the psychic plane, for she was undoubtedly a medium of unusual powers, and sometimes in actual fact ; the dances, feasting, music, songs, of the Sabbat ; her copulation with " the Devil " ; the worship of Satan ; all these may be paralleled by the details of the Sabbat given in my previous study, and mere repetition were superfluous. In the Nogaredo trials and confessions we certainly find some of the most valuable and interesting witch material Italian archives afford.

In 1647 Fra Brognoli, a Franciscan of much experience, was called in by Father Carlo de Velitri, Vicar of the Holy Office at Treviso, to assist him in reclaiming a Manichæan Satanist, who in agonies of remorse had voluntarily placed himself in the Inquisitor's hands for reconciliation. Fra Brognoli was so impressed by the revelations of the penitent that he composed a treatise, *Alexicacon*, in which he discusses with great acumen the exact boundaries between medicine and theology in such cases. His work is of no little value, since it is a record of first-hand evidence.

Perhaps even more important is the *De Dæmonialitate* of Sinistrari, which was first published from the original manuscript by the well-known bibliophile Isidore Liseux, Paris, 8vo, 1875. Ludivico Maria Sinistrari was born at Ameno, a small town in the diocese of Novara, on 26 February, 1622. In the year 1647 he entered the Franciscan Order, and for fifteen years he professed first Philosophy and then Theology at the University of Pavia. He was a scholar of immense erudition, *omnium scientiarum uir*, and an eloquent preacher. At Rome he was appointed Consultor to the Supreme Tribunal of the Holy Office, and later he acted as Vicar-General of the Archbishop of Avignon. For many years also he was Theologian to the Cardinal-Archbishop of Milan. Full of honours he died on 6 March, 1701, at the age of seventy-nine. His works were published in three folio volumes, Rome, Giannini, 1753–54.

Although there are a few passages which may, perhaps, be accused of some slight extravagance the *De Dæmonialitate* is of great value, especially as showing the belief in witches, and the modification of that belief which persisted throughout the seventeenth century. With regard to the penalties for Witchcraft he writes as follows : " Quantum ad pœnas *Dæmonialitatis*, nulla lex ciuilis, aut canonica, quam legerim, reperitur, quæ pœnam sanciat contra crimen huiusmodi. Tamen, quia crimen hoc supponit pactum, ac societatem cum Dæmone, ac apostasiam a fide, ultra ueneficia, atque alia infinita propemodum damna, quæ a Maleficis inferuntur, regulariter extra Italiam, suspendio et incendio punitur. In Italia autem, rarissime traduntur huiusmodi Malefici ab Inquisitoribus Curiæ sæculari."

During the whole of the eighteenth century the belief in Witchcraft was universal throughout Italy. Many cases were tried by the Inquisition behind closed doors, but often mob law prevailed, and doting beldames, whom the popular voice declared to be witches, were stoned or beaten to death in the streets by some frenzied rout. There also flourished sibyls of superior wit, if not of superior rank, who traded upon vulgar credulity, told fortunes, and supplied both " love-philtres " and, it was whispered, more dangerous medicaments, for which they were handsomely fee'd. The lessons of Hieronyma Spara, a notorious witch and poisoner, who was hanged 5 July, 1659, under Alexander VII (Fabio Chigi, 1655–67), and of her successor, La Toffania, the Neapolitan Locusta, were not forgotten. The more innocent charlatans used to display their wares and tell fortunes in the Piazza Navona.

There is a tale told of a certain Madame T.M. who some sixty years ago went to one of these vagrant sorceresses for a charm, by means of which she might extract admiration and money from Cardinal Antonelli (died 6 November, 1876). The witch declared that in order to confect an efficacious charm she must have His Eminence's red berretta. Servants were heavily bribed, and the berretta was forthcoming. Presently the lady presented herself before the Cardinal, but the spell did not work and she met with a chilling reception.[73]

In May, 1789, there arrived in Rome the notorious Joseph Balsamo, who now dubbed himself Alexander, Count Cagliostro, with his wife Lorenza. Expelled from half a dozen countries, mixed up in half a hundred discreditable transactions, more than suspected of fraud, forgery, peculation, sorcery, and half a score knaveries, he was none the less received with kindness by several great nobles and even by some prelates of no mean rank. Thus encouraged he took a private house in the Piazza Farnese, and before long he had the inconceivable folly to give an exhibition of his so-called occult powers in the presence of a large audience whom he had assembled there one evening in September. The Abate Benedetti writes an account of this gathering. Among those who assisted were the French ambassador, Cardinal Bernis ; the Abate Ennio Visconti ; the Princess Rezzonico ; the Princess Santacroce ; the Marchese Vivaldi and her secretary Father Tanganelli ; the Marchese Massimi attended by a Capuchin, Fra Francesco da San Maurizio ; and a large number of the Roman nobility. At the end of the salon had been erected a kind of altar, on which were placed skulls, stuffed monkeys, serpents who writhed and coiled as in life, owls, musty parchments, amulets, crucibles, and other strange furniture. Incense was burning before the images of fantastic Chinese and Egyptian idols. Cagliostro, wrapped in a Chaldean robe, appeared followed by his wife. He passed—or pretended to pass—into trance, and gave a lively description of the Marriage at Cana of Galilee. He then seized a glass beaker of pure water and crying " Ego sum qui sum " poured therein two drops from a small vial he kept in his bosom, whereupon the liquid seemed to be transformed into a sparkling wine, cups of which were handed to the guests who pronounced it delicious. Psychometry and crystal-gazing followed, and anon Cagliostro addressed them on the subject of a mysterious society, which the Capuchin most indiscreetly announced that he was willing to join. " He certainly did many things which greatly surprised me," says the Abate Benedetti, " but in all his actions there is much imposture. . . . Sooner or later I believe that his true object will be discovered, and that he will be denounced to the Governor or the Holy Office."

The séances continued for a while, but on 27 December, Cagliostro, his wife, and Fra Francesco were all arrested by the Inquisition ; a sequel which was only to be expected. When brought before the tribunal Cagliostro denied the charges, but his wife confessed all. On 7 April, 1791, the Holy Office promulgated sentence and adjudged him worthy " of all the pains and penalties inflicted by the Canons of the Church, and the laws of the land, whether civil or municipal, upon heretics, astrologers, and magicians," that is to say, death. But Pius VI commuted the punishment into perpetual imprisonment in the fortress of S. Leo, after he had made public abjuration of his errors in S. Maria sopra Minerva. The Capuchin was assigned to his Order to be visited with exemplary discipline, whilst Cagliostro's wife was relegated to the convent of Santa Appollonia in Trastevere, where she languished forgotten and in obscurity. Cagliostro himself died, impenitent, on 28 August, 1795.

He appears to have been in some way connected with Satanism, but whether he participated in these abominations from any serious motive, or whether his charlatanry saw therein a way of getting money, by threats and blackmail, must remain an open question. It is certain that bands of Satanists, who, however, only dared to practise their rites in circumstances of the utmost secrecy, existed in Italy all through the eighteenth century and have, indeed, continued to the present day. Monseigneur de Ségur definitely states that in 1848 a Satanist chapel was discovered in Rome, where an altar had been placed with six black candles. The mass of the Devil was celebrated before a congregation of men and women, each one of whom spat and defiled a crucifix, and deposited in a ciborium a consecrated Host either stolen from a church or purchased. The whole assembly stabbed the Hosts with horrid imprecations, and an orgy followed similar to " Pagan mysteries and Manichæan reunions." Even more recently, about some ten years ago, another chapel arranged for diabolic worship was accidentally discovered at Rome, great scandal ensued, and this haunt of the infernal cult was speedily suppressed.

There is also a link, although far more innocent, and, indeed, comparatively harmless, between many obsolescent superstitions, that yet covertly linger in modern Italy, and the Witchcraft of three centuries ago. Rhymed spells and doggerel formulas such as were used by the sixteenth-century *streghe* have been handed down for generations, but happily they have for the most part lost their ill-omened names and evil motives to take a more honest turn, and many such a magic rune has become strangely identified or connected with some Christian Saint.

Even to-day in Italy certain Saints are regarded as *folletti*, goblin Saints. The chief of these is S. Antony, the first hermit. Probably the fact that this Saint was so tormented by demons and won such tremendous power over them gave rise to this traditional superstition. " San Antonio and San Simeone cannot be saints," said a *strega* to Leland,[74] " because we always perform incantations in a cellar to them at night." For S. Antony the Great is often confounded with S. Antony of Padua. So when you have lost anything you say a double paternoster to S. Antony, thus :

> Pater noster—Pater noster !
> Qui es in cœlis—Qui es in cœlis !

But the *Pater-noster a doppio* is decidedly a matter of Witchcraft, at least this is what every peasant believes. " Ma dire il paternoster così e della stregheria, e non della vera religione Cattolica." So said one who had received a liberal education in magic. S. Antony the Great protects his votaries from sorcery and spells. Therefore they say to him in Romagnola :

> Sant' Antogne, Sant' Antogne
> Sopre eame, liberez dai sase !
> Edal streghi chliùvengu,
> In camia a stregem.

In Italian :

> Santo Anton sopra il cammino
> Liberati ci dagli assassini !
> Edalle Streghe che non vengano
> In casa mia a stregare.

San Elia and San Eliseo are also Saints by whose invocation charms may be rendered effective. Both, it may be remembered, are venerated by the Carmelites as founders of that august Order, the feast of S. Elias the Prophet, " Dux ac Pater noster," being observed on 20 July as a Double of the First Class with an Octave, the feast of S. Eliseus, " Propheta Pater noster," being celebrated on 14 June as a Double of the Second Class. The statues of these two Saints may often be seen in Carmelite churches,[75] and in S. Peter's S. Elias stands amongst the Founders of Religious Orders. S. Eliseus is especially appealed to by maidens whose lovers seem fickle. The name of S. Elias occurs in connexion with a harmless enough little rhyme used by those with weak eyes :

" To cure an affliction of the eyes, take three roots bound with a red ribbon, three leaves of trefoil, and then say :

' Stacco queste trefoglie per Santo Elia,
Che il mal d'occhio mi mandi via.' "

Perhaps the most popular of these Saints is Il Vecchio Simeone Santo. The *Libretto di Stregonerie*, a halfpenny chapbook, has the following curious piece of old-world lore.

Il Buon Vecchio Simeone.

" Procure a picture or statue in plaster of this great Saint, who presided at the Circumcision of our Lord Jesus Christ with the old Saint Joseph and our Immaculate Lady, both being the dearly beloved progenitors of the Lord God the Redeemer.

It makes no difference whether it be a picture of the Saint or a plaster Statue if we repeat the marvellous Novena dedicated to him, and if according to the instructions in it we recite the customary prayer.

And it is certain that soon after the Novena, the good old man will appear in some form, and grant the one praying his request ; but what he principally bestows is lucky numbers in the lottery.

There is no need to fear, for the Saint generally appears in a dream while you sleep, and his look is so good and benevolent that there is no danger of awaking in a fright.

The whole difficulty is to know how to decipher the exact meaning of the words and signs which the Saint will give. Many people mistake his meaning, such is the experience of many, so difficult is it to decipher and unravel his gestures and figurations."

The novena is merely the following grayer : " O glorio-
sissimo S. Vecchio Simeone che meritaste ed aveste la bella
sorte di ricevere e portare nella vostre fortunate braccie il
Divin Pargoletto Gesù—E le annunziaste e profetiziaste e le
vostre Profezie furono sante verità. O Santo concedetomi
la grazia che vi addomando. *Amen.*"

An old woman (a witch) told Leland to repeat this prayer
three nights in succession at midnight. The Saint will then
appear. He may assume any figure. A priest clad all in
white, a friar with a long beard, an old man wrapped in a
mantle. He will inquire what it is you demand, and you must
answer promptly, asking three lucky numbers in the lottery,
where a certain treasure is hidden, just what you will. But
if you are not fearless, and do not reply immediately and
boldly, he will give you a sound cuff on the head, so that the
marks of his five fingers can be plainly seen in the morning.
Sometimes, indeed, they never disappear. Above all in
repeating the prayer you must not err in a single syllable.
If you are without fear, however, you will get what you want.

Holy Simeon may be considered to be commemorated on
2 February, Candlemas, but his particular Feast is on
21 October,[76] when he was formerly honoured at Venice
with a special office and proper antiphons, the collect being :
" Omnipotens sempiterne Deus, qui Unigenitum tuum ulnis
Sancti Simeonis in templo sancto tuo suscipiendum præ-
sentasti, tuam supplices deprecamen clementiam ; ut, eo inter-
ueniente, in templo sancto gloriæ tuæ præsentari mereamur.
Per eundem Dominum." The Venetian *Calendarium* for
the current year (1925) omits Holy Simeon, so I presume his
Feast is now only kept in his own church, the green-domed
S. Simeone Grande, which to me, for its intimate associations
and its masses, will always be one of the dearest and loveliest
of Venice's churches. Beside the high-altar is the recumbent
statue of S. Simeone, a masterpiece of the Roman artist,
Marco Romano, 1317. In Lent there is a Station at S. Simeone
on the Tuesday after the First Sunday. The Greeks honour
Holy Simeon and the aged Prophetess Anna on 3 February.

Even yet the idea among rustic folk in Italy that Witchcraft runs in families is deep rooted. In January, 1891, there
was a priest at Florence, an excellent and even holy man,

who was none the less said to be a *stregone* since his mother
had always been reputed to be a *strega*.

Old women in the Tuscan Romagna will tell you still that
the witches meet for their Sabbat on Tuesdays and Fridays.
Unfortunately the darker superstitions yet lurk in dusty
corners, foul obscene things dreading the light. The Neapolitan *Sfruttata*, whose lover has deserted her, will take a
lemon and with horrid imprecations stick it full of long black
pins that as the fruit withers and dies, so may he who has forsaken her sicken and pine, so may her rival be burned with
fever and racked with aches till she drop into the grave.

There are modern charms which recall the horrors of the
sixteenth century, the love pastes of Guibourg, the elixirs of
Le Franc and Davot. For one enchantment " si deve
prendere del sangue menstruale chi viene alla donna," rue
and cummin boiled in pure water, which are all fashioned into
comfits, a curse being declaimed during this strange cookery.
To rouse bitter strife between persons on their wedding-day,
and to cause impotency in a husband whilst inflaming the
wife's desires, the witch takes an orange flower pounded with
salt, pepper, cummin, and the herb *sconcordia* (literally
variance), and this she scatters secretly over the bride's dress,
muttering meanwhile : " Tu sia maladetta, Tu non possa
avere un giorno di pace, E quando vai, Inginnochiarti, Avanti
l'altare, Tu possa essere gia peniti, Del passa che tu fai."
There are hideous stories of the mutilation of animals for
purposes of sorcery, too sickening to relate, too loathsome for
thought. There is also *la ghirlanda delle streghe*, a long cord
tied in elaborate knots with the feathers of a black hen
inserted in the strands. This is hidden away in some secret
place with appropriate maledictions, and the person at whom
the bane is launched will be consumed with a swift disease
no doctor can cure. Strangely enough one of these enchanted
ropes was in 1886 found in the belfry of an English country
church. All were puzzled, for it was evidently twined and
twisted for some specific purpose. An old woman in the
village identified it as a " witch's ladder," but it was not
until an engraving had been published in *The Folk Lore
Journal* that full information was received and the purport
of the mysterious charm completely understood. This is a
most singular occurrence, and proves that less than forty

years ago there were some who held firmly enough to witch-craft even in enlightened England.

It is true that even in Italy here and there Satanism still lingers in obscure corners, and yet persist dark practices and hidden deeds of shameless blasphemy. Speaking of the South a modern writer with more force than truth says :

" Naples abounds in persons who profess to be inspired by the Devil or by the Saints, and for a few halfpence will give you aforehand the winning numbers at the lottery, and it is to these prophets that the Neapolitans—who I dare not swear believe in God, but most assuredly believe in the Saints and in the Devil—are continually resorting. . . . There is one most curious belief which still holds : If an unscrupulous and accommodating priest can be found who is willing to recite the Canon and celebrate Mass in honour of the Devil and give Satan's body in communion, the fiend—*noblesse oblige*—will immediately reward the inquirer by gaining him a trey. This Mass is known as the *Black Mass*, and those deboshed priests, dirty and unkempt as the lazzaroni of the harbour, who can easily be seen any day walking about the narrow and muddy slums of old Naples, are continually being asked to do folk the favour of celebrating this Mass. They, modern Talley-rands that they are, seldom make much difficulty about giving God the cold shoulder by saying the *Black Mass*. . . . Auri sacra fames."[77]

The faults and vices of the Neapolitan are primitive and flamboyant. None the less there are at this very day great saints living in Naples, and these not only in the cloister. The devotion of the crowded churches at Holy Mass is truly wonderful ; their love for the Madonna beautiful as only a true love romance can be. It is notorious that the colder nations of the North do not understand such things.

In parts of Sicily strange barbaric beliefs may yet be found. On 3 September, 1896, near Messina a young boy was lost, and it was discovered upon official inquiry that certain ignorant peasants, dreaming they were on the track of a buried treasure, had stolen the child whom they actually sacrificed alive, since they were assured that human blood would infallibly secure for them what they sought. I can well remember the thrill of horror that ran throughout all Italy at the disclosure of this monstrous crime.

Needless to say all superstitions are forbidden by the Church, and evil or baneful practices, intending harm and often combined with some filthy circumstance, would fall beneath a particular ban. With regard to idle and empty charms, in which to simple folk the events might often seem to justify the performance, it may be said that the universality of such incongruous beliefs and observances, though not always inducing inculpable ignorance, may possibly obscure the knowledge and weaken the will to a degree incompatible with mortal sin, nay, formal guilt may often be reduced to a vanishing point by easy credulity.

NOTES TO CHAPTER VII

[1] *Mystères de la Chevalerie et de l'amour platonique*, 1858. The views expressed in *Dante Hérétique*, 1854, do not commend themselves to my judgement.

[2] Alexander IV showed great favour to the Greyfriars, and among his earliest official acts was the canonization of S. Clare.

[3] Vaissette, *Histoire du Languedoc*, IX, p. 39.

[4] Of which see the Pontiff himself had formerly (1300–10) been bishop.

[5] " Diuinationibus et sortilegiis se immiscuerunt, perperam *dianis* nonnunquam utentes." It has been suggested that *Diani* are succubi, but I would rather understand " familiars." The familiar was often employed for purposes of divination. In the confession of Silvain Nevillon, who was tried at Orleans in 1614 (De Lancre, *L'Incredulité*, pp. 801–3), we have : " Qu'il y a des Sorciers qui nourrissent des Marionettes, qui sont de petits Diableteaux en forme de Crapaux. . . . Et quand ils veulent aller en marchandise on coüer, & sçauoir s'il y fera bon ils regardent si les-dites Marionettes sont ioyeuses, en ce cas ils vont en marchandise, ou ioüer : mais si elles sont maussades & tristes, ils ne bougent de la maison. Gentilon Gentiĕ le Clere dit qu'il auoit plus d'acquest en sa Marionette qu'en Dieu."

[6] [*Johannes*, XXII.] Uenerabili fratri Bartholomeo episcopo Foroiuliens i et dilecto filio magistro Petro Textoris doctori decretorum priori monasterii Sancti Antonini diocesis Ruth[enensis] per priorem soliti gubernari ac Petro de Pratis iuris ciuilis professori preposito ecclesie Claromontensis, capellanis nostris.

Romanus pontifex, ad quem ex officii debito principaliter pertinet saluti animarum intendere, eo uacare debet instantius circa corrigendos filios exorbitantes a fide, quo cercius ad salutem aliquid ualere non posse dinoscitur, si non in fidei radice fundatur. Ad nostrum siquidem assertio fide digna et sonorum quoddam uulgaris fame preloquium nouiter perduxit auditum, quod Iohannes de Lemouicis, Iacobus dictus Brabantinus, Iohannes de Amanto medicus, Radulphus Penchaclau, Gualterus Loflamene, Guillelmus Marini, Conradus Alamannus, et quondam Thomas dictus Alamannus, clerici et Innocentius barbitonsor uenerabilis fratris nostri . . . archiepiscopi Lugdunensis diocesum et nonnulli alii in nostra curia residentes, nolentes iuxta doctrinam apostoli sobrie sapere, sed nimie uanitatis ebrietate desipere reprobis ausibus appetentes, se nigromancie, geomancie et aliarum magicarum artium moliminibus implicarunt et implicant, scripta et libros habentes huiusmodi artium, que quidem, cum sint artes demonum ex quadam pestifera societate hominum et angelorum malorum exorte, uitande forent cuilibet christiano et omni penitus execratione dampnande, speculis et ymaginibus secundum oritum suum execrabilem consecratis usi fuere frequenter ac in circulis se ponentes malignos spiritus sepius inuocarunt, ut per eos contra salutem hominum molirentur aut eos interimendo uiolentia carminis aut eorum abreuiando uitam uiolentia immissa langoris, demones in speculis, circulis seu anulis interdum incluserunt, ut eos nedum de preteritis set et de futuris inquirerent, futura ipsa, que prescire solius dei est, ex illorum consultationibus predicturi, diuinationibus et sortilegiis se immiscuerunt, perperam dianis nonnunquam utentes. Sed et experimenta quam plurima quandoque fecerunt circe hec et alia per eos demonibus inuocatis. Nec uerentur asserere, quod nedum potus uel cibi propinatione, quin etiam solius uerbi prolatione hominum abreuiare seu prorogare uitam aut prorsus perimere et ab omni possent infirmitate curare, talibus se usos fuisse firmiter affirmantes. Relicto preterea creatore suo in huiusmodi demonum suffragiis confidentes eosque dignos arbitrantes, quibus seruiant et quibus honores diuinos impendant, illos ydolatrarum more adorare cum exhibitione cultus et reuerentie presumpserunt. Hiis et aliis superstitionibus detestandis et aduersantibus catholice fidei prefati clerici et barberius et eorum quilibet, necnon aliqui alii residentes in curia non semel sed pluries institisæ feruntur, nedum in suarum sed in quamplurium aliarum periculum animarum. Quia igitur pestem superstitionum huiusmodi, quarum reprobos sectatores ciuilis ratio comunis salutis hostes reputat et humani generis inimicos, nec uolumus nec ualemus conniuentibus oculis pertransire, presertim cum labem sapiant heretice prauitatis, super predictis omnibus et singulis zelo fidei, cuius negotium est ubique fauorabiliter prosequendum, ad inquisitionem contra clericos barberium et alios memoratos censuimus procedendum, non obstante quod predictus quondam Thomas in fata decesserit, cum de talibus agatur criminibus, de·quibus etiam licet memoriam accusare defuncti, cuius post mortem comprobata perfidia debite plecti debet. Quocirca uobis et uestrum cuilibet in solidum, de quorum discretione plenam in domino fiduciam gerimus, auctoritate presentium committimus et mandamus, quatinus super premissis omnibus et singulis specificatis ac dependentibus ex eisdem nec non super quibuslibet, de quibus predictos clericos, barberium et alios quoslibet in ipsa curia existentes inueneritis publice diffamatos, cum ipsis et cum personis aliis, quas ad id uideritis expedientes et utiles, summarie et de plano sine strepitu et figura iudicii ac omni appellatione cessante solum deum habendo pre oculis inquiratis exacta diligentia ueritatem et inquisicionem exinde factam, prout iustum fuerit, fine debito terminetis. Nos enim uobis et uestrum cuilibet in solidum, ita quod non sit melior condicio occupantis, sed quod unus uestrum, quandocunque et quocienscunque incepit, alter resumere seu continuare valeat et finire, premissa omnia et singula faciendi testes et personas alias ad hoc oportunas, prout et quociens uobis expediens esse uidebitur, super hiis admittendi, euocandi et ad partes personaliter citandi, contradictores et rebelles per censuram ecclesiasticam auctoritate apostolica compellendi et alia faciendi et exequendi, que pro predictis uel ea tangentibus expedientia fuerint, tam de dualus dictis in concilio generali quam aliis quibuscunque contrariis constitutionibus per predecessores nostros Romanos pontifices editis nequaquam obstantibus, plenam et liberam tenore presentium concedimus potestatem. Dat. Auinione iii kl. Martii.

[7] To be distinguished from William Durandus the Younger (ob. 1328), nephew of the famous ritualist and canonist with whom he is often confounded; as also from the Dominician Durandus of Saint-Pourçain, Doctor Resolutissimus (ob. 1332).

[8] Pastor, *History of the Popes* (London, 1891), I, 190, and Hergenröther, *Kirchengeschichte*, II, 1, 65, deny the legitimacy of this papacy. But the name of Alexander V occurs in the Roman *Gerarchia Cattolica*, which prior to 1906 gave a chronological list of the popes, and in 1889 the tomb of Alexander V at S. Francis in Bologna was magnificently restored by order of Leo XIII.

[9] He was elected 11 November, 1417, at Constance, which city he left for Rome, 16 May, 1418.

[10] It must be remembered that in mediæval times the archdiocese of

ITALY 581

Narbonne was of the greatest importance. Bernard de Fargues founded the Narbonne College at Paris.

[11] Elected 20 December, 1334 ; died at Avignon 24 April, 1342.

[12] Notwithstanding his defence, *Apologia J. Pici Mirandolani Concordiœ comitis*, 1480.

[13] It is now venerated in S. Peter's.

[14] The alleged permission granted by Innocent VIII to the Norwegians to celebrate Mass without wine is a forgery. *Bullarium Romanum*, III, 111 (Rome, 1743), 190–225.

[15] The idle stories about the Jewish doctor and the infusion of blood, culled from the shameless liar Infessura, may be ignored. It is a pity that these and other trattles should be graphically retailed in the pages of so brilliant a writer as John Addington Symonds.

[16] His own youth was loose enough, and his *Caccia d'Amore* (Venice, 1526 and 1537) is not particularly puritan.

[17] His works were published at Florence, 1497, *Hymni et Epigrammata Marulli.* Poliziano, who loathed him, has some stinging epigrams which lash him well. Incidentally Poliziano's sapphics *Innocentio Pontifici Max.* are exceedingly fine.

[18] *Leo the Tenth*, 4th ed., London, 1846, Vol. I, p. 81.

[19] Innocentius episcopus, seruus seruorum dei, ad perpetuam rei memoriam. Summis desiderantes affectibus, prout pastoralis sollicitudinis cura requirit, ut fides catholica nostris potissime temporibus ubique augeatur et floreat ac omnis hæretica prauitas de finibus fidelium procul pellatur, ea libenter declaramus ac etiam de nouo concedimus, per quæ huiusmodi pium desiderium nostrum uotiuum sortiatur effectum, cunctisque propterea per nostræ operationis ministerium, quasi per prouidi operationis sarculum erroribus extirpatis, eiusdem fidei zelus et obseruantia in ipsorum corda fidelium fortius imprimatur.

Sane nuper ad nostrum non sine ingenti molestia peruenit auditum, quod in nonnullis partibus Alemaniæ superioris necnon in Maguntinensi, Coloniensi, Treuirensi, Saltzburgensi et Bremensi prouinciis, ciuitatibus, terris, locis et diocesibus quamplures utriusque sexus personæ, propriæ salutis immemores et a fide catholica deuiantes, cum dæmonibus incubis et succubis abuti ac suis incantationibus, carminibus et coniurationibus aliisque nefandis superstitiis et sortilegiis, excessibus, criminibus et delictis mulierum partus, animalium fœtus, terræ fruges, uinearum uuas et arborum fructus necnon homines, mulieres, iumenta, pecora, pecudes et alia diuersorum generum animalia, uineas quoque, pomeria, prata, pascua, blada, frumeuter et alia terræ legumine perire, suffocari et extingui facere et procurare, ipsosque homines, mulieres, iumenta, pecora, pecudes et animalia diris tam intrinsecis quam extrinsecis doloribus et tormentis afficere et excruciare, ac eosdem homines ne gignere, et mulieres ne concipere, uirosque ne uxoribus, et mulieres ne uiris actus coniugiales reddere ualeant, impedire ; fidem præterea ipsam, quam in sacri susceptione baptismi susceperunt, ore sacrilego abnegare, aliaque quamplurima nefanda, excessus et crimina, instigante humani generis inimico, committere et perpetrare non uerentur, in animarum suarum periculum, diuinæ maiestatis offensam ac perniciosum exemplum ac scandalum plurimorum. Quodque licet dilecti filii Henricus Institoris, in prædictis partibus Alemaniæ superioris, in quibus etiam prouinciæ, ciuitates, terræ, diœceses et alia loca huiusmodi comprehensa fore censentur, necnon Jacobus Sprenger, per certas partes lineæ Rheni, ordinis fratrum Prædicatorum et theologiæ professores, hæreticæ prauitatis inquisitores per literas apostolicas deputati fuerint, prout adhuc existunt, tamen nonnulli clerici et laici illarum partium, quærentes plura sapere quam oporteat, pro eo quod in literis deputationis huiusmodi prouinciæ, ciuitates, diœceses, terræ et alia loca prædicta illarum que personæ ac excessus huiusmodi nominatim et specifice expressa non fuerunt, illa sub eisdem partibus minime contineri et propterea præfatis inquisitoribus in prouinciis, ciuitatibus, diœcesibus, terris et locis prædictis huiusmodi inquisitionis officium exequi non licere et ad personarum earundem super excessibus et criminibus antedictis punitionem, incarcerationem et correctionem admitti non debere, pertinaciter asseuere non erubescunt. Propter quod in prouinciis, ciuitatibus, diœcesibus, terris et locis prædictis excessus et crimina huiusmodi non sine animarum earundem euidenti iactura et æternæ salutis dispendio remanent impunita.

Nos igitur impedimenta quælibet, per quæ ipsorum inquisitorum officii executio quomodo libet retardari posset, de medio submouere, et ne labes hæreticæ prauitatis aliorumque excessuum huiusmodi in perniciem aliorum innocentium sua uenena diffundat, opportunis remediis, prout nostro incumbit officio, providere uolentes, fidei zelo ad hoc maxime nos impellente, ne propterea continget prouincias, ciuitates, diœceses, terras et loca prædicta sub eisdem partibus Alemaniæ superioris debito inquisitionis officio carere, eisdem inquisitoribus in illis officium inquisitionis huiusmodi exequi licere et ad personarum earundem super excessibus et criminibus prædictis correctionem, incarcerationem et punitionem admitti debere, perinde in omnibus et per omnia acsi in literis predictis prouinciæ, ciuitates, diœceses, terræ et loca ac personæ et excessus huiusmodi nominatim et specifice expressa forent, auctoritate apostolica tenore præsentium statuimus.   Proque potiori cautela literas et deputationem prædictas ad prouincias, ciuitates, diœceses, terras et loca necnon personas et crimina huiusmodi extendentes, præfatis inquisitoribus, quod ipsi et alter eorum, accersito secum dilecto fitio Ioanne Cremper, clerico Constantiensis diœcesis, magistro in artibus, eorum moderno seu quouis alio notario publico, per ipsos et quemlibet eorum pro tempore deputando in prouinciis, ciuitatibus, diœcesibus, terris et locis prædictis contra quascumque personas, cuiuscumque conditionis et præ-eminentiæ fuerint, huiusmodi inquisitionis officium exequi ipsasque personas, quas in præmissis culpabiles repererint, iuxta eorum demerita corrigere, incarcerare, punire et mulctare, necnon in singulis prouinciarum huiusmodi parochialibus ecclesiis uerbum dei fideli populo quotiens expedierit ac eis uisum fueirt, proponere et prædicare, omniaque alia et singula in præmissis et circa ea necessaria et opportuna facere et similiter exequi libere et licite ualeant, plenam ac liberam eadem auctoritate de nouo concedimus facultatem.

Et nihilominus uenerabili fratri nostro episcopo Argentinensi per apostolica scripta mandamus, quatenus ipse per se uel alium seu alios præmissa, ubi, quando et quotiens expedire cognouerit fueritque pro parte inquisitorum huiusmodi seu alterius eorum legitime requisitus, solemniter publicans, non permittat eos per quoscunque super hoc contra prædictarum et præsentium literarum tenorem quauis auctoritate molestari seu alias quomodolibet impediri ; molestatores et impedientes et contradictores quoslibet et rebelles, cuiuscumque dignitatis, status, gradus, præeminentia, nobilitatis et excel-lentiæ aut conditionis fuerint et quocunque exemptionis priuilegio sint muniti, per excommunicationis, suspensionis et interdicti ac alias etiam formidabiliores, de quibus sibi uidebitur, sententias, censuras et pœnas, omni appellatione postposita, compescendo, et etiam legitimis super his per eum seruandis processibus, sententias ipsas, quotiens opus fuerit, aggrauare et reaggrauare auctoritate nostra procuret, inuocato ad hoc, si opus fuerit, auxilio brachii sæcularis.

Non obstantibus præmissis ac constitutionibus et ordinationibus apostolicis contrariis quibuscunque, etc.

Nulli ergo omnino hominum liceat, etc. Si quis, etc.

Datum Romæ apud S. Petrum, anno incarnationis dominicæ millesimo quadringentesimo octuagesimo quarto, nonis Decembris, pontificatus nostri anno primo.

[20] Relatum est nobis, quod feruenter defensionem fidei suscipis aduersus hereticos quantumque opere et fauoris inquisitoribus prestas. Commendamus itaque deuotionem tuam et animi tui religionem ac probitatem, Fungeres enim officio boni et catholici prelati.

[21] The month and day are not found.

[22] Cum acceperimus, in prouincia Lombardiæ diuersas utriusque sexus personas diuersis incantationibus et diabolicis superstiticionibus operam dare suisque ueneficiis et uariis obseruationibus multa refanda scelera procurare,

homines et iumenta ac campos destruere et diuersos errores inducere magnaque
inde scelere exoriri, decreuimus pro pastoralis officii nobis exalto commissi
ministerio scelere huiusmodi compescere ac scandalis et erroribus præmissis,
quantum cum deo possumus, occurrere.

²³ Dilecto filio Modesto Uincentino ord. Præd. Dudum, uti nobis exponi
fecisti, per fel. rec. Iulium papam II prædecessorem nostrum non sine magna
tune animi sui displicentia accepto, quod per quendam Georgium de Casali,
ordinis fratrum Prædicatorum professorem et in ciuitate Cremonensi hæreticæ
prauitatis inquisitorem deputatum, in nonnullis Lombardiæ partibus et
præsertim in locis, in quibus dictus Georgius inquisitor deputatus erat,
repertæ fuerunt quamplures utriusque sexus personæ, propriæ salutis
immemores et a fide catholica deuiantes, certam sectam facientes, fidem,
quam in sacri susceptione baptismatis susceperant, abnegantes, sanctam
crucem pedibus conculcantes et opprobria super eam perpetrantes, ecclesiasticis et præsertim eucharistiæ sacramentis abutentes, diabolum in suum
dominum et patronum assumentes eique obedientiam et reuerentiam
exhibentes, et suis incantationibus, carminibus, sortilegiis, aliisque nefandis
superstitionibus homines, animalia et fructus terræ multipliciter lædentes,
aliaque quamplurima nefanda, excessus et crimina eodem diabolo instigante
committentes et perpetrantes, in animarum suarum periculum, diuinæ
maiestatis offensam, perniciosum quoque exemplum et scandalum plurimorum.
Contra quas, cum (ut prædictus Georgius tunc asserebat) in dictis locis suæ
inquisitioni deputatis, quod ipsius Georgii incumbebat officio, ipse processisset,
nonnulli autem tam clerici quam laici illarum partium, quærentes plus sapere
quam oporteret, præmissa delicta ad eiusdem Georgii inquisitionis officium
non pertinere temere asserere præsumentes, in populo odiosum reddere et
dicti Georgii officium impedire conati fuerant, prout etiam tunc impediebant,
ita quod propter præmissa personæ prædictæ delicta huiusmodi perpetrantes
remanebant impunitæ et aliæ earum exemplo ad similia perpetranda
quotidie inducebantur, in non modicum fidei opprobrium, animarum
periculum et scandalum plurimorum. Dictus prædecessor uolens, ne inquisitionis officii executio quomodolibet retarderetur et labes hæreticæ prauitatis
longius uenena diffunderet, prouidere, dicto Georgio per quasdam suas in forma
breuis literas commisit et mandauit, quatenus in locis eiusdem Georgii inquisitioni deputatis de excessibus huiusmodi cognoscere, et contra quascunque
personas cuiuscunque conditionis et præeminentiæ fuerint inquisitionis
officium exercere et exequi, ipsasque personas, quas in præmissis culpabiles
reperiret, una cum locurum ordinariorum uicariis, quatenus uoluissent
interesse, iuxta dictarum personarum demerita corrigere et punire deberet
et ualeret, secundum modum contra alios hæreticos a iure et sacris
canonibus statutum, contradictores quoscunque per censuras ecclesiasticas
et alia iuris remedia compescendo. Eos uero, qui in præmissis consilium,
auxilium vel fauorem præstarent, præfatus prædecessor noster eisdem
indulgentiis ubi et gaudere decreuit, quibus crucesignati contra alios hæreticos,
ex indulto apostolico eis concesso, tunc gaudebant et utebantur, prout in
dictis litteris plenius contineri dicitur. Et sicut eadem expositio subiungebat,
non solum delicta et crimina huiusmodi contra fidem catholicam et christianam
religionem sub iurisdictione inquisitoris Cremonensis committuntur et perpetrantur, sed in omnibus aliis locis et diœcesibus sub iurisdictione aliorum
inquisitorum dicti ordinis congregationis Lombardiæ in dies perpetrantur et
committuntur. Et cum eadem sint delicta, eadem profecto prouisione et
castigatione eis est iuxta earundem literarum tenorem prouidendum. Quare
tu, [qui] sicut asseris, in ciuitate Comensi dictæ prauitatis inquisitor deputatus
existis, tam tuo, quam aliorum omnium dictorum ordinis et congregationis
hæreticæ prauitatis inquisitorum ubilibet consistentium et deputatorum
nominibus fecisti nobis similiter supplicari, ut literas prædictas ad uos
extendere et ampliare aliasque desuper opportune prouidere dignaremur.
Nos igitur huiusmodi supplicationibus inclinati, literas prædictas cum omnibus
in eis contentis clausulis in omnibus et per omnia, prout in eisdem literis
continetur, ad te et alios ordinis et congregationis huiusmodi inquisitores,
tam in præsentiarum deputatos quam in futuram perpetuis futuris temporibus

deputandos, ac si tibi et cuilibet dictorum inquisitorum dirigerentur et directæ fuissent, apostolica auctoritate tenore præsentium extendimus ipsas que literas tibi et illis, ut præmittitur, eisdem auctoritate et tenore concedimus. Non obstantibus omnibus illis, quæ idem Iulius prædecessor in dictis literis uoluit non obstare, cæterisque contrariis quibuscunque. Et quia difficile foret, præsentes literas ad singula loca, in quibus de eis fides forsan fuerit facienda, deferre, uolumus et apostolica auctoritate decernimus, quod ipsarum trans-sumptis manu cuiuscunque notarii publici subscriptis et sigillo alicuius curiæ ecclesiasticæ seu personæ in dignitate ecclesiasticæ constitutæ munitis in iudicio et alibi, ubi opus fuerit, eadem prorsus fides adhibeatur, quæ adhiberetur eisdem præsentibus, si forent exhibitæ vel ostensæ. Datum Romæ apud sanctum Petrum sub annulo piscatoris die 20. Iulii, 1523, pontificatus nostri anno primo primo.

²⁴ Hoc autem non narrasset neque talia iussisset sanctissimus dominus noster, si tales personæ sc. Striges, quæ indicantur hæreticæ, non uero essent hæreticæ, uel si ea, quæ per ipsas fiunt, propter quæ iudicentur hæreticæ, solum essent illusiones diaboli.

²⁵ MS. Sixtus V, Pontifex Maximus, Bibl. Altien., 80 pages.

²⁶ I have used the original publication, "Anno a Natiuitate Domini, Millesimo quingentesimo Octuagesimo sexto," with signature " H. Proilat. Ioannes Baptista Canobius." The *Bullarium Romanum*, " Taurinensis editio " (ed. Sebastian and Henry Dalmazza), 1863, gives this Constitution in Vol. VIII, pp. 646 *sqq.*

²⁷ Cotgrave (1611) has, *Mathematicien :* a Mathematician . . . a caster of nativities.

²⁸ Contra Exercertes Iudiciariæ Astrologiæ Artem Et alia quæcunque diuinationum genera, librosque de eis legentes ac tenentes. Fallaces et uanæ, improborum hominum astutia et dæmonum fraudibus introductæ, ex quorum operatione, consilio uel auxilio omnis diuinatio dimanat. . . . Quæ quidem ipsis cognita sunt, non diuinitate aliqua nec uera futurarum rerum scientia sed naturæ subtilioris acumine, et aliis quibusdam modis, quos hominum obtusior intelligentia ignorat. Quambrem dubitandum non est, in huiusmodi futurorum contingentium et fortuitorum euentuum inquisitione et præcognitione, diaboli operationem se fallaciter immiscere, ut sua fraude ac dolis miseros homines a uia salutis auertat, et laqueo damnationis inuoluat. . . . tales in primis sunt Astrologi, olim Mathematici, Genethliaci, et Planetarij uocati. . . . Alij enim Geomãtiæ, Hydromantiæ, Aeromantiæ, Pyromantiæ, Onomantiæ, Chiromantiæ, Necromantiæ, alijsq ; sortilegijs & superstitionibus, non sine Dæmonũ saltem occulta societate, aut tacita pactione, operam dare, seu illis, ac sortibus illicitis taxillorum, granorum triticeorum, uel fabarum iactu vti non uerentur. Alij item sunt, qui eũ Morte fedus ineunt, & pactũ faciunt cũ Inferno, qui similiter ad occultorũ diuinationem ad inueniendos thesauros, uel ad alia facinora perpetranda, etiã expressa cũ Diabolo pactione facta, in manifestã suarũ perniciem animarũ, nefarias magicæ artis incãtationes, instrumẽta, & ueneficia, adhibent circulos, & diabolicos characteres describunt Dæmones inuocant aut consulunt, ab eis responsa petunt, aut accipiunt, eis preces & thuris, aut aliarum rerum suffimenta, seu fumicationes, aliaue sacrificia offerunt, candelas accendunt, aut rebus sacris, uel Sacramentis, aut Sacramentalibus, sacrilegè abutuntur, adorationis, genuflexionis, aut quæuis alia impietatis obsequia præstant, cultum uenerationemue tribuunt, aut anulum, uel speculum, aut ¹ paruas phyalas sibi fabricant, aut fabricari curant ad Dæmones in eis alligandos, seu includendos, vt putant, ad responsa ab ipsis inde petenda, aut habenda . . . etiamsi in plerisque ex his casibus antea non præcedebant aut procedere non ualebant . . . omnes & singulos libros, opera, & tractatus huiusmodi iudiciariæ Astrologiæ, Geomantiæ, Hydro-mantiæ, Pyromantiæ, Onomantiæ, Chiromantiæ, Necromantiæ, Artis Magicæ, aut in quibus sortilegia, ueneficia, auguria, auspicia, execrabiles incantationes ac superstitiones continentur.

²⁹ *Instruttione al padre Don Tobia Corona, de' chierici regolari, mandato da*

---

¹ S. and H. Dalmazzo, the editors of the *Bullarium Romanum*, VIII, Turin, 1863, omit " aut anulum, uel speculum, aut."

Papa Gregorio XV al re di Francia e prima al duca di Servoia per l'impreso della città di Ginevra. MS. 26 leaves, 4to, Frankfort Library.

[30] S.mi D. N. D. Gregorii, Papæ XV. Constitutio Aduersus Maleficia, se Sortilegia committentes. [Romæ, ex Typographia Reuerenda Cameræ Apostolicæ, MDCXXIII.] Gregorius Papa XV. Ad perpetuam rei memoriam. Omnipotentis Dei Saluatoris Nostri, qui, ut hominem a laqueis Diaboli liberaret, Crucem subire dignatus est, uices, quamquam immeriti, gerentes in terris, in id summo studio, iuxta creditum Nobis desuper Apostolicæ seruitutis officium, incumbimus, ut gregem Dominicum, inæstimabili pretio redemptum, aduersus Sathanæ fraudes defendamus, ciusdem officii partes desuper interponendo, prout conspicimus in Domino salubriter expedire. Sane nonnulli suæ conditionis obliti, et solemnis sponsionis ab iis factæ, cum in Christi gregem per Sacrum regenerationis lauacrum adsciti fuerunt, Sathanæ, cui renunciarunt, artibus, maleficiis, superstitionibus, ac nefariis inventis operam dare non uetentur, quinimo Magistrum imitantes, qui capitali odio, quo humanum genus prosequitur, hominibus insidiari nunquam cessat, proximum uariis modis lædere, animas uero suas perdere, non timent. Quapropter, ut tam exitiosa scelera a Christifidelibus arceantur, grauioribus pœnis uindicanda duximus. Motu itaque proprio, et ex certa scientia, ac matura deliberatione, nostræ deque Apostolicæ potestatis plenitudine, tenore præsentium decernimus, præcipimus, et mandamus, ut constito, quod aliquis pactum cum Diabolo fecerit, et a fide apostatando, maleficiis, siue sortilegiis unam, seu plures personas ita læserit, ut ex maleficio, uel sortilegio mors secuta sit, etiam pro primo lapsu, Curiæ seculari tradatur, debitis pœnis puniendus : Qui uero, similiter apostatando pactum cum Diabolo, ut præfertur fecerit, et maleficium, seu sortilegium commiserit, ex quo, licet mors secuta non sit, infirmitas tamen, diuortia, impotentia generandi, sive animalibus, frugibus, uel aliis fructibus damnum notabile prouenerit, muro claudi, sive perpetuis carceribus in Sancto Inquisitionis officio, ubi illud existit, fabricandis, mancipari debeat : Qui uero similium delinquentium notitiam habuerint, eos Episcopo, sive Inquisitori denunciare teneantur. Non obstantibus constitutionibus, et ordinationibus Apostolicis, ceterisque, contrariis quibuscunque. Uolumus autem, quod præsentium transumptis, etiam impressis, manu alicuius Notarii publici subscriptis, et sigillo alicuius personæ in dignitate Ecclesiastica constitutæ munitis eadem prorsus, fides ubique adhibeatur, quæ eisdem praesentibus adhiberetur, si forent exhibitæ, vel ostensæ ; quodque eædem præsentes, postquam in ualuis Basilicarum Sancti Ioannis Lateranensis, ac Principis Apostolorum de Urbe, et Cancellariæ Apostolicæ, necnon in acie Campi Floræ affixæ fuerint, omnes, et singulos, ad quos spectat, arctent, et efficiant, perinde acsi unicuique personaliter intimatæ fuissent. Dat. Romæ apud Sanctum Petrum sub annulo piscatoris, die 20 Martii MDCXXIII, Pontificatus nostri Anno Tertio. S. Card. S. Susannæ

[31] E.g. Dom Michael Ott, o.s.b., Professor of the History of Philosophy, S. John's University Collegeville, Minnesota, *Gregory XV.*

[32] Romæ, MDCXXXI, Ex Typographia Reu. Cam. Apost. Et Uenetiis, Apud Andream Baba, *Si vende à S. Marco sotto li Portici delle Procuratie noue.* It has been reprinted in the *Bullarium Romanum,* Vol. XIV, 1868, under the supervision of Cardinal Bilio, pp. 211–14.

[33] I, 20. The lines have been translated into Latin by Alciat in his *Emblems.* It is curious that since the walnut tree had so unfortunate a name nuts were scattered among the crowd at a wedding whilst the Fescennines were sung. But so Pliny says, and calls " nuces iuglandes . . . nuptialium Fescenninorum comites." *Historia Naturalis,* XV, 86. One may compare the commentary of Servius on Vergil's *Eclogue VIII,* 29 and 30, where he explains that the nuts were scattered to boys on these occasions " ut significarent se puerilia cuncta iam spernere." In the exquisite *Epithalamium* of Catullus we have :

> Da nuces pueris iners
> Concubine : satis diu
> Lusisti nucibus : lubet
> Iam seruire Thalassio.
> Concubine, nucas da.

[34] J. A. Symonds, *Italian Literature*, XIV.

[35] " Huc illuc uagari solitum fuisse uerosimile putamus. . . . Theophili animus continuis fluctibus iactabatur." *De Theophili Folengi Rebus Gestis et Scriptis*, 3.

[36] I have used the edition Amstelodami, 1769 and 1771, 2 vols., 4to. Amsterdam is doubtless Mantua. My copy was that of the late John Addington· Symonds, and his pencilled notes in the margins are very interesting and valuable.

[37] Folengo jestingly relates that this poem owed its inspiration to a witch of Val Camonica.

[38] Dies Jouis, quibus unctæ Sagæ, ad maleficia peragenda noctu per ærem ferri credunt nimiæ credulitatis mulieres.

[39] Obsequium coram exhibere.

[40] Cum in maleficiis detegerentur Sagæ flammis tradebantur.

[41] *Macaronea XX*.

[42] De spuma quam Rubeta ab ore emittit. *Zatto* in the Mantuan dialect is a toad,

[43] Detestabili sane sacrilegio, qui magicis se artibus addicunt, rebus sacris ad maleficia peragenda abutuntur.

[44] Arcana, quæ in magicis libris, reperiuntur.

[45] Marcidæ.

[46] Parua uasa fictilia.

[47] Dandolo, *La Signora di Monza*, Milano, 1855.

[48] Decrepitæ, quæ terebratis nucibus, et uacuis comparantur.

[49] Sagarum præcepta.

[50] Medullas extrahant.

[51] Sensus est, quomodo efficiant, ut Diabolus formam induat Amasii.

[52] *The Wonderfull Discoverie of Witches* . . . by Thomas Potts, Esq., London, 1613, reprinted by the Chetham Society, J. Crossley, ed., 1845.

[53] Thomas Cooper, *Mystery of Witchcraft*, London, 1617, pp. 90–2.

[54] But the Decretal, for the full text of which see *supra*, p. 583, was issued in 1523, four years after the first edition of Folengo's poem.

[55] I cannot agree with Symonds that " under the allegory of witchcraft, in which at the same time he seems to have believed firmly, Folengo meant to satirise the secret corruption of Society." In 1519 Italian society was notoriously not secretly corrupt. Folengo believed in witchcraft, and every detail is authentic.

[56] Cantù, *Storia della città e della diocesi di Como*, 2 vols, Milan, 1829–31.

[57] *De Strigibus*, c. xiii.

[58] One of the most important and fullest MSS. (Vaticanus 3870) had been brought to Rome, 1428–9.

[59] In ancient days it was the custom to execute criminals here and bury them on the spot. The Esquiline long bore an ugly reputation as witch-haunted, a belief which persisted until the Middle Ages. One may compare Horace, *Sermonum*, I, viii, the traditional rubric to which ran " Conqueritur Priapus Esquilinum montem ueneficarum incantationibus infestari."

[60] There is a pertinent allusion in Folengo, *Macaronea XXI* : Qualiter ad stagnum Nursæ sacrare quadernos.

[61] *Novelle di Antonfrancesco Grazzini detto Il Lasca*, in Londra, 1756, pp. 200–34.

[62] *Compendio delli casi più degni e memorandi occorsi nelli pontificati da Gregorio XIII fino alla creatione di Clemente IX* (1590–1667), MS., 50 leaves. The record would seem to be by more than one hand. It is a collection of notable events and happenings.

[63] A number of witches were burned at Bologna by order of Pope Paul IV (Giovanni Pietro Caraffa), 1555–9.

[64] *Racconto delle cose più considerabili che sono occorso nel governo di Roma in tempo di Monsʳ Gio. Batt. Spada*.

[65] Ripamonte, *De Peste Mediolani*.

[66] *Relazione di Roma in Tempo di Pio IV e V*, Paolo Tiepolo.

[67] *L'Incredulité et Mescreance du Sortilège*, De Lancre, Paris, 1622.

⁶⁸ *La Tradition*, V, p. 215, Van Elven, 1891.
⁶⁹ *Akhelarre* literally means " goat pasture."
⁷⁰ *Basque Legends*, p. 66, Rev. Wentworth Webster, London, 1879, 2nd ed.
⁷¹ *Discoverie of Witches*, Thomas Potts.
⁷² *Welsh Folklore*, J. Ceredig Davies, Aberystwith, 1911, p. 231.
⁷³ *La Corte a la Societa Romana rei XVIII e XIX secoli*, David Silvagni.
⁷⁴ *Etruscan Roman Remains*, p. 238.
⁷⁵ E.g. the Carmelite convent at San Remo. S. Elias is greatly honoured in the Greek Church.
⁷⁶ " Dies assign. ex 8 huius," says the *Officia Sanctorum Pro Ciuitate et Dioccsi Uenetiarum usque nunc Concessa*, 1864.
⁷⁷ Napoli è ricchissima di individui che dicendosi ispirati dal diavolo o dai santi, dànno per pochi soldi i numeri per giocare al lotto e il popolo napoletano—il quale non giureremmo che creda in Dio, ma certamente crede ai santi e al diavolo—ricorre sempre a costoro. . . . Una credenza originalissima di questo popolo . . . è questa : se si trova un prete poco scrupoloso, disposto a leggere il canone e dir la messa in onore del diavolo e a darir la comunione del corpo di Satana, lo spirito maligno—*noblesse oblige*—vi ricompenserà subito dandovi un terno. Questa messa si chiama *messa nera*, e quei preti affamati, sporchi come lazzoroni del porto, che facilmente voi vedrete in giro per le strette e fangose vie della Napoli vecchia, sono continuamente pregati di tal favori. Essi, Talleyrands in sessantaquattresimo, voltanto senza troppa difficoltà le spalle al buon Dio per recitare la *messa nera*. . . . *Auri sacra fames*. Alfredo Niceforo, *L'Italia Barbara Contemporanea*, Milano, 1898, pp. 81–3. An interesting but exaggerated book.

CHAPTER VIII

Spain

The origin of Spanish Christianity is apostolic, and there exists a venerable tradition that not only S. James but also S. Paul visited the Peninsula, which under Roman domination had attained a high estate of culture and civilization. The Spanish calendar boasts a remarkable number of early martyrs, and Prudentius tells us that very many fervent souls witnessed their faith even to blood in every one of the persecutions. During this period, too, important Councils were held in Spain, and in 380 at the Council of Saragossa Priscillianism was expressly condemned. This heresy was derived from the Gnostic. Manichæan doctrines taught by Marcus, an Egyptian from Memphis, one of whose disciples, the rhetorician Helpidius, contrived to seduce Priscillian, "a man of noble birth and great riches, bold, restless, eloquent."[1] In a short time the neophyte became the leader of the party and an ardent propagator of strange and extravagant errors. The foundation of the Priscillianist heresy was the Dualism of Mani, a belief in a kingdom of Darkness which rivalled and might overcome the kingdom of Light. It was taught that the death of Our Lord was phantasmal, and there was much obscure and involved angelology, in which allegory became dogma, and fancy fact. Thus S. Gregory the Great tells us that the Priscillianists imagined that every man was born under the influence of a star, and that his lot was mysteriously fixed by that star, since a new Star was seen when Our Lord was born. "The Boy, however," says the Saint, "was not guided by the star, but the star by the Boy."[2] It is not necessary to pursue these exoteric and esoteric tenets, which in practice led to repellent asceticism on the one hand, such as fasting on Sundays and on Christmas Day, and on the other hand to flagrant indecencies and unashamed immorality of life.

In defiance of the Synod Priscillian was ordained to the priesthood and consecrated Bishop of Avila. The Emperor Gratian, however, issued a decree depriving the Priscillianists of their churches, and the new-made prelate accompanied by certain of his followers presently journeyed to Rome to plead his cause with Pope S. Damasus I, only to find an audience denied. At Milan S. Ambrose refused to receive them or to use his influence on their behalf. They then resorted to bribery and intrigue, and thus won over certain imperial officials by whose offices they were reinstated in at least some of the Spanish cities, whereupon Bishop Ithacius of Ossanova, a strong opponent of the heretics, appealed to Gratian, who, as it happened, was treacherously slain at Lyons 25 August, 383. Maximus, his successor, who had revolted against him, was extremely anxious to gain a secure position, and deeming that it was necessary to placate the orthodox party, gave orders for a synod at Bordeaux in 384. Instantius, one of the leaders of the Priscillianists, was condemned to deposition by the assembly, whereupon Priscillian himself appealed to the Emperor at Treves. The accusations brought against the heretics were so many and so well founded that a sentence of imprisonment was passed whilst future steps should be considered. S. Martin of Tours, who was then at Treves, intervened, and having justly expressed his disapproval of bringing ecclesiastical cases before a civil court, obtained from Maximus a promise that no blood should be shed. After the Saint had left the town, the Emperor appointed the Prefect Evodius, a severe and unyielding magistrate, to try the cause. Ithacius seeing the inevitable sequel now declined to press the charge, but Evodius after a long and careful hearing found Priscillian guilty of lewd imposture, of professing an obscene philosophy, and of black magic.[3] This judgement was reported to the Emperor, who following the rigour of the statute at once ordered Priscillian and some other of his followers to be executed by the headsman on the count of sorcery. In a little while S. Martin, hearing of what had happened, protested energetically and upon his return to Treves rebuked the Emperor face to face; S. Ambrose was equally stern in his denunciation of the proceedings; whilst Pope S. Siricius (elected December, 384) gravely censured both the Emperor and Ithacius, actually excommunicating

Bishop Felix of Treves who pertinaciously defended their proceedings.

A period of some difficulty followed, for the Spanish followers of the heretics increased in numbers and zeal. There can be no doubt that the secret doctrines of the Priscillianists comprised initiation into the lower forms of magic ; Priscillian himself was known to have devoted himself to the close study of occult arts from his earliest years.[4] The upheaval in the Peninsula consequent on the invasion of the Vandals and the Suevi enormously helped the sect, which was not wholly eradicated until the end of the sixth century.

After the sack of Rome by Alaric (410), the Visigoths, or Western Goths, turned towards Spain, and before many years began to extend their rule throughout the country, almost entirely confining the Suevi to Galicia, the independence of which territory was stoutly maintained, although Euric (466), who gave the earliest written laws to the Visigoths, may be considered the first monarch of Spain. The Visigoths were Arians, and in the following reigns the Catholic kings of France appeared as protectors of the Hispano-Roman Catholics. Religious unity was at last obtained by Recared, the brother of S. Hermengild, who had suffered martyrdom for rejecting communion with those who denied the divinity of Christ. Recared accepted the Catholic Faith in the Third Council of Toledo, 589.

One hundred years later saw the decay of the Gothic kingdom. The fanatical hordes of Mahomet were already advancing through North Africa. The last Gothic King of Spain, Roderic, son of Theodofridus, the thirty-third of that line, reigned from 710 to 714. Legend has it that he violated Florinda, La Cara, the beautiful daughter of Count Julian, governor of Ceuta, who in revenge for this dishonour opened to the Moslems the gates of the Peninsula.[5] The battle of Guadelete, when Roderic faced the foe, seems to have been lost through the treachery of the partisans of Witiza, his predecessor on the throne. The Arabs spread rapidly through Andalusia, soon reaching Toledo, the Gothic capital, whilst the Jews, who were numerous in the cities, facilitated their advance. Musa, governor of Barbary, came to share the triumph of the infidel, and in 714 he captured Saragossa, and the period of the domination of the Crescent began.

The Mussulmen occupied Toledo for three hundred and seventy-three years, and Saragossa for rather more than four centuries.[6] Especially in these two cities did they establish their schools of medicine and philosophy, which latter included judicial astrology and other occult lore. Ere long Toledo and Saragossa, as well as the University of Salamanca[7] (at a later date), became notorious throughout Europe as nurseries of the black art. Blessed Gil of Santarem, a Portuguese Dominican, in his youth excelled in scholarship. Whilst on his way from Coimbra to the University of Paris he fell into company with a courteous stranger who offered to teach him magic at Toledo. As payment the stranger, a Satanist, required that Gil should make over his soul to the Devil, and sign the contract with his blood. After complying with these conditions he devoted seven years to goetism and hermetics at Toledo, whence he proceeded to Paris and enjoyed a brilliant career. Repentance, however, came ; he burned his grimoires, and returning to Portugal took the habit of S. Dominic. After a long life of penitence and prayer he died at Santarem, 14 May, 1295, and here his body is still venerated. His cult was ratified by Benedict XIV, 9 March, 1748. His feast is observed 14 May.[8]

The old French romance[9] of the Christian enchanter Maugis (the Malagigi of Ariosto) and his brother Vivian, the sons of Beuves, count of Aigremont, contains some very singular adventures. Maugis acquires the rudiments of magic with supreme ease from the brother of a benevolent fairy, who has rescued him when a babe stolen by a Moorish slave. His first experiment is remarkable. Disguised as the Devil he reaches the isle of Boucault, where he subdues and tames the horse Bayardo, an exploit incidentally which Tasso assigns to Rinaldo. This masquerade as a demon is interesting ; it may hint at the dress and vizard assumed by the Grand Master of a district when he was to preside over a Sabbat in the person of Satan. After various other adventures Maugis gains admittance to the necromantic societies of Toledo, and here he completes his researches into wizardry, ultimately obtaining the professor's chair of sorcery in that occult University.[10]

This almost casual introduction of Toledo in a popular romance as the headquarters of goetic lore and practice is extremely significant. Luigi Pulci (1432–74) also has a pointed reference in the *Morgante Maggiore*, where he writes :

> The city of Toledo erst
> Fostered the lore of necromancy,
> Professors there, in magic versed,
> From public chair taught pyromancy,
> Or geomancy ; or rehearsed
> Experiments in hydromancy.[11]

In the Middle Ages the ignorance of the common folk attached superstitious traditions to many of the greatest names. Blessed Albert Magnus, O.P., " Magnus in magia, maior in philosophia, maximus in theologia " was reported to be an occultist advanced in goetic lore, and even S. Thomas bore the reputation of a magician and a thaumaturge.[12] Thus Blessed Ramón Lull,[13] Doctor Illuminatus, the sweet Catalán poet and profoundest mystic, was vulgarly bruited to be an adept in hidden sciences, a master of secret arts, both lawful and unlawful. No doubt his romantic life, his travels to and fro, and many missionary adventures were utilized to give some colour to the rumour, and so thickly had legend and myth invested his name that even amongst the collected editions of his works which appeared at Mainz from 1734 onwards in ten magnificent folios are included various alchemical treatises. Between alchemy and sorcery popular credulity drew a very thin line of distinction, and it has been well said that " the history of alchemy is, in the first place, a history of fabulous ascriptions."

Official proceedings against Witchcraft are comparatively rare in Spanish history. This is, perhaps, because necromancy and black magic were definitely associated with, if not almost entirely merged in, heresy, and heresy fell under the cognizance of the Holy Inquisition. Thus Nicolas Eymeric, the famous theologian and inquisitor, who was born at Gerona about 1320 and died there 4 January, 1399, in his *Directorium Inquisitorum*, written as early as 1376 (published Barcelona, 1503), particularly emphasizes that any fortune-telling, the fashioning of love amulets, brewing of philtres, or the like must be regarded as coming within the jurisdiction of the Holy Office, more especially as Holy Water and other Sacramentals, the Holy Oils, nay even the Blessed Sacrament itself, are used to confect charms, and this constitutes sacrilege in the highest degree. Sorcerers who give manifest signs of repentance are to be treated leniently and reconciled, but none the less they must always be regarded as suspect of heresy.

It is noticeable that in Spain the regulations of the Papal Bulls dealing with magic were adhered to very closely, and prosecutions were conducted upon the prescribed lines. In 1507 the Inquisition of Calahorra was long busied with an important case, at the conclusion of which thirty women were burned as proven witches. Seemingly no details of the trials are recorded, but in 1512 the assembly of the Cortes at Monzon in Aragon memorialized Ferdinand V, asking him to confine the authority of the Holy Office in charges of sorcery to those issues enumerated in the Apostolic Constitution *Super illius specula* of John XXII (1326). Nor were these representations ineffectual, for an important trial for sorcery which took place in 1527 at Estella in Navarre was relegated to a civil tribunal composed of members of the Royal Council administering that province.

The facts are curious. Two little girls, the elder aged eleven and the younger but nine, presented themselves of their own accord at a sitting of the Council and demanded that their story should be heard. Such insistence seeming unusual their depositions were taken. Both declared they belonged to a sect to which they gave the name *Jurginas*. They were stricken in conscience, and vowed that if their lives were spared and mercy shown them they would deliver over to justice a large number of persons belonging to this secret society of sorcerers who were known to them. There existed a certain occult sign[14] whereby they could recognize any witch who was a member of the coven. In this connexion it is assuredly not impertinent to recall the fact that the Manichæans had " signa oris, manus, et sinus," and Epiphanius gives us particulars of the Grip used by various Gnostic bodies : " On the arrival of any stranger belonging to the same sect, they have a sign given by the man to the woman and *vice versa*. In holding out the hand under the pretence of saluting each other, they feel and tickle it in a particular manner, underneath the palm, and by that means discover whether the new-comer belongs to the same organization." The Albigenses and other dark brotherhoods had words and signs by which they could recognize their fellows without betraying themselves to the uninitiate.[15]   Ivan du Narbonne, a convert from these horrid sects, in a letter to Giraldus, Archbishop of Bordeaux, as cited by Matthew of Paris, says that in every city where he travelled he was always known by cryptic signs.[16]

The Court, then, appointed a Commissary, who, with an escort of fifty well-armed and mounted guardsmen, should bear letters to the provosts and magistrates of the various localities indicated by the two girls.   They were to accompany this band, and any persons whom they pointed out as suspect must be forthwith examined by the authorities and questioned as to their adherence to the infamous *Jurginas*.   A number of wretched hags were thus arrested and when interrogated freely avowed their guilt.   They confessed that they had assisted at the Sabbat, that there they adored the Devil who appeared to them as a monstrous buck-goat, black and loathly.   After having renounced Christ and His Immaculate Mother, Holy Baptism and the Sacraments, they danced an infernal saraband to the shrill skirl of a Zamora cornemuse. The President of the Sabbat obliged them to salute him in an obscene manner, the *osculum infame*, after which disgusting ceremony food was provided.   In Germany, France, and England the banquet at these meetings seems to have been plentiful and rich, the sorcerers gorging and cramming to drunkenness and beastly repletion.   At this repast, on the contrary, only bread and cheese and wine were set before the company.   This homely fare has a parallel in the account given by Goodwife Foster of Salem of the light collation partaken with the Andover coven : " I enquired what she did for Victuals ; She answered that she carried Bread and Cheese in her pocket, and that she and the Andover Company came to the Village before the Meeting began, and sat down together under a tree, and eat their food, and that she drank water out of a Brook to quench her thirst."[17]

The number of persons who acknowledged their guilt is unknown, but there were more than one hundred and fifty witches in the district of Estella alone.   In some few cases the accused confessed that they had destroyed their enemies by secret poisoning, a very common method amongst the members of these dark orders to ensure a complete and speedy fulfilment of their threats and curses. For, as Professor A. J. Clark points out, "the society of witches had a very creditable knowledge of the art of poisoning."[18]

There can, I think, be no doubt in the face of the accumulated evidence that Satanism was fairly extensively spread in the North of Spain. There is no reason to question the truth of these turpitudes, attendance at the Sabbat, renunciation of the Christian Faith, self-devotion to the powers of evil. That various extravagances were boasted and idle fictions born of hysteria and egomania mingled with the tale of actual happenings in no wise discredits the main tenor of the revelations. The Holy Office certainly considered that the crime of sorcery was amply proven, and this judgement seems eminently proper and just. But the Commissary of the Royal Council studiously refrained from exacting the penalty of death. Fifty of the accused were punished with two hundred stripes at the hands of the common hangman and terms of imprisonment extending over several years.

In the same year, however, 1527, as these trials had taken place Charles V, alarmed at the fearful increase of Witchcraft in Biscay, addressed an urgent letter to the Bishop of Calahorra with the Provincials of the Friars Minor and Dominicians bidding them select eloquent and well-approved preachers to travel the country-side from end to end in order that the people might be warned, fortified, and, if need be, converted.

In 1536 the Inquisition of Saragossa arrested and brought to trial a large number of witches who were found to belong to the *Jurginas* and to be assiduously propagating their abominable tenets. Upon examination these wretches were convicted of demonism and every impiety, whereupon by a majority of votes the Tribunal condemned them to suffer at the stake. A minority, however, were for penance and perpetual imprisonment. According to the Constitutions of the Holy Office, which comprise twenty-eight articles, drawn up by the general assembly of Spanish Inquisitors under the presidency of Tomás de Torquemada at Seville, 29 November, 1484, in a case where there is a difference of opinion of this kind among the members of a local Tribunal the matter must be referred to the Suprema. But in this instance after some further discussion the minority agreed to the capital judgement, and the gangs of Satanists were forthwith executed according to law.   None the less so exact was the Inquisition in the observance of its statutes and codes that when a report of the proceedings reached the Suprema, this, the highest court, addressed a circular letter to all the local Tribunals in Spain, sharply reproving the Tribunal of Saragossa, which by not submitting the sentence and the divergement of a minority to the Central Authority for a ruling and direction, had autonomously preferred to settle the question, thus committing a very grave dereliction from duty and obedience. The incident is illuminating, and serves to show that contrary to vulgar opinion and legend a very strict adherence to the Constitutions of the Holy Office was enforced throughout Spain, and that any transgression, however minute or technical, on the part of a local body would promptly meet with animadversion and coercive censure from the Suprema. The reproof administered to Saragossa was not without its effect, since on 12 June the Tribunal of Toledo wrote to the Suprema asking for detailed directions to be followed in the cases of sorcery, and a reply was received which emphasized the provision that if no formal pact with the Devil could be clearly proved the accused was to be remitted to the civil courts for examination and trial.

The parish priest of Bargota, near Viana, in the diocese of Calahorra, who bore a great name for learning and wizardry at the beginning of the sixteenth century, is a very shadowy figure.   Story says that he had the power of transporting himself from place to place in the twink of an eye.   Thus he was invisibly present at many of the engagements of both Ferdinand V and Charles V.   He publicly announced in the streets of Viana and Logrogno the victories gained by these monarchs on the very days their triumphs had been won, news which was afterwards confirmed by couriers from the field.   In fine, the Inquisition of Logrogno took cognizance of these wonders, but he seems to have convinced the Tribunal that his was only white magic, and to have gone scot-free.

A far more illustrious and important person was the *Doctor graduado* Eugenio Torralba.   Born of a good family[19] at Cuenca towards the end of the fifteenth century, at the age of eleven he was sent to Rome where he entered the household of the Bishop of Volterra, Francesco Soderini, a noble prelate who received his hat in May, 1503. Here Torralba studied medicine under the famous physician Cipion and other masters of their art, himself soon attaining no mean skill. Amongst those who frequented the episcopal palace was a certain Fra Pictro, a Dominican. Presently an unusual intimacy based upon similar pursuits was formed between the young doctor and the friar, who in close confidence imparted to his friend that he was attended by an angel or genius named Zequiel (Ezechiel). He was bound by no pact or vow, however, to this spirit upon whom he merely had to call for help to be relieved in any necessity and advised as to his future undertakings. Fra Pietro promised to present Torralba to Zequiel, and at a fitting opportunity the form of a young man with fair hair and a mild countenance stood before them. Addressing the doctor the spirit said : " I will hold myself at your service so long as you live, and I will follow you faithfully wheresoever you go." There was no other suggestion of any bond or agreement between the two. Henceforward Zequiel appeared to the doctor at the quarterly changes of the moon, and more often, whenever he was summoned, 'if there was need of him. Torralba expressly stated that the spirit had never uttered a word contrary to religion, never given him bad counsel, never inspired evil thoughts, and not infrequently even accompanied him to Holy Mass, so that he verily thought an angel was his monitor and guide.

By the time that the Bishop of Volterra was raised to the cardinalate Doctor Torralba already enjoyed a high reputation as a physician, and the new dignity of his patron yet further increased his clientele, whose numbers swelled more and more when it was found he secretly practised chiromancy and could with no small cunning cast a horoscope.

In 1510 Torralba returned to Spain and for a while was held in much esteem at the court of Ferdinand the Catholic. One day Zequiel announced that the King would shortly receive bad news, whereupon the doctor lost no time in warning the first Minister of State and Primate, Cardinal Ximénez de Cisneros, Archbishop of Toledo, as also the famous general Gonzalvo Hernández de Córdova. A few hours later a post arrived in hot haste to announce the crushing disaster which had overwhelmed the expedition against the Moors and that Don Garcia of Toledo, son of Fadrique de Toledo, Duke of Alva, had fallen at the head of his troops. It would almost seem that Torralba made no great secret of his communications with Zequiel. The story goes that Cardinal Ximénez manifested a keen desire to see Zequiel, and that Torralba endeavoured to persuade the spirit to comply with this request, which was, however, denied, the refusal being something mitigated by the prophecy that one day Ximénez would be lord of all Spain, and this proved true six years later, in 1516, when the Cardinal was appointed Regent upon the death of Ferdinand, pending the arrival of Charles V from Flanders. It is true that relying on the authority of a document previously signed by Charles, Adrian Dedel,[20] Dean of the Collegiate Church of S. Peter, at Louvain, claimed the appointment, but the jurists were unanimous in favour of Ximénez, and the Emperor, realizing that he would be more acceptable of the two, confirmed him in the regency whilst Adrian was gratified with the Bishopric of Tortona and the honour of Grand Inquisitor of Aragon. Whilst acting as regent Cardinal Ximénez not only greatly improved the conditions of the army and navy, initiated a new system of taxation and other reforms, but also forced several rebellious cities and nobles to do him homage as the representative of the Emperor. It is in the highest degree unlikely that so pious and rigorous a man should have countenanced any commerce with a spirit, or that he should have expressed a wish to see this supernatural visitor. He was acknowledged even by his opponents to be a prince of the most unstained probity, in public life he was sternly conscientious, whilst in private he carried his austerities and mortifications so far as to endanger his health. The cause of his canonization has been introduced, and indeed he has been for many centuries honoured as a Saint in various districts of the Peninsula. I have no hesitation in dismissing the story that he would have discoursed with Zequiel as an idle and baseless canard.

Many other events are said to have been revealed to Torralba by Zequiel, such as the fearful conspiracy in 1517 of the Cardinal of Siena, Alfonso Petrucci, who had plotted to take the life by poison of the Supreme Pontiff.[21]

The doctor, who had been residing in Rome for some three

years, returned to Spain during 1516, and was at once consulted by Cardinal Bernardino Lopez de Carvajal,[22] a theologian of acknowledged eminence, concerning a dark and mysterious business. A lady of wealth and position had with great trepidation and alarm informed the Cardinal that she was nightly disturbed by the phantom of a man, completely unknown to her, who declared that he had been murdered and unavailingly sought rest. The Cardinal had directed his body-physician Morales to watch with the lady and to report what occurred. Morales for several nights had remained in the chamber but could discern nothing, although at a certain hour he felt a chill as if of the grave, accompanied by a loathly smell of corruption which filled him with no ordinary horror and fear, whilst the lady cried out that the ghost had appeared. Cardinal Carvajal, knowing Torralba's deep studies in occultism, prayed him to join Morales at the next opportunity, and accordingly the two doctors took their station in the haunted room. About one o'clock they heard an anguished cry, the air grew deathly cold and was foul with the stench of human decay. Torralba saw by the bed the figure of a man covered with wounds, the countenance distorted and pale with pain. A little further there lurked an even more terrifying apparition, the half-formed shadow of an evil woman, her vile face leering horribly from the darkness. " What would you ? " demanded the scryer. " The treasure ! the treasure ! " moaned the vision. Upon being questioned, Zequiel informed Torralba that in a cellar long years before had been buried the body of a miser, assassinated, all unshriven and unhouseled, for the vast sums it was known he had concealed in the house. The woman, whose spectre had been seen, was his servant who had admitted the ruffians with whom she was in league, but after the murder they could not find the hiding-place of the money-bags, and so perforce remained unsatisfied. The crime had never been discovered. Zequiel revealed the sliding panel which gave access to the secret room where the wealth was stored, and which actually opened out of the lady's bed-chamber. The money was thus recovered, a part was devoted to masses for the dead man's soul, the remainder to other pious and charitable uses, and so the unhappy and unquiet house found rest.

In 1517 Torralba returned to Rome, and here he formed ties of closest intimacy with Don Diego de Zugniga, a near relation of the Duke de Bejar, and brother of Don Antonio de Zugniga, Grand Chancellor of the Order of Saint John in Castile.[23]   Only two years had passed when the two friends together returned to Spain.   On their journey they halted for some time at Barcelonnette, then a town of Savoy, where they became acquainted with Azevedo, an officer of some distinction, who had been adjutant-general of the Spanish forces in Italy.   One day whilst they were sitting and talking of hermetic philosophy Zugniga and Azevedo thought that they saw a shadow, as it were, swiftly pass into the room and after a moment as swiftly disappear.   Torralba at the same instant informed them that Zequiel had just conveyed to him certain news.   From that moment Zugniga continually pressed the doctor to allow him an interview with the spirit, but his most earnest entreaties were withstood, and at last as he became over-importunate smartly rebuffed, a check which, although at the time he showed disappointment rather than displeasure, rankled sourly and was to have its consequences.   When Barcelona was reached Torralba and Zugniga held many secret interviews with a canon of the Cathedral, Don Juan Garcia, a mysterious personage, in whose library were several books of necromancy, on the margin of a leaf of one of which Torralba perceived a magic formula enabling him who wore it about his person infallibly to gain at cards, hazard, or any game of chance.   This the doctor transcribed and presented to Zugniga, bidding him make a copy thereof in his own hand on a Wednesday (miércoles),[24] the day dedicated to Mercury,[25] god of sharpers and thieves.[26]   The story goes that Zugniga was in truth supremely lucky at the tables and won large sums of money at ombre, raffle, and other games, although some attributed his fortune to high-running dice and sleight-o'-hand rather than to mystic runes and sigils.

Upon one occasion, in 1527, Torralba announced to Zugniga that he was about to pay a visit to Rome, and when the latter inquired how long he purposed to be absent from Valladolid,[27] where they were then residing, he answered but a few hours as he had a means of aerial transport that would convey him to and fro with supernatural speed.   This journey,

which was asserted to have taken place on 4–5 May, enabled
the doctor actually to be present at the sack of Rome by the
Lutheran hordes under their bandit leaders, and as he made
no secret, but rather boasted, of the remarkable journey
it is not surprising that it was widely discussed on every side
and is perhaps the most notorious of his exploits. So curious
is the narrative that it is worth while giving Torralba's own
account which he naïvely detailed when examined before the
Tribunal of the Holy Inquisition.[28] " Interrogated whether
the same spirit, ZEQUIEL, had ever corporally removed him
from one place to another, and in what manner, he made
answer in the affirmative ; that being in Valladolid, in the
month of May last (1527), the said Zequiel had told him that
Rome was sacked and entered the very hour that event
happened, and that he had repeated what Zequiel told him,
and the Emperor had heard of it ; but he did not himself
believe it ; and that the following night, Zequiel perceiving
that he would not believe it, persuaded him to go with him,
and that he would carry himself to Rome, and bring him home
again the same evening. And it was so ; for at four o'clock
they both went out of the gates of Valladolid, and being
without the city, the said spirit thus enjoined him : ' Have
no fear, no ill shall befall you ; take this in your hand.'
(*No haber paura ; fidate de me ; que yo te prometo que no
tiendras ningun displacer ; per tanto piglia aquesto in mano.*)
And it appeared to him that the thing which was put into
his hand was a knotty stick ; and the spirit said : ' Shut
your eyes, Torralba,' (*cerra occhi*) and he did so ; and when he
opened his eyes again, he saw the sea as if it were so near that
he could touch it with his hands ; and when he opened them
again he perceived a great obscurity, as if it had been a cloud,
and then again a great brightness, from which he was filled
with dread and alarm, and the spirit said to him : ' Fear not,
ignorant beast ' (*Noli timere, bestia fiera*), and he did so.
And they went on, and in about the space of half an hour he
found himself in Rome upon the streets ; and the spirit asked
him where he thought he was (*dove pensate che state adesso ?*)
and that he told him. That he stood on the *Torre di Nona*,[29]
and heard the clock on the Castle of S. Angelo strike five ;
and that they talked and walked together as far as the *Torre
Sant Ginian*, where he saw the Bishop Copis, a German ; and

that they saw many houses sacked and pillaged, and observed everything that was passing in Rome,[30] and then came back in the same manner to Valladolid (from which he thought he might have been absent in all an hour and a half), and so he betook himself to his own lodging, which is near the monastery of San Benito." Torralba immediately published abroad all that he had done and seen to the universal astonishment of the city.

It will be remembered that Cervantes alludes to this celebrated voyage in *Don Quixote* (Part II, Chapter XLI) where the Knight and Sancho, blindfold, are mounted on Clavileno, the wooden horse, and apparently whisking through the upper air. " I remember," says the don, " the strange, but true story, of Doctor Torralba, whom the devil carried to Rome hoodwinked, and, bestriding a reed, in twelve hours' time setting him down in the tower of Nona, in one of the streets of that city. There he saw the dreadful tumult, assault, and death of the Constable of Bourbon ; and, the next morning, he found himself at Madrid, where he related the whole story. Among other things, he said, as he went through the air, the devil bid him open his eyes, which he did, and then he found himself so near the moon, that he could touch him with his finger ; but durst not look towards the earth, lest the distance should make his brains turn round."[31]

In 1528 Torralba was at Cuenca where also Don Diego Zugniga happened to be sojourning. This latter, stricken in conscience, and ashamed of his long life of trickery and flat cheating at the gaming tables, began very seriously to examine his estate. He realized that he had been the sport of evil influences, and made full confession of his guilty practices, denouncing the doctor to the Inquisition as a sorcerer. The nets must have been drawing around Torralba for some time, and an explicit accusation at once fast tightened the cords. The doctor was arrested, thrown into prison, and examined before the tribunal. The process lasted many months. Torralba frankly acknowledged his intercourse with Zequiel, who was, he maintained, a good spirit, perhaps an angel. In May, 1525, however, the proceedings suddenly ceased, and for some reason were held in abeyance for a full year. After this fresh charges were brought. It was deposed that the doctor whilst at Rome had expressed doubts as to the divinity of Christ and the immortality of the soul. The case took on a far more serious aspect, and was reported by the Tribunal of Cuenca to the Suprema, at whose appointment Fray Agustin Barragan, Prior of the Dominican house at Cuenca, and Don Diego Manriquez, a canon of the Cathedral, with some two of three assessors sat to try the prisoner. After a patient hearing, on 6 March, 1531, he was condemned to make a formal and public abjuration of all heresy and magic, to strict confinement, and to wear the *san-benito* at the good pleasure of the Grand Inquisitor. A clause was particularly inserted whereby he swore to hold no further communication with the spirit Zequiel. At the time of his arrest Torralba had newly been appointed body-physician to the Admiral of Castile, Don Federico Enriquez, and there can be no doubt that his patron intervened on his behalf, since no long while after sentence we find that the Grand Inquisitor, "in view of his sincere and sore repentance," allowed Torralba to be set at liberty and reinstated in the Admiral's household.

It is true that Pellicer, the famous editor of Cervantes, has a note to the effect that Doctor Eugenio Torralba was condemned to death as a sorcerer by the Holy Office, and executed 6 May, 1531. This, however, is certainly erroneous.

It was this sounding scandal that caused Don Alfonso Manriquez, the Grand Inquisitor, to publish certain articles detailing crimes which every good Christian was bound to denounce to the local tribunal. Don Alfonso had been elected to his high office on 10 September, 1523, his predecessor having been Adrian, Bishop of Tortosa, who as Adrian VI ascended the papal throne on 9 January, 1522. The offences which a man was in duty required to make known were as follows :

1. If he knew or heard of any person who entertained and rewarded familiars and flies,[32] who invoked spirits by describing goetic circles and asked them questions, who had made any agreement, tacit or explicit, with a demon ; who sought to use holy objects for purposes of divination, who in a word gave the creature that honour due to the Creator alone.

2. If any person in order to discover either secrets or the future employed geomancy, hydromancy, aeromancy, pyro-

mancy, anthropomancy, theriomancy, kleromancy, oneiro-
mancy, kapnomancy, knissomancy, koskinomancy, astragalomancy, krithomancy, alphitomancy, tessaromancy, necromancy, or any other magic craft,

3. If any person made use of circles, partagons, or any other
such sign and symbol for purposes of invoking demons ; if he
offered them incense or the fume of other burning substances ;
if he should sacrifice unto them ; if he should abuse in their
honour the Sacraments ; if he should adore them, or pay them
any homage in any manner whatsoever.

4. If any person employed judicial astrology to discover
the future by those stars which had been in conjunction at the
conception or birth of any individual consulting him, or if he
should foretell good and evil from planetary influences.

5. If any person made or caused to be made mirrors, rings,
phials of glass or other vessels in order thereby to control or
therein to contain some spirit who should reply to his
inquiries and aid his projects ; if he should invoke a spirit
even under the name of an Angel with prayer and fasting ;
if he should practise superstitious ceremonies with basins of
fair water and blessed tapers ; if he should inspect the nails
or the palm of the hand after rubbing it with vinegar ; if he
should reveal the future by phantom shows or images in a
mirror.

6. If any person should keep and read grimoires or books
of magic, or manuscripts of this kind, excepted always such
volumes as might appertain to medicine and surgery.

In the face of these injunctions we are not surprised to read
in *Don Quixote*, Part II, Chapter LXII, that when at Barcelona Don Antonio Moreno shows the knight the Enchanted
Head, fashioned by a disciple of the famous wizard Michael
Scot, he exacts a vow of solemn secrecy. The Head, which
resembled the bust of a Roman Emperor, is supposed to
answer all questions which are put to it, and when interrogated by a small and select company it indeed replies in a
most surprising manner. The trick is, of course, that the
Head and the table whereupon it stands are hollow, and
through the cavities is conveyed a pipe, which piercing the
floor enters another room. Thence Don Antonio's nephew,
a clever youth, who has been previously well coached, returns
the answers and is able to hit upon some smart and apt

sentences. The whole thing is a jest, " but, at last, the noise of Don Antonio's having an Enchanted Head in his house that gave answers to all questions began to fly about the city ; and, as he feared this would reach the ears of the watchful sentinels of our faith, he thought fit to give an account of the whole matter to the reverend Inquisitors, who advised him to break it to pieces, lest it should give occasion of scandal among the ignorant vulgar." This entertaining episode in Cervantes' immortal romance is interesting for the accidental light it throws upon the caution it was necessary to observe when one even feigned a magic feat for the sake of a practical joke.

With reference to the belief that spirits could be imprisoned in vessels of glass[33] it may be remembered that Don Cleofas, the hero of *El Diabolo Coxuelo* by Luis Velez de Guevara (first printed in 1641), having accidentally entered the abode of an astrologer delivers from a bottle wherein he had been confined by a potent charm el diabolo coxuelo who richly rewards his liberator. Perhaps the situation is even better known owing to *Le Diable Boiteux* and the release of Asmodée, all of which Le Sage has amply borrowed from the Spanish work. In Guevara's romance we also have the sketch of the hypocrite who is rubbing himself with grease " in order to go to a meeting of sorcerers this night between San Sebastian and Fontarabia." The familiar adds : " I would carry you thither this minute, to oblige you with so pleasant a diversion, if I was not afraid of being known by the Devil, who personates the goat there." Such are the sorcerers who appear in Goya's pictures of the Sabbat, or that loathly bloated witch whom he has drawn as she stands with uplifted finger, menacing and horrible to see, by the bedside of the trembling peasants in the dead of night.

As in France we find the possession of the Ursulines of Aix, the Brigittines of Lille, the Ursulines of Loudun ; in Germany the terrible story of the Nobertines of Unterzell; so in Spain we have a record of diabolic attacks upon religious, convents being the strongholds of the faith, against which evil influences may assuredly concentrate their malice. Magdalena de la Cruz was born in 1487 of poor parents at Aguilar de la Frontera. From her earliest years her tender devotion was admired by all, and when she was but a maid of twelve she passed for a saint, a little later miracles even were attributed to her prayers. In 1504, when scarce seventeen, she took the Franciscan habit in the strict house of S. Elizabeth at Cordova, and in 1533 she became Abbess of the community. At two successive Councils in 1536 and 1539 she was re-elected, since for nearly forty years there was no name so venerated throughout Cordova, and indeed all Spain, as her own. Not only the poor and the citizens of the town thronged to see her, but also professors, doctors, other religious, lords and great nobles, bishops, archbishops, and cardinals themselves. The Cardinal of Seville, Don Alfonso Manriquez, Inquisitor-General, journeyed to Cordova expressly to converse with her, and in letters saluted her as *dearest daughter in Christ*, earnestly recommending himself to her prayers. The Inquisitors of Cordova showed her high honour, and the holy Francisco de Quiñones, to be one of the most famous members of the Sacred College, traversed many miles solely to obtain a sight of the Abbess of S. Elizabeth. Even the papal nuncio Giovanni da Reggio came to Cordova in great pomp on the same errand, and the Empress Isabel, proudest of queens, wrote to Magdalena, addressing her as *my dearest Mother*, sending her portrait as a gift to the community who had it hung in the parlour, and at the birth of the Infante Philip (afterwards Philip II) requesting the nun to bless her baby's chrisom cloth and baptismal robes of white.[34] Indeed, so many persons of high estate and widest influence flocked to Cordova to consult the Abbess that it was said her convent resembled an imperial chancellery.[35]

On every side nothing was heard but her praises. People talked loudly of her rapts, her ecstasies, her gift of prophecy. She foretold his approaching death to the Marquis de Vilena when he was in robust health and seemed to have many more years of life ; she announced to the General of her Order, Francisco de Quiñones, that he would one day receive the scarlet hat, and years after, in September, 1528, he was created Cardinal of S. Croce in Gerusalemme ; she predicted the captivity of Francis I and his marriage with Leonor, Queen of Portugal, the sister of Charles V.

Magdalena had been re-elected Abbess of S. Elizabeth in 1539, but in 1542 at the triennial council it was seen that a certain section of the community was opposed to her and endeavoured not without success to deprive her of the superiorship. It had been bruited and was piously believed by many that the holy nun neither ate nor drank, living only upon the Blessed Sacrament, a phenomenon which is not altogether rare in the lives of the Saints. In the eighth century S. Walburga, who had the reputation of only existing on the Eucharistic species, was placed under supervision for many days and nights and it was seen that the report was true. In 1225 Hugh de Wells, Bishop of Lincoln (1209–35) and Chancellor of England, having heard that a nun of Leicester had been sustained seven years by Holy Communion alone, refused to believe it and deputed not one, but fifteen ecclesiastics, to watch her for a fortnight without losing sight of her for a moment. It was only after this severe trial that the prelate declared himself amply convinced. S. Angela of Foligno remained twelve years without any nourishment save the Bread of Heaven ; S. Catherine of Siena eight years ; S. Lydwine of Scheidam twenty-eight ; Blessed Elizabeth of Reute more than fifteen years ; Blessed Catherine of Racconigi ten years ; Domenica of Paradise twenty ; and in recent times Rosa Andriani twenty-eight years ; Domenica Lazzari and Louise Lateau fourteen years. During his sojourn at Perugia Pope Innocent VIII caused a searching judicial inquiry to be made into the case of Blessed Colomba of Rieti, who had taken no nourishment save the Host for more than twenty years. In 1659 the famous shepherdess of Laus was taken to the Bishop's house at Ernbrun and guarded strictly for fifteen days every minute of the twenty-four hours, her inedia was then adjudged supernatural. In 1813 that wonderful mystic Anne Catherine Emmerich, whose abstinence was no less remarkable, was watched closely for ten days, and a report drawn up by the famous Dr. Overberg. In 1868 the abstinence of Sister Espérance of Jesus was officially confirmed by the Bishop of Ottawa assisted by two physicians, one, Dr. Baubien, a Catholic, the other, Dr. Ellis, a Protestant. She was rigorously guarded for six weeks by nurses who never left her. From 25 October to 7 December, 1877, the abstinence of Josephine Reverdy was examined in like manner. She was guarded by relays of five trained matrons, and the authenticity of the fact recognized.[36]

Not only do these abstaining saints eat nothing secretly, but often they can no longer receive food without throwing it up again immediately. They are so advanced in the paths of perfection that the Bread of Angels is the only nourishment they desire or can sustain.[37]

It was to this extraordinary gift that Magdalena de la Cruz laid claim, and many hailed the phenomenon as a mark of unusual sanctity. However, it was discovered in the convent that she privily obtained bread and water and other refreshments. As was inevitable, she was sharply rebuked and penanced in chapter for venturing so audaciously to foster a fraud. She retaliated by diverting the rich stream of alms and bequests which was constantly flowing in upon her and which she had employed upon the house to other and exterior purposes. The new Abbess, a superior of singular acuteness and perception, soon began to entertain shrewd suspicions concerning the reputed saint, but she prudently hesitated before she took action or gave any indication that she guessed all was not fair and well. It was natural, too, that many among the Sisters should be troubled at the flagrant deception in which Magdalena had been discovered, and where peace had formerly reigned mistrust made its sinuous way. Better the truth, however harsh and cruel, than a false painted show, a mockery and a mumming.

During the year 1543 Magdalena was seized with an unusual sickness, and before long it was clear that no ordinary guilt laid heavy upon her soul. A letter, dated 30 January, 1544, written by a Sister of the same community, gives us ample details of the terrible story. The physicians who had been called in to consult upon the invalid pronounced her state to be desperate and bade her prepare for death. Thereupon her confessor presented himself to shrive his penitent and otherwise encourage her in good dispositions to receive the last Sacraments. To the amazement and terror of those who were kneeling by her bed convulsions suddenly seized the unhappy woman. She writhed and twisted her limbs with the most indecent acrobatism so that she could hardly be held in her place, all the while she yelled and screeched the foulest obscenities, blaspheming like a maniac, biting and snapping at those who approached, her eyes blazing with fury, and foam dripping from her swelled and champing lips. The priest retired appalled at the sight. On the morrow and on the third day when he entered the room the same fits were renewed with increased violence. At length realizing that here was some diabolic disorder he exorcized the sick nun. The contortions passed, to be succeeded by what seemed an attack of chorea, when she presently made a long and awful confession.

She had been debauched and given over to evil from her earliest years ; when she was as yet but a child of five a strange apparition, much like an Angel, visited her without awaking any alarm, and by announcing that she was destined to become a great saint fanned the smoky fires of the sin of presumption. Two years later further apparitions encouraged her in her folly and pride, and in spite of her secret malpractices she beheld the form of the Crucified, to whom she was wedded, as it were, with spiritual espousals. The source of these appearances was none other than the Demon. It is the constant teaching and tradition of the Catholic Church that the Devil has the power of transforming himself into an Angel of light, and that he has dared to assume the sensible exterior of Our Lord or the Saints. There are numberless instances which testify to this : such are especially remarkable in the life of S. Antony written by S. Athanasius, that of S. Benedict by S. Gregory the Great, and other Fathers. Among more recent occurrences of the nineteenth century, it is enough to call to mind the apparitions and other diabolical delusions of Pierre-Michel Ventras at Tilly (Calvados), and their condemnation by that saintly Pontiff Gregory XVI in 1843. Fraudulent phenomena can, however, always be detected by the person thus visited. S. Teresa gives holy humility as a sure test of this, for she teaches : " I look upon it as a most certain truth that the Devil will never deceive, and that God will not suffer him to deceive the soul which has no confidence whatsoever in itself . . . seeking for further light on this side and on that."[38] Benedict XIV also has many shrewd directions which will infallibly distinguish a false vision from a true and divine manifestation.[39] If it be the former some mark of its evil origin may assuredly be discerned by close observation, some hideous trait will be shown beneath the mask of goodness and beauty.

The appearances which visited Magdalena carefully coached her in trickery and deception so that she was enabled to perform seeming miracles, wonders which she herself knew were mere cozenage and therefore must have had an origin more than suspect. She became puffed up with pride and rejoiced to hear herself everywhere saluted as a Saint. When the sin of pride had wholly possessed her heart, lust soon followed. The Demon showed himself to her as a handsome youth and informed her that he was one of those angels who had fallen from Heaven. The name by which he desired to be known was Balban, and yet another spirit Pithon, his comrade, also desired her. He promised her that if she would consent to their solicitations he would ensure her the reputation of a saint upon earth. The wretched girl consented, and actually entered into an explicit contract with the familiars, devoting her body to every excess of lechery whereby they chose to defile and abuse her. After she had taken the veil it was Balban who helped her to carry out her infamous and profane mummery throughout the convent years. He threw her into trances, such as modern mediums use, and hypnotic slumbers which were taken to be ecstasies and rapts. He informed her of events to come[40] so that she could ape the gift of prophecy. It was he who raised her from the earth when it was believed she was levitated. He further manifested himself so as to be seen by the entire community, once even under the form of a baby in her arms, when she declared she was fondling the Infant Jesus, and occasionally as some good angel or Saint. In fine, her life for many long years had been a tissue of blasphemies, licentiousness, and imposture. She had not infrequently availed herself of her position in the house to leave the enclosure secretly at night in order to attend meetings of Satanists in the town.

As has been stated the first suspicions were aroused when it was discovered that her claim to live upon the Blessed Sacrament alone was a mere pretence, and that she was well supplied with food which she devoured in private at times she deemed herself unseen. So vile an imposture wrecked her opinion for sanctity. Upon hearing the hideous truth the confessor enjoined her to make an open acknowledgement before the community to whom such scandal had been given.

This she did, and shortly afterwards the Provincial of the Franciscans with his socius and other reverend assessors made a special journey to Cordova in order that they might fully investigate these terrible businesses. Magdalena, whose health after her confession had suddenly and surprisingly improved, now retracted all she had said, and denied with horrid imprecations that she had ever consorted with demons and Satanists. It seemed as if she had again fallen under the thrall of the Evil One, but owing to the exhortations and pious prayers of her confessor, who assured her that only by an open discovery of her guilt and due penitence could she hope for pardon, she at length reiterated on the 24 December, 1543, in the presence of the Provincial and his colleagues, the representatives of the Holy Office, and other priests of honour and learning, all she had admitted and avowed. She was accordingly placed under formal arrest and lodged in the prisons of the Inquisition. Her trial and examination were conducted with extraordinary patience and care. On 13 May, 1546, she was obliged to walk in an *auto-da-fé*. Clad in her religious habit but without the veil, a cord about her neck, and a lighted candle in her hand, she was conducted to the Cathedral of Cordova,[41] and here she was placed upon a high scaffold whilst the sentence was read aloud. This was followed by a sermon denouncing her crimes, as was usual in such circumstances. She was condemned to spend the rest of her days in a cloister of the strictest Franciscans, situate a few miles beyond the town. She was deprived of all rights and privileges as a member of the community, she might not wear the veil, and every Friday she fasted on bread and water. She was not to speak to any save her confessor, or in case of grave necessity the superiors. Holy Communion was granted her but once in every three years, unless a serious illness rendered advisable the Viaticum. When one considers her blasphemies and Satanic impostures, her debaucheries and ninefold guilt, the scandal given to all Spain and all the faithful, the sentence cannot be pronounced severe.

No doubt in the case of Dr. Torralba, as in the case of Magdalena la Cruz, there is much which may be explained by hallucination, coincidence, hysteria. There is much exaggeration, and a quota of legend. That Dr. Torralba played—perhaps half-unconsciously—the rôle of wise man and even magician in order to impress the vulgar seems very certain. With regard to the Abbess of S. Elizabeth I agree with Simon Maiolo[42] that there are many proven facts in this history it seems impossible to account for unless one allow that there was some connexion or communication with dark influences and entities. If we read her confession in view of the more secret, and I will add loathly, phenomena of modern spiritism much may be understood and accepted which at first sight might be pronounced incomprehensible and impossible. We are hardly surprised to learn that even after Magdalena had been imprisoned and when she was confined according to her sentence in the remote convent, the cloisters of S. Elizabeth were disturbed by uncanny sounds, and the nuns scared by strange sights and shadowy figures lurking in those haunted walls.

Throughout the records of the Holy Office some infrequent cases of sorcery are to be found, but these are almost without exception resolved into trials for heresy, and a condemnation for Witchcraft alone is of the rarest.

At the present day, as in England, France, Italy, Germany, and indeed all countries of the world, old beliefs and old superstitions linger among the peasantry of Spain in the smaller and more distant villages. Reputed witches may be found everywhere the whole world over, and everywhere are there those who lack not the will if they have not the power to maim and kill by Witchcraft, for, as S. Augustine says, in many more ways than one does man sacrifice to the evil angels.

NOTES TO CHAPTER VIII

[1] Sulpicius Severus, *Historia Sacra* (*Chronicorum Libri duo*), II, 46. Migne, *Pat. Latini*, XX.

[2] Priscillianistæ hæretici nasci unumquemque hominem sub constitutionibus stellarum putant : et hoc in adiutorium sui erroris assumunt, quod noua stella exiit cum Dominus in carne apparuit : . . . Non Puer ad stellam, sed stella ad Puerum cucurrit. *Homilia X in Euangelium secundum Matthæum.*

[3] Jacob Bernays, *Uber die Chronik des Sulpicius Severus*, Berlin, 1861, pp. 13–17.

[4] " Idem [Priscillianus] uanissimus et plus iusto inflatior prophanarum rerum scientia : quin et magicas artes ab adolescentia eum exercuisse creditum est." Sulpicius Severus, *Hist. Sacra*, II, 47.

[5] This is the subject of William Rowley's tragedy *All's Lost by Lust*, 4to, 1633, but acted a decade or more earlier.

[6] Saragossa was reconquered by Alfonso I of Aragon, 18 December, 1118.

[7] Founded in the twelfth century.

[8] Bollandists, 14 May. Touron, *Histoire des hommes illustres de l'ordre de Saint Dominique*, Paris, 1743.

[9] *La, tres playsante hystorye de Maugist Daygremont et de Uiuian son frere, en laquelle est contenu cóment Maugist a layde de Orlande la Face samye alla en lysle de Boucault ou il schabilla en diable. Et puis commét il enchanta le deable Raouart, et occist le serpent qui gardoit la roche par laquelle chose il conquist le cheual Bayard et aussi conquesta le grant Geant Sorgalant.* A. Lotrain, Paris, 4to. Brunet gives no date, but considers that an impression of the romance by T. Trepperel, Paris, which bibliographers have recorded, is even earlier. There are numerous subsequent issues.

[10] Maugis continues his enchantments in *La cōsqueste du trespuissant empire de Tresbisonde et de la spacieuse Asie.* He also plays a great part in *Quatre fils Aymon*, whilst the concluding scenes of his life are told in the *Histoire singuliere & fort recreatiue Cótenát la reste des faits & Gestes des quatre fils Aymon. . . . Et de leur cousin Maugis,* . . . a work usually known as the *History of Mabrian.*

[11]   Questa città di Tolletto solea,
  Tenere studio di Negromanzia,
  Quivi di magica arte si leggea
  Publicamente, e di Piromanzia ;
  E molti Geomanti sempre avea
  E sperimenti assai di Hidromanzia.
                Canto XXV.

[12] See Gabriel Naudé, *Apologie pour tovs les grands hommes* . . . Paris, 1625, and William Godwin's *Lives of the Necromancers*, 1835.

[13] The feast of the Beato Ramón, Martyr, is celebrated by the Order of S. Francis on 4 July, as a semiduplex.

[14] This is said to have been a peculiar cast (known in France as *pathe de crapaud*) in the left eye. But it was obviously some grip or motion with the hand, no mere blemish or disfigurement. See *Historia de la Vida y hechos del emperador Carlos V*, by Bishop Prudencio Sandoval.

[15] Muratori, *Antiquitates italicæ medii œui*, V.

[16] Gabriele Rossetti, *Disquisitions*, Vol. I, p. 27.

[17] G. L. Burr, *Narratives of the Witchcraft Cases*, p. 418.

[18] *Apud* Miss M. A. Murray's *The Witch-Cult in Western Europe*, Appendix V, p. 279.

[19] Zapata in his *Carlos famoso* calls him *familiar del admirante*, which would seem to imply that he was in some way distantly connected with the Admiral of Castille.

[20] Who succeeded Pope Leo X and reigned from 9 January, 1522, to 14 September, 1523. Adrian VI (the last *Pontefice barbaro*, Guiccardini, XIV, v) is the only Pope of modern times, except Marcellus II (1555), who retained his baptismal name when crowned. Marcellus II was Marcello Cervini degli Spannochi.

[21] For details of these terrible happenings see Guiccardini, XIII ; and Paolo Giovio, *Uita Leonis X.* Roscoe, *Leo the Tenth*, chap. 14, gives a trustworthy account of the proceedings.

[22] Born at Plasencia, Estremadura, 1455 ; died at Rome, 16 December, 1523.

[23] The Hospitallers of S. John of Jerusalem, a very ancient Order. Known as Hospitallers of Jerusalem until 1309, the members were called Knights of Rhodes from 1309–1522, and have been named Knights of Malta since 1530. The Knights of Rhodes comprised eight chief nations, and one of the eight supreme dignities was reserved to each several nation, to Italy admiral, to England turcopolier, to Aragon standard-bearer, to Castile grand chancellor, etc.

[24] *Dies Mercurii*, or, *dies Mercuris*, Wednesday. *Inscriptiones Muratorii*, 402, 7.

[25] Mercurius a mercibus est dictus. Hunc etenim negotiorum omnium æstimabant esse deum. *Apud* the abstract from Sextus Pompeius Festus, the grammarian, made by Paulus, Ed. K. O. Müller (1839), p. 124.

[26] Cf. Dryden's *Amphitryon ; Or, The Two Socia's*, produced 1690, 4to 1690, II. *Mercury :* Suppose I were *Mercury*, the God of Merchandise ? *Phœdra :* What, the God of small Wares, and Fripperies, of Pedlars and Pilferers ? V.—*Phœdra :* Begin, begin ; Heads of Articles to be made, &c. betwixt *Mercury*, God of Thieves——

[27] Zapata says that Torralba was at Medina de Riosseo, but in his own confession before the tribunal of the Holy Office the doctor said Valladolid.

[28] In 1528. The record has been printed by Pellicer, whence this translation is made.

[29] One of the towers on the walls. It was fortified by Alexander VI, who thus protected the Eternal City from naval attacks. Later the Torre di Nona served as a strong prison. In 1567 the heretic Pietro Carneseechi—executed in October of that year—was incarcerated here.

[30] A vivid description of the unexampled horrors of the pillage of Rome may be read in Valeriano's dialogue *De Literatorum Infelicitate.* I have used the Venice edition of 1620.

[31] Translation by Motteux. I quote from Lockhart's edition, 4 vols., 1885.

[32] A fly is a familiar. Cf. Jonson, *The Alchemist*, acted 1610, 4to 1612, I 2 :

Subtle : If I do give him a familiar,
　　Give you him all you play for ; never set him :
　　For he will have it.
Face :　Y'are mistaken, Doctor.
　　Why, he do's aske one but for cups, and horses,
　　A rifling flye : none o' your great familiars.

[33] In the *Uinculum Spirituum* it is related that Solomon imprisoned three millions of infernal spirits with seventy-two of their kings in a bottle of black glass, which he cast into a deep well near Babylon. The Babylonians, however, hoping to find a treasure in the well, descended, and broke the bottle, thus releasing these legions of darkness. The story of the Djin and the Fisherman in *The Thousand and One Nights* is familiar to all. As the idea of enclosing demons in phials is Oriental it has been pertinently suggested that the Moors introduced this fantasy into Spain.

[34] The Empress was profoundly assured of the great destiny which awaited her son. She deemed that any manifestation of pain or weakness during her delivery might detract from the dignity of the occasion. One of her Portuguese ladies, fearing that this effort of self-control on the part of the Empress would add to her sufferings, begged her to give natural vent to her feelings as she lay in the agonies of labour.—" Silence ! " said the mother, " die I may, but lament and make womanly moan I will not." She then ordered that her face should be hidden from the light, that no involuntary sign of pain should be seen.

[35] Llorente, *Histoire critique de l'Inquisition d'Espagne*, II, p. 104.

[36] *Apparitions de Boullent*, chap. v, where full details are given.

[37] These fasts are clearly different from the feats performed by certain *fasting men* who have attracted considerable notice from time to time in European and American capitals, such performers as Tanner, Succi, Merlatti. Succi constantly boasted that he had provided for his nourishment by means of compressed foods. Merlatti abstained from solids, but he drank three litres of water daily, and took other liquids. In any case these exhibitions are wholly and entirely another thing from the supernatural inedia of the mystics.

[38] *Castle*, 6th M., ch. iv.

[39] *De canonizatione sanctorum*, Lib. III, c. iii.

[40] The demons have no knowledge of the future, but these spirits by their nature enjoy great intellectual illumination, as Maiolo explains, " In shrewdness, knowledge, perspicuity, they far excel mankind, and they can look much further into the future by logical deduction."

[41] The Mosque, begun by Ard-Er-Rahman I in 786, and completed in 1001, which was converted into a Christian church.

[42] *Dicrum canicularium.*

INDEX

Library of the Mystic Arts

A LIBRARY OF ANCIENT AND MODERN CLASSICS

BARTON, R. F. Autobiographies of Three Pagans in the Philippines. intro. by Dr. Nancy Oestreich Lurie. ill. index bibliog. 320 pp. 5½" x 8¼" 62-19195. $7.50   ANTHROP
"It is difficult to realize that the people in these autobiographies, two men and a woman live on the same planet that we do. Head-hunting and spearing your enemy are everyday occurrences. Anyone who knows your kin is an enemy, unless he is your kin. It is the savage eye for an eye and tooth for a tooth of Biblical times, even though coming of the Americans has discouraged some of the practices. R. F. Barton was among the Ifugaos long enough to select three representatives of the tribe. In the autobiographies he gives their life history before marriage, including many of their ceremonies and customs. It is an interesting and inform- ative anthropological study." — WICHITA EAGLE & BEACON

BERNHEIM, H. Hypnosis and Suggestion in Psychotherapy: The Nature and Uses of Hypnotism. intro. by Ernest R. Hilgard. index. 428 pp. 6⅛" x 9¼" 63-22664. $10.00   PSYCH
Hypnosis has had a checkered career over a period of centuries, going through cycle after cycle of general approval and total eclipse. The fate of this book indicates how fragile the reputation of hypnosis has been; written almost eighty years ago, and translated into English a few years later, it has always been acknowledged as a great classic. Yet it has been out of print for some seventy years. It was not obsolete; nor was it suppressed. It has simply been neglected — as has hypnotism itself. It was the Second World War that reintro- duced hypnosis in psychotherapy, and the widespread contemporary interest dates from that time. Today its potential is recognized by practically all medical societies over the world, and courses in hypnotism are appearing in medical school curricula and in training programs for psychiatric residents. Numerous psychologists are also turning to hypnosis as a fertile field for research and therapy.

BULLOUGH, Vern L. The History of Prostitution. index. 320 pp. 6⅛" x 9¼" 64-16619. $7.50   HIST
Prostitution, like the weather, has often been talked about, but very rarely has any scholar bothered to do any research on the topic. Few serious studies on prostitution have been undertaken by social scientists over the past fifty years. Although an occasional sociologist, psychologist, psychiatrist, or anthropologist has concerned himself, the historian has totally neglected the subject. As a result this book is the first attempt at a serious history of prostitution in English in this century.

The author, Dr. Vern L. Bullough, is a historian who has specialized in the history of medicine and science. He has published numerous articles, primarily on medical history, in various learned journals. He was assisted in his researches by his wife, Bonnie L. Bullough.

COOMARASWAMY, Ananda Kentish. Buddha and the Gospel of Buddhism. intro. by John C. Wilson. ill. index. bibliog. glossary. 370 pp. 6⅛" x 9¼" 64-16160. $10.00   REL
A classic introduction to Buddhism, Coomaraswamy's book was originally pub- lished in England in 1916. It was reprinted without change in 1927, and it is now finally available in its original form in an American edition. The author was revered both in the East and the West for his unique contributions to art

and philosophy as well as religion. An ardent Indian nationalist, his life work became the preservation of India's heritage and the monumental task of teaching the West to respect and revere the great civilization of India. When Coomaraswamy died, Aldous Huxley spoke of his "unique importance as a mediator between East and West." The author was fond of calling himself a traditionalist and often emphasized the virtues of orthodoxy. He was always suspicious of the Western fashionable interest in Buddhism and frequently spoke with considerable irony of the contemporary offbeat Zen enthusiasts. "The suspicious popularity of 'Buddhism' in Europe," he wrote in 1938, "has rested upon a very thorough misunderstanding of what Buddhism really means. The essential doctrines of Buddhism, like those of all orthodox relgions, are in radical opposition to our modern individualism." The book continues to be a solid exposition of Buddhistic thought and its reissue should be timely in view of current rapprochment between the West and Eastern religious systems. Some twenty plates add interest and value.—VIRGINIA KIRKUS SERVICE.

FEILDING, Everard. Sittings with Eusapia Palladino and other Studies. intro. by E. J. Dingwall. 324 pp. 6⅛″ x 9¼″ 63-18682. $10.00   PARAPSYCH
"The author, well known as an objective observer of psychical phenomena, presents primarily a detailed report of 13 seances with the noted Italian medium of the 20th Century. There are included accounts of other mediums and of the stigmata of a French abbe. Facts are given; conclusions are left for the reader." — JOURNAL OF THE AMERICAN MEDICAL ASSOCIATION
"William James deplored the cheating and the vulgarity connected with the mediumship of Eusapia Palladino, but he believed that there was a residuum of phenomena in her performances which could not be explained. So did Everard Feilding of the Society for Psychic Research. He put her through the most rigid tests possible early in this century and concluded that she possessed some inexplicable power which caused tables to levitate, bells to ring, and lights to flash. In this most interesting collection of Feilding's writings we find that although he was a serious researcher, he always retained a sense of humor and a healthy skepticism. Eric Dingwall, who was his friend, has contributed a witty and appreciative introduction which reinforces the impression one gets from these papers that Feilding was a "most acute and well-balanced investigator" of ESP. Recommended for all libraries interested in this field of research." — LIBRARY JOURNAL

GUIGNEBERT, Charles. Jesus fwd. by Joel Carmichaël. index. bibliog. xv + 560 pp. 6⅛″ x 9¼″ 56-7837. $10.00   REL
This historical study of the life of Jesus and the origins of Christianity has received the highest possible praise from biblical scholars of the status of Niebuhr, Barth and Pfeiffer. Its author, Charles Guignebert, is generally considered one of the finest examples of European scholarship. He spent a lifetime of research into the genesis of all forms of religious belief; toward the end of his life he held the chair of the History of Christianity at the Sorbonne.
REINHOLD NIEBUHR: "The virtue of Professor Guignebert's venture lies in his comprehensive analysis of the scholarship of the past decades in this field. The specialists are acquainted with all the evidence which he analyzes. But there is no book of recent years which will give the interested layman a more comprehensive account of what has been written and said about the life of Jesus and a fairer estimate of conflicting evidence. Naturally the author has a position of his own to maintain, but the reader is permitted to see how he arrived at it, and with what cogency and plausibility he defends it against contrasting views."
ROBERT H. PFEIFFER: "Aside from Guignebert's JESUS, only Goguel's LIFE may be regarded as a serious attempt to write a critical and objective historical work.

Guignebert furnishes an excellent introduction to the subject, a reliable guide to beginners, and an informing manual for scholars. We need to be reminded again by Guignebert of the strict and sober discipline required of the true historian."

JAFFE, Aniela. Apparitions and Precognitions: A study from the Point of View of C. G. Jung's Analytical Psychology. intro. by C. G. Jung. index. 224 pp. 6⅛" x 9¼". 63-19744. $7.50   PSYCH
The author, well known for her valuable contributions to the literature of analytical psychology, was specifically selected by Dr. Jung to write this book. The book represents a psychological evaluation of more than 1500 personal accounts elicited in response to a series of articles by Dr. Jung, dealing with prophetic dreams, coincidences, premonitions, apparitions. The articles appeared in the popular Swiss magazine, *Schweizerische Beobachter,* and the astonishing response to it came from all social classes — farmers, workmen, tradesmen, office employees and various professions.
One of the notable things to come to light in Dr. Jaffe's book is the fact that among the Swiss, who are commonly regarded as stolid, unimaginative, rationalistic and materialistic, there are just as many ghost stories and strange tales as is likely to be found in any other land; bewitching, sorcery, magic spells, as practiced in the Middle Ages and remoter times have by no means died out, but presently flourish among the Swiss as rampantly as they did centuries ago.
The author leaves aside the questioner of ultimate truth; instead she tries to inquire into the psychological questions: Exactly who is it that sees a ghost? Under what psychic conditions does he see it? What does a ghost signify when examined for its content as a symbol?

KING, C. Daly. The States of Human Consciousness. fwd. by Roy Finch. index. v-xiii + 176 pp. 6⅛" x 9¼" 63-10385. $7.50
PSYCH
The crucial thesis of this book is that in addition to the forms of consciousness known to all human beings (Sleep and Waking) there exist two further forms not yet widely known (Awakeness and Objective Consciousness).
What led such an extremely skeptical man as Dr. King to accept the unorthodox idea that additional states of human consciousness are possible? There were four main lines of evidence which convinced him: These were: 1) the neurological and physiological teachings of the Guardjieff Institute; 2) his personal psychological experiments and experiences; 3) his historical studies of ancient civilizations; 4) his studies in behavioral patterns.

LEARY, Timothy; ALPERT, Richard; Metzner, Ralph. A Guide to Psychedelic Experience. 150 pp. 8" x 9" 64-19705. $5.00
PSYCH
During the past few years newspapers and magazines have poured out unrestrained criticism on the subject of psychedelic drugs. Meanwhile certain technical journals have simultaneously dealt out unrestrained praise. Whom are we to believe?
Perhaps the most objective evidence available on these important new drugs comes from recent studies made by four scientific research groups, which administered LSD and psilocybin to 462 persons — among them physicians, lawyers, writers, ministers, psychologists, artists, musicians, engineers and housewives. The percentage of these persons reporting it was a pleasant experience was 73%; the percentage reporting they wished to try it again was 82%; a total of 67% reported the experience brought them greater regard for other human beings; 67% felt a sense of relaxation and freedom from anxiety and tension; 65% felt it was of lasting benefit; 38% said it increased their interest in nature, art, music; and 64% felt the experience had changed their lives.
Drs. Leary, Alpert and Metzner have for years been among the most prominent names in the research of psychedelics. They were engaged in a program of experiments with the drugs at Harvard University, until sensational national

publicity, unfairly concentrating on student interest in the drugs, led to the suspension of the experiments. Since then, the authors have continued their work without academic auspices.

Like other scientists involved with psychedelic research, the authors maintain that the drug is only one component of the psychedelic session. Equally important is the mental and spiritual preparation, both before and in the course of taking the drug. The authors find no need to invent new mental and spiritual materials for this purpose. The great literature of meditation lends itself very well to this use. This particular guide uses preparation material from THE TIBETAN BOOK OF THE DEAD.

LEGMAN, G. The Horn Book; Studies in Erotic Folklore and Bibliography. index. bibliog. 565 pp. 6⅛" x 9¼" 63-19743. $12.50 REF

The author is probably the most learned and most controversial figure in the field of American folklore. He is also the principal living specialist in erotic folklore. A former bibliographer for the Kinsey Institute, he enjoys repute as a lecturer and as the editor of *Neurotica* magazine. He is also the author of *Love and Death: A Study in Censorship*, now in its second edition. In his present work, the author's intention is to give the real facts about erotic literature and folklore. Eloquently, he attacks the substitution of fakelore for folklore in the mass communications media of America today. After establishing the value of unfettered folk-art, Mr. Legman analyzes with penetrating psychological discernment the displacement of sexual symbolism in our society and makes a strong case for authentic, unexpurgated collections. He attacks the patently illogical and insensible idea that sex must be expunged — while allowing the sadistic programs, books and plays an uncriticized place in our society. Murder, torture, cannibalism freely appear in our mass media, while the healthy normality of sexual intercourse between man and woman is deprecated or silently omitted. And the author points a serious warning: "The substitution of allowed sadism for prohibited sexuality in folk literature and mass communications can only result in the most sinister abnormalization of the whole psychic structure of future generations."

The book's table of contents follows:

I. STUDIES IN EROTIC BIBLIOGRAPHY
    1. The Bibliography of Prohibited Books: Pisanus Fraxi
    2. The Horn Book, and Other Bibiliographical Problems
    3. Great Collectors of Erotica
II. THE REDISCOVERY OF BURNS' MERRY MUSES OF CALEDONIA
    4. The Cunningham Manuscript
    5. *The Merry Muses* as Folklore
III. PROBLEMS OF EROTIC FOLKLORE
    6. Folklore and Fakelore
    7. Misconceptions in Erotic Folklore
    8. The Bawdy Song...In Fact and In Print
    9. The Limerick: A History and Critique
    10. Toward a Motif-Index of Erotic Humor
    11. Folksongs, Fakelore, Folkniks and Cash
    12. Who Owns Folklore?

MARTIN, Eva. Reincarnation: The Ring of Return. index. bibliog. v-xi + 306 pp. 5½" x 8¼" 63-18492. $5.00 REL

The idea of reincarnation has always appealed powerfully to man's innate sense of justice, to his yearning for eternal progress. Yet, strangely enough, there are not many books to be found in English on the subject. Nor are any of them likely to be, as the present volume is, an anthology of the great writings on reincarnation.

"This first American edition of what is regarded as a standard work in its field, is comprehensive in that it covers the pre-Christian era, the early Christian era and other writings of the first five centuries. Miscellaneous sources are drawn upon and material from the first three decades of the Twentieth Century is also included. Almost exclusively, the author in her quotations, turns to the poets. Such a book as this, as the publisher remarks, 'whatever its shortcomings is not likely to become dull reading.'" — CHRISTIAN HERALD

PODMORE, Frank. From Mesmer to Christian Science: A Short History of Mental Healing; intro. By E. J. Dingwall. index. xxi + 306 pp. 6⅛" x 9¼" 63-21599. $10.00   PSYCH
"This short history of mental healing covers broadly and impressively just about everything from Mesmer to Christian Science. Certainly, spiritual healing has become an important part of our everyday life. In medicine there are psychoanalysts and an entire new school of therapy along with the use of hypnosis as an anesthesia; and in religion, not only Christian Science and New Thought, but many movements within the established churches and synagogues. More and more it brings into sharp focus the miraculous therapy' of Jesus. In these pages one follows the steady march of mental healing from quackery and chicanery to respectability, with something added." — *Dr. Daniel A. Poling,* CHRISTIAN HERALD

"Since the first appearance of this book in 1909, no publication has superseded Podmore's critical and detailed study. An outstanding member of the British Society for Psychical Research, he traced the subject from the hectic days of pre-Revolutionary Paris to the beginning of the 20th Century. Obsessed with the idea of fraud, the medical profession obstinately rejected all evidence of the validity of these investigations, abandoning the field to amateurs and fanatics. Eventually the phenomena which Mesmer attributed solely to a material fluid came to be explained as a purely spiritual process. The progeny of Mesmerism therefore include not only hypnotism and aspects of experimental psychology, but also Spiritualism, New Thought, and Mental Healing, of which Christian Science is most prominent. Recommended for most psychology collections." — LIBRARY JOURNAL

PRINCE, Walter Franklin. The Case of Patience Worth. intro. by John C. Wilson. 509 pp. 6⅛" x 9¼" 63-23268. $10.00   PARAPSYCH
The author, a renowned psychologist and a pioneer in scientific psychic research, regards the case of Patience Worth as one of the most fascinating and enigmatic psychic manifestations of all time. In the conclusion of his book, Dr. Prince states that he could offer no rational explanation to the riddle of Patience Worth, despite years of impartial scientific investigation.
Patience Worth identified herself as a spirit from 17th Century England and she communicated through a medium, Mrs. Pearl Curran, an unlettered Missouri housewife. Over a period of five years, Patience created and communicated through Mrs. Curran an enormous quantity of poetry and prose of astonishing quality. Her literary creations displayed original genius, enormous erudition, familiarity with classic literature and history, piercing wit and penetrating wisdom; in brief, creations which could not conceivably have come from the simple, unlettered Mrs. Curran, who had never been out of the Mid-West and who had managed to complete a grammar school education only after considerable difficulty.

ROSSMAN, Joseph. Industrial Creativity: The Psychology of the Inventor. intro. by Gardner Murphy. index. bibliog. 288 pp. 6⅛" x 9¼" 64-16161. $7.50   PSYCH
In this scholarly and painstaking study of the mental processes of creativity, Dr. Rossman, long associated with the U.S. Patent Office, presents many startling conclusions developed after a long and careful analysis of source material obtained from 700 active and important inventors. Dr. Rossman, a chemical engineer, a member of the bar practicing before both the U.S. Supreme Court and the Court of Customs and Patent Appeals, a famous patent attorney, and a doctor of psychology, is perhaps the only man who could have undertaken such a study.

Popular fantasy pictures the inventor as a wild-eyed, impractical dreamer. But the cumulative portrait that emerges in this book reveals an ability for keen analysis, a mind strikingly original and observant, an astonishing perseverance in the face of apparently insurmountable obstacles.

Dr. Rossman's book was first published primarily to help inventors understand all the implications of the inventive process. That was thirty years ago. Today it is published anew, with new material by Dr. Rossman. This time he addresses his book to all those interested in the nature of creativity. For those more specifically interested in scientific invention, there is a considerable body of original information.

SMITH, Susy. The Mediumship of Mrs. Leonard, photographs. bibliog. 256 pp. 6⅛" x 9¼" 64-17317. $7.50   PARAPSYCH

This is the first comprehensive study taking in the entire life work of Mrs. Leonard, the last of the great trance mediums of the golden age. She is now well into her eighties. This important new work is destined to endure as a classic in the search for psychic truth; it presents the strongest evidence ever obtained of the survival of the human spirit — of earthly memories abiding beyond the grave.

The scientific evidence in the case of Mrs. Leonard is the most documented in psychic history. No trance medium has ever been more thoroughly investigated and researched. Most of her career was spent not as a private medium but under the exclusive control of the Society of Psychical Research. The Society established a framework of painstaking supervision and kept exact records of everything said at Mrs. Leonard's sittings.

This book continues the series from University Books dealing with the great mediums. The two outstanding physical mediums, D. D. Home and Eusapia Palladino, are already represented. Of the three great trance mediums, Mrs. Piper was introduced in *William James On Psychic Research* and Helene Smith in Flournoy's *From India To The Planet Mars*. The third trance medium is Gladys Osborne Leonard.

APOCRYPHA. Introduction by Morton Enslin, Professor of Biblical Languages and Literature, St. Lawrence University. Bound in white and gold, 3-color slipcase. xv + 239 pp. 7¼" x 11" 62-12335. $15.00   REL

"In 1924 the Nonesuch edition of the Apocrypha appeared, limited to 1325 copies. This new edition is an almost exact facsimile of that very beautiful work, bound in a most attractive cover with stamped gilt design, and boxed. Most marked of its changes from the original, and one that enhances the value of the work considerably, is an Introduction by the editor of this Journal, Dr. Morton S. Enslin, who in brief, concise paragraphs provides excellent prefaces to the work as a whole and to each of the books individually. He places the Apocrypha in its proper context in biblical literature, indicates the inappropriateness of the name when applied to the books as a whole, and shows how it was that Luther split off these writings and placed them 'in the limbo between the Old Testament and the New.' The individual introductions serve to provide the backgrounds, probable datings, and general contents of each of the fourteen pieces. This is a valuable work for both the biblical scholar and the lover of fine books." — *J. Calvin Keene,* JOURNAL OF BIBLICAL LITERATURE

BIRREN, Faber. Color: A Survey in Words and Pictures: From Ancient Mysticism to Modern Science. ill. index. 250 pp. 7⅝" x 10½" 62-18889. $15.00   PSYCH

"This book is a compilation of information concerning color, from the physiology of the eye and theories of color vision to the ancients' belief in magical qualities of color, and even current theories of color and personality. The author has written several books on color and color psychology, particularly relating color to commercial purposes." — LIBRARY JOURNAL

"An introduction to the history of color, both ancient and modern, and to its

various uses. This book is highly recommended." — PSYCHIATRIC QUARTERLY
"All in all, an absorbing book in an uncrowded field, and one which does credit
to the author's erudition and intuition." — ST. LOUIS POST-DISPATCH

BIRREN, Faber. Color Psychology and Color Therapy: A Factual Study of the Influence of Color on Human Life. intro by Felix Morrow. ill. photogs. index. biblio. xv + 302 pp. 6⅛" x 9¼" 61-14266. $7.50
PSYCH
"Faber Birren is a consultant on the use of color in industrial and other applications, and perhaps without peer in this field. The book, however, goes much
farther than the mere applications and their psychology. There is fascinating
detail from historical, medical, occult, physiological sources as well — fascinating
and documented... Recommended." — LIBRARY JOURNAL

THE BOOK OF THE DEAD: the Hieroglyphic Transcript of the Papyrus of ANI. tr. and intro. by E. A. Wallis Budge. ill. index. appendixes. xiv + 704 pp. 6⅛" x 9¼" 60-12165. $12.50   REL
This is the collection of texts which the ancient Egyptian scribes composed for
the benefit of the dead. A book-length introduction by Sir Wallis Budge, late
Keeper of the Egyptian and Assyrian Antiquities in the British Museum, gives
us its history and theology. This is an exact reproduction of the famous Medici
Society edition of 1911 except that the original two volumes are here bound
as one.

BUCKE, Richard Maurice, M.D. Cosmic Consciousness; A Study in the Evolution of the Human Mind. bibliog. xvii + 326 pp. 7¼" x 9¾" 61-11100. $5.95   PSYCH
One of the great classics of mystical experience, this work was first published in
1901. The author saw the emergence of a new faculty, the natural outgrowth of
our present level of consciousness to a level as far above it as it is above the
simple consciousness of animals. William James read the work when it appeared
and wrote to the author: "I believe that you have brought this kind of consciousness 'home' to the attention of students of human nature in a way so
definite and inescapable that it will be impossible henceforward to overlook it
or ignore it... But my total reaction on your book, my dear Sir, is that it is an
addition to psychology of first rate importance, and that you are a benefactor of
us all."

BUDGE, E. A. Wallis. Amulets and Talismans. ill. b/w 22 plates, 300 ill. index. xxxix + 543 pp. 6⅛" x 9¼" 61-7163. $10.00   REL/ARCHEOL
"This encyclopedic volume represents years of research and an extensive knowl-
edge of ancient civilizations. The author, as teacher at Cambridge University
and curator of the British Museum, has accumulated a wealth of data dealing
with demonology, divination, astrology, numerology and the belief in the
prophylactic properties of the gems prevalent among the people of the ancient
civilizations of Sumer, Babylon, Persia, Egypt and others. The author throws
new light on many passages in early biblical writings which will give the student
of the Old Testament often a clearer meaning of the archaic sense of the text.
'Amulets and Talismans' is a reliable reference book of lasting value." — THE
LUTHERAN

BUDGE, E. A. Wallis. Osiris; the Egyptian Religion of Resurrection; 2 vs. bound in one; intro. by Jane Harrison. ill. 14 b/w plates, 212 line cuts. index. appendix. xliii + 440 pp. 6⅛" x 9¼" 61-10531. $15.00
REL
"In this full-length study, Dr. Wallis Budge, the late Keeper of the Egyptian
and Assyrian Antiquities in the British Museum, interprets Osiris as a year-god
who dies and lives again. In contradistinction to Frazer, he dwells on the native
African origins of this ancient Egyptian cult and avoids the obvious parallels
with the Mid-Eastern gods Attis and Adonis... His work will be read with profit
and enjoyment by all students of comparative religion." — LIBRARY JOURNAL